CASES AND MATERIALS

LAW OF TORTS

Second Edition

John Lewthwaite LLB, LLM, ACIS
Senior Lecturer in Law, Nottingham Law School

and

John S. Hodgson, MA, LLM, Solicitor
Principal Lecturer in Law, Nottingham Law School

b BLACKSTONE
PRESS LIMITED

First published in Great Britain 1996 by Blackstone Press Limited,
Aldine Place, London W12 8AA.   Telephone 0181–740 2277

© Nottingham Law School, Nottingham Trent University, 1996

First edition 1996
Reprinted 1997
Second edition 1998

ISBN: 1 85431 823 3

British Library Cataloguing in Publication Data
A CIP catalogue record for this book is available from the British Library.

Typeset by Style Photosetting Limited, Mayfield, East Sussex
Printed by Livesey Limited, Shrewsbury, Shropshire

FOREWORD

The books in the LLB series have been written for students studying law at undergraduate level. There are two books for each subject. The first is the *Learning Text* which is designed to teach you about the particular subject in question. However, it does much more than that. By means of Activities, Self Assessment and End of Chapter Questions, the *Learning Text* allows you to test your knowledge and understanding as you work. Each chapter starts with 'Objectives' which indicate what you should be able to do by the end of it. You should use these Objectives in your learning — check them frequently and ask yourself whether you have attained them.

The second book is a volume of *Cases and Materials*. This is cross-referenced from the *Learning Text*. It contains the primary sources of law such as statutes and cases plus subsidiary sources such as extracts from journals, law reform papers and textbooks. This is your portable library. Although each volume can stand alone, they are designed to be complementary.

The two-volume combination aims to support your learning by challenging you to demonstrate your mastery of the principles and application of the law. They are appropriate whatever your mode of study — full-time or part-time.

CONTENTS

PREFACE

The division of labour between the authors is as for the Learning Text. John Lewthwaite is responsible for Negligence in all its branches and Breach of Statutory Duty, John Hodgson for Product Liability, Nominate Torts and Remedies. Again there is a difference of approach present, reflecting the different nature of the subject matter.

Tort remains the common law subject par excellence. It is thus inevitable that most of the contents of a Cases and Materials book will be cases. The House of Lords never seems to tire of improving the law, particularly, of Negligence, and there are many recent cases of the first importance.

Statute is important in specific areas. There is a temptation, both for students and lecturers, to ignore this. That temptation must be resisted. For instance, the statutory liability for defective products under the Consumer Protection Act 1987 has virtually supplanted the common law liability under *Donoghue* v *Stevenson*. Analysis of the statute and its parent EC Directive is therefore essential. Indeed, although there must have been many claims relying on the Act, it has yet to generate its first reported decision.

Negligence has also generated very substantial academic literature, and this is reflected here. This is less true of the nominate torts, and here the emphasis has been kept firmly on primary materials.

Some case are briefly excerpted for the sake of a specific ratio or dictum. In many cases longer extracts have been provided, although only rarely has space allowed the full judgment to be given. We hope that this will give readers a better idea of the style and form of a judgment, providing more of a context, and less editorialising than is the case where only the bare essentials are selected. Usually later cases have been selected rather than the older 'leading' cases. This is because the later judges themselves discuss and criticise the earlier judgments, providing, we hope, a richer legal experience.

ACKNOWLEDGMENTS

Nottingham Law School and the publishers would like to thank the following for permission to reproduce copyright material:

Butterworth & Co. (Publishers) Ltd: extracts from the All England Law Reports, Commercial Cases and the Law Times Reports.

Canada Law Book Company: extracts from the Dominion Law Reports.

Eclipse Group Ltd: extracts from the Industrial Relations Law Reports.

Incorporated Council of Law Reporting for England & Wales: extracts from the Law Reports and the Weekly Law Reports.

Law Book Company of Australia: extracts from the Commonwealth Law Reports.

Lloyd's of London Press: extracts from the Lloyd's Law Reports.

Sweet & Maxwell Ltd: extracts from Miller 'Felthouse v Bindley Re-visited' (1972) 35 MLR 489; Treitel, Law of Contract, 8th ed, pp. 8, 24, 27 and 42; and the English Reports.

T & T Clark and Times Newspapers Ltd: extracts from the Times Law Reports.

TABLE OF CASES

Cases reported in full are shown in heavy type. The page at which the report is printed is shown in heavy type.

TABLE OF STATUTES

Statutes, and sections thereof, which are set out in full or in part are shown in heavy type. The page at which the statute or section is printed is shown in heavy type.

CHAPTER ONE

LIABILITY IN TORT

1.1   Vicarious Liability

1.1.1   AN EMPLOYER'S VICARIOUS LIABILITY FOR THE TORTS OF HIS EMPLOYEE

McKendrick, E., *Tort Textbook*, 6th edn, HLT Publications, 1992, pp. 21–2

The rationale of vicarious liability
. . . It is probably true to say that there is no one justification for the imposition of vicarious liability. The best conclusion may be that of Professor Williams when he said in his article Vicarious Liability and the Master's Indemnity ((1957) 20 MLR 220, 232):

> . . . that vicarious liability owes its explanation, if not its justification, to the search for a solvent defendant. It is commonly felt that when a person is injured . . . he ought to be able to obtain recompense from someone; and if the immediate tortfeasor cannot afford to pay, then he is justified in looking around for the nearest person of substance who can plausibly be identified with the disaster. Where there is no immediate tortfeasor at all, the same sentiment works itself out through rules of strict liability.

. . . This lack of a coherent rationale for the doctrine does not appear to have troubled the judiciary. Lord Pearce in *Imperial Chemical Industries Ltd* v *Shatwell* [1965] AC 656, 685 said: 'The doctrine of vicarious liability has not grown from any very clear, logical or legal principle but from social convenience and rough justice.' Despite this apparent lack of concern on the part of the judiciary, we shall note at various stages of this chapter that the issue is an important one and that its resolution would help to stabilise the law and give it greater coherence.

ALCOCK v *WRAITH AND OTHERS*, The Times, 23 December 1991 (CA)

It was held that an employer is not generally liable for the torts of an independent contractor, but there is an exception where the contractor has been employed to carry out a task which is 'extra hazardous'.

The plaintiff was the neighbour (the parties lived in terraced houses) of the Swinhoes who had employed Wraith (subsequently declared bankrupt) to carry out roofing work on their house.

The Swinhoes had concrete interlocking roof tiles installed, to replace slates. Before this work was carried out, each house in the terrace was roofed with slates extending as a continuous roof, uninterrupted by the party walls between the neighbouring properties. The interlocking tiles had encroached onto Alcock's premises, and newspaper, which had been stuffed in the joint between the new tiles and Alcock's slates, had become saturated allowing damp to penetrate into the upper floors of his house.

At first instance the Swinhoes were found liable to Alcock in trespass, nuisance and negligence, and their appeal against this judgment was dismissed. According to Neill LJ: 'Mr and Mrs Swinhoe had the right to interfere with the joint between the two roofs but if they exercised that right, they were under a duty to see that reasonable skill and care was used in the operation. That duty could not be delegated to an independent contractor.'

The Court applied the decision in *Honeywill and Stein Ltd* v *Larkin Bros Ltd* [1934] 1 KB 191.

1.1.1.1   The tests

SIME v SUTCLIFFE CATERING (SCOTLAND) LTD [1990] IRLR 228 (Scotland)

In this case the plaintiff worked in a canteen and was injured when she slipped on some food which had been dropped by a fellow worker. The plaintiff's employer, a manufacturer, had contracted out the management of the canteen to a firm of caterers, the defendant, but had kept the existing canteen staff, including the plaintiff, on its payroll. Thus the plaintiff was not directly employed by the caterers.

The evidence was such that it could not be established whether or not the person who had dropped the food was in the **actual** employment of the caterers; the accident could have been caused by the negligence of an existing member of the canteen staff, who would have been in the employment of the manufacturer.

It then became necessary for the court to decide whether the caterers could be held vicariously liable for someone they might not employ. They held that the deciding factor in the present circumstances was **control**: '. . . [did] the substitute employer (the caterer) (have) sufficient power of control and supervision purely to be regarded as the effective employer at the critical time(?)' Since the caterers had taken on the 'whole day-to-day management of the catering operation and staff . . . the canteen manager had complete control over the way in which all the canteen workers did their job . . .' they were vicariously liable to the plaintiff for her injuries. In the event, however, her damages were reduced by 25 per cent for contributory negligence. The court said it was quite predictable that food might be spilt in or near a kitchen, where a number of people were working with food or dirty dishes, and it was therefore necessary that the plaintiff should keep a look out for reasonably foreseeable dangers, such as slippery patches on the floor.

LANE v SHIRE ROOFING CO. (OXFORD) LTD, *The Times*, 17 February 1995 (CA)

HENRY LJ: In this case the plaintiff was a builder/roofer/carpenter who had since 1982 traded as a one-man firm. He had obtained self-employed fiscal status with a right to tax exemption certificates. He had found work through advertisements and when engaged by clients would be responsible for the estimating and buying of materials. But that work had dried up.

The defendants, a newly established roofing business, did not want to take on employees. They considered it prudent and advantageous to hire for individual jobs. They had advertised for men to work on a large roofing job in Marlow. The plaintiff was employed by them at the daily rate of £45.

That job was nearly over when the defendants' requested the plaintiff to re-roof the porch at Sonning Common. He had visited the site with a representative of the defendants and had discussed what was necessary in the way of plant, ladders and scaffolding, to do the job.

It was agreed that the defendants would pay the plaintiff an all-in fee for the job. The plaintiff had taken all his personal roofing and carpentry tools but had provided no materials. He took his own ladder. While carrying out the work he had fallen from the ladder and suffered the injuries which had caused serious brain damage . . . There were reasons on both sides to avoid the employee label. But there were good policy reasons in the safety at work field to ensure that the law properly discriminated between employees and independent contractors. Many factors had to be taken into account and with different priority being given to those factors certain principles emerged.

First the element of control was important: who laid down what was to be done, the way in which it was to be done, the means by which it was to be done and the time when it was to be done? Who provided, hired and fired, the team by which it was done, and the materials, plant, machinery and tools used?

The control test might not be decisive, for instance in the case of skilled employees with discretion to decide how their work should be done. In such cases the question was broadened to whose business was it? Was the workman carrying on his own business, or was he carrying on his employer's?

The answer to that question might involve looking to see where the financial risk lay and whether and how far the workman had an opportunity of profiting from sound management in the performance of his task.

Those questions had to be asked in the context of who was responsible for the overall safety of the men doing the work. Here the defendants had agreed that they were. That answer was not decisive, although it might be indicative, because ultimately the question was one of law and the defendants could be wrong as to where the legal responsibility lay.

The defendants rightly distinguished between a *Ferguson* v *Dawson* [1976] 1 WLR 1213 situation where an employer engaged men on 'the lump' to do labouring work, where the men were clearly employees whatever their tax status, and when a specialist subcontractor was employed to perform some part of a general building contract. That individual clearly would be an independent contractor.

Mr Matthews submitted that the plaintiff fell somewhere in between. That was correct but this case was substantially nearer 'the lump' than the specialist sub-contractor, although the degree of control the defendants would use would depend on the need they felt to supervise and direct the plaintiff.

The question 'whose business was it?' in relation to the Sonning Common job could only be answered by saying that it was the defendants' business and not the plaintiff's. They owed the duties of employers to the plaintiff.

With the concurrence of Lord Justice Nourse and Lord Justice Auld the defendants were held liable for breach of statutory duty but the plaintiff's damages were reduced for contributory negligence.

1.1.1.2 Borrowed employees

McCONKEY v *AMEC PLC AND OTHERS* (1990) 27 Construction LR 88

BALCOMBE LJ: On 17 December 1984 the plaintiff, Mr Edward McConkey, a scaffolder employed by Stirling Scaffolding Ltd, was working at Hadrian Yard, Wallsend, Tyne and Wear, of which the first defendants, Amec plc, were the occupiers. At the yard was an NCK Andes crawler crane, owned by the second defendants, G W Sparrow and Sons plc (Sparrow) and hired by them under a contract dated 10 December 1984 to the third party, William Press Production Systems Ltd (Press), a subsidiary of Amec. The plaintiff was walking at ground level beneath the crane, which was in the process of lifting four metal plates with a total weight of some 7.68 tons. The fly jib of the crane buckled and the plates fell, striking the plaintiff and causing him serious injury. In due course he sued both Amec and Sparrow: Amec for breach of duty under the Factories Act 1961 and the Construction (Lifting Operations) Regulations 1961, SI 1961/1581 (the 1961 regulations) and negligence; Sparrow for negligence. Sparrow then brought in Press as a third party. The action came on for trial before Alliott J at Newcastle on 28 November 1988 and at the outset of the trial he gave judgment by consent for the plaintiff against both defendants in the sum of £140,000. He then proceeded to hear the issue between Sparrow and Press. Although there was no formal claim by Amec for contribution from Sparrow, or vice versa, it appears to have been common ground that Amec was entitled to be indemnified by Sparrow, and that the real issue was the effect of the contract between Sparrow and Press. By a reserved judgment delivered on 1 December 1988 the judge held that Sparrow was entitled to be indemnified by Press. From that judgment Press has appealed to this court.

The contract between Sparrow (called 'the owner') and Press (called 'the hirer') was on a standard form provided by Sparrow and incorporated the Model Conditions agreed between the Contractors' Plant Association and the Federation of Civil Engineering Contractors . . .

The judge did find that Farrelly was not, at the relevant time, a competent operator for the purposes of cl 8 of the Model Conditions. This finding is challenged in this court by Press under a respondent's notice under RSC Ord 59, r. 6(2)(b). However, the judge went on to hold that cll 8 and 13 were to be read 'disjunctively' and that, notwithstanding that cl 8 did not pass vicarious liability for Farrelly's acts and omissions to Press, cl 13 did provide

Sparrow with a full and complete indemnity from Press in respect of the claim, which arose out of the use of the plant.

So the issues before us are: (1) Was there evidence before the judge which entitled him to find that Farrelly was not a competent operator within the meaning of cl 8? (2) Was there evidence before the judge which would have entitled him to find that there was a defect in the condition of the crane which was causative of the accident? (3) If so, was this a breach of the owner's obligations under cl 5? (4) In the absence of any finding by the judge under (2) and (3) above, should we make such a finding? (5) What is the effect of cl 13 in the circumstances of the present case?

I consider these issues separately below.

1. *Farrelly's competence*

It hardly needs saying that incompetence is not the same as negligence and, indeed, this was common ground in the argument before us. Mr Samuels QC sought to maintain that Farrelly was not even negligent, but in the light of the undisputed fact that the accident was caused by his operating the crane with a substantial overload, and with no explanation being offered for that, I have no hesitation in saying that he was plainly negligent. Nevertheless even a competent operator may on occasion be negligent, and if the judge had based his finding of Farrelly's incompetence merely on the circumstances of the accident then there might well be grounds for challenging that finding. But in my judgment there was ample evidence to justify the judge's finding that Farrelly was not a competent operator. There was the fact that he had either fitted the wrong cam for the Wylie indicator or, if he had not himself fitted the cam, had failed to check that the right cam for the length of the main boom was fitted. There was the evidence of Errington and Spencer which clearly impressed the judge, even though he did not feel able to make specific findings of what was said. That evidence clearly suggested that Farrelly was unaware of what was his safe load, and also that he wholly misunderstood the function of the load radius indicator. Then, if it be the case that the Wylie safe load indicator failed to operate at the time of the accident, it is possible (to put it no higher) that Farrelly had failed to test it at the beginning of his shift. Finally there is the damning report of January 1985 that Farrelly 'still had very little knowledge about his Wylie safe load indicator or the correct use of his fly jib'. I know of no reason why this should not be material which the judge was entitled to take into account in deciding whether Farrelly was a competent operator when Sparrow supplied him to Press with the crane just one month previously. In my judgment the judge's finding that Farrelly was not at the relevant time a competent operator for the purposes of cl 8 cannot be faulted.

2. *The defective condition of the crane*

I have already mentioned the effect of the expert evidence on this issue. The experts' evidence was not shaken in cross-examination and there was no evidence to the contrary called by Sparrow. Accordingly there was evidence before the judge which would have entitled him to find that the defective condition of the fly jib was causative of the accident.

3. *The effect of cl 5*

Clause 5 is headed 'Delivery in Good Order . . .' It provides that, unless complaint is made by the hirer within a specified time, the plant shall be deemed to be in good order, save for either an inherent fault or a fault not ascertainable by reasonable examination. Curiously, cl 5 imposes no explicit obligation upon the owner to supply plant which is in good order, but the deeming provision make no sense unless that is the owner's primary obligation, and that is in any event his obligation under the general law: see *Hyman* v *Nye* (1881) 6 QBD 685, Clause 2 cannot operate to negative this only sensible construction of the phrase 'save for either an inherent fault or a fault not ascertainable by reasonable examination' is apt grammatically to qualify only the deeming provision of cl 5(a), but even if it were to be construed as qualifying the owner's primary obligation to supply plant which is in good order, there was no evidence called by Sparrow to establish that the defects in the jib were not ascertainable by reasonable examination—clearly rust and bad welding are not inherent faults.

So if the crane was defective then in my judgment Sparrow was in breach of its obligations to Press under cl 5, and is liable to Press for any damage caused by that breach.

4. *Our finding under cl 5*

It would have been helpful to us if there had been a finding by the judge on this issue. Fortunately, however, there is no need for us to remit the present case, since the evidence on the condition of the crane was all one way. In my judgment, therefore, we can and should find that Sparrow was in breach of its obligations to Press under cl 5.

5. *The effect of cl 13*

The judge held that cl 13 was to be read 'disjunctively', a phrase which appears to have originated with Mr Samuels for Sparrow, and was used to mean that, on the facts of this case, cl 13 provided Sparrow with an indemnity from Press against the plaintiff's claim, notwithstanding the provisions of cll 5 and 8. In my judgment this is an untenable construction of the Model Conditions. Apart altogether from the basic rule that a contract is to be construed as a whole, so as to give full and proper effect to all its various terms, cl 13 starts with these express words: '(a) For the avoidance of doubt it is hereby agreed and declared that nothing in this clause affects the operation of cll 5, 8 and 9 of this Agreement'. So I turn to consider what, apart from cl 13, would be the operation of cl 8 of the agreement on the facts of this case.

Mr Farrelly was the employee of Sparrow who prima facie would be vicariously liable for any damage caused by his negligence. However, if the owner supplies a competent operator: 'such [operator] shall for all purposes in connection with [his] employment in the working of the plant be regarded as the [servant] or [agent] of the Hirer . . . who alone shall be responsible for all claims arising in connection with the operation of the plant by the said [driver] or [operator].' If the owner supplies an incompetent operator, then such operator is not to be regarded as the servant or agent of the hirer and the owner remains vicariously liable for his negligence. So the operation of cl 8 on the facts of this case is that Sparrow remains vicariously liable for the negligence of Farrelly, and nothing in cl 13 is to affect that operation of cl 8. The construction which found favour with the judge would be correct if cl 13(a) were changed to read: 'nothing in cll 5, 8 and 9 of this Agreement affects the operation of this Clause'.

Even without the express words of cl 13(a), there is ample internal evidence that cl 13 does not have an independent existence of its own but is to be read so as to make a coherent whole with the other clauses of the Model Conditions. Thus cl 8, in deeming a competent operator to be the servant or agent of the hirer, expressly provides that that is to be without prejudice to any of the provisions of cl 13. This is a clear reference to cl 13(c), which sets out in detail certain circumstances where the owner accepts liability for damage to the plant or arising out of its use. Thus if the plant is travelling to or from a site under its own power with a driver supplied by the owner and is involved in an accident in which third parties are injured, the owner remains liable, notwithstanding that he has supplied a competent operator. There is a similar cross-reference to cl 9 in cl 13(b).

By a process of reasoning similar to that which applies to cl 8, if the owner supplies a crane which is not in good order, and as a result is liable in damages to the hirer for breach of the owner's obligation under cl 5(a), nothing in cl 13 is to affect that operation of cl 5—see cl 13(a).

In my judgment this construction of cl 13 is not only in accordance with the literal wording of the Model Conditions, but also accords with what the parties may be assumed to have intended. If the owner supplies a defective crane, or an incompetent operator, and an accident happens which is caused by that defect, or by the negligence of that operator, why should the hirer be liable rather than the owner? Such a construction would accord with neither reason nor justice. It is possible to imagine many circumstances in which cl 13(b) will be applicable so as to require the hirer to indemnify the owner, and the reminder to the hirer in the contract form to insure against his liabilities under cll 8 and 13 makes perfectly good sense without interpreting it to mean that the hirer must insure against liability arising from the owner's breaches of its obligations under the Model Conditions.

In the circumstances it becomes unnecessary to consider whether, if cl 13 were otherwise relevant to the present case, its operation is excluded by s. 2(1) of the Unfair Terms Contract Act 1977. Before the judge it was accepted that he was bound by the decision of this court in *Thompson* v *T Lohan (Plant Hire) Ltd* [1987] 2 All ER 631, [1987] 1 WLR 649. That was a decision which on its terms was concerned only with the effect of cl 8 of the Model Conditions, following as it did the decision of the House of Lords in *Arthur White*

(Contractors) Ltd v *Tarmac Civil Engineering Ltd* [1967] 3 All ER 586, [1967] 1 WLR 1508, and
it is arguable that it does not decide that cl 13 taken alone is unaffected by the 1977 Act. For
similar reasons it is also unnecessary to consider whether cl 13 taken alone is wide enough
to indemnify the owner from the consequences of its own negligence: see *Smith* v *South
Wales Switchgear Ltd* [1978] 1 All ER 18, [1978] 1 WLR 165.

I would allow this appeal, discharge the judgment of 1 December 1988, and substitute in
its place declarations that Amec is entitled to be indemnified by Sparrow against any
liability towards the plaintiff on his judgment in the action and that Sparrow is not entitled
to any indemnity from Press is respect of the plaintiff's judgment.

[The concurring judgments of Stocker LJ, and Sir Edward Eveleigh are omitted.]

1.1.2 COURSE OF EMPLOYMENT

SMITH v *STAGES* [1989] 1 All ER 833 (HL)

X was employed by the defendant (appellant) to install insulation in power stations.
Together with the plaintiff (respondent) who was a colleague, X was on an urgent job in
Wales.

The plaintiff and X were paid for eight hours' travelling time from the Midlands to Wales
and the same amount for the return journey. They were also paid the appropriate rail fare.

X used his car for the trip and on the way back the plaintiff was badly injured in an
accident caused by X's negligence. The plaintiff sued X, who was uninsured, and the
defendant, alleging vicarious liability on their part for X's negligence committed in the
course of his employment.

At first instance the judge found for the defendant on the ground that X was not acting
in the course of his employment at the time of the accident.

The Court of Appeal, however, found for the plaintiff on the issue of vicarious liability
and the House of Lords confirmed this decision unanimously.

LORD GOFF: The fundamental principle is that an employee is acting in the course of his
employment when he is doing what he is employed to do, to which it is sufficient for
present purposes to add, or anything which is reasonably incidental to his employment. . . .

As usual, it is comparatively easy to state the principle; but it is more difficult to apply it
to the facts of individual cases. Even so, it is important always to keep the principle in
mind.

As I have already observed, we are here concerned with a case which may be seen as one
of those cases concerned with travelling to or from work. I have used guarded language in
so describing it, because (as will appear) I do not consider the present case to fall strictly
within that category of case. Even so, it is helpful to use the cases in that category as a
starting point. We can begin with the simple proposition that, in ordinary circumstances,
when a man is travelling to or from his place of work, he is not acting in the course of his
employment. So a bank clerk who commutes to the City of London every day from
Sevenoaks is not acting in the course of his employment when he walks across London
Bridge from the station to his bank in the City. This is because he is not employed to travel
from his home to the bank: he is employed to work at the bank, his place of work, and so
his duty is to arrive there in time for his working day. Nice points can arise about the
precise time, or place, at which he may be held to have arrived at work; but these do not
trouble us in the present case. Likewise, of course, he is not acting in the course of his
employment when he is travelling home after his day's work is over. If, however, a man is
obliged by his employer to travel to work by means of transport provided by his employer,
he may be held to be acting in the course of his employment when doing so.

These are the normal cases. There are, however, circumstances in which, when a man is
travelling to (or from) a place where he is doing a job for his employer, he will be held to
be acting in the course of his employment. Some of these are listed by Lord Atkin in *Blee* v
London and North Eastern Rly Co. [1938] AC 126 at 131–132. So, if a man is employed to do
jobs for his employer at various places during the day, such as a man who goes from door
to door canvassing for business, or who distributes goods to customers, or who services
equipment like washing machines or dishwashers, he will ordinarily be held to be acting

in the course of his employment when travelling from one destination to another, and may also be held to do so when travelling from his home to his first destination and home again after his last. Again, it has been held that, in certain circumstances, a man who is called out from his home at night to deal with an emergency may be acting in the course of his employment when travelling from his home to his place of work to deal with the emergency: see *Blee* v *London and North Eastern Rly Co*. There are many other cases.

But how do we distinguish the cases in this category in which a man is acting in the course of his employment from those in which he is not? The answer is, I fear, that everything depends on the circumstances. . . .

For example, the fact that a man is being paid by his employer in respect of the relevant period of time is often important, but cannot of itself be decisive. A man is usually paid nowadays during his holidays; and it often happens that an employer may allow a man to take the afternoon off, or even a whole day off, without affecting his wages. In such circumstances, he will ordinarily not be acting in the course of his employment despite the fact that he is being paid. Indeed, any rule that payment at the relevant time is decisive would be very difficult to apply in the case of a salaried man. Let me, however, give an example concerned with travelling to work. Suppose that a man is applying for a job, and it turns out that he would have a pretty arduous journey between his home and his new place of work, lasting about an hour each way, which is deterring him from taking the job. His prospective employer may want to employ him, and may entice him by offering him an extra hour's pay at each end of the day, say ten hours' pay a day instead of eight. In those circumstances he would not, I think, be acting in the course of his employment when travelling to or from work. This is because he would not be employed to make the journey: the extra pay would simply be given to him in recognition of the fact that his journey to and from work was an arduous one.

That example serves, I think, to point up the two alternative solutions under consideration in the present case. For to me, the question is this. Was Mr Stages employed to travel to and from Pembroke? Or was the pay given to him in recognition of the fact that he had lost two days' work at Drakelow because, in order to work at the power station at Pembroke, he would have to make his own way to Pembroke and back again to the Midlands? If we can solve that problem, we can answer the question whether Mr Stages was acting in the course of his employment when, worn out, he crashed his car on the A40 near Llandeilo.

I propose first to consider the problem not in relation to his journey back from Pembroke when the accident in fact happened, but in relation to his journey out to Pembroke. I shall do so because I find it easier to consider the problem uncomplicated by the fact that Monday, 29 August, was a bank holiday or by the fact that Mr Stages was being paid eight hours' sleeping time because he had worked through the night of Sunday, 28 August, although, as will appear, I consider both facts to be irrelevant. I should add that Mr Stages's contract of service was not apparently in evidence before the judge; and so, although that is normally a material document, sometimes a highly material document, in these cases, your Lordships' House has (like the courts below) to reach a conclusion unassisted by the terms of the relevant contract.

I approach the matter as follows. I do not regard this case an an ordinary case of travelling to work. It would be more accurate to describe it as a case where an employee, who has for a short time to work for his employers at a different place of work some distance away from his usual place of work, has to move from his ordinary base to a temporary base (here lodgings in Pembroke) from which he will travel to work at the temporary place of work each day. For the purpose of moving base, a normal working day was set aside for Mr Stages's journey, for which he was paid as for an eight-hour day. In addition to his day's pay he was given a travel allowance for his journey, and an allowance for his lodgings at his temporary base in Pembroke. In my opinion, in all the circumstances of the case, Mr Stages was required by the employers to make this journey, so as to make himself available to do his work at the Pembroke power station, and it would be proper to describe him as having been employed to do so. The fact that he was not required by his employer to make the journey by any particular means, nor even required to make it on the particular working day made available to him, does not detract from the proposition that he was employed to make the journey. Had Mr Stages wished, he could have driven down on the afternoon of Sunday, 21 August, and have devoted the Monday to (for example) visiting friends near Pembroke. In such circumstances it could, I suppose, be said that Stages was not travelling 'in his employers' time'. But this would not matter; for the fact remains that the Monday, a normal working day, was made available for the journey, with full pay for that day to perform a task which he was required by the employers to perform.

I have it very much in mind that Mr Machin and Mr Stages were described by counsel for the employers as peripatetic laggers working at such sites as were available. This may well be an accurate description of their work. If so, their contracts of service may have provided at least an indication as to how far they would be acting in the course of their employment when changing from one power station to another. Indeed, accepting the description as correct, it is difficult to know how much weight to give it in the absence of their contracts of service. However, the present case can in any event be differentiated on the basis that it was a departure from the norm in that it was concerned with a move to a temporary base to deal with an emergency, on the terms I have described.

I turn to Mr Stages's journey back. Another ordinary working day, Tuesday, 30 August, was made available for the journey, with the same pay, to enable him to return to his base in the Midlands to be ready to travel to work on the Wednesday morning. In my opinion, he was employed to make the journey back, just as he was employed to make the journey out to Pembroke. If he had chosen to go to sleep on the Monday morning and afternoon for eight hours or so, and then to drive home on the Monday evening so that he could have Tuesday free (as indeed Mr Pye expected him to do), that would not have detracted from the proposition that his journey was in the course of his employment. For this purpose, it was irrelevant that Monday was a bank holiday. Of course, it was wrong for him to succumb to the temptation of driving home on the Monday morning, just after he had completed so long a spell of work; but once again that cannot alter the fact that his journey was made in the course of his employment.

For these reasons, I would dismiss the appeal.

1.1.2.1 Expressly forbidden acts

ROSE v *PLENTY* [1976] 1 WLR 141 (CA)

LORD DENNING MR: . . . The judge found that Mr Plenty was negligent, but he felt that young Leslie was old enough to bear some part of the blame himself. He assessed the responsibility for the accident at 75 per cent to Mr Plenty and 25 per cent to the boy. He assessed the total damages at £800. He gave judgment against Mr Plenty for three-quarters of it, £600. But he exempted the employers from any liability. He held that Mr Plenty was acting outside the scope of his employment and that the boy was a trespasser on the float. The boy, through his father, now appeals to this court. He says the employers, Co-operative Services, are liable for the acts of their milk roundsman . . .

Applying the first question in *Young* v *Box* [1951] 1 TLR 789, it is quite clear that the driver, Mr Plenty, was liable to the boy, Leslie Rose, for his negligent driving of the milk float. He actually invited the boy to ride on it. So the second question arises, whether his employers, Co-operative Services, are liable for the driver's negligence. That does not depend on whether the boy was a trespasser. It depends, as I said in *Young* v *Box* on whether the driver, in taking the boy on the milk float, was acting in the course of his employment.

In considering whether a prohibited act was within the course of the employment, it depends very much on the purpose for which it is done. If it is done for his employers' business, it is usually done in the course of his employment, even though it is a prohibited act. That is clear from *Limpus* v *London General Omnibus Co.* [1862] 1 H & C 526, *Young* v *Box* and *Ilkiw* v *Samuels* [1963] 2 All ER 879. But if it is done for some purpose other than his master's business, as, for instance, giving a lift to a hitchhiker, such an act, if prohibited, may not be within the course of his employment. Both *Twine* v *Bean's Express Ltd* (1946) 175 LT 131 and *Conway* v *George Wimpey & Co. Ltd* [1951] 2 KB 266 are to be explained on their own facts as cases where a driver had given a lift to someone else contrary to a prohibition and not for the purposes of the employers. *Iqbal* v *London Transport Executive* [1973] KIR 329 seems to be out of line and should be regarded as decided on its own special circumstances. In the present case it seems to me that the course of Mr Plenty's employment was to distribute the milk, collect the money and to bring back the bottles to the van. He got or allowed this young boy, Leslie Rose, to do part of that business which was the employers' business. It seems to me that although prohibited, it was conduct which was within the course of the employment; and on this ground I think the judge was in error. I agree it is a nice point in these cases on which side of the line the case falls; but, as I understand the authorities, this case falls within those in which the prohibition affects only the conduct within the sphere of the employment and did not take the conduct outside the sphere altogether. I would hold this conduct of Christopher Plenty to be within the course of his employment and the master is liable accordingly, and I would allow the appeal.

In parting with the case, it may be interesting to notice that this type of case is unlikely to arise so much in the future, since a vehicle is not to be used on a road unless there is in force an insurance policy covering, inter alia, injury to passengers.

LAWTON LJ: [dissenting] Ever since 1946 employers of drivers have been entitled to arrange their affairs on the assumption that if they gave clear and express instructions to their drivers that they were not to carry passengers on the employers' vehicles, the employers would not be liable in law for any injury sustained by such passengers. They were entitled to make that assumption because of the decision of this court in *Twine* v *Bean's Express Ltd*. No doubt since 1946 employers when negotiating with their insurers have sought to get reductions in premiums and have done so because of the assumption which, so it seems to me, they were entitled to make about freedom from liability to unauthorised passengers. It may well be that the judgment of Lord Greene MR, as reported, is not as clear as the judgments of that great judge normally were; but it was the judgment of the Master of the Rolls and it was accepted by the other two members of the court, both judges of very great distinction who were later to go to the House of Lords: Morton and Tucker LJJ. If between 1946 and 1951 any employers had the kind of doubts about *Twine's* case which in more recent years have been expressed by academic writers, their minds would have been put at rest by another decision of this court in 1951, namely *Conway* v *George Wimpey & Co. Ltd*. That was a case in which a lorry driver employed by a firm of contractors on a site where many other contractors were working, contrary to his express instructions, gave an employee of another firm of contractors a lift in his lorry. This man was injured whilst a passenger. The problem for the court was whether the injured man could claim against the employers of the lorry driver who had given him a lift. This court, in a unanimous decision, adjudged that the injured man could not claim. The leading judgment was given by Asquith LJ; he gave his reason for saying that what the lorry driver had done had not been done in the course of his employment. He said:

> ... I should hold that taking men other than the defendants' employees on the vehicle was not merely a wrongful mode of performing an act of the class which the driver ... was employed to perform, but was the performance of an act of a class which he was not employed to perform at all.

These two cases have not been overruled by the House of Lords. Insurers have proceeded ever since on the assumption that these cases are properly decided. It would I think be most unfortunate if this court departed from clear decisions save on good and clear grounds. What has been submitted is that those two judgments should not be followed; because when the first defendant, the driver of the milk float, employed the plaintiff to carry bottles for him, he was employing him to do acts which furthered the second defendants' business interests. In my judgment he was doing nothing of the sort. The first defendant had been employed to drive the milk float and deliver the milk. He had not been authorised to sub-contract his work. What he was doing was setting the plaintiff to do the job for which he had been employed and for which he was getting paid. In my judgment in so doing he was acting outside the scope of his employment—just as in the same way as was the driver in *Conway* v *George Wimpey & Co. Ltd*.

If a general principle should be needed to support my opinion in this case, I would adopt the same approach as Lord Greene MR in *Twine's* case. What duty did the second defendants owe to the plaintiff? Counsel for the plaintiff says: 'Oh well, they put the driver with the milk float on the road; they put him into a position to take passengers if he were minded to disobey his instructions and therefore it is socially just that they should be responsible.' I do not agree. When they put the first defendant with his float on the road they put him into a position where he had to take care not to injure those with whom he was reasonably likely to have dealings or to meet, that is all other road users and his customers. They expressly excluded anyone travelling as a passenger on his milk float. He was instructed expressly that he was not to carry passengers. Had he obeyed his instructions, he would not have had a passenger to whom he owed a duty of care. It was his disobedience which brought the injured plaintiff into the class of persons to whom the second defendants vicariously owed a duty of care. He had not been employed to do anything of the kind. In my judgment, the plaintiff has failed to establish that the second defendants owed him any duty of care.

I appreciate that in *Ilkiw* v *Samuels*, to which Lord Denning MR has already referred, Diplock LJ, did say that a broad approach must be made to this problem. But the broad approach must not be so broad that it obscures the principles of law which are applicable. Therein lies the danger of too broad an approach. That can be illustrated by examining Diplock LJ's suggested general question, namely, what was the job on which he, the employee, was engaged for his employer? If that general question is asked without reference to the particular circumstances, the answer in *Twine* v *Bean's Express Ltd* would have been to make Bean's Express liable for his injuries. The van driver in that case had been employed to drive carefully. He had not been employed to drive negligently. When Twine was injured the driver was doing the job he had been employed to do, namely to drive. Unless this court is prepared to say that *Twine* v *Bean's Express Ltd* was wrongly decided, for my part I cannot see how that case can be distinguished from this. In the course of the argument an illustrative example was put to counsel for the plaintiff. He was asked whether if in *Twine's* case the driver had asked the passenger to do some map reading for him in order that he could get more quickly to the place where in the course of his employment he wanted to go, whether that fact would have made the employers liable. Counsel for the plaintiff said it would. In my judgment fine distinctions of that kind should have no place in our law, particularly in a branch of it which affects so many employers and their insurers. Having regard to what has been decided in the past, in my judgment it would be wrong now, without the authority either of the House of Lords or of Parliament, not to follow the 1946 and 1951 cases.

I would dismiss the appeal.

SCARMAN LJ: Should there be an attentive visitor from Mars sitting in court at this moment, he might be forgiven for thinking that he was witnessing the exposure of an irreconcilable breach between two lines of authority in the English common law. But in my judgment no such breach has in fact been opened and the two lines of authority that have led Lawton LJ to differ from the judgment of Lord Denning MR are perfectly well capable, when properly analysed, of being reconciled with the principles of the law as asserted, not for the first time, by Lord Denning MR in his judgment in this case.

Let me begin with a statement of the general principle of vicarious liability, as I understand it in its application to compensation for accidental damage. In words which have frequently been quoted both in the courts and in the universities, Salmond on Torts refers to the basis of vicarious liability for accidental damage as being one of public policy. That view is supported by quotations (dated no doubt, but still full of life) of a dictum of Lord Brougham and of another, one hundred years or more earlier, of Sir John Holt. That it is 'socially convenient and rough justice' to make an employer liable for the torts of his servant in the cases to which the principle applies, was recognised in *Limpus* v *London General Omnibus Co*; see the judgment of Willes J. I think it important to realise that the principle of vicarious liability is one of public policy. It is not a principle which derives from a critical or refined consideration of other concepts in the common law, eg the concept of trespass or indeed the concept of agency. No doubt in particular cases it may be relevant to consider whether a particular plaintiff was or was not a trespasser. Similarly, when, as I shall indicate, it is important that one should determine the course of employment of the servant, the law of agency may have some marginal relevance. But basically, as I understand it, the employer is made vicariously liable for the tort of his employee not because the plaintiff is an invitee, nor because of the authority possessed by the servant, but because it is a case in which the employer, having put matters into motion, should be liable if the motion that he has originated leads to damage to another. What is the approach which the cases identify as the correct approach in order to determine this question of public policy? First, as Lord Denning MR has already said, one looks to see whether the servant has committed a tort on the plaintiff. In the present case it is clear that the first defendant, the servant of the dairy company, who are the second defendants, by the negligent driving of the milk float, caused injury to the plaintiff, a boy 13½ years old, who was on the float at his invitation. There was therefore a tort committed by the servant. The next question, as Lord Denning MR has said, is whether the employer should shoulder the liability for compensating the person injured by the tort. With all respect to the points developed by Lawton LJ, it does appear to me to be clear, since the decision of *Limpus* v *London General Omnibus Co*, that that question has to be answered by directing attention to what the first defendant was employed to do when he committed the tort that has caused damage to the plaintiff. The first defendant was, of course, employed at the time of the accident to do a whole number of operations. He was certainly not employed to give the plaintiff a lift, and if one confines one's analysis of the facts to the incident of injury to the plaintiff, then no doubt one would say that carrying the plaintiff on the float—giving him a lift—was not in the course of the first defendant's employment. But in *Ilkiw* v *Samuels* Diplock LJ indicated that the proper approach to the nature of the servant's employment is a broad one. He said:

> As each of these nouns implies [he is referring to the nouns used to describe course of employment, sphere, scope and so forth] the matter must be looked at broadly, not dissecting the servant's task into its component activities—such as driving, loading, sheeting and the like—by asking: What was the job on which he was engaged for his employer? and answering that question as a jury would.

Applying those words to the employment of the first defendant, I think it is clear from the evidence that he was employed as a roundsman to drive his float round his round and to deliver milk, to collect empties and to obtain payment. That was his job. He was under an express prohibition—a matter to which I shall refer later—not to enlist the help of anyone doing that work. And he was also under an express prohibition not to give lifts on the float to anyone. How did he choose to carry out the task which I have analysed? He chose to disregard the prohibition and to enlist the assistance of the plaintiff. As a matter of common sense, that does seem to me to be a mode, albeit a prohibited mode, of doing the job with which he was entrusted. Why was the plaintiff being carried on the float when the accident occurred? Because it was necessary to take him from point to point so that he could assist in delivering milk, collecting empties and, on occasions, obtaining payment. The plaintiff was there because it was necessary that he should be there in order that he could assist, albeit in a way prohibited by the employers, in the job entrusted to the first defendant by his employers . . .

It is for those reasons that I agree with Lord Denning MR, and if that visitor from Mars is still in court after this long judgment, he will return to his planet conscious that one member of the court sees no irreconcilable difference opening up in the common law.

1.1.2.2   Connection with employer's business

FAULKNER v CHIEF ADJUDICATION OFFICER, The Times, 8 April 1994 (CA)

The Court of Appeal, following *Ex parte Michael* held that a police officer who was injured while playing for his police football team could not claim industrial injury benefit because his injury was not suffered in the course of his employment.

NEILL LJ: It made no difference whether he was on duty or not. The question was whether at the time he was doing his job.

The appellant argued that *Ex parte Michael* should be viewed in the light of changes in society, in the police and in the community's perception of the role of the police. Reference was made to riots in 1981 and 1985 and to the miners' strike in 1984. The whole ethos of policing had changed since those dates. It was no longer enough to say that such things as football amounted to recreation for the police. The price to pay for that was that the police had to be protected by industrial injuries benefit.

In *Nancollas* v *Insurance Officer* [1985] 1 All ER 833 the court said that 'in a changed social matrix, the foundation of the employment relationship is no longer so much based on orders and instructions as on requests and information and contractual rights and duties are supplemented by mutual expectations of cooperation . . . We cannot overemphasise the importance of looking at the factual picture as a whole and rejecting any approach based on the fallacious concept that any one factor is conclusive.'

To the extent that *Ex parte Michael* conflicted with *Nancollas* Mr Hand submitted that the social matrix approach was to be preferred in deciding what was or was not reasonably incidental to the employment of the police officer in that context.

In his Lordship's judgment, the question whether, when playing football for the police team, the appellant had been in the course of his employment could not be answered by considering whether he had been doing something reasonably incidental to that work.

The first question was what was the extent of the appellant's employment? Implication of a contractual term was not to be made because it seemed sensible or reasonable to the appeal tribunal that such a term should be implied, or because the chief police officer, the Police Federation representative or the appellant regarded community policing as a good and useful policy, as no doubt it was, but according to ordinary legal principle which was that an obligation might be read into a contract 'if it is such as the nature of the contract itself implicitly requires, no more, no less: a test, in other words, of necessity': see *Liverpool City Council* v *Irwin* [1977] AC 239, 254.

The decision in *Nancollas* provided no basis upon which the court could depart from or distinguish *Ex parte Michael*. In *Nancollas* the question had been whether the claimant was at the relevant time engaged on an activity which had been in the course of his employment or whether he was going from his home to another place in order to resume the course of his employment.

It was for the purpose of answering that question that the court had emphasised the importance of looking at the factual picture as a whole and rejecting any approach based on the fallacious concept that any one factor was conclusive.

In his Lordship's judgment, the commissioner had been right to hold as he did. There had been no evidence before the tribunal upon which it could properly have held that the appellant had been injured in the course of his employment.

Lord Justice Farquharson and Lord Justice Hoffmann gave concurring judgments.

MORRIS v C W MARTIN & SONS LTD [1965] 2 All ER 725 (CA)

The plaintiff sent her fur coat to be cleaned by the defendants, who entrusted their employee with the task. He stole the coat, and the defendants were found liable on two grounds viz. the goods had been entrusted to him, therefore the theft was committed in the course of employment; and the defendants as bailees of the coat, owed the plaintiff a duty to take reasonable care of it. The theft by the employee, to whom they had delegated responsibility, was a breach of that duty.

LORD DENNING MR: The case raises the important question of how far a master is liable for theft or dishonesty by one of his servants. If the master has himself been at fault in not employing a trustworthy man, of course he is liable. But what is the position when the master is not himself at fault at all?

The law on this subject has developed greatly over the years. During the nineteenth century it was accepted law that a master was liable for the dishonesty or fraud of his servant if it was done in the course of his employment *and* for his master's benefit. Dishonesty or fraud by the servant for his *own* benefit took the case out of the course of his employment. The judges took this simple view: No servant who turns thief and steals is acting in the course of his employment. He is acting outside it altogether. But in 1912 the law was revolutionised by the case of *Lloyd v Grace, Smith & Co.* [1912] AC 716, where it was held that a master was liable for the dishonesty or fraud of his servant if it was done within the course of his employment, no matter whether it was done for the benefit of the master or for the benefit of the servant. Nevertheless there still remains the question: What is meant by the phrase 'in the course of his employment'? When can it be said that the dishonesty or fraud of a servant, done for his *own* benefit, is in the course of his employment?

On this question the cases are baffling. In particular those cases, much discussed before us, where a bailee's servant dishonestly drives a vehicle for his own benefit. These stretch from *The Coupé Co.* v *Maddick* to the present day. Let me take an illustration well fitted for a moot. Suppose the owner of a car takes it to a garage to be repaired. It is repaired by a garage-hand who is then told to drive it back to the owner. But instead, he takes it out on a 'frolic of his own' (to use the nineteenth-century phrase) or on a 'joy-ride' (to come into the twentieth century). He takes it out, let us say, on a drunken escapade or on a thieving expedition. Nay more, for it is all the same, let us suppose the garage-hand steals the car himself and drives off at speed. He runs into a motor-cyclist. Both the car and the motor-cycle are damaged. Both owners sue the garage proprietor for the negligence of his servant. The motor-cyclist clearly cannot recover against the garage proprietor for the simple reason that at the time of the accident the servant was not acting in the course of his employment; see *Storey* v *Ashton* [1869] LR 4 QB 476. You might think also that the owner of the car could not recover, and for the self-same reason, namely, that the servant was *not* acting in the course of his employment. Before 1912 the courts would undoubtedly have so held; see *Sanderson* v *Collins*, *Cheshire* v *Bailey*, as explained by Lord Shaw of Dunfermline in *Lloyd* v *Grace, Smith & Co.* itself. But since 1912 it seems fairly clear that the owner of the damaged car could recover from the garage proprietor; see *Central Motors (Glasgow), Ltd* v *Cessnock Garage and Motor Co.*, on the ground that, although the garage-hand was using the car for his own private purposes, 'he should be regarded as still acting in the course of his employment' (see *Aitchison* v *Page Motors, Ltd*): and even if he stole the car on the journey, it was a conversion 'in the course of the employment' (see *United Africa Co., Ltd* v *Saka Owoade*). I ask myself, how can this be? How can the servant, on one and the same journey, be acting both within and without the course of his employment? Within *qua* the car owner. Without *qua* the motor-cyclist. It is time we got rid of this confusion. And the only way to do it, so far as I can see, is by reference to the duty laid by the law on the master. The duty of the garage proprietor to the owner of the car is very different from his duty to the motor-cyclist. He owes to the owner of the car the duty of a bailee for reward, whereas he owes no such duty to the motor-cyclist on the road. He does not even owe him a duty to use care not to injure him.

If you go through the cases on this difficult subject, you will find that in the ultimate analysis, they depend on the nature of the duty owed by the master towards the person whose goods have been lost or damaged. If the master is under a duty to use due care to keep goods safely and protect them from theft and depredation, he cannot get rid of his responsibility by delegating his duty to another. If he entrusts that duty to his servant, he is answerable for the way in which the servant conducts himself therein. No matter whether the servant be negligent, fraudulent, or dishonest, the master is liable. But not when he is under no such duty . . .

From all these instances we may deduce the general proposition that when a principal has in his charge the goods or belongings of another in such circumstances that he is under a duty to take all reasonable precautions to protect them from theft or depredation, then if he entrusts that duty to a servant or agent, he is answerable for the manner in which that servant or agent carries out his duty. If the servant or agent is careless so that they are stolen by a stranger, the master is liable. So also if the servant or agent himself steals them or makes away with them . . .

DIPLOCK LJ: One of the common law duties owed by a bailee of goods to his bailor is not to convert them, i.e., not to do intentionally in relation to the goods an act inconsistent with the bailor's right of property therein (see *Caxton Publishing Co., Ltd* v *Sutherland Publishing Co., Ltd, per* Lord Porter). This duty, which is common to all bailments as well as to other relationships which do not amount to bailment, is independent of and additional to the other common law duty of a bailee for reward to take reasonable care of his bailor's goods. Stealing goods is the simplest example of conversion; but, perhaps because in his classic judgment in *Coggs* v *Bernard*, Sir John Holt CJ discusses the circumstances in which bailees are liable to their bailors for the loss of goods stolen not by the servant of the bailee but by a stranger, some confusion has, I think, arisen in later cases through failure to recognise the co-existence of the two duties of a bailee for reward: to take reasonable care of his bailor's goods and not to convert them—even by stealing.

If the bailee in the present case had been a natural person and had converted the plaintiff's fur by stealing it himself, no one would have argued that he was not liable to her for its loss; but the defendant bailees are a corporate person. They could not perform their duties to the plaintiff to take reasonable care of the fur and not to convert it otherwise than vicariously by natural persons acting as their servants or agents. It was one of their servants, to whom they had entrusted the care and custody of the fur for the purpose of doing work on it, who converted it by stealing it. Why should they not be vicariously liable for this breach of their duty by the vicar whom they had chosen to perform it? Sir John Holt, I think, would have answered that they were liable 'for seeing that someone must be the loser by this deceit it is more reason that he who employs and puts a trust and confidence in the deceiver should be the loser than a stranger' (*Hern* v *Nichols*) . . .

The judgments in *Cheshire* v *Bailey* seem to me, with great respect, to show a confusion between two distinct lines of authority; that of the frolicsome coachman and that of the dishonest servant. A coachman had a tendency, well-recognised in the nineteenth century, to drive off with his master's vehicle on a 'frolic of his own' and sometimes to injure a passer-by while indulging in this foible. The only connection between the injury to the passer-by and the master's act in employing the coachman was that, but for such employment, the coachman would probably not have had the opportunity of driving off with the vehicle at all. At a period when judges themselves commonly employed coachmen, this connection was regarded as too tenuous to render the master vicariously liable to the passer-by for the injury caused by the coachman, at any rate if the master had exercised reasonable care in selecting him for employment. The immunity of the master from vicarious liability for tortious acts of a servant while engaged on a frolic can be rationalised in a variety of ways. The master's employment of the servant was only a *causa sine qua non* of the injury: it was not the *causa causans*. It was not 'foreseeable' by the master that his employment of the servant would cause injury to the person who sustained it. The master gave no authority to the servant to create an Atkinian proximity relationship between the master and the person injured by the servant's acts. One or other of these relationships underlies the common phrase in which the test of the master's liability is expressed: 'Was the servant's act within the scope or course of his employment?' . . . .

If the principle laid down in *Lloyd* v *Grace, Smith & Co.* is applied to the facts of the present case, the defendants cannot in my view escape liability for the conversion of the plaintiff's fur by their servant Morrissey. They accepted the fur as bailees for reward in order to clean it. They put Morrissey as their agent in their place to clean the fur and to take charge of it while doing so. The manner in which he conducted himself in doing that work was to convert it. What he was doing, albeit dishonestly, he was doing in the scope or course of his employment in the technical sense of that infelicitious but time-honoured phrase. The defendants as his masters are responsible for his tortious act.

I should add that we are not concerned here with gratuitous bailment. That is a relationship in which the bailee's duties of care in his custody of the goods are different from those of a bailee for reward. It may be that his duties being passive rather than active, the concept of vicarious performance of them is less apposite. However this may be, I express no views as to the circumstances in which he would be liable for conversion of the goods by his servant. Nor are we concerned with what would have been the liability of the defendants if the fur had been stolen by another servant of theirs who was not employed by them to clean the fur or to have the care or custody of it. The mere fact that his employment by the defendants gave him the opportunity to steal it would not suffice. The crucial distinction between *Lloyd* v *Grace, Smith & Co.* and *Ruben and Ladenburg* v *Great Fingall Consolidated* is that in the latter case the dishonest servant was neither actually nor ostensibly employed to warrant the genuineness of certificates for shares in the company which employed him. His fraudulent conduct was facilitated by the access which he had to the company's seal and documents in the course of his employment for another purpose: but the fraud itself which was the only tort giving rise to a civil liability to the plaintiffs was not committed in the course of doing that class of acts which the company had put the servant in his place to do.

I base my decision in this case on the ground that the fur was stolen by the very servant whom the defendants as bailees for reward had employed to take care of it and to clean it.

Salmon LJ concurred with Diplock LJ.

ILKIW v SAMUELS [1963] 2 All ER 879

A lorry (truck) driver, employed by the defendants, was loading up on a third party's premises and allowed an employee of that third party to assist him in his work by driving the vehicle. The lorry driver's employers, the defendants, had given him strict instructions not to allow any one else to drive the lorry.

The lorry driver knew nothing about his 'assistant's' ability in driving; in fact, the latter had never driven a lorry before that occasion and did not possess a driving licence. The plaintiff was injured as a result of the 'assistant's' incompetent handling of the vehicle.

At first instance the defendants were found liable for the negligence of their lorry driver in allowing this person to drive his vehicle, and the Court of Appeal affirmed this decision. It was found that the lorry driver was negligent **either**.

■ in allowing the person to drive without first checking his ability to handle the vehicle; **or**

■ because the lorry was driven negligently while it was in his control;

and in **either** case

■ that this negligence arose in the course of his employment.

His employer's prohibition against unauthorised persons driving the vehicle affected only the **mode** of doing his job. Thus, his disobedience did not take his behaviour outside the course of his employment.

WILMER, LJ: . . . the mere fact that the act complained of was done in disobedience to express instructions is of no necessary materiality in deciding whether or not the act was within the course of the employment. It seems to me that those authorities to which I have referred leave no doubt whatsoever as to the principle which is involved in this case. Once again, as is not uncommon, the difficulty is to apply the principle to the unusual facts of the case.

In the end I have come to the conclusion without any hesitation that the judge was right in the conclusion at which he arrived, and for the reasons which he gave. The driver of the vehicle . . . as I see it, was employed, not only to drive, but also to be in charge of his vehicle in all circumstances during any such times as he was on duty. That means to say that, even when he was not himself sitting at the controls, he remained in charge of the lorry, and in charge as his employers' representative. His employers must remain liable for his negligence so long as the vehicle was being used in the course of their business. As I understand the authorities, the employers escape liability if, but only if, at the time of the negligent act, the vehicle was being used by the driver for the purpose of what has been called a 'frolic' of his own. That is not this case. Here, at the material time, this vehicle was in fact being used in the course of the defendants' business. In those circumstances it appears to me that there is no ground on which the defendants can escape liability . . .

Many authorities have been cited about the vicarious liability of a master for the torts of his servants, for the law is nearly always most obscure in those fields in which judges say: 'The principle is plain, but the difficulty lies in its application to particular facts.' The principle as set out in Salmond on Torts in the passages already cited by my lord is clear; and in approving those passages in Canadian *Pacific Rail. Co.* v *Lockhart* Lord Thankerton also cited with approval the dictum of Lord Dunedin in *Plumb* v *Cobden Flour Mills Co., Ltd.* that '. . . there are prohibitions which limit the sphere of employment, and prohibitions which only deal with conduct within the sphere of employment'. In cases such as this, where there is an express prohibition, the decision into which of these two classes the prohibition falls seems to me to involve first determining what would have been the sphere, scope, course (all these nouns are used) of the servant's employment if the prohibition had not been imposed. As each of these nouns implies, the matter must be looked at broadly, not dissecting the servant's task into its component activities—such as driving, loading, sheeting and the like—by asking: What was the job on which he was engaged for his employer? and answering that question as a jury would.

In the present case it appears to me that the job on which [the lorry driver] was engaged for his employers was to collect a load of sugar at the sugar factory and transport it to its destination, using for that purpose his employers' lorry of which he was put in charge. The express prohibition was against permitting anyone else to drive the lorry in the course of performing this job. This, it seems to me, was a prohibition on the mode in which he was to do that which he was employed to do, a prohibition dealing with conduct within the sphere of employment.

A & W HEMPHILL LTD v WILLIAMS [1966] 2 Lloyd's Rep 101

The plaintiff was a member of the Boys' Brigade which had been camping in Argyllshire. At the conclusion of the camp the boys were to be taken back to Glasgow in the defendants' coach. The boys persuaded the defendants' driver to leave the more direct route and drive through Stirling, though the driver had been refused permission to do this. Later, the driver was persuaded to make another detour and on the way an accident occurred due to the negligence of the driver, and the plaintiff was injured. The House of Lords held that the defendants were liable because the driver remained in the course of his employment as he was primarily employed to drive the boys to Glasgow, and this he was still doing at the time of the accident.

KAY v ITW LTD [1967] 3 All ER 22

An employee employed by the defendants to drive a fork-lift truck, was unable to get into the warehouse which was obstructed by a lorry. The driver of the lorry could easily have been asked to move it, but the employee got into the lorry to move it himself. In doing so he negligently injured the plaintiff. Although the act was foolhardy and unnecessary, it was still held to be within the course of the employee's employment, as it was in the course of his employment to move certain obstacles, e.g. a packing case obstructing the path of his fork-lift truck. To do what he did, therefore, was a wrong mode of doing what he was employed to do, rather than something which he was not employed to do.

1.2 Contributions between Tortfeasors

CIVIL LIABILITY (CONTRIBUTION) ACT 1978

1. Entitlement to contribution

(1)   Subject to the following provisions of this section, any person liable in respect of any damage suffered by another person may recover contribution from any other person liable in respect of the same damage (whether jointly with him or otherwise).

(2)   A person shall be entitled to recover contribution by virtue of subsection (1) above notwithstanding that he has ceased to be liable in respect of the damage in question since the time when the damage occurred, provided that he was so liable immediately before he made or was ordered or agreed to make the payment in respect of which the contribution is sought.

(3)   A person shall be liable to make contribution by virtue of subsection (1) above notwithstanding that he has ceased to be liable in respect of the damage in question since the time when the damage occurred, unless he ceased to be liable by virtue of the expiry of a period of limitation or prescription which extinguished the right on which the claim against him in respect of the damage was based.

(4)   A person who has made or agreed to make any payment in bona fide settlement or compromise of any claim made against him in respect of any damage (including a payment into court which has been accepted) shall be entitled to recover contribution in accordance with this section without regard to whether or not he himself is or ever was liable in respect of the damage, provided, however, that he would have been liable assuming that the factual basis of the claim against him could be established.

(5)   A judgment given in any action brought in any part of the United Kingdom by or on behalf of the person who suffered the damage in question against any person from whom contribution is sought under this section shall be conclusive in the proceedings for contribution as to any issue determined by that judgment in favour of the person from whom the contribution is sought.

(6)   References in this section to a person's liability in respect of any damage are references to any such liability which has been or could be established in an action brought

against him in England and Wales by or on behalf of the person who suffered the damage; but it is immaterial whether any issue arising in any such action was or would be determined (in accordance with the rules of private international law) by reference to the law of a country outside England and Wales.

2. Assessment of contribution

(1)   Subject to subsection (3) below, in any proceedings for contribution under section 1 above the amount of the contribution recoverable from any person shall be such as may be found by the court to be just and equitable having regard to the extent of that person's responsibility for the damage in question.

(2)   Subject to subsection (3) below, the court shall have power in any such proceedings to exempt any person from liability to make contribution or to direct that the contribution to be recovered from any person shall amount to a complete indemnity.

(3)   Where the amount of the damages which have or might have been awarded in respect of the damage in question in any action brought in England and Wales by or on behalf of the person who suffered it against the person from whom the contribution is sought was or would have been subject to—

(a)   any limit imposed by or under any enactment or by any agreement made before the damage occurred;

(b)   any reduction by virtue of section 1 of the Law Reform (Contributory Negligence) Act 1945 or section 5 of the Fatal Accidents Act 1976; or

(c)   any corresponding limit or reduction under the law of a country outside England and Wales;

the person from whom the contribution is sought shall not by virtue of any contribution awarded under section 1 above be required to pay in respect of the damage a greater amount than the amount of those damages as so limited or reduced.

3. Proceedings against persons jointly liable for the same debt or damage

Judgment recovered against any person liable in respect of any debt or damage shall not be a bar to an action, or to the continuance of an action, against any other person who is (apart from any such bar) jointly liable with him in respect of the same debt or damage.

4. Successive actions against persons liable (jointly or otherwise) for the same damage

If more than one action is brought in respect of any damage by or on behalf of the person by whom it was suffered against persons liable in respect of the damage (whether jointly or otherwise) the plaintiff shall not be entitled to costs in any of those actions, other than that in which judgment is first given, unless the court is of the opinion that there was reasonable ground for bringing the action.

5. Application to the Crown

Without prejudice to section 4(1) of the Crown Proceedings Act 1947 (indemnity and contribution), this Act shall bind the Crown, but nothing in this Act shall be construed as in any way affecting Her Majesty in Her private capacity (including in right of Her Duchy of Lancaster) or the Duchy of Cornwall.

6. Interpretation

(1)   A person is liable in respect of any damage for the purposes of this Act if the person who suffered it (or anyone representing his estate or dependants) is entitled to recover compensation from him in respect of that damage (whatever the legal basis of his liability, whether tort, breach of contract, breach of trust or otherwise).

(2)   References in this Act to an action brought by or on behalf of the person who suffered any damage include references to an action brought for the benefit of his estate or dependants.

(3)   In this Act 'dependants' has the same meaning as in the Fatal Accidents Act 1976.

(4)   In this Act, except in section 1(5) above, 'action' means an action brought in England and Wales.

7. Savings

(3)   The right to recover contribution in accordance with section 1 above supersedes any right, other than an express contractual right, to recover contribution (as distinct from

indemnity) otherwise than under this Act in corresponding circumstances; but nothing in this Act shall affect—

(a)   any express or implied contractual or other right to indemnity; or

(b)   any express contractual provision regulating or excluding contribution; which would be enforceable apart from this Act (or render enforceable any agreement for indemnity or contribution which would not be enforceable apart from this Act).

1.3   Summary

SALSBURY v WOODLAND AND OTHERS [1969] 3 All ER 863 (CA)

The first defendant, D1, employed the second defendant, D2, who was an apparently competent independent contractor, to fell a large tree in his front garden, which was near the highway. Due to D2's negligence the tree fouled some telephone wires as it fell, bringing the wires down across the highway. The third defendant, D3, negligently drove his vehicle into the wires. As a result of all this the plaintiff was injured, and the question of D1's liability for D2's negligence arose for consideration by the court.

WIDGERY LJ: . . . The first defendant appreciated that the felling of this tree was not a job for an amateur like himself, and his wife was considering how expert assistance might be acquired. Some days before 5th July she had seen in an adjacent road a party of men felling trees. She asked the foreman whether one of his men would come and take down this hawthorn tree for her. The foreman said that he would enquire and next day told the first defendant's wife that a Mr Coombe, the second defendant, was prepared to do this work. The first defendant's wife, quite properly, accepted the second defendant as a man of competence and experience for the job. . . .

At the trial, as is understandable, many difficult questions of causation and foreseeability were considered. The case against the three defendants, in a nutshell, was this. It was said that the second defendant (the tree-feller) had been negligent in felling the tree and that that negligence was the cause of foreseeable injury to the plaintiff. It was said, and was found by the learned judge, that the first defendant was liable for that injury because in the circumstances of this case the judge held that he was liable for the negligence of the second defendant. Thirdly, it was said that the third defendant was negligent in that when driving up the road he either saw the telephone wires and failed to take evasive action or alternatively was negligent in that he ought to have seen the telephone wires and ought again to have taken evasive action but failed to do so.

Any question of causation resulting from the negligence of the third defendant is a matter which does not arise in this appeal and I am therefore spared the necessity of going into it in any detail. So far as the second defendant is concerned, judgment was obtained against him, I think in default of defence. No issue of his liability was raised here. The appeals of the first and third defendants respectively raise quite different questions and therefore they can conveniently be dealt with separately . . .

[Further references to the case against the third defendant, whose appeal was dismissed, are omitted, since they are not relevant to the topic of vicarious liabilty.]

It is, of course, trite law that an employer who employs an independent contractor is not vicariously responsible for the negligence of that contractor. He is not able to control the way in which the independent contractor does the work and the vicarious obligation of a master for the negligence of his servant does not arise under the relationship of employer and independent contractor. I think it is entirely accepted that these cases—and there are some—in which an employer has been held liable for injury done by the negligence of an independent contractor are in truth cases where the employer owes a direct duty to the person injured, a duty which he cannot delegate to the contractor on his behalf. The whole question in this case is whether, in the circumstances which I have briefly outlined, the first defendant is to be judged by the general rule, which would result in no liability, or whether he comes within one of the somewhat special exceptions—cases in which a direct duty to see that care is taken rests on the employer throughout the operation. . . .

In truth, according to the authorities there are a number of well-determined classes of case in which this direct and primary duty on an employer to see that care is taken exists. Two such classes are directly relevant for consideration in this case. The first class concerns what have sometimes been described as 'extra hazardous acts'—acts commissioned by an employer which are so hazardous in their character that the law has thought it proper to impose this direct obligation on the employer to see that care is taken. . . .

I do not propose to add to the wealth of authority on this topic by attempting further to define the meaning of 'extra hazardous acts'; but I am confident that the act commissioned in the present case cannot come within that category. The act commissioned in the present case, if done with ordinary elementary caution by skilled men, presented no hazard to anyone at all.

The second class of case which is relevant for consideration of the present dispute concerns dangers created in a highway. There are a number of cases on this branch of the law, a good example of which is *Holliday* v *National Telephone Co.* [1899] 2 QB 392 . . . These, on analysis, will all be found to be cases where work was being done in a highway and was work of a character which would have been a nuisance unless authorised by statute. It will be found in all these cases that the statutory powers under which the employer commissioned the work were statutory powers which left on the employer a duty to see that due care was taken in the carrying out of the work, for the protection of those who passed on the highway. In accordance with principle, an employer subject to such a direct and personal duty cannot excuse himself if things go wrong merely because the direct cause of the injury was the act of the independent contractor.

This again is not a case in that class. It is not a case in that class because in the instant case no question of doing work in the highway, which might amount to a nuisance if due care was not taken, arises. In my judgment, the present case is clearly outside the well-defined limit of the second class to which I have referred. Counsel for the plaintiff accordingly invited us to say that there is a third class into which the instant case precisely falls and he suggested that the third class comprised those cases where an employer commissions work to be done *near* a highway in circumstances in which, if due care is not taken, injury to passers-by on the highway may be caused. If that be a third class of case to which the principle of liability of the employer applies, no doubt the present facts would come within the description. The question is, is such a third class?

Reliance is placed primarily on three authorities. The first is *Holliday's* case, to which I have already referred. *Holliday's* case was a case of work being done in a highway by undertakers laying telephone wires. The injury was caused by the negligent act of a servant of the independent contractor who was soldering joints in the telephone wires. The cause of the injury was the immersion of a defective blow-lamp in a pot of solder, and the pot of solder was physically on the highway—according to the report, on the footpath. The Earl of Halsbury, LC, holding the employers responsible for that negligence, in my view, on a simple application of the cases applicable to highway nuisance to which I have already referred, put his opinion in these words: 'Therefore, works were being executed in proximity to a highway, in which in the ordinary course of things an explosion might take place.' Counsel for the plaintiff draws our attention to the phrase 'in proximity to a highway' and submits that that supports his contention on this point. I am not impressed by this argument, because the source of danger in *Holliday's* case was itself on the highway and also because I do not think it follows (although one need not decide the point today) that in the true highway cases to which I have referred the actual source of injury must arise on the highway itself. Counsel for the plaintiff said that in *Holliday's* case it would have been ridiculous if there had been liability because the pot of solder was on the highway but no liability if it was two feet off the highway. That is an observation with which I entirely sympathise; but I can find nothing in Lord Halsbury's use of the word 'proximity' to justify the view that there is therefore a special class of case on the lines submitted by counsel.

The second case relied on is *Tarry* v *Ashton*, where a building adjoining the highway had attached to it a heavy lamp which was suspended over the footway and which was liable to be a source of injury to passers-by if allowed to fall into disrepair. It fell into disrepair, and injury was caused. The defendant sought to excuse himself by saying that he had employed a competent independent contractor to put the lamp into good repair and that the cause of the injury was the fault of the independent contractor. Counsel for the plaintiff argues that that case illustrates the special sympathy which with the law regards passers-by on the highway. He says this demonstrates that the law has always been inclined to give special protection to persons in that category and so supports his argument that any action adjacent to the highway may be subject to special rights. But in my judgment that is not so. *Tarry* v *Ashton*, seems to me to be a perfectly ordinary and straightforward example of a case where the employer was under a positive and continuing duty to see that the lamp was kept in repair. That duty was imposed on him before the contractor came and after the contractor had gone; and on the principle that such a duty cannot be delegated the responsibility of the employer in that case seems to me to be fully demonstrated. I cannot find that it produces on a side-wind, as it were, anything in support of counsel for the plaintiff's contention.

The last one to which I will refer on this point is *Walsh* v *Holst & Co., Ltd* a decision of this court. In that case the occupier of premises adjoining the highway was carrying out works of reconstruction which involved knocking out large areas of the front wall. He employed for this purpose a contractor, and the contractor employed a sub-contractor. It was obvious to all, no doubt, that such an operation was liable to cause injury to passers-by by falling bricks unless special precautions against that eventuality were taken. Indeed very considerable precautions were so taken. However, on a day when the only workman employed was an employee of the sub-contractor one brick escaped the protective net, fell in the street and injured a passer-by. The passer-by-plaintiff brought his action against the occupier, the contractor, and the sub-contractor, relying on the doctrine of res ipsa loquitur. In my judgment, the only thing that was really decided by that case was that on those facts the precautions which had been taken against such an injury rebutted the presumption of negligence which might otherwise have arisen under the doctrine of res ipsa loquitur. No attempt appears to have been made in argument to distinguish the liability of the occupier as compared with that of the contractor or sub-contractor, and it certainly was not material to the decision; but counsel for the plaintiff relies on it for dicta which unquestionably are helpful to him. . . . this decision was obiter because the case turned on the absence of negligence and not on any nice question of which of the defendants might have been liable if negligence had been proved.

Accordingly, in my judgment, there is no third class of cases of the kind put forward by counsel for the plaintiff; and it was for those reasons that I concurred in the court's decision, already announced, that the appeal of the first defendant should be allowed and the judgment against him set aside. . . .

Sachs LJ and Harman LJ concurred.

1.4 End of Chapter Assessment Question

Chris lends to his friend, Ray, a van driver, Geoff, as a temporary replacement for Ray's own driver who is ill. While making deliveries in Ray's van one day, Geoff decides to pull in for lunch at a café, and in so doing negligently knocks down and injures Liz. He is so upset by this that he drives to a pub some miles away and proceeds to get drunk. At the pub he meets Michelle and offers to drive her home, but on the way he negligently collides with another vehicle and Michelle is injured.

Advise Liz and Michelle on any claims they may have for damages in the law of tort.

1.5 End of Chapter Assessment Outline Answer

Geoff (G) has been negligent in driving a vehicle and as a result Liz (L) and Michelle (M) have been injured. Another vehicle has been damaged in the accident, but the question seeks advice only with regard to personal injuries of L and M.

There would probably be little difficulty in establishing a legal duty to take care on the facts: *Donoghue* v *Stevenson* 'neighbour principle' (see, e.g., *Nettleship* v *Weston*). This duty would be that owed by a road user to other road users. Duty—to drive without carelessness; to observe the standard of care of the reasonable man in the circumstances. We are told in the question that G has been negligent.

G is probably **personally** liable in respect of the damage. The question arises, however, whether Ray (R) would also be liable. There being no evidence of personal fault, or other tortious behaviour on his part, the issue of his **vicarious liability** for the tortious act(s) of G arises for discussion.

A 'master' or employer may be vicariously liable for the tort(s) of his 'servant' or employee, committed **in the course of the latter's employment**. Who, in law, is a servant? Various tests have been formulated in the cases. (A brief summary of these tests should be given at this point.) The traditional 'control' test may be appropriate in this case. It would be necessary to look at the nature of G's job, which is the fairly uncomplicated task of driving a van.

However, Chris (C) normally employs G and on this occasion has loaned G to R. Is G the servant of C or R or of both? In the case of a 'borrowed' servant there is a strong **presumption** that the servant concerned remains in the service of the usual employer (C in this case) in which case the servant will be the transferee's independent contractor. Much depends on the circumstances of each case. The question to be answered is: Has the servant been so completely 'taken over' that he becomes the servant of the borrower?

The leading authority on this issue is *Mersey Docks & Harbour Board* v *Coggins*, in which the borrowed crane driver was held by the House of Lords to be the servant of the general employer because of the following factors: he continued to be paid by the Board which alone had the power to dismiss him, the borrower could give him directions as to the work to be done but could not instruct him in the operation of the crane. These factors outweighed the fact that the contract of hire (is there such a contract in the present case?), provided that the driver should be the servant of the borrowers or hirers since this, as far as vicarious liability was concerned, was for judicial rather than contractual determination.

Factors which **may affect a decision** are: whether the servant lent is technically skilled (since the service of an unskilled servant is more easily transferred) and whether the servant is lent for a specified task or for the general purposes of the transferee.

In the present case, the question of whether R is the master of G is difficult to determine because insufficient facts are given. It is, however, reasonable to assume that a van driver is unskilled and this factor, together with other relevant facts (see above) **may** indicate that G is, for present purposes, R's servant, so distinguishing the problem from that presented to the court in *Coggins* (above); but the **presumption** must be that he remains in the employment of C. (Their Lordships in *Coggins* were of the opinion that the **lender** has the burden of rebutting this presumption in each case.)

Has C obtained an **indemnity** from R?

It is essential that the servant's tortious act must have been committed in the **course of the latter's employment**. What lies within a particular servant's employment is essentially a question of **fact** in each case. The authorities indicate the following factors as relevant for the purpose of determining issues of 'course of employment':

(i)   time, space (authorised expressly/implied) e.g., detours (degree and purpose will be important here), 'frolics' of the servant's own;

(ii)   any prohibitions issued by master;

(iii)   acts reasonably incidental to work, though not strictly part of it;

(iv)   criminal/deliberate conduct of the servant;

(v)   job performed in unauthorised way/not doing job at all.

The following are some of the authorities which illustrate such matters:

> *Smith* v *Stages*; *Limpus* v *London General Omnibus Co.*, *Century Insurance Co.* v *Northern Ireland Road Transport Board*; *Whatman* v *Pearson*; *Hilton* v *Burton*; *Rose* v *Plenty*; *Elleanor* v *Cavendish Woodhouse*; *Heasemans* v *Clarity Cleaning Co. Ltd.*

With respect to L's injuries, it is arguable that G was acting within the course of his employment at the time she was injured. A lunch break (we do not know the precise terms of G's employment) would probably be regarded as incidental to his job; it would be difficult to classify this as a 'frolic'. Whether the servant is on a frolic of his own is often a question of degree.

It is probably the case that G, in visiting the pub, is acting outside the course of his employment. This might well be a 'frolic' of his own. He is probably **not** doing his job at this stage and is still on the 'frolic' when he picks up M and takes her home, injuring her and damaging the other vehicle. Furthermore, as regards M's injuries, the giving of lifts to unauthorised persons (in this case there appear to be no express prohibitions) have in the past been regarded as outside the scope of a servant's employment. In *Rose* v *Plenty* the court was able to distinguish on the facts, and found the act to be within the relevant course of employment, because the plaintiff was engaged in the employer's business. M may therefore have only a personal action against G (as may anyone bringing an action in respect of the damaged vehicle).

The driver of the other vehicle may have been responsible, together with G, for the collision. In that case, he/she will be regarded as 'several concurrent tortfeasor' with G and the provisions of the Civil Liability (Contributions) Act 1978 are applicable.

Where R and/or C may be vicariously liable for G's negligence, he and/or C will be regarded as a joint tortfeasor with G for the purposes of the 1978 Act (above). R and/or C may also have available a claim for an indemnity from G: *Lister* v *Romford Ice*.

The possibility of an alternative claim against R on the basis of the ruling in *Ormrod* v *Crosville Motors* and *Morgans* v *Launchbury* ('principal and agent') should also be considered. However, the problem of **unauthorised** behaviour, connected with the principal's 'purposes', would arise again in respect of the trip to and from the pub. Liability on the part of R in respect of this incident may be doubtful.

If G were found to be R's independent contractor rather than his servant, the court might be persuaded that R should be personally liable for the consequences of choosing an incompetent driver. This argument would, however, depend on evidence of G's incompetency (e.g., a history of drunkenness, to take an extreme example of relevant evidence) and R's knowledge of this fact. No such evidence is apparent on the facts of the problem.

If M were to have a claim, and she **would** have a possible claim against G, at least, the question of her possible contributory negligence under the provisions of the Law Reform (Contributory Negligence) Act 1945 would arise: *Owens* v *Brimmell*. This defence would be stronger than *volenti*, because of the terms of the RTA 1988: e.g., *Pitts* v *Hunt*.

CHAPTER TWO

GENERAL DEFENCES

2.1 Introduction

2.1.1 SELF-DEFENCE

MURPHY v *CULHANE* [1976] 3 All ER 533 (CA)

This was an action for damages brought under the Fatal Accidents legislation by the widow of Murphy against Culhane, who had killed Murphy. The facts are set out in the judgment of Lord Denning MR:

> On or about the nineteenth day of September 1974, near Grove Place, in the area of Greater London, the Defendant assaulted and beat the Deceased by striking him on the head with a plank. The said assault was unlawful. The Plaintiff intends to adduce evidence pursuant to section 11 of the Civil Evidence Act 1968, that the Defendant was on the 25th day of April 1975, convicted on his own plea of guilty before the Central Criminal Court of manslaughter of the Deceased.

The defence admits those allegations and further admits that, by reason of the assault, Mr Murphy was killed. It then says:

> The said assault occurred during and as part of a criminal affray which was initiated by the Deceased and others who had together come to 20 Grove Place on the occasion in question with the joint criminal intent of assaulting and beating the Defendant.

That is followed by legal contentions of *ex turpi causa non oritur actio, volenti non fit injuria*, and that the deceased's said death was caused in part by his own aforesaid fault.

... There are two cases which seem to show that, in a civil action for damages for assault, damages are not to be reduced because the plaintiff was himself guilty of provocation. Provocation, it was said, can be used to wipe out the element of exemplary damages but not to reduce the actual figure of pecuniary damages. It was so said by the High Court of Australia in 1962 in *Fontin* v *Katapodis* and followed by this court in 1967 in *Lane* v *Holloway*. But those were cases where the conduct of the injured man was trivial—and the conduct of the defendant was savage—entirely out of proportion to the occasion. So much so that the defendant could fairly be regarded as solely responsible for the damage done. I do not think they can or should be applied where the injured man, by his own conduct, can fairly be regarded as partly responsible for the damage he suffered. So far as general principle is concerned, I would like to repeat what I said in the later case of *Gray* v *Barr*:

> In an action for assault, in awarding damages, the judge or jury can take into account, not only circumstances which go to aggravate damages, but also those which go to mitigate them.

That is the principle I prefer rather than the earlier cases. Apart altogether from damages, however, I think there may well be a defence on liability. If Murphy was one of a gang which set out to beat up Culhane, it may well be that he could not sue for damages if he got more than he bargained for. A man who takes part in a criminal affray may well be said to have been guilty of such a wicked act as to deprive himself of a cause of action or, alternatively, to have taken on himself the risk. . . .

There is another point, too even if Mrs Murphy were entitled to damages under the Fatal Accidents Acts, they fall to be reduced under the Law Reform (Contributory Negligence) Act 1945 because the death of her husband might be the result partly of his own fault and partly of the default of the defendant: see s. 1(1) and (4) of the 1945 Act. On this point I must explain a sentence in *Gray* v *Barr* where the widow of the dead man was held to be entitled to full compensation without any reduction. Her husband had not been guilty of any 'fault' within s. 4 of the 1945 Act because his conduct had not been such as to make him liable in an action of tort or, alternatively, was not such that he should be regarded as responsible in any degree for the damage. So also in *Lane* v *Holloway*, as Winn LJ pointed out. But in the present case the conduct of Mr Murphy may well have been such as to make him liable in tort.

It seems to me that this is clearly a case where the facts should be investigated before any judgment is given. It should be open to Mr Culhane to be able to put forward his defences so as to see whether or not and to what extent he is liable in damages.

I would therefore allow the appeal. The judgment should be set aside and the case go for trial accordingly.

Orr and Waller LJJ concurred.

2.2 The Remaining, Major Defences

2.2.1 *VOLENTI NON FIT INJURIA*

2.2.1.1 Consent

GILLICK v WEST NORFOLK AND WISBECH AREA HEALTH AUTHORITY
[1985] 3 All ER 402

A circular issued to Area Health Authorities by the Department of Health and Social Security, advising them that a doctor, consulted by a girl under 16, would be acting lawfully if he prescribed contraceptives for her use, was found by the House of Lords to be lawful. The girl's mother had asked the court for a declaration that the advice was unlawful. Their Lordships said that a person under 16 could consent to such advice and treatment without the need for any parental consent, provided the child had the ability to appreciate the situation.

LORD BRIDGE: My Lords, the memorandum, in expressing the view that in exceptional and unusual cases it may be proper for a doctor to offer contraceptive advice and treatment to a girl under 16 without the knowledge or consent of her parent, guardian or other person in loco parentis, implies that the law does not prohibit the doctor from so acting. The exceptional and unusual cases contemplated are clearly not confined to cases of children abandoned by their parents and not yet taken into care by a local authority or to cases of 'emergency', whatever meaning one may give to that word in this context. I am content to assume, without deciding, that Mrs Gillick, in view of her dispute with the health authority, has sufficient locus standi to contest the issue of the lawfulness of the memorandum. To succeed in her action against the DHSS she must at least establish that, leaving aside cases of abandoned children or emergencies, the law does absolutely prohibit the prescription of contraception for a girl under 16 without parental consent or an order of the court.

The most direct support for that proposition is to be found in the opinion of my noble and learned friend Lord Brandon that to prescribe contraception for a girl under 16, with or without parental consent, is either to aid and abet the offence which will be committed by the man with whom she has intercourse, or at least so far to facilitate his criminal conduct as to be contrary to public policy. I appreciate the logical cogency of my noble and learned friend's reasoning, but I cannot agree with his conclusion. With reference to the possible criminal complicity of the doctor I am content gratefully to adopt the relevant passage from the judgment of Woolf J (see [1984] QB 581 at 593–595), with which I fully agree. On the issue of public policy, it seems to me that the policy consideration underlying the criminal sanction imposed by statute on men who have intercourse with girls under 16 is the protection of young girls from the untoward consequences of intercourse. Foremost among these must surely be the risk of pregnancy leading either to abortion or the birth of a child to an immature and irresponsible mother. In circumstances where it is apparent that the criminal sanction will not, or is unlikely to, afford the necessary protection it cannot, in my opinion, be contrary to public policy to prescribe contraception as the only effective means of avoiding a wholly undesirable pregnancy. On the facts presented to Butler-Sloss J in *Re P* (a minor) (1981) LGR 301, I think, if I may respectfully say so, that she took an eminently sensible and entirely proper course.

The alternative and more extensively argued ground on which Mrs Gillick challenges the lawfulness of the memorandum depends on the two closely related propositions: (a) that no girl under 16 can have the capacity in law to give a valid consent to submit to contraceptive treatment; (b) that the prescription of such treatment without parental consent is an unlawful invasion of parental rights. Both these propositions are comprehensively examined in the speeches of my noble and learned friends Lord Fraser and Lord Scarman. I fully agree with the reasons expressed by both my noble and learned friends for reaching the conclusion that neither proposition is well founded in law.

Accordingly I would allow the appeal of the DHSS to the extent of setting aside the declaration made by the Court of Appeal that the memorandum was contrary to law.

F v WEST BERKSHIRE HEALTH AUTHORITY AND ANOTHER (MENTAL HEALTH ACT COMMISSION INTERVENING) [1989] 2 All ER 545 (HL)

LORD GOFF: It is against this background that I turn to consider the question whether, and if so when, medical treatment or care of a mentally disordered person who is, by reason of his incapacity, incapable of giving his consent can be regarded as lawful. As is recognised in Cardozo J's statement of principle, and elsewhere (see eg *Sidaway* v *Bethlem Royal Hospital Governors* [1985] AC 871 at 882 *per* Lord Scarman), some relaxation of the law is required to accommodate persons of unsound mind. In *Wilson* v *Pringle* [1986] 2 All ER 440 the Court of Appeal considered that treatment or care of such persons may be regarded as lawful, as falling within the exception relating to physical contact which is generally acceptable in the ordinary conduct of everyday life. Again, I am with respect unable to agree. That exception is concerned with the ordinary events of everyday life, jostling in public places and such like, and affects all persons, whether or not they are capable of giving their consent. Medical treatment, even treatment for minor ailments, does not fall within that category of events. The general rule is that consent is necessary to render such treatment lawful. If such treatment administered without consent is not to be unlawful, it has to be justified on some other principle.

On what principle can medical treatment be justified when given without consent? We are searching for a principle on which, in limited circumstances, recognition may be given to a need, in the interests of the patient, that treatment should be given to him in circumstances where he is (temporarily or permanently) disabled from consenting to it. It is this criterion of a need which points to the principle of necessity as providing justification.

That there exists in the common law a principle of necessity which may justify action which would otherwise be unlawful is not in doubt. But historically the principle has been seen to be restricted to two groups of cases, which have been called cases of public necessity and cases of private necessity. The former occurred when a man interfered with another man's property in the public interest, for example (in the days before we could dial 999 for the fire brigade) the destruction of another man's house to prevent the spread of a catastrophic fire, as indeed occurred in the Great Fire of London in 1666. The latter cases occurred when a man interfered with another's property to save his own person or property from imminent danger, for example when he entered on his neighbour's land without his consent in order to prevent the spread of fire onto his own land.

There is, however, a third group of cases, which is also properly described as founded on the principle of necessity and which is more pertinent to the resolution of the problem in the present case. These cases are concerned with action taken as a matter of necessity to assist another person without his consent. To give a simple example, a man who seizes another and forcibly drags him from the path of an oncoming vehicle, thereby saving him from injury or even death, commits no wrong. But there are many emanations of this principle, to be found scattered through the books. These are concerned not only with the preservation of the life or health of the assisted person, but also with the preservation of his property (sometimes an animal, sometimes an ordinary chattel) and even to certain conduct on his behalf in the administration of his affairs. Where there is a pre-existing relationship between the parties, the intervener is usually said to act as an agent of necessity on behalf of the principal in whose interests he acts, and his action can often, with not too much artificiality, be referred to the pre-existing relationship between them. Whether the intervener may be entitled either to reimbursement or to remuneration raises separate questions which are not relevant to the present case.

We are concerned here with action taken to preserve the life, health or well-being of another who is unable to consent to it. Such action is sometimes said to be justified as arising from an emergency; in Prosser and Keeton *Torts* (5th edn, 1984) p 117 the action is said to be privileged by the emergency. Doubtless, in the case of a person of sound mind, there will ordinarily have to be an emergency before such action taken without consent can be lawful; for otherwise there would be an opportunity to communicate with the assisted person and to seek his consent. But this is not always so; and indeed the historical origins of the principle of necessity do not point to emergency as such as providing the criterion of lawful intervention without consent. The old Roman doctrine of negotiorum gestio presupposed not so much an emergency as a prolonged absence of the dominus from home as justifying intervention by the gestor to administer his affairs. The most ancient group of cases in the common law, concerned with action taken by the master of a ship in distant parts in the interests of the shipowner, likewise found its origin in the difficulty of communication with the owner over a prolonged period of time, a difficulty overcome today by modern means of communication. In those cases, it was said that there had to be an emergency before the master could act as agent of necessity; though the emergency could well be of some duration. But, when a person is rendered incapable of communication either permanently or over a considerable period of time (through illness or accident or mental disorder), it would be an unusual use of language to describe the case as one of 'permanent emergency', if indeed such a state of affairs can properly be said to exist. In truth, the relevance of an emergency is that it may give rise to a necessity to act in the interests of the assisted person without first obtaining his consent. Emergency is however not the criterion or even a prerequisite; it is simply a frequent origin of the necessity which impels intervention. The principle is one of necessity, not of emergency....

In a sense, these statements overlap. But from them can be derived the basic requirements, applicable in these cases of necessity, that, to fall within the principle, not only (1) must there be a necessity to act when it is not practicable to communicate with the assisted person, but also (2) the action taken must be such as a reasonable person would in all the circumstances take, acting in the best interests of the assisted person. . . .

I have said that the doctor has to act in the best interests of the assisted person. In the case of routine treatment of mentally disordered persons, there should be little difficulty in applying this principle. In the case of more serious treatment, I recognise that its application may create problems for the medical profession; however, in making decisions about treatment, the doctor must act in accordance with a responsible and competent body of relevant professional opinion, on the principles set down in *Bolam* v *Friern Hospital Management Committee* [1957] 2 All ER 118, [1957] 1 WLR 582. No doubt, in practice, a decision may involve others besides the doctor. It must surely be good practice to consult relatives and others who are concerned with the care of the patient. Sometimes, of course, consultation with a specialist or specialists will be required; and in others, especially where the decision involves more than a purely medical opinion, an inter-disciplinary team will in practice participate in the decision. It is very difficult, and would be unwise, for a court to do more than to stress that, for those who are involved in these important and sometimes difficult decisions, the overriding consideration is that they should act in the best interests of the person who suffers from the misfortune of being prevented by incapacity from deciding for himself what should be done to his own body in his own best interests.

In the present case, your Lordships have to consider whether the foregoing principles apply in the case of a proposed operation of sterilisation on an adult woman of unsound mind, or whether sterilisation is (perhaps with one or two other cases) to be placed in a separate category to which special principles apply. Again, counsel for the Official Solicitor assisted your Lordships by deploying the argument that, in the absence of any parens patriae jurisdiction, sterilisation of an adult woman of unsound mind, who by reason of her mental incapacity is unable to consent, can never be lawful. He founded his submission on a right of reproductive autonomy or right to control one's own reproduction, which necessarily involves the right not to be sterilised involuntarily, on the fact that sterilisation involves irreversible interference with the patient's most important organs, on the fact that it involves interference with organs which are functioning normally, on the fact that sterilisation is a topic on which medical views are often not unanimous and on the undesirability, in the case of a mentally disordered patient, of imposing a 'rational' solution on an incompetent patient. Having considered these submissions with care, I am of the opinion that neither singly nor as a whole do they justify the conclusion for which counsel for the Official Solicitor contended. Even so, while accepting that the principles which I have stated are applicable in the case of sterilisation, the matters relied on by counsel provide powerful support for the conclusion that the application of those principles in such a case calls for special care. There are other reasons which support that conclusion. It appears, for example, from reported cases in the United States that there is a fear that those responsible for mental patients might (perhaps unwittingly) seek to have them sterilised as a matter of administrative convenience. Furthermore, the English case of *Re D (a minor) (wardship: sterilisation)* [1976] 1 All ER 326, [1976] Fam 185 provides a vivid illustration of the fact that a highly qualified medical practitioner, supported by a caring mother, may consider it right to sterilise a mentally retarded girl in circumstances which prove, on examination, not to require such an operation in the best interests of the girl. Matters such as these, coupled with the fundamental nature of the patient's organs with which it is proposed irreversibly to interfere, have prompted courts in the United States and in Australia to pronounce that, in the case of a person lacking the capacity to consent, such an operation should only be permitted with the consent of the court. Such decisions have of course been made by courts which have vested in them the parens patriae jurisdiction, and so have power, in the exercise of such jurisdiction, to impose such a condition. They are not directly applicable in this country, where that jurisdiction has been revoked; for that reason alone I do not propose to cite passages from the American and Australian cases although, like my noble and learned friend Lord Brandon, I have read the judgments with great respect and found them to be of compelling interest. I refer in particular to *Re Grady* (1981) 85 NJ 235 in the United States and, in Australia, to the very full and impressive consideration of the matter by Nicholson CJ in *Re Jane* (22 December 1988, unreported), who in particular stressed the importance of independent representation by some disinterested third party on behalf of the patient (there a minor).

Although the parens patriae jurisdiction in the case of adults of unsound mind is no longer vested in courts in this country, the approach adopted by the courts in the United States and in Australia provides, in my opinion, strong support for the view that, as a matter of practice, the operation of sterilisation should not be performed on an adult person who lacks the capacity to consent to it without first obtaining the opinion of the court that the operation is, in the circumstances, in the best interests of the person concerned, by seeking a declaration that the operation is lawful. (I shall return later in this speech to the appropriateness of the declaratory remedy in cases such as these.) In my opinion, that guidance should be sought in order to obtain an independent, objective and authoritative view on the lawfulness of the procedure in the particular circumstances of the relevant case, after a hearing at which it can be ensured that there is independent representation on behalf of the person on whom it is proposed to perform the operation. This approach is consistent with the opinion expressed by Lord Templeman in *Re B (a minor) (wardship: sterilisation)* [1988] AC 199 at 205–206 that, in the case of a girl who is still a minor, sterilisation should not be performed on her unless she has first been made a ward of court and the court has, in the exercise of its wardship jurisdiction, given its authority to such a step . . .

I am satisfied that, for the reasons so clearly expressed by the judge, he was right to grant the declarations sought by the plaintiff in the present case. I would therefore dismiss the appeal. . . .

LORD GRIFFITHS: We have been taken through many authorities in the United States, Australia and Canada which stress the danger that sterilisation may be proposed in circumstances which are not truly in the best interests of the woman but for the convenience of those who are charged with her care. In the United States and Australia the solution has been to declare that, in the case of a woman who either because of infancy or mental incompetence cannot give her consent, the operation may not be performed without the consent of the court. In Canada the Supreme Court has taken an even more extreme stance and declared that sterilisation is unlawful unless performed for therapeutic reasons, which I understand to be as a life-saving measure or for the prevention of the spread of disease: see *Re Eve* (1986) 31 DLR (4th). This extreme position was rejected by this House in *Re B (a minor) (wardship: sterilisation)* [1988] AC 199, which recognised that an operation might be in the best interests of a woman even though carried out in order to protect her from the trauma of a pregnancy which she could not understand and with which she could not cope. Nevertheless Lord Templeman stressed that such an operation should not be undertaken without the approval of a High Court judge of the Family Division. In this country *Re D (a minor) (wardship: sterilisation)* [1976] 1 All ER 326, [1976] Fam 185 stands as a stark warning of the danger of leaving the decision to sterilise in the hands of those having the immediate care of the woman, even when they genuinely believe that they are acting in her best interests.

I have had the advantage of reading the speeches of my noble and learned friends Lord Brandon and Lord Goff and there is much therein with which I agree. I agree that those charged with the care of the mentally incompetent are protected from any criminal or tortious action based on lack of consent. Whether one arrives at this conclusion by applying a principle of 'necessity' as do Lord Brandon and Lord Goff or by saying that it is in the public interest as did Neill LJ in the Court of Appeal, appear to me to be inextricably interrelated conceptual justifications for the humane development of the common law. Why is it necessary that the mentally incompetent should be given treatment to which they lack the capacity to consent? The answer must surely be because it is in the public interest that it should be so. . . .

But I cannot agree that it is satisfactory to leave this grave decision with all its social implications in the hands of those having the care of the patient with only the expectation that they will have the wisdom to obtain a declaration of lawfulness before the operation is performed. In my view the law ought to be that they must obtain the approval of the court before they sterilise a woman incapable of giving consent and that it is unlawful to sterilise without that consent. I believe that it is open to your Lordships to develop a common law rule to this effect. Although the general rule is that the individual is the master of his own fate the judges through the common law have, in the public interest, imposed certain constraints on the harm that people may consent to being inflicted on their own bodies. Thus, although boxing is a legal sport, a bare knuckle prize fight in which more grievous injury may be inflicted is unlawful (see *R v Coney* (1882) 8 QBD 534), and so is fighting which may result in actual bodily harm (see *Re A-G's Reference (No 6 of 1980)* [1981] QB 715). So also it is unlawful to consent to the infliction of serious injury on the body in the course of the practice of sexual perversion (see *R v Donovan* [1934] 2 KB 498). Suicide was unlawful at common law until Parliament intervened by the Suicide Act 1961.

The common law has, in the public interest, been developed to forbid the infliction of injury on those who are fully capable of consenting to it. The time has now come for a further development to forbid, again in the public interest, the sterilisation of a woman with healthy reproductive organs who, either through mental incompetence or youth, is incapable of giving her fully informed consent unless such an operation has been inquired into and sanctioned by the High Court. Such a common law rule would provide a more effective protection than the exercise of parens patriae jurisdiction which is dependent on some interested party coming forward to invoke the jurisdiction of the court. The parens patriae jurisdiction is in any event now only available in the case of minors through their being made wards of court. I would myself declare that on grounds of public interest an operation to sterilise a woman incapable of giving consent on grounds of either age or mental incapacity is unlawful if performed without the consent of the High Court. I fully recognise that in so doing I would be making new law. However, the need for such a development has been identified in a number of recent cases and in the absence of any parliamentary response to the problem it is my view that the judges can and should accept responsibility to recognise the need and to adapt the common law to meet it. If such a development did not meet with public approval it would always be open to Parliament to reverse it or to alter it by perhaps substituting for the opinion of the High Court judge the second opinion of another doctor as urged by counsel for the Mental Health Act Commission.

As I know that your Lordships consider that it is not open to you to follow the course I would take I must content myself by accepting, but as second best, the procedure by way of declaration proposed by Lord Brandon and agree to the dismissal of this appeal.

Lords Brandon, Bridge and Jauncey agreed in dismissing the appeal of the Official Solicitor (and others) against the granting of a declaration that it was lawful for F to be sterilised without her consent.

RE J, *The Times*, 10 June 1992 (CA)

The court will not exercise its wardship jurisdiction by ordering a doctor to treat a minor in a manner contrary to the doctor's clinical judgment.

RE W [1992] 4 All ER 627 (CA)

The court, in its wardship jurisdiction, can, in the minor's own best interests, objectively considered, override the wishes of a mentally competent child who seeks to refuse medical treatment in circumstances which will in all probability lead to the child's death or to severe permanent injury. The court should, however, have 'a strong predilection' to give effect to the minor's wishes.

RE T [1992] 4 All ER 649 (CA)

Prima facie, every adult has the right and capacity to decide whether or not he/she will accept medical treatment even if such refusal may risk permanent injury to his/her health; or even lead to premature death; and regardless of whether the reasons for the refusal are rational or irrational, unknown or even non-existent. However, if an adult patient did not have the capacity to decide at the time of the purported refusal and still does not have that capacity, or if his/her capacity to make a decision has been overborne by others, it is the duty of the doctors concerned to treat him/her in whatever way they consider (in accordance with their clinical judgment) to be in his/her best interests.

RE S [1992] 4 All ER 671

The court will exercise its inherent jurisdiction to grant a declaration authorising the surgeons and staff of a hospital to carry out an emergency caesarean operation and necessary consequential treatment upon a patient, contrary to her religious beliefs, if the operation is in the best interests of the patient and is necessary to protect the vital interest so the unborn child, and will declare that the operation will be lawful despite the patient's refusal of consent: Sir Stephen Brown P in the Family Division of the High Court.

AIREDALE NHS TRUST v BLAND [1993] 1 All ER 821 (HL)

Artificial feeding and antibiotic drugs may lawfully be withheld from an insensate patient with no hope of recovery when it is known that the result will be that the patient will shortly thereafter die, if responsible and competent medical opinion is of the view that it would be in the patient's best interests not to prolong his life by continuing that form of medical treatment.

RE B (A MINOR) (WARDSHIP: STERILISATION)[1988] 1 AC 199 (HL)

The House of Lord held that in the case of a mentally handicapped minor the court (in its hardship jurisdiction) could consent to the sterilisation of a minor if that was in the minor's best interests.

Where a child under 16 is competent to consent the consent will be valid in law: s. 8(3) Family Reform Act 1969. A person who has attained the age of 16 can consent as if he or she is no longer a minor: s. 8(1) of the 1969 Act (above).

A parent or guardian may consent on behalf of a minor who is not capable of consenting personally, although the general principle in relation to medical treatment is that only the patient himself can consent.

The Children Act 1989, ss. 44 and 45, is also relevant in this context but the provisions of the Act are beyond the scope of this book.

T v T [1988] 1 All ER 613

The parent of a 19 year old woman (epileptic and severely mentally handicapped) was granted a declaration by Wood J in the Family Division of the High Court, in relation to the termination of a pregnancy, in order to protect those performing the operation—even though the declaration related to future actions.

FRENCHAY HEALTHCARE NHS TRUST v S [1994] 2 All ER 403 (CA)

SIR THOMAS BINGHAM MR: This appeal comes before the court at very short notice and raises an acute dilemma. The question for decision put very shortly is whether the plaintiffs in the action, who are a hospital trust, should in effect be given leave not to embark on a surgical procedure, the result of that decision being (if they do not carry out the procedure) that a patient, a young man aged 24, will die within a couple of days . . .

I am conscious that in the course of this judgment I have already referred on a number of occasions to the authority of *Airedale NHS Trust* v *Bland* [1993] 1 All ER 821 . . . [There] the ethical guidelines which were before the court all pointed the same way. There was, despite this unanimity of judicial opinion, widespread and understandable concern, both among lawyers and amongst the public, at the implications of the decision. This is not in any way surprising since it touched on values which are literally fundamental to our view of society and of the world. The courts were of course alive to, and I would hope responsive to, this concern. They were certainly anxious that their decision should not be in any way misunderstood or misapplied. So it was that various rules and principles were laid down in that case to try and prevent abuse and reassure the public. First of all, it was suggested, at any rate in the short term, that those seeking to discontinue treatment in . . . the *Bland* situation should come to court and obtain a declaration from the court that it was proper to do so. Secondly, it was envisaged that such applications should be preceded by full investigation with an opportunity for the Official Solicitor, as the representative of the unconscious patient, to explore the situation fully, to obtain independent medical opinions of his own, and to ensure that all proper material was before the court before such a momentous decision was taken. Thirdly, the courts made plain that their decisions were to be understood as strictly applying to the *Bland* situation and no other. A number of judges were at pains to emphasise that they should not be taken as approving anything falling outside the factual situation which was then before the court.

It is against that background that we have heard the submissions made on behalf of the Official Solicitor today . . .

I go on then to what is Mr Munby's second major submission which is that on the face of the plaintiff's own evidence there is reason to question the diagnosis of PVS. This is of course an important submission because, as I have emphasised, in *Bland's* case the courts were at pains to emphasise that their decision applied only to the facts which were before them. Mr Munby raises an important question as to whether the facts of *Bland's* case are the facts of the present case for legal purposes. He draws attention to a number of features of the evidence which in his submission raise doubts as to whether the cases are truly comparable . . . I think it is plain that the evidence in this case is not as emphatic and not as unanimous as that in *Bland's* case. That certainly causes one to look critically and anxiously at the evidence that is before us. In particular we have to ask ourselves whether the respects in which the evidence is not the same throws doubt on the decision which the consultant has taken and invited the court to approve. For my part there appears to be very little doubt in the evidence, particularly the evidence of the doctors who know S best, that he is in a persistent vegetative state, that there is no prospect of recovery, and that he has no cognitive function worth the name. It is not suggested that one is dealing here with a brain damaged patient who has some significant cognitive function. The evidence to which I have already referred in some detail presents S as a person who has no conscious being at all. That being the case it does not seem to me that in the acute emergency which has arisen the court should attach great weight to the points of distinction that have been raised between the two cases.

I come on, therefore, to the third major submission that Mr Munby has laid before the court which is . . . that the judge erred in attaching too much importance to the judgment of doctors as to what was in the patient's best interests. Mr Munby submits that the House of Lords' decision in *Bland* left open whether the judgment was finally to be made by the doctors or by the court, his submission being that in the last resort it must be made by the court, albeit with great regard to the opinions of responsible medical men. It is true that the judge paid close attention to what members of the House of Lords had said about the subject in the course of their speeches in *Bland* and did express the view that the conclusion at which S's consultant had arrived was reasonable and bona fide. He regarded the judgments which had been expressed by the doctors in this case as being fully in accord with criteria which their Lordships had laid down. It is, I think, important that there should not be a belief that what the doctor says is the patient's best interest *is* the patient's best interest. For my part I would certainly reserve to the court the ultimate power and duty to review the doctor's decision in the light of all the facts. But in a case such as this the question which must be asked is I think clear, and the question is: what is in the best interests of the patient? The plaintiff's answer to that question is clear, and it is that given by the consultant to whom I have repeatedly referred. The answer given on behalf of S, through the Official Solicitor, is that a declaration should not be made. That would leave the doctors in this position: either they would feel obliged to embark upon the surgical procedure necessary to reinsert the tube, which the consultant has made quite clear is contrary in a profound sense to his judgment of what is in the patient's best interests, and which he is himself unwilling to authorise, or they would simply do nothing and persist in the course of conduct on which they have embarked, uncertain whether at the end of the day the law would condemn that decision or not. That may sometimes be the right course for the court to adopt, but it seems to me a highly unsatisfactory position into which one should be reluctant to lead doctors unless the court has real doubt about the reliability, or bona fides, or correctness of the medical opinion in question. Here we have, as it seems to me, a careful, professional and clearly very thoughtful conclusion expressed by a consultant of the highest standing with a knowledge of this patient acquired over a period of years. It is an opinion shared by other doctors who have had the opportunity of seeing the patient, again over a period of years. It is an opinion which no medical opinion contradicts. It is strictly correct, as Mr Munby points out, that there are not two independent medical opinions supporting that of the consultant who in effect makes this application. That is partly a reflection of the emergency which has given rise to the application. But we have, as I have said, two opinions, both to the same effect as the consultant's, and no contrary opinion.

Returning, therefore, to the fundamental question, what is in the best interests of the patient, I find no reason to question the answer which the consultant has given and the answer which the plaintiff hospital trust propounds. I accordingly find myself in agreement with the judge in the decision to which he came and I would for my part dismiss the appeal.

Waite and Peter Gibson LJJ concurred.

2.2.1.2 Exclusion of liability/agreements not to sue

UNFAIR CONTRACT TERMS ACT 1977

1. Scope of Part I

(1)   For the purposes of this Part of this Act, 'negligence' means the breach—

(a)   of any obligation, arising from the express or implied terms of a contract, to take reasonable care or exercise reasonable skill in the performance of the contract;

(b)   of any common law duty to take reasonable care or exercise reasonable skill (but not any stricter duty);

(c)   of the common duty of care imposed by the Occupiers' Liability Act 1957 or the Occupiers' Liability Act (Northern Ireland) 1957.

(2)   This Part of this Act is subject to Part III; and in relation to contracts, the operation of sections 2 to 4 and 7 is subject to the exceptions made by Schedule 1.

(3)   In the case of both contract and tort, sections 2 to 7 apply (except where the contrary is stated in section 6(4)) only to business liability, that is liability for breach of obligations or duties arising—

(a)   from things done or to be done by a person in the course of a business (whether his own business or another's); or

(b)   from the occupation of premises used for business purposes of the occupier; and references to liability are to be read accordingly [but liability of an occupier of premises for breach of an obligation or duty towards a person obtaining access to the premises for recreational or educational purposes, being liability for loss or damage suffered by reason of the dangerous state of the premises, is not a business liability of the occupier unless granting that person such access for the purposes concerned falls within the business purposes of the occupier].

(4)   In relation to any breach of duty or obligation, it is immaterial for any purpose of this Part of this Act whether the breach was inadvertent or intentional, or whether liability for it arises directly or vicariously.

2.   Negligence liability

(1)   A person cannot by reference to any contract term or to a notice given to persons generally or to a particular persons exclude or restrict his liability for death or personal injury resulting from negligence.

(2)   In the case of other loss or damage, a person cannot so exclude or restrict his liability for negligence except in so far as the term or notice satisfies the requirement of reasonableness.

(3)   Where a contract term or notice purports to exclude or restrict liability for negligence a person's agreement to or awareness of it is not of itself to be taken as indicating his voluntary acceptance of any risk.

3.   Liability arising in contract

(1)   This section applies as between contracting parties where one of them deals as consumer or on the other's written standard terms of business.

(2)   As against that party, the other cannot by reference to any contract term—

(a)   when himself in breach of contract, exclude or restrict any liability of his in respect of the breach; or

(b)   claim to be entitled—

(i)   to render a contractual performance substantially different from that which was reasonably expected of him, or

(ii)   in respect of the whole or any part of his contractual obligation, to render no performance at all,

except in so far as (in any of the cases mentioned above in this subsection) the contract term satisfies the requirement of reasonableness.

. . .

9.   Effect of breach

(1)   Where for reliance upon it a contract term has to satisfy the requirement of reasonableness, it may be found to do so and be given effect accordingly notwithstanding that the contract has been terminated either by breach or by a party electing to treat it as repudiated.

(2)   Where on a breach the contract is nevertheless affirmed by a party entitled to treat it as repudiated, this does not of itself exclude the requirement of reasonableness in relation to any contract term.

10.   Evasion by means of secondary contract

A person is not bound by any contract term prejudicing or taking away rights of his which arise under, or in connection with the performance of, another contract, so far as those rights extend to the enforcement of another's liability which this Part of this Act prevents that other from excluding or restricting.

11.   The 'reasonableness' test

(1)   In relation to a contract term, the requirement of reasonableness for the purposes of this Part of this Act, section 3 of the Misrepresentation Act 1967 and section 3 of the

Misrepresentation Act (Northern Ireland) 1967 is that the term shall have been a fair and reasonable one to be included having regard to the circumstances which were, or ought reasonably to have been, known to or in the contemplation of the parties when the contract was made.

(2)   In determining for the purposes of section 6 or 7 above whether a contract term satisfies the requirement of reasonableness, regard shall be had in particular to the matters specified in Schedule 2 to this Act; but this subsection does not prevent the court or arbitrator from holding, in accordance with any rule of law, that a term which purports to exclude or restrict any relevant liability is not a term of the contract.

(3)   In relation to a notice (not being a notice having contractual effect), the requirement of reasonableness under this Act is that it should be fair and reasonable to allow reliance on it, having regard to all the circumstances obtaining when the liability arose or (but for the notice) would have arisen.

(4)   Where by reference to a contract term or notice a person seeks to restrict liability to a specified sum of money, and the question arises (under this or any other Act) whether the term or notice satisfies the requirement of reasonableness, regard shall be had in particular (but without prejudice to subsection (2) above in the case of contract terms) to—

(a)   the resources which he could expect to be available to him for the purpose of meeting the liability should it arise; and

(b)   how far it was open to him to cover himself by insurance.

(5)   It is for those claiming that a contract term or notice satisfies the requirement of reasonableness to show that it does.

12.   'Dealing as consumer'

(1)   A party to a contract 'deals as consumer' in relation to another party if—

(a)   he neither makes the contract in the course of a business nor holds himself out as doing so; and

(b)   the other party does make the contract in the course of a business; and

(c)   in the case of a contract governed by the law of sale of goods or hire-purchase, or by section 7 of this Act, the goods passing under or in pursuance of the contract are of a type ordinarily supplied for private use or consumption.

(2)   But on a sale by auction or by competitive tender the buyer is not in any circumstances to be regarded as dealing as consumer.

(3)   Subject to this, it is for those claiming that a party does not deal as consumer to show that he does not.

13.   Varieties of exemption clause

(1)   To the extent that this Part of this Act prevents the exclusion or restriction of any liability it also prevents—

(a)   making the liability or its enforcement subject to restrictive or onerous conditions;

(b)   excluding or restricting any right or remedy in respect of the liability, or subjecting a person to any prejudice in consequence of his pursuing any such right or remedy;

(c)   excluding or restricting rules of evidence or procedure;

and (to that extent) sections 2 and 5 to 7 also prevent excluding or restricting liability by reference to terms and notices which exclude or restrict the relevant obligation or duty.

(2)   But an agreement in writing to submit present or future differences to arbitration is not to be treated under this Part of this Act as excluding or restricting any liability.

14.   Interpretation of Part I

In this Part of the Act—

'business' includes a profession and the activities of any government department or local or public authority;

'goods' has the same meaning as in [the Sale of Goods Act 1979];

'hire-purchase agreement' has the same meaning as in the Consumer Credit Act 1974;

'negligence' has the meaning given by section 1(1);

'notice' includes an announcement, whether or not in writing, and any other communication or pretended communication; and

'personal injury' includes any disease and any impairment of physical or mental condition.

SCHEDULE 2
'GUIDELINES' FOR APPLICATION OF REASONABLENESS TEST

The matters to which regard is to be had in particular for the purposes of sections 6(3), 7(3) and (4), 20 and 21 are any of the following which appear to be relevant—

(a) the strength of the bargaining positions of the parties relative to each other, taking into account (among other things) alternative means by which the customer's requirements could have been met;

(b) Whether the customer received an inducement to agree to the term, or in accepting it had an opportunity of entering into a similar contract with other persons, but without having to accept a similar term;

(c) whether the customer knew or ought reasonably to have known of the existence and extent of the term (having regard, among other things, to any custom of the trade and any previous course of dealing between the parties);

(d) where the term excludes or restricts any relevant liability if some condition is not complied with, whether it was reasonable at the time of the contract to expect that compliance with that condition would be practicable;

(e) whether the goods were manufactured, processed or adapted to the special order of the customer.

NORWICH CITY COUNCIL v HARVEY [1989] 1 All ER 1180 (CA)

MAY LJ: . . . The case concerns a building contract and a sub-contract. I take the facts of the case from the judge's judgment in which they are clearly set out. The plaintiffs, the building owners, own and operate a swimming pool complex at St Augustines in Norwich. In March 1981 they entered into a contract with main contractors, called Bush Buildings (Norwich) Ltd, for an extension to the complex. The latter sub-contracted certain felt roofing work to the second defendants. Unfortunately one of the latter's employees, the first defendant, while using a gas blowtorch, set fire to both the existing buildings and the new extension causing damage, which gave rise to the claim in these proceedings.

The judge held that any duty of care which would otherwise have been owed by the defendants to the plaintiffs had been qualified by the terms of the respective contracts between the parties, whereby the plaintiffs accepted the risk of damage by fire and other perils to their property and that consequently it would not be just and reasonable to hold that the defendants owed any duty to the plaintiffs to take reasonable care to avoid such damage. This is the fundamental issue in this case.

The contract between the plaintiffs and Bush Builders, to which I shall refer as the 'main contract', was in the familiar JCT Standard Form of Building Contract, Local Authorities' Edition with Quantities, 1963 edn (July 1977 revision). The material clauses of that contract for present purposes are cll 17, 18, 19 and 20[C] . . .

The judge held that there was no privity of contract between the employer and the sub-contractors, and also that there was no question of the main contractor acting either as the agent or trustee for the sub-contractors (see his Honour Judge David Smout QC in *Southern Water Authority* v *Carey* [1985] 2 All ER 1077). The judge further declined to act on any analogy with the bailment cases where, as in *Leigh & Sillavan Ltd* v *Aliakmon Shipping Co. Ltd, The Aliakmon* [1986] AC 785, the contractual exemption is in the defendant sub-bailee's contract with the bailee. . . .

I trust I do no injustice to the plaintiffs argument in this appeal if I put it shortly in this way. There is no dispute between the employer and the main contractor that the former accepted the risk of fire damage: see *James Archdale & Co. Ltd* v *Comservices Ltd* [1954] 1 All ER 210 and *Scottish Special Housing Association* v *Wimpey Construction UK Ltd* [1986] 2 All ER 957. However cl 20[C] does not give rise to any obligation on the employer to indemnify the sub-contractor. That clause is primarily concerned to see that the works were completed. It was intended to operate only for the mutual benefit of the employer and the main contractor. If the judge and sub-contractors are right, the latter obtain protection which the rules of privity do not provide. Undoubtedly the sub-contractors owed duties of care in respect of damage by fire to other persons and in respect of other property (for instance the lawful visitor, employees of the employer or other buildings outside the site); in those circumstances it is impracticable juridically to draw a sensible line between the plaintiffs on the one hand and others on the other to whom a duty of care was owed. The employer had no effective control over the terms on which the relevant sub-contract was let and no direct contractual control over either the sub-contractors or any employee of theirs.

In addition, the plaintiffs pointed to the position of the first defendant, the sub-contractors' employee. Ex hypothesi he was careless and, even if his employers are held to have owed no duty to the building employers, on what grounds can it be said that the employee himself owed no such duty? In my opinion, however, this particular point does not take the matter very much further. If in principle the sub-contractors owed no specific duty to the building owners in respect of damage by fire, then neither in my opinion can any of their employees have done so.

In reply the defendants contend that the judge was right to hold that in all the circumstances there was no duty of care on the sub-contractors in this case. Alternatively they submit that the employers' insurers have no right of subrogation to entitle them to maintain this litigation against the sub-contractors. . . .

In my opinion the present state of the law on the question whether or not a duty of care exists is that, save where there is already good authority that in the circumstances there is such a duty, it will only exist in novel situations where not only is there foreseeability of harm, but also such a close and direct relation between the parties concerned, not confined to mere physical proximity, to the extent contemplated by Lord Atkin in his speech in *Donoghue* v *Stevenson* [1932] AC 562. Further, a court should also have regard to what it considers just and reasonable in all the circumstances and facts of the case.

In the instant case it is clear that as between the employer and the main contractor the former accepted the risk of damage by fire to its premises arising out of and in the course of the building works. Further, although there was no privity between the employer and the sub-contractor, it is equally clear from the documents passing between the main contractors and the sub-contractors to which I have already referred that the sub-contractors contracted on a like basis. In *Scottish Special Housing Association* v *Wimpey Construction UK Ltd* [1986] 2 All ER 957, [1986] 1 WLR 995 the House of Lords had to consider whether, as between the employer and main contractors under a contract in precisely the same terms as those of the instant case, it was in truth intended that the employer should bear the whole risk of damage by fire, even fire caused by the contractor's negligence. The position of sub-contractors was not strictly in issue in the *Scottish Housing* case, which I cannot think the House did not appreciate, but having considered the terms of cll 18, 19 and 20[C] of the same standard form as was used in the instant case Lord Keith, in a speech with which the remainder of their Lordships agreed, said ([1986] 2 All ER 957 at 959, [1986] 1 WLR 995 at 999):

> I have found it impossible to resist the conclusion that it is intented that the employer shall bear the whole risk of damage by fire, including fire caused by the negligence of the contractor or that of sub-contractors . . .

In these circumstances the overall burden of the authorities to which our attention was drawn in my opinion supports the view taken by the judge below and, accordingly, I do not think it necessary to consider the question of the insurance position and subrogation rights as between the parties and their respective insurers.

For the reasons that I have given I would dismiss this appeal.

Croom-Johnson and Glidewell LJJ concurred.

2.2.1.3   Voluntary assumption of risk

NETTLESHIP v *WESTON* [1971] 3 All ER 581 (CA)

LORD DENNING MR: *The responsibility of a learner-driver towards his instructor*
The special factor in this case is that Mr Nettleship was not a mere passenger in the car. He was an instructor teaching Mrs Weston to drive. Seeing that the law lays down, for all drivers of motor cars, a standard of care to which all must conform, I think that even a learner-driver, so long as he is the sole driver, must attain the same standard towards all

passengers in the car, including an instructor. But the instructor may be debarred from claiming for a reason peculiar to himself. He may be debarred because he has voluntarily agreed to waive any claim for any injury that may befall him. Otherwise he is not debarred. He may, of course, be guilty of contributory negligence and have his damages reduced on that account. He may, for instance, have let the learner take control too soon, he may not have been quick enough to correct his errors, or he may have participated in the negligent act himself: see *Stapley* v *Gypsum Mines Ltd* [1953] AC 663. But, apart from contributory negligence, he is not excluded unless it be that he had voluntarily agreed to incur the risk.

This brings me to the defence of volenti non fit injuria. Does it apply to the instructor? In former times this defence was used almost as an alternative defence to contributory negligence. Either defence defeated the action. Now that contributory negligence is not a complete defence, but only a ground for reducing the damages, the defence of volenti non fit injuria has been closely considered, and, in consequence, it has been severely limited. Knowledge of the risk of injury is not enough. Nor is a willingness to take the risk of inury. Nothing will suffice short of an agreement to waive any claim for negligence. The plaintiff must agree, expressly or impliedly, to waive any claim for any injury that may befall him due to the lack of reasonable care by the defendant: or more accurately, due to the failure of the defendant to measure up to the standard of care that the law requires of him. That is shown in England by *Dann* v *Hamilton* and *Slater* v *Clay Cross Co. Ltd* [1939] 1 KB 509; and in Canada by *Lehnert* v *Stein*; and in New Zealand by *Morrison* v *Union Steamship Co. of New Zealand Ltd*. The doctrine has been so severely curtailed that in the view of Diplock LJ: '. . . the maxim, in the absence of express contract, has no application to negligence simpliciter where the duty of care is based solely on proximity or "neighbourship" in the Atkinian sense': see *Wooldridge* v *Sumner* [1963] 2 QB 43.

Applying the doctrine in this case, it is clear that Mr Nettleship did not agree to waive any claim for injury that might befall him. Quite the contrary. He enquired about the insurance policy so as to make sure that he was covered. If and insofar as Mrs Weston fell short of the standard of care which the law required of her, he has a cause of action. But his claim may be reduced insofar as he was at fault himself—as in letting her take control too soon or in not being quick enough to correct her error.

I do not say that the professional instructor—who agrees to teach for reward—can likewise sue. There may well be implied in the contract an agreement by him to waive any claim for injury. He ought to insure himself, and may do so, for aught I know. But the instructor who is just a friend helping to teach never does insure himself. He should, therefore, be allowed to sue. . . .

Final conclusion

In my opinion when a learner-driver is being taught to drive a car under the instruction of an experienced driver, then if the car runs off the road and there is an accident in which one or other, or both of them are injured, it should be regarded as the fault of one or other or both of them. In the absence of any evidence enabling the court to draw a distinction between them, they should be regarded as equally to blame, with the result that the injured one gets damages from the other, but they are reduced by one-half owing to his own contributory negligence. The only alternative is to hold that the accident is the fault of neither, so that the injured person gets no compensation from anyone. To my mind, that is not an acceptable solution, at any rate in these days of compulsory insurance.

I would, therefore, allow the appeal and hold the damages (now agreed) be divided half-and-half.

SALMON LJ: I need not recite the facts which have been so lucidly stated by Lord Denning MR. I entirely agree with all he says about the responsibility of a learner-driver in criminal law. I also agree that a learner-driver is responsible and owes a duty in civil law towards persons on or near the highway to drive with the same degree of skill and care as that of the resonably competent and experienced driver. The duty in civil law springs from the relationship which the driver, by driving on the highway, has created between himself and persons likely to suffer damage by his bad driving. This is not a special relationship. Nor, in my respectful view, is it affected by whether or not the driver is insured. On grounds of public policy, neither this criminal nor civil responsibility is affected by the fact that the driver in question may be a learner, infirm or drunk. The onus, of course, lies on anyone claiming damages to establish a breach of duty and that it has caused the damages which he claims.

Any driver normally owes exactly the same duty to a passenger in his car as he does to the general public, namely to drive with reasonable care and skill in all the relevant circumstances. As a rule, the driver's personal idiosyncracy is not a relevant circumstance. In the absence of a special relationship what is reasonable care and skill is measured by the standard of competence usually achieved by the ordinary driver. In my judgment, however, there may be special facts creating a special relationship which displaces this standard or even negatives any duty, although the onus would certainly be on the driver to establish such facts. With minor reservations I respectfully agree with and adopt the reasoning and conclusions of Sir Owen Dixon in his judgment in *Insurance Comr v Joyce*. I do not however agree that the mere fact that the driver has, to the knowledge of his passenger, lost a limb or an eye or is deaf can affect the duty which he owes the passenger to drive safely. It is well known that many drivers suffering from such disabilities drive with no less skill and competence than the ordinary man. The position, however, is totally different when, to the knowledge of the passenger, the driver is so drunk as to be incapable of driving safely. Quite apart from being negligent, a passenger who accepts a lift in such circumstances clearly cannot expect the driver to drive other than dangerously.

The duty of care springs from relationship. The special relationship which the passenger has created by accepting a lift in the circumstances postulated surely cannot entitle him to expect the driver to discharge a duty of care or skill which ex hypothesi the passenger knows the driver is incapable of discharging. Accordingly in such circumstances, no duty is owed by the driver to the passenger to drive safely, and therefore no question of volenti non fit injuria can arise. . . .

Such a case seems to me to be quite different from *Smith v Baker & Sons* [1891] AC 325 and *Slater* v *Clay Cross Co. Ltd*. Like Sir Owen Dixon, I prefer to rest on the special relationship between the parties displacing the prima facie duty on the driver to drive safely rather than on the ground of volenti non fit injuria. Whichever view is preferable, it follows that, in spite of the very great respect I have for any judgment of Lord Asquith, I do not accept that *Dann v Hamilton* [1939] 1 KB 509 was correctly decided. Although Sir Owen Dixon's judgment was delivered in 1948, I cannot think of anything which has happened since which makes it any less convincing now than it was then.

I should like to make it plain that I am not suggesting that whenever a passenger accepts a lift knowing that the driver has had a few drinks, this displaces the prima facie duty ordinarily resting on a driver, let alone that it establishes volenti non fit injuria. Indeed, Sir Owen Dixon dissented in *Joyce's* case, because he did not agree that the evidence was capable of establishing that the plaintiff passenger knew that the driver was so drunk as to be incapable of exercising ordinary care and skill. In practice it would be rare indeed that such a defence could be established. . . .

For the reasons I have stated, I would, but for one factor, agree with the learned judge's decision in favour of the defendant, Mrs Weston. I have, however, come to the conclusion, not without doubt, that this appeal should be allowed. Mr Nettleship when he gave evidence was asked:

> *Q* Was there any mention made of what the position would be if you were involved in an accident? *A* I had checked with Mr and Mrs Weston regarding insurance, and I was assured that they had fully comprehensive insurance, which covered me as a passenger in the event of an accident.

Mrs Weston agreed, when she gave evidence, that this assurance had been given before Mr Nettleship undertook to teach her. In my view this evidence completely disposes of any possible defence of volenti non fit injuria. Moreover, this assurance seems to me to be an integral part of the relationship between the parties. In *Hedley Byrne & Co. Ltd v Heller & Partners Ltd*, the House of Lords decided that the relationship which there existed between the parties would have imposed a duty of care on the defendants in giving the plaintiffs information but for the fact that the defendants gave the information 'without responsibility'. This disclaimer of responsibility was held to colour the whole relationship between the parties by negativing any duty of care on the part of the defendants. Much the same result followed when a passenger accepted a lift in a car which exhibited a notice stating:

'Warning. Passengers travelling in this vehicle do so *at their own risk*': *Bennett* v *Tugwell* [1971] 2 QB 267. This case is perhaps the converse of the cases of *Hedley Byrne* and *Bennett* v *Tugwell*.

On the whole, I consider, although with some doubt, that the assurance given to Mr Nettleship altered the nature of the relationship which would have existed between the parties but for the assurance. The assurance resulted in a relationship under which Mrs Weston accepted responsibility for any injury which Mr Nettleship might suffer as a result of any failure on her part to exercise the ordinary driver's standards of reasonable care and skill.

As for contributory negligence, I agree with Lord Denning MR that the learned judge's finding on this issue should not be disturbed. . . .

Megaw LJ also delivered a judgment in favour of allowing the appeal.

2.2.1.4   The consent or agreement must be real

VIDEAN v *BRITISH TRANSPORT COMMISSION* [1963] 2 All ER 860 (CA)

A young child wandered on to a railway track and was exposed to the danger of being run down by a motor-trolley (used on the track for maintenance work) when he was saved by his father, the stationmaster. The latter was killed in the successful rescue of his son.

The court held that since a stationmaster's presence on the line was foreseeable, and the duty owed to a rescuer was of an independent nature ie it was not derived from any duty owed to the person in danger, it was irrelevant that the boy in this case was a trespasser to whom the defendant owed no legal liability.

LORD DENNING MR: . . . I turn now to the widow's claim in respect of the death of her husband. In order to establish it, the widow must prove that the trolley driver owed a duty of care to the stationmaster, that he broke that duty, and that, in consequence of the breach, the stationmaster was killed. Counsel for the defendants says that the widow can prove none of these things. All depends, he says, on the test of foreseeability; and, applying that test, he puts the following dilemma: If the trolley driver could not reasonably be expected to foresee the presence of the child, he could not reasonably be expected to foresee the presence of the father. He could not foresee that a trespasser would be on the line. So how could he be expected to foresee that anyone would be attempting to rescue him? Counsel for the defendants points out that, in all the rescue cases that have hitherto come before the courts, such as *Haynes* v *Harwood* [1935] 1 KB 146, and (*Ward and*) *Baker* v *T. E. Hopkins & Sons, Ltd*, the conduct of the defendant was a wrong to the victim or the potential victim. How can he be liable to the rescuer when he is not liable to be rescued?

I cannot accept this view. The right of the rescuer is an independent right, and is not derived from that of the victim. The victim may have been guilty of contributory negligence—or his right may be excluded by contractual stipulation—but still the rescuer can sue. So, also, the victim may, as here, be a trespasser and excluded on that ground, but still the rescuer can sue. Foreseeability is necessary, but not foreseeability of the particular emergency that arose. Suffice it that he ought reasonably to foresee that, if he did not take care, some emergency or other might arise, and that someone or other might be impelled to expose himself to danger in order to effect a rescue. Such is the case here. The trolley driver ought to have anticipated that some emergency or other might arise. His trolley was not like an express train which is heralded by signals and whistles and shouts of 'Keep clear'. His trolley came silently and swiftly on the unsuspecting quietude of a country station. He should have realised that someone or other might be put in peril if he came too fast or did not keep a proper look-out; and that, if anyone was put in peril, then someone would come to the rescue. As it happened, it was the stationmaster trying to rescue his child; but it would be the same if it had been a passer-by. Whoever comes to the rescue, the law should see that he does not suffer for it. It seems to me that, if a person by his fault creates a situation of peril, he must answer for it to any person who attempts to rescue the person who is in danger. He owes a duty to such a person above all others. The rescuer may act instictively out of humanity or deliberately out of courage. But whichever it is, so long as it not wanton interference, if the rescuer is killed or injured in the attempt, he can recover damages from the one whose fault has been the cause of it . . .

MEGAW LJ: It is submitted on behalf of Mrs Weston that even if the standard of care be, as I think it is, the same for a learner-driver vis-à-vis a passenger as it is vis-à-vis a member of the public outside the car, yet in this case the doctrine of *volenti non fit injuria* applies and provides a defence. If there were special facts and circumstances which showed that the passenger not merely was aware of, but accepted for himself the risk of injury caused by the driver's lack of skill or experience, that doctrine would provide a defence. But the mere fact that the passenger knows of the driver's inexperience is not enough.

In the present case, so far from there being such special facts and circumstances, the indications are all the other way. I have no doubt that the proper inference of fact to be drawn from the care which Mr Nettleship took to investigate the comprehensiveness of Mr Weston's insurance policy is that he would have declined to undertake the task of teaching Mrs Weston if he had been told: 'If you are injured as a result of Mrs Weston's lack of skill or experience, you will have to bear your loss without remedy against anyone.' That is not a case of *volenti non fit injuria*.

On the question of contributory negligence, with all respect to Lord Denning MR and Salmon LJ and to the learned judge, I find myself unable, having read and re-read the evidence, to see in what respect Mr Nettleship fell below the standard of care and skill of a competent instructor supervising a learner-driver. There is no conceivable reason why, having regard to what he had seen of Mrs Weston's driving during the three lessons, he should not have permitted her to undertake the manoeuvre which she undertook, at the time and place where she undertook it. From the first warning of trouble to the collision with the lamp-post, on the uncontradicted evidence of distance and speed, the time which elapsed could not have exceeded three seconds. Only one wheel of the car went over the kerb, and that by a matter of inches only. The suggestion that Mr Nettleship could and should have switched off the ignition, as well as using his hands on the brake and the steering wheel during those three seconds, is, I venture to think, quite unrealistic. Apart altogether from the well known factor of 'thinking time', any sudden or dramatic action in such circumstances may well accentuate the panic and thus actually increase the danger. In short, I can see nothing done by him which he ought not to have done, and nothing left undone by him which he ought to have done. Moreover, Mrs Weston herself said, in examination-in-chief, that Mr Nettleship 'did all he could to stop the vehicle before it crashed'. Where, as here, the only participants and the only eye witnesses say that the plaintiff did all he could, how can that evidence be overridden?

I would allow the appeal in full and hold that Mr Nettleship is entitled to the whole of the agreed amount of damages.

HARMAN LJ: . . . It is, to my mind, most significant that it is an instruction to trolley drivers that they must approach stations with care. The inference from this is that they must take care that there are no persons on the line, more especially railway servants engaged in maintenance and like duties. One of these servants was the dead stationmaster. He was a person whose presence on the track was well within the contemplation of the driver. He could not be said to be a trespasser. If the infant had suffered nothing and action had been brought on behalf of the father alone, I do not see what answer the defendants could have to a claim for vicarious liability for the negligent act of their servant, the trolley driver. The fact that the father acted rather as a father than as stationmaster seems to me to obscure the issue. The infant might not have been his son but a child of a passenger. It would clearly be within the scope of the stationmaster's employment to take all steps to rescue such a child. It is not necessary that the exact event should be foreseeable. The presence of the stationmaster, one of the defendant's employees, on the track was within the sphere of contemplation. Whether, if the rescuer had been a member of the public, there would have been liability, I leave out of account.

It is, perhaps, rather a different point of view to hold that the emergency justified the father's presence on the line. In the policeman's case, *Haynes* v *Harwood*, the policeman dashed into the highway to stop the horse which was a menace to children on the highway. It may be said to be different in that such children were lawfully on the highway and were not trespassers, but the emergency is the like and the rescuer has an independent right. . . .

Pearson LJ concurred with Harman LJ.

HARRISON v BRITISH RAILWAYS BOARD AND OTHERS [1981] 3 All ER 679

BOREHAM J: This action arises out of events which occurred on the afternoon of Saturday, 30th November 1974, at Weybridge station on the Southern Region of British Rail. As a result of these events the plaintiff sustained severe and permanent injury in the course of his employment by the first defendants, as a passenger train guard. The plaintiff was then aged 34. He had joined British Rail in the previous June. His ambition was to become a train ticket inspector and, as a step in that direction, in August and September he had undergone a course of instruction as a train guard. He completed the course in September, and qualified as a guard with good marks. Thus by 30th November he had comparatively short experience as a guard but he had the advantage of having the lessons of his recent training still fresh in his mind.

On the day in question the plaintiff was the guard on the 1352 hrs passenger train from Waterloo to Portsmouth. It was a stopping train comprising two 4-coach electric units, eight coaches in all. There was a guard's van in the second coach and another in the sixth. The plaintiff used the latter. The driver of the train was Mr John Dean, the third defendant, a driver of some twelve years' experience. He and the plaintiff had worked together on a few occasions prior to 30th November.

The respective duties of guard and driver, so far as they are relevant to this action, were as follows. The driver's duty was to observe and obey the signals along his road and to stop at the appropriate stations; it was also his duty to observe and obey the guard's proper signals. The safety of the train and its passengers was to a substantial extent the guard's responsibility. In particular it was his duty to ensure that it was safe to start from a station and then to give the driver the ready-to-start signal. It was also his duty to give the driver the signal to stop in an emergency and/or to apply the emergency air-brake, the lever control for which was in his van. On some trains, particularly suburban trains, the guard's ready-to-start signal was given by hand, a flag during ordinary daylight, a hand-held light during the hours of darkness or in foggy conditions. The emergency stop signal was given by applying the emergency air-brake. On the longer-distance Southern Region trains, such as the 1352 hrs Waterloo to Portsmouth, the signals from guard to driver were given by electric bell: two rings to start, one ring to stop. Whatever the bell signal given by the guard, it was the driver's duty to acknowledge it by repeating it on the Loudaphone call button (see r. 4.3.2 of the rules for drivers and guards on the Southern Region).

The Loudaphone is an intercommunication system which enables the driver and the guard to converse or to communicate by audible signals. The rules expressly forbade its use (a) for speech when the train was in motion, except in an emergency, and (b) for starting passenger trains from stations. If the starting-bell apparatus was unserviceable the guard's ready-to-start signal had to be given by hand (see r. 4.3.3). In such circumstances the emergency stop signal would be given by the application of the emergency air-brake in order to attract the driver's attention. The driver's duty then was to shut off the power and bring the train to a stop with the brakes. I am satisfied that at the material time the plaintiff and Mr Dean were familiar with the equipment to which reference has been made and with the rules relating to its use.

When the time came to leave Waterloo on 30th November it became apparent that the starting-bell apparatus was unserviceable, and so the plaintiff and Mr Dean took counsel together over the Loudaphone. There is an important dispute as to what occurred. They both accept that they agreed (a) that at stations where the driver was on the platform side the plaintiff would give the ready-to-start signal by hand, in accordance with the rules and (b) that at other stations, where the driver was not on the platform side, the plaintiff would give the ready-to-start signal by two buzzes on the Loudaphone call button. They both acknowledge that this was in breach of the rules. It was agreed in order to save time because they were already several minutes late. The plaintiff's case is that they also agreed that the signal for an emergency stop should be one buzz on the Loudaphone, again in breach of the rules. Mr Dean denies that there was any discussion or agreement as to the use of the Loudaphone in an emergency. The difference is of prime importance . . .

I find that what happened was this. When the plaintiff's train arrived at Weybridge the station foreman on duty was Mr Howard, the second defendant, who had been employed by British Rail since about 1935. For 22 years from 1949 he had been a passenger train guard and since 1971 he had been station foreman at Weybridge. On Saturday, 30th November, he was on early turn, that is from 7 am until 3 pm. For some time, however, there had been an arrangement between himself and the late-turn foreman, Mr Butler, that the latter would relieve him at 1415 hrs instead of 1500 hrs. This arrangement was entirely unofficial. On Saturday, 30th November, Mr Howard had a particularly pressing personal reason for catching the 1423 hrs down train, the plaintiff's train. Unhappily Mr Butler was late, and, although the train was running four minutes late, it was already in the station at the down platform when Mr Butler arrived in the car park. Mr Howard was in his office on the up side of the station waiting to leave. On seeing Mr Butler he ran across the footbridge, his raincoat over his left arm and his food bag in his left hand. When he reached the down platform the train had just started to move. He was determined to catch it if he possibly could. His approach had been observed by Mr Foxon, who shouted to the plaintiff, 'Stop the train for my mate.' At this moment the plaintiff was still in the doorway of his van. I have no doubt that he heard Mr Foxon shout and that he saw Mr Howard. The plaintiff then went into the van, gave one buzz on the Loudaphone and returned to the doorway of the van. In the plaintiff's absence from the doorway Mr Howard, the second defendant, had managed to grasp the rearmost vertical rail at the side of the guard's door. His intention was to board the train. The train quickly gathered speed and by the time the plaintiff returned to the doorway Mr Howard could no longer keep his feet. He was in grave danger and the plaintiff realised it. He, the plaintiff, therefore reached out to take hold of Mr Howard, whose ability to hang on with one hand without support from his feet was nearly at an end. His feet then went between the platform and the train, he was compelled to release his handhold and fell into what is called the cess, and was very badly injured. His fall pulled the plaintiff from the doorway. He, too, fell, between the train and the platform, and the train went on. The plaintiff was unconscious for a short time only. Soon after the train had gone he was seen by Mr Massey to climb up onto the platform. It was a commendable effort by the plaintiff to try to save Mr Howard. He paid dearly for it . . .

I turn now to the case against the second defendant. It is unnecessary to repeat the facts. They leave me in no doubt that the second defendant was negligent to the extent that he acted with a reckless disregard for his own safety. As a very experienced railwayman, and in particular as an ex-train guard, he was well aware of the rule against attempting to board a moving train, and he was well aware of the reasons for making that rule . . .

One might perhaps be forgiven for thinking that in those circumstances Mr Howard the second defendant, must be liable to the plaintiff. Counsel for Mr Howard says, 'Not so', though in the end he said it somewhat tentatively. Much of his argument was based on the plaintiff's evidence that he deliberately jumped from the moving train to go to Mr Howard's assistance. That account I have been unable to accept. But he also argued that even on the facts as I have found them Mr Howard is not liable because he, being the person rescued, owed no duty to the plaintiff. In presenting this argument counsel has helpfully and responsibly referred me to the relevant authorities. It was this review, indeed, that, in the end, sapped some of his confidence in the argument.

By refraining from a detailed review of the relevant authorities, I intend no disrespect for counsel's careful argument. The question that has to be considered is this: is a man who, through lack of care for his own safety, puts himself into a situation of danger, and who ought, as a reasonable person, to have foreseen that another might endanger himself by attempting to rescue him, liable to his rescuer for injuries sustained in the course of the rescue, or attempted rescue? In the absence of authority I should have answered Yes. It has long been established that a duty of care arises whenever a reasonable person would foresee that if he did not take care he would put another in danger. That duty is owed to all who are within the sphere of the danger thus created. It is also owed to a rescuer, provided that the defendant ought, as a reasonable man, to have foreseen that someone would, or might, come to the rescue of the person imperilled by the defendant's negligence: see *Haynes v Harwood* [1935] 1 KB 146. For some time there appeared to be room for the argument that the duty owed to the rescuer was what was called a derivative, or secondary, duty, namely a duty which arose only when the defendant owed a duty to the person being rescued: see *Dupuis v New Regina Trading Co.* [1943] 4 DLR 275. There was, however, another school of thought; see, for instance, *Baker v Hopkins* [1958] 3 All ER 147, [1958] 1 WLR 993, *per* Barry J.

So far as this court is concerned, the principle has now been established that a duty will be owed to the rescuer if his intervention is reasonably foreseeable, albeit that the defendant owes no duty to the person being rescued: see *Videan v British Transport*

Commission [1963] 2 QB 650. The remaining question, namely whether or not a duty is owed to the rescuer when the person being rescued is he who created the dangerous situation, has, so far as I am aware, not previously been decided in this country. If however, as we decided in *Videan* v *British Transport Commission*, the duty may be owed to the rescuer, although no duty is owed to the person in danger, I see no reason in principle why it should not be owed to the rescuer when the person being rescued is the person who created the peril. Why should the defendant, who, by lack of reasonable care for his own safety, creates a dangerous situation which invites rescue, be in a better position than he who creates a similar situation by lack of reasonable care for another's safety? I can think of no reason, nor has any been suggested to me. In each case, of course, liability will attach only if the defendant ought, as a reasonable man, to have foreseen the likelihood of intervention by a rescuer. I am comforted by the thought that this approach is in line with the most recent decision of the Supreme Court of Canada in *Horsley* v *MacLaren, The Ogopogo* [1971] 2 Lloyd's Rep 410 . . .

Thus, two questions arise: had the second defendant, Mr Howard, by a lack of reasonable care for his own safety, created a situation of danger? I have no doubt that he had. The second question: ought he, as a reasonable man, to have foreseen that the plaintiff might very well come to his aid? I have said enough already to indicate that in my view he should have foreseen, and he probably did foresee, the probability of the plaintiff's intervention. In these circumstances I hold that the second defendant is liable in negligence to the plaintiff.

On this finding counsel for the plaintiff, pursuant to a very late amendment of the statement of claim, urged that at the material time the second defendant was acting in the course of his employment, so that the first defendants are vicariously liable for his negligence. As I understand it, his argument is this: it was by reason of his employment that the second defendant, Mr Howard, was authorised to board the train. Thus he was doing something which he was authorised to do, albeit that he was doing it in an unauthorised manner. Even assuming this to be acceptable, it is by no means conclusive of the question whether or not he was at the material time acting in the course of his employment. Counsel for the first defendants submits that the crucial question is this: at the material time was Mr Howard doing his work, or had he finished for the day? I agree that that is the essential question and I think the answer is clear. Mr Howard was no longer at work. He should have been, but he was not. That is why he was running for the train. It follows that what he did was not done in the course of his employment. In my judgment, the first defendants are not liable to the plaintiff for the second defendant's negligence.

Finally, so far as liability is concerned, the second defendant contends that the plaintiff was guilty of contributory negligence. Counsel for the second defendant argues that the plaintiff failed to observe the rules by failing to apply the emergency brake. The plaintiff's case is that he considered applying the brake but refrained from doing so because he was afraid that the sudden deceleration of the train would make matters worse for the second defendant, Mr Howard, in that it would almost inevitably have made him lose his grip and fall between the train and the platform. The difficulty I have in accepting this explanation is that I am satisfied that Mr Howard was not hanging onto the train when the plaintiff went into the guard's van to try and bring the train to a stop. Had Mr Howard by then grabbed the rail I am sure the plaintiff would have tried to help him aboard. On the other hand, Mr Howard's intentions must have been clear to the plaintiff and I am prepared to accept that he assumed at the time he was in the van that Mr Howard had, or might well have, grasped and hung onto some part of the train. But the fact remains that if he had wished to stop the train (and I accept that he did) the only proper means of doing so was by the emergency brake. I accept the evidence of Mr Girling that the brake may be applied slowly and thus a too-sudden deceleration would be avoided. Indeed, that is the proper way to apply it. It was the plaintiff's duty, according to the rules, to apply the brake in an emergency; he knew it and I think he was negligent in not doing so. Had he done so, the speed of the train would have been reduced. He should have known it was his duty, and I believe he did know it. As it was, he gave (no doubt in the heat of the moment) a meaningless signal and the train continued to accelerate. In these circumstances, I have come to the conclusion that had he acted as he should have done it is probable, though not certain, that both the chance of his being injured at all and the severity of his injuries would have been reduced. He should, therefore, bear some of the blame for those injuries.

One has a feeling of distaste about finding a rescuer guilty of contributory negligence. It can rarely be appropriate to do so, in my judgment. Here, however, the contributory negligence which is alleged does not relate to anything done in the course of the actual rescue. What is alleged is the failure by the man in authority to reduce the danger by doing what he was duty-bound to do. The major responsibility must, of course, be borne by the second defendant. I assess the plaintiff's share at 20 per cent . . .

HORSLEY AND OTHERS v MACLAREN (THE 'OGOPOGO')
[1971] 2 Lloyd's Report 410 (Canada Supreme Court)

The facts are set out in the judgment of Mr Justice Laskin (with whom Mr Justice Hall concurred):

. . . On a cool evening in early May, 1966, an invited guest on board a cabin cruiser, which was on its way to its home port, Oakville, from Port Credit, accidentally fell into the lake. In the course of rescue operations, another invited guest dived into the water to help him. The effort was without avail. The rescuer was pulled from the water by others on board, could not be resuscitated and was later pronounced dead. The body of the rescuee was never recovered. These are the bare bones of two fatal accident actions brought against the boat owner, who was in charge of his craft at the time, for the benefit of the widows and dependants of the two deceased. The rescuer's family succeeded at the trial but their claim was dismissed on appeal, and they now seek restoration by this Court of the favourable trial judgment. The other claim failed at trial and was not pursued farther.

Various theories of the liability of the boat owner MacLaren were explored at trial and on appeal. Mr Justice Lecourcière founded himself on the following conclusions: (1) MacLaren was under a duty to aid the passenger Matthews who had accidentally fallen overboard and, in any event, he had affirmatively undertaken to effect a rescue; (2) he was negligent in the way in which he attempted the rescue; (3) he thus induced the rescuer Horsley to court the danger of effecting a rescue and was, accordingly, liable for the resulting injury and damage; (4) there was no contributory negligence on Horsley's part, nor any voluntary assumption of the risk created by MacLaren's negligence. . . .

In this Court, Counsel for the appellants relied on three alternative bases of liability. There was, first, the submission that in going to the aid of Matthews, as he did, MacLaren came under a duty to carry out the rescue with due care in the circumstances, and his failure to employ standard rescue procedures foreseeably brought Horsley into the picture with the ensuing fatal result. The second basis of liability was doubly founded as resting (a) on a common-law duty of care of a private carrier to his passengers, involving a duty to come to the aid of a passenger who has accidentally fallen overboard, or (b) on a statutory duty under sect. 526(1) of the Canada Shipping Act, RSC 1952, cap. 29, to come to the aid of a passenger who has fallen overboard. There was failure, so the allegation was, to act reasonably in carrying out these duties or either of them, with the foreseeable consequence of Horsley's encounter of danger. The third contention was the broadest, to the effect that where a situation of peril, albeit not brought about originally by the defendant's negligence, arises by reason of the defendant's attempt at rescue, he is liable to a second rescuer for ensuing damage on the ground that the latter's intervention is reasonably foreseeable.

None of the bases of liability advanced by the appellants is strictly within the original principle on which the 'rescue' cases were founded. That was the recognition of a duty by a negligent defendant to a rescuer coming to the aid of the person imperilled by the defendant's negligence. The evolution of the law on this subject, originating in the moral approbation of assistance to a person in peril, involved a break with the 'mind your own business' philosophy. Legal protection is now afforded to one who risks injury to himself in going to the rescue of another who has been foreseeably exposed to danger by the unreasonable conduct of a third person. The latter is now subject to liability at the suit of the rescuer as well as at the suit of the imperilled person provided, in the case of the rescuer, that his intervention was not so utterly foolhardy as to be outside of any accountable risk and thus beyond even contributory negligence.

Moreover, the liability to the rescuer, although founded on the concept of duty, is now seen as stemming from an independent and not a derivative duty of the negligent person.

As Fleming on Torts, 3rd ed. (1965) has put it (at p. 166), the cause of action of the rescuer, in arising out of the defendant's negligence, is based

> . . . not in its tendency to imperil the person rescued, but in its tendency to induce the rescuer to encounter the danger. Thus viewed, the duty to the rescuer is clearly independent . . .

This explanation of principle was put forward as early as 1924 by Professor Bohlen (see his Studies in the Law of Torts, at p. 569) in recognition of the difficulty of straining the notion of foreseeability to embrace a rescuer of a person imperilled by another's negligence. Under this explanation of the basis of liability, it is immaterial that the imperilled person does not in fact suffer any injury or that, as it turns out, the negligent person was under no liability to him either because the injury was not caused by the negligence or the damage was outside the foreseeable risk of harm to him: cf *Videan* v *British Transport Commission*, [1963] 2 QB 650. It is a further consequence of the recognition of an independent duty that a person who imperils himself by his carelessness may be as fully liable to a rescuer as a third person would be who imperils another. In my opinion, therefore, *Dupuis* v *New Regina Trading Company Ltd* [1943] 4 DLR 275, ought no longer to be taken as a statement of the common law in Canada in so far as it denies recovery because the rescuer was injured in going to the aid of a person who imperilled himself. The doctrinal issues are sufficiently canvassed by the late Dean Wright in (1943) 21 Can Bar Rev 758; and see also *Baker* v *T. E. Hopkins & Son Ltd* [1959] 3 All ER 225.

I realise that this statement of the law invites the conclusion that Horsley's estate might succeed against that of Matthews if it was proved that Matthews acted without proper care for his own safety so that Horsley was prompted to come to his rescue. This issue does not, however, have to be canvassed in these proceedings since the estate of Matthews was not joined as a co-defendant.

The thinking behind the rescue cases, in so far as they have translated a moral impulse into a legally protectible interest, suggests that liability to a rescuer should not depend on whether there was original negligence which created the peril and which therefore, prompted the rescue effort. It would appear that the principle should be equally applicable if, at any stage of the perilous situation, there was negligence on the defendant's part which induced the rescuer to attempt the rescue or which operated against him after he had made the attempt. If this be so, it indicates the possibility of an action by a second rescuer against a first. On one view of the present case, this is what we have here. It is not, however, a view upon which, under the facts herein, the present case falls to be decided.

The reason is obvious. MacLaren was not a random rescuer. As owner and operator of a boat on which he was carrying invited guests, he was under a legal duty to take reasonable care for their safety. This was a duty which did not depend on the existence of a contract of carriage, nor on whether he was a common carrier or a private carrier of passengers. Having brought his guests into a relationship with him as passengers on his boat, albeit as social or gratuitous passengers, he was obliged to exercise reasonable care for their safety. That obligation extends, in my opinion, to rescue from perils of the sea where this is consistent with his duty to see to the safety of his other passengers and with concern for his own safety. The duty exists whether the passenger falls overboard accidentally or by reason of his own carelessness. . . .

It follows from this assessment that MacLaren cannot be regarded as simply a Good Samaritan. Rather it is Horsley who was in that role, exposing himself to danger upon the alleged failure of MacLaren properly to carry out his duty to effect Matthews' rescue.

The present case is thus reduced to the question of liability on the basis of (1) an alleged breach of a duty of care originating in the relationship of carrier and passenger; (2) whether the breach, if there was one, could be said to have prompted Horsley to go to Matthews' rescue; and (3) whether Horsley's conduct, if not so rash in the circumstances as to be unforeseeable, nonetheless exhibited want of care so as to make him guilty of contributory negligence.

Whether MacLaren was in breach of his duty of care to Matthews was a question of fact on which the trial Judge's affirmative finding is entitled to considerable weight. That finding was, of course, essential to the further question of a consequential duty to Horsley. Lecourcière, J., came to his conclusion of fact on the evidence, after putting to himself the following question:

What would the reasonable boat operator do in the circumstances, attributing to such person the reasonable skill and experience required of the master of a cabin cruiser who is responsible for the safety and rescue of his passengers [*see* [1969] 2 OR 137, at p. 144; [1969] 1 Lloyd's Rep 374, at p. 379].

It was the trial Judge's finding that MacLaren, as he himself admitted, had adopted the wrong procedure for rescuing a passenger who had fallen overboard. He knew the proper procedure, and had practised it. Coming bow on to effect a rescue was the standard procedure and was taught as such . . .

I do not see how it can be said that the trial Judge's finding against MacLaren on the issue of breach of duty is untenable . . .

I turn to the question whether the breach of duty to Matthews could properly be regarded in this case as prompting Horsley to attempt a rescue. Like the trial Judge, I am content to adopt and apply analogically on this point the reasoning of Cardozo, J, as he then was in *Wagner* v *International Railway Co.* (1921) 133 NE 437 and of Lord Denning, MR in *Videan* v *British Transport Commission sup.* To use Judge Cardozo's phrase, Horsley's conduct in the circumstances was 'within the range of natural and probable'. The fact, moreover, that Horsley's sacrifice was futile is no more a disabling ground here than it was in the *Wagner* case, where the passenger thrown off the train was dead when the plaintiff went to help him, unless it be the case that the rescuer acted wantonly.

In responding as he did, and in circumstances where only hindsight made it doubtful that Matthews could be saved, Horsley was not wanton or foolhardy. Like the trial Judge, I do not think that his action passed the point of brave acceptance of a serious risk and became a futile exhibition of recklessness for which there can be no recourse. There is, however, the question whether Horsley was guilty of contributory negligence. This was an alternative plea of the respondent based, *inter alia*, on Horsley's failure to put on a life-jacket or secure himself to the boat by a rope or call on the other passengers to stand by, especially in the light of the difficulties of Matthews in the cold water. . . .

. . . However, in concern of the occasion, and having regard to MacLaren's breach of duty, I do not think that Horsley can be charged with contributory negligence in diving to the rescue of Matthews as he did. I point out as well that the evidence does not indicate that the failure to put on a life-jacket or secure himself to a lifeline played any part in Horsley's death.

I would allow the appeal.

The majority judgment, given by Mr Justice Richie (with whom Judson and Spence JJ concurred) dismissed the plaintiffs' appeal:

. . . The duty, if any, owing to the late Mr Horsley stands on an entirely different footing. If, upon Matthews falling overboard, Horsley had immediately dived to his rescue and lost his life, as he ultimately did upon contact with the icy water, then I can see no conceivable basis on which the respondent could have been held responsible for his death.

There is, however, no suggestion that there was any negligence in the rescue of Horsley and if the respondent is to be held liable to the appellants, such liability must in my view stem from a finding that the situation of peril brought about by Matthews falling into the water was thereafter, within the next three or four minutes, so aggravated by the negligence of MacLaren in attempting his rescue as to induce Horsley to risk his life by diving in after him . . .

In the present case a situation of peril was created when Matthews fell overboard, but it was not created by any fault on the part of MacLaren and before MacLaren can be found to have been in any way responsible for Horsley's death it must be found that there was such negligence in his method of rescue as to place Matthews in an apparent position of increased danger subsequent to and distinct from the danger to which he had been initially exposed by his accidental fall. In other words, any duty owing to Horsley must stem from the fact that a new situation of peril was created by MacLaren's negligence which induced Horsley to act as he did.

In assessing MacLaren's conduct in attempting to rescue Matthews, I think it should be recognised that he was not under a duty to do more than take all reasonable steps which would have been likely to effect the rescue of a man who was alive and could take some action to assist himself. While there is no express finding that Matthews died upon contact with the icy water because his body was never found, there is nevertheless unanimous agreement amongst all those who saw him that he was from the moment he entered the water, inert and rigid with his torso out of the water, his arms outstretched and his eyes staring, and the learned trial Judge reached the conclusion on the balance of probabilities that it had not been shown that his life could have been saved. The added difficulties in rescuing an inert body from the water as opposed to the body of a man who was alive and could assist himself do not need to be stressed, but as will hereafter appear, the difficulties entailed in retrieving a dead body undoubtedly increase the time involved in effecting its rescue . . .

I share the view expressed by my brother Laskin when he says, in the course of his reasons for judgment, that

> Encouragement by the common law of the rescue of persons in danger would, in my opinion, go beyond reasonable bounds if it involved liability of one rescuer to a succeeding one where the former has not been guilty of any fault which could be said to have induced a second rescue attempt.

In the present case, however, although the procedure followed by MacLaren was not the most highly recommended one, I do not think that the evidence justifies the finding that any fault of his induced Horsley to risk his life by diving as he did. In this regard I adopt the conclusion reached by Mr Justice Schroeder in the penultimate paragraph of his reasons for judgment where he says [1970] 1 Lloyd's Rep at p 264:

> . . . if the appellant erred in backing instead of turning the cruiser and proceeding towards Matthews 'bow on', the error was one of judgment and not negligence, and in the existing circumstances of emergency ought fairly to be excused.

I think it should be made clear that in my opinion the duty to rescue a man who has fallen accidentally overboard is a common-law duty the existence of which is in no way dependent upon the provisions of s. 526 (1) of the Canada Shipping Act, RSC 1952, cap. 29.

I should also say that, unlike Mr Justice Jessup, the failure of Horsley to heed MacLaren's warning to remain in the cockpit or cabin plays no part in my reasoning.

For all these reasons I would dismiss this appeal with costs.

2.2.2   ILLEGALITY

2.2.2.1   Comparison with *volenti*

PITTS v HUNT AND ANOTHER [1990] 3 All ER 344 (CA)

After drinking alcohol together the defendant (deceased) gave the plaintiff a lift home on his motor-bike. The deceased, whose alcohol level was twice over the legal limit, was encouraged by the plaintiff to drive too fast and to intimidate other road users. To the plaintiff's knowledge the deceased did not have a licence and was not insured. In a collision with an oncoming vehicle whose driver was not to blame, the defendant was killed and the plaintiff was badly injured.

The plaintiff's claim in negligence against the deceased's estate failed because the defence invoked successfully *ex turpi causa non oritur actio*. It was found that *volenti non fit injuria* would have applied but for the effect of s. 149 of the Road Traffic Act 1988 (formerly s. 148(3) of the 1972 Act).

BELDAM LJ: The first two grounds on which the judge rejected the plaintiff's claim arose from the first defendant's reliance on public policy and, in particular, the policy expressed in the Latin maxim *ex turpi causa non oritur actio* . . .

The particular sphere of social behaviour and activity arising from the use of motor vehicles in modern conditions is one in which Parliament has been continuously active during this century. It has produced codes designed to regulate and control the behaviour of drivers and for the construction, maintenance and use of vehicles for the purpose of securing the safety of road users. It has also produced a code of requirements for motor insurance designed to make provision for compensating those who suffer injury from the use of vehicles on the road. Thus it seems to me that the primary source of public policy in this sphere must be the Acts of Parliament themselves. That policy is properly supplement- ed by taking into account the reasons given by the courts of this country for refusing to enforce rights based on conduct which has been regarded as sufficiently anti-social and contrary to the policy of the Acts. I would regard decisions in other jurisdictions which may have different social attitudes as of but secondary guidance, though of course entitled to respect and consideration. Although it is part of that policy that passengers carried on or in vehicles who sustain injury should be compensated, it is clear that Parliament did not regard it as essential that the driver of a vehicle who by his own fault injures himself should be required to insure against that risk. Parliament did however provide that, of the various offences specifically relating to the use of motor vehicles, causing death by reckless driving, reckless driving itself and driving when under the influence of drink and drugs were to be regarded as among the most serious of offences and were to be punishable by imprisonment. Parliament did not expressly provide that a passenger who took part with the driver in the commission of such offences should not be entitled to the benefit of the provisions designed to secure that he should receive compensation.

The policy underlying the provisions for compulsory insurance for passengers and others injured in road accidents is clearly one intended for their benefit; it does not follow that if an offence is committed jointly by the driver and passenger of a kind not regarded as so serious as to disentitle the driver from claiming indemnity for the benefit of an innocent passenger, the passenger who is a joint offender can, subject to questions of contributory negligence, recover compensation from the driver. If, however, the offence, or series of offences, is so serious that it would preclude the driver on grounds of public policy from claiming indemnity under a policy required to be effected under the Act for the benefit of a passenger, that public policy would in my judgment also preclude the passenger jointly guilty of that offence from claiming compensation.

On the facts found by the judge in this case the plaintiff was playing a full and active part in encouraging the young rider to commit offences which, if a death other than that of the young rider himself had occurred, would have amounted to manslaughter. And not just manslaughter by gross negligence on the judge's findings. It would have been man- slaughter by the commission of a dangerous act either done with the intention of frightening other road users or when both the plaintiff and the young rider were aware or but for self-induced intoxication would have been aware that it was likely to do so and nevertheless they went on and did the act regardless of the consequences. Thus on the findings made by the judge in this case I would hold that the plaintiff is precluded on grounds of public policy from recovering compensation for the injuries which he sustained in the course of the very serious offences in which he was participating. On a question on which, as Bingham LJ said, the courts have tended to adopt a pragmatic approach, I do not believe that it is desirable to go further in an attempt to categorise the degree of seriousness involved in offences which will not preclude recovery of compensation. I would, however, add that the public attitude to driving a motor vehicle on a road when under the influence of drink has, I believe, changed markedly with the increasing number of serious accidents and the dreadful injuries which are the consequence of such driving. The public conscience is ever-increasingly being focussed not only on those who commit the offence but, in the words of recent publicity, those who ask the driver to drink and drive.

The second ground on which the judge held that the plaintiff's claim failed was because in the circumstances of the case the law would not recognise the existence of a duty of care owed by the rider to the plaintiff. As this ground is also based on public policy, it is not I think in the circumstances of this case significant. That both the plaintiff and rider owed a duty to other road users to exercise reasonable care is clear. I am not convinced of the wisdom of a policy which might encourage a belief that the duty to behave responsibly in driving motor vehicles is diminished even to the limited extent that they may in some circumstances not owe a duty to each other, particularly when those circumstances involve conduct which is highly dangerous to others.

As to the defence raised that the plaintiff voluntarily undertook to run the risk of injury by taking part in such a foolhardy, risky and illegal activity, I would have been prepared to say that it was obvious from the description of the plaintiff's behaviour whilst he was participating that he had done so. However the judge accepted that the effect of s. 148(3) of the Road Traffic Act 1972 was that any agreement or understanding that the risk of injury would be the plaintiff's was of no effect . . .

Although it is unnecessary in view of the decision to which I have come to express an opinion on the judge's decision that the plaintiff should have his damages reduced to nil by reason of his own fault, I would say that I was quite unpersuaded by the argument for the plaintiff that this was a correct apportionment of responsibility. Although the court when apportioning liability between two tortfeasors is given express power under s 6 of the Law Reform (Married Women and Tortfeasors) Act 1935 to exempt a person from liability to make contribution, or to direct that a contribution to be recovered from any person liable in respect of the damage should amount to a complete indemnity, it seems to me that the wording of s. 1 of the Law Reform (Contributory Negligence) Act 1945 is incapable of a similar interpretation. Section 1 begins with the premise that the person suffers damage as a result partly of his own fault and partly of the fault of any other person or persons. Thus before the section comes into operation, the court must be satisfied that there is fault on the part of both parties which has caused damage. It is then expressly provided that the claim shall not be defeated by reason of the fault of the person suffering the damage. To hold that he is himself entirely responsible for the damage effectively defeats his claim. It is then provided that the damages recoverable in respect thereof (that is the damage suffered partly as a result of his own fault and partly the fault of any other person) shall be reduced. It therefore presupposes that the person suffering the damage will recover some damage. Finally reduction is to be to such extent as the court thinks just and equitable, having regard to the claimant's share in the responsibility for the damage. To hold that the claimant is 100% responsible is not to hold that he shared in the responsibility for the damage.

For these reasons I would not support the judge's conclusion. In the circumstances of this case in which arguments can be advanced on the question of blameworthiness which might suggest a greater degree of fault on the older as opposed to the younger boy, or as to the rider as opposed to the passenger, I would not myself take any view which attributed a greater share of responsibility to one or the other. They participated equally in the illegal and dangerous escapade regardless of the safety of others and of themselves and had they been jointly charged with the criminal offences they were jointly committing they would have been charged and convicted as principals.

Subject to the question of their ages, I doubt whether any distinction would have been drawn for the purpose of any sentence imposed on them. In the circumstances, had the plaintiff been entitled to damages, I would have held that they should have been reduced by 50%. For the reasons I have given, however, I would dismiss the appeal.

BALCOMBE LJ: In a case of this kind I find the ritual incantation of the maxim *ex turpi causa non oritur actio* more likely to confuse than to illuminate. I prefer to adopt the approach of the majority of the High Court of Australia in the most recent of the several Australian cases to which we were referred, *Jackson v Harrison* (1978) 138 CLR 438. That is to consider what would have been the cause of action had there been no joint illegal enterprise, that is the tort of negligence based on the breach of a duty of care owed by the deceased to the plaintiff, and then to consider whether the circumstances of the particular case are such as to preclude the existence of that cause of action. I find myself in complete agreement with the following passage from the judgment of Mason J in *Jackson v Harrison* (at 455–456):

If a joint participant in an illegal enterprise is to be denied relief against a co-participant for injury sustained in that enterprise, the denial of relief should be related not to the illegal character of the activity but rather to the character and incidents of the enterprise and to the hazards which are necessarily inherent in its execution. A more secure foundation for denying relief, though more limited in its application—and for that reason fairer in its operation—is to say that the plaintiff must fail when the character of the enterprise in which the parties are engaged is such that it is impossible for the court to determine the standard of care which is appropriate to be observed. The detonation of an explosive device is a case of this kind. But the driving of a motor vehicle by an unlicensed and disqualified driver, so long as it does not entail an agreement to drive the car recklessly on the highway (see *Bondarenka v Sommers* ((1968) 69 SR(NSW) 269), stands in a somewhat different position. In this case the evidence indicates that the participants contemplated that the vehicle would be driven carefully—an accident or untoward event might, as in fact it did, lead to discovery of their breach of the law. It is not suggested that either party lacked the experience or ability to drive carefully—that they were unlicensed was due to their having been disqualified as a result of earlier traffic offences . . . A plaintiff will fail when the joint illegal enterprise in which he and the defendant are engaged is such that the court cannot determine the particular standard of care to be observed. It matters not whether this in itself provides a complete answer to the plaintiff's claim or whether it leads in theory to the conclusion that the defendant owes no duty of care to the plaintiff because no standard of care can be determined in the particular case. . . .

This approach seems to me to enable the court to differentiate between those joint enterprises which, although involving a contravention of the criminal law and hence illegal, eg the use of a car by an unlicensed and disqualified driver as in *Jackson* v *Harrison* are not such as to disable the court from determining the standard of care to be observed and those, such as the use of a get-away car as in *Ashton* v *Turner* [1981] QB 137, where it is impossible to determine the appropriate standard of care.

Counsel for the plaintiff submitted that, however reprehensible the plaintiff's conduct may have been, his culpability involved neither dishonesty nor violence nor any moral turpitude such as is inherent in crimes of dishonesty or violence. Although an assessment of the degree of moral turpitude becomes unnecessary if one adopts, as I do, the approach of the majority of the High Court of Australia in *Jackson* v *Harrison*, I would not wish to be thought that I accept this submission. It was only by good fortune that no innocent third party was injured by this disgraceful piece of motor cycle riding, in which the judge found on the facts that the plaintiff was an active participant. If moral turpitude were relevant, here was moral turpitude of a high degree.

However, I prefer to found my judgment on the simple basis that the circumstances of this particular case were such as to preclude the court from finding that the deceased owed a duty of care to the plaintiff.

I agree with Dillon LJ, and for the reasons which he gives, that s. 148(3) of the Road Traffic Act 1972 does not affect the position under this head.

Volenti and s. 148(3)

Counsel for the first defendant sought to persuade us that the application of the volenti doctrine is to extinguish liability and, if liability has already been extinguished, there is nothing on which s. 148(3) of the Road Traffic Act 1972 can bite. As Dillon LJ says, if this argument were to be accepted, it would mean that s. 148(3) could never apply to a normal case of *volenti*, although that was clearly its intention. For the reasons given by the judge below, by both Beldam and Dillon LJJ and by the Inner House of the Court of Session in *Winnik* v *Dick* 1984 SLT 185, I agree that the effect of s. 148(3) is to exclude any defence of volenti which might otherwise be available. On this issue I agree with the judge below that Ewbank J's decision in *Ashton* v *Turner* [1981] QB 137 at 148 was incorrect.

Contributory negligence

I agree that the judge's finding that the plaintiff was 100% contributorily negligent is logically unsupportable and, to use his own words, 'defies common sense'. Such a finding is equivalent to saying that the plaintiff was solely responsible for his own injuries, which he clearly was not. For my part I prefer to express no opinion on how the liability should have been apportioned, had that been material.

I agree that this appeal should be dismissed.

DILLON LJ: I find a test that depends on what would or would not be an affront to the public conscience very difficult to apply, since the public conscience may well be affected by factors of an emotional nature, eg that these boys by their reckless and criminal behaviour happened to do no harm to anyone but themselves. Moreover, if the public conscience happened to think that the plaintiff should be compensated for his injuries it might equally think that the deceased driver of the motor cycle, had he survived and merely been injured, ought to be compensated, and that leads into the much-debated question whether there ought to be a universal scheme for compensation for the victims of accidents without regard to fault.

Beyond that, appeal to the public conscience would be likely to lead to a graph of illegalities according to moral turpitude, and I am impressed by the comments of Mason J in *Jackson* v *Harrison* (1978) 138 CLR 438 at 455, where he said:

> ... there arises the difficulty, which I regard as insoluble, of formulating a criterion which would separate cases of serious illegality from those which are not serious. Past distinctions drawn between felonies and misdemeanours, malum in se and malum prohibitum, offences punishable by imprisonment and those which are not, non-statutory and statutory offences offer no acceptable discrimen.

Bingham LJ's dichotomy between cases where the plaintiff's action in truth arises directly *ex turpi causa* and cases where the plaintiff has suffered a genuine wrong to which allegedly unlawful conduct is incidental avoids this difficulty, in that it does not involve grading illegalities according to moral turpitude. ...

That a defence of illegality can be pleaded to a case founded in tort is, in my judgment, clear, whether or not the defence is correctly called *ex turpi causa*. *Thackwell* v *Barclays Bank plc* [1986] 1 All ER 676 is one instance. Another is *Murphy* v *Culhane* [1977] QB 94. There the plaintiff as the widow and administratix of the estate of her deceased husband claimed damages from the defendant on the ground that the defendant had unlawfully assaulted the deceased by beating him about the head with a plank by which assault he was killed. The plaintiff did not have to plead any illegality as part of her case, but on a preliminary issue the defendant was allowed by this court to plead that the assault alleged occurred during and as part of a criminal affray initiated by the deceased and others with the joint criminal purpose of assaulting and beating the defendant. Lord Denning MR considered that a man who took part in a criminal affray might well be said to have been guilty of such a wicked act as to deprive himself of a cause of action; alternatively, even if the plaintiff were entitled to damages, they might fall to be reduced under the Law Reform (Contributory Negligence) Act 1945. Since the case came before this court on a preliminary issue, it was unnecessary to decide between these alternatives.

I find it, at this stage, both necessary and helpful to examine the principal Australian cases. ...

I feel unable to draw any valid distinction between the reckless riding of the motor cycle in the present case by the deceased boy, Hunt, and the plaintiff under the influence of drink, and the reckless driving of the cars, albeit stolen, in *Smith* v *Jenkins* and *Bondarenko* v *Sommers*. The words of Barwick CJ in *Smith* v *Jenkins* (1970) 119 CLR 397 at 399–400:

> The driving of the car by the appellant, the manner of which is the basis of the respondent's complaint, was in the circumstances as much a use of the car by the respondent as it was a use by the appellant. That use was their joint enterprise of the moment.

apply with equal force to the riding of the motor cycle in the present case. This is a case which, in Bingham LJ's words, the plaintiff's action in truth arises directly *ex turpi causa*.

It remains, however, to consider whether the agreement or understanding between the plaintiff and the deceased to ride the motor cycle recklessly while under the influence of drink falls within s. 148(3) of the Road Traffic Act 1972 and so is of no effect so far as it purports or might be held to negative or restrict any such liability of the deceased in respect of persons carried in or on the vehicle as is required by the Act to be covered by a policy of insurance.

It is fundamental to the distinction by the Australian courts between *Smith* v *Jenkins* and *Bondarenko* v *Sommers* (and the decision of the Full Court of the Supreme Court of New South Wales in *Godbolt* v *Fittock* [1963] SR (NSW) 617 on the one hand and *Jackson* v *Harrison* and *Progress and Properties Ltd* v *Craft* (1976) 51 ALJR 184 on the other hand) that the joint illegal purpose on which the parties were engaged at the time of the accident must have displaced the ordinary standard of care. Does s. 148(3) have the effect that an express or tacit agreement by the parties to engage in such a joint illegal venture cannot be relied on to negative or restrict liability for negligent driving in the ordinary sense of those words?

My answer to that question is 'No' because s. 148(3) is concerned to preclude a defence of *volenti*, but it is not concerned with any defence of illegality. The words 'agreement or understanding' in s. 148(3) do not contemplate an illegal agreement, express or tacit, to carry out an illegal purpose, otherwise, since the words in s. 148(3) are 'negative or restrict' liability, the passenger in the stolen getaway car driven recklessly from the scene of a robbery in order to escape interception and capture would be able to recover full damages from the Motor Insurers' Bureau, as representing the uninsured driver, without even any reduction or restriction of the damages for contributory negligence.

For the foregoing reasons I would dismiss this appeal.

2.2.3   CONTRIBUTORY NEGLIGENCE

LAW REFORM (CONTRIBUTORY NEGLIGENCE) ACT 1945

1.   Apportionment of liability in case of contributory negligence

(1)   Where any person suffers damage as the result partly of his own fault and partly of the fault of any other person or persons, a claim in respect of that damage shall not be defeated by reason of the fault of the person suffering the damage, but the damages recoverable in respect thereof shall be reduced to such extent as the court thinks just and equitable having regard to the claimant's share in the responsibility of the damage: Provided that—

(a)   this subsection shall not operate to defeat any defence arising under a contract;

(b)   where any contract or enactment providing for the limitation of liability is applicable to the claim, the amount of damages recoverable by the claimant by virtue of this subsection shall not exceed the maximum limit so applicable.

(2)   Where damages are recoverable by any person by virtue of the foregoing subsection subject to such reduction as is therein mentioned, the court shall find and record the total damages which would have been recoverable if the claimant had not been at fault.

. . .

(5)   Where, in any case to which subsection (1) of this section applies, one of the persons at fault avoids liability to any other such person or his personal representative by pleading the Limitation Act, 1939, or any other enactment limiting the time within which proceedings may be taken, he shall not be entitled to recover any damages [. . .] from that other person or representative by virtue of the said subsection.

(6)   Where any case to which subsection (1) of this section applies is tried with a jury, the jury shall determine the total damages which would have been recoverable if the claimant had not been at fault and the extent to which those damages are to be reduced.

. . .

4.   Interpretation
The following expressions have the meanings hereby respectively assigned to them, that is to say—

'court' means, in relation to any claim, the court or arbitrator by or before whom the claim falls to be determined;
'damage' includes loss of life and personal injury; [. . .]
'fault' means negligence, breach of statutory duty or other act or omission which gives rise to liability in tort or would, apart from this Act, give rise to the defence of contributory negligence.

CORPORACION NACIONAL DEL COBRE DE CHILE v SOGEMIN METALS LTD AND OTHERS [1997] 2 All ER 917

CARNWATH J: . . . What [the paragraphs in the defences which the plaintiff sought to strike out] come down to is a plea that simply because (i) officers and employees of Codelco were aware of a relationship between the UK-based commodity broker and Codelco, and (ii) D's trading was overseen by a committee within Codelco, Codelco is at least partly responsible for its own losses; in effect, that they had the opportunity to investigate and failed to take it, but not that they were put on notice in any way of any irregularity.

The plaintiff submits in short that such an assertion does not add up to a defence to a claim based on fraud, whether at law or in equity. It relies principally on *Alliance & Leicester*

Building Society v *Edgestop Ltd* [1994] 2 All ER 38 . . . Mummery J held that . . . contributory negligence of a plaintiff suing in deceit could not be pleaded as a defence. He gave three reasons for this (at 50–51). . . . The first was that: 'At common law contributory negligence of a plaintiff is no defence in the case of an intentional tort.' For this he referred to Lord Lindley in *Quinn* v *Leathem* [1901] AC 495 at 537: 'The intention to injure the plaintiff negatives all excuses . . .' Secondly, he said: 'At common law a successful plea of contributory negligence would have startling consequences in the context of deceit' because it would have defeated the plaintiff's entire claim. Thirdly, he said it would have offended against the general principles stated by Sir George Jessel MR in *Redgrave* v *Hurd* (1881) 20 Ch D 1 at 13–14, in misrepresentation cases: '. . . that the effect of false representation is not got rid of on the ground that the person to whom it was made has been guilty of negligence.'

The defendants criticised certain aspects of this judgment [in *Alliance & Leicester*], but it seems to me to have been a fully argued and considered judgment and it would not be appropriate for me to depart from it. In any event, it seems to be entirely consistent with the tenor of the text books and the other authorities to which I have been referred . . . The *Alliance and Leicester* case is cited [in *Clerk & Lindsell on Tort* (17th edn, 1995), at para 3–19] as authority for [the proposition that a defence of contributory negligence was not available in an action for deceit]. The note indicates that contributory negligence is available in a claim under s. 2(1) of the Misrepresentation Act 1967 and refers to *Gran Gelato Ltd* v *Richcliff (Group) Ltd* [1992] 1 All ER 865 . . . As to *Gran Gelato Ltd* v *Richcliff (Group)*, I agree with Mummery J in *Alliance & Leicester* (at 52–53), that that decision rests on analogy with negligence and does not affect arguments in respect of deceit. He also noticed that in fact in that case, although holding that a plea of contributory negligence was possible, the court declined to make any reduction of the plaintiff's damages, on the ground that 'in principle, carelessness in not making inquiries provides no answer to a claim that the plaintiff has done that which the representor intended that he should do.'

A number of cases have been referred to dealing with trespass to the person but I do not find these helpful since the subject matter is so different. There does appear to be a difference between the United Kingdom, where contributory negligence has been recognised as a defence in such cases (see *Murphy* v *Culhane* [1976] 3 All ER 533) and other common law jurisdictions (see *Horkin* v *North Melbourne Football Club Social Club* [1983] 1 VR 153 where *Murphy* was not followed in Australia).

If *Murphy* is right, it shows that the statement by Lord Lindley in *Quinn* v *Leathem* (at 537) that the 'intention to injure negatives all excuses' cannot be taken without qualification, but that does not, to my mind, undermine Mummery J's conclusion with respect to deceit. His conclusion is, as I have said, in line with the consistent strand in the authorities in law and equity.

I was referred by the plaintiff to an interesting summary of dicta on this point in *Day* v *Bank of New South Wales* (1978) 18 SASR 163 at 176, in which it was held that contributory negligence is not available as a defence to a claim for misappropriation of cheques. I was also referred to an important decision of the Privy Council in *Barton* v *Armstrong* [1975] 2 All ER 465 [where it was held, inter alia] '(1) that the equitable rule, which enabled a contract entered into as a result of fraudulent misrepresentation to be set aside, applied in cases of duress . . .'

. . . There appears to be no direct authority on the availability of contributory negligence, or its equivalent in equity, as a defence to a claim based on bribery, as opposed to deceit or duress, but I can see no sensible reason for drawing a distinction. If a defendant has dishonestly induced the plaintiff's employee to act to the plaintiff's disadvantage, it should not matter whether he has done so by deception, by threats, or by bribery. As in the case of deceit, in my view, the defendant cannot reduce his responsibility merely because the plaintiff had the opportunity to intervene but failed to take it.

. . . There needs to be something more, something to put him on notice of the dishonesty and a consequent failure by him of 'reasonable prudence'. There is nothing of that kind pleaded in the defence. There is no allegation that the plaintiff knew or had reason to suspect dishonesty, no allegation of conduct 'so egregious' that he is the author of his own misfortune. If that sort of allegation is to be made, in my view it must be pleaded.

. . . In my view, the mere fact that the plaintiff had the opportunity to discover the fraud and failed to take it is not a defence or a ground for reducing the damages. As I have explained, the impugned paragraphs of the defence amount to no more than that. In my view they should be struck out. The same applies to the equivalent paragraphs to the second and third defendants' defences . . .

2.3 Summary

KIRKHAM v CHIEF CONSTABLE OF THE GREATER MANCHESTER POLICE
[1990] 3 All ER 246 (CA)

LLOYD LJ: I turn last to *ex turpi causa non oritur actio*. This is the most difficult part of the case. Prior to 1961 suicide was a crime. Although there appears to be no reported case directly in point, I do not doubt that a claim based on the failure of the authorities to prevent a suicide would have failed. The courts would have declined to lend their aid to enforce such a claim. But by s. 1 of the Suicide Act 1961 the rule of law whereby it was a crime for a person to commit suicide was abrogated. The question is whether that Act, by abrogating the criminal nature of suicide, has taken away the defence of *ex turpi causa*. The judge took the straightforward line that the defence depends on some causally related criminal activity. He referred to *Hardy* v *Motor Insurers' Bureau* [1964] 2 QB 745 and *Murphy* v *Culhane* [1977] QB 94 and considered that, since suicide is no longer a crime, the defence *ex turpi causa* is no longer available.

Unfortunately, the judge was not referred to three recent cases in which the scope of the defence has been considered: *Thackwell* v *Barclays Bank plc* [1986] 1 All ER 676, *Saunders* v *Edwards* [1987] 2 All ER 651, [1987] 1 WLR 1116 and *Euro-Diam Ltd* v *Bathurst* [1990] QB 1. The last two cases contain an elaborate analysis of the relevant principles by Kerr LJ. It would be superfluous to summarise the principles here. It is sufficient to quote two sentences from Kerr LJ's judgment in the *Euro-Diam* case [1988] 2 All ER 23 at 28–29, [1990] QB 1 at 35:

> The *ex turpi causa* defence ultimately rests on a principle of public policy that the courts will not assist a plaintiff who has been guilty of illegal (or immoral) conduct of which the courts should take notice. It applies if, in all the circumstances, it would be an affront to the public conscience to grant the plaintiff the relief which he seeks because the court would thereby appear to assist or encourage the plaintiff in his illegal conduct or to encourage others in similar acts . . .

It is apparent from these authorities that the *ex turpi causa* defence is not confined to criminal conduct. So we cannot adopt the simple approach favoured by the judge. We have to ask ourselves the much more difficult question whether to afford relief in such a case as this, arising, as it does, directly out of a man's suicide, would affront the public conscience, or, as I would prefer to say, shock the ordinary citizen. I have come to the conclusion that the answer should be No. I would give two reasons.

In the first place the Suicide Act 1961 does more than abolish the crime of suicide. It is symptomatic of a change in the public attitude to suicide generally. It is no longer regarded with the same abhorrence as it once was. It is, of course, impossible for us to say how far the change in the public attitude has gone. But that there has been a change is beyond doubt. The fact that aiding and abetting suicide remains a crime under s. 2 of the 1961 Act does not diminish the force of the argument.

The second reason is that in at least two decided cases courts have awarded damages following a suicide or attempted suicide. In *Selfe* v *Ilford and District Hospital Management Committee* (1970) 114 SJ 935 Hinchcliffe J awarded the plaintiff damages against a hospital for failing to take proper precautions when they knew that the plaintiff was a suicide risk. In *Pigney* v *Pointers Transport Services Ltd* [1957] 2 All ER 807, [1957] 1 WLR 1121, to which I have already referred, Pilcher J awarded damages to the dependants of a suicide under the Fatal Accidents Act 1846. Moreover, in *Hyde* v *Tameside Area Health Authority*, another hospital case, the judge awarded £200,000 damages in respect of an unsuccessful suicide attempt. The Court of Appeal allowed the defendant's appeal on the ground that the plaintiff's cause of action arose *ex turpi causa*; the appeal was allowed. *Selfe's* case and *Pigney's* case are not binding on us. But they are important for this reason. They show, or appear to show, that the public conscience was not affronted. It did not occur to anyone to argue in either case that the granting of a remedy would shock the ordinary citizen; nor did it occur to the court.

For the above reason I would hold that the defence of *ex turpi causa* is not available in these cases, at any rate where, as here, there is medical evidence that the suicide is not in full possession of his mind. To entertain the plaintiff's claim in such a case as the present would not, in my view, affront the public conscience, or shock the ordinary citizen. I thus reach the same conclusion as the judge on this aspect of the case, but for somewhat different reasons. . . .

Farquharson LJ and Sir Denys Buckley concurred. The Chief Constable's appeal was dismissed.

TINSLEY v *MILLIGAN* [1993] 3 All ER 65 (HL)

This case was concerned with the effect of illegality in contract, and on claims to property between contracting parties. The 'public conscience' test was rejected by their Lordships in this context.

In many instances claims in the torts of deceit (fraud) and conversion spring from contract.

LORD GOFF: Before the Court of Appeal it was the submission of the appellant that there was a principle of law, binding on the Court of Appeal, that the court will not give effect to an equitable interest arising from a transaction which is unlawful by reason of a claimant's unlawful purpose; and that accordingly the respondent was unable to establish any equitable interest in 141 Thomas Street, or to defeat the appellant's claim to possession. This principle was said to be well recognised in a number of authorities; but reliance was placed in particular on *Gascoigne* v *Gascoigne* [1918] 1 KB 223 and *Tinker* v *Tinker* [1970] 1 All ER 540, [1970] P 136, the former a decision of a Divisional Court and the latter a decision of the Court of Appeal. It was this line of authority which ultimately persuaded Ralph Gibson LJ in his dissenting judgment, that the appellant's appeal should be allowed. But Nicholls LJ was not so persuaded. He first invoked a group of recent Court of Appeal decisions, which point to a more flexible approach than has been adopted in the past in cases of illegality under which, according to Nicholls LJ ([1992] 2 All ER 391 at 398, [1992] Ch 310 at 319):

> . . . the underlying principle is the so-called public conscience test. The court must weigh, or balance, the adverse consequences of granting relief against the adverse consequences of refusing relief. The ultimate decision calls for a value judgment . . .

It is against the background of these established principles that I turn to consider the judgments of the majority of the Court of Appeal. As I have recorded, Nicholls LJ in particular invoked a line of recent cases, largely developed in the Court of Appeal, from which he deduced the proposition that, in cases of illegality, the underlying principle is the so-called public conscience test, under which the court must weigh, or balance, the adverse consequences of respectively granting or refusing relief. This is little different, if at all, from stating that the court has a discretion whether to grant or refuse relief.

2.4   End of Chapter Assessment Question

Rex, and his fiancée, Portia, after drinking alcohol at lunchtime, stole a car for a joyride. Portia, not wearing her seat belt, drove the car at speed along a cliff top road, skidded on a bend and the car crashed into a boulder before coming to a stop, and hanging precariously over the edge of the cliff. Rex was injured but managed to get out of the car.

Sam, a passing motorist, stopped at the scene of the accident and, together with Rex, climbed into the car to help Portia. The car tipped up under the combined weight of them all and fell down the cliff. Rex and Sam were seriously injured and Portia was killed, but it transpired that she would in any event probably have died from her initial injuries.

Discuss the tortious issues arising from these events.

2.5   End of Chapter Assessment Outline Answer

P = Portia, R = Rex, S = Sam

P and R are injured whilst P is driving a car which they have stolen following a lunchtime 'drink'. Later, P is killed and R suffers, **apparently**, *further* injury ('serious' injury is mentioned, but **not** in relation to the *first* incident) when the car, still containing P, falls over a cliff during an unsuccessful rescue attempt by R, and S, a passing motorist. S is also injured in the second incident.

In the first instance it should be noted that P and R have committed the torts of trespass to goods and conversion by stealing the car. It is, however, mainly in relation to **other** tortious liability that the problem directs us viz. liability arising in the tort of negligence and liability to rescuers.

P's injuries

Up until the point at which the car falls over the cliff P would seem to have been the author of her own misfortune – she was driving the car at speed and not wearing a seat belt; there being no evidence that R was to blame, other than as a participant in the illegal joyride. No evidence is given on the point, but presumably it was – or could have been – a combination of bad driving and a failure to wear a seat beat which contributed to her injuries. Even if only one of these 'agents' was the cause the fact remains that it was her own fault. (There would be no point in considering the failure to wear a seat belt – statutory regulations require seat belts to be worn – as evidence of contributory negligence under the Law Reform (Contributory Negligence) Act 1945 because she could hardly have a 'defence' against her **own** wrongdoing.)

It might be said that P has caused her own death: *McWilliams* v *Arrol*.

If the later event of the car falling over the cliff is taken into account we see that P was in fact 'killed'. The evidence tells us, however, that she would have probably died anyway – as the result of her initial injuries. Thus, on the basis of the 'but for' test of causation (see e.g. *Barnett* v *Chelsea Hospital)* any tortious acts that R and/or S might have committed would not be causatively potent in connection with her death.

It must be the case that R and S could only be liable to P if their acts, **assuming** at this point that these acts are tortious in nature, have caused **further** damage to an already injured person and this is not clear from the information given. Authorities such as *Cutler* v *Vauxhall Motors; Baker* v *Willoughby* (and *Jobling* v *Associated Dairies*) would be relevant here.

R's injuries

R is injured initially as the result of the car crash. It must be clear that P owes a duty of care in negligence to R, her passenger – see *Nettleship* v *Weston*. There should be little difficulty in establishing the **general** criteria set out in *Caparo* v *Dickman*.

R would have to prove negligence on the facts i.e. that P was in breach of her duty of care. According to *Nettleship* v *Weston* the standard of a qualified, competent driver would be

applied. Evidence of negligence would have to be introduced e.g. her level of intoxication at the time.

P (or her **estate**, to be precise) would not be able to plead *volenti non fit injuria* (as in *Morris v Murray*) because of the Road Traffic Act 1988. Contributory negligence, however, under the provisions of the 1945 Act, might be available as a partial defence as in *Owens v Brimmell*.

Ex turpi causa non oritur actio might also be pleaded, as in *Pitts v Hunt*, since both R and P were engaged in an illegal enterprise at the time, quite apart from the matter of drinking alcohol in the context of using a vehicle on the highway.

In the present circumstances, however, is R sufficiently *in pari delicto* with P? Will the court refuse to set a duty of care/standard of care/is the injury an integral part of the activity or are the two inextricably intertwined? Would the public find it 'distateful' if the court allowed the action to proceed? Relevant authorities are *Saunders v Edwards*; *Euro-Diam v Bathurst*; *Kirkham v Chief Constable of the Greater Manchester Police*; *Revill v Newbery*. In simpler terms, would the court exercise its **discretion** against R (*per* Lord Goff in *Tinsley v Milligan*)?

More evidential detail is required of the 'partnership' (if such it be) between P and R, and of what transpired during the fateful journey, in order to arrive at a fully considered resolution. In *prima facie* terms, however, R may be so far implicated in the venture that the court would refuse to aid him in any litigation he wished to pursue.

R is presumably further injured in the attempted rescue of P. (At this point it may be noted, although only for the purpose of pursuing a moot point, since an argument on causation has already been advanced, that R may, because of his involvement in the accident (more detail is required of the degree and nature of this involvement), owe an obligation to rescue P – see *Horsley v MacLaren* ('The Ogopogo').)

'Danger invites rescue': *Haynes v Harwood*. A rescuer, however, may be obliged to be as careful as possible in carrying out the rescue and not to make the situation worse: *Horsley v MacLaren*. It **may** be that the **way in which** the rescue is performed in the present circumstances is negligent, though the reasonable man **in the heat and danger of rescue** will presumably be excused much that would attract the censure of the court in different circumstances.

Otherwise, P will, in principle, owe a duty to R as a rescuer. On the other hand, *ex turpi causa non oritur actio* may apply – see above. Furthermore, the defence of contributory negligence under the 1945 Act is available against a rescuer: *Harrison v BRB*. Has R been sufficiently careless of his own safety on the facts? In *Harrison* the court was reluctant to apply this defence against a rescuer, but on the present facts R may himself be partly responsible (see argument advanced above) for the state of affairs.

S's injuries

On the present facts it is submitted that S's rescue attempt is probably foreseeable: *Haynes v Harwood* and P and R are **jointly** responsible for creating the situation of danger. In that sense, P and R are joint tortfeasors with regard to S's injuries. (The provisions of the Civil Liability (Contributions) Act 1978 will apply as between P and R.)

Thus, P and R are responsible in tort for S's injuries. In principle, as we have seen, the defence of contributory negligence (1945 Act) is available against a rescuer: *Harrison v BRB*. Depending on the evidence, the court may accordingly reduce S's damages.

(It has been noted that rescuers may owe a duty to proceed as carefully as possible with the rescue. The spectre of S and R as joint tortfeasors with regard to P could, no doubt, materialise were it not for the argument on **causation** referred to above.)

It might be argued that R and S owe a duty to each other as fellow rescuers, as *Donoghue v Stevenson* neighbours, and that they should have each other's safety in mind during the rescue attempt. The respective parties might have difficulty in persuading the court that there has been negligence on the facts, however, bearing in mind the 'heat of the moment', etc.

On this point, it is not so clear that R's initial illegality would still have potency; it might be spent as a causative force. It could be said that the initial illegality only created the opportunity for the rescue attempt and that this should be regarded as a separate incident.

The court might, however, decide to exercise its discretion against any action by R, under the cloak of 'public disapproval'.

CHAPTER THREE

NEGLIGENCE

3.1 Duty

3.1.1 THE NEIGHBOUR TEST AS A GENERAL PRINCIPLE OF LIABILITY

HOME OFFICE v DORSET YACHT CO. LTD [1970] 2 All ER 294 (HL)

LORD REID: The case for the Home Office is that under no circumstances can Borstal officers owe any duty to any member of the public to take care to prevent trainees under their control or supervision from injuring him or his property. If that is the law, then inquiry into the facts of this case would be a waste of time and money because whatever the facts may be the respondents must lose. That case is based on three main arguments. First it is said that there is virtually no authority for imposing a duty of this kind. Secondly it is said that no person can be liable for a wrong done by another who is of full age and capacity and who is not the servant or acting on behalf of that person. And thirdly it is said that public policy (or the policy of the relevant legislation) requires that these officers should be immune from any such liability.

The first would at one time have been a strong argument. About the beginning of this century most eminent lawyers thought that there were a number of separate torts involving negligence, each with its own rules, and they were most unwilling to add more. They were of course aware from a number of leading cases that in the past the courts had from time to time recognised new duties and new grounds of action. But the heroic age was over; it was time to cultivate certainty and security in the law; the categories of negligence were virtually closed. The Attorney-General invited us to return to those halcyon days, but, attractive though it may be, I cannot accede to his invitation.

In later years there has been a steady trend towards regarding the law of negligence as depending on principle so that, when a new point emerges, one should ask not whether it is covered by authority but whether recognised principles apply to it. *Donoghue* v *Stevenson* [1932] AC 562 may be regarded as a milestone, and the well-known passage in Lord Atkin's speech should I think be regarded as a statement of principle. It is not to be treated as if it were a statutory definition. It will require qualification in new circumstances. But I think that the time has come when we can and should say that it ought to apply unless there is some justification or valid explanation for its exclusion. For example, causing economic loss is a different matter; for one thing, it is often caused by deliberate action. Competition involves traders being entitled to damage their rivals' interests by promoting their own, and there is a long chapter of the law determining in what circumstances owners of land can and in what circumstances they may not use their proprietary rights so as to injure their neighbours. But where negligence is involved the tendency has been to apply principles analogous to those stated by Lord Atkin: cf. *Hedley Byrne & Co. Ltd* v *Heller & Partners Ltd* [1964] AC 465. And when a person has done nothing to put himself in any relationship with another person in distress or with his property mere accidental propinquity does not require him to go to that person's assistance. There may be a moral duty to do so, but it is not practicable to make it a legal duty. And then there are cases, e.g., with regard to landlord and tenant, where the law was settled long ago and neither

Parliament nor this House sitting judicially has made any move to alter it. But I can see nothing to prevent our approaching the present case with Lord Atkin's principles in mind . . . I would dismiss this appeal.

LORD DIPLOCK: . . . Is any duty of care to prevent the escape of a Borstal trainee from custody owed by the Home Office to persons whose property would be likely to be damaged by the tortious acts of the Borstal trainee if he escaped?

This is the first time that this specific question has been posed at a higher judicial level than that of a county court. Your Lordships in answering it will be performing a judicial function similar to that performed in *Donoghue* v *Stevenson* [1932] AC 652 and more recently in *Hedley Byrne & Co. Ltd* v *Heller & Partners Ltd* [1964] AC 465 of deciding whether the English law of civil wrongs should be extended to impose legal liability to make reparation for the loss caused to another by conduct of a kind which has not hitherto been recognised by the courts as entailing any such liability.

This function, which judges hesitate to acknowledge as law-making, plays at most a minor role in the decision of the great majority of cases, and little conscious thought has been given to analysing its methodology. Outstanding exceptions are to be found in the speeches of Lord Atkin in *Donoghue* v *Stevenson* and of Lord Devlin in *Hedley Byrne & Co. Ltd* v *Heller & Partners Ltd*. It was because the former was the first authoritative attempt at such an analysis that it has had so seminal an effect upon the modern development of the law of negligence.

It will be apparent that I agree with the Master of the Rolls that what we are concerned with in this appeal 'is . . . at bottom a matter of public policy which we, as judges, must resolve.' He cited in support Lord Pearce's dictum in *Hedley Byrne & Co. Ltd* v *Heller & Partners Ltd* [1964] AC 465, 536:

> How wide the sphere of the duty of care in negligence is to be laid depends ultimately upon the courts' assessment of the demands of society for protection from the carelessness of others.

The reference in this passage to 'the courts' in the plural is significant, for

> As always in English law, the first step in such an inquiry is to see how far the authorities have gone, for new categories in the law do not spring into existence overnight (*per* Lord Devlin, at p. 525).

The justification of the courts' role in giving the effect of law to the judges' conception of the public interest in the field of negligence is based upon the cumulative experience of the judiciary of the actual consequences of lack of care in particular instances. And the judicial development of the law of negligence rightly proceeds by seeking first to identify the relevant characteristics that are common to the kinds of conduct and relationship between the parties which are involved in the case for decision and the kinds of conduct and relationships which have been held in previous decisions of the courts to give rise to a duty of care.

The method adopted at this stage of the process is analytical and inductive. It starts with an analysis of the characteristics of the conduct and relationship involved in each of the decided cases. But the analyst must know what he is looking for, and this involves his approaching his analysis with some general conception of conduct and relationships which ought to give rise to a duty of care. This analysis leads to a proposition which can be stated in the form:

> In all the decisions that have been analysed a duty of care has been held to exist wherever the conduct and the relationship possessed each of the characteristics A, B, C, D, etc, and has not so far been found to exist when any of these characteristics were absent.

For the second stage, which is deductive and analytical, that proposition is converted to: 'In all cases where the conduct and relationship possess each of the characteristics A, B, C, D, etc, a duty of care arises.' The conduct and relationship involved in the case for decision is then analysed to ascertain whether they possess each of these characteristics. If they do the conclusion follows that a duty of care does arise in the case for decision.

But since ex hypothesi the kind of case which we are now considering offers a choice whether or not to extend the kinds of conduct or relationships which give rise to a duty of care, the conduct or relationship which is involved in it will lack at least one of the characteristics A, B, C or D, etc. And the choice is exercised by making a policy decision as to whether or not a duty of care ought to exist if the characteristic which is lacking were absent or redefined in terms broad enough to include the case under consideration. The policy decision will be influenced by the same general conception of what ought to give rise to a duty of care as was used in approaching the analysis. The choice to extend is given effect to by redefining the characteristics in more general terms so as to exclude the necessity to conform to limitations imposed by the former definition which are considered to be inessential. The cases which are landmarks in the common law, such as *Lickbarrow* v *Mason* (1787) 2 Term Rep 63, *Rylands* v *Fletcher* (1868) LR 3 HL 330, *Indermaur* v *Dames* (1866) LR 1 CP 274, *Donoghue* v *Stevenson* [1932] AC 562, to mention but a few, are instances of cases where the cumulative experience of judges has led to a restatement in wide general terms of characteristics of conduct and relationships which give rise to legal liability.

The plaintiff's argument in the present appeal . . . seeks to treat as a universal not the specific proposition of law in *Donoghue* v *Stevenson* which was about a manufacturer's liability for damage caused by his dangerous products but the well-known aphorism used by Lord Atkin to describe a 'general conception of relations giving rise to a duty of care' [1932] AC 562, 580:

> You must take reasonable care to avoid acts or omissions which you can reasonably foresee would be likely to injure your neighbour. Who, then, in law is my neighbour? The answer seems to be—persons who are so closely and directly affected by my act that I ought reasonably to have them in contemplation as being so affected when I am directing my mind to the acts or omissions which are called in question.

Used as a guide to characteristics which will be found to exist in conduct and relationships which give rise to a legal duty of care this aphorism marks a milestone in the modern development of the law of negligence. But misused as a universal it is manifestly false. . . .

In the present appeal the place from which the trainees escaped was an island from which the only means of escape would presumably be a boat accessible from the shore of the island. There is thus material fit for consideration at the trial for holding that the plaintiff, as the owner of a boat moored off the island, fell within the category of persons to whom a duty of care to prevent the escape of the trainees was owed by the officers responsible for their custody.

If, therefore, it can be established at the trial of this action (1) that the Borstal officers in failing to take precautions to prevent the trainees from escaping were acting in breach of their instructions and not in bona fide exercise of a discretion delegated to them by the Home Office as to the degree of control to be adopted and (2) that it was reasonably foreseeably by the officers that if these particular trainees did escape they would be likely to appropriate a boat moored in the vicinity of Brownsea Island for the purpose of eluding immediate pursuit and to cause damage to it, the Borstal officers would be in breach of a duty care owed to the plaintiff and the plaintiff would, in my view, have a cause of action against the Home Office as vicariously liable for the 'negligence' of the Borstal officers.

I would accordingly dismiss the appeal on the preliminary issue of law and allow the case to go for trial on those issues of fact.

Lord Morris also agreed that the appeal should be dismissed, but Viscount Dilhorne argued that the appeal should be allowed.

ANNS v LONDON BOROUGH OF MERTON [1977] 2 All ER 492 (HL)

LORD WILBERFORCE: Through the trilogy of cases in this House—*Donoghue* v *Stevenson* [1932] AC 562, *Hedley Byrne & Co. Ltd* v *Heller & Partners Ltd* [1964] AC 465, and *Dorset Yacht Co. Ltd* v *Home Office* [1970] AC 1004, the position has now been reached that in order to establish that a duty of care arises in a particular situation, it is not necessary to bring the facts of that situation within those of previous situations in which a duty of care has been held to exist. Rather the question has to be approached in two stages. First one has to ask whether, as between the alleged wrongdoer and the person who has suffered damage there is a sufficient relationship of proximity or neighbourhood such that, in the reasonable contemplation of the former, carelessness on his part may be likely to cause damage to the latter—in which case a prima facie duty of care arises. Secondly, if the first question is answered affirmatively, it is necessary to consider whether there are any considerations which ought to negative, or to reduce or limit the scope of the duty or the class of person to whom it is owed or the damages to which a breach of it may give rise . . . .

What then is the extent of the local authority's duty towards these persons? Although, as I have suggested, a situation of 'proximity' existed between the council and owners and occupiers of the houses, I do not think that a description of the council's duty can be based upon the 'neighbourhood' principle alone or upon merely any such factual relationship as 'control' as suggested by the Court of Appeal. So to base it would be to neglect an essential factor which is that the local authority is a public body, discharging functions under statute: its powers and duties are definable in terms of public not private law. The problem which this type of action creates, is to define the circumstances in which the law should impose, over and above, or perhaps alongside, these public law powers and duties, a duty in private law towards individuals such that they may sue for damages in a civil court. It is in this context that the distinction sought to be drawn between duties and mere powers has to be examined.

Most, indeed probably all, statutes relating to public authorities or public bodies, contain in them a large area of policy. The courts call this 'discretion' meaning that the decision is one for the authority or body to make, and not for the courts. Many statutes also prescribe or at least presuppose the practical execution of policy decisions: a convenient description of this is to say that in addition to the area of policy or discretion, there is an operational area. Although this distinction between the policy area and the operational area is convenient, and illuminating, it is probably a distinction of degree; many 'operational' powers or duties have in them some element of 'discretion.' It can safely be said that the more 'operational' a power or duty may be, the easier it is to superimpose upon it a common law duty of care.

I do not think that it is right to limit this to a duty to avoid causing extra or additional damage beyond what must be expected to arise from the exercise of the power or duty. That may be correct when the act done under the statute *inherently* must adversely *affect* the interest of individuals. But many other acts can be done without causing any harm to anyone—indeed may be directed to preventing harm from occurring. In these cases the duty is the normal one of taking care to avoid harm to those likely to be affected.

Let us examine the Public Health Act 1936 in the light of this. Undoubtedly it lays out a wide area of policy. It is for the local authority, a public and elected body, to decide upon the scale of resources which it can make available in order to carry out its functions under Part II of the Act—how many inspectors, with what expert qualifications, it should recruit, how often inspections are to be made, what tests are to be carried out, must be for its decision. It is no accident that the Act is drafted in terms of functions and powers rather than in terms of positive duty. As was well said, public authorities have to strike a balance between the claims of efficiency and thrift (du Parcq LJ in *Kent* v *East Suffolk Rivers Catchment Board* [1940] 1 KB 319, 338): whether they get the balance right can only be decided through the ballot box, not in the courts. It is said—there are reflections of this in the judgments in *Dutton* v *Bognor Regis Urban District Council* [1972] 1 QB 373—that the local authority is under no duty to inspect, and this is used as the foundation for an argument, also found in some of the cases, that if it need not inspect at all, it cannot be liable for negligent inspection: if it were to be held so liable, so it is said, councils would simply decide against inspection. I think that this is too crude an argument. It overlooks the fact that local authorities are public bodies operating under statute with a clear responsibility for public health in their area. They must, and in fact do, make their discretionary decisions responsibly and for reasons which accord with the statutory purpose . . .

If they do not exercise their discretion in this way they can be challenged in the courts. Thus, to say that councils are under no duty to inspect, is not a sufficient statement of the position. They are under a duty to give proper consideration to the question whether they should inspect or not. Their immunity from attack, in the event of failure to inspect, in other words, though great is not absolute. And because it is not absolute, the necessary premise for the proposition 'if no duty to inspect, then no duty to take care in inspection' vanishes.

Passing then to the duty as regards inspection, if made. On principle there must surely be a duty to exercise reasonable care. The standard of care must be related to the duty to be performed—namely to ensure compliance with the byelaws. It must be related to the fact that the person responsible for construction in accordance with the byelaws is the builder, and that the inspector's function is supervisory. It must be related to the fact that once the inspector has passed the foundations they will be covered up, with no subsequent opportunity for inspection. But this duty, heavily operational though it may be, is still a duty arising under the statute. There may be a discretionary element in its exercise—discretionary as to the time and manner of inspection, and the techniques to be used. A plaintiff complaining of negligence must prove, the burden being on him, that action taken was not within the limits of a discretion bona fide exercised, before he can begin to rely upon a common law duty of care. But if he can do this, he should, in principle, be able to sue.

Is there, then, authority against the existence of any such duty or any reason to restrict it? It is said that there is an absolute distinction in the law between statutory duty and statutory power—the former giving rise to possible liability, the latter not, or at least not doing so unless the exercise of the power involves some positive act creating some fresh or additional damage.

My Lords, I do not believe that any such absolute rule exists . . .

In [*Dorset Yacht Co. Ltd* v *Home Office* [1970] AC 1004] the Borstal officers, for whose actions the Home Office was vicariously responsible, were acting, in their control of the boys, under statutory powers. But it was held that, nevertheless they were under a duty of care as regards persons who might suffer damage as the result of their carelessness—see *per* Lord Reid, at pp. 1030–1031, Lord Morris of Borth-y-Gest, at p. 1036, Lord Pearson, at p. 1055: 'The existence of the statutory duties does not exclude liability at common law for negligence in the performance of the statutory duties.' Lord Diplock in his speech gives this topic extended consideration with a view to relating the officers' responsibility under public law to their liability in damages to members of the public under private, civil law: see pp. 1064 et seq. My noble and learned friends points out that the accepted principles which are applicable to Powers conferred by a private Act of Parliament, as laid down in *Geddis* v *Bann Reservoir Proprietors*, 3 App Cas 430, cannot automatically be applied to public statutes which confer a large measure of discretion upon public authorities. As regards the latter, for a civil action based on negligence at common law to succeed, there must be acts or omissions taken outside the limits of the delegated discretion: in such a case 'Its actionability falls to be determined by the civil law principles of negligence': see [1970] AC 1004, 1068.

It is for this reason that the law, as stated in some of the speeches in *East Suffolk Rivers Catchment Board* v *Kent* [1941] AC 74, but not in those of Lord Atkin or Lord Thankerton, requires at the present time to be understood and applied with the recognition that, quite apart from such consequence as may flow from an examination of the duties laid down by the particular statute, there may be room, once one is outside the area of legitimate discretion or policy, for a duty of care at common law. It is irrelevant to the existence of this duty of care whether what is created by the statute is a duty or a power: the duty of care may exist in either case. The difference between the two lies in this, that, in the case of a power, liability cannot exist unless the act complained of lies outside the ambit of the power. In *Dorset Yacht Co. Ltd* v *Home Office* [1970] AC 1004 the officers may (on the assumed facts) have acted outside any discretion delegated to them and having disregarded their instruction as to the precautions which they should take to prevent the trainees from escaping: see *per* Lord Diplock, at p. 1069. So in the present case, the allegations made are consistent with the council or its inspector having acted outside any delegated discretion either as to the making of an inspection, or as to the manner in which an inspection was made. Whether they did so must be determined at the trial. . . .

Lords Diplock, Russell and Simon agreed with Lord Wilberforce in allowing the appeal, whilst Lord Salmon argued that it be dismissed.

3.1.2   A DIFFERENT VIEW

GOVERNORS OF THE PEABODY DONATION FUND v SIR LINDSAY PARKINSON & CO. LTD [1984] 3 All ER 529 (HL)

LORD KEITH: Lord Atkin's famous enunciation of the general principle of negligence in *Donoghue* v *Stevenson* [1932] AC 562 at 580 has long been recognised as not intended to afford a comprehensive definition, to the effect that every situation which is capable of falling within the terms of the utterance and which results in loss automatically affords a remedy in damages. Lord Reid said in *Home Office* v *Dorset Yacht Co. Ltd* [1970] AC 1004 at 1027:

> It is not to be treated as if it were a statutory definition. It will require qualification in new circumstances. But I think that the time has come when we can and should say that it ought to apply unless there is some justification or valid explanation for its exclusion. For example, causing economic loss is a different matter; for one thing it is often caused by deliberate action. Competition involves traders being entitled to damage their rivals' interests by promoting their own, and there is a long chapter of the law determining in what circumstances owners of land can, and in what circumstances they may not, use their proprietary rights so as to injure their neighbours. But where negligence is involved the tendency has been to apply principles analogous to those stated by Lord Atkin (cf *Hedley Byrne & Co. Ltd* v *Heller & Partners Ltd* [1964] AC 465). And when a person has done nothing to put himself in any relationship with another person in distress or with his property mere accidental propinquity does not require him to go to that person's assistance. There may be a moral duty to do so, but it is not practicable to make it a legal duty.

Lord Wilberforce spoke on similar lines in *Anns* v *Merton London Borough Council* [1978] AC 728. There has been a tendency in some recent cases to treat these passages as being themselves of a definitive character. This is a temptation which should be resisted. The true question in each case is whether the particular defendant owed to the particular plaintiff a duty of care having the scope which is contended for, and whether he was in breach of that duty with consequent loss to the plaintiff. A relationship of proximity in Lord Atkin's sense must exit before any duty of care can arise, but the scope of the duty must depend on all the circumstances of the case. In *Home Office* v *Dorset Yacht Co. Ltd* [1970] AC 1004 at 1038–1039 Lord Morris, after observing that at the conclusion of his speech in *Donoghue* v *Stevenson* [1932] AC 562 at 599 Lord Atkin said that it was advantageous if the law 'is in accordance with sound common sense' and expressing the view that a special relation existed between the prison officers and the yacht company which gave rise to a duty on the former to control their charges so as to prevent them doing damage, continued:

> Apart from this I would conclude that in the situation stipulated in the present case it would not only be fair and reasonable that a duty of care should exist but that it would be contrary to the fitness of things were it not so. I doubt whether it is necessary to say, in cases where the court is asked whether in a particular situation a duty existed, that the court is called on to make a decision as to policy. Policy need not be invoked where reasons and good sense will at once point the way. If the test whether in some particular situation a duty of care arises may in some cases have to be whether it is fair and reasonable that it should so arise the court must not shrink from being the arbiter. As Lord Radcliffe said in his speech in *Davis Contractors Ltd* v *Fareham Urban District Council* [1956] AC 696 at 728 the court is 'the spokesman of the fair and reasonable man'.

Lords Bridge, Brandon, Scarman and Templeman agreed.

YUEN KUN-YEU v A-G OF HONG KONG [1987] 2 All ER 705 (PC)

It was held that the Commissioner of Deposit Taking Companies in Hong Kong had not voluntarily assumed responsibility to members of the public who had invested in companies he had admitted to the official register. It was not reasonable for the investors to rely on mere registration of the companies as proof of their financial probity: thus the relationship between the parties was insufficiently proximate.

The Commissioner did not owe a duty of care in negligence to the investors.

LORD KEITH: This passage [in *Anns*] has been treated with some reservation in subsequent cases in the House of Lords, in particular by Lord Keith of Kinkel in *Governors of the Peabody Donation Fund* v *Sir Lindsay Parkinson & Co. Ltd* [1985] AC 210, 240, by Lord Brandon of Oakbrook in *Leigh & Sillavan Ltd* v *Aliakmon Shipping Co. Ltd* [1986] AC 785, 815, and by Lord Bridge of Harwich in *Curran* v *Northern Ireland Co-ownership Housing Association Ltd* [1987] AC 718. The speeches containing these reservations were concurred in by all the other members of the House who were party to the decisions. In *Council of the Shire of Sutherland* v *Heyman* (1985) 59 ALJR 564 Brennan J, in the High Court of Australia, indicated his disagreement with the nature of the approach indicated by Lord Wilberforce, saying, at p. 588:

> Of course, if foreseeability of injury to another were the exhaustive criterion of a prima facie duty to act to prevent the occurrence of that injury, it would be essential to introduce some kind of restrictive qualification—perhaps a qualification of the kind stated in the second stage of the general proposition in *Anns*. I am unable to accept that approach. It is preferable, in my view, that the law should develop novel categories of negligence incrementally and by analogy with established categories, rather than by a massive extension of a prima facie duty of care restrained only by indefinable 'considerations which ought to negative, or to reduce or limit the scope of the duty or the class of persons to whom it is owed.' The proper role of the 'second stage', as I attempted to explain in *Jaensch* v *Coffey* [(1984) 58 ALJR 426, 437, 438], embraces no more than 'those further elements [in addition to the neighbour principle] which are appropriate to the particular category of negligence and which confine the duty of care within narrower limits than those which would be defined by an unqualified application of the neighbour principle.

Their Lordships venture to think that the two stage test formulated by Lord Wilberforce for determining the existence of a duty of care in negligence has been elevated to a degree of importance greater than it merits, and greater perhaps than its author intended. Further, the expression of the first stage of the test carries with it a risk of misinterpretation. As Gibbs CJ pointed out in *Council of the Shire of Sutherland* v *Heyman*, 59, ALJR 564, 570, there are two possible views of what Lord Wilberforce meant. The first view, favoured in a number of cases mentioned by Gibbs CJ, is that he meant to test the sufficiency of proximity simply by the reasonable contemplation of likely harm. The second view, favoured by Gibbs CJ himself, is that Lord Wilberforce meant the expression 'proximity or neighbourhood' to be a composite one, importing the whole concept of necessary relationship between plaintiff and defendant described by Lord Atkin in *Donoghue* v *Stevenson* [1932] AC 562, 580. In their Lordships' opinion the second view is the correct one. As Lord Wilberforce himself observed in *McLoughlin* v *O'Brian* [1983] 1 AC 410, 420, it is clear that foreseeability does not of itself, and automatically, lead to a duty of care. There are many other statements to the same effect. The truth is that the trilogy of cases referred to by Lord Wilberforce in *Anns* v *Merton London Borough Council* [1978] AC 728, 751, each demonstrate particular sets of circumstances, differing in character, which were adjudged to have the effect of bringing into being a relationship apt to give rise to a duty of care. Foreseeability of harm is a necessary ingredient of such a relationship, but it is not the only one. Otherwise there would be liability in negligence on the part of one who sees another about to walk over a cliff with his head in the air, and forbears to shout a warning.

Donoghue v *Stevenson* [1932] AC 562 established that the manufacturer of a consumable product who carried on business in such a way that the product reached the consumer in the shape in which it left the manufacturer, without any prospect of intermediate examination, owed the consumer a duty to take reasonable care that the product was free from defect likely to cause injury to health. The speech of Lord Atkin stressed not only the requirement of foreseeability of harm but also that of a close and direct relationship of proximity....

In view of the direction in which the law has since been developing, their Lordships consider that for the future it should be recognised that the two-stage test in *Anns* v *Merton*

London Borough Council [1978] AC 728, 751–752, is not to be regarded as in all circumstances a suitable guide to the existence of a duty of care.

This case is also of importance in the context of Chapter 5 of the Text.

CAPARO INDUSTRIES PLC v *DICKMAN* [1990] 1 All ER 568 (HL)

LORD BRIDGE: . . . since the *Anns* case a series of decisions of the Privy Council and of your Lordships' House, notably in judgments and speeches delivered by Lord Keith of Kinkel, have emphasised the inability of any single general principle to provide a practical test which can be applied to every situation to determine whether a duty of care is owed and, if so what is its scope: see *Governors of Peabody Donation Fund* v *Sir Lindsay Parkinson & Co. Ltd* [1985] AC 210, 239F–241C, *Yuen Kun Yeu* v *Attorney-General of Hong Kong* [1988] AC 175, 190E–194F; *Rowling* v *Takaro Properties Ltd* [1988] AC 473, 501 D–G; *Hill* v *Chief Constable of West Yorkshire* [1989] AC 53, 60B–D. What emerges is that, in addition to the foreseeability of damage, necessary ingredients in any situation giving rise to a duty of care are that there should exist between the party owing the duty and the party to whom it is owed a relationship characterised by the law as one of 'proximity' or 'neighbourhood' and that the situation should be one in which the court considers it fair, just and reasonable that the law should impose a duty of a given scope upon the one party for the benefit of the other. But it is implicit in the passages referred to that the concepts of proximity and fairness embodied in these additional ingredients are not susceptible of any such precise definition as would be necessary to give them utility as practical tests, but amount in effect to little more than convenient labels to attach to the features of different specific situations which, on a detailed examination of all the circumstances, the law recognises pragmatically as giving rise to a duty of care of a given scope. Whilst recognising, of course, the importance of the underlying general principles common to the whole field of negligence, I think the law has now moved in the direction of attaching greater significance to the more traditional categorisation of distinct and recognisable situations as guides to the existence, the scope and the limits of the varied duties of care which the law imposes. We must now, I think, recognise the wisdom of the words of Brennan J in the High Court of Australia in *Sutherland Shire Council* v *Heyman* (1985) 60 ALR 1, 43–44, where he said:

> It is preferable, in my view, that the law should develop novel categories of negligence incrementally and by analogy with established categories, rather than by a massive extension of a prima facie duty of care restrained only by indefinable 'considerations which ought to negative, or to reduce or limit the cope of the duty or the class of person to whom it is owed.'

One of the most important distinctions always to be observed lies in the law's essentially different approach to the different kinds of damage which one party may have suffered in consequence of the acts or omissions of another. It is one thing to owe a duty of care to avoid causing injury to the person or property of others. It is quite another to avoid causing others to suffer purely economic loss. . . .

LORD ROSKILL: . . . I agree with your Lordships that it has now to be accepted that there is no simple formula or touchstone to which recourse can be had in order to provide in every case a ready answer to the questions whether, given certain facts, the law will or will not impose liability for negligence or in cases where such liability can be shown to exist, determine the extent of that liability. Phrases such as 'foreseeability,' 'proximity,' 'neighbourhood,' 'just and reasonable,' 'fairness,' 'voluntary acceptance of risk,' or 'voluntary assumption of responsibility' will be found used from time to time in the different cases. But, as your Lordships have said, such phrases are not precise definitions. At best they are but labels or phrases descriptive of the very different factual situations which can exist in particular cases and which must be carefully examined in each case before it can be pragmatically determined whether a duty of care exists and, if so, what is the scope and extent of that duty. If this conclusion involves a return to the traditional categorisation of cases as pointing to the existence and scope of any duty of care, as my noble and learned friend Lord Bridge of Harwich, suggests, I think this is infinitely preferable to recourse to somewhat wide generalisation which leave their practical application matters of difficulty and uncertainty. This conclusion finds strong support from the judgment of Brennan J in *Sutherland Shire Council* v *Heyman*, 60 ALR 1, 43–44 in the High Court of Australia in the passage cited by my noble and learned friends.

LORD OLIVER: . . . Thus the postulate of a simple duty to avoid any harm that is, with hindsight, reasonably capable of being foreseen becomes untenable without the imposition of some intelligible limits to keep the law of negligence within the bounds of common sense and practicality. Those limits have been found by the requirement of what has been called a 'relationship of proximity' between plaintiff and defendant and by the imposition of a further requirement that the attachment of liability for harm which has occurred be 'just and reasonable.' But although the cases in which the courts have imposed or withheld liability are capable of an approximate categorisation, one looks in vain for some common denominator by which the existence of the essential relationship can be tested. Indeed it is difficult to resist a conclusion that what have been treated as three separate requirements are, at least in most cases, in fact merely facets of the same thing, for in some cases the degree of foreseeability is such that it is from that alone that the requisite proximity can be deduced, whilst in others the absence of that essential relationship can most rationally be attributed simply to the court's view that it would not be fair and reasonable to hold the defendant responsible. 'Proximity' is, no doubt, a convenient expression so long as it is realised that it is no more than a label which embraces not a definable concept but merely a description of circumstances from which, pragmatically, the courts conclude that a duty of care exists.

There are, of course, cases where, in any ordinary meaning of the words, a relationship of proximity (in the literal sense of 'closeness') exists but where the law, whilst recognising the fact of the relationship, nevertheless denies a remedy to the injured party on the ground of public policy. *Rondel* v *Worsley* [1969] 1 AC 191 was such a case, as was *Hill* v *Chief Constable of West Yorkshire* [1989] AC 53, so far as concerns the alternative ground of that decision. But such cases do nothing to assist in the identification of those features from which the law will deduce the essential relationship on which liability depends and, for my part, I think that it has to be recognised that to search for any single formula which will serve as a general test of liability is to pursue a will-o'-the-wisp. The fact is that once one discards, as it is now clear that one must, the concept of foreseeability of harm as the single exclusive test—even a prima facie test—of the existence of the duty of care, the attempt to state some general principle which will determine liability in an infinite variety of circumstances serves not to clarify the law but merely to bedevil its development in a way which corresponds with practicality and common sense. In *Sutherland Shire Council* v *Heyman*, 60 ALR 1, 43–44, Brennan J in the course of a penetrating analysis, observed:

> Of course, if foreseeability of injury to another were the exhaustive criterion of a prima facie duty to act to prevent the occurrence of that injury, it would be essential to introduce some kind of restrictive qualification—perhaps a qualification of the kind stated in the second stage of the general proposition in *Anns* [1978] AC 728. I am unable to accept that approach. It is preferable, in my view, that the law should develop novel categories of negligence incrementally and by analogy with established categories, rather than by a massive extension of a prima facie duty of care restrained only by indefinable 'considerations which ought to negative, or to reduce or limit the scope of the duty or the class of person to whom it is owed.'

Perhaps, therefore, the most that can be attempted is a broad categorisation of the decided cases according to the type of situation in which liability has been established in the past in order to found an argument by analogy. Thus, for instance, cases can be classified according to whether what is complained of is the failure to prevent the infliction of damage by the act of the third party (such as *Dorset Yacht Co. Ltd* v *Home Office* [1970] AC 1004, *P. Perl (Exporters) Ltd* v *Camden London Borough Council* [1984] QB 342, *Smith* v *Littlewoods Organisation Ltd* [1987] AC 241 and, indeed, *Anns* v *Merton London Borough Council* [1978] AC 728 itself), in failure to perform properly a statutory duty claimed to have been imposed for the protection of the plaintiff either as a member of a class or as a member of the public (such as the *Anns* case, *Ministry of Housing* and *Local Government* v *Sharp* [1970] 2 QB 223, *Yuen Kun Yeu* v *Attorney-General of Hong Kong* [1988] AC 175) or in the making by the defendant of some statement or advice which has been communicated, directly or indirectly, to the plaintiff and upon which he has relied. Such categories are not, of course, exhaustive. Sometimes they overlap as in the *Anns* case, and there are cases which do not readily fit into easily definable categories (such as *Ross* v *Caunters* [1980] Ch 297). Nevertheless, it is, I think, permissible to regard negligent statements or advice as a separate category displaying common features from which it is possible to find at least guidelines by which a test for the existence of the relationship which is essential to ground liability can be deduced.

Lords Ackner and Jauncey agreed.

This decision is also important in the context of **Chapter 5** of the *Learning Text*.

T. Weir, *A Casebook on Tort*, 7th edn, Butterworths, 1992, p. 80

In 1985 Goff LJ said: 'Once proximity is no longer treated as expressing a relationship founded simply on foreseeability of damage it ceases to have an ascertainable meaning, and it cannot therefore provide a criterion for liability.' (*The Aliakmon* [1985] 2 All ER 44, 74.) Do you agree? If the existence of a legal duty depends on the presence or absence of a variable number of different factors which can only be determined *ex post facto*, can there be said to be any rule at all? Six relevant factors are listed by Neil LJ in *McNaughton Papers Group* v *Hicks Anderson* [1991] 1 All ER 134.

HILL v CHIEF CONSTABLE OF WEST YORKSHIRE [1988] 2 All ER 238 (HL)

LORD KEITH: It has been said almost too frequently to require repetition that foreseeability of likely harm is not in itself a sufficient test of liability in negligence. Some further ingredient is invariably needed to establish the requisite proximity of relationship between the plaintiff and defendant, and all the circumstances of the case must be carefully considered and analysed in order to ascertain whether such an ingredient is present. The nature of the ingredient will be found to vary in a number of different categories of decided cases.

TOPP v LONDON COUNTRY BUS (SOUTH WEST) LTD [1993] RTR 279 (CA)

A bus belonging to the defendant had been left unattended, with the key in the ignition lock for about 9 hours. The vehicle was stolen by a third party for whom the defendant was not responsible, and the thief killed a cyclist whilst driving the bus.
    Relying on the decision in *Perl* v *Camden LBC* [1984] QB 342, the court held that the defendant did not owe a duty of care in negligence to protect the deceased from the actions of third parties.

LONRHO PLC v TEBBITT [1992] 4 All ER 280 (CA)

DILLON LJ: . . . Mr Richards for the defendants in the present case says—as he has to—that Lonrho's claim in these proceedings against these defendants is obviously doomed to failure whatever facts may emerge at a trial, and that Browne-Wilkinson V-C was wrong to hold, as he did, that Lonrho had an arguable case fit to go to trial, that it has rights in private law against the defendants in relation to the release of the undertaking. Browne-Wilkinson V-C said in the present case that both the principal points that arise in the present case are in developing fields of law involving new and uncertain principles of law and public policy. That, in my judgment, is plainly right.
    Mr Richards urges, and urges it as plain and obvious, that the defendants owed no duty in private law to Lonrho, that all the matters that arise are matters of public law and that the release of the undertaking was a matter for the discretion of the Secretary of State exercising his powers under the 1973 Act in the public interest. He also urges—and in this brief summary I am doing scant justice to a carefully thought out and skilfully deployed argument—that there is no precedent for holding a minister to owe a duty of care in private law as a result of his exercise of public law powers, and no precedent for holding a minister or department of state liable in damages, and particularly for mere economic damages, because in good faith they have misconstrued their legal position—if indeed they have misconstrued it.

The relevance of the latter point is that there is, as I have said, no allegation of bad faith against the defendants, but it is alleged that they acted *ultra vires*, that is to say beyond their powers, in deferring the release of the undertaking until 14 March 1985 when the MMC report had become available on or about 14 February. If that is so, the likely conclusion is that the defendants acted as they did in good faith, believing that they were entitled to time for consideration and to look at the matter in the round and consider at the same time whether the undertaking given by Lonrho should be released, and whether the bid by Holdings for House of Fraser should be referred to the MMC. Reference was made to an apparently unlimited dictum of Nourse LJ in *Bourgoin SA* v *Ministry of Agriculture Fisheries and Food* [1986] QB 716 at 790:

In this country the law has never allowed that a private individual should recover damages against the Crown for an injury caused to him by an *ultra vires* order made in good faith.

But the fields of law with which we are concerned in this case are difficult and developing. Mr Richards gave us an admirable summary of the principal authorities. In the law of negligence he referred us to the two-stage test suggested by Lord Wilberforce in *Anns* v *Merton London Borough* [1978] AC 728 at 754, and showed how that had been rejected in later authorities and particularly in *Murphy* v *Brentwood DC* [1991] 1 AC 398. The preferred approach is now what is called 'the incremental approach' as stated by Brennan J in *Sutherland Shire Council* v *Heyman* (1985) 60 ALR 1 at 43–44:

It is preferable . . . that the law should develop novel categories of negligence incrementally and by analogy with established categories, rather than by a massive extension of a *prima facie* duty of care restrained only by indefinable 'considerations which ought to negative, or reduce or limit the scope of the duty or the class of person to whom it is owed'.

Mr Richards referred us also to authorities which show that a civil action for damages cannot be brought as a result of a 'policy decision' of a public authority and to judgments where a distinction is suggested between 'policy decisions' which cannot be justiciable and 'operational decisions' which may be justiciable. But in *Rowling* v *Takaro Properties Ltd* [1988] AC 473, to which Mr Richards also referred us, some of the difficulties of that approach are explored in the opinion of Lord Keith and the conclusion of their Lordships seems to be that the question whether a duty of care should be imposed is a question of an intensely pragmatic character, well-suited for gradual development but requiring most careful analysis (see [1988] 1 All ER 163 at 172, [1988] AC 473 at 501). That is in line with the incremental approach to the development of the tort of negligence.

The imposition of the undertaking on Lonrho in 1981 was of course a matter of public law in the public interest when the MMC had considered that the acquisition by Lonrho of the share capital of House of Fraser might be expected to operate against the public interest. The public interest in having the undertaking released when the acquisition by Lonrho of the share capital of House of Fraser was no longer expected to operate against the public interest is considerably more remote and sophisticated. But the private interest of Lonrho in having the undertaking released as soon as it was no longer needed in the public interest is obvious. It does not therefore appal me that it should be suggested that, if the Secretary of State imposes the restrictions of the undertaking on Lonrho in the public interest, the Secretary of State should thereby assume a private law duty to Lonrho to release the undertaking when it is no longer needed and the restriction on Lonrho's freedom to conduct its business no longer has a rationale. There is an arguable case for Lonrho, therefore, against which may have to be set the sort of considerations militating against the imposition of liability which Lord Keith rehearses in *Rowling* v *Takaro Properties Ltd* [1988] AC 473 at 501–502. These raise questions which the court in *Rowling* v *Takaro* did not have to resolve. Moreover, the nature of any private law duty would have to be carefully defined. Is it, for instance, an absolute duty to release the undertaking when no longer required in the public interest, or is it only a duty of care, within the field of the tort of negligence—with the result in the latter case that there would be no liability on the defendants if delay in releasing the undertaking was due to an error of law which was not negligent?

In these circumstances, I agree with Browne-Wilkinson V-C that Lonrho's claim should not be struck out as disclosing no reasonable cause of action. Lonrho faces considerable difficulties, and others may arise on the facts as the evidence emerges at trial, but I cannot say that Lonrho has no arguable case, or, in Lord Bridge's words, that the claim is obviously foredoomed to fail.

I turn to the final question whether, if Lonrho's claim is not struck out on the ground that it discloses no reasonable cause of action, it ought none the less to be struck out as an abuse of the process of the court on the ground that Lonrho ought to be required to get a ruling by way of judicial review before it starts any proceedings by way of writ and civil action against the defendants.

Mr Richards founds this submission on *Cocks v Thanet DC* [1983] 2 AC 286. He says in effect that it is a matter of public law for the plaintiff to establish the necessary public law basis on which it can ground a private right, as in *Cocks*'s case. Therefore the plaintiff must obtain a declaration in proceedings for judicial review on which to found a claim to a private right or for breach of a private law duty.

I see the matter differently. The plaintiff is asserting a private law right, albeit arising out of a background of public law. That can be asserted in an action by writ as in *Roy v Kensington and Chelsea and Westminster Family Practitioner Committee* [1992] 1 AC 624. If the plaintiff fails to establish the private law right claimed, the action will fail. But it is not necessary to apply for judicial review before bringing the action.

I would accordingly dismiss this appeal.

Stocker LJ and Sir Michael Kerr agreed; the defendant's appeal was dismissed.

SKINNER v SECRETARY OF STATE FOR TRANSPORT, *The Times*, 3 January 1995

The plaintiff, who had survived a fishing boat tragedy, claimed damages against the Department of Transport for the Coastguard's failure to react promptly to an emergency radio message. The plaintiff, who suffered personal injury, was in the sea for over 9 hours before he was rescued.

Evidence showed that a faint radio message had been received by a Coastguard Auxiliary, but he had not reported it. The word 'Mayday' (an internationally recognised distress call) had not been used.

In the High Court, Judge Gareth Edwards held that the Coastguard did not owe a duty of care in negligence to individual mariners when exercising its every-day activities of

- watching
- listening; and
- rescue co-ordination,

even in emergencies.

It was found that the Coastguard Act 1925 created an administrative, rather than a directive, framework and this did not place a statutory duty on the coastguard. The coastguard could not be equated with a state body, because it was not *created* by state and its functions were not statutorily defined.

His Lordship looked to *Caparo v Dickman* [1990] 1 All ER 568 for guidance; this authority favoured an *incremental* approach to the development of legal responsibility in negligence. The scope of 'duty of care' could be widened only through the process of reasoning by *analogy*.

ELGUZOULI-DAF v COMMISSIONER OF THE METROPOLIS AND ANOTHER McBREARTY v MINISTRY OF DEFENCE AND OTHERS [1995] 1 All ER 833 (CA)

It was held that the Crown Prosecution Service (the CPS) did not owe a duty of care in negligence to individuals it prosecuted unless its conduct indicated that it had assumed responsibility for a competent prosecution in the case of a particular defendant.

STEYN LJ: While Mr Richards, who appeared for the CPS, disputed that even the element of foreseeability of harm is established, I would be prepared to accept that the plaintiffs can satisfy this requirement. For my part the matter turns on a combination of the element of proximity and the question whether it is fair, just and reasonable that the law should impose a duty of care. It does not seem to me that these considerations can sensibly be considered separately in this case: inevitably they shade into each other.

Recognising that individual justice to private individuals, or trading companies, who are aggrieved by careless decisions of CPS lawyers, militate in favour of the recognition of a duty of care, I conclude that there are compelling considerations, rooted in the welfare of the whole community, which outweigh the dictates of individualised justice. I would rule that there is no duty of care owed by the CPS to those it prosecutes. In so ruling I have considered whether a distinction between operational and discretionary lapses, with potential liability in the former but not the latter, should be made. Whatever the merit of such a distinction in other areas of the law, I would reject it in regard to the CPS as impractical, unworkable and not capable of avoiding the adverse consequences for the CPS on which I have rested my decision. Subject to one qualification, my conclusion that there is no duty of care owed by the CPS to those it prosecutes is intended to be of general application. The qualification is that there may be cases, of which *Welsh* was an example, where the CPS assumes by conduct a responsibility to a particular defendant: see *Spring* v *Guardian Assurance plc* [1994] 3 All ER 129 *per* Lord Goff. And it is trite law that such an assumption of responsibility may generate legal duties. But that qualification has no relevance to the cases before us . . .

I would dismiss both appeals.

Rose and Morritt LJJ agreed.

OLOTU v *HOME OFFICE* [1997] 1 All ER 385 (CA)

The decision in *Elguzouli-Daf* (above) was applied in *Olotu* v *Home Office*. It was held that no action for breach of statutory duty or damages for false imprisonment can be made against the Home Office or the CPS where a person is remanded in custody even though the custody time limit under s. 22 of the Prosecution of Offences Act 1985 (and Regulations made thereunder) has expired. The court said in such cases it was possible to apply for release on bail or *habeas corpus* and *mandamus* and it could not, therefore, have been the intention of Parliament to confer a private law right of action in such circumstances. (See also **Chapter 8** of both the *Learning Text* and *Cases and Materials*.)

BARRETT v *MINISTRY OF DEFENCE* [1995] 3 All ER 87 (CA)

BELDAM LJ: It should be said that there was no evidence that the deceased had consumed brandy on the night he died or that anyone knew he had a bottle of brandy in his cabin. The appellant challenged the grounds on which the judge held that it was in breach of duty to the deceased. The judge had likened the disciplinary codes to the Highway Code or even pamphlets relating to safety in factories, describing them as 'a practical guide to a standard the defendant aimed at'. In this the appellant says he misdirected himself. Queen's Regulations and standing orders are not comparable to the Highway Code or safety regulations, still less to pamphlets relating to safety in factories. The purpose of Queen's Regulations and standing orders is the maintenance of good order and discipline in the service. In so far as the standing orders extend to conduct by personnel ashore, they are confined to actions calculated to bring the Royal Navy into disrepute.

The judge also held that once the deceased had collapsed, the appellant had assumed responsibility for him and had taken inadequate steps to care for him. No medical officer or medical attendant was informed and supervision of the deceased was wholly inadequate by the standard which the appellant's own officers accepted were necessary.

The appellant does not challenge the judge's findings that it was in breach of duty to take care of the deceased once he had collapsed and it had assumed responsibility for him.

The appellant's principal ground of appeal is that the judge was wrong to hold that it was under any duty to take care to see that the deceased, a mature man thirty years of age, did not consume so much alcohol that he became unconscious. If the deceased himself was to be treated as a responsible adult, he alone was to blame for his collapse. On this basis the judge's apportionment of liability was plainly wrong. Even if the judge's finding of this duty were to stand, the deceased ought to have been regarded as equally responsible for his own death.

In my view the judge was wrong to equate the Queen's Regulations and standing orders with guidance given in the Highway Code or in pamphlets relating to safety in factories.

The purpose of Queen's Regulations and standing orders is to preserve good order and discipline in the service and to ensure that personnel remain fit for duty and while on duty obey commands and off duty do not misbehave bringing the service into disrepute. All regulations which encourage self-discipline, if obeyed, will incidentally encourage service personnel to take greater pride in their own behaviour but in no sense are the regulations and orders intended to lay down standards or to give advice in the exercise of reasonable care for the safety of the men when off duty drinking in the bars.

The judge placed reliance on the fact that it was foreseeable that if the regulations and standing orders were not properly enforced in this particular environment the deceased would succumb to heavy intoxication. He also said it was just and reasonable to impose a duty in these circumstances . . .

There are now many judicial pronouncements of high authority that mere foreseeability of harm is not a sufficient foundation for a duty to take care in law. Since *Anns v Merton London Borough* [1978] AC 728 the House of Lords has preferred the approach of the High Court of Australia in *Sutherland Shire Council v Heyman* (1985) 157 CLR 424 that the imposition of additional duties to take care for the safety of others should develop incrementally and by analogy with established categories, an approach which involves consideration of whether it is fair, just and reasonable that the law should impose a duty of a given scope upon one party for the benefit of another. The mere existence of regulatory or other public duties does not of itself create a special relationship imposing a duty in private law.

In the present case the judge posed the question whether there was a duty at law to take reasonable steps to prevent the deceased becoming unconscious through alcohol abuse. He said his conclusion that there was such a duty was founded on the fact that:

> It was foreseeable in the environment in which the defendant grossly failed to enforce their regulations and standing orders that the deceased would succumb to heavy intoxication.

And in these circumstances that it was just and reasonable to impose a duty.

The respondent argued for the extension of a duty to take care for the safety of the deceased from analogous categories of relationship in which an obligation to use reasonable care already existed. For example employer and employee, pupil and schoolmaster and occupier and visitor. It was said that the appellant's control over the environment in which the deceased was serving and the provision of duty free liquor, coupled with the failure to enforce disciplinary rules and orders were sufficient factors to render it fair, just and reasonable to extend the duty to take reasonable care found in the analogous circumstances. The characteristic which distinguishes those relationships is reliance expressed or implied in the relationship which the party to whom the duty is owed is entitled to place on the other party to make provision for his safety. I can see no reason why it should not be fair, just and reasonable for the law to leave a responsible adult to assume responsibility for his own actions in consuming alcoholic drink. No one is better placed to judge the amount that he can safely consume or to exercise control in his own interest as well as in the interest of others. To dilute self-responsibility and to blame one adult for another's lack of self-control is neither just nor reasonable and in the development of the law of negligence an increment too far.

Should the individual members of the senior rates' mess who bought rounds of drinks for a group of mess mates and the deceased each be held to have had a share in the responsibility for his death? Or should responsibility only devolve on two or three of them who bought the last rounds? In the course of argument Mr Nice QC for the respondent experienced great difficulty in articulating the nature of the duty. Eventually he settled on two expositions. It was a duty owed by the defendant to any serviceman at this base in this environment to take into account group behaviour and arising from a duty to provide for the servicemen's accommodation and welfare there was a duty to take reasonable care to prevent drunkenness/drinking: '(a) To a level which endangered his safety or (b) Such as to render him unconscious.'

The impracticality of the duty so defined is obvious. The level of drink which endangers safety depends upon the behaviour of the person affected. The disinhibiting effects of even two or three drinks may on occasions cause normally sober and steady individuals to behave with nonchalant disregard for their own and others' welfare and safety.

The respondent placed reliance on *Crocker v Sundance Northwest Resorts Ltd* [1988] 1 SCR 1186, a decision of the Supreme Court of Canada, and on another Canadian case, *Jordan House Ltd* v *Menow* [1974] SCR 239. In the first case the defendant was held liable to an intoxicated plaintiff for permitting him to take part in a dangerous ski hill race which caused him to be injured. The defendant had taken the positive step of providing him with the equipment needed for the race knowing that he was in no fit state to take part. The plaintiff had consumed alcohol in the defendant's bars. Liability was based not on permitting him to drink in the bars but in permitting him to take part in the race. In the *Jordan House* case the plaintiff was an habitual customer of the defendant. He became intoxicated from drinking heavily. The defendant proprietor evicted him knowing he was unsteady and incapable in spite of the fact that he would have to cross a busy thoroughfare. The court held that these circumstances, including the fact that at the time he was evicted the plaintiff's relationship with the defendant was that of invitee/invitor, were sufficient to justify the imposition of a duty to take care for the safety of the customer.

In each of these cases the court founded the imposition of a duty on factors additional to the mere provision of alcohol and the failure strictly to enforce provisions against drunkenness.

In the present case I would reverse the judge's finding that the appellant was under a duty to take reasonable care to prevent the deceased from abusing alcohol to the extent he did. Until he collapsed I would hold that the deceased was in law alone responsible for his condition. Thereafter, when the appellant assumed responsibility for him, it accepts that the measures taken fell short of the standard reasonably to be expected. It did not summon medical assistance and its supervision of him was inadequate.

The final question is how far the deceased should be regarded as responsible for his death. Mr Nice argued that once the deceased had become unconscious his fault was virtually spent and the whole responsibility for his death ought to fall on the appellant, though he did not seek to disturb the judge's assessment of 25%.

The immediate cause of the deceased's death was suffocation due to inhalation of vomit. The amount of alcohol he had consumed not only caused him to vomit, it deprived him of the spontaneous ability to protect his air passages after he had vomited. His fault was therefore a continuing and direct cause of his death. Moreover, his lack of self-control in his own interest caused the appellant to have to assume responsibility for him. But for his fault, it would not have had to do so. How far in such circumstances is it just and equitable to regard the deceased as the author of his misfortune? The deceased involved the appellant in a situation in which it had to assume responsibility for his care and I would not regard it as just and equitable in such circumstances to be unduly critical of the appellant's fault. I consider a greater share of blame should rest upon the deceased than on the appellant and I would reduce the amount of the damages recoverable by the respondent by two-thirds holding the appellant one third to blame. Accordingly I would allow the appeal, set aside the judgment in the sum of £160,651·16 and order judgment for the plaintiff in the sum of £71,400·51 with interest to be assessed.

Saville and Neil LJJ agreed.

3.2   Liability in Contract and Tort

JOHNSTONE v BLOOMSBURY HEALTH AUTHORITY [1991] 2 All ER 293 (CA)

The plaintiff argued that the specific term in his contract, requiring him to work up to 88 hours a week (on average) was excessive and injurious to his health. This term, he said, should be read subject to his employer's common law obligation (see Chapter 8 of the Text) to safeguard his health from reasonably foreseeable risks.

It was argued that the employer could ask only for those hours of work which did not conflict with the employer's common law duty: this duty requires the employer to take account of the needs of the *individual* employee. In the instant use, said the plaintiff, the hours of work required were injurious to *his* health.

The Court of Appeal, on balance, agreed with the plaintiff's argument though only Stuart-Smith LJ fully agreed. Browne Wilkinson LJ was reluctant to see such obligations as a mixture of contract and tort, but did agree that the obligation to safeguard the employee's health did, in the circumstances, override the specific contractural requirement. Leggatt LJ did not at *all* agree that 'tort could trump contract', his Lordship regarded the case as turning entirely on the terms of the contract of employment. On the facts, the defendant was not in breach of contract and that ended the matter.

Sir Nicholas Browne-Wilkinson V-C agreed with Stuart-Smith LJ in dismissing the Health Authority's application (on appeal) struck out as an unarguable case, although his Lordship differed in his reasoning.

All three judges allowed the plaintiff's cross-appeal to the effect that it could be argued part of the contract of employment was contrary to s. 2(1) of the Unfair Contract Terms Act 1977. Discussion on this point is omitted here.

3.3   Public Bodies and Negligence

ROWLING v TAKARO PROPERTIES [1988] AC 473 (PC)

Certain statutory regulations in New Zealand required persons wishing to issue shares to foreign concerns to first obtain the consent of the Minister of Finance. Takaro, who had applied for consent, claimed that the Minister owed them a duty of care in negligence in relation to the construction of the relevant regulations and that on the facts he had committed a breach of that duty. The judge at first instance found that the minister did owe a prima facie duty but Takaro had failed to establish (a) a breach of that duty; nor was there any evidence of (b) a malicious exercise of statutory powers:

The judge said:

The distinction between the policy and the operational areas can be both fine and confusing. Various expressions have been used instead of operational eg: 'adminstrative' or 'business powers'. It may not be easy to attach any of these labels to the decision of the minister in this case, but what appears to me to emerge clearly enough is that for the reasons I have indicated his decision was the antithesis of policy or 'discretion'. I therefore equate it with having been operational. The result of that conclusion is that I consider the prima facie existence of a duty of care has been established.

The Court of Appeal found negligence proved on the facts. Takaro appealed to the Privy Council.

According to their Lordships in the Privy Council the Minister was not in breach of any assumed duty of care and therefore the New Zealand Court of Appeal was not entitled to interfere with the trial judge's decision and findings.

LORD KEITH: The Court of Appeal found no difficulty in holding that a duty of care rested upon the minister; indeed, Cooke J [1986] 1 NZLR 22, 67, went so far as to observe that the question of liability to the plaintiff seemed to him to be relatively straightforward.

For reasons which will appear, their Lordships do not find it necessary to reach any final conclusion on the question of the existence, or (if it exists) the scope, of the duty of care resting upon a minister in a case such as the present; and they have come to the conclusion that it would not be right for them to do so, because the matter was not fully exposed before them in argument. In particular, no reference was made in argument to the extensive academic literature on the subject of the liability of public authorities in negligence, study of which can be of such great assistance to the courts in considering areas of the law which, as in the case of negligence, are in a continuing state of development. Even so, such is the importance of the present case, especially in New Zealand, that their Lordships feel that it would be inappropriate, and perhaps be felt to be discourteous, if they were to make no reference to the relevant considerations affecting the decision whether a duty of care should arise in a case such as the present.

Quilliam J considered the question with particular reference to the distinction between policy (or planning) decisions and operational decisions. His conclusion was expressed [1986] 1 NZLR 22, 35:

The distinction between the policy and the operational areas can be both fine and confusing. Various expressions have been used instead of operational, e.g., 'administrative' or 'business powers.' It may not be easy to attach any of these labels to the decision of the minister in this case, but what appears to me to emerge clearly enough is that for the reasons I have indicated his decision was the antithesis of policy or discretion. I therefore equate it with having been operational. The result of that conclusion is that I consider the prima facie existence of a duty of care has been established.

Their Lordships feel considerable sympathy with Quilliam J's difficulty in solving the problem by simple reference to this distinction. They are well aware of the references in the literature to this distinction (which appears to have originated in the United States of America), and of the critical analysis to which it has been subjected. They incline to the opinion, expressed in the literature, that this distinction does not provide a touchstone of liability, but rather is expressive of the need to exclude altogether those cases in which the decision under attack is of such a kind that a question whether it has been made negligently is unsuitable for judicial resolution, of which notable examples are discretionary decisions on the allocation of scarce resources or the distribution of risks: see especially the discussion in *Craig on Administrative Law* (1983), pp. 534–538. If this is right, classification of the relevant decision as a policy or planning decision in this sense may exclude liability; but a conclusion that it does not fall within that category does not, in their Lordships' opinion, mean that a duty of care will necessarily exist.

[Their Lordships] recognise that the decision of the minister is capable of being described as having been of a policy rather than an operational character; but, if the function of the policy/operational dichotomy is as they have already described it, the allegation of negligence in the present case is not, they consider, of itself of such a character as to render the case unsuitable for judicial decision. Be that as it may, there are certain considerations which militate against imposition of liability in a case such as the present.

Their Lordships wish to refer in particular to certain matters which they consider to be of importance. The first is that the only effect of a negligent decision, such as is here alleged to have been made, is delay. This is because the processes of judicial review are available to the aggrieved party; and, assuming that the alleged error of law is so serious that it can properly be described as negligent, the decision will assuredly be quashed by a process which, in New Zealand as in the United Kingdom, will normally be carried out with promptitude. The second is that, in the nature of things, it is likely to be very rare indeed that an error of law of this kind by a minister or other public authority can properly be categorised as negligent. As is well known, anybody, even a judge, can be capable of misconstruing a statute; and such misconstruction, when it occurs, can be severely criticised without attracting the epithet 'negligent.' Obviously, this simple fact points rather to the extreme unlikelihood of a breach of duty being established in these cases, a point to which their Lordships will return; but it is nevertheless a relevant factor to be taken into account when considering whether liability in negligence should properly be imposed.

The third is the danger of overkill. It is to be hoped that, as a general rule, imposition of liability in negligence will lead to a higher standard of care in the performance of the relevant type of act; but sometimes not only may this not be so, but the imposition of liability may even lead to harmful consequences. In other words, the cure may be worse than the disease. There are reasons for believing that this may be so in cases where liability is imposed upon local authorities whose building inspectors have been negligent in relation to the inspection of foundations, as in *Anns* v *Merton London Borough Council* [1978] AC 728 itself; because there is a danger that the building inspectors of some local authorities may react to that decision by simply increasing, unnecessarily, the requisite depth of foundations, thereby imposing a very substantial and unnecessary financial burden upon members of the community. A comparable danger may exist in cases such as the present, because, once it became known that liability in negligence may be imposed on the ground that a minister has misconstrued a statute and so acted ultra vires, the cautious civil servant may go to extreme lengths in ensuring that legal advice, or even the opinion of the court, is obtained before decisions are taken, thereby leading to unnecessary delay in a considerable number of cases.

Fourth, it is very difficult to identify any particular case in which it can properly be said that a minister is under a duty to seek legal advice. . . .

WOOD v THE LAW SOCIETY, *The Times*, 30 July 1993

The plaintiff, aged 77, alleged that the Law Society was negligent and in breach of its statutory duty (the general topic of breach of statutory duty is dealt with in **Chapter 8** of the *Learning Text*) in failing to investigate properly her complaints against her former solicitors. She had first complained to the defendant in 1979 that her former solicitor had arranged a loan for her from another client, 'Mobile Homes', without disclosing that the company was part-owned by the solicitor's husband who was also the senior partner of the solicitors' practice.

The plaintiff had no income and was hoping to develop her cottage and land, but the solicitor demanded payment of the loan on behalf of Mobile Homes. The Law Society refused to investigate the plaintiff's complaint, claiming there was no evidence of professional misconduct. Later, the solicitors sued her on behalf of another client who had lent her money and she was evicted from her home and re-housed in council accommodation.

Otton J held that while its conduct in initially dismissing her complaint, fell far enough short of a proper standard of care to amount to negligence, the Law Society did not owe the plaintiff a duty of care, and was therefore not liable for her loss. His Lordship said that the plaintiff's misfortune stemmed from her inability to pay her creditors and prompt action on her complaint would not in any case have prevented her from losing her home.

OTTON J: Miss Wood seeks to establish a novel duty of care, namely, that a body vested with a power and duty to investigate complaints against and to control its members owes a duty of care to a complainant the breach of which entitles the complainant to damages . . . I have come to the following conclusions.

(1)   The Law Society, although not a statutory body in origin, is subject to statutory duties and through its Council exercises statutory powers including those under the Solicitors Act 1974 as amended in relation to disciplinary and investigative proceedings.

(2)   The primary consideration is whether there exists between the Law Society and complainants such close and direct relations as to place the Law Society, in the exercise of its powers and functions under a duty of care towards complainants. I have come to the conclusion that such proximity did not exist between Miss Wood and the Law Society.

(3)   She was a member of an unascertained class. The class is wide and diffuse and includes, for example, but not exhaustively: (i) those complaining about their own solicitors in non-contentious business and civil litigation; (ii) unsuccessful defendants and victims of injustice (as they see it) in civil and criminal proceedings; (iii) those who complain about solicitors acting for third parties. It is impossible to identify or ascertain within the class those sections or particular persons who could be afforded a duty of care and those who would be denied. Even the heart-rending story of Miss Wood does not permit a special relationship to be spelt out.

(4)   The investigative function of the Law Society in dealing with the complaints against the plaintiff's former solicitors were discretionary and quasi-judicial acts in the exercise of a statutory power and called for the exercise of discretion and judgment on the part of the officials concerned. The fact that Miss Wood's complaints were inefficiently handled without due diligence would not alter the quasi-judicial character of the function.

(5)   The duty owed by the Law Society was not to safeguard the plaintiff against loss, but rather to sanction conduct unbecoming a solicitor. The powers conferred on the Law Society are not to prevent or avoid loss to individuals such as Miss Wood.

(6)   The Law Society had no power to control the day-to-day activities of solicitors who by their activities caused the loss. This is in contra-distinction to the borstal officers in the *Dorset Yacht* case and more akin to the statutory body in *Curran's* case, where the absence of control and supervision exercised by the officials was the determining factor.

(7)   I do not consider it essential or in the public interest for the Law Society to have the immunity from suit afforded to the police in *Hill v Chief Constable of West Yorkshire* [1989] AC 53. The role of the police in investigating crime, maintaining order and their responsibility for security is different from that of a professional body regulating its members. Clearly public policy carries great weight in the former. I am not persuaded that public policy considerations arise when the Law Society is carrying out its investigative and disciplinary functions. If the plaintiff could bring herself within the principles of

proximity and foreseeability and the only other consideration was immunity based on public policy I would not decline to find that a duty of care existed.

(8) It is not unreasonable to require a plaintiff who has suffered loss to look for redress to the person who caused the loss by their conduct, i.e. the solicitors about whose conduct the complaint is made. Miss Wood sued Hubbard & Co. for negligence and conspiracy. She compromised the action for £2,500 with costs. It is unreasonable for her now to be able to sue the regulatory body of the solicitors' profession.

(9) A complainant in the position of the plaintiff has alternative remedies if dissatisfied with the manner in which the complaint is handled: (i) reference to the lay observer under s. 45 of the 1974 Act; (ii) to apply directly to the Solicitors Complaints Tribunal; (iii) an action for negligence against the solicitors concerned; (iv) to apply directly to the High Court under s. 51 of the Solicitors Act 1984. Bearing in mind Mr Hansen's arguments about the ineffectiveness of alternative remedies and giving such weight to them as I can, I am satisfied that the alternative remedies are of such a character that this is a legitimate consideration to take into account when considering whether it is just and reasonable to impose a duty of care upon the Law Society.

(10) Finally, to paraphrase Lord Bridge in *Curran's* case, the dictates of good sense and consideration of what is fair and reasonable point clearly against the imposition of any duty of care. If there was no duty of care, then the allegation that the Law Society mishandled Miss Wood's complaints cannot assist her.

Thus Miss Wood's claim must fail in negligence. However, another court hereafter may find to the contrary. Thus I must consider the case in negligence in detail. . . .

The plaintiff appealed to the Court of Appeal which affirmed the decision of Otton J (1995) 145 NLJ 8.

Ms Wood applied for relief to the **European Commission of Human Rights**, but the Commission upheld the decision of the English courts: New Law Journal, 5 September 1997, p. 1267.

X (MINORS) v *BEDFORDSHIRE COUNTY COUNCIL, M (A MINOR) AND ANOTHER* v *NEWHAM LONDON BOROUGH COUNCIL AND OTHERS, E (A MINOR)* v *DORSET COUNTY COUNCIL, CHRISTMAS* v *HAMPSHIRE COUNTY COUNCIL, KEATING* v *BROMLEY LONDON BOROUGH COUNCIL* [1995] 3 All ER 353 (HL)

It was found unanimously that a breach of statutory duty did not of itself create a cause of action in private law (tort). Such a cause of action might well arise where the traditional conditions for the common law action for breach of statutory duty were met (see **Chapter 8** of the *Learning Text*) for example, where there was an allegation of abuse against someone appointed by the local authority to care for a child. There might also be the possibility of *vicarious* liability on the part of an authority in an appropriate case.

If an allegation was made of a careless exercise of a statutory duty, the plaintiff would have to show that a duty of care in negligence arose in *those* circumstances.

An exercise by a public authority of its statutory discretion at the policy-making level was not actionable of common law.

Their Lordships said that it was neither just not reasonable to 'superimpose' a common law duty of care on a local authority in relation to its performance of statutory duties to protect children, otherwise the system set up to protect children at risk would be upset.

Professionals retained by local authorities to advise them did not owe any duty of care to the children involved; not was any such duty owed to their parents.

The results of the appeals are set out in the following speech.

LORD BROWNE-WILKINSON: . . . The basic proposition is that in the ordinary case a breach of statutory duty does not, by itself, give rise to any private law cause of action but such a cause would arise if it could be shown, as a matter of construction of the statute, that the statutory duty was imposed for the protection of a limited class of the public and that Parliament intended to confer on members of that class a private right of action for breach of duty.

There is no general rule by reference to which it can be decided whether a statute does create such a right of action but there are a number of indicators.

If the statute provides no other remedy for its breach and the parliamentary intention to protect a limited class is shown that indicates that there might be a private right of action since otherwise there is no method of securing the protection the statute was intended to confer.

If the statute does provide some other means of enforcing the duty, that will normally indicate that the statutory right is intended to be enforceable by those means and not by private right of action: *Cutler* v *Wandsworth Stadium Ltd* [1994] AC 398 and *Lonrho Ltd* v *Shell Petroleum Co. Ltd* [1982] AC 173.

However, it is possible to show that on its true construction the statute intended a protected class to have a private remedy, for instance, where specific duties were imposed on employers in respect of factory premises: *Groves* v *Lord Wimborne* [1898] 2 QB 402.

There are cases in which the plaintiff alleged (a) the statutory duty and (b) the negligent breach of that duty but did not allege that the defendant was under a common law duty of care to the plaintiff.

It is the use of the word 'negligent' in that context which gives rise to confusion: it is sometimes used to connote mere carelessness, where there is no common law duty of care, and sometimes to import the concept of a common lay duty of care.

It is important to distinguish between the two concepts. The careless performance of a statutory duty does not in itself give rise to any cause of action in the absence of either a statutory right of action or a common law duty of care.

The correct view is that in order to found a cause of action flowing from the careless exercise of statutory powers or duties, the plaintiff has to show that the circumstances were such as to raise a duty of care at common law. The mere assertion of the careless exercise of a statutory power or duty is not sufficient: see *Dorset Yacht Co. Ltd* v *Home Office* [1970] AC 1004.

A common duty of care might arise in the performance of statutory functions. But a broad distinction has to be drawn beween (a) cases in which it is alleged that the authority owed a duty of care in the manner in which it exercised a statutory discretion and (b) cases in which a duty of care is alleged to arise from the manner in which the statutory duty had been implemented in practice.

Where Parliament has conferred a statutory discretion on a public authority, it is for that authority, not for the courts, to exercise the discretion. Nothing which the authority does within the ambit of the discretion can be actionable at common law.

Where the decision complained of falls outside the statutory discretion, it can give rise to common law liability but where the factors relevant to the exercise of the discretion include matters of policy, the court cannot adjudicate on such policy matters and therefore cannot reach the conclusion that the decision was outside the ambit of the statutory discretion.

Therefore, a common law duty of care in relation to the taking of decisions involving policy matters cannot exist.

Where such matters are justifiable the ordinary principles of negligence apply namely, whether the damage to the plaintiff is reasonably foreseeable, whether the relationship between the plaintiff and the defendant is sufficient proximate and whether it is just and reasonable to impose a duty of care: *Rowling* v *Takaro Properties Ltd* [1988] AC 473, *Hill* v *Chief Constable of West Yorkshire* [1989] AC 53, *Caparo Industries plc* v *Dickman* [1990] 2 AC 605 and *Henderson* v *Merrett Syndicates Ltd* [1994] 3 WLR 761.

But where a common law duty of care is inconsistent with, or has a tendency to discourage, the due performance by the authority of its statutory duties it cannot be imposed.

Even where there is no allegation of a separate duty of care owed by a servant of the defendant authority to the plaintiff the negligent acts of that servant are capable of constituting a breach of the duty of care, if any, owed directly by the authority to the plaintiff.

Although those basic principles are not only applicable to pure economic loss cases but are also applicable to claims for physical damage it is not just and reasonable to superimpose a common law duty of care on the local authority in relation to performance of its statutory duties to protect children.

That would cut across the whole statutory system, which is an inter-disciplinary system, set up for the protection of children at risk. The task of the local authority and its servants in dealing with children at risk is extraordinarily delicate and statutory provisions, such as s. 17 of the Children Act 1989, required the local authority to have regard not only to the physical well being of the child but also to the advantages of not disrupting the child's family environment.

When as in Bedfordshire and Newham the social workers and psychiatrists are retained by the local authority to advise it, not the plaintiffs, even though the subject matter of their advice and activities is the child and tendering of advice involved interviewing and examining the child, such relationship with the child cannot alter the extend of their duty owed under the retainer from the local authority.

Even where the advice tendered by such professionals comes to the knowledge of the child and his parents and they would not regulate their conduct in reliance on the report, those professionals do not assume any general professional duty of care to the plaintiffs.

The professionals involved are under no separate duty of care to the plaintiffs for breach of which the local authorities could be vicariously liable: see *Everett* v *Griffiths* [1920] 3 KB 163, *Hill* v *Chief Constable of West Yorkshire* [1989] AC 53 and *Smith* v *Eric S Bush* [1990] 1 AC 831.

In Newham alone, the psychiatrist was instructed to carry out the examination of the child for the specific purpose of discovering whether the child had been sexually abused and, if possible, the identify of the abuser.

The psychiatrist must have known that if such an abuse was discovered proceedings by the local authority for the protection of the child would ensue and that her findings would be the evidence on which those proceedings would be based.

Therefore, such investigations, as having such an immediate link with possible proceedings in pursuance of a statutory duty cannot be made the basis of subsequent claims: *Evans* v *London Hospital Medical College (University of London)* [1981] 1 WLR 184.

In the Dorset case the defendant authority is under no liability at common law for the negligent exercise of the statutory discretion conferred on it by the Education Acts 1944 to 1981 but can be liable, both directly and vicariously, for negligence in the operation of the psychology service and negligent advice given by its officers.

Where the authority offers a service, such as psychological advice to the public, even though it obtains its powers from a statute, it is in the same position as any private individual or organisation holding itself out as offering such a service. It comes under a duty of care to those who use the service to exercise care in its conduct: *Gold* v *Essex County Council* [1942] KB 293.

The educational psychologists held themselves out as having special skills. They are like any other professional, bound both to possess such skills and to exercise them carefully: *Bolam* v *Friern Hospital Management Committee* [1957] 1 WLR 582. The defendant authority, therefore, can be shown to be directly or vicariously liable for them.

In the Hampshire care the plaintiff's claim is based solely on an allegation that the defendant authority was vicariously liable for the breaches of a duty of care owed by its employees, the headmaster and the member of the advisory service. The claim is a pure common law claim based on a duty of care owed by a headmaster and educational adviser to a pupil.

Although it is impossible to impose a common law duty of care which is inconsistent with, or which fetters, a statutory duty, there is no legal or common sense principle which requires one to deny a common law of duty of care which would otherwise exist just because there is a statutory scheme which addresses the same problem.

A school which accepts a pupil accepts responsibility not only for his physical well being but also for his educational needs. The head teacher being responsible for the school, himself came under a duty of care to exercise the reasonable skills of a headmaster in relation to such educational needs.

If it came to the attention of the headmaster that a pupil was under-performing, he did owe a duty to take such steps as a reasonable teacher would consider appropriate to try to deal with such under performance.

To hold that, in such circumstances, the head teacher could properly ignore the matter and make no attempt to deal with it would fly in the face, not only of society's expectations of what a school would provide, but also the fine traditions of the teaching profession itself.

If such head teacher gave advice to the parents then he must exercise the skills and care of a reasonable teacher in giving such advice. Similarly, an advisory teacher, in giving advice, owes a duty to the child to exercise the skill and care of a reasonable advisory teacher.

As to the Bromley case, no statutory right of action for damages for breach of s. 8 of the 1944 Act exists. The plaintiff's claim depends on alleged breaches of the duties imposed by ss. 8(2)(c), 33 and 34 of the 1944 Act and of ss. 4, 5 and 7 of the 1981 Act.

Assuming that the plaintiff, as a child having special educational needs, is a member of a class for whose protection the statutory provisions were enacted, there is nothing in the statutory provisions which demonstrates a parliamentary intention to give that class a statutory right of action for damages.

Those provisions indicate that Parliament did not intend to confer a private right of action. Accordingly, the plaintiff's claim based on breach of statutory duty was rightly struck out by the judge.

But as the present stage it would not be right to disregard a possible claim founded on vicarious liability. The defendant expressly accepted for the purposes of the appeal that the plaintiff alleged negligence against unidentified professionals or other officials of the defendant.

It is right, therefore, to assume that, at trial, the plaintiff would be able to allege and prove that one or more professionals employed by the defendant came into a relationship with the plaintiff which gave rise to a normal professional duty of care. In law such duty of care is capable of existing.

Lords Ackner, Jauncey, Lane and Nolan agreed with Lord Browne-Wilkinson in finding that the appeal of the minors in *X* and *M* should be dismissed, and that the claims for *direct* and/or *vicarious* liability in the tort of *negligence* in E and for *vicarious* liability (again in relation to common law negligence) *only* in *Christmas* and *Keating* should go ahead for trial on the facts.

STOVIN v WISE (NORFOLK COUNTY COUNCIL, THIRD PARTY)
[1996] 3 All ER 801 (HL)

S was injured when W turned right, across his path, at a road junction where visibility was restricted by a bank of land owned by X. Accidents had occurred at the junction in the past, but not often enough to warrant giving the site the title of an accident 'blackspot'.

Nevertheless, the council got in touch with X with a view to removing the bank, and eventually asked for permission to enter on to the land to do the necessary work. At that point, however, neither party took the matter any further and the bank remained in place: the accident between S and W occurred nearly a year later. S sued W in the tort of negligence, and W (or rather her **insurance company**) joined the council as third party, claiming negligence and breach of statutory duty in failing to take reasonable steps to remedy a known road hazard. Both the court at first instance and the Court of Appeal found that the council owed a duty of care in negligence, superimposed on its statutory obligations, to road users and assessed its share of blame for the accident at 30 per cent.

The council did not dispute its negligence (via its surveyor) but claimed that it did not owe a duty to take care on the facts in the first place. In the House of Lords, a majority found in favour of the council (W's liability was not in doubt).

LORD HOFFMANN:
Acts and omissions

Omissions, like economic loss, are notoriously a category of conduct in which Lord Atkin's generalisation in *Donoghue* v *Stevenson* [1932] AC 562 offers limited help . . . There are sound reasons why omissions require different treatment from positive conduct. It is one thing for the law to say that a person who undertakes some activity shall take reasonable care not to cause damage to others. It is another thing for the law to require that a person who is doing nothing in particular shall take steps to prevent another from suffering harm from the acts of third parties (like Mrs Wise) or natural causes. One can put the matter in political, moral or economic terms. In political terms it is less of an invasion of an individual's freedom for the law to require him to consider the safety of others in his actions than to impose upon him a duty to rescue or protect. A moral version of this point may be called the 'why pick on me?' argument. A duty to prevent harm to others or to render assistance to a person in danger or distress may apply to a large and indeterminate class of people who happen to be able to do something. Why should one be held liable rather than another? In economic terms, the efficient allocation of resources usually requires an activity should bear its own costs. If it benefits from being able to impose some of its costs on other people (what economists call 'externalities') the market is distorted because the activity appears cheaper than it really is. So liability to pay compensation for loss caused by negligent conduct acts as a deterrent against increasing the cost of the activity to the community and reduces externalities. But there is no similar justification for requiring a person who is not doing anything to spend money on behalf of someone else. Except in special cases (such as marine salvage) English law does not reward someone who voluntarily confers a benefit on another. So there must be some special reason why he should have to put his hand in his pocket . . .

There may be a duty to act if one has undertaken to do so or induced a person to rely upon one doing so. Or the ownership or occupation of land may give rise to a duty to take positive steps for the benefit of those who come upon the land and sometimes for the benefit of neighbours. In *Goldman* v *Hargrave* [1966] 2 All ER 989 the High Court of Australia held that the owner and occupier of a 600 acre grazing property in Western Australia had a duty to take reasonable steps to extinguish a fire, which had been started by lightning striking a tree on his land, so as to prevent it from spreading to his neighbour's land. This is a case in which the limited class of persons who owe the duty (neighbours) is easily identified and the political, moral and economic arguments which I have mentioned are countered by the fact that the duties are mutual. One cannot tell where the lightning may strike and it is therefore both fair and efficient to impose upon each landowner a duty to have regard to the interests of his neighbour. In giving the advice of the Privy Council . . . Lord Wilberforce underlined the exceptional nature of the liability when he pointed out that the question of whether the landowner had acted reasonably should be judged by reference to the resources he actually had at his disposal and not by some general or objective standard. This is quite different from the duty owed by a person who undertakes a positive activity which carries the risk of causing damage to others. If he does not have the resources to take such steps as are objectively reasonable to prevent such damage, he should not undertake that activity at all . . .

Of course it is true that the conditions necessary to bring about an event always consist of a combination of acts and omissions. Mr Stovin's accident was caused by the fact that Mrs Wise drove out into Station Road and omitted to keep a proper look-out. But this does not mean that the distinction between acts and omissions is meaningless or illogical. One must have regard to the purpose of the distinction as it is used in the law of negligence, which is to distinguish between regulating the way in which all activity may be conducted and imposing a duty to act upon a person who is not carrying on any relevant activity. To hold the defendant liable for an act, rather than an omission, it is therefore necessary to be able to say, according to common sense principles of causation, that the damage was caused by something which the defendant did . . .

Public authorities

The argument that the council had a positive duty to take action giving rise to a claim for compensation in tort must therefore depend . . . upon the public nature of its powers, duties and funding. The argument is that while it may be unreasonable to expect a private landowner to spend money for the benefit of strangers who have the right to cross his land, the very purpose of the existence of a public authority like the council is to spend its resources on making the roads convenient and safe . . . It is certainly true that some of the arguments against liability for omissions do not apply to public bodies like a highway authority. There is no 'why pick on me?' argument . . . the highway authority alone had the financial and physical resources, as well as the legal powers, to eliminate the hazard. But this does not mean that the distinction between acts and omissions is irrelevant to the duties of a public body or that there are not other arguments, peculiar to public bodies, which may negative the existence of a duty of care.

(a) *Negligent conduct in the exercise of statutory powers*

Since *Mersey Docks and Harbour Board Trustees* v *Gibbs* (1866) LR 1 HL 93 it has been clear law that in the absence of express statutory authority, a public body is in principle liable for torts in the same way as a private person. But its statutory powers or duties may restrict its liability . . . In the case of positive acts, therefore, the liability of a public authority in tort is in principle the same as that of a private person but may be *restricted* by its statutory powers and duties. The argument in the present case, however, is that whereas a private person would have owed no duty of care in respect of an omission to remove the hazard at the junction, the duty of the highway authority is *enlarged* by virtue of its statutory powers. The existence of the statutory powers is said to create a 'proximity' between the highway authority and the highway user which would not otherwise exist.

(b)   *Negligent omission to use statutory powers*

Until the decision of this House in *Anns* v *Merton London BC* [1977] 2 All ER 492 there was
no authority for treating a statutory power as giving rise to a common law duty of care.
Two cases in particular were thought to be against it [ie] *Sheppard* v *Glossop Corporation*
[1921] 3 KB 132 [and] *East Suffolk Rivers Catchment Board* v *Kent* [1940] 4 All ER 527 [where]
Lord Romer cited *Sheppard* v *Glossop Corporation* and stated the principle which he said it
laid down: 'Where a statutory authority is entrusted with a mere power it cannot be made
liable for any damage sustained by a member of the public by reason of a failure to exercise
that power' . . . What the majority found impossible was to derive such a duty [of care] from
the existence of a statutory power: to turn a statutory 'may' into a common law 'ought' . . .

Anns v *Merton London BC*

This brings me to *Anns* . . . it is now necessary to ask whether the reasoning can support
the existence of a duty of care owed by a public authority in respect of foreseeable physical
injury which is founded upon the existence of statutory powers to safeguard people
against that injury.

Lord Wilberforce . . . first stated the well known two stage test for the existence of a duty
of care. This involves starting with a prima facie assumption that a duty of care exists if it
is reasonably foreseeable that carelessness may cause damage and then asking whether
there are any considerations which ought to 'negative, or to reduce or limit the scope of the
duty or the class of person to whom it is owed or the damages to which a breach of it may
arise'. Subsequent decisions in this House and the Privy Council have preferred to
approach the question the other way round, starting with situations in which a duty has
been held to exist and then asking whether there are considerations of analogy, policy,
fairness and justice for extending it to cover a new situation: see for example Lord Bridge
of Harwich in *Caparo Industries plc* v *Dickman* [1990] 1 All ER 568. It can be said that,
provided that the considerations of policy etc are properly analysed, it should not matter
whether one starts from one end or the other.

On the other hand the assumption from which one starts makes a great deal of difference
if the analysis is wrong. The trend of authorities has been to discourage the assumption
that anyone who suffers loss is prima facie entitled to compensation from a person
(preferably insured or a public authority) whose act or omission can be said to have caused
it. The default position is that he is not . . .

It is clear, however, that [a] public law duty cannot in itself give rise to a duty of care. A
public body almost always has a duty in public law to consider whether it should exercise its
powers, but that does not mean that it necessarily owes a duty of care which may require that
the power should actually be exercised . . . A mandamus can require future consideration of
the exercise of a power. But an action for negligence looks back to what the council ought to
have done. Upon what principles can one say of a public authority that not only did it have a
duty in public law to consider the exercise of the power but that it would thereupon have
been under a duty in private law to act, giving rise to a claim in compensation against public
funds for its failure to do so? . . . The only tool which the *Anns* case provides for defining these
circumstances is the distinction between policy and operations . . .

Policy and operations

Since *Anns* there have been differing views, both in England and the Commonwealth, over
whether it was right to breach the protection which the *East Suffolk* principle gave to public
authorities . . . What has become clear, however, is that the distinction between policy and
operations is an inadequate tool with which to discover whether it is appropriate to impose
a duty of care or not [see] *Rowling* v *Takaro Properties Ltd* [1988] 1 All ER 163 . . . There are
at least two reasons why the distinction is inadequate. The first is that, as Lord Wilberforce
himself pointed out, the distinction is often elusive. This is particularly true of powers to
provide public benefits which involve the expenditure of money. Practically every decision
about the provision of such benefits, no matter how trivial it may seem, affects the budget
of the public authority in either timing or amount . . . But another reason is that even if the
distinction is clear cut, leaving no element of discretion in the sense that it would be
irrational (in the public law meaning of that word) for the public authority not to exercise
its power, it does not follow that the law should superimpose a common law duty of care.
This can be seen if one looks at cases in which a public authority has been under a statutory

or common law *duty* to provide a service or other benefit for the public or a section of the public. In such cases there is no discretion but the courts have nevertheless not been willing to hold that a member of the public who has suffered loss because the service was not provided to him should necessarily have a cause of action, either for breach of statutory duty or for negligence at common law.

There are many instances of this principle being applied to statutory duties, but perhaps the most relevant example of the dissociation between public duty and a liability to pay compensation for breach of that duty was the ancient common law duty to repair the highway . . . In terms of public finance, this is a perfectly reasonable attitude. It is one thing to provide a service at the public expense. It is another to require the public to pay compensation when a failure to provide the service has resulted in loss. Apart from cases of reliance, which I shall consider later, the same loss would have been suffered if the service had not been provided in the first place. To require payment of compensation increases the burden on public funds. Before imposing such an additional burden, the courts should be satisfied that this is what Parliament intended . . .

The same is true of omission to perform a statutory duty. If such a duty does not give rise to a private right to sue for breach, it would be unusual if it nevertheless gave rise to a duty of care at common law which made the public authority liable to pay compensation for foreseeable loss caused by the duty not being performed. It will often be foreseeable that loss will result if, for example, a benefit or service is not provided. If the policy of the act is not to create a statutory liability to pay compensation, the same policy should ordinarily exclude the existence of a common law duty of care.

In the case of a mere statutory power, there is the further point that the legislature has chosen to confer a discretion rather than create a duty. Of course there may be cases in which Parliament has chosen to confer a power because the subject matter did not permit a duty to be stated with sufficient precision. It may nevertheless have contemplated that in circumstances in which it would be irrational not to exercise the power, a person who suffered loss because it had not been exercised, or not properly exercised, would be entitled to compensation. I therefore do not say that a statutory 'may' can never give rise to a common law duty of care. I prefer to leave open the question of whether the *Anns* case was wrong to create any exception to Lord Romer's statement of principle in the *East Suffolk* case and I shall go on to consider the circumstances (such as 'general reliance') in which it has been suggested that such a duty might arise. But the fact that Parliament has conferred a discretion must be some indication that the policy of the Act conferring the power was not to create a right to compensation. The need to have regard to the policy of the statute therefore means that exceptions will be rare.

In summary therefore, I think that the minimum pre-conditions for basing a duty of care upon the existence of a statutory power, if it can be done at all, are, first, that it would in the circumstances have been irrational not to have exercised the power, so that there was in effect a public law duty to act, and secondly, that there are exceptional grounds for holding that the policy of the statute requires compensation to be paid to persons who suffer loss because the power was not exercised.

Particular and general reliance
This ground for imposing a duty of care has been called 'general reliance'. It has little in common with the ordinary doctrine of reliance; the plaintiff does not need to have relied upon the expectation that the power would be used or even known that it existed. It appears rather to refer to general expectations in the community, which the individual plaintiff may or may not have shared. A widespread assumption that a statutory power will be exercised may affect the general pattern of economic and social behaviour. For example, insurance premiums may take into account the expectation that statutory powers of inspection or accident prevention will ordinarily prevent certain kinds of risk from materialising. Thus the doctrine of general reliance requires all inquiry into the role of a given statutory power in the behaviour of members of the general public, of which an outstanding example is the judgment of Richardson J in *Invercargill CC v Hamlin* [1994] 3 NZLR 513.

It appears to be essential to the doctrine of general reliance that the benefit or service provided under statutory powers should be of a uniform and routine nature, so that one can describe exactly what the public authority was supposed to do. Powers of inspection for defects clearly fall into this category. Another way of looking at the matter is to say that if a particular service is provided as a matter of routine, it would be irrational for a public authority to provide it in one case and arbitrarily withhold it in another. This was obviously the main ground upon which this House in *Anns* considered that the power of the local authority to inspect foundations should give rise to a duty of care.

But the fact that it would be irrational not to exercise the power is, as I have said, only one of the conditions which has to be satisfied. It is also necessary to discern a policy which confers a right to financial compensation if the power has not been exercised ... I do not propose to explore further the doctrine of general reliance because, for reasons which I shall explain, I think that there are no grounds upon which the present case can be brought within it. I will only note in passing that its application may require some very careful analysis of the role which the expected exercise of the statutory power plays in community behaviour. For example, in one sense it is true that the fire brigade is there to protect people in situations in which they could not be expected to be able to protect themselves. On the other hand, they can and do protect themselves by insurance against the risk of fire. It is not obvious that there should be a right to compensation from a negligent fire authority which will ordinarily ensure by right of subrogation to an insurance company. The only reason would be to provide a general deterrent against inefficiency. But there must be better ways of doing this than by compensating insurance companies out of public funds ...

Duties of a highway authority

I return to consider whether the council owed a duty of care which required it to take steps to improve the junction ... I will start by asking whether in the light of what the council knew or ought to have known about the junction, it would have had a duty in public to undertake the work. This requires that it would have been irrational not to exercise its discretion to do so ... It seems to me therefore that the question of whether anything should be done about the junction was at all times firmly within the area of the council's discretion. As they were therefore not under a public law duty to do the work, the first condition for the imposition of a duty of care was not satisfied.

But even if it were, I do not think that the second condition would be satisfied. Assuming that the highway authority ought, as a matter of public law, to have done the work, I do not think that there are any grounds upon which it can be said that the public law duty should give rise to an obligation to compensate persons who have suffered loss because it was not performed. There is no question here of reliance on the council having improved the junction. Everyone could see that it was still the same. Mr Stovin was not arbitrarily denied a benefit which was routinely provided to others. In respect of the junction, he was treated in exactly the same way as any other road user. The foundation for the doctrine of general reliance is missing in this case, because we are not concerned with provision of a uniform identifiable benefit or service. Every hazardous junction, intersection or stretch of road is different and requires a separate decision as to whether anything should be done to improve it ...

In my view the creation of a duty of care upon a highway authority, even on grounds of irrationality in failing to exercise a power, would inevitably expose the authority's budgetary decisions to judicial inquiry. This would distort the priorities of local authorities, which would be bound to try to play safe by increasing their spending on road improvements rather than risk enormous liabilities for personal injury accidents. They will spend less on education or social services. I think that it is important, before extending the duty of care owed by public authorities, to consider the cost to the community of the defensive measures which they are likely to take in order to avoid liability. It would not be surprising if one of the consequences of the *Anns* case and the spate of cases which followed was that local council inspectors tended to insist upon stronger foundations than were necessary. In a case like this, I do not think that the duty of care can be used as a deterrent against low standards in improving the road lay-out. Given the fact that the British road network largely antedates the highway authorities themselves, the court is not in a position to say what an appropriate standard of improvement would be. This must be a matter for the discretion of the authority. On the other hand, denial of liability does not leave the road user unprotected. Drivers of vehicles must take the highway network as they find it. Everyone knows that there are hazardous bends, intersections and junctions. It is primarily the duty of drivers of vehicles to take due care. And if, as in the case of Mrs Wise, they do not, there is compulsory insurance to provide compensation to the victims. There is no reason of policy or justice which requires the highway authority to be an additional defendant. I would therefore allow the appeal.

Lord Goff and Lord Jauncey agreed; Lord Slynn and Lord Nicholls dissented.

ALEXANDROU v *OXFORD* [1993] 4 All ER 328 (CA)

It was found that the police are not liable for negligence to individual members of the public who suffer loss through the activities of criminals. In order to create a duty of care in such circumstances there must exist some 'special relationship' between the police and a member of the public. Thus, when an occupier of premises installs a burglar alarm system which is connected to a police station, that does not of itself create a 'special relationship' between him and the police. The plaintiff's loss in this case had not been caused directly by any act or omission on the part of the police; it had been caused by burglars. According to Glidewell LJ it was not sufficient for a plaintiff, seeking to establish that a defendant owed him a duty of care to see that he did not suffer loss through the activities of another person, to show only that the loss was foreseeable; it must also be shown that he had a special relationship with the defendant. In some cases, for instance, the police might owe a contractual duty to an occupier in such circumstances. In the present case, however, the communication with the police was by a 999 call and any duty owed was to the public at large (not redressable in negligence).

SLADE LJ: As Glidewell LJ has pointed out, it is possible to envisage an agreement between an occupier of a property protected by a burglar alarm and the police which would impose on the police a contractual liability, but no such contractual liability has been suggested in the present case. As things are, I cannot see that the duty in tort (if any) owed by the police to this plaintiff can have been any greater than the duty in tort (if any) owed by them to any ordinary member of the public who by means of a 999 call warns them that a crime is being or is about to be committed against his person or property. By common law police officers owe to the general public a duty to enforce the criminal law. This duty may in an appropriate case be enforced at the instance of one having title to sue by mandamus (see *Hill's case* [1989] AC 53 at 59 *per* Lord Keith). In my judgment, however, on public policy grounds similar to those given by Lord Keith (see [1988] 2 All ER 238 at 243, [1989] AC 53 at 63), it is unthinkable that the police should be exposed to potential actions for negligence at the suit of every disappointed or dissatisfied maker of a 999 call. I can see no sufficient grounds for holding that the police owed a duty of care to this plaintiff on or after receipt of the 999 call on 26 January 1986 if they would not have owed a duty of care to ordinary members of the public who made a similar call.

For these and the further reasons given by Glidewell LJ, I consider that the police owed no duty of care to the plaintiff of the kind here alleged, and would allow the appeal on this ground.

Appeal allowed.

OSMAN AND ANOTHER v *FERGUSON AND ANOTHER* [1993] 4 All ER 344 (CA)

There *was* close proximity between the plaintiff and the police, creating a 'special relationship' between all parties, yet the court decided that public policy dictated that no duty of care in negligence to individuals sprang from that relationship.

McCOWAN LJ: Mr Freeland submits that the facts in the present case are indistinguishable from those in *Hill* v *Chief Constable of West Yorkshire* so far as public policy is concerned. Mr Hendy QC, however, argues that there are the following distinctions. First, he says that in the *Hill* case the culprit had at the relevant time not yet been identified, while here he had. I do not find that a satisfactory distinction. It is one thing for the police to say, 'We believe that a particular man has committed or has threatened to commit a crime', but it is another matter for them to bring it home to him. Here the police were still in the process of gathering evidence against Paget-Lewis which would include evidence of what he said when found and interviewed. Searching for him for that purpose was all part of the investigation.

When one looks at the particulars of negligence one sees, among other things, failure to apprehend him, failure to interview him, failure to search his home, failure to trace him through cars he hired and failure to link the theft of the shotgun with him. These all appear to me to be properly described as failures in investigation. Mr Hendy argues, however, than no further investigation was needed. All the police had to do was arrest him and keep him in custody and thereby suppress the crime that he in fact went on to commit. In fact Lord Keith speaks of the police function 'in the investigation and suppression of crime'. Mr Hendy says, however, that it is significant that Lord Keith does not refer to 'investigation or suppression' and that Lord Templeman does not use the word 'suppression' at all. I am afraid I am quite unable to accept that any of that is significant. In particular Lord Templeman is plainly thinking in terms of suppression of crime when he says ([1988] 2 All ER 238 at 245, [1989] AC 53 at 65): 'If the policeman does not arrest on suspicion a suspect with previous convictions, the police force may be held liable for subsequent crimes.' In my judgment investigation of crime is not meant to be narrowly interpreted and suppression includes the prevention of crime.

Secondly, Mr Hendy submits that the ratio of *Hill's* case is that policy decisions are protected by public policy immunity but operational decisions are not and that, whereas the failures in *Hill's* case were of a policy nature, those in the present case were of an operational nature. In my judgment, such a distinction is not to be supported by the speeches in *Hill's* case. Indeed I consider such a dividing line to be utterly artificial and impossible to draw in the present case. I should add that Mr Hendy placed reliance on the judgment of Henry J in the Canadian case of *Doe* v *Metropolitan Toronto (Municipality) Comrs of Police* (1989) 58 DLR 396. This does contain material supporting Mr Hendy's argument, but I do not find it helpful, first, because it seems to me to be directly contrary to the reasoning in *Hill's* case which is of course binding on us and, secondly, because the principle of public policy has not yet been introduced into the law of Canada.

Mr Hendy's final point is that, if the class of victim is sufficiently proximate (as he says the victims here were) and sufficiently small, the public policy argument may not apply. I cannot accept this submission. Lord Keith plainly treats public policy as a separate point which is not reached at all unless there is a duty of care. If Mr Hendy were right, public policy would not be a separate argument at all because if a plaintiff were proved to be sufficiently proximate and a member of a sufficiently small class, public policy would not arise. . . .

. . . In my judgment the House of Lords decision on public policy in *Hill's* case dooms this action to failure as against the second defendant.

As a last resort, Mr Hendy sought to place reliance on the words of Browne-Wilkinson V-C in *Lonrho* v *Tebbit* [1991] 4 All ER 973 at 979:

A claim should only be struck out in a plain and obvious case. The difficulty arises where, as in the present case, a claim to strike out depends upon the decision of one or more difficult points of law. In such a case, the judge should normally refuse to entertain such a claim to strike out. But, if in a particular case the judge is satisfied that the decision of the point of law at that stage will either avoid the necessity for trial altogether or render the trial substantially easier and cheaper, he can properly determine such [a] difficult point of law on the striking-out application . . .

Mr Hendy submitted that the present was a case depending on the decision of one or more difficult points of law and that we should therefore refuse to entertain the claim to strike out. I cannot agree. I consider this a plain and obvious case falling squarely within a House of Lords decision. I would therefore allow the appeal.

Beldam and Simon Brown LJJ agreed.

ANCELL AND ANOTHER v MCDERMOTT AND OTHERS [1993] 4 All ER 355 (CA)

As a result of the alleged negligence of other parties diesel fuel was present on the highway, and the police were aware of this fact. The first and second plaintiffs were passengers in a car driven by the first plaintiff's wife; the car skidded on the diesel fuel and collided with another vehicle.

The two plaintiffs were injured and the first plaintiff's wife was killed in the accident.

It was held that the police were under no general duty of care to protect or warn road users in respect of hazards discovered by the police in the course of carrying out their duties on the highway, because it would be against public policy to impose a duty in the absence of exceptional circumstances creating a special relationship between the police and the plaintiffs where the danger had been created by other persons for whom the police were not responsible.

CAPITAL AND COUNTIES PLC v HAMPSHIRE COUNTY COUNCIL AND OTHERS
[1997] 2 All ER 565 (CA)

In *Capital and Counties plc v Hampshire County Council and others; Digital Equipment Co. Ltd v Hampshire County Council and others; John Munroe (Acrylics) Ltd v London Fire and Civil Defence Authority and others; Church of Jesus Christ of Latter Day Saints (Great Britain) v West Yorkshire Fire and Civil Defence Authority* [1997] 2 All ER 865, the Court of Appeal heard several appeals together because they all raised a common issue of public and legal importance, viz. the question of whether a fire brigade could be liable in the tort of negligence for a fire the brigade had attended in response to an emergency call. In other words, the question for the court to consider was whether a fire brigade owed **a duty of care** to the owners/occupiers of buildings damaged or destroyed by fire.

It was held that a fire brigade is not under a common law duty to answer a call for help and is not under any duty to take care to do so. If firefighters fail to turn up or fail to turn up in time because they have carelessly misunderstood the message, got lost on the way or run into a tree (for example), they are not liable.

The court then considered the question of whether a duty of care is owed by a fire brigade to the owner/occupier after arriving at the scene of the fire. It was held that the fire brigade does not enter into a sufficiently proximate relationship with the owner or occupier of premises merely by attending at the site and fighting the fire, even though the senior officer actually assumes control of the operation.

With regard to a fire brigade's statutory duties under the Fire Services Act 1947, although a breach of statutory duty does not, in ordinary cases, give rise to any private law cause of action, a private law cause of action will arise if it can be shown, as a matter of construction of the statute, that the statutory duty was imposed for the protection of a limited class of the public and that Parliament intended to confer on members of that class a private right of action for breach of duty. On the facts no action for breach of duty lay under s. 13, Fire Services Act 1947. The duties laid down in ss. 1 and 13 are in the nature of statutory provisions establishing a regulatory system or scheme of social welfare for the benefit of the public at large, conferring no right of private action. Accordingly, the West Yorkshire and the London Fire Brigade appeals (by the plaintiff owners/occupiers against the first instance decisions in favour of the fire authorities) were dismissed.

In the *Hampshire* case, following *Hill v Chief Constable of West Yorkshire*, the court found that there was no question that a fire officer, like anyone else, could be liable in tort to a person who is injured as a direct result of his actions or omissions. It was held, therefore, that in finding the senior fire officer negligent in turning off water sprinklers (the building had its own fire prevention/containment system), the judge at first instance had found that no reasonably well informed and competent fireman (*Bolam* applied) could have made such a decision. Although the defendant's fire expert said there were occasions when he had known sprinklers to be turned off, the judge gave unassailable reasons for not accepting the reasons which were given for turning them off in the instant case. The decision to turn off the sprinkler system had increased the risk of fire spreading, and the defendant fire authority could not show that the building would have been destroyed in any case, i.e. even without the fire officer's negligent action. Accordingly this appeal, by the fire authority, was dismissed.

Four further points may be made:

(a)   the appeals were in fact brought by the injured parties' **insurance companies** which had paid out on various policies (insurance companies which indemnify insured persons against losses can use the doctrine of **subrogation** – i.e. the companies can 'step into the shoes' of the insured persons to bring actions against persons who are legally liable for the damage – in order to recoup their losses);

(b)   the issues raised in relation to **the action for breach of statutory duty** are pertinent to the discussion in **Chapter 8**;

(c)   the Court of Appeal considered the decision in *Stovin v Wise*, and applied the majority opinion in that case;

(d)   this is a case in which a rescuer (albeit a **professional rescuer**) was found liable for making the situation worse.

DALY v SURREY COUNTY COUNCIL, The Times, 25 October 1997

In *Daly* v *Surrey County Council*, Mrs Daly became the first person to sue a rescuer for damages in English law – in claiming that a fireman caused the death of her husband, a building-site foreman, by preventing colleagues of the deceased from trying to dig him free from a collapsed trench.

Mr Daly died after he became trapped in a trench on a construction site: he had climbed in the trench to repair a broken drainage pipe. A driver of a mechanical digger began a rescue attempt, but the fire officer in question ordered him to stop so that his men could take over the rescue.

It was the contention of the plaintiff that, had the fire officer not prevented the site workers from continuing with their efforts to free Mr Daly, they would have reached the deceased (who died from suffocation within an hour of the trench collapsing) more quickly and his life would have been saved. The fire brigade, on the other hand, argued that (a) it owed no duty of care to the deceased, (b) there was no negligence on the facts, and (c) Mr Daly would probably have died anyway even if the construction workers' attempts had been allowed to continue.

May J found that the fire brigade had not been negligent in the circumstances, i.e. there had been no breach of duty – therefore there was no liability in respect of the death. His Lordship added, however, that Mr Daly had acted foolishly and that **if** the fire brigade **had** been negligent, any award of damages would have been substantially reduced because of the deceased's contributory negligence.

BARRETT v ENFIELD LONDON BC [1997] 3 All ER 171 (CA)

The plaintiff had been in care between the ages of 10 and 18 and claimed damages in the tort of negligence for psychiatric and psychological difficulties allegedly caused by incidents occurring while he was in care. It was decided that where a local authority takes a decision about the future of a child in its care, and this is a decision which would in normal circumstances be taken by a **parent**, the authority does **not** owe a duty of care to the child.

The authority can, however, be vicariously liable where the decision concerns an 'operational' matter, e.g. where a social worker is negligent in relation to an interdisciplinary assessment (i.e. an assessment made by the various professionals involved in the child's case) of what action should be taken in relation to the child.

Lord Woolf MR said that in *X (Minors)* v *Bedfordshire CC* the court was concerned with the extent of the duty owed by local authorities to children prior to their being taken into care. The present appeal, however, concerned the extent of any duty owed by local authorities **after** children had been placed in care.

Therefore, since there was no previous decision establishing a common law duty of care in negligence in the present circumstances, the court had to consider whether it was just and reasonable to extend the common law duty of care to a local authority when it was performing its statutory duties to protect and promote the welfare of children in its care.

The court was of the opinion that it would be contrary to the public interest to impose a duty in the present context. Where the local authority was in the position of a **parent** to the plaintiff, and was considering his future in those terms, decisions would often require 'a difficult and delicate balancing of conflicting interests'. Parents made decisions on a daily basis about their children's future and it would be 'wholly inappropriate' that **those** decisions should give rise to a liability for damages – even if they could be shown to be wrong.

The possibility of litigation years afterwards could cause a more defensive and cautious approach to taking positive decisions with regard to a child's future. In any event, said his Lordship, the ombudsman complaints procedure could be used in such circumstances.

CLUNIS v CAMDEN AND ISLINGTON HEALTH AUTHORITY [1998] 3 All ER 180 (CA)

At first instance it was found that where a plaintiff alleges that a hospital was negligent in failing to provide appropriate treatment to the plaintiff for his mental disorder, and seeks damages for self-inflicted harm and an indemnity for damages the plaintiff has to pay to others because he has harmed those other persons, there is no reason in law why those claims should be struck out of the plaintiff's **pleadings**.

The Court of Appeal struck out the claim for damages. Beldam LJ said it would not be just and reasonable to impose a common law duty of care on a health authority in relation to its statutory responsibility to provide after-care. Nor would it be fair to hold the authority responsible for the plaintiff's actions. His Lordship said: 'The court ought not to allow itself to be made an instrument to enforce obligations alleged to arise out of the plaintiff's own criminal act.'

HARRIS v EVANS (AND THE HEALTH AND SAFETY EXECUTIVE) [1998] 3 All ER 522 (CA)

In a striking out action (a **pleadings** case) it was held that a health and safety inspector (and his employer vicariously) did not owe a duty of care in the tort of negligence to the plaintiff, who ran a bungee-jumping business.

The defendant gave advice (in accordance with his powers under the Health and Safety at Work Act 1974) to certain local authorities concerning the safety of equipment used by the plaintiff in his business, as a result of which the local authorities used their statutory powers (also under the 1974 Act) to prevent the use of this equipment. Consequently the plaintiff suffered 'pure' economic loss because of the loss of trade caused by this ban.

The court, adopting the *Caparo* incremental approach, said *X* v *Bedfordshire County Council* was the leading authority on the question of whether *Hedley Byrne/White* v *Jones/Spring* v *Guardian Assurance* applied in the present context. As in *X*, there was here a statutory scheme: the defendant advised the local authorities and they acted within the terms of the 1974 Act. It was implicit in the Act that economic loss might be caused when prohibition orders (against the use of equipment) were issued – whether by the local authorities acting on the advice of the defendant or by the defendant himself – and the Act itself provided remedies for the erroneous use of its powers by inspectors or local (enforcing) authorities. (In *X*, it was pointed out by Lord Browne-Wilkinson that the Children Act 1989 provided procedures for the resolution of grievances.)

Sir Richard Scott, V-C, giving the judgment of the court, said that a further factor to be considered (as it had been in *X*, above) was whether the imposition of a duty of care in negligence on inspectors such as the defendant would 'engender untoward caution' on their part in the performance of their statutory duties – in the present case their 'vital safety role' had to be considered. His Lordship said that had the defendant in the present case imposed some particular requirement which introduced 'a new risk or danger not present in the [plaintiff's] business activity as previously conducted' and this risk or danger materialised, causing damage to the business as well as physical damage to person or property, it was possible that that damage might be compensated via an action in negligence; but that was not so here: all that the alleged negligence of the defendant had done in the present case was to lead to **statutory** restraints being placed on the plaintiff's ability to carry on his business. **That** alleged negligence was **not** actionable, whether the notices had been issued by the inspector himself or by an enforcing authority acting on his advice.

OLL LTD v SECRETARY OF STATE FOR TRANSPORT [1997] 3 All ER 897

Following *Capital and Counties plc* v *Hampshire County Council*, it was found that the coastguard service owes no private law duty to respond to an emergency call; nor is it liable if its response to such a call is negligent – although it might be different if it commits a **positive** act which directly causes greater injury than would have occurred if it had not intervened at all. The service is also not liable in negligence if it is guilty of issuing misdirection to other rescue organisations.

PALMER v TEES HEALTH AUTHORITY AND HARTLEPOOL AND EAST DURHAM NHS TRUST, The Times, 19 February 1998

The High Court struck out a claim for damages in negligence brought against hospital authorities by the mother of a child who was murdered by a psychopath who had been released from hospital. The psychopath was under the hospital's care from 1992 until being rehoused on the estate where the plaintiff lived. He abducted and murdered her daughter, aged 3, in 1994. It was alleged that the hospital authorities owed the plaintiff, and her (deceased) daughter a duty of care.

At first instance, it was ruled that the psychopath had made no **direct** threat against the child and her family; there was, therefore, a lack of 'proximity' in legal terms.

PHELPS v HILLINGDON LONDON BOROUGH COUNCIL, *The Times*, 10 October 1997

It was held, at first instance, that an educational psychologist (employed by a local authority) owes a duty of care in negligence to a child whom he or she is assessing.

Thus, two findings were made on the facts of this case, viz. (i) a psychologist who fails to diagnose dyslexia in circumstances where a competent psychologist would diagnose the condition will be negligent (*Bolam* applied); (ii) the local authority employing the psychologist is vicariously liable for that negligence (*X* v *Bedfordshire* CC followed).

Garland J said that children, and their parents, in normal circumstances have no access to educational psychological advice other than that provided by the local authority which runs both the school and educational psychological services. It follows that their reliance on this type of advice is so much the greater.

W v COMMISSIONER OF POLICE OF THE METROPOLIS, *The Times*, 21 July 1997 (CA)

A woman police officer complained to her employer that she was subjected to serious sexual attacks from a fellow officer and then brought an action in negligence claiming that senior police officers were negligent in dealing with her allegations. It was held that no duty of care was owed to individual police officers, enabling them to claim damages for the negligent performance of internal disciplinary procedures.

W v ESSEX COUNTY COUNCIL [1998] 3 All ER 111

The Ws fostered a fifteen-year-old youth and he allegedly abused the Ws' children. The Ws claimed that the defendant local authority, and one of its social workers (who was in charge of the case) knew that the youth was an active sexual abuser. It was held by Hooper J – **on the pleadings** – that a case could be argued, to go to full trial, on the basis (i) that a social worker placing a child with foster parents has a duty to provide them with such information about the child as a reasonable social worker would provide in the circumstances; (ii) a local authority is **vicariously** liable for the conduct of its social worker in this respect.

The Ws claimed that they were told only that the boy could be a bully and a liar and that his father, a convicted paedophile, had abused him. They said they would not have fostered the youth had they known he had gone into care at the age of 12 after abusing his sister.

This ruling gave the Ws' children permission to start full proceedings in negligence against the social worker and the council. His Lordship did, however, **strike out** the parents' claim for the post-traumatic stress disorder they developed after discovering the abuse because, like the parents in *Alcock* (see **Chapter 6**) who had not been at the football ground in that case, they were barred from claiming on the ground that they had not personally seen or heard 'a horrifying event'.

This decision was **confirmed** by a majority in the Court of Appeal (*The Times*, 3 April 1998). Stuart-Smith LJ, in his dissenting judgment, was of the opinion that the council's only duty was to do the best it could for the foster child.

He said: 'Almost by definition, adolescent children in care are likely to have serious problems, and there may often be a conflict of interest between foster child and foster parents.'

In his Lordship's opinion local authorities and social workers 'might err on the side of caution', and might give too much information — 'perhaps some of it based on rumour and hearsay' — to potential foster parents against the child's interest should a duty of care in negligence be imposed. The abused children in this case could, he said, make a claim under the criminal injuries compensation scheme.

Judge LJ, delivering the majority judgment, however, said the local authority had introduced a 'potential menace' into the plaintiffs' home. This case was different from other cases which had been struck out because here the victims were not children for whom the council had any care responsibilities. Indeed, for the benefit of the W's four children the council had accepted the W's express condition of 'no sexual abusers'.

Furthermore, if it were known that local authorities might withhold information from foster parents they, the foster parents, 'might very well be discouraged from . . . offering to provide homes for children'. In the circumstances, the local authority had assumed responsibility for the accuracy of its positive assurance to the parents about G [the fostered boy in this case]'.

The court **unanimously** struck out the parents' claim for damages for their own psychological trauma.

WELTON v NORTH CORNWALL DISTRICT COUNCIL, The Times, 19 July 1996 (CA)

It was held that where an environmental health officer negligently required the owner of food premises to undertake works which were **unnecessary** to secure compliance with regulations made under the Food Safety Act 1990, and the owner of the premises incurred substantial and **unnecessary** expenditure in carrying out the works, the local authority (the local food authority for present purposes) was liable for breach of its common law duty of care to the owner for the economic loss suffered.

The plaintiff took on the works because of the insistence of the officer, who knew that what he said would be relied upon by the plaintiff without independent inquiry. In the circumstances, it was found that the fact that the relationship between the parties arose out of the **purported exercise of statutory functions** was no reason why the local authority should not be liable in the tort of negligence.

3.4 Specific Issues in Relation to Duty

3.4.1 THE UNBORN CHILD

CONGENITAL DISABILITIES (CIVIL LIABILITY) ACT 1976

1. Civil liability to child born disabled.

(1) If a child is born disabled as the result of such an occurrence before its birth as is mentioned in subsection (2) below, and a person (other than the child's own mother) is under this section answerable to the child in respect of the occurrence, the child's disabilities are to be regarded as damage resulting from the wrongful act of that person and actionable accordingly at the suit of the child.

(2) An occurrence to which this section applies is one which—

(a) affected either parent of the child in his or her ability to have a normal, healthy child; or

(b) affected the mother during her pregnancy, or affected her or the child in the course of its birth, so that the child is born with disabilities which would not otherwise have been present.

(3) Subject to the following subsections, a person (here referred to as 'the defendant') is answerable to the child if he was liable in tort to the parent or would, if sued in due time, have been so; and it is no answer that there could not have been such liability because the parent suffered no actionable injury, if there was a breach of legal duty which, accompanied by injury, would have given rise to the liability.

(4) In the case of an occurrence preceding the time of conception, the defendant is not answerable to the child if at that time either or both of the parents knew the risk of their child bring born disabled (that is to say, the particular risk created by the occurrence); but should it be the child's father who is the defendant, this subsection does not apply if he knew of the risk and the mother did not.

(5) The defendant is not answerable to the child, for anything he did or omitted to do when responsible in a professional capacity for treating or advising the parent, if he took reasonable care having due regard to then received professional opinion applicable to the particular class of case; but this does not mean that he is answerable only because he departed from received opinion.

(6) Liability to the child under this section may be treated as having been excluded or limited by contract made with the parent affected, to the same extent and subject to the same restrictions as liability in the parent's own case; and a contract term which could have been set up by the defendant in an action by the parent, so as to exclude or limit his liability to him or her, operates in the defendant's favour to the same, but no greater, extent in an action under this section by the child.

(7)   If in the child's action under this section it is shown that the parent affected shared the responsibility for the child being born disabled, the damages are to be reduced to such extent as the court thinks just and equitable having regard to the extent of the parent's responsibility.

[1A.   Extension of section 1 to cover infertility treatments
   (1)   In any case where—
      (a)   a child carried by a woman as the result of the placing in her or an embryo or of sperm and eggs or her articial insemination is born disabled,
      (b)   the disability results from an act or omission in the course of the selection, or the keeping or use outside the body, of the embryo carried by her or of the gametes used to bring about the creation of the embryo, and
      (c)   a person is under this section answerable to the child in respect of the act or omission,
the child's disabilities are to be regarded as damage resulting from the wrongful act of that person and actionable accordingly at the suit of the child.
   (2)   Subject to subsection (3) below and the applied provisions of section 1 of this Act, a person (here referred to as 'the defendant') is answerable to the child if he was liable in tort to one or both of the parents (here referred to as 'the parent or parents concerned') or would, if sued in due time, have been so; and it is no answer that there could not have been such liability because the parent or parents concerned suffered no actionable injury, if there was a breach of legal duty which, accompanied by injury, would have given rise to the liability.
   (3)   The defendant is not under this section answerable to the child if at the time the embryo, or the sperm and eggs, are placed in the woman or the time of her insemination (as the case may be) either or both of the parents knew the risk of their child being born disabled (that is to say, the particular risk created by the act or omission).
   (4)   Subsections (5) to (7) of section 1 of this Act apply for the purposes of this section as they apply for the purposes of that but as if references to the parent or the parent affected were references to the parent or parents concerned.]

2.   Liability of woman driving while pregnant
A woman driving a motor vehicle when she knows (or ought reasonably to know) herself to be pregnant is to be regarded as being under the same duty to take care for the safety of her unborn child as the law imposes on her with respect to the safety of other people; and if in consequence of her breach of that duty her child is born with disabilities which would not otherwise have been present, those disabilities are to be regarded as damage resulting from her wrongful act and actionable accordingly at the suit of the child.

3.   Disabled birth due to radiation
   (1)   Section 1 of this Act does not affect the operation of the Nuclear Installations Act 1965 as to liability for, and compensation in respect of, injury or damage caused by occurrences involving nuclear matter or the emission of ionising radiations.
   (2)   For the avoidance of doubt anything which—
      (a)   affects a man in his ability to have a normal, healthy child; or
      (b)   affects a woman in that ability, or so affects her when she is pregnant that her child is born with disabilities which would not otherwise have been present,
is an injury for the purposes of that Act.
   (3)   If a child is born disabled as the result of an injury to either of its parents caused in breach of a duty imposed by any of sections 7 to 11 of that Act (nuclear site licensees and others to secure that nuclear incidents do not cause injury to persons, etc.), the child's disabilities are to be regarded under the subsequent provisions of that Act (compensation and other matters) as injuries caused on the same occasion, and by the same breach of duty, as was the injury to the parent.
   (4)   As respects compensation to the child, section 13(6) of that Act (contributory fault of person injured by radiation) is to be applied as if the reference there to fault were to the fault of the parent.
   (5)   Compensation is not payable in the child's case if the injury to the parent preceded the time of the child's conception and at that time either or both of the parents knew the

risk of their child being born disabled (that is to say, the particular risk created by the injury).

4. Interpretation and other supplementary provisions

(1)   References in this Act to a child being born disabled or with disabilities are to its being born with any deformity, disease or abnormality, including predisposition (whether or not susceptible or immediate prognosis) to physical or mental defect in the future.

(2)   In this Act—

(a)   'born' means born alive (the moment of a child's birth being when it first has a life separate from its mother), and 'birth' has a corresponding meaning; and

(b)   'motor vehicle' means a mechanically propelled vehicle intended or adapted for use on roads.

[and references to embryos shall be construed in accordance with section 1 of the Human Fertilisation and Embryology Act 1990].

(3)   Liability to a child under section 1 [1A] or 2 of this Act is to be regarded—

(a)   as respects all its incidents and any matters arising or to arise out of it; and

(b)   subject to any contrary context or intention, for the purpose of construing references in enactments and documents to personal or bodily injuries and cognate matters,

as liability for personal injuries sustained by the child immediately after its birth.

(4)   No damages shall be recoverable under [any] of those sections in respect of any loss of expectation of life, nor shall any such loss be taken into account in the compensation payable in respect of a child under the Nuclear Installations Act 1965 as extended by section 3, unless (in either case) the child lives for at least 48 hours.

[(4A) In any case where a child carried by a woman as the result of the placing in her of an embryo or of sperm and eggs or her artificial insemination is born disabled, any reference in section 1 of this Act to a parent includes a reference to a person who would be a parent but for sections 27 to 29 of the Human Fertilisation and Embryology Act 1990.]

(5)   This Act applies in respect of births after (but not before) its passing, and in respect of any such birth it replaces any law in force before its passing, whereby a person could be liable to a child in respect of disabilities with which it might be born; but in section 1(3) of this Act the expression 'liable in tort' does not include any reference to liability by virtue of this Act or to liability by virtue of any such law.

5.   Crown application
This Act binds the Crown

BURTON v ISLINGTON HEALTH AUTHORITY [1992] 3 All ER 833 (CA)

It was held that a child born suffering from disabilities caused as a result of medical negligence before birth can maintain an action for damages in negligence. Although not a 'person' in law at the time when the injury took place, an unborn child is deemed for the purposes of such an action to be born whenever its interests require and therefore has all the rights of action when born which he or she would have had if actually in 'existence' at the date of the accident to the mother. (There were **two** plaintiffs in this case: both were born before the Congenital Disabilities (Civil Liability) Act 1976 came into effect.)

3.5   Breach of Duty

3.5.1   GENERAL OBSERVATIONS

3.5.1.1   Consent

CONDON v BASI [1985] 2 All ER 453 (CA)

SIR JOHN DONALDSON MR: This is an appeal from a decision of his Honour Judge Wooton in the Warwick County Court given in March 1984. It arose out of a football match played on a Sunday between Whittle Wanderers and Khalsa Football Club. They are both clubs in the Leamington local league. The plaintiff was playing for Whittle Wanderers and the defendant for the Khalsa Football Club. Most unfortunately, during the game the defendant tackled the plaintiff in such a manner as to lead to the plaintiff breaking his leg. The county court judge found that he had been negligent, and awarded a sum of £4,900 in damages.

It is said that there is no authority as to what is the standard of care which governs the conduct of players in competitive sports generally and, above all, in a competitive sport whose rules and general background contemplate that there will be physical contact between the players, but that appears to be the position. This is somewhat surprising, but appears to be correct. For my part I would completely accept the decision of the High Court of Australia in *Rootes* v *Shelton* [1968] ALR 33. I think it suffices, in order to see the law which has to be applied, to quote briefly from the judgment of Barwick CJ and from the judgment of Kitto J. Barwick CJ said (at 34):

> By engaging in a sport or pastime the participants may be held to have accepted risks which are inherent in that sport or pastime: the tribunal of fact can make its own assessment of what the accepted risks are: but this does not eliminate all duty of care of the one participant to the other. Whether or not such a duty arises, and, if it does, its extent, must necessarily depend in each case upon its own circumstances. In this connexion, the rules of the sport or game may constitute one of those circumstances; but, in my opinion, they are neither definitive of the existence nor of the extent of the duty; nor does their breach or non-observance necessarily constitute a breach of any duty found to exist.

Kitto J said (at 37):

> . . . in a case such as the present, it must always be a question of fact, what exoneration from a duty of care otherwise incumbent upon the defendant was implied by the act of the plaintiff joining in the activity. Unless the activity partakes of the nature of a war or of something else in which all is notoriously fair, the conclusion to be reached must necessarily depend, according to the concepts of the common law, upon the reasonableness, in relation to the special circumstances, of the conduct which caused the plaintiff's injury. That does not necessarily mean the compliance of that conduct with the rules, conventions or customs (if there are any) by which the correctness of conduct for the purposes of the carrying on of the activity as an organised affair is judged; for the tribunal of fact may think that in the situation in which the plaintiff's injury was caused a participant might do what the defendant did and still not be acting unreasonably, even though he infringed the 'rules of the game'. Non-compliance with such rules, conventions or customs (where they exist) is necessarily one consideration to be attended to upon the question of reasonableness; but it is only one, and it may be of much or little or even no weight in the circumstances.

I have cited from those two judgments because they show two different approaches which, as I see it, produce precisely the same result. One is to take a more generalised duty of care and to modify it on the basis that the participants in the sport or pastime impliedly consent to taking risks which otherwise would be a breach of the duty of care. That seems to be the approach of Barwick CJ. The other is exemplified by the judgment of Kitto J, where he is saying, in effect, that there is a general standard of care, namely the Lord Atkin approach that you are under a duty to take all reasonable care taking account of the circumstances in which you are placed (see *Donoghue* v *Stevenson* [1932] AC 562 at 580; which, in a game of football, are quite different from those which affect you when you are going for a walk in the countryside.

For my part I would prefer the approach of Kitto J, but I do not think it makes the slightest different in the end if it is found by the tribunal of fact that the defendant failed to exercise that degree of care which was appropriate in all the circumstances, or that he acted in a way to which the plaintiff cannot be expected to have consented. In either event, there is liability.

Having set out the test, which is the test which I think was applied by the county court judge, I ought to turn briefly to the facts, adding before I do so that it was submitted by counsel on behalf of the defendant that the standard of care was subjective to the defendant and not objective, and if he was a wholly incompetent football player, he could do things without risk of liability which a competent football player could not do. For my part I reject that submission. The standard is objective, but objective in a different set of circumstances. Thus there will of course be a higher degree of care required of a player in a First Division football match than of a player in a local league football match.

But none of these sophistications arise in this case, as is at once apparent when one looks at the facts. . . .

The judge said that he entirely accepted the 'value judgements' of the referee. He said:

[The tackle] was made in a reckless and dangerous manner not with malicious intent towards the plaintiff but in an 'excitable manner without thought of the consequences'.

The judge's final conclusion was:

It was not for me in this court to attempt to define exhaustively the duty of care between players in a soccer football game. Nor, in my judgment, is there any need because there was here such an obvious breach of the defendant's duty of care towards the plaintiff. He was clearly guilty, as I find the facts, of serious and dangerous foul play which showed a reckless disregard of the plaintiff's safety and which fell far below the standards which might reasonably be expected in anyone pursuing the game.

For my part I cannot see how that conclusion can be faulted on its facts, and on the law I do not see how it can possibly be said that the defendant was not negligent. Accordingly I would dismiss the appeal.

Stephen Brown and Glidewell LJJ agreed.

SMOLDEN v WHITWORTH, *The Times*, 23 April 1996

Curtis J applied the decision in *Condon v Basi* in finding that the defendant, a referee in a rugby match, was liable in negligence to the plaintiff who had been severely injured when the scrum, in which he was the hooker, collapsed upon him. His Lordship, in a judgment carefully tailored to fit the actual facts of the case, said 'the duty of referees is to exercise that degree of care for the safety of players which is appropriate in the circumstances.' In his Lordship's opinion the referee wears a 'preventive mantle'.

It was found that collapsing a scrum was contrary to the rules of the game and dangerous. In the particular game, a 'Colts' game, for players under 19 years of age and who were consequently not fully mature, the risk of injury was greater than it would have been in other circumstances. There was a finding of fact that the defendant was not fully cognisant of the purpose of some rules and was thus of poor judgment.

The Court of Appeal (*The Times*, 18 December 1996) upheld this decision. It was emphasised that a referee owes a duty of care to his players; indeed the referee, the defendant, did not contest this issue. Thus, the case was argued on the **content** of the duty, i.e. the **relevant standard of care**.

Lord Bingham LCJ, giving the judgment of the court, said that since the game of rugby was involved, with all its dangerous consequences and fast-moving and competitive nature, the referee's job was 'difficult and demanding' and he could not reasonably be expected to be in 'all parts of the field at the same time'; furthermore, the job was usually, as in the present case, 'performed out of goodwill by a devotee of the game'. In such circumstances, said his Lordship: 'The threshold of liability is a high one. It will not easily be crossed.'

On **the facts of the present case** viz. it was a 'Colts' game, involving **young and inexperienced** players, the defendant had not measured up to the degree of care and skill expected of him. In the opinion of the court the defendant had been properly found to be in breach of his duty of care by failing to take appropriate steps to prevent a collapse of the scrum; and one of the players, the plaintiff, suffered spinal injuries of a kind that the rules of the game were designed to prevent, i.e. the defendant was liable for the foreseeable result of his breach of duty – even though in statistical terms it was a very unlikely eventuality.

The defendant had also argued that the defence of *volenti non fit injuria* applied but the court rejected this plea. Although it was true that as a player the plaintiff had consented to the ordinary incidents of a game of rugby football of the kind in which he was taking part, it could not be said that he had consented to a breach of duty on the part of the very official who was duty bound to apply the rules of the game (which were meant to protect the plaintiff) and take reasonable care to see that those rules were observed by others.

His Lordship said that if the plaintiff had been the 'prime culprit' in causing the collapse of the scrum, *volenti* and contributory negligence might well have had to be considered, but that was not so on the facts of the case.

McCORD v SWANSEA CITY AFC, *The Times*, 11 February 1997

A football player carried out an **intentional** foul on another player. It was held that where a player in a football match makes a serious mistake or misjudgment when tackling another player, the tackler is liable to his or her opponent where that mistake is inconsistent with a player's duty to take reasonable care for the safety of his or her fellow players.

3.5.1.2   The usual practice in the trade, profession or calling in question

GOLD v HARINGEY HEALTH AUTHORITY [1987] 2 All ER 888 (CA)

The plaintiff in this case became pregnant after a sterilisation operation and sued the defendant in negligence on the basis that she had been given insufficient information on the risk of the operation not being a success. At first instance, the plaintiff succeeded, the judge found that the plaintiff should have been warned that the operation might not succeed and that vasectomy (for her husband) which had a better record of success, was an alternative to sterilisation.

The defendant appealed.

LLOYD LJ: How, then, I ask again, did it come about that the judge found the defendants guilty of negligence, when he accepted that there was a substantial body of responsible medical opinion in 1979 who would not have given any warning? The answer is that he drew a distinction between advice or warning in a therapeutic context and advice or warning in a contraceptive context. In a therapeutic context there was a body of responsible medical opinion which would not have warned of the failure rate. But in a contraceptive context there was no such body of responsible medical opinion. Even if there had been, he would still have found the defendants negligent, since in his view the *Bolam* test does not apply to advice given in a non-therapeutic context. . . .

So the judge decided against the defendants on two grounds. First, he held that the *Bolam* test did not apply at all in a contraceptive context. Instead he applied his own judgment as to what should have been mentioned in that context. Second, if the *Bolam* test did apply, then he found as a fact that there was no body of responsible medical opinion, which would not, in a contraceptive context, have warned of the risk of failure. I have reversed these two grounds, since the first ground raises a question of considerable general importance.

Was the judge right when he held that the *Bolam* test is an exception to the ordinary rule in actions for negligence? If by an 'exceptional rule' the judge meant that the *Bolam* test is confined to actions against doctors, then I would respectfully disagree. I have already quoted a passage from McNair J's summing up in *Bolam's* case. In an earlier passage he had said ([1957] 2 All ER 118 at 121, [1957] 1 WLR 582 at 586):

> . . . where you get a situation which involves the use of some special skill or competence, then the test whether there has been negligence or not is not the test of the man on top of a Clapham ominibus, because he has not got this special skill. The test is the standard of the ordinary skilled man exercising and professing to have that special skill.

So far as I know that passage has always been treated as being of general application whenever a defendant professes any special skill. It is so treated in *Charlesworth on Negligence* (7th edn, 1983) para. 6–17. The *Bolam* test is not confined to a defendant exercising or professing the particular skill of medicine. If there had been any doubt on the question, which I do not think there was, it was removed by the speech of Lord Diplock in the *Sidaway* case [1985] AC 871 at 892 where Lord Diplock made it clear that the *Bolam* test is rooted in an ancient rule of common law applicable to all artificers. In *Saif Ali* v *Sydney Mitchell & Co. (a firm)* [1980] AC 198 at 220. Lord Diplock treated the same test as applicable to barristers, although he did not mention the *Bolam* case by name. The question in that case was whether a barrister is immune from an action in negligence in relation to advice given out of court. It was held that he is not. Lord Diplock said:

> No matter what profession it may be, the common law does not impose on those who practise it any liability for damage resulting from what in the result turned out to have been errors of judgment, unless the error was such as no reasonably well informed and competent member of that profession could have made.

Counsel for the plaintiff did his best to argue that the *Bolam* test is confined to doctors. For the reasons I have given, I cannot accept that argument. I can see no possible ground for distinguishing between doctors and any other profession or calling which requires special skill, knowledge or experience. To be fair to the judge, it was not, I think, on this ground that he regarded the *Bolam* test as exceptional.

In passing, I should mention that the *Bolam* test is often thought of as limiting the duty of care. So in one sense it does. But it also extends the duty of care, as the second of the two passages I have quoted from McNair J's summing up in the *Bolam* case makes clear. The standard is not that of the man on the top of the Clapham ominibus, as in other fields of negligence, but the higher standard of the man skilled in the particular profession or calling.

Why then did the judge think that it would be an extension of the *Bolam* test to apply it in the present case? The reason can only have been that which I have already mentioned, namely the distinction between therapeutic and non-therapeutic advice. Counsel for the plaintiff took us through the *Sidaway* case speech by speech, and paragraph by paragraph, in order to point the distinction. But I remain unconvinced. In the first place the line between therapeutic and non-therapeutic medicine is elusive. A plastic surgeon carrying out a skin graft is presumably engaged in therapeutic surgery; but what if he is carrying out a facelift, or some other cosmetic operation? Counsel found it hard to say . . .

The principle does not depend on the context in which any act is performed, or any advice given. It depends on a man professing skill or competence in a field beyond that possessed by the man on the Clapham ominubs. If the giving of contraceptive advice required no special skill, then I could see an argument that the *Bolam* test should not apply. But that was not, and could not have been, suggested. The fact (if it be the fact) that giving contraceptive advice involves a different sort of skill and competence from carrying out a surgical operation does not mean that the *Bolam* test ceases to be applicable. It is clear from Lord Diplock's speech in *Sidaway* that a doctor's duty of care in relation to diagnosis, treatment and advice, whether the doctor be a specialist or general practitioner, is not to be dissected into its component parts. To dissect a doctor's advice into that given in a therapeutic context and that given in a contraceptive context would be to go against the whole thrust of the decision of the majority of the House of Lords in that case. So I would reject the argument of counsel for the plaintiff under this head, and hold that the judge was not free, as he thought, to form his own view of what warning and information ought to have been given, irrespective of any body or responsible medical opinion to the contrary . . .

The judge accepted in his judgment that the distinction between advising in a contraceptive and non-contraceptive context was not 'crystal clear' on the evidence. With respect, that is an understatement. The witnesses were never asked to distinguish between the two cases. There was therefore only one finding open on the evidence, namely that there was a body of responsible medical opinion which would not have given any warning as to the failure of female sterilisation, and the possible alternatives, in the circumstances in which the defendants actually found themselves. So I would not accept the second of the two grounds on which the judge decided against the defendants.

That makes it unnecessary to consider whether, if the defendants had been under a duty to warn, they were entitled to assume that an adequate warning had been given by Dr Gomez, the general practitioner. We know form his letter of 31 July 1979 that he warned the plaintiff that the operation was irreversible. But since he was not called, we do not know what other warning, if any, he may have given.

Counsel for the plaintiff referred us in passing to *Thake* v *Maurice* [1986] QB 644, where it was held to have been negligent on the part of a surgeon undertaking a vasectomy not to warn of the risk of failure in accordance with his usual practice. But in that case, Kerr LJ pointed out, there was no independent medical evidence called by either side (see [1986] QB 644 at 679–80). So, as counsel for the plaintiff sensibly agreed, it does not help him in the present case. Nor does he get any help from *Jones* v *Berkshire Health Authority* (2 July 1986, unreported), for in that case the duty to warn was admitted.

Finally, I should mention the plaintiff's claim for negligent misrepresentation. In para 7A of the statement of claim it is pleaded by amendment as follows:

By reason of the matters pleaded . . . above, the defendants negligently misrepresented to the plaintiff that the operation would render her permanently sterile and/or that sterilisation was her only contraceptive option and in reliance upon which representation the plaintiff agreed to undergo the said operation.

The judge deals with that allegation at the end of his judgment, and does so in a very few words for the sake, as he puts it, of completeness. He makes no finding as to the terms of the representation, or whether it was express or implied. All he says is: 'I find that allegation proved.'

The only possible justification for the judge's finding on the evidence is that it is to be inferred from the fact that the plaintiff was told that the operation was irreversible. But to draw that inference from the use of the work 'irreversible' would be inconsistent with the decision of this court in *Eyre* v *Measday* [1986] 1 All ER 488, where a similar argument was advanced. Slade LJ said (at 494):

There has been some discussion in the course of argument on the meaning of the phrase 'irreversible' and as to the relevance of the statement, undoubtedly made by the defendant to the plaintiff, that the proposed operation must be regarded as being irreversible. However, I take the reference to irreversibility as simply meaning that the operative procedure in question is incapable of being reversed, that what is about to be done cannot be undone. I do not think it can reasonably be construed as a representation that the operation is bound to achieve its acknowleded object, which is a different matter altogether.

So I would reject the plaintiff's claim for negligent misrepresentation.

For the reasons I have given the plaintiff has failed to make good her claim for negligence. Accordingly, I would allow this appeal.

Watkins and Stephen Brown LJJ agreed.

Khan, M. and Robson, M., 'What is a responsible group of medical opinion?', *Professional Negligence*, Vol. 11, No. 4, 1995 (p. 122)

In all other [i.e. non-medical] negligence cases the courts look at the risk, and examine the precautions that could have been adopted to minimise the risk and the practicality of these precautions. Accepted practice comes far down the table and is only used as an evidential tool of what is often done, not as a binding rule of what should have been done. The time when plaintiffs can rely on the courts to actually judge the issues . . . and not be forced to try and side-step the *Bolam* rule by attempting to find loopholes in its definition as in *Defreitas* seems to be light years away.

Jones M.A., Textbook on Torts, 5th edn, pp. 156–7

. . . Despite the authority with which the *Bolam* test has been imbued it contains an inherent ambiguity. It could mean that negligence is a departure from the practices which *in fact* are commonly adopted by the profession (the standards of the 'ordinary skilled man'). Alternatively negligence may be a departure from standards that *ought* to be adopted by the profession, whether or not they are in fact practised (the standards of the 'reasonably competent' man). This distinction was identified at the time of *Bolam* (see Montrose (1958)

21 MLR 259 – 'is negligence an ethical or a sociological concept?') and can be seen in some cases, although it is often overlooked or conflated (see *Jackson and Powell* para. 1.68). The question is most likely to arise in the context of the second limb of the *Bolam* test: does compliance with a common practice of the profession absolve the defendant from a finding of negligence or may the court condemn a common professional practice as unreasonable and therefore negligent? Lord Scarman, for example, has suggested that a practitioner whose actions have received the seal of approval of distinguished professional opinion, 'truthfully expressed, honestly held' is not negligent (*Maynard* v *West Midlands Regional Health Authority* [1984] 1 WLR 634, 639G; see also the same judge in *Sidaway* v *Bethlem Royal Hospital Governors* [1985] 1 All ER 643, 649e, commenting that the *Bolam* test 'leaves the determination of a legal duty to the judgment of doctors'). Nonetheless, it is submitted that the second alternative is the correct approach. A professional person must conform to the standards of a reasonably competent individual exercising and professing to have that professional skill (*Jackson and Powell* para. 1.69; *Dugdale and Stanton* para. 15.22). What is reasonable is ultimately a question of law to be determined by the court, but not surprisingly the courts place heavy reliance on expert evidence which is usually crucial to the outcome of an action. (Codified professional standards may also be significant evidence of what constitutes reasonable care; see Gwilliam (1986) 2 PN 175.) Once a body of professional opinion supporting the defendant's conduct is characterised as a 'responsible' body of opinion the court will not choose between conflicting views (see, e.g., *Ashcroft* v *Mersey Regional Health Authority* [1983] 2 All ER 245; *Maynard* v *West Midlands Regional Health Authority*) . . .

On the other hand, the number of cases in which it can be said that the court has declared a professional practice to be negligent is comparatively small, and there is a suggestion that the judges tend to be particularly deferential to the views of medical experts in medical negligence cases in comparison to the approach adopted in other jurisdictions . . .

BOLITHO v *CITY AND HACKNEY HEALTH AUTHORITY* [1997] 4 All ER 771 (HL)

This is an important case in the context of medical negligence. A boy aged two was admitted to hospital after an attack of croup. He suffered respiratory failure and a senior registrar was called on two occasions by the nursing staff, but she failed to attend (it seems that she 'bleeped' a junior doctor on the second occasion to go in her place, but he did not get the message).

The boy suffered catastrophic brain damage, and died. Negligence, in failing to attend, was admitted, but legal liability for the brain damage and death was denied on the ground that there was a lack of causal connection between that negligence and the damage suffered: i.e. *Barnett* v *Chelsea and Kensington Hospital Management Committee* [1969] 1 All ER 428 (see *Learning Text* (4.2)) applied.

There is nothing remarkable in such an argument, provided the defence can show that the patient would have died anyway (as in *Barnett*); the point about this case is the **legal basis** of the argument about causation. The defence used *Bolam* in this context: i.e. the '*Bolam* test', it was argued, was a determining factor in any decision on **causative links** – it was not restricted merely to the issue of breach of duty.

On the facts, the patient would probably have survived if he had been 'intubated' (i.e. if a tube had been inserted to provide a clear airway) and the question the court was asked to decide was whether the doctor **would** have intubated **had** she been in attendance. If the answer was 'no', her (admitted) negligence was not a cause of the death.

The doctor said she would **not** have intubated even if she had attended the patient, and used the *Bolam* test to justify her argument. Since the court was willing to accept this use of *Bolam*, legal argument then turned on the question of what a 'responsible body' of doctors would/would not have done in the circumstances.

Five medical experts gave evidence for the plaintiff to the effect that the child had been in such a state that **total** respiratory failure was inexorable; intubation was therefore recommended. The defence's three experts, however, disputed this by arguing that the risk of total failure was small; and the nurses' evidence also gave support to the defence. Thus, on the facts, the failure to attend and to intubate were not material factors and the plaintiff failed to prove causation.

Although the court accepted that *Bolam* could be used in this way, so creating another hurdle for plaintiffs in medical litigation, their Lordships did say that judges must not

simply accept the word of medical experts who give evidence for doctors that a particular course of action was acceptable. Lord Browne-Wilkinson, giving the judgment of the court, said judges have to be satisfied that the experts' opinion has a logical basis, that they have directed their minds to the risks and benefits of a particular course of action, and that they have reached a 'defensible conclusion'. On the facts, the court was satisfied that it was reasonable not to subject the child to such an invasive procedure as intubation bearing in mind the small risk of total respiratory failure.

It may be thought that the advice from the House of Lords to judges concerning their assessment of expert evidence might indicate a potential weakening of *Bolam's* grip, but their Lordships did also say that it will only be in **rare** cases that it will be correct for a judge to conclude that the views held by a competent medical expert are unreasonable.

3.5.2   SOME CONCLUSIONS

KNIGHT AND OTHERS v *THE HOME OFFICE AND ANOTHER* [1990] 3 All ER 237

This case concerned the standard of care required in a prison hospital towards a prisoner who was mentally ill, and who was known to have suicidal tendencies. It was alleged that the prison authorities were negligent in not preventing the prisoner from committing suicide.

PILL J: It is for the court to consider what standard of care is appropriate to the particular relationship and in the particular situation. It is not a complete defence for a government department any more than it would be for a private individual or organisation to say that no funds are available for additional safety measures.

I cannot accept what was at one time submitted by counsel for the defendants that the plaintiffs only remedy would be a political one. To take an extreme example, if the evidence was that no funds were available to provide any medical facilities in a large prison there would be a failure to achieve the standard of care appropriate for prisoners. In a different context, lack of funds would not excuse a public body which operated its vehicles on the public roads without any system of maintenance for the vehicles if an accident occurred because of lack of maintenance. The law would require a higher standard of care towards other road users.

In making the decision as to the standard to be demanded the court must, however, bear in mind as one factor that resources available for the public service are limited and that the allocation of resources is a matter for Parliament.

I am unable to accept the submission that the law requires the standard of care in a prison hospital to be as high as the standard of care for all purposes in a psychiatric hospital outside prison. I am unable to accept that the practices in a prison hospital are to be judged in all respects by the standard appropriate to a psychiatric hospital outside prison. There may be circumstances in which the standard of care in a prison falls below that which would be expected in a psychiatric hospital without the prison authority being negligent. Even in a medical situation outside prison, the standard of care required will vary with the context. The facilities available to deal with an emergency in a general practitioner's surgery cannot be expected to be as ample as those available in the casualty department of a general hospital, for example.

Psychiatric hospitals perform a specialist function in treating mental illness and, where possible, effecting a cure. Interaction with skilled staff is, on the evidence, a vital part of the treatment in cases such as the present. The prison's central function is to detain persons deprived of their liberty by operation of law. The prison authorities have a duty to provide medical care where physical or mental illness is present. That includes a duty to protect a mentally ill patient against himself. I bear in mind the statutory provisions, but in my judgment the law should not and does not expect the same standard across the entire spectrum of possible situations, including the possibility of suicide, as it would in a psychiatric hospital outside prison. The duty is tailored to the act and function to be performed.

There was no negligence in the failure to provide in the hospital wing of the prison the patient/staff ratio present at Bethlem Royal Hospital and other psychiatric hospitals. I am unable to find for the plaintiffs on the ground that the same facilities should have been available in prison as would have been available in a psychiatric hospital.

Since no intermediate standard between that of a specialist psychiatric hospital and that at Brixton has been advocated either in evidence or submissions, I do not consider that it is open to me to speculate on what an appropriate standard might be. If necessary, I would, however, be prepared to hold on the evidence before me as to conditions in 1981 and 1982 that even bearing in mind the number of prisoners and the condition of many of them, the general standard of care was, on the information available, appropriate to the function to be performed. . . .

SURTEES v KINGSTON-UPON-THAMES BOROUGH COUNCIL [1991] 2 FLR 559 (CA)

The plaintiff, Kathy, was fostered with the defendants (D2), the Hughes family, at the age of two and suffered injury from scalding. At the time of the incident the plaintiff had been standing in a sink into which very hot water ran from an immersion heater above the sink: the evidence assumed that the plaintiff had accidentally knocked the tap on the heater to the 'on' position. On reaching her legal majority (18 years of age) the plaintiff claimed damages in negligence against her foster parents and the local authority (D1) in whose care she was at the time.

At first instance Legatt J said that from the evidence he was sure Kathy's injury was not caused deliberately. The Hughes looked after Kathy as they did their own children; and although they no doubt had feelings of conscience when they decided to return Kathy, that did not affect the way they behaved towards her so long as she remained with them.

Before Kathy was fostered the child care officer had visited the Hughes home and the Hughes had visited the council office and Kathy. The omens were good and there was no reason why Kathy should not have been boarded with the Hughes.

The 'warning signs' relied on were incidents showing the Hughes indecision. But what decided them against adoption and continuation of fostering was the realisation that Mrs Hughes, contrary to what they had planned, was pregnant again. The Hughes prevarication only warned of a breakdown in long-term fostering. It did not warn of any defect in the short-term.

It was probable that the child care officer had not visited the Hughes between June 26 and August 19 1986 but that failure was immaterial when considering the accident. No matter how many visits had been made, it would not have altered the events because there would have been no occasion to remove Kathy urgently from the Hughes' care. What eventually happened was not caused by stress, pressure or uncertainty on the Hughes part. The child care officer did all that was expected and exhibited no want of care. The case against the council failed.

On the case against the Hughes, the question was whether Mrs Hughes was negligent to leave Kathy on a laundry box high enough to allow her access to the hot tap. It was foreseeable that Kathy might succeed in clambering into the basin and Mrs Hughes must have known that the water from the tap would be very hot. But Mrs Hughes believed that Kathy could not deliberately turn on the tap unaided. On balance of probabilities she did not do so and Mrs Hughes' belief was reasonable.

It was not foreseeable that Kathy would be exposed to risk or injury from the hot water. It was a mystery how she succeeded in releasing the tap, but to hold Mrs Hughes negligent in those circumstances would be to impose an impossibly high standard to which few parents would habitually measure up.

It was doubtful whether breach of the Boarding Out of Children Regulations 1995 (SI No: 1377) afforded a child affected by it any civil remedy, because they were passed to provide for the welfare of children rather than to prevent injury to them. But even if that was wrong the only breach in this case consisted of a failure to visit the child and that did risk of injury to Kathy: there was no causative link between that breach and her injury.

His Lordship expressed sympathy for Kathy, but said that in law not every accident is remediable in damages. This accident had happened without fault and the actions were dismissed.

The decision was affirmed by a majority of the Court of Appeal. Beldam LJ dissented from Sir Nicholas Browne-Wilkinson and Stocker LJ, on the ground that it would have been relatively easy for Mrs Hughes to have prevented the plaintiff from getting to the taps.

MORRELL v OWEN, *The Times*, 14 December 1993

It was held in this case that organisers of a sporting event for disabled persons owed a greater standard of care in the tort of negligence than would be the case in relation to organising a similar event for able-bodied participants.

HEDLEY v CUTHBERTSON, *The Times*, 21 June 1997

According to the evidence given in this case, it was quite usual for wealthy amateur mountain climbers to pay guides, who often became friends, to accompany them on difficult climbs. The guides would help with safety and provide companionship and moral support.

In this case the court was asked to decide whether the more experienced climber took **legal** responsibility for the safety of his amateur companion. Dyson J found that he did, and held the defendant liable in negligence for the death of his friend, whom he had accompanied for a fee of £50 on a climb in the French Alps.

It was found that the deceased (this action was brought in the name of his six-year-old son) would not have fallen to his death had the defendant taken 30 seconds to hammer in a second ice screw, thereby securely anchoring Mr Hedley to the ice face of the Tour Ronde mountain: the use of only one screw by the defendant had been 'a serious mistake' said the judge. In his judgment the use of two ice screws in belays and the installation of running belays was the 'universally accepted practice' in climbing, and there had to be 'overriding reasons' for departing from the normal safety measure.

His Lordship said the threat of a rock-fall in this case (the defendant had argued that his actions – performed in a hurry – were due to such a threat) was a real one, but it had been only 'slight' and did not justify the use of only one screw. Indeed the defendant's negligence in this respect was compounded by his failure to install running belays.

LEWISHAM INVESTMENT PARTNERSHIP LTD v MORGAN, *The Times*, 25 November 1997

An expert valuer valued a lease on the basis of legal advice as to the principles to be applied in the valuation process. He was found **not** to be negligent, however, in following this advice even though the judge in the case thought that that advice was wrong.

MULLIN v RICHARDS AND ANOTHER [1998] 1 All ER 920 (CA)

HUTCHISON LJ: On 29 February 1988 at Perry Beeches Secondary School in Birmingham two 15-year-old schoolgirls, Teresa Jane Mullin and Heidi Richards, who were friends and were sitting side by side at their desk, were engaged in playing around, hitting each other's white plastic 30 cm rulers as though in a play sword fight, when one or other of the rulers snapped and a fragment of plastic entered Teresa's right eye with the very unhappy result that she lost all useful sight in that eye, something that must be a source, I am sure, of great distress to her and her family.

Teresa brought proceedings against Heidi and the Birmingham City Council, who were the education authority, alleging negligence. It is worth noting that her pleaded case involved facts quite different from those that I summarised a moment ago. My summary reflects the learned judge's unchallenged findings of fact as well as the case pleaded by Heidi in her defence. The judge dismissed the claim against the authority, holding that the mathematics teacher, Miss Osborne, whose class was coming to an end when the mishap occurred, had not been guilty of negligence and the plaintiff does not appeal against that decision. The case against the local authority was based only on lack of proper supervision in the classroom on the day in question. However, the judge having rejected Teresa's and accepted Heidi's version of how the accident occurred, concluded that each had been guilty of negligence, that Teresa's injury was the foreseeable result and that, accordingly, her claim against Heidi succeeded subject to a reduction of 50% for contributory negligence.

From that decision Heidi now appeals to this court . . .

So far as negligence is concerned, the relevant principles are well settled and I do not understand there to be any real difference between the views of counsel for the parties to this appeal. I would summarise the principles that govern liability in negligence in a case such as the present as follows. In order to succeed the plaintiff must show that the defendant did an act which it was reasonably foreseeable would cause injury to the plaintiff, that the relationship between the plaintiff and the defendant was such as to give rise to a duty of care, and that the act was one which caused injury to the plaintiff. In the present case, as it seems to me, no difficulty arose as to the second and third requirements because Teresa and Heidi were plainly in a sufficiently proximate relationship to give rise to a duty of care and the causation of the injury is not in issue. The argument centres on foreseeability. The test of foreseeability is an objective one; but the fact that the first defendant was at the time a 15-year-old schoolgirl is not irrelevant. The question for the judge is not whether the actions of the defendant were such as an ordinarily prudent and reasonable adult in the defendant's situation would have realised gave rise to a risk of injury, it is whether an ordinarily prudent and reasonable 15-year-old schoolgirl in the defendant's situation would have realised as much. In that connection both counsel referred us to, and relied upon, the Australian decision in *McHale* v *Watson* (1966) 115 CLR 199 esp at 213–214 in the judgment of Kitto J. I cite a portion of the passage I have referred to, all of which was cited to us by Mr Lee on behalf of the appellant, and which Mr Stephens has adopted as epitomising the correct approach:

> The standard of care being objective, it is no answer for him [that is a child], any more than it is for an adult, to say that the harm he caused was due to his being abnormally slow-witted, quick-tempered, absent-minded or inexperienced. But it does not follow that he cannot rely in his defence upon a limitation upon the capacity for foresight or prudence, not as being personal to himself, but as being characteristic of humanity at his stage of development and in that sense normal. By doing so he appeals to a standard of ordinariness, to an objective and not a subjective standard.

Mr Stephens also cited to us a passage in the judgment of Owen J (at 234):

> . . . the standard by which his conduct is to be measured is not that to be expected of a reasonable adult but that reasonably to be expected of a child of the same age, intelligence and experience.

I venture to question the word 'intelligence' in that sentence, but I understand Owen J to be making the same point essentially as was made by Kitto J. It is perhaps also material to have in mind the words of Salmon LJ in *Gough* v *Thorne* [1966] 3 All ER 398 at 400, [1966] 1 WLR 1387 at 1391, which is cited also by Mr Stephens, where he said:

> The question as to whether the plaintiff can be said to have been guilty of contributory negligence depends on whether any ordinary child of $13\frac{1}{2}$ can be expected to have done any more than this child did. I say 'any ordinary child'. I do not mean a paragon of prudence; nor do I mean a scatter-brained child; but the ordinary girl of $13\frac{1}{2}$.

. . . Applying those principles to the facts of the present case the central question to which this appeal gives rise is whether on the facts found by the judge and in the light of the evidence before him he was entitled to conclude that a ordinary, reasonable 15-year-old schoolgirl in the first defendant's position would have appreciated that by participating to the extent that she did in a play fight, involving the use of plastic rulers as though they were swords, gave rise to a risk of injury to the plaintiff of the same general kind as she sustained. In that connection I emphasise that a mere possibility is not enough as passages in the well-known case of *Bolton* v *Stone* [1951] 1 All ER 1078, [1951] AC 850 . . .

I do not propose, in the light of the conclusion to which I have come without hesitation in this case, to deal individually with all the grounds of appeal, though I should mention in relation to the third ground, which asserts that the judge treated the first defendant as an adult and not as a 15-year-old child, that I reject that contention. It seems to me that his reference to the age of the two girls in the passage which I have cited from his judgment shows that he had in mind the correct principles. Accordingly I would hold that he approached the matter in that respect in the correct way.

However the question of actual foreseeability (that is to say the application of that correct approach in law to the facts) raises, in my judgment, great difficulties . . .

The judge, it seems to me, found negligence without there being material on which he could properly do so. He seems indeed from the language he used to have regarded it as axiomatic that if there was a fight going on, such as he found there was, a play fight, that imported that injury was reasonably foreseeable and from his finding that the ruler broke that there was necessarily dangerous or excessive violence. For my part, I would say that in the absence of evidence one simply does not know why the ruler broke, whether because it was unusually weak, unlike other rulers; whether because it had been damaged in some way; or whether because rulers of this sort are particularly prone to break; one does not know. What certainly one cannot infer, and the judge was, I consider, not entitled to infer, was that there was here excessive violence or inappropriate violence over and above that which was inherent in the play fencing in which these two girls were indulging. This was in truth nothing more than a schoolgirls' game such as on the evidence was commonplace in this school and there was, I would hold, no justification for attributing to the participants the foresight of any significant risk of the likelihood of injury. They had seen it done elsewhere with some frequency. They had not heard it prohibited or received any warning about it. They had not been told of any injuries occasioned by it. They were not in any sense behaving culpably. So far as foresight goes, had they paused to think they might, I suppose, have said: 'It is conceivable that some unlucky injury might happen', but if asked if there was any likelihood of it or any real possibility of it, they would, I am sure, have said that they did not foresee any such possibility. Taking the view therefore that the learned judge – who, as I have said, readily and almost without question accepted that on his findings of fact there was negligence on the part of both these young ladies – was wrong in his view and there was no evidence on which he could come to it, I would allow the appeal and direct that judgment be entered for the first defendant I have to say that I appreciate that this result will be disappointing to the plaintiff for whom one can have nothing but sympathy, because she has suffered a grave injury through no fault of her own. But unfortunately she has failed to establish in my view that anyone was legally responsible for that injury and, accordingly, her claim should have failed.

SIR JOHN VINELOTT: I agree . . .

BUTLER-SLOSS LJ: I agree with both judgments and since there has been little earlier authority on the proper approach to the standard of care to be applied to a child, I would like to underline the observations of Hutchison LJ and rely upon two further passages in the persuasive judgment of Kitto J in the High Court of Australia in *McHale* v *Watson* (1966) 115 CLR 199 at 213:

> In regard to the things which pertain to foresight and prudence experience, understanding of causes and effects, balance of judgment, thoughtfulness – it is absurd, indeed it is a misuse of language, to speak of normality in relation to persons of all ages taken together. In those things normality is, for children, something different from what normality is for adults; the very concept of normality is a concept of rising levels until 'years of discretion' are attained. The law does not arbitrarily fix upon any particular age for this purpose, and tribunals of fact may well give effect to different views as to the age at which normal adult foresight and prudence are reasonably to be expected in relation to particular sets of circumstances. But up to that stage the normal capacity to exercise those two qualities necessarily means the capacity which is normal for a child of the relevant age, and it seems to me that it would be contrary to the fundamental principle that a person is liable for harm that he causes by falling short of an objective criterion of 'propriety' in his conduct – propriety, that is to say, as determined by a comparison with the standard of care reasonably to be expected in the circumstances from the normal person to hold that where a child's liability is in question the normal person – to be considered is someone other than a child of corresponding age.

I would respectfully indorse those observations as entirely appropriate to English law and I would like to conclude with another passage of Kitto J (at 216) particularly relevant today:

> . . . in the absence of relevant statutory provision, children, like everyone else, must accept as they go about in society the risks from which ordinary care on the part of others

will not suffice to save them. One such risk is that boys of twelve may behave as boys of twelve . . .

– and I would say that girls of 15 playing together may play as somewhat irresponsible girls of 15. I too would allow this appeal.

Appeal allowed.

3.5.3 BURDEN OF PROOF OF NEGLIGENCE ON THE FACTS

CIVIL EVIDENCE ACT 1968

11. Convictions as evidence in civil proceedings

(1) In any civil proceedings the facts that a person has been convicted of an offence by or before any court in the United Kingdom or by a court-martial there or elsewhere shall (subject to subsection (3) below) be admissible in evidence for the purpose of proving whether to do so is relevant to any issue in those proceedings, that he committed that offence, whether he was so convicted upon a plea of guilty or otherwise and whether or not he is a party to the civil proceedings; but no conviction other than a subsisting one shall be admissible in evidence by virtue of this section.

(2) In any civil proceedings in which by virtue of this section a person is proved to have been convicted of an offence by or before any court in the United Kingdom or by a court-martial there or elsewhere—

(a) he shall be taken to have committed that offence unless the contrary is proved; and

(b) without prejudice to the reception of any other admissible evidence for the purpose of identifying the facts on which the conviction was based, the contents of any documents which is admissible as evidence of the conviction, and the contents of the information, complaint, indictment or charge-sheet on which the person in question was convicted, shall be admissible in evidence for that purpose.

(3) Nothing in this section shall prejudice the operation of section 13 of this Act or any other enactment whereby a conviction or a finding of fact in any criminal proceedings is for the purposes of any other proceedings made conclusive evidence of any fact.

(4) Where in any civil proceedings the contents of any document are admissible in evidence by virtue of subsection (2) above, a copy of that document, or of the material part thereof, purporting to be certified or otherwise authenticated by or on behalf of the court or authority having custody of that document shall be admissible in evidence and shall be taken to be a true copy of that document or part unless the contrary is shown.

. . .

13. Conclusiveness of convictions for purposes of defamation actions

(1) In an action for libel or slander in which the question whether a person did or did not commit a criminal offence is relevant to an issue arising in the action, proof that at the time when that issue falls to be determined, that person stands convicted of that offence shall be conclusive evidence that he committed that offence, and his conviction thereof shall be admissible in evidence accordingly.

(2) In any such action as aforesaid in which by virtue of this section a person is proved to have been convicted of an offence, the contents of any document which is admissible as evidence of the conviction, and the contents of the information, complaint, indictment or charge-sheet on which that person was convicted, shall, without prejudice to the reception of any other admissible evidence for the purpose of identifying the facts on which the conviction was based, be admissible in evidence for the purpose of identifying those facts.

(3) For the purposes of this section a person shall be taken to stand convicted of an offence if but only if there subsists against him a conviction of that offence by or before a court in the United Kingdom or by a court-martial there or elsewhere.

(4) Subsections (4) to (6) of section 11 of this Act shall apply for the purposes of this section as they apply for the purposes of that section, but as if in the said subsection (4) the reference to subsection (2) were a reference to subsection (2) of this section.

HENDERSON v HENRY E JENKINS & SONS & EVANS [1969] 3 All ER 756 (HL)

In this case an action in negligence was brought by the widow of a man who had been killed when the brakes on the defendant's lorry failed suddenly as it went down a hill. A pipe carrying hydraulic fluid for the brakes had corroded, causing a hole to form through which fluid had escaped. *That* part of the pipe could not have been seen without the whole of the pipe being removed. The action was brought against the owners of the lorry *and* their driver.

Since the evidence showed that sudden, complete brake failure from corrosion was unusual the defendants claimed a 'latent defect' which would not have been discovered by the taking of reasonable care. They said they had followed usual practice by regularly inspecting only those parts of the pipe which could be seen without removing the pipe itself, and by doing this they were following the advice of the Ministry of Transport and the manufacturers of the lorry.

The plaintiff's action was dismissed at first instance as was her appeal to the Court of Appeal. She now appealed to the House of Lords.

LORD REID: If there were nothing in the evidence to indicate a probability that something unusual must have happened to this lorry to cause the very unusual type of brake failure which the learned trial judge has held in fact occurred here, then undoubtedly the respondents would have proved that they had exercised all proper care in this case. But if the evidence indicates a likelihood that something unusual has occurred to cause a break-down, then I do not see how the owner can say that he has exercised all proper care unless he can prove that he neither knew nor ought to have known of any such occurrence. For if he did know of it he would have been bound to take adequate steps to prevent any resulting break-down. It may well be that it would be sufficient for him to prove that he had a proper system for drivers reporting all unusual occurrences and that none had been reported to him . . . this appeal should be allowed.

LORD DONOVAN: . . . The plea of 'latent defect' made by the respondents had to be made good by them. It was for them to show all reasonable care, and that despite this, the defect remained hidden.

They proved that the pipe in question was visually inspected in situ once a week; that the brake pedal was on these occasions depressed to check for leaks from the pipe and one seen; that nothing more than such visual inspection of the pipe was required by the Ministry of Transport rules or the maker's advice. On the question of the likelihood of corrosion of the pipe they produced two expert witnesses, the first of whom said that was nothing unusual about it, and the second of whom said it was extremely unusual. The appellant's expert witness had testified without challenge that corrosion occurred quite often. The trial judge did not resolve this discord by any finding of his own. The respondents second expert witness considered that the pipe had been subjected to some unusual treatment from outside by some chemical agent.

It is obvious that visual inspection of the pipe in situ, however frequest, could not disclose corrosion on the hidden part of it. The question, therefore, suggests itself at once: did not reasonable care require the removal of the pipe at suitable intervals so that the whole of it could be inspected? It is equally obvious that the answer to this question must depend party on the age of the vehicle, party on the mileage it had done, and partly on the load it had been carrying. All these things affected the measure of reasonable care which the respondents had to exercise.

The lorry was an Albion lorry, five years old. The speedometer showed that it had done 52,000 miles, but since speedometers begin again at nought once they have registered 100,000 miles, nobody has suggested that reliance could be placed on the reading of 52,000. But no evidence was tendered as to mileage. So that the lorry might have done either 150,000 or 250,000 miles in its five years of life. As to the loads it carried, we know no more than that on the day of the accident it was carrying 9 ½ tons of concrete pipes.

Yet the kind of load this lorry had been carrying in the past was something which had to be known in order to assess the measure of the duty of reasonable care resting on the respondents. For the corrosion of the pipe was caused by some chemical agent. Had the lorry, therefore, been carrying chemicals of any kind? Or had it operated under conditions where salt (also a corrosive agent) might come in contact with the pipe? Or had it at some time been adapted for carrying cattle and done so? If any of these things were the case then clearly visual inspection of the pipe in situ would not have been enough. It should have been removed at intervals so that the whole of it, and not merely part of it, could be examined.

It was for the respondents to deal with these matters by evidence. They were asserting, and had to prove, that they exercised all reasonable care, but whether they had or not depended on what the facts were in the foregoing respects. Yet on these matters they chose to give no evidence at all. The result was that they failed to establish their defence and should have lost the case.

Nield J, however, decided in their favour . . .

I differ from Nield J with regret. But the tenor of his judgment suggests that he dealt with this case as though it were the more usual type where the onus of proof lay on the appellant; whereas in fact the burden of proof that they had taken all reasonable care rested on the respondents. For these reasons, which are substantially those given by Sachs LJ in his dissenting judgment below, I am of the opinion that the appeal should be allowed and the appellant should recover from the respondents the agreed damages of £5,700. . . .

LORD PEARSON: My Lords, in my opinion, the decision in this appeal turns on what is sometimes called 'the evidential burden of proof', which is to be distinguished from the formal (or legal or technical) burden of proof. . . . For the purposes of the present case the distinction can be simply stated in this way. In an action for negligence the plaintiff must allege, and has the burden of proving, that the accident was caused by negligence on the part of the defendants. That is the issue throughout the trial, and in giving judgment at the end of the trial the judge has to decide whether he is satisfied on a balance of probabilities that the accident was caused by negligence on the part of the defendants, and if he is not so satisfied the plaintiff's action fails. The formal burden of proof does not shift. But if in the course of the trial there is proved a set of facts which raises a prima facie inference that the accident was caused by negligence on the part of the defendants, the issue will be decided in the plaintiff's favour unless the defendants by their evidence provide some answer which is adequate to displace the prima facie inference. In this situation there is said to be an evidential burden of proof resting on the defendants. I have some doubts whether it is strictly correct to use the expression 'burden of proof' with this meaning, as there is a risk of it being confused with the formal burden of proof, but it is a familiar and convenient usage.

. . . The respondents and the driver were, by this plea . . . alleging and, therefore, admitting that the accident was caused by a sudden brake failure resulting from corrosion of the brake fluid pipe, and were assuming an evidential burden of proving that the corrosion occured without any fault on their part and that its existence was not discoverable by the exercise of reasonable care by them.

That was the effect of the pleading of the respondents and the driver, but in any case the physical facts of the case raise a strong prima facie inference that the respondents and the driver were at fault and that their fault was a cause of the acident . . . From these facts it seems to me clear, as a prima facie inference, that the accident must have been due to default of the respondents in respect of inspection or maintenance or both. Unless they had a satisfactory answer, sufficient to displace the inference, they should have been held liable.

The respondents' answer was that they had followed a practice of relying solely on visual inspection of the pipes, and that this was a general and proper practice. The learned judge's finding was that 'it is plainly the custom in the ordinary course of things not to remove these fluid pipes.' This may be a general and proper practice for an ordinary case in which there are no special circumstances increasing the risk. But I think the respondents' answer should not have been accepted without evidence from the respondents sufficiently showing that this was an ordinary case without special circumstances increasing the risk.

. . . The respondents might perhaps have been able to show by evidence that the lorry had not been used in any way, or involved in any incident, that would cause abnormal corrosion or require special inspection or treatment, or at any rate that they neither knew nor ought to have known of any such use or incident. But they did not call any such evidence. Their answer was incomplete. They did not displace the inference, arising from the physical facts of the case, that the accident must have been due to their default in respect of inspection or maintenance or both.

While fully accepting the learned judge's findings of primary fact. I am of opinion that he drew a wrong conclusion in holding that the accident was not caused by negligence of the respondents. I would allow the appeal.

Viscount Dilhorne and Lord Guest were agreed that the appeal should be *dismissed*.

WARD v TESCO STORES LTD [1976] 1 All ER 219 (CA)

LAWTON LJ: On 29 June 1974, at about midday, the plaintiff went to the defendants' supermarket. It is a large one and is carried on in premises which used to be a cinema. Inside, the premises were laid out in the way which is usual nowadays in supermarkets. On duty there was a total of about 30 to 35 staff; but in the middle of the day that number was reduced because staff had to be relieved in order to enable them to get their midday meals.

The plaintiff went round the store, carrying a wire basket, as shoppers are expected to do in supermarkets. She was doing her shopping at the back of the store when she felt herself slipping. She appreciated that she was slipping on something which was sticky. She fell to the ground, and sustained minor injuries. She had not seen what had caused her to slip. It was not suggested, either at the trial or in this court, that she had in any way been negligent in failing to notice what was on the floor as she walked along doing her shopping. When she was picking herself up she appreciated that she had slipped on some pink substance which looked to her like yoghurt. Later, somebody on the defendants' staff found a carton of yoghurt in the vicinity which was two-thirds empty.

A member of the staff helped to pick the plaintiff up. The manager was called. The plaintiff was taken to his office. She was dealt with there in a kindly and considerate way. The defendants offered to, and did, arrange for such of her clothes as had been soiled by the fall to be cleaned.

That is all the plaintiff was able to prove, save for one additional fact. About three weeks later when she was shopping in the same store she noticed that some orange squash had been spilt on the floor. She kept an eye on the spillage for about a quarter of an hour. During that time nobody came to clear it up.

The trial judge was of the opinion that the facts which I have related constituted a prima facie case against the defendants. . . .

In this case the floor of this supermarket was under the management of the defendants and their servants. The accident was such as in the ordinary course of things does not happen if floors are kept clean and spillages are dealt with as soon as they occur. If an accident does happen because the floors are covered with spillage, then in my judgment some explanation should be forthcoming from the defendants to show that the accident did not arise from any want of care on their part; and in the absence of any explanation the judge may give judgment for the plaintiff. Such burden of proof as there is on defendants in such circumstances is evidential, not probative. The trial judge thought that prima facie this accident would not have happened had the defendants taken reasonable care. In my judgement he was justified in taking that view because the probabilities were that the spillage had been on the floor long enough for it to have been cleaned up by a member of the staff.

The next question is whether the defendants by their evidence gave any explanation to show that they had taken all reasonable care. . . . The judge weighted the evidence and decided as a matter of fact from which in this case there can be no appeal that the precautions taken were not enough, and that the plaintiff in consequence had proved her case . . . I would dismiss this appeal.

MEGAW LJ: . . . It is for the plaintiff to show that there has occurred an event which is unusual and which, in the absence of explanation, is more consistent with fault on the part of the defendants than the absence of fault; and to my mind the learned judge was wholly right in taking that view of the presence of this slippery liquid on the floor of the supermarket in the circumstances of this case: that is that the defendants knew or should have known that it was a not uncommon occurence; and that if it should happen, and should not be promptly attended to, it created a serious risk that customers would fall and injure themselves. When the plaintiff has established that, the defendants can still escape from liability. They could escape from liability if they could show that the accident must have happened, or even on balance of probability would have been likely to have happened, irrespective of the existence of a proper and adequate system, in relation to the circumstances, to provide for the safety of customers. But, if the defendants wish to put forward such a case, it is for them to show that on balance of probability either by evidence or by inference from the evidence that is given or is not given, this accident would have been at least equally likely to have happened despite a proper system designed to give reasonable protection to customers. That, in this case, they wholly failed to do. . . .

ORMROD LJ: I have the misfortune to disagree with the judgment of Lawton LJ. Starting from the beginning, I do not think that it was established that this accident was caused by any want of care on the part of the defendants. The accident described by the plaintiff—and she did no more than describe the accident, namely that she slipped in some yoghurt which was on the floor of the supermarket—could clearly have happened no matter what degree of care these defendants had taken. The crucial question is how long before the accident the yoghurt had been on the floor. Had some customer knocked it off the shelf a few moments before, then no reasonable system which the defendants could be expected to operate would have prevented this accident. So I think that the plaintiff fails at the outset.

So far as the proposition which Lawton LJ has cited from Erle CJ is concerned, all I would say is that, since this accident could quite easily have happened without any want of care on the part of the defendants, I do not think that that broad proposition is applicable. . . .

The appeal was dismissed.

NG CHUN PUI AND OTHERS v LEE CHUEN TAT AND OTHERS [1988] RTR 298

A motor coach owned by D2 but driven by D1 left one side of dual carriageway, crossed the central reservation and collided with a public bus travelling on the other side of the dual carriageway. The plaintiffs were injured in the accident.

No oral evidence was submitted by the plaintiffs at trial; they relied merely on the fact of the accident (*res ipsa loquitur*). In this approach they were justified because in the ordinary course of events a well maintained and properly driven coach would not collide with other traffic in the circumstances outlined. The plaintiffs would be entitled to succeed in the absence of any evidence by the defendants.

In other words . . . according to Lord Griffiths in the Privy Council: '. . . the proper inference was that the coach was not being driven with the standard of care required by the law and that the driver was negligent.'

The defendants, however, did call evidence explaining how the driver came to lose control of the coach and this evidence was accepted by the trial judge but he found that because the plaintiffs had relied on the doctrine of *res ipsa loquitur* the burden of disproving negligence remained on the defendants, and in the circumstances they had failed in their task.

The Privy Council said that it is not entirely correct to regard the burden of proof as shifting to the defendant on an application of the *res ipsa loquitur* maximum since it is up to the plaintiff to establish negligence on the facts and he must bear this burden throughout the case. The so-called doctrine of *res ipsa loquitur* is no more than a legal maxim to describe a state of evidence from which it is proper to draw an inference of negligence. In an appropriate case the plaintiff can establish a prima facie case by relying on the fact of the accident; if the defendant adduces no evidence, there is nothing to rebut the inference of negligence, but, if he does, that evidence has to be evaluated to see if it is still reasonable to draw the inference of negligence from the mere fact of the accident.

The Privy Council dismissed an appeal by the plaintiffs from the decision of the Court of Appeal in Hong Kong.

LORD GRIFFITHS: That was a misunderstanding of the so-called doctrine, which is no more than a legal maxim to describe a state of the evidence from which it is proper to draw an inference of negligence.

Where the plaintiff has suffered injuries as a result of an accident which ought not to have happened if the defendant had taken due care, it will often be possible for the plaintiff to discharge the burden of proof by inviting the court to draw the inference that on the balance of probabilities, the defendant must have failed to exercise due care even though the plaintiff does not know in what respects.

In an appropriate case the plaintiff establishes a prima facie case by relying on the fact of the accident. If the defendant adduces no evidence there is nothing to rebut the inference of negligence, but if he does, that evidence has to be evaluated to see if it is still reasonable to draw the inference of negligence from the mere fact of the accident.

Resort to the burden of proof is a poor way to decide a case but in so far as resort is had to it, the burden remains at the end as it was at the beginning i.e. on the plaintiff to prove that his injury was caused by the defendant's negligence.

The true meaning and effect of the so-called doctrine is expressed most clearly in *Henderson* v *Henry E Jenkins & Sons* [1970] AC 282, 301 and *Lloyde* v *West Midlands Gas Board* [1971] 1 WLR 749, 755.

The [trial] judge also failed to give effect to the authorities which establish that a defendant placed in a position of peril and emergency is not to be judged by too critical a standard when he acted on the spur of the moment to avoid an accident.

The Court of Appeal rightly rejected the judge's approach and appreciated that once the first defendant's explanation of the accident was accepted, his driving had to be judged in the light of the emergency he had been placed in by the driver of the blue car.

Weir, Tony, *A Casebook on Tort*, 7th edn, London: Sweet & Maxwell 1992, pp. 162–3

Section 5.—Proof of Breach
At the trial itself, the plaintiff must lead some evidence . . . For example, from the fact that a well-made machine worked badly one may infer that it was not very well maintained; whether that lack of maintenance, if one infers it, amounts to a shortfall in the defendant depends on how expert and frequent the maintenance incumbent on him, as a matter of law is. But one may not infer bad maintenance at all. The machine may have been badly handled. If the person responsible for maintenance is also responsible for the faults of the operator of the machine, it does not matter which is inferred, and it is enough that it is more likely than not that it must have been one or the other.

When one can infer from the facts proved that the defendant was careless in some respect not specifically shown, then it is said that *res ipsa loquitur*. People have tried to say under what circumstances such an inference is possible or permissible or unavoidable, but it appears from the nature of the matter that there can be no real rules about it. If there are few rules to tell us when a defendant was careless, there must be even fewer to tell us when he must have been careless. We may, with Megaw LJ in *Lloyde* v *West Midlands Gas Board* [1971] 1 WLR 719, 755, doubt whether it is right to describe *res ipsa loquitur* as a 'doctrine'.

If *res ipsa loquitur*, a matter which need not be specifically pleaded (*Bennett* v *Chemical Construction (GB) Ltd* [1971] 1 WLR 1571), the defendant will lead evidence. His aim is to show that he behaved properly. He may try to prove the physical cause of the accident and that it is not attributable to his fault; but it is enough, even if he cannot do that, to clear himself of fault by showing that he behaved properly throughout. If the facts he proves make it appear less likely than not that there are unproved facts suggesting that he was at fault, then the plaintiff loses . . .

SCOTT v *LONDON AND ST KATHERINE DOCKS CO.*
(1865) 3 H & C 596 (Court of Exchequer Chamber)

The plaintiff was standing near the door of the defendants warehouses when he was injured by some bags of sugar which fell on him. The judge at first instance had directed a verdict for the defendants on the ground that there was no evidence of negligence. The Court of Exchequer Chamber (the forerunner of the Court of Appeal) however, directed a new trial by relying on the doctrine of *res ipsa loquitur*.

ERLE CJ: There must be reasonable evidence of negligence. But where a thing is shown to be under the management of the defendant or his servants, and the accident is such as in the ordinary course of things do not happen if those who have the management use proper care, it affords reasonable evidence, in the absence of explanation by the defendants, that the accident arose from want of care.

MORRIS v *WINSBURY-WHITE* [1937] 4 All ER 494

The defendant had operated on the plaintiff, and the post-operative treatment involved the insertion into his body of tubes and their frequent replacement.

The tubes were originally inserted by the defendant during the operation but replacements were made subsequently by resident doctors and nurses. Sometime after his discharge from hospital a portion of a tube was found in the plaintiff's bladder.

In an action for negligence against the defendant, it was held that *res ipsa loquitur* did not apply because, in hospital, he was treated by numerous doctors and nurses and was not in the control or charge of the defendant for the whole period.

MAHON v *OSBORNE* [1939] 1 All ER 535 (CA)

SCOTT LJ: But to treat the maxim as applying in every case where a swab is left in the patient seems to me an error of law. The very essence of the rule when applied to an action for negligence is that on the mere fact of the event happening, for example, an injury to the plaintiff, there arise two presumptions of fact: (1) that the event was caused by a breach by somebody of the duty of care towards the plaintiff, and (2) that the defendant was that somebody. The presumption of fact only arises because it is an inference which the reasonable man knowing the facts would naturally draw, and that is in most cases for two reasons: (1) because the control over the happening of such an event rested solely with the defendant, and (2) that in the ordinary experience of mankind such an event does not happen unless the person in control has failed to exercise due care. The nature even of abdominal operations varies widely, and many considerations enter it—the degree of urgency, the state of the patient's inside, the complication of his disorder or injury, the condition of his heart, the effects of the anaesthetic, the degree and kind of help which the surgeon has (for example, whether he is assisted by another surgeon), the efficiency of the theatre team of nurses, the extent of the surgeon's experience, the limits of wise discretion in the particular circumstances (for example, the complications arising out of the operation itself, and the fear of the patient's collapse). In the present case, all the above considerations combined together to present a state of things of which the ordinary experience of mankind knows nothing, and therefore to make it unsafe to beg the question of proof. I cannot see how it can be said that the first essentials of the rule, if it can be called a rule, apply . . . In Goddard LJ's article on *Negligence*, in vol. 23 of Halsbury's Laws of England, 2nd ed., on pp. 671 *et seq.*, there is a very clear exposition of the law. His initial sentence indicates the necessary limitation of the rule: An exception to the general rule that the burden of proof of the alleged negligence is in the first instance on the plaintiff occurs wherever the facts already established are such that the proper and natural inference immediately arising from them is that the injury complained of was caused by the defendant's negligence, or where the event charged as negligence 'tells its own story' of negligence on the part of the defendant, the story so told being clear and unambiguous. To these cases the maxim '*res ipsa loquitur* applies.' . . . The person to draw 'the proper and natural inferrence immediately arising' when the defendant's counsel submits there is no case, is the judge, not the jury. How can the ordinary judge have sufficient knowledge of surgical operations to draw such an inference, or, to apply the phrase in the judgment in *Scott* v *London and St Katherine Docks Co.* (1865) 3 H & C 596, what does he know of 'the ordinary course of things' in a complicated abdominal operation? And if he does not know, is expert evidence admissible to supply the judicial lack of knowledge? But, even if the rule can apply in more surgical cases than I think, there is an additional reason why it cannot apply in the present case. The action was brought not only against the surgeon, but also against the nurse, and a hospital operation depends on the joint efforts of surgeon and nursing staff. Against which defendant, surgeon or theatre sister, did the presumption arise? There is a further point, also. In the present case counsel for the plaintiff put in the defendant surgeon's answers to interrogatories, and in so far as they described the operation the plaintiff made the description part of her case. How can it be said the the rule continued to apply after that?

For these various reasons I do not think that the principle, if it be one, had any application in the present case. As, however, the defendant's counsel did not elect to stand on his submission that there was no case, it is unnecessary to express any final opinion on the questions involved in his submission . . .

GODDARD LJ . . . The plaintiff, beyond proving facts necessary to establish damage and putting in answers to interrogatories, called no further evidence. She proved by the interrogatories that the swab had been left in at the operation performed by the defendant, and that was enough to call upon him for an explanation. And here, as I understand the Court is not unanimous on the point, I think it right to say that in my opinion the doctrine of *res ipsa loquitur* does apply in such a case as this, at least to the extent I mention below.

The surgeon is in command of the operation, it is for him to decide what instruments, swabs and the like are to be used, and it is he who uses them. The patient, or, if he dies, his representatives, can know nothing about this matter. There can be no possible question but that neither swabs nor instruments are ordinarily left in the patient's body, and no one would venture to say that it is proper, although in particular circumstances it may be excusable, so to leave them. If, therefore, a swab is left in the patient's body, it seems to me clear that the surgeon is called on for an explanation, that is, he is called on to show not necessarily why he missed it but that he exercised due care to prevent it being left there. It is no disparagement of the devoted and frequently gratuitous service which the profession of surgery render to mankind to say that its members may on occasion fall short of the standard of care which they themselves, no less the law, require, and, if a patient on whom had befallen such a misfortune as we are now considering were not entitled to call on the surgeon for an explanation, I cannot but feel that an unwarranted protection would be given to carelessness, such as I do not believe the profession itself would either expect or desire . . .

Mackinnon LJ agreed with Goddard LJ on the application of *res ipsa loquitur*.

EASSON v LONDON AND NORTH EASTERN RAILWAY [1944] 2 KB 421

The plaintiff, aged four, fell through the door of a passenger train. At the time of the accident the train was seven miles from its last stopping place. It was held that *res ipsa loqitur* was not applicable because the defendants did not have sufficient control over the door at that time. Anyone in the train corridor could have meddled with the door.

BARKWAY v SOUTH WALES TRANSPORT CO. LTD [1950] 1 All ER 393 (HL)

The plaintiff was injured when the bus he was travelling in burst a tyre, mounted the pavement and fell down an embankment. The tyre had burst owing to a defect in its wall which could not have been discovered beforehand. The House of Lords held that *res ipsa loquitur* did not apply here, because there was evidence of the circumstances of the accident, and a negligent system of tyre inspection at the defendants garage.

A plaintiff who is able to present a partial account of what happened, however, is not prevented from relying on the principle of *res ipsa loquitur*.

LORD PORTER: The doctrine is dependent on the absence of explanation, and, although it is the duty of the defendants, if they desire to protect themselves, to give an adequate explanation of the cause of the accident, yet, if the facts are sufficiently known, the question ceases to be one where the facts speak for themselves, and the solution is to be found by determining whether, on the facts as established, negligence is to be inferred or not.

CASSIDY v MINISTRY OF HEALTH [1951] 2 KB 343 (CA)

The plaintiff, who was injured as a result of the negligence of hospital staff, could not bring evidence to show which member of the hospital staff had been negligent. However, it was held that in such circumstances i.e. where the plaintff cannot point to the particular servant who is in control, the principle of *res ipsa loquitur* will apply so as to render the employer vicariously liable.

ROE v MINISTRY OF HEALTH [1954] 2 All ER 131 (CA)

DENNING LJ: If an injured person shows that one or other of two persons injured him, but cannot say which of them it was, he is not defeated altogether. He can call on each of them for an explanation.

WALSH v HOLST & CO. LTD [1958] 1 WLR 800

Contractors were carrying out work on a building when a brick from the building fell on and injured the plaintiff who was walking along the street. It was held that *res ispa loquitur* did apply, so that a defendant's duty is so extensive that he is responsible for the negligence of an independent contractor. However, on the facts, it was held that the contractors were not liable as it was shown that they had not been negligent having taken precautions.

PEARSON v NORTH-WESTERN GAS BOARD [1968] 2 All ER 669 (CA)

The plaintiff's husband was killed and her home destroyed by a gas explosion. This was found to be due to a fractured main caused by a very severe frost. In such weather, the defendants had men standing by to deal with reports of gas leaks, but there was no way of preventing or predicting such an explosion. On this evidence it was held that, assuming *res ipsa loquitur* applied, the defendants had rebutted the presumption of negligence.

LLOYDE v WEST MIDLANDS GAS BOARD [1971] 2 All ER 1240 (CA)

MEGAW LJ: . . . I doubt whether it is right to describe *res ipsa loquitur* as a 'doctrine'. I think it is no more than an exotic, though convenient, phrase to describe what is in essence no more than a common sense approach, not limited by technical rules, to the assessment of the effect of evidence in certain circumstances. It means that a plaintiff prima facie establishes negligence where: (i) it is not possible for him to prove precisely what was the relevant act or omission which set in train the events leading to the accident; but (ii) on the evidence as it stands at the relevant time it is more likely than not that the effective cause of the accident was *some* act or omission of the defendant or of someone for whom the defendant is responsible, which act or omission constitutes a failure to take proper care for the plaintiff's safety.

I have used the words 'evidence as it stands at the relevant time'. I think this can most conveniently be taken as being at the close of the plaintiff's case. On the assumption that a submission of no case is then made, would the evidence, as it then stands, enable the plaintiff to succeed because, although the precise cause of the accident cannot be established, the proper inference on balance of probability is that that cause, whatever it may have been, involved a failure by the defendant to take due care for the plaintiff's safety? If so, *res ipsa loquitur*. If not, the plaintiff fails. Of course, if the defendant does not make a submission of no case, the question still falls to be tested by the same criterion, but evidence for the defendant, given thereafter, may rebut the inference. The res, which previously spoke for itself, may be silenced, or its voice may, on the whole of the evidence, become too weak or muted. . . .

WIDDOWSON v NEWGATE MEAT CORPORATION, The Times, 4 December 1997 (CA)

The plaintiff suffered from a severe mental disorder, and he was injured in a road accident. At the trial of the action he gave no evidence, relying on *res ipsa loquitur*. In these circumstances the defendant called no evidence, claiming that there was no case to answer.

At first instance the court found in favour of the plaintiff, and the Court of Appeal held that where a judge could not find out what actually happened, because there was no evidence on which to form an opinion, *res ipsa loquitur* applies. If the defendant cannot give a plausible explanation for what happened, the plaintiff is entitled to succeed in his claim.

Wright, Cecil, *Cases on the Law of Torts*, 4th edn, 1967, London: Butterworths pp. 245–7

It is significant that in England, where juries have practically disappeared in negligence cases, *res ipsa loquitur* has, in effect, operated to shift the burden of disproof of negligence to a defendant. Perhaps this is inevitable in light of the fact that the same person who decides that the facts are such as to make the principle of *res ipsa loquitur* applicable, is also faced with the additional problem of determining the actual outcome of the issue of liability on those facts. Once having decided that the facts give rise to an interference of negligence, it is understandable that a judge would require something in the way of proof in order that his mind should be changed. The situation, however, in jurisdictions with juries is entirely different. There, it is the jury which assesses the weight of the inference to be drawn and the jury should, in theory, not be bound by the inference which a judge may initially have drawn. This distinction may explain the difference between many English and Canadian cases. If it does, it is an additional indication of a move towards liability without fault, since an onus of disproof of negligence automatically gives a benefit to a plaintiff at the expense of a defendant who must bear that burden.

If, as Maine said, substantive law was in the early days 'secreted in the interstices of procedure' it is no less true today that under the guise of procedure courts are able to shift imperceptibly into forms of liability without fault, while speaking the language of negligence. In the tradition of the common law, effect is frequently given to policies without mentioning them or, perhaps even recognising them. The cases in the present section, therefore, while exploring some of the problems of proof in negligence actions, provide further material for a study of the basic objectives and policies of loss-shifting—or loss distribution. Further, difficult problems of proof are a salutary check on the naive but common belief of students that 'black-letter' law is more important than the facts to which it must be applied.

Milner, M.A., *Negligence in Modern Law*, 1967,
London: Butterworths pp. 89–93

. . . On the orthodox analysis of a *res ipsa loquitur* case, the onus remains throughout on the plaintiff. His failure to dispel doubt is as fatal to him as though the probabilities positively favour the defendant's case. On the other hand, if, in a *res ipsa loquitur* case, the legal onus passes to the defendant, failure to dispel doubt reacts on the defendant and entitles the plaintiff to judgment, just as though the probabilities were positively adverse to the defendant's case.

There is not inconsiderable judicial support for this latter interpretation of *res ipsa loquitur* in English courts. The effect is to transform *res ipsa loquitur* from a convenient descriptive term for evidence of a certain type of event which is ordinarily indicative of negligence in the defendant, into a rule of law which, in the absence of affirmative proof of innocence by the defendant cogent enough to exculpate him, compels the court to find for the plaintiff. The plaintiff in a *res ipsa loquitur* case is thereby more favourably placed than is the plaintiff in an ordinary case of *prima facie* negligence, in which the plaintiff would fail if the evidence as a whole left the issue of negligence and causation in doubt. This view of the English authorities has, however, been rejected by the High Court of Australia in *Mummery v Irvings (Pty) Ltd*, in which Dixon CJ, said that the rule itself was merely descriptive of a method by which, in appropriate cases, a *prima facie* case of negligence might be made out, and the court could see no reason why the plaintiff in such a case should be in any different position from one making out a *prima facie* case in any other way. Any analogy to the supposed rule in a trespass action that the *defendant* must show inevitable accident has been vitiated by the assimilation of trespass to negligence in matters of onus of proof.

If then the *res ipsa loquitur* rule is confined to the modest role assigned to it by the orthodox theory, it cannot openly operate to introduce into the class of negligence case to which it applies a stricter rule of liability than otherwise governs negligence actions, a rule approximating the position in *Rylands* v *Fletcher* and nuisance cases, in so far as it would throw upon the defendant the onus to show a specific cause of the event of such a nature as to exclude the negligence or default of himself or those under his control. Furthermore the resemblance to *Rylands* v *Fletcher* and nuisance breaks down at the point where the defendant, being unable to explain the cause of the injurious event, relies simply upon proof of his own conformity with the standard of conduct of a reasonable man. *Rylands* v *Fletcher* and nuisance are alike in treating the defence that the defendant had taken all reasonable precautions as inadequate.

This deflation of the theoretical significance of *res ipsa loquitur* even if it be good law, is nevertheless capable of grossly minimising the role of the maxim in the actual operation of the law today. *Res ipsa loquitur* is an immensely important vehicle for importing strict liability into negligence cases. In practice, there are many cases where *res ipsa loquitur* is properly invoked in which the defendant is unable to show affirmatively either that he took all reasonable precautions to avoid injury or that the particular cause of the injury was not associated with negligence on his part. Industrial and traffic accidents, and injuries caused by defective merchandise, are so frequently of this type that the theoretical limitations of the maxim are quite overshadowed by its practical significance. The result is a certain disparity between the theory of fault liability underlying negligence and the actual functioning of the remedy, which could best be resolved by the open recognition of certain spheres of conduct as carrying an 'insurance' against risk. Injuries sustained in the sphere of such guaranteed safety would then cease to be governed by negligence considerations, and the incipient tendency of *res ipsa loquitur* towards strict liability would, in a defined class of case, be consummated by appropriate legislation.

3.6 Summary

Tony Weir, *A Casebook on Tort*, 4th edn, Sweet and Maxwell 1979, p. 21

This great case [*Donoghue* v *Stevenson*] with its bare majority, finally established negligence as a tort, by pointing to the common element of the relationships which give rise to the duty to take reasonable care and by extending them to include that of manufacturer and consumer. The 'neighbour' formula, however, must not be taken *au pied de la lettre*, as being a conclusive test of the existence of a duty to take care, for, as the succeeding cases demonstrate, there are many situations where a person has no claim, though he is quite blameless, in respect of damage foreseeably caused to him by the carelessness of another . . .

Furthermore, although the foreseeability formula may well be the highest common factor of all the relationships which do give rise to a duty to take reasonable care, there are many relationships which are not at all adequately described in terms of foreseeability. One of these is that of manufacturer and consumer.

If one asked a manufacturer about his consumers, he would not answer in terms of *foreseeing* but of *aiming*. He launches his product at the consumer, he identifies him in advance by expensive research techniques, and he designs his product and arranges his advertising so as to lure the consumer to use it. The consumer is not a person of whom the manufacturer *ought* to be thinking; he is a person of whom the manufacturer *is* thinking. The relationship is quite different from that between strangers in a public or private place as between whom a relationship is set up for the first time when one injures the other (e.g., *Booker* v *Wenborn* [1962] 1 WLR 162; *Johnson* v *Rea* [1962] 1 QB 373). In subsuming both under a common formula, Lord Atkin risked making them appear similar.

Now in the principal case no evidence was ever led, and the question of the specificity of proof did not and could not arise, though Lord Macmillan (above, p. 20) said that the plaintiff must prove carelessness. Four years later, in *Grant* v *Australian Knitting Mills* [1936] AC 85, the plaintiff complained of dermatitis resulting from the use of underpants manufactured by the defendant which contained excess sulphites. The defendant led evidence that he had manufactured 4,737,600 pairs of underpants with never a complaint. Yet the plaintiff succeeded. No one can reasonably say that a manufacturer with a failure rate of only one in a million is not a reasonably careful manufacturer; it is, indeed, an astonishing performance which should earn a prize. And one cannot say that he was not reasonably careful with the pants in question, since there was no evidence as to them, save their defect. He was in fact made to pay because the pants were defective when they left his factory. Thus the principal case, though it expresses the duty in terms of taking reasonable care, virtually results in a guarantor's liability [**in manufacturer's liability cases**].

D. Howarth, *Textbook on Tort*, 1995, London: Butterworths, pp. 65–7

One of the most serious temptations for those coming across the tort of negligence for the first time is to be drawn into answering all questions with the words 'reasonable foreseeability'. Indeed, some students seem to believe that the evil necessity of detailed analysis can be kept at bay in negligence by the pious chanting of 'foreseeability' as a kind of mantra.

The courts themselves are partly responsible for this almost comical state of affairs. For example, in *Surtees* v *Kingston-upon-Thames Borough Council*, the trial judge, Stocker LJ and

Sir Nicholas Browne-Wilkinson all attempt to show that it is not 'reasonably foreseeable' at all that a child left next to a hot tap might scald itself, an intellectual enterprise so ludicrous that the two appeal judges, at least, eventually give up the attempt and slide back into admitting that the proper ground for their decision is the general knock-on effects of holding busy parents to standards of near perfection in childcare. Judges are perhaps influenced by the fact that by stressing foreseeability rather than reasonableness itself, it might be possible to give the appearance of avoiding the inherent conflicts about value that judgments about fault involve, and to concentrate solely on an issue that sounds as if it is objectively measurable. But, in reality, there is no way, in a tort based on fault, of avoiding substantive judgments of value. Foreseeability should be seen for what it is, not the philosopher's stone of the tort of negligence, but instead a shorthand way of stating a simple but important aspect of the test for fault, namely the tense of the verb to be used in judgments about fault.

That tense is the conditional perfect – *would have*. What matters is how the situation *would have* seemed to a reasonable person at the time. It would be possible to construct other tests in negligence that might still be called fault-based liability but which would use a different tense. There could be, for example, a test based on the simple conditional 'would a reasonable person do this again, knowing now what the outcome would be?' Such a test would be different from foreseeability because it would allow the judgment about whether the defendant acted reasonably to take into account facts that have only come to light since the accident, including the fact that the accident happened. As Sir Nicholas Browne-Wilkinson V-C said in *Strover* v *Harrington*, in negligence 'the question is not what [the defendant] will think is desirable in the future as a result of the perhaps bitter experience of this case, but whether on 4 March 1968 he fell below the then standards [applicable to him] . . .

Foreseeability therefore rules out anything that could not have been relevant to the defendant's decision about how to act. If, for example, technology has moved on, or scientific knowledge has accumulated, since the time of the defendant's injury-causing act, the new knowledge may not be taken into account . . .

Note that often the reasonably foreseeable risk is no different from the risk as it seems now. Sometimes it is less. It may even be greater (if, for example, new scientific evidence shows that the event in question is very much rarer than previously believed). But it is always the risk as it *would have appeared at the time* that counts.

Note also that if the risk would have appeared at the time to be zero, or next to zero, the injury may be said to be 'unforeseeable' or 'not reasonably foreseeable'. If this is the case the defendant cannot be liable – but not for some mysterious reason to do with the magic of foreseeability, but because if the risk of injury is to be counted as zero, then there is nothing to balance against the costs of the precautions, and so the defendant cannot have been at fault.

It is in this sense alone that foreseeability can be said to be a necessary element of liability in negligence. But, of course, it is clearly never sufficient by itself for liability, since a foreseeable risk may be so small that a reasonable person might ignore it (*Bolton* v *Stone*) or the cost of eliminating the foreseeable risk might be unreasonable (*Wagon Mound No. 2*).

3.7 End of Chapter Assessment Questions

1   '... the well known passage in Lord Atkin's speech [in *Donoghue* v *Stevenson*] should I think be regarded as a statement of principle. It is not to be treated as if it were a statutory definition. It will require qualification in new circumstances. But I think that the time has come when we can and should say that it ought to apply unless there is some justification or valid explanation for its exclusion.' (*Home Office* v *Dorset Yacht Company*, *per* Lord Reid.)

Discuss.

2   Mandy was driving her car home one night, when a tyre punctured as a result of an invisible structural defect in its wall. She attempted to change the wheel, but without success. Nick, a passing motorist, saw her plight and offered his assistance. He changed the wheel but forgot to tighten the wheel-nuts. As a result the wheel came off soon afterwards, the car crashed and Mandy was injured.

Advise her on any claim she may have in tort against Nick. Would your answer be different if Nick were an AA patrolman, whom Mandy had summoned to help her?

NB: **two** questions are given here because questions on duty of care in negligence often take the form of **essay** questions; and **Chapter 3** covers **breach** of duty, as well as duty.

3.8 End of Chapter Assessment Outline Answers

QUESTION 1

'We often speak today of the "duty of care" which must exist before negligence is actionable, but the problem facing a modern judge is not a new one. In every Action on the Case the court in effect recognised a duty of care, e.g. of innkeeper to guest, surgeon to patient, without using the phrase. The main extension has in reality been from duties arising out of some antecedent relationships, such as contract or local proximity, to duties towards casual strangers as in highway accidents, or towards sub-purchasers with whom the manufacturer does not come in contact. "Who is my neighbour?" takes on a constantly wider meaning.' Kiralfy in *The English Legal System*, 9th edn 1990.

Lord Atkin's 'neighbour principle', expressed in terms of 'foreseeability' and 'proximity' and formulated in *Donoghue* v *Stevenson*, has been acknowledged since 1932 as the general starting point in any discussion relating to the duty of care factor in the tort of negligence. It assumes a role of particular significance within the context of 'hard cases' i.e. where there is a paucity of authority on the point in issue.

His Lordship expressed his opinion as follows:

The rule that you are to love your neighbour becomes in law, you must not injure your neighbour; and the lawyer's question, Who is my neighbour? receives a restricted reply. You must take reasonable care to avoid acts or omissions which you can reasonably foresee would be likely to injure your neighbour. Who then in law is my neighbour? The answer seems to be – persons who are so closely and directly affected by my act that I ought reasonably to have them in contemplation as being so affected when I am directing my mind to the acts or omissions which are called in question.

This is the 'passage' referred to by Lord Reid in his speech in *Dorset Yacht*, and it is clearly the case that Lord Atkin is expressing himself in language of considerably open texture.

Before *Donoghue* v *Stevenson* the courts had fixed categories of situations or relations in which it was possible to establish a duty of care in the tort of negligence. A plaintiff's case had to fit into a 'pigeon hole', and the courts were reluctant to acknowledge new situations. The significance of *Donoghue* lies in the fact that not only did the House of Lords establish a duty of care owed by a manufacturer to his consumer in the tort of negligence; the case also gave birth to the neighbourhood principle. This embodied a duty to avoid causing foreseeable injury, and it eventually led to the expansion of the tort of negligence because it stated a general principle, not merely another classification.

The courts were slow to adopt Lord Atkin's principle because of a reluctance to undermine established rules of law. 'There continued to be no duty of care in making statements or in disposing of tumbledown houses – words were not like deeds and a dwelling was inherently different from a ginger beer bottle' (*Winfield & Jolowicz*).

Nevertheless, Lord Atkin's test was employed, eventually, to extend the boundaries of the tort of negligence; though it could be argued that the courts tended on the whole to take an approach on the development of the law based on the existence of 'duty situations'. These 'duty situations' post-*Donoghue*, however, became more flexible and capable of adaptation and extension to meet new claims for compensation. As Lord MacMillan observed in *Donoghue*, 'the categories of negligence are never closed.'

As Lord Wilberforce observed in *Anns*, however, '. . . it may well be that full recognition of the impact of *Donoghue* v *Stevenson* . . . only came with the decision of this House in *Home Office* v *Dorset Yacht Co*. . .'

The Atkinian test has traditionally been regarded as too wide because merely causing foreseeable damage is not regarded as actionable in negligence in all circumstances. An obvious example is 'pure' economic loss.

The requirement of 'proximity', in **addition** to 'foreseeability', was an early attempt to qualify the 'neighbour' test. There have, also, always been traditional 'exemptions' from the application of the Atkinian 'test' (e.g. 'Omissions': e.g. Lord Goff in *Smith* v *Littlewoods*). For this reason, and partly because of Lord Atkin's choice of words in his formulation of the 'neighbour principle', particular problems have been encountered in certain areas of damage.

It can be argued, however, that by establishing a common factor in the majority of cases where the court imposed liability for negligent behaviour, the neighbour principle did entrench negligence as a tort in its own right. (In *Donoghue* itself, the contract 'fallacy' in connection with the liability of a manufacturer to his ultimate consumer was laid to rest.) It allowed lawyers to argue that there should be a duty of care in situations where there had never been a duty of care before, basing their arguments on the point that the damage was foreseeable. The increase in liability was, however, **incremental**, built upon existing case law. There was no runaway expansion in the tort of negligence.

The Atkinian formula in other words was accepted as a necessary, though not necessarily sufficient, determinant of liability in relation to 'duty' in 'hard cases'. (Thus, even in *Dorset Yacht* Lord Reid said the test was **not** 'a statutory definition'.) As time went on, however, the neighbour principle achieved greater acceptance. In *Hedley Byrne & Co.* v *Heller & Partners Ltd* [1964] the House of Lords confirmed the neighbour principle as 'a flexible test which could be applied in any fact situation.' (It was only **then** that real inroads were made into the 'inviolability' of 'pure' economic loss.)

The *Dorset Yacht* case in 1970 was another major landmark. *Donoghue* had identified the person to whom a duty of care may be owed, but had not said in what circumstances that duty should be owed: in *Dorset Yacht* Lord Reid attempted to rectify this. Whilst admitting that Lord Atkin's neighbour principle should not be treated as if it were a statutory definition and acknowledging that it would need qualification in new circumstances, he said: 'We can and should say that it ought to apply unless there is some justification or valid explanation for its exclusion.'

For the first time the neighbourhood principle was acknowledged by an appellate court as a general principle which should give rise to a *prima facie* duty of care, unless there was a reason for saying that it should not.

Lord Reid's statement was taken up by the House of Lords in *Anns* (1978) when Lord Wilberforce reformulated it as a two stage test:

> First one has to ask whether, as between the alleged wrong-doer and the person who has suffered the damage, there is a sufficient relationship of proximity or neighbourhood such that, in the reasonable contemplation of the former, carelessness on his part may be likely to cause damage to the latter, in which case a *prima facie* duty of care arises. Secondly, if the first question is answered affirmatively, it is necessary to consider whether there are any considerations which ought to negative or to reduce or limit the scope of the duty or the class of persons to whom it is owed, or the damages to which a breach of it may give rise.

In the late 1970s and early 1980s the test was widely relied upon and was used by some judges to attack previously well entrenched principles of non-liability. It was the basis for the expansion of the law of negligence in relation to nervous shock (*McLoughlin* v *O'Brian* [1983] and 'pure' economic loss (*Junior Books* v *Veitchi* [1982]).

Lord Reid in *Dorset Yacht* and Lord Wilberforce in *Anns* v *Merton* took what might be regarded as a more **principled** approach to the question of applying the Atkinian formulation of 'neighbourliness'. These speeches show a difference in **emphasis** from earlier approaches to the problem: a 'presumptive' or '*prima facie*' duty would arise where parties were in close proximity to each other. The Atkinian approach was elevated to a more prominent position; there was something of a movement towards a **general principle of liability** for careless conduct. (See e.g. Lord Bridge in *Curran* v *N I Co-Ownership Housing Assoc. Ltd* and *Caparo plc* v *Dickman*.) The traditional 'exceptions' and 'special cases' consequently assumed lesser importance.

As Lord Wilberforce said, in *Anns*, it was not necessary in order to found liability to bring the facts of a case within the precise terms of a previously decided case.

This position, however, came under sustained attack from 1985; a reaction perhaps to the application of the two-stage test in such cases as *Junior Books* (above) which is a decision regarded widely at the time as threatening to 'open the floodgate of litigation'. This reaction is manifest most particularly in the so-called 'pure economic loss' cases, e.g. *Leigh & Sillavan* v *Aliakmon Shipping Co.* (see especially Lord Brandon's speech: his Lordship thought that there was even a danger of **established** authority being disregarded). In general, see *Peabody* v *Parkinson, Sutherland Shire Council* v *Heyman (Aust.)*, *Yuen Kun Yeu* v *A-G for Hong Kong*; *Rowling* v *Takaro Properties*; *Curran* (in which the Wilberforce test was criticised as blurring the distinction between 'omissions' and 'acts'; and contract and tort); *Muirhead* v *Industrial Tank Specialities*; *Candlewood* v *Mitsui*; *D & F Estates* v *Church Commissioners*; **and** *Murphy* v *Brentwood DC* (in which *Anns* was overruled on its facts).

The move towards a more general, principled approach to the establishment of a duty of care (if that is what had been taking place as the result of Lord Wilberforce's elegant rationalisation) was halted.

This approach, though laudable in principle (it accords more with the French solution to the problem, for example) was not without its dangers: 'It is twenty years since Dr Stevens (no timid conservative) complained that the Law Lords in *Hedley Byrne* had led people out into the wilderness and left them there. Since then the Law Lords have led the caravan even further into the desert; the decisions in *Anns* and *Junior Books* have left us staring out over a featureless plain in which all the traditional landmarks have been obliterated.' (JC Smith 'Liability in Negligence'.)

It may be pointed out in reply that the Reid/Wilberforce approach led only to a **presumptive** duty of care: see *Hill* v *West Yorks Police*; *Rigby* v *Chief Constable of Northants*. Policy might then dictate a different answer on the facts.

Lord Keith has criticised the high profile given to 'policy' in the Wilberforce approach – see e.g. *Yuen Kun Yeu*, in which he reinterpreted the 'two-stage test'. He and other judges, emphasise **'foreseeability'**, **'proximity'** and **'just and reasonable'** as the factors to be considered and applied in the light of **established** authority. An **incremental** approach is now evident in the context of the development of the duty of care: pre-existing authority must be followed and, where possible, adapted or extended to meet new demands.

Caparo is acknowledged generally as the leading authority for the 'new' three-stage test, and *Marc Rich and Co.* v *Bishop Rock Marine* says that **all** cases of negligence (**regardless** of the nature of the damage suffered) must satisfy this test.

Is this a return to 'duty situations', as some claim? Does 'authority' once again offer the security in certainty which lawyers crave? It is surely too early to arrive at a settled conclusion.

'Foreseeability', 'proximity' (and 'just and reasonable') in their application often mask policy decisions, and Lord Roskill in *Caparo* described these expressions as mere 'labels which **defined** nothing'. Consider also the different approaches taken to the problem of 'pure economic loss' by Lord Keith and Lord Oliver in *Murphy* (above). In truth, is not much legal argument concerned merely with litigated policy whatever form is given to the test for determining liability?

Much of the criticism of the two stage test was based on the fact that it had been treated as though it were a statutory definition. It seems, however, that the courts also felt the *Anns* approach was opening the floodgates to areas of new liability: it seemed that the first stage of the *Anns* test was quite easy to pass and that the courts in the period immediately after *Anns* had used the second stage to find liability where previously there had been none, with only scant regard to case law. The courts seem to have perceived this development as an alarming trend, concerned that insurance companies and the public coffers would be unable to finance a dramatically expanded tort of negligence, and wanting to ensure that negligence did not overshadow other legal rules established by the courts and by Parliament.

Lord Templeman summed up the problem in *CBS Songs Ltd* v *Amstrad Consumer Electronics plc* when he said that *Anns* had left the 'floodgates on the jar' and that since *Anns* 'we are all neighbours now, Pharisees and Samaritans alike, that foreseeability is a reflection of hindsight and that for every mischance in an accident-prone world someone solvent must be liable in damages.'

The three stage test, which signifies a pragmatic approach to the problem, contains its difficulties viz. the test is still confusing because there is so much overlap between its three limbs, as Lord Oliver acknowledged in *Caparo*; the test still represents an attempt to set down a general principle, with all the problems that brings; replacing the policy stage of the *Anns* test with criteria of 'fair, just and reasonable' could be regarded as a step backwards. *Anns* at least allowed the courts to be more open about the policy considerations they were applying to the facts in a particular case. Now, with the three stage test, the courts are still applying policy considerations but they are doing so less openly. Policy decisions are couched in the language of 'proximity' and 'just and reasonable' and not always explained openly.

In *Caparo* and *Murphy* the courts spoke of a return to 'traditional categories'. This seems to imply a rejection of any general principle which decides that there is a duty of care unless policy dictates one should not exist, whether it be phrased as a two stage test or a three stage test. As Lord Roskill said in *Caparo Industries*:

It has now to be accepted that there is no simple formula or touchstone to which recourse can be had in order to provide in every case a ready answer to the questions whether, given certain facts, the law will or will not impose liability for negligence or in cases where such liability can be shown to exist, determine the extent of that liability. Phrases such as foreseeability, proximity, neighbourhood, just and reasonable, fairness . . . [are] at best . . . but labels or phrases descriptive of the very different factual situations which can exist in particular cases and which must be carefully examined in each case before it can be pragmatically determined whether a duty of care exists and, if so, what is the scope and extent of that duty.

In practice then, what we have today in the tort of negligence is a traditional approach in which the courts recognise certain distinct categories in which a duty of care arises. When they are trying to decide whether a duty of care will exist in a new situation they take a step by step approach to the problem, placing great emphasis on decided cases.

Jones (*Textbook on Torts*) sums this up as 'an incremental development by analogy with established categories, rather than by a sweeping extension of a prima facie duty of care restrained only by vague considerations which ought to negative or to reduce or limit the scope of duty'.

This is indeed a far more conservative and cautious approach than the one which prevailed in the immediate post-*Anns* period. It is, however, debatable whether the aim of keeping the floodgates shut has succeeded.

QUESTION 2

M = Mandy and N = Nick

The incident is caused, *prima facie*, by the punctured tyre and M's inability to change it. There is **no evidence of negligence** on the part of **anyone** concerned. **In any event**:

(a) The law looks to the most immediate cause of an accident: in the circumstances this would probably be the negligent(?) changing of the wheel by N, and possibly M's negligence in not checking the job, i.e. there may be contributory negligence on her part, under the Law Reform (Contributory Negligence) Act 1945. On **this** reasoning the puncture and M's inability to do anything about it merely presented the **opportunity** for N's negligence (if any).

(b)   The puncture did not directly cause any injury to person or property – this is a requirement in both negligence (e.g. *Aswan Engineering* v *Lupdine*) and under the terms of the strict liability regime introduced by the **Consumer Protection Act 1987, s. 1.**

In **each** case damages for **mere repair** are **not** available. There can be little doubt that N owes a duty of care in negligence to M. It is likely that the usual requirements – 'foreseeability'/'proximity'/'just and reasonable' – will be satisfied (*Caparo; Marc Rich*). In any event, there is a contractual relationship between M and the **AA**.

Liability in contract and the question of concurrent liability in contract and tort are not explored in this answer. Issues arising under the Supply of Goods and Services Act 1982 (in connection with the possible liability of the AA) are not considered.

The only real problem would arise in relation to the **standard of care** expected of N in the circumstances. In the case of the **AA**, what does the contract say, if anything, on the matter? (It is assumed that the wheel comes off as a result of the loose nuts and that M's injury was caused by this accident.) Has N been negligent on the facts? In the absence of provision in the contract, it may be argued that the standard is likely to be high, i.e. that of a skilled mechanic. The task is simple; N was doing his job at the time – an everyday event. *Winfield* (14th edn, p. 114): '. . . anyone [who] practises a profession or is engaged in a transaction in which he holds himself out as having skill [is expected] to show the amount of competence associated with the proper discharge of the duties of that profession, trade or calling, and if he falls short of that and injures someone in consequence, he is not behaving reasonably.' (*Bolam* and analogous cases can be used at this point.)

There is much to be said, therefore, for the argument that N has been negligent. (Is N the agent for the AA in the discharge of their contractual obligation; or is it a case of their **vicarious** liability for his negligence? There **may** be evidence that N is incompetent and that the AA is therefore **personally** liable for employing such a person: authority on 'servants' and 'independent contractors' and 'primary' and 'vicarious liability' can be given at this point.)

If N is merely a **passing motorist** different considerations may apply. Does he owe a duty of care? He has voluntarily taken on this task it is true (outside the case of a mere omission *per* **Lord Keith** in *Yuen Kun Yeu*) but is it just and reasonable in the circumstances for the law to impose a duty? (Foreseeability and proximity are unlikely to cause problems.) There appears to be little direct authority on the topic; something of a 'novel' situation? Question of insurance cover? Strictly speaking, of course, inability to pay is not a reason for refusing to find liability. If a duty were found to exist on a 'simple' *Donoghue* v *Stevenson* basis, the question of **standard of care** would then arise.

Perhaps **not too much would be expected** of a motorist in a hurry? On the other hand, the task undertaken by N is of a fairly simple nature. In *Wells* v *Cooper* a householder who took on a relatively minor job of repair in his house was not expected to apply the skill of 'a professional carpenter for reward' – but he was expected to show the skill of a reasonably competent carpenter doing the job in question. It may be argued that it would not be expecting too much of an ordinary motorist (he holds himself out as nothing more; surely he does not give assurances about safety?) to apply to the job in hand the skill of a typical motorist, doing that job. However, would he be expected to show the skill of a reasonably competent mechanic or repairer? Would that be expecting too much?

It could be said that M has agreed, by accepting N's help (he is a 'mere' motorist) to accept a lower standard of care than could be expected from a professional: e.g. *Phillips* v *Whiteley; Condon* v *Basi.*

Is N a 'rescuer'? Would such persons be deterred from helping stranded motorists (perhaps in situations of peril) were the law to impose an onerous burden of responsibility for casual acts of negligence? 'Rescue' could be explained, briefly, at this point.

In any event, has M been **contributorily negligent** in (apparently) failing to make sure the job was properly performed by a stranger (N)? The provisions of the 1945 Act might apply. N could have been asked by M whether the job was secured properly, bearing in mind the relatively simple nature of the task and the potential risks involved. (This argument could be advanced in relation to the AA but with, perhaps, less potential for success because of the contractual relationship and the professionalism involved.)

CHAPTER FOUR

CAUSATION AND REMOTENESS

4.1 Introduction

ROE v *MINISTER OF HEALTH* [1954] 2 All ER 131 (CA)

DENNING LJ: . . . the three questions, duty, causation and remoteness, run continually into one another. It seems to me that they are simply three different ways of looking at one and the same problem. Starting with the proposition that a negligent person should be liable, within reason, for the consequences of his conduct, the extent of his liability is to be found by asking the one question: Is the consequence fairly to be regarded as within the risk created by the negligence? If so the negligent person is liable for it: but otherwise not.

SPARTAN STEEL & ALLOYS LTD v *MARTIN & CO.* [1972] 3 All ER 557 (CA)

LORD DENNING MR: . . . In many cases where economic loss has been held not to be recoverable, it has been put on the ground that the defendant was under no *duty* to the plaintiff. Thus where a person is injured in a road accident by the negligence of another, the negligent driver owes a duty to the injured man himself, but he owes no duty to the servant of the injured man: see *Best* v *Samuel Fox & Co. Ltd*; nor to the master of the injured man: *Inland Revenue Comrs* v *Hambrook*; nor to anyone else who suffers loss because he had a contract with the injured man: see *Simpson & Co.* v *Thomson*; nor indeed to anyone who only suffers economic loss on account of the accident: see *Kirkham* v *Boughey*. Likewise when property is damaged by the negligence of another the negligent tortfeasor owes a duty to the owner or possessor of the chattel, but not to one who suffers loss only because he had a contract entitling him to use the chattel or giving him a right to receive it at some later date: see *Elliott Steam Tug Co.* v *Shipping Controller* and *Margarine Union GmbH* v *Cambay Prince Steamship Co. Ltd*.

In other cases, however, the defendant seems clearly to have been under a duty to the plaintiff but the economic loss has not been recovered because it is too remote. Take the illustration given by Blackburn J in *Cattle* v *Stockton Waterworks Co*: when water escapes from a reservoir and floods a coalmine where many men are working; those who had their tools or clothes destroyed could recover, but those who only lost their wages could not. Similarly when the defendants' ship negligently sank a ship which was being towed by a tug, the owner of the tug lost his renumeration, but he could not recover it from the negligent ship although the same duty (of navigation with reasonable care) was owed to both tug and tow: see *Société Remorquage à Hélice* v *Bennetts*. In such cases if the plaintiff or his property had been physically injured, he would have recovered; but, as he only suffered economic loss he is held not entitled to recover. This is, I should think, because the loss is regarded by the law as too remote: see *King* v *Phillips*.

On the other hand, in the cases where economic loss by itself has been held to be recoverable, it is plain that there was a duty to the plaintiff and the loss was not too remote. Such as when one ship negligently runs down another ship, and damages it with the result that the cargo has to be discharged and reloaded. The negligent ship was already under a duty to the cargo-owners; and they can recover the cost of discharging and reloading it, as it is not too remote: see *Morrison Steamship Co. Ltd* v *Greystoke Castle (Owners of Cargo lately laden on)*. Likewise, when a banker negligently gives a reference to one who acts on it, the duty is plain and the damage is not too remote: see *Hedley Byrne & Co. Ltd* v *Heller & Partners Ltd*.

The more I think about these cases, the more difficult I find it to put each into its proper pigeon-hole. Sometimes I say: 'There was no duty.' In others I say: 'The damage was too remote.' So much so that I think the time has come to discard those tests which have proved so elusive. It seems to me better to consider the particular relationship in hand, and see whether or not, as a matter of policy, economic loss should be recoverable. Thus in *Weller & Co.* v *Foot and Mouth Disease Research Institute* [1966] 1 QB 569 it was plain that the loss suffered by the auctioneers was not recoverable no matter whether it is put on the ground that there was no duty or that the damage was too remote. Again, in *Electrochrome Ltd* v *Welsh Plastics Ltd* [1968] 2 All ER 205, it is plain that the economic loss suffered by the plaintiffs' factory (due to the damage to the fire hydrant) was not recoverable, whether because there was no duty or that it was too remote.

4.2 Causation

JOBLING v ASSOCIATED DAIRIES LTD [1981] 2 All ER 752 (HL)

LORD WILBERFORCE: 1. Causation arguments. The unsatisfactory character of these is demonstrated by the case of *Baker* v *Willoughby* [1970] AC 467; [1969] 3 All ER 1528. I think that it can now be seen that Lord Reid's theory of concurrent causes even if workable on the particular facts of *Baker* v *Willoughby* (where successive injuries were sustained by the same limb) is as a general solution not supported by the authority he invokes (*Harwood* v *Wyken Colliery Co.* [1913] 2 KB 158) or workable in other cases. . . .

2. The 'vicissitudes' argument. This is that since, according to accepted doctrine, allowance, and if necessary some discount, has to be made in assessing loss of future earnings for the normal contingencies of life, amongst which 'illness' is normally enumerated, so, if one of these contingencies becomes actual before the date of trial, this actuality must be taken into account. Reliance is here placed on the apophthegm 'the court should not speculate when it knows'. This argument has a good deal of attraction. But it has its difficulties: it raises at once the question whether a discount is to be made on account of all possible 'vicissitudes' or only on account of 'non-culpable' vicissitudes (ie such that if they occur there will be no cause of action against anyone, the theory being that the prospect of being injured by a tort is not a normally foreseeable vicissitude) or only on account of 'culpable' vicissitudes (such as per contra). And if this distinction is to be made how is the court to act when a discounted vicissitude happens before trial? Must it attempt to decide whether there was culpability or not? And how is it to do this if, as is likely, the alleged culprit is not before it?

This actual distinction between 'culpable' and 'non-culpable' events was made, with supporting argument, in the Alberta case of *Penner* v *Mitchell* [1978] 5 WWR 328. One may add to it the rider that, as pointed out by Dickson J in the Supreme Court of Canada in *Andrews* v *Grand & Toy Alberta Ltd* (1978) 83 DLR (3d) 452 at 470, there are in modern society many public and private schemes which cushion the individual against adverse circumstances. One then has to ask whether a discount should be made in respect of (a) such cases or (b) cases where there is no such cushion. There is indeed in the 'vicissitude' argument some degree of circularity, since a discount in respect of possible events would only be fair if the actual event, discounted as possible, were to be taken into account when happening. But the whole question is whether it should be. One might just as well argue from what happens in 'actual' cases to what should happen in discountable cases.

In spite of these difficulties, the 'vicissitude' argument is capable in some, perhaps many, cases of providing a workable and reasonably just rule, and I would certainly not discountenance its use, either in the present case or in others.

The fact, however, is that to attempt a solution of these and similar problems, where there are successive causes of incapacity in some degree, on classical lines ('the object of damages for tort is to place the plaintiff in as good a position as if etc'; 'the defendant must compensate for the loss caused by his wrongful act, no more'; 'the defendant must take the plaintiff as he finds him etc') is, in many cases, no longer possible. We do not live in a world governed by the pure common law and its logical rules. We live in a mixed world where a man is protected against injury and misfortune by a whole web of rules and dispositions, with a number of timid legislative interventions. To attempt to compensate him on the basis of selected rules without regard to the whole must lead either to logical inconsistencies or to over or under compensation. As my noble and learned friend Lord Edmund-Davies has pointed out, no account was taken in *Baker* v *Willoughby* of the very real possibility that the plaintiff might obtain compensation from the Criminal Injuries Compensation Board. If he did in fact obtain this compensation he would, on the ultimate decision, be over-compensated.

In the present case, and in other industrial injury cases, there seems to me no justification for disregarding the fact that the injured man's employer is insured (indeed since 1972 compulsorily insured) against liability to his employees. The state has decided, in other words, on a spreading of risk. There seems to me no more justification for disregarding the fact that the plaintiff (presumably; we have not been told otherwise), is entitled to sickness and invalidity benefit in respect of his myelopathy, the amount of which may depend on his contribution record, which in turn may have been affected by his accident. So we have no means of knowing whether the plaintiff would be over-compensated if he were, in addition, to receive the assessed damages from his employer, or whether he would be under-compensated if left to his benefit. It is not easy to accept a solution by which a partially incapacitated man becomes worse off in terms of damages and benefit through a greater degree of incapacity. Many other ingredients, of weight in either direction, may enter into individual cases. Without any satisfaction I draw from this the conclusion that no general, logical or universally fair rules can be stated which will cover, in a manner consistent with justice, cases of supervening events, whether due to tortious, partially tortious, non-culpable or wholly accidental events. The courts can only deal with each case as best they can in a manner so as to provide just and sufficient but not excessive compensation, taking all factors into account. I think that this is what *Baker* v *Willoughby* did, and indeed that Lord Pearson reached his decision in this way; the rationalisation of the decision, as to which I at least have doubts, need and should not be applied to other cases. In the present case the Court of Appeal reached the unanswerable conclusion that to apply *Baker* v *Willoughby* to the facts of the present case would produce an unjust result, and I am willing to accept the corollary that justice, so far as it can be perceived, lies the other way and that the supervening myelopathy should not be disregarded. If rationalisation is needed, I am willing to accept the 'vicissitudes' argument as the best available. I should be more firmly convinced of the merits of the conclusion if the whole pattern of benefits had been considered, in however general a way. The result of the present case may be lacking in precision and rational justification, but so long as we are content to live in a mansion of so many different architectures this is inevitable.

I would dismiss the appeal.

LORD BRIDGE: . . . The vicissitudes principle itself, it seems to me, stems from the fundamental proposition of law that the object of every award of damages for monetary loss is to put the party wronged so far as possible in the same position, no better and no worse, as he would be in if he had not suffered the wrong in respect of which he claims. To assume that an injured plaintiff, if not injured, would have continued to earn his full wages for a full working life, is very probably to over-compensate him. To apply a discount in respect of possible future loss of earnings arising from independent ca[u]ses may be to under-compensate him. When confronted by future uncertainty, the court assesses the prospects and strikes a balance between these opposite dangers as best it can. But, when the supervening illness or injury which is the independent cause of loss of earning capacity has manifested itself before trial, the event has demonstrated that, even if the plaintiff had never sustained the tortious injury, his earnings would now be reduced or extinguished. To hold the tortfeasor, in this situation, liable to pay damages for a notional continuing loss of earnings attributable to the tortious injury is to put the plaintiff in a better position than he would be in if he had never suffered the tortious injury. Put more shortly, applying well-established principles for the assessment of damages at common law, when a plaintiff injured by the defendant's tort is wholly incapacitated from earning by supervening illness or accidental injury, the law will no longer treat the tort as a continuing cause of any loss of earning capacity. . . .

LORD KEITH: . . . the majority in *Baker* v *Willoughby* were mistaken in approaching the problems common to the case of a supervening tortious act and to that of supervening illness wholly from the point of view of causation. While it is logically correct to say that in both cases the original tort and the supervening event may be concurrent causes of incapacity, that does not necessarily, in my view, provide the correct solution. In the case of supervening illness, it is appropriate to keep in view that this is one of the ordinary vicissitudes of life, and when one is comparing the situation resulting from the accident with the situation, had there been no accident, to recognise that the illness would have overtaken the plaintiff in any event, so that it cannot be disregarded in arriving at proper compensation, and no more than proper compensation.

Additional considerations come into play when dealing with the problems arising where the plaintiff has suffered injuries from two or more successive and independent tortious acts. In that situation it is necessary to secure that the plaintiff is fully compensated for the aggregate effects of all his injuries. As Lord Pearson noted in *Baker* v *Willoughby* [1970] AC 467 at 495 it would clearly be unjust to reduce the damages awarded for the first tort because of the occurrence of the second tort, damages for which are to be assessed on the basis that the plaintiff is already partially incapacitated. I do not consider it necessary to formulate any precise juristic basis for dealing with this situation differently from the case of supervening illness. It might be said that a supervening tort is not one of the ordinary vicissitudes of life, or that it is too remote a possibility to be taken into account, or that it can properly be disregarded because it carries its own remedy. None of these formulations, however, is entirely satisfactory. The fact remains that the principle of full compensation requires that a just and practical solution should be found. In the event that damages against two successive tortfeasors fall to be assessed at the same time, it would be highly unreasonable if the aggregate of both awards were less than the total loss suffered by the plaintiff. The computation should start from an assessment of that total loss. The award against the second tortfeasor cannot in fairness to him fail to recognise that the plaintiff whom he injured was already to some extent incapacitated. In order that the plaintiff may be fully compensated, it becomes necessary to deduct the award so calculated from the assessment of the plaintiff's total loss and award the balance against the first tortfeasor. If that be a correct approach, it follows that, in proceedings against the first tortfeasor alone, the occurrence of the second tort cannot be successfully relied on by the defendant as reducing the damages which he must pay. That, in substance, was the result of the decision in *Baker* v *Willoughby*, where the supervening event was a tortious act, and to that extent the decision was, in my view, correct.

Before leaving the case, it is right to face up to the fact that, if a non-tortious supervening event is to have the effect of reducing damages but a subsequent tortious act is not, there may in some cases be difficulty in ascertaining whether the event in question is or is not of a tortious character, particularly in the absence of the alleged tortfeasor. Possible questions of contributory negligence may cause additional complications. Such difficulties are real, but are not sufficient, in my view, to warrant the conclusion that the distinction between tortious and non-tortious supervening events should not be accepted. The court must simply do its best to arrive at a just assessment of damages in a pragmatical way in the light of the whole circumstances of the case.

My Lords, for these reasons I would dismiss the appeal.

The rest of the House were in favour of dismissing the plaintiff's appeal.

**Hepple, M. H., and Matthews, B. A., *Tort: Cases and Materials*,
4th edn, Butterworths, 1996, p. 319**

One of Lord Keith's suggestions for reconciling *Baker* v *Willoughby* with *Jobling*—that a supervening tort is not one of the ordinary vicissitudes of life—met with some support from Lord Russell who was 'prepared to suggest' that physical damage from such an event would not be a 'relevant vicissitude'. Compare the approach of Lord Wilberforce and Lord Bridge set out ante.

To distinguish the situation in *Baker* v *Willoughby* is one thing, but the question of the justification for such a distinction must also be considered. It does seem unfair to allow a person such as the plaintiff in *Baker* v *Willoughby* to be worse off because he has been the victim of two torts rather than of one; and of course the decision obviates that result. However, it should be borne in mind that, as Lord Wilberforce made clear in *Jobling*, tort is not the only system of compensation. See T. Hervey (1981) 97 LQR 210 at 211–212 who, in commenting on the Court of Appeal's decision in *Jobling*, points out that an injured person can suffer, not just from 'falling between' two tortfeasors (which *Baker* v *Willoughby* does manage to avoid), but also from 'falling between' tort and another compensation system. See e.g. reg. 11(3) of the Social Security (General Benefit) Regulations S.I. 1982, No. 1408. In the light of this should a distinction be drawn between tortious and non-tortious supervening events?

4.3   Proof of Causation

McGHEE v *NATIONAL COAL BOARD* [1972] 3 All ER 1008 (HL)

LORD REID: It has always been the law that a pursuer [plaintiff] succeeds if he can show that the act of the defender [plaintiff] caused or materially contributed to his injury. There may have been two separate causes but it is enough if one of the causes arose from fault of the defender. The pursuer does not have to prove that this cause would of itself have been enough to cause him injury. That is well illustrated by the decision of this House in *Bonnington Castings Ltd* v *Wardlaw* [1956] AC 613. There the pursuer's disease was caused by an accumulation of noxious dust in his lungs. The dust which he had inhaled over a period came from two sources. The defenders were not responsible for one source but they could and ought to have prevented the other. The dust from the latter source was not in itself sufficient to cause the disease but the pursuer succeeded because it made a material contribution to his injury. The respondents . . . distinguish *Wardlaw's* case by arguing that then it was proved that every particle of dust inhaled played its part in causing the onset of the disease whereas in this case it is not proved that every minor abrasion played its part.

In the present case the evidence does not show—perhaps no one knows just how dermatitis of this type begins. It suggests to me that there are two possible ways. It may be than an accumulation of minor abrasions of the horny layer of skin is a necessary precondition for the onset of the disease. Or it may be that the disease starts at one particular abrasion and then spreads, so that multiplication of abrasions merely increases the number of places where the disease can start and in that way increases the risk of its occurrence.

I am inclined to think that the evidence points to the former view. But in a field where so little appears to be known with certainty I could not say that that is proved. If it were then this case would be indistinguishable from *Wardlaw's* case. But I think that in cases like this we must take a broader view of causation. The medical evidence is to the effect that the fact that the man had to cycle home caked with grime and sweat added materially to the risk that this disease might develop. It does not and could not explain just why that is so. But experience shows that it is so. Plainly that must be because what happens while the man remains unwashed can have a causative effect, although just how the cause operates is uncertain. I cannot accept the view expressed in the Inner House that once the man left the brick kiln he left behind the causes which made him liable to develop dermatitis. That seems to me quite inconsistent with a proper interpretation of the medical evidence. Nor can I accept the distinction drawn by the Lord Ordinary between materially increasing the risk that the disease will occur and making a material contribution to its occurrence.

LORD SALMON: I, of course, accept that the burden rests on the appellant to prove, on a balance of probabilities, a causal connection between his injury and the respondents' negligence. It is not necessary, however, to prove, that the respondents' negligence was the only cause of injury. A factor, by itself, may not be sufficient to cause injury but if, with other factors, it materially contributes to causing injury, it is clearly a cause of injury. Everything the present case depends on what constitutes a cause. I venture to repeat what I said in *Alphacell Ltd* v *Woodward*:

The nature of causation has been discussed by many eminent philosophers and also by a number of learned judges in the past. I consider, however, that what or who has caused a certain event to occur is essentially a practical question of fact which can best be answered by ordinary common sense rather than abstract metaphysical theory.

In the circumstances of the present case it seems to me unrealistic and contrary to ordinary common sense to hold that the negligence which materially increased the risk of injury did not materially contribute to causing the injury . . .

I think that the approach by the courts below confuses the balance of probability test with the nature of causation. Moreover, it would mean that in the present state of medical knowledge and in circumstances such as these (which are by no means uncommon) an employer would be permitted by the law to disregard with impunity his duty to take reasonable care for the safety of his employees.

My Lords, I would suggest that the true view is that, as a rule, when it is proved, on a balance of probabilities, that an employer has been negligent and that his negligence has materially increased the risk of his employee contracting an industrial disease, then he is liable in damages to that employee if he contracts the disease notwithstanding that the employer is not responsible for other factors which have materially contributed to the disease: *Bonnington Castings Ltd* v *Wardlaw* (above) and *Nicholson* v *Atlas Steel Foundry & Engineering Co. Ltd* [1957] 1 All ER 776. I do not find the attempts to distinguish those authorities from the present case at all convincing.

In the circumstances of the present case, the possibility of a distinction existing between (a) having materially increased the risk of contracting the disease, and (b) having materially contributed to causing the disease may no doubt be a fruitful source of interesting academic discussions between students of philosophy. Such a distinction is, however, far too unreal to be recognised by the common law. I would accordingly allow the appeal.

[See also the speeches of Lord Simon and Lord Kilbrandon to the same effect. Note, however, the approach taken by Lord Wilberforce. He explicitly acknowledged that the court was bridging the gap between 'materially increasing the risk' to the plaintiff and 'materially contributing' to his injury.]

KAY v AYRSHIRE AND ARRAN HEALTH BOARD [1987] 2 All ER 417 (HL)

An overdose of penicillin was negligently administered to treat a child suffering from meningitis. The child went into convulsions and suffered a degree of paralysis but remedial treatment had a positive effect. However, on discharge from hospital he was found to be suffering from profound deafness. The defendants denied liability for the deafness, which they claimed was due to the meningitis; it was argued that the disease commonly had this effect. Medical knowledge indicated that deafness occurred in approximately one third of all cases of pneumococcal meningitis (the type contracted by the boy in the present case). Lord Keith found that McGhee offered no assistance in the circumstances. 'Had there been acceptable medical evidence than an overdose of penicillin administered by lumbar puncture [as in the present case] was known to increase the risk that the meningitis, which the penicillin was intended to treat, would cause deafness the decision [in McGhee] would have been in point. It would be immaterial that medical science was unable to demonstrate the precise mechanism whereby the risk was increased.' It was found that no firm inferences could be drawn from the evidence and on the balance of probabilities the deafness was caused by the meningitis.

PAGE v SMITH (No. 2) [1996] 3 All ER 272 (CA)

This case was remitted from the House of Lords, to determine issues of **causation**. The court ruled that the test applicable in causation cases (determined on the 'balance of probabilities') was whether the defendant's negligence had caused or materially contributed to the development or the prolongation of the plaintiff's symptoms. A 'material' cause was one which was **more than** 'minimal' or 'trivial' or 'insignificant'. On the present facts, the **balance** of medical opinion regarded the defendant's negligence as a factor that could have materially contributed to the re-emergence of the plaintiff's condition and 'converted it from a mild and sporadic state to one of chronic intensity and permanence' (Sir Thomas Bingham MR, with whom Morritt LJ and Auld LJ agreed).

The court found that, since the trial judge, who had listened to all the evidence, was satisfied (**in the plaintiff's favour**) on this issue it would not be appropriate to disagree with him. The defendant's appeal was accordingly **dismissed**.

HILL v WILLIAM TOMKINS LTD, *The Guardian*, 18 October 1997

The plaintiff, a farmworker, was found by Mrs Justice Smith to have suffered ill-effects from organophosphate poisoning via exposure to the insecticide 'Actellic D' in the course of his employment with the defendant company. However, her Ladyship said that it was impossible for her to say, on the issue of legal **causation**, that she had found either for the plaintiff or against him:

> My findings are in general that he has suffered ill-effects from his exposure to Actellic D in 1993, and some of his continuing symptoms are attributable to that exposure.
>
> But some are in part attributable to psychological factors and have, at times, been exaggerated by him and his wife in description to doctors – and have also on occasions been affected by the frequency with which he has been examined by doctors ...
>
> I think that there have been times when he has needed the wheelchair, but I think his acceptance of it owed more to psychological factors than physical ones. I think that by then he had begun to accept the role of a sick man.

The defendant admitted that the exposure of the plaintiff to 'Actellic D' was tortious and that he suffered an adverse reaction to it, but argued that the effects of that exposure were short-lived and that any long-term ill-health he had suffered, since 1993, had not been caused or contributed to by the exposure.

It was stated, however, that the two sides were likely to come to an **agreement** on damages.

HOTSON v BERKSHIRE AREA HEALTH AUTHORITY [1987] 2 All ER 909 (HL)

The plaintiff was injured in an accident when he was 13 and he was sent to hospital. Due to an incorrect diagnosis damage to one of his hips was not discovered until several days later; the injury was of such severity that a major disability was likely in the future. He did in fact develop a major permanent disability at the age of 20. The defendants admitted negligence in relation to the original examination but claimed that the resultant delay had had no adverse effect on the plaintiff's long-term future. At first instance the judge found that there was a 75% risk of the plaintiff's condition developing as a result of his accident but the negligent diagnosis by the defendants had made his disability inevitable, thus preventing his 25% chance of health. The defendants claimed that though damages for a lost chance might be recoverable in contract (e.g. *Chaplin v Hicks* [1911] 2 KB 786) this was not the case in tort.

The Court of Appeal held that provided a loss of chance or benefit could be identified and valued a plaintiff could recover for it in tort—provided causation could be established. According to Sir John Donaldson and Croom-Johnson LJ possibly only nominal damages would be payable where a plaintiff was uninjured or otherwise unaffected by a loss of chance.

According to Sir John Donaldson, *McGhee* (above) shows that it is enough if a plaintiff proves on the balance of probabilities that a lack of washing facilities contributed materially to dermatitis. It is NOT necessary to prove that such facilities and their use by the plaintiff would have prevented the disease from developing. In loss of chance cases the court will look for a higher degree of substantiality. According to Sir John although it is always better specifically to ascertain the loss, calculate damages in full and discount accordingly, if the *extent* of a proved loss is unascertainable the plaintiff is entitled to damages.

He said that there were passages in *McGhee* suggesting that where an employer is in breach of a statutory duty and the injury suffered is that which the duty is intended to prevent but, in the current state of medical knowledge it is not possible to prove how effective the statutory precautions would have been in the particular circumstances, the burden of proof is reversed and it is up to the employer to prove no causal connection. The more orthodox interpretation would be this: in such circumstances, where there is a claim for breach of statutory duty, a prima facie inference of causation arises. 'However that might be, it is clear that no one suggested that it was possible to assess the likelihood that the provision of washing facilities would have prevented or reduced the severity of the dermatitis and that damages should be awarded on the basis of a discount reflecting such likelihood.'

In the House of Lords *Hotson* was decided in favour of the Health Authority on the basis that the plaintiff had failed to establish a causal link between his injury and the negligent diagnosis; on the balance of probabilities his damage was due to his accident. Questions concerning the loss of a chance could not arise where it had been found on the state of the evidence that before the defendant's duty arose the damage complained of had already been sustained or had become inevitable. The judge at first instance had found that even correct diagnosis and treatment would not have prevented the onset of the disability; the issue of *quantification* of damages therefore never arose.

Their Lordships left open the question whether loss of a chance (in the present case the lost chance of a better medical result) could be recovered in tort. Lord Bridge thought that [there] were 'formidable difficulties in the way of accepting the analogy [with *Chaplin* v *Hicks* (above)]'. According to Lord Mackay . . . unless and until this House departs from the decision in *McGhee* your Lordships

> cannot affirm the proposition that in no circumstances can evidence of loss of a chance . . . found a successful claim of damages.

LORD BRIDGE: In analysing the issue of law arising from his findings the judge said ([1985] 3 All ER 167 at 175, [1985] 1036 at 1034–1044):

> In the end the problem comes down to one of classification. Is this on true analysis a case where the plaintiff is concerned to establish causative negligence or is it rather a case where the real question is the proper quantum of damage? Clearly the case hovers near the border. Its proper solution in my judgment depends on categorising it correctly between the two. If the issue is one of causation then the defendants succeed since the plaintiff will have failed to prove his claim on the balance of probabilities. He will be lacking an essential ingredient of his cause of action. If, however, the issue is one of quantification then the plaintiff succeeds because it is trite law that the quantum of a recognised head of damage must be evaluated according to the chances of the loss occurring.

He reached the conclusion that the question was one of quantification and thus arrived at his award to the plaintiff of one quarter of the damages appropriate to compensate him for the consequences of the avascular necrosis.

It is here, with respect, that I part company with the judge. The plaintiff's claim was for damages for physical injury and consequential loss alleged to have been caused by the authority's breach of their duty of care. In some cases, perhaps particularly medical negligence cases, causation may be shrouded in mystery that the court can only measure statistical chances. But that was not so here. On the evidence there was a clear conflict as to what had caused the avascular necrosis. The authority's evidence was that the sole cause was the original traumatic injury to the hip. The plaintiff's evidence . . . was that the delay in treatment was a material contributory cause. This was a conflict, like any other about some relevant past event, which the judge could not avoid resolving on a balance of probabilities. Unless the plaintiff proved on a balance of probabilities that the delayed treatment was at least a material contributory cause of the avascular necrosis he failed on the issue of causation and no question of quantification could arise. But the judge's findings of fact, as stated in the numbered paragraphs (1) and (4) which I have set out earlier in this opinion, are unmistakably to the effect that on a balance of probabilities the injury caused by the plaintiff's fall left insufficient blood vessels intact to keep the epiphysis alive. This amounts to a finding of fact that the fall was the sole cause of the avascular necrosis.

The upshot is that the appeal must be allowed on the narrow ground that the plaintiff failed to establish a cause of action in respect of the avascular necrosis and its consequences. Your Lordships were invited to approach the appeal more broadly and to decide whether, in a claim for damages for personal injury, it can ever be appropriate, where the cause of the injury is unascertainable and all the plaintiff can show is a statistical chance which is less than even that, but for the defendant's breach of duty, he would not have suffered the injury, to award him a proportionate fraction of the full damages appropriate to compensate for the injury as the measure of damages for the lost chance.

There is a superficially attractive analogy between the principle applied in such cases as *Chaplin* v *Hicks* [1911] 2 KB 786 (award of damages for breach of contract assessed by reference to the lost chance of securing valuable employment if the contract had been performed) and *Kitchen* v *Royal Air Forces Association* [1958] 2 All ER 241 (damages for solicitors' negligence assessed by reference to the lost chance of prosecuting a successful civil action) and the principle of awarding damages for the lost chance of avoiding personal injury or, in medical negligence cases, for the lost chance of a better medical result which might have been achieved by prompt diagnosis and correct treatment. I think there are formidable difficulties in the way of accepting the analogy. But I do not see this appeal as a suitable occasion for reaching a settled conclusion as to whether the analogy can ever be applied.

As I have said, there was in this case an inescapable issue of causation first to be resolved. But if the plaintiff had proved on a balance of probabilities that the authority's negligent failure to diagnose and treat his injury promptly had materially contributed to the development of avascular necrosis, I know of no principle of English law which would have entitled the authority to a discount from the full measure of damage to reflect the chance that, even given prompt treatment, avascular necrosis might well still have developed. The decisions of this House in *Bonnington Castings Ltd* v *Wardlaw* [1956] AC 613 and *McGhee* v *National Coal Board* [1972] 3 All ER 1008 give no support to such a view.

I would allow the appeal to the extent of reducing the damages awarded to the plaintiff by £11,500 and the amount of any interest on that sum which is included in the award.

The rest of their Lordships agreed in allowing the appeal.

Hill, T., 'A Lost Chance for Compensation in the Tort of Negligence by the House of Lords' (1991) 54 *Modern Law Review* 511

Recently, the doctrine of compensation for a 'lost chance' has been subjected to detailed judicial and academic attention. Although the House of Lords in *Hotson* v *East Berkshire AHA* [1987] 2 All ER 909 denied recovery in the instant case, reversing the adoption of such a doctrine by the Court of Appeal, their Lordships unfortunately left open the question of whether, when a lost chance of recovery or of avoiding loss could be proved to result from a breach of duty, compensation for that 'lost chance' was recoverable in tort.

The term 'lost chance' is an ambiguous one. It is the aim of this article to show that there are in fact two types of chance, namely *personal chances* and *statistical chances*, and any claim based upon a 'lost chance' involves either a question of past or a future hypothetical question. Only in cases involving a future hypothetical question can there be a lost chance of any value. That is a lost 'personal' chance.

An appreciation of these two points is vital to an analysis of a loss of chance doctrine, and such an analysis shows that a loss of chance argument has no real substance in the way it has been hitherto applied. The loss of a statistical chance, standing alone, should not be considered a compensatable loss . . .

The traditional approach, simply put, is as follows. The damage which forms the 'gist of the negligence action' is the physical injury suffered by a plaintiff. Once it has been decided that the defendant has breached the required duty of care, the courts focus on determining whether there is a causative link between the breach of duty and the physical injury suffered, the traditional test being the 'but-for' test. The traditional effect has been that any physical injury, 'more likely than not' caused by the defendant's breach, will be recoverable.

But what if the physical injury suffered by a plaintiff is not, on the balance of probabilities, likely to have been caused by the defendant's breach? Can one reformulate the damage suffered, not as the physical injury, but rather as the 'lost chance' of avoiding the physical injury? Dr Stapleton argues in 'The Gist of Negligence' that this would not violate the traditional approach. The damage suffered would still have to be 'more likely that not' caused by the defendant's breach. Dr Stapleton argues that it is the traditional effects which are bypassed by such a reformulation of the destroyed interest. The gist of the negligence action becomes the 'lost chance'.

When examining such an argument, an important consideration has to be borne in mind. It is in fact possible to distinguish between two types of chances: 'statistical' and 'personal'. A statistical chance can only be an assessment, based on data collected from previous unconnected outcomes, giving a probability of that outcome in any non-individual case. The average life expectancy of a man is 68 years. This does not mean that Hotson had a personal chance, assessed at 50%, of living for 68 years or more. The average is a mere statistic. The length of Hotson's life is dependent on genetic and environmental preconditions. The statistics are irrelevant to Hotson as an individual; only a *personal* chance would be peculiar to a particular individual and would reflect these preconditions.

The significance of this distinction lies in the value that one may attribute to each chance. Should one, as a matter of policy, compensate for a lost statistical chance? . . . From the decision of the House of Lords in *Hotson*, at first glance it would appear that the doctrine of compensation for a 'lost chance' has been thrown out. However, a closer reading of the speeches by their Lordships, reveals that the House of Lords unfortunately left open the question of whether a loss of chance may form the gist of an action in the tort of negligence.

Lord Bridge found himself unable to reach a 'settled conclusion' regarding a 'loss of chance' doctrine generally. Although he saw a 'superficially attractive analogy' between the principles applied in cases such as *Chaplin* v *Hicks* and *Kitchener* v *RAFA* and the principle of awarding damages for the lost chance of avoiding personal injury, he considered that 'formidable difficulties' stood in the way of accepting such an analogy, and that this was not a suitable case in which to reach a settled conclusion whether the analogy could be applied.

However, *Chaplin* v *Hicks* is distinguishable from such medical cases of 'lost chance'. In *Chaplin*, a contract gave the plaintiff a right to belong to a limited class of competitors for a prize; a right of considerable value, as Fletcher Moulton LJ explained. To use Dr Stapleton's words, the 'gist' of the negligence was the lost right under the contract, not a lost chance. Causation must still be proved; that is, on the balance of probabilities, that the defendant's negligence resulted in a loss of that right. Then to value that right, once causation has been proved, one must take probabilities into account. Equally, in *Kitchen* v *RAFA*, another often quoted analogy, a clear breach of contract by the defendant solicitors deprived the plaintiff of a worthwhile action. Again, the 'gist' of the negligence was the action, not a lost chance.

> It is, of course, obvious that it is not only actions that are bound to succeed that have a value. Every action with a prospect of success has a value and it is a familiar task for the court to assess that value where negligence has prevented such an action being brought.

Lord Mackay in *Hotson* felt that it would be unwise to say that a plaintiff could never succeed by proving loss of a chance in a medical case. He quoted *McGhee* v *National Coal Board*, which he said stood for the following proposition: where it was proved the failure to provide washing facilities for the plaintiff at the end of his shift had materially increased the risk of dermatitis, 'it was proper to hold' that the failure to provide such facilities was a cause, to a material extent, of his developing dermatitis and thus entitled him to damages from his employers for their negligent failure, measured by his loss resulting from dermatitis. Material increase in the risk of developing dermatitis is equivalent to a material decrease in the chance of avoiding dermatitis . . .

The decision of the House of Lords in *Wilsher* was that the burden of proof remains on the plaintiff to prove the causative link between the defendant's negligence and *his injury*, although that link could legitimately be inferred from the evidence. This lends support to Lord Mackay's dictum in the earlier case of *Hotson*, which concerned the possibility of a loss of chance doctrine (as discussed). Such dictum can therefore be considered as standing. Consequently, from Lord Mackay's illustration one concludes that it was not a loss of chance case and the question of whether one can compensate for a lost chance, necessarily statistical, is still unresolved . . .

The emotive speech and obvious feelings of sympathy for a 'loss of chance' plaintiff must not let us colour or obscure the real issue—the existence of an 'evidentiary gap.' Proof of causation should not be accepted on anything less than the balance of probabilities, as is common with all civil actions. A loss of chance does not, by any means, always denote the loss of 'personal chance'; what is necessary is an unresolved future hypothetical question.

English courts cannot, at present, compensate for the 'loss of chance' when the essential question of past fact involved in the determination of causation concludes that the plaintiff in essence possessed no personal chance.

The House of Lords did not use the opportunity afforded in *Hotson* to clarify any limited loss of chance doctrine. It is urged that they do so at the earliest appropriate juncture, before variant 'loss of chance' arguments are advanced and accepted by the lower courts, as anticipated by Lord Mackay. It should be for Parliament to decide whether such rules are to be dispensed with, the casual question bypassed, and the policy of compensating for statistical chances begun. It is, in any case, argued that such a step would be wrong; the loss of a 'statistical chance' has no individual value and would lead to an unmanageable influx of 'loss of chance' actions.

Scott, W., 'Causation in Medico-Legal Practice—A Doctor's Approach to the "Lost Opportunity" Cases' (1992) 55 *Modern Law Review* 521

Advances in modern medicine increasingly provide patients with opportunities of cure which would hitherto have been impossible. If a patient can show that the doctor's negligence caused him to lose that opportunity, the question arises of how to quantify the damage in a way that is just for both parties. In this type of case, it is in the defendant's interest to show that the damage was caused by the disease process and was inevitable, regardless of the treatment; and it is in the plaintiff's interest to show that it was caused by the doctor's negligent failure to treat that illness. In other words, the plaintiff will attempt to show that the doctor's shortcoming caused him to lose the opportunity of cure. This difficulty is peculiar to medical negligence cases because, even with the best treatment available, some disease processes may not have a successful outcome. This means that the best that any plaintiff can achieve is to show that he lost the opportunity of being cured . . .

Hill supports the 'all or none' approach by drawing a distinction between what he calls *personal chances* and *statistical chances*. He argues that a statistical chance, with a figure taken from a series of medical cases, is irrelevant to the chance which any individual patient would have had. Using the example of negligent failure to diagnose cancer in good time, he rightly points out that we cannot know whether the patient with whom we are concerned belonged to the group which would have died anyway, or to the group which would have survived if it had been treated properly. Hill points out that we are dealing with a question of past fact. In reality, the patient must have belonged to one group or to the other, and he argues that it is artificial to base a decision on statistics. To do so means calculating the chances of a favourable outcome from a series of perhaps hundreds of other cases. Hill distinguishes this from future hypothetical questions which involve events which have not yet happened and where it is acceptable to think in terms of percentage chances. Hill attempts to justify the unacceptability of using a statistical chance in relation to a particular plaintiff, on the basis that the statistics do not take sufficient account of the facts of the individual's case.

However, there are two reasons why it is not unreasonable to use statistical chances when considering an individual plaintiff's case. The first reason is that when a series of medical cases is being designed for research purposes, the members of the cohort are matched as closely as possible to ensure that results are not vulnerable to accusations that they have been distorted by factors which are unrelated to the one which is being studied. For example, if a surgeon wishes to compare the benefits of surgery, radiotherapy and chemotherapy in breast cancer, he will ensure that the patients whom he puts into his study are as closely matched as possible as far as all the variables are concerned. These variables would be matters such as age of the patient, size of the tumour, evidence of distant spread of the tumour, treatment which has already been given, and the presence or absence of other unrelated illnesses. Furthermore, when the figures from the study are subjected to analysis, the statistician will calculate whether or not any advantage of one treatment over another is statistically significant. This ensures that one treatment is not allowed the claim of being superior to another because of marginal differences which may have occurred even between patients who belonged to the same group. For this reason, a well designed and modern series of medical statistics will be a fairly accurate reflection of the chances that any individual patient would have had of a good outcome.

There is a second reason why a statistical approach helps to promote justice. The 'all or none' approach is reasonably fair to patients who, statistically, would have had chances somewhere near 0 per cent or 100 per cent of the predicted outcome, but it tends to be unfair to those patients whose chances were nearer the 50 per cent borderline. If a patient had a fifty-fifty chance of survival without the doctor's negligence, both parties are more likely to be content with a settlement of 50 per cent of full damages: the patient whose case reached a 49 per cent probability will at least feel that he has recovered something and the doctor, faced with a patient whose case reached a 51 per cent chance, will feel that he has not paid out unduly. Thus, justice will have been seen to have been done to both sides . . .

Lewis, C., 'A Last Chance' [1986] *Professional Negligence* **119**

After arguing that it is unclear **when** the courts will regard a case as one to be examined on the basis of liability or on the basis of lost chance, the author concludes:

> In the final analysis it may be that one can do no better than say that whether one will be awarded proportionate damages for a lost chance, rather than all or nothing on the probabilities, will depend on the court's being willing to see an injury in the lost chance itself.

Hotson is an example of a decision on the basis of 'all or nothing'.

WILSHER v ESSEX AREA HEALTH AUTHORITY [1988] 1 All ER 871 (HL)

A prematurely born baby had developed a condition, typically found in premature babies who have been given too much oxygen, known as retrolental fibroplasia (RLF), which had had serious consequences for his sight. The Court of Appeal in *Wilsher* appeared to extend the decision in *McGhee*. Mustill LJ said: 'If it is an established fact that conduct of a particular kind creates a risk that injury will be caused to another or increases an existing risk that injury will ensue; and if the two parties stand in such a relationship that one party owes a duty not to conduct himself in that way; and if the first party does conduct himself in that way; and if the other party does suffer injury of the kind to which the risk related; then the first party is taken to have caused the injury by breach of duty, even though the existence and extent of the contribution made by the breach cannot be ascertained.'

However, their Lordships held that in cases of negligence it is for the plaintiff to establish causation. The two important points decided in this case were (1) that in law the trainee/learner medical doctor has to be judged by the same standard as that which would be applied to more experienced colleagues; and (2) that, contrary to the attempt by Peter Pain J in *Clark* v *MacLennan* [1983] 1 All ER 416 (which he had accepted as trial judge in this case) to allow it, a plaintiff cannot shift the burden of proof on to the defendant doctor (or the doctor's employer) merely by showing that a particular step in specific treatment which was designed to accept a risk, or to minimise it, has not been taken in the circumstances of the case. Therefore, even where the defendant creates the risk of a particular injury (and this amounts to a breach of duty) and the plaintiff suffers that injury, the burden of proof remains with the plaintiff.

In the opinion of Lord Bridge *McGhee* did not lay down any new principle of law 'whatever'. On the contrary, it affirmed the principle that the onus of proving causation lies on the plaintiff.

It was found that *McGhee's* case was 'wholly different' from the present one in that in the former there was only one possible 'agent' which could have caused the plaintiff's injury; in *Wilsher* there were several possible 'agents' which could have caused the plaintiff's condition and a casual link was not established. A breach of duty plus injury could not raise a presumption of causation. Their Lordships allowed the Authority's appeal against the decision of the trial judge (affirmed by a majority of the Court of Appeal) and ordered a retrial on the causation issue.

4.3.1 INTERVENING CAUSES

LAMB v LONDON BOROUGH OF CAMDEN [1981] 2 All ER 408 (CA)

LORD DENNING MR: The truth is that all these three, duty, remoteness and causation, are all devices by which the courts limit the range of liability for negligence or nuisance. As I said recently in *Campania Financiera Soleada SA* v *Hamoor Tanker Corpn Inc, The Borag* [1981] 1 All ER 856 at 861 '. . . it is not every consequence of a wrongful act which is the subject of compensation. The law has to draw a line somewhere.'

Sometimes it is done by limiting the range of the persons to whom duty is owed. Sometimes it is done by saying that there is a break in the chain of causation. At the other times it is done by saying that the consequence is too remote to be a head of damage. All these devices are useful in their way. But ultimately it is a question of policy for the judges to decide. . . .

Looking at the question as one of policy, I ask myself: whose job was it to do something to keep out the squatters? And, if they got in, to evict them? To my mind the answer is clear. It was the job of the owner of the house, Mrs Lamb, through her agents. That is how everyone in the case regarded it. It has never been suggested in the pleadings or elsewhere that it was the job of the council. No one ever wrote to the council asking them to do it. The council were not in occupation of the house. They had no right to enter it. All they had done was to break the water main outside and cause the subsidence. After they had left the site, it was Mrs Lamb *herself* who paved the way for squatters by moving out all her furniture and leaving the house unoccupied and unfurnished. There was then, if not before, on the judge's findings, a reasonably foreseeable risk that squatters might enter. She ought to have taken steps to guard against it. She says that she locked the doors and pulled the shutters. That turned out to be insufficient, but it was her responsibility to do more. At any rate, when the squatters did get in on the first occasion in 1974, it was then her agents who acted on her behalf. They got the squatters out. Then, at any rate, Mrs Lamb or her agents ought to have done something effective. But they only put up a few boards at a cost of £10. Then there was the second invasion in 1975. Then her agents did recognise her responsibility. They did what they could to get the squatters out. They eventually suceeded. But no one ever suggested throughout that it was the responsibility of the council.

In her evidence Mrs Lamb suggested that she had not the money to do more. I do not think the judge accepted the suggestion. Her agents could well have made the house secure for a modest sum which was well within her capabilities.

On broader grounds of policy, I would add this: the criminal acts here, malicious damage and theft, are usually covered by insurance. By this means the risk of loss is spread throughout the community. It does not fall too heavily on one pair of shoulders alone. The insurers take the premium to cover just this sort of risk and should not be allowed, by subrogation, to pass it on to others. . . . It is commonplace nowadays for the courts, when considering policy, to take insurance into account. . . .

So here, it seems to me, that, if Mrs Lamb was insured against damage to the house and theft, the insurers should pay the loss. If she was not insured, that is her misfortune.

Taking all these policy matters into account, I think the council are not liable for the acts of these squatters.

I would dismiss this appeal.

WATKINS LJ: It seems to me that if the sole exclusive test of remoteness is whether the fresh damage has arisen from an event or act which is reasonably foreseeable, or reasonably foreseeable as a possibility, or likely or quite likely to occur, absurd, even bizarre, results might ensue in actions for damages for negligence. Why, if this test were to be rigidly applied to the facts in the *Dorset Yacht* case, one can envisage the Home Office being found liable for the damage caused by an escaped borstal boy committing a burglary in John o'Groats. This would plainly be a ludicrous conclusion.

I do not think that words such as, among others, 'possibility', 'likely' or 'quite likely' assist the application of the test of reasonable foreseeability. If the crisply stated test which emanates from *The Wagon Mound (No. 2)* is to be festooned with additional words supposedly there for the purpose of amplification or qualification, an understandable application of it will become impossible.

In my view the *Wagon Mound* test should always be applied without any of the gloss which is from time to time being applied to it.

But when so applied it cannot in all circumstances in which it arises conclude consideration of the question of remoteness, although in the vast majority of cases it will be adequate for this purpose. In other cases, the present one being an example of these in my opinion, further consideration is necessary, always providing, of course, a plaintiff survives the test of reasonable foreseeability.

This is because the very features of an event or act for which damages are claimed themselves suggest that the event or act is not on any practical view of it remotely in any way connected with the original act of negligence. These features will include such matters as the nature of the event or act, the time it occurred, the place where it occurred, the identity of the perpetrator and his intentions, the responsibility, if any, for taking measures to avoid the occurrance and matters of public policy.

A robust and sensible approach to this very important area of the study of remoteness will more often than not produce, I think, an instinctive feeling that the event or act weighed in the balance is too remote to sound in damages for the plaintiff. I do not pretend that in all cases the answer will come easily to the inquirer. But that the question must be asked and answered in all these cases I have no doubt.

To return to the present case, I have the instinctive feeling that the squatters' damage is too remote. I could not possibly come to any other conclusion, although on the primary facts I, too, would regard that damage or something like it as reasonably foreseeable in these times.

We are here dealing with unreasonable conduct of an outrageous kind. It is notorious that squatters will take the opportunity of entering and occupying any house, whether it be damaged or not, which is found to be unoccupied for more than a very temporary duration. In my opinion this kind of antisocial and criminal behaviour provides a glaring example of an act which inevitably, or almost so, is too remote to cause a defendant to pay damages for the consequences of it.

Accordingly, I would hold that the damge caused by the squatters in the present case is too remote to be recovered from these defendants....

The plaintiff's appeal was dismissed unanimously.

WARD v CANNOCK CHASE DISTRICT COUNCIL [1985] 3 All ER 537

SCOTT J: Although the three judgments in *Lamb v Camden London Borough* [1981] QB 625 give different reasons for coming to the same conclusion, a common ratio is, to my mind, identifiable at least in the judgments of Oliver and Watkins LJJ. Both start with the reasonable foreseeable test as expressed in *The Wagon Mound (No. 2)*. Both, where damage caused by independent third parties in concerned, require something more than merely the foreseeable possibility of the occurrence of the damage. Oliver LJ would ask what the reasonable man, if he thought about the consequences of the negligent act or omission, would actually foresee. Unless a reasonable man would actually foresee the intervening acts in question, Oliver LJ would hold the damage too remote. Watkins LJ would exclude the damage if, on a practical view, it did not seem sufficiently connected with the negligent act or omission. Lord Reid [in *Dorset Yacht*] would ask whether the intervening acts were the very kind of thing likely to happen.

I do not think there is any real difference between Lord Reid's and Oliver LJ's formulations. Each, in my view, expresses in different language the same essential requirements. There is, however, a difference between their approach and that of Watkins LJ. Both Lord Reid and Oliver LJ would examine the nature of the damage in question from the anterior moment when the negligent act or omission took place. From that standpoint they would ask whether the damage would be actually foreseen by a reasonable man, or would be regarded as the very kind of thing likely to happen. Watkins LJ's approach, however, would start with the damage under review and look back to the negligent act or omission in order to find some sufficient connection. In most cases, this difference of approach would I think make no difference to the result.

Salmond and Heuston, *The Law of Torts*, 20th edn, Sweet & Maxwell, 1992, pp. 522–525

Common sense and causation

This doctrine of remoteness of damage is one of very considerable obscurity and difficulty. Questions of causation 'have vexed the best of human intellects for 2,400 years.' Yet 'In the varied web of affairs, the law must abstract some consequences as relevant, not perhaps on ground of pure logic but simply for practical reasons.' There are many judicial statements praising the value of common-sense principles and stating that in any case the question of issue can be determined by applying common-sense to the facts of the particular case. There are also many judicial warnings against too ready a reliance on 'philosophy' or the 'grave danger of being led astray by scholastic theories of causation and their ugly and barely intelligible jargon'. Some judges and writers go so far as to say that it is impossible to characterise any principles on which common-sense proceeds. 'This seems a counsel of despair which we should hesitate to accept. . . . Common sense is not a matter of inexplicable or arbitrary assertions, and the casual notions which it employs, though flexible and complex and subtly influenced by context, can be shown to rest, at least in part, on stateable principles; though the ordinary man who uses them may not, without assistance, be able to make them explicit.' Nor should it be assumed (as it seems sometimes to have been done) that philosophy is equivalent to that department of it called metaphysics: much can be learnt from the empiricists of the past and their influential descendants of the present day.

An attempt has been made to state more explicitly those common-sense principles of causation according to which the courts have consistently said that causal questions must be decided. These principles cannot provide conclusive answers to the complex causal questions which the courts are sometimes obliged to answer, but serve rather as an organising framework within which a choice may be made according to whatever considerations of policy the law may consider to be relevant. At the outset it should be noted that a question as to the cause of an event may lead to answers which vary according to the context of the inquiry. 'A car skids while cornering at a certain point, turns turtle, and bursts into flames. From the car-driver's point of view, the cause of the accident was cornering too fast, and the lesson is that one must drive more carefully. From the county surveyor's point of view, the cause was a defective road surface, and the lesson is that one must make skid-proof roads. From the motor-manufacturers' point of view, the cause was defective design, and the lesson is that one must place the centre of gravity lower.' The conclusion is that the word 'cause' can hardly be defined, but is one 'to which converging limits can be assigned in its context as concrete cases come to be decided.'

So the basic principle in the common-sense notion of cause is that '*the cause*' is one condition selected from a complex set of conditions which, according to known generalisations, are together jointly sufficient for the occurrence of the consequence in question. For, even though the road surface is defective, a car will not skid unless certain other conditions are satisfied—e.g. the car must be of a certain weight and construction and be moving at a certain minimum speed. Within this jointly sufficient set of conditions common sense (like the law) distinguishes mere conditions from causes, and the principal criterion for this distinction lies in the contrast between (1) a voluntary human action and other conditions, (2) an abnormal contingency (e.g. an act of God or a coincidence) and other conditions. The legal distinctions of *novus actus interveniens*, superseding cause, and proximate cause may be defined in terms of these contrasts. It should be noted that although either an abnormal contingency or a voluntary human act may negative causal connection, there are differences between them. Thus an abnormal contingency only negatives causal connection if it intervenes in time between the wrongful act and the consequence; whereas a voluntary act may negative causal connection even though it precedes in time both the wrongful act and the harm.

Finally, it is worth noting that the broad open question 'What is the cause of this event?' is more suited to those inquiries in which we are seeking to discover the explanation of how or why some contingency happened. But when an explanation has been provided (or when none is needed) the more circumscribed question 'Given this wrongful act (or other designated event) and given this loss or harm, is the latter the consequence of the former?' is appropriate. To ask the question in this way makes it plain that we are not seeking to understand what has happened but to allocate responsibility. This form of question is helpful when we are considering a case which raises the issue of *novus actus interveniens*, for it makes it plain that the real problem is whether some third factor (which may be the act or omission of a human being, or the act of an animal, or a natural event or state of affairs) prevents the attribution of given harm to a given action or contingency as its consequence.

Weir, T., *A Casebook on Torts*, 7th edn, Sweet & Maxwell, 1992, p. 232

These opinions are pretty desperate. Watkins LJ relies on intuition like a lay-judge in medieval Germany; Lord Denning, as usual, where law and sense deviate, opts for sense;

Oliver LJ is reduced to semantics. The difficulties inherent in remoteness have certainly been enhanced as liability in tort has been imposed ever more widely, but the despair comes, it is fair to say, from the delusive simplicity of *The Wagon Mound*. 'Foreseeability rules, O.K.?' is simply inadequate to cope with the complexities of life and litigation. Given the trouble caused by the foreseeability formula in this area, we may be glad that it has been abandoned as the sole determinant of the existence of a duty to take care. The substitution of 'proximity' in that context reminds us that in the United States it is only if a tortfeasor's conduct is a 'proximate cause' of harm that he is responsible for it.

The decision in *Lamb* and its readings of Lord Reid's words in *Dorset Yacht* are considered along with other cases in which the defendant was sued for damage done by thieves and vandals in *Smith* v *Littlewoods Organisation* [1987] 1 All ER 710, 723–727, *per* Lord Mackay LC and also by Scott J in *Ward* v *Cannock Chase DC* [1985] 3 All ER 537, where the local authority which rendered the plaintiff's house uninhabitable was held liable for the damage done to it by vandals, but not for the damage they caused to his chattels in it.

4.3.1.1 Duty approach

SMITH v LITTLEWOODS ORGANISATION LTD (CHIEF CONSTABLE, FIFE CONSTABULARY, THIRD PARTY) [1987] 1 All ER 710 (HL)

LORD GOFF: My Lords, the Lord President founded his judgment on the proposition that the defenders, who were both owners and occupiers of the cinema, were under a general duty to take reasonable care for the safety of premises in the neighbourhood.

Now if this proposition is understood as relating to a general duty to take reasonable care *not to cause damage* to premises in the neighbourhood (as I believe that the Lord President intended it to be understood) then it is unexceptionable. But it must not be overlooked that a problem arises when the pursuer is seeking to hold the defender responsible for having failed to *prevent* a third party from causing damage to the pursuer or his property by the third party's own deliberate wrongdoing. In such a case, it is not possible to invoke a general duty of care: for it is well recognised that there is no *general* duty of care to prevent third parties from causing such damage. The point is expressed very clearly in Hart and Honore, *Causation in the Law*, 2nd ed. (1985), when the authors state, at pp. 196–197:

> The law might acknowledge a general principle that, whenever the harmful conduct of another is reasonably foreseeable, it is our duty to take precautions against it . . . But, up to now, no legal system has gone so far as this . . .

The same point is made in Fleming, *The Law of Torts*, 6th ed. (1983), where it is said, at p. 200: 'there is certainly no *general* duty to protect others against theft or loss.' I wish to add that no such general duty exists even between those who are neighbours in the sense of being occupiers of adjoining premises. There is no general duty upon a householder that he should act as a watchdog, or that his house should act as a bastion, to protect his neighbours house. . . .

Another statement of principle, which has been much quoted, is the observation of Lord Sumner in *Weld-Blundell* v *Stephens* [1920] AC 956, when he said, at p. 986: 'In general . . . even though A is in fault he is not responsible for injury to C which B, a stranger to him, deliberately chooses to do.' This dictum may be read as expressing the general idea that the voluntary act of another, independent of the defender's fault, is regarded as a novus actus interveniens which, to use the old metaphor, 'breaks the chain of causation.' But it also expresses a general perception that we ought not to be held person or property of those in the vicinity, should be held liable to such a person for damage so caused to him. It is useful to take the example of a fire hazard, not only because that is the relevant hazard which is alleged to have existed in the present case, but also because of the intrinsically dangerous nature of fire hazards as regards neighbouring property. Let me give an example of circumstances in which an occupier of land might be held liable for damage so caused. Suppose that a person is deputed to buy a substanial quantity of fireworks for a village fireworks display on Guy Fawkes night. He stores them, as usual, in an unlocked garden shed abutting onto a neighbouring house. It is well known that he does this.

Mischievous boys from the village enter as trespassers and, playing with the fireworks, cause a serious fire which spreads to and burns down the neighbouring house. Liability might well be imposed in such a case; for, having regard to the dangerous and tempting nature of fireworks, interference by naughty children was the very thing which, in the circumstances, the purchaser of the fireworks ought to have guarded against.

But liability should only be imposed under this principle in the cases where the defender has negligently caused or permitted the creation of a source of danger on his land, and where it is foreseeable that third parties may trespass on his land and spark it off, thereby damaging the pursuer or his property. Moreover it is not to be forgotten that, in ordinary households in this country, there are nowadays many things which might be described as possible sources of fire if interfered with by third parties, ranging from matches and firelighters to electric irons and gas cookers and even oil-fired central heating systems. These are common places of modern life; and it would be quite wrong if householders were to be held liable in negligence for acting in a socially acceptable manner. No doubt the question whether liability should be imposed on defenders in a case where a source of danger on his land has been sparked off by the deliberate wrongdoing of a third party is a question to be decided on the facts of each case, and it would, I think, be wrong for your Lordships' House to anticipate the manner in which the law may develop: but I cannot help thinking that cases where liability will be so imposed are likely to be very rare.

There is another basis upon which a defender may be held liable for damage to neighbouring property caused by a fire started on his (the defender's) property by the deliberate wrongdoing of a third party. This arises where he has knowledge or means of knowledge that a third party has created or is creating a risk of fire, or indeed has started a fire, on his premises, and then fails to take such steps as are reasonably open to him (in the limited sense explained by Lord Wilberforce in *Goldman* v *Hargrave* [1967] 1 AC 645, 663–664) to prevent any such fire from damaging neighbouring property. If, for example, an occupier of property has knowledge, or means of knowledge, that intruders are in the habit of tresspassing upon his property and starting fires there, thereby creating a risk that fire may spread to and damage neighbouring property, a duty to take reasonable steps to prevent such damage may be held to fall upon him. He could, for example, take reasonable steps to keep the intruders out. He could also inform the police; or he could warn his neighbours and invite their assistance. If the defender is a person of substantial means, for example a large public company, he might even be expected to employ some agency to keep a watch on the premises. What is reasonably required would, of course, depend on the particular facts of the case. I observe that, in *Goldman* v *Hargrave*, such liability was held to sound in nuisance; but it is difficult to believe that, in this respect, there can be any material distinction between liability in nuisance and liability in negligence. . . .

I wish to emphasise that I do not think that the problem in these cases can be solved simply through the mechanism of foreseeability. When a duty *is* cast upon a person to take precautions against the wrongdoing of third parties, the ordinary standard of foreseeability applies and so the possibility of such wrongdoing does not have to be very great before liability is imposed. I do not myself subscribe to the opinion that liability for the wrongdoing of others is limited because of the unpredictability of human conduct. So, for example, in *Haynes* v *Harwood* [1935] 1 KB 146, liability was imposed although it cannot have been at all likely that a small boy would throw a stone at the horses left unattended in the public road; and in *Stansbie* v *Troman* [1948] 2 KB 48, liability was imposed although it cannot have been at all likely that a thief would take advantage of the fact that the defendant left the door on the latch while he was out. Per contra, there is at present no general duty at common law to prevent persons from harming others by their deliberate wrongdoing, however foreseeable such harm may be if the defender does not take steps to prevent it . . .

I wish to emphasise that I do not think that the problem in these cases can be solved simply through the mechanism of foreseeability. When a duty *is* cast on a person to take precautions against the wrongdoing of third parties, the ordinary standard of foreseeability applies; and so the possibility of such wrongdoing does not have to be very great before liability is imposed. I do not myself subscribe to the opinion that liability for the wrongdoing of others is limited because of the unpredictability of human conduct. So, for example, in *Haynes* v *Harwood* [1935] 1 KB 146 liability was imposed although it cannot have been at all likely that a small boy would throw a stone at the horses left unattended in the public road, and in *Stansbie* v *Troman* [1948] 2 KB 48 liability was imposed although it cannot have been at all likely that a thief would take advantage of the fact that the defendant left the door on the latch while he was out. Per contra, there is at present no general duty at common law to prevent persons from harming others by their deliberate wrongdoing, however foreseeable such harm may be if the defender does not take steps to prevent it.

Of course, if persons trespass on the defender's property and the defender either knows or has the means of knowing that they are doing so and that in doing so they constitute a danger to neighbouring property, then the defender may be under an affirmative duty to take reasonable steps to exclude them, in the liited sense explained by Lord Wilberforce in *Goldman* v *Hargrave* [1967] 1 AC 645 at 663–664, but that is another matter. I incline to the opinion that this duty arises from the fact that the defender, as occupier, is in exclusive control of the premises on which the danger has arisen.

In preparing this opinion, I have given careful consideration to the question whether *P Perl (Exporters) Ltd* v *Camden London BC* [1984] QB 342, in which I myself was a member of the Court of Appeal, was correctly decided. I have come to the conclusion that it was, though on rereading it I do not think that my own judgment was very well expressed. But I remain of the opinion that to impose a general duty on occupiers to take reasonable care to prevent others from entering their property would impose an unreasonable burden on ordinary householders and an unreasonable curb on the ordinary enjoyment of their property; and I am also of the opinion that to do so would be contrary to principle. It is very tempting to try to solve all problems of negligence be reference to an all-embracing criterion of foreseeability, thereby effectively reducing all decisions in this field to questions of fact. But this comfortable solution is, alas, not open to us. The law has to accommodate all the untidy complexity of life; and there are circumstances where considerations of practical justice impel us to reject a general imposition of liability for foreseeable damage. An example of this phenomenon is to be found in cases of pure economic loss . . . As the present case shows, another example of this phenomenon is to be found in cases where the plaintiff has suffered damage through the deliberate wrongdoing of a third party; and it is not surprising that once again we should find the courts seeking to identify specific situations in which liability can properly be imposed. Problems such as these are solved in Scotland, as in England, by means of the mechanism of the duty of care . . .

For these reasons I would dismiss these appeals.

The House was agreed in dismissing the pursuers' appeals (from the Scottish courts).

4.3.1.2   Intervening medical negligence

R v *CHESHIRE* [1991] 3 All ER 670 (CCA)

BELDAM LJ: In the criminal law, and in particular in the law of homicide, whether the death of a deceased was the result of the accused's criminal act is a question of fact for the jury, but it is a question of fact to be decided in accordance with legal principles explained to the jury by the judge. We think the matter cannot be better put than it was by Goff LJ in *R* v *Pagett* (1983) 76 Crim App R 279 at 288 . . .

Goff LJ went on to express his indebtedness to Hart and Honore *Causation in the law*. We too are indebted to section IV of Chapter 12 of that work. Under the heading 'Doctor's or Victim's Negligence' the authors deal with the cases in which an assult or wounding is followed by improper medical treatment or by refusal of treatment by the victim or failure on his part to take proper care of the wound or injury. The authors trace from Hale's *Pleas of the Crown* and Stephen's *Digest of the Criminal Law* the emergence of a standard set by Stephen of common knowledge or skill which they suggest appears to require proof of something more than ordinary negligence in order that one who inflicts a wound may be relieved of liability for homicide. And they refer to most American authorities as requiring at least gross negligence to negative causal connection. English decisions, however, have not echoed these words. In conclusion the authors state: 'Our survey of the place of doctor's and victim's negligence in the law of homicide, where differences of policy between civil and criminal law might be expected to make themselves felt, yields a meagre harvest . . . On Stephen's view, which has some modern support, there is no difference between civil and criminal law as regards the effect of medical negligence; in each case gross negligence (want of common knowledge or skill) is required to negative responsibility for death.'

Whatever may be the differences of policy between the approach of the civil and the criminal law to the question of causation there are we think reasons for a critical approach when importing the language of the one to the other.

Since the apportionment of responsibility for damage has become commonplace in the civil law, judges have sought to distinguish the blameworthiness of conduct from its causative effect. Epithets suggestive of degrees of blameworthiness may be of little help in deciding how potent the conduct was in causing the result. A momentary lapse of concentration may lead to more serious consequences than a more glaring neglect of duty. In the criminal law the jury considering the factual question, did the accused's act cause the deceased's death, will we think derive little assistance from figures of speech more appropriate to conveying degrees of fault or blame in questions of apportionment. Unless authority suggests otherwise, we think such figures of speech are to be avoided in giving guidance to a jury on the question of causation. Whilst medical treatment unsuccessfully given to prevent the death of a victim with the care and skill of competent medical practitioner will not amount to an intervening cause, it does not follow that treatment which falls below that standard of care and skill will amount to such a cause. As Professors Hart and Honore comment, treatment which falls short of the standard expected of the competent medical practitioner is unfortunately only too frequent in human experience for it to be considered abnormal in the sense of extraordinary. Acts or omissions of a doctor treating the victim for injuries he has received at the hands of an accused may conceivably be so extraordinary as to be capable of being regarded as acts independent of the conduct of the accused but it is most unlikely that they will be . . .

It seems to us that [this case] demonstrates the difficulties in formulating and explaining a general concept of causation but what we think does emerge from this and the other cases is that when the victim of a criminal attack is treated for wounds or injuries by doctors or other medical staff attempting to repair the harm done, it will only be in the most extraordinary and unusual case that such treatment can be said to be so independent of the acts of the accused that it could be regarded in law as the cause of the victim's death to the exclusion of the accused's acts.

Where the law requires proof of the relationship between an act and its consequences as an element of responsibility, a simple and sufficient explanation of the basis of such a relationship has proved notoriously elusive.

In a case in which the jury have to consider whether negligence in the treatment of injuries inflicted by the accused was the cause of death, we think it is sufficient for the judge to tell the jury that they must be satisfied that the Crown have proved that the acts of the accused caused the death of the deceased, adding that the accused's acts need not be the sole cause or even the main cause of the death, it being sufficient that his acts contributed significantly to that result. Even though negligence in the treatment of the victim was the immediate cause of his death, the jury should not regard it as excluding the responsibility of the accused unless the negligent treatment was so independent of his acts and in itself so potent in causing death that they regard the contribution made by his acts as insignificant.

It is not the function of the jury to evaluate competing causes or to choose which is dominant provided they are satisfied that the accused's acts can fairly be said to have made a significant contribution to the victim's death. We think the word 'significant' conveys the necessary substance of a contribution made to the death which is more than negligible . . .

In the present case . . . although . . . we think that the judge erred when he invited the jury to consider the degree of fault in the medical treatment rather than its consequences, we consider that no miscarriage of justice has actually occurred. Even if more experienced doctors than those who attended the deceased would have recognised the rare complication in time to have prevented the deceased's death, that complication was a direct consequence of the appellant's acts which remained a significant cause of his death. We cannot conceive that on the evidence given any jury would have found otherwise. Accordingly we dismiss the appeal.

4.4 Remoteness

4.4.1 DIRECTNESS

4.4.1.1 Reasonable foreseeability

OVERSEAS TANKSHIP (UK) LTD v MORTS DOCK AND ENGINEERING CO. LTD
(THE WAGON MOUND) [1961] AC 388 (PC)

VISCOUNT SIMONDS: Enough has been said to show that the authority of *Polemis* has been severely shaken though lip-service has from time to time been paid to it. In their Lordships' opinion it should no longer be regarded as good law. It is probable that many cases will for that reason have a different result, though it is hoped that the law will be thereby simplified, and that in some cases, at least, palpable injustice will be avoided. For it does not seem consonant with current ideas of justice or morality that for an act of negligence, however slight or venial, which results in some trivial foreseeable damage the actor should be liable for all consequences however unforeseeable and however grave, so long as they can be said to be 'direct', It is a principle of civil liability, subject only to qualifications which have no present relevance that a man must be considered to be responsible for the probable consequences of his act. To demand more of him is too harsh a rule, to demand less is to ignore that civilised order requires the observance of a minimum standard of behaviour.

This concept applied to the slowly developing law of negligence has led to a great variety of exprosssions which can, as it appears to their Lordships, be harmonised with little difficulty with the single exception of the so-called rule in *Polemis*. For, if it is asked why a man should be responsible for the natural or necessary or probable consequences of his act (or any other similar description of them) the answer is that it is not because they are natural or necessary or probable, but because, since they have this quality, it is judged by the standard of the reasonble man that he ought to have foreseen them. Thus it is that over and over again it has happened that in different judgments in the same case, and sometimes in a single judgment, liablity for a consequence has been imposed on the ground that it was reasonably foreseeable or, alternatively, on the ground that it was natural or necessary or probable. The two grounds have been treated as coterminous, and so they largely are. But, where they are not, the question arises to which the wrong answer was given in *Polemis*. For, if some limitation must be imposed upon the consequences for which the negligent actor is to be held responsible—and all are agreed that some limitation there must be—why should that test (reasonable foreseeability) be rejected which, since he is judged by what the reasonable man ought to foresee, corresponds with the common conscience of mankind, and a test (the 'direct' consequence) be substituted which leads to nowhere but the never-ending and insoluble problems of causation. 'The lawyer,' said Sir Frederick Pollock, 'cannot afford to adventure himself with philosophers in the logical and metaphysical controversies that beset the idea of cause.' Yet this is just what he has most unfortunately done and must continue to do if the rule in *Polemis* is to prevail. A conspicuous example occurs when the actor seeks to escape liability on the ground that the 'chain of causation' is broken by a 'nova causa' or 'novus actus interveniens.' . . .

At an early stage in this judgment their Lordships intimated that they would deal with the proposition which can best be stated by reference to the well-known dictum of Lord Sumner: 'This however goes to culpability not to compensation.' It is with the greatest respect to that very learned judge and to those who have echoed his words, that their Lordships find themselves bound to state their view that this proposition is fundamentally false.

It is, no doubt, proper when considering tortious liability for negligence to analyse its elements and to say that the plaintiff must prove a duty owed to him by the defendant, a breach of that duty by the defendant, and consequent damage. But there can be no liability until the damage has been done. It is not the act but the consequences on which tortious liability is founded. Just as (as it has been said) there is no such thing as negligence in the air, so there is no such thing as liability in the air. Suppose an action brought by A for damage caused by the carelessness (a neutral word) of B, for example, a fire caused by the careless spillage of oil. It may, of course, become relevant to know what duty B owed to A, but the only liability that is in question is the liability for damage by fire. It is vain to isolate the liability from its context and to say that B is or is not liable, and then to ask for what damage he is liable. For his liability is in respect of that damage and no other. If, as admittedly it is, B's liability (culpability) depends on the reasonable foreseeability of the consequent damage, how is that to be determined except by the foreseeability of the damage which in fact happened—the damage in suit? And, if that damage is unforeseeable so as to displace liability at large, how can the liability be restored so as to make compensation payable?

But, it is said, a different position arises if B's careless act has been shown to be negligent and has caused some foreseeable damage to A. Their Lordships have already observed that to hold B liable for consequences however unforeseeable of a careless act, if, but only if, he is at the same time liable for some other damage however trivial, appears to be neither logical nor just. This becomes more clear if it supposed that similar unforeseeable damage is suffered by A and C but other foreseeable damage, for which B is liable, by A only. A system of law which would hold B liable to A but not to C for the similar damage suffered by each of them could not easily be defended. Fortunately, the attempt is not necessary. For the same fallacy is at the root of the proposition. It is irrelevant to the question whether B is liable for unforeseeable damage that he is liable for foreseeable damage, as irrelevant as would the fact that he had trespassed on Whiteacre be to the question whether he has trespassed on Blackacre. Again, suppose a claim by A for damage by fire by the careless act of B. Of what relevance is it to that claim that he has another claim arising out of the same careless act? It would surely not prejudice his claim if that other claim failed: it cannot assist it if it succeeds. Each of them rests on its own bottom, and will fail if it can be established that the damage could not reasonably be foreseen. We have come back to the plain common sense stated by Lord Russell of Killowen in *Bourhill* v *Young* [1943] AC 92, 101. As Denning LJ said in *King* v *Phillips* [1953] 1 QB 429: 'there can be no doubt since *Bourhill* v *Young* that the test of *liability for shock* is foreseeability of *injury by shock*.' Their Lordships substitute the word 'fire' for 'shock' and endorse this statement of the law.

McKendrick, E., *Tort Textbook*, **6th edn, HLT Publications, 1992, pp. 144–7**

So it appears the kind of damage is divided into a narrower category than damage to property simpliciter. It is submitted that there are two major policy reasons behind this narrower approach in the case of damage to property. The first policy reason is that the plaintiff whose property is damaged is much more likely to be insured against such damage than is the person who is injured as the result of the defendant's negligence. So the plaintiff, in the case of property damage, is often in a better position to bear the loss. The second policy reason is that the measure of damage in a case of property damage can be far greater than in a case of personal injury, for example where, as in *The Wagon Mound*, the negligence leads to extensive damage to a ship. Where this is the case there is a reluctance on the part of the court to find the defendant liable for the whole of the loss, especially when, as we have already noted, the plaintiff is likely to be insured against such a loss.

So it is submitted that there are good reasons behind the courts' narrower approach to damage to property. The difficult question which remains is how we divide up property damage. We could say that the vital question is whether the events which have occurred are within the 'risk' which has been created by the defendant. This does not take us very far unless a definition is provided of the risk which was created by the defendant. For example what was the risk created by the defendants in the *Wagon Mound* cases? Another approach is to say that the distinction depends on the nature of the impact of the damage. This approach can explain *The Wagon Mound (No 1)* because it can be said that the damage was done by the impact of fire whereas the foreseeable impact was damage by fouling. But it is doubtful whether or not it is applicable to all cases and again much depends on how impact is defined.

It is submitted that the instability here is reflective of the insecure terminology which is used in this area. According to the test laid down in *The Wagon Mound (No 1)* the kind of damage must be foreseeable but neither the manner nor the extent need be foreseeable. This view was reiterated by the House of Lords in *Hughes* v *Lord Advocate*. However it is submitted that there is no clear-cut distinction between the kind of damage and the manner by which the damage occurs. For example it could be said that in *The Wagon Mound (No 1)* the kind of damage was damage to property and that the manner of damage was by fire rather than by fouling and so the defendants were liable. Equally it could be said that in *Hughes* the kind of damage was damage by fire and that damage by explosion was different in kind from damage by fire and so the defendants were not liable. What the courts do not tell us is how they go about defining the 'kind' of damage as opposed to the 'manner' in which the damage has occurred. Until we know how the courts set about that task the present test appears to be capable of almost infinite expansion or contraction as the courts enjoy considerable discretion in deciding what is the kind of damage. However it is submitted that the courts are correct in taking a narrower approach in the case of damage to property because tort law is generally less assiduous of interests in property than it is in a person's interest in his personal security and because of the availability of insurance in cases of damage to property . . .

The traditional explanation of the difference between *Polemis* and *Wagon Mound* is that the former only requires that the damage be a direct result of the defendant's negligence whereas the latter requires that the damage be a reasonably foreseeable consequence of the defendant's negligence. The analysis offered here suggests that the traditional explanation is not entirely accurate . . .

There does not appear to be any difference between the two rules in relation to damage to the person. The difference appears to lie in the rules applicable to damage to property because *Wagon Mound* adopts a narrower approach than the one which was adopted in *Polemis* . . .

Stanton, K. M., *The Modern Law of Tort***, Sweet & Maxwell, 1994, pp. 96–7**

. . . This result is one of the major triumphs of the principle of fault liability. On the facts of the *Wagon Mound* the new test narrowed the range of consequences for which the admittedly negligent defendant was held liable. It was possible to view the result as producing an internally consistent body of law: all three stages of the negligence test, duty, breach and damage had been made subject to tests based on the concept of foreseeability.

Although the *Wagon Mound* principle has clearly been accepted by English law the reasoning on which it is based is not unassailable. As a matter of policy it is not immediately apparent why the law should opt for a rule which limits the liability of a defendant who has broken a legally recognised duty at the expense of an innocent victim of this act. If it is an important part of the deterrent role of tort that the costs of accidents should fall on the least cost avoider it is presumably the case that it is the real rather than notional costs which should be placed in the equation. In addition, in efficiency terms the cost of obtaining additional insurance cover against unlikely marginal risks is likely to be cheaper for the person who bears the cost of insuring the standard risks.

It is also arguable that the vagueness of the criterion of reasonable foreseeability coupled with the exceptions to the rule which have been recognised has meant that few, if any, cases have been decided differently as a result of the change. The concept of reasonable foreseeability is difficult to define and any search for internal consistency in the theory underlying negligence is almost certain to be fruitless. Foreseeability is not the sole determinant of liability at any stage of the negligence process. As a test of the existence of a duty of care it has been heavily qualified by notions of policy and proximity and can have little role to play in an era of incremental development of the law. Foreseeability is relevant, but not central, to issues of breach of a negligence duty; of more relevance are questions of the likelihood of the risk, its magnitude, the ease of protecting against it and the advantages of running it. In any event it is by no means certain that foreseeability bears the same meaning in all three contexts. The view has been expressed in Chapter 3 that foreseeability in the context of the standard of care in negligence is the equivalent of the word conceivable. This places a person who is under a duty of care in a position of having to take reasonable care to avoid remote risks. The word may not bear so wide a meaning when it is used to test the existence of a duty of care as notions such as proximity and a special relationship may be used to restrict its meaning.

In the context of remoteness of damage, to use foreseeability as the equivalent of conceivable may produce results which are wider than would be achieved under *Re Polemis* . . .

4.4.1.2   The way in which the damage occurs

HUGHES v LORD ADVOCATE [1963] 1 All ER 705 (HL)

LORD JENKINS: It is true that the duty of care expected in cases of this sort is confined to reasonably foreseeable dangers, but it does not necessarily follow that liability is escaped because the danger actually materialising is not identical with the danger reasonably foreseen and guarded against. Each case must depend on its own particular facts. For example (as pointed out in the opinions), in the present case the paraffin did the mischief by exploding, not burning, and it is said that, while a paraffin fire (caused, e.g. by the upsetting of the lighted lamp or otherwise allowing its contents to leak out) was a reasonably foreseeable risk so soon as the pursuer got access to the lamp, an explosion was not. To my mind the distinction drawn between burning and explosion is too fine to warrant acceptance. Supposing the pursuer had on the day in question gone to the site and taken one of the lamps, and upset it over himself, thus setting his clothes alight, the person to be considered responsible for protecting children from the dangers to be found there would presumably have been liable. On the other hand, if the lamp, when the boy upset it, exploded in his face, he would have had no remedy, because the explosion was an event which could not reasonably be foreseen. This does not seem to me to be right. I think that in these imaginary circumstances the danger would be a danger of fire of some kind, e.g. setting alight to his clothes or causing him bodily hurt. If there is a risk of such a fire as that I do not think that the duty of care prescribed in *Donoghue* v *Stevenson* [1932] AC 562 is prevented from coming into operation by the presence of the remote possibility of the more serious event of an explosion.

Lords Guest, Morris, Pearce and Reid agreed in allowing the pursuer's (plaintiff's) appeal. *The Wagon Mound* (1961) was not discussed by the House in this case.

DOUGHTY v TURNER MANUFACTURING CO. LTD [1964] 1 All ER 98 (CA)

DIPLOCK LJ: There is no room today for mystique in the law of negligence. It is the application of common morality and common sense to the activities of the common man. He must take reasonable care to avoid acts or omissions which he can reasonably foresee would be likely to injure his neighbours; but he need do no more than this. If the act which he does is not one which he could, if he thought about it, reasonably foresee would injure his neighbour it matters not whether he does it intentionally or inadvertently. The learned judge's finding, uncontested on appeal, that in the state of knowledge as it was at the time of the accident the defendants could not reasonably have foreseen that the immersion of the asbestos cement cover in the liquid would be likely to injure anyone, must lead to the conclusion that they would have been under no liability to the plaintiff if they had intentionally immersed the cover in the liquid. The fact that it was done inadvertently cannot create any liability, for the immersion of the cover was not an act which they were under any duty to take any care to avoid.

It was, however, argued by counsel for the plaintiff that, even though the risk of explosion on immersion of the cover was not one which the defendants could reasonably foresee, the plaintiff can, nevertheless, recover because one of the defendants' servants inadvertently either knocked the cover into the liquid or allowed it to slip in, thus giving rise to a foreseeable risk of splashing the hot liquid onto the plaintiff and injuring him by burning. The actual damage sustained by the plaintiff was damage of the same kind, that is by burning, as could be foreseen as likely to result from knocking the cover into the liquid or allowing it to slip in, and his counsel contended that this was sufficient to impose a duty on the defendants owed to the plaintiff to take reasonable care to avoid knocking the cover into the liquid, or allowing it to slip in, and that the plaintiff's damage flowed from their breach of this duty. Such a proposition might, before *The Wagon Mound*, have been supported by *Re Polemis*, but that decision of the Court of Appeal is no longer law; and counsel for the plaintiff relied principally on *Hughes* v *Lord Advocate* [1963] AC 837, a case in which the House of Lords treated *The Wagon Mound* as correctly stating the law, but distinguished it on the facts. I do not think that this authority assists him. In *Hughes* v *Lord Advocate* the breach of duty by the defendant on which reliance was placed was his omission to guard a dangerous allurement to children, which was liable to cause them injury (*inter alia*) by burning. The infant plaintiff, to whom the duty was owed, was allured and was injured by burning, although the particular concatenation of circumstances which resulted in his burns being more serious than they would have been expected to be could not reasonably have been foreseen. They were, nevertheless, the direct consequence of the defendant's breach of duty and the injury was of the same kind as could reasonably have been foreseen, although of unforeseen gravity. But in the present case the defendants' duty owed to the plaintiff in relation to the only foreseeable risk, that is of splashing, was to take reasonable care to avoid knocking the cover into the liquid or allowing it to slip in such a way as to cause a splash which would injure the plaintiff. Failure to avoid knocking it into the liquid, or allowing it to slip in, was of itself no breach of duty to the plaintiff. It is not clear on the evidence whether the dropping of the cover onto the liquid caused any splash at all. The judge made no finding on this. The reasoning in his judgment is not sufficiently explicit to make it clear whether the point argued by counsel for the plaintiff, with which I am now dealing, formed part of his ratio decidendi, though some of his observations in the course of the hearing suggest that it was not. However that may be, it is incontrovertible that, even if there was some slight splash when the cover fell onto the liquid, the plaintiff was untouched by it and it caused him no injury. There was thus, in the circumstances of this case, no breach of duty to the plaintiff involved in inadvertently knocking the cover into the liquid or inadvertently allowing it to slip in.

4.4.1.3 Extent of harm

Dias, R.W.M., 'Remoteness of Liability and Legal Policy'
[1962] *Cambridge Law Journal* 178

Much of the foregoing analysis has been directed to underlining the part played by policy in the evolution of the rules of remoteness. It is evident that the course of history has witnessed a complete reversal of attitude from one of concern for the plaintiff to one of concern for the defendant. Neither of these should predominate, and it would be in keeping with the traditions of the judicial office to ensure a just balance between these two opposing considerations, as between others. It might be supposed that in view of the legislative creation of strict liability in the interest of plaintiffs the balance is restored by bending the common law principles so that they favour defendants. This is potentially dangerous. Redressing a balance should not mean the creation of tension, and such there will inevitably be between statute and common law if they came to be based on such sharply conflicting ideals. This in itself may not be considered too serious, but there is some cause for disquiet when one appreciates the fact that the overwhelming majority of statutory torts are found in the sphere of industrial law. It is undoubtedly the case that workmen are generally plaintiffs and employers defendants. If the policy of statute law were to favour the former and common law the latter, such an aggravation of the existing tension between these two groups and between statute and common law in this context is wholly deplorable.

The law of tort ought to pay due regard to the point of view of both plaintiff and defendant, and this will best be accomplished if its principles are such as to leave room for the exercise of discretion. The balance can be kept readjusted in accordance with fluctuating circumstances. A good deal is possible even within the framework of the fault principle as now declared by the Judicial Committee, and that is by varying far more the 'standard of care' as occasion demands. This could be indulgently low or stringent to the utmost degree. In this way, in the first place, it might be possible to effect some compromise between statutory torts and common law negligence through a concept of 'statutory negligence', that is, by treating the standard and scope of the conduct required of the defendant as having been fixed by the statute. More might also be done by raising the standards of care in common law negligence to the verge even of strictness when the interests of plaintiffs demand that there should be liability. The concept of reasonable foresight itself appears to be capable of the most catholic interpretations.

The fault principle could thus in large measure be made even now to apply in favour of plaintiffs as well as defendants, but whether this is done or not will entirely depend on judicial sympathies. What has not always been realised is that the *Polemis* principle could likewise have yielded a comparable range of results. Inclined though it was in favour of plaintiffs, it was sufficiently broad as to enable a tribunal, if it so wished, to find for the defendant in a great many instances. It was never understood or presented in a sense that would have enabled all this, and perhaps more, to be accomplished. 'I am not sure it has been everywhere understood': so concluded one of the greatest of modern judges. It has now had to suffer the fate of Desdemona.

4.4.1.4   Relative nature of foreseeability

THE WAGON MOUND (No. 2) [1966] 2 All ER 709 (PC)

LORD REID: The findings of the learned trial judge are as follows:
(1) Reasonable people in the position of the officers of the *Wagon Mound* would regard the furnace oil as very difficult to ignite upon water. (2) Their personal experience would probably have been that this had very rarely happened. (3) If they had given attention to the risk of fire from the spillage, they would have regarded it as a possibility, but one which could become an actuality only in very exceptional circumstances. (4) They would have considered the chances of the required exceptional circumstances happening whilst the oil remained spread on the harbour waters as being remote. (5) I find that the occurrence of damage to the plaintiff's property as a result of the spillage was not reasonably foreseeable by those for whose acts the defendant would be responsible. (6) I find that the spillage of oil was brought about by the careless conduct of persons for whose acts the defendant would be responsible. (7) I find that the spillage of oil was a cause of damage to the property of each of the plaintiffs. (8) Having regard to those findings, and because of finding (5), I hold that the claim of each of the plaintiffs, framed in negligence, fails . . .

The crucial finding of Walsh J in this case is in finding (5): that the damage was 'not reasonably foreseeable by those for whose acts the defendant would be responsible.' That is not a primary finding of fact but an inference from the other findings, and it is clear from the learned judge's judgment that in drawing this inference he was to a large extent influenced by his view of the law. The vital parts of the findings of fact which have already been set out in full are (1) that the officers of the *Wagon Mound* [1961] AC 388 'would regard furnace oil as very difficult to ignite upon water'—not that they would regard this as impossible; (2) that their experience would probably have been 'that this had very rarely happened'—not that they would never have heard of a case where it had happened, and (3) that they would have regarded it as a 'possibility, but one which could become an actuality only in very exceptional circumstances'—not, as in *The Wagon Mound (No. 1)*, that they could not reasonably be expected to have known that this oil was capable of being set afire when spread on water. The question which must now be determined is whether these differences between the findings in the two cases do or do not lead to different results in law.

In *The Wagon Mound (No. 1)* the Board were not concerned with degrees of foreseeability because the finding was that the fire was not foreseeable at all. So Lord Simonds had no cause to amplify the statement that the 'essential factor in determining liability is whether the damage is of such a kind as the reasonable man should have foreseen.' But here the findings show that some risk of fire would have been present to the mind of a reasonable man in the shoes of the ship's chief engineer. So the first question must be what is the precise meaning to be attached in this context to the words 'foreseeable' and 'reasonably foreseeable.'

Before *Bolton* v *Stone* [1951] AC 850 the cases had fallen into two classes: (1) those where, before the event, the risk of its happening would have been regarded as unreal either because the event would have been thought to be physically impossible or because the possibility of its happening would have been regarded as so fantastic or far-fetched that no reasonable man would have paid any attention to it—'a mere possibility which would never occur to the mind of a reasonable man' (*per* Lord Dunedin in *Fardon* v *Harcourt-Rivington* (1932) 146 LT 391) — or (2) those where there was a real and substantial risk or chance that something like the event which happens might occur, and then the reasonable man would have taken the steps necessary to eliminate the risk.

Bolton v *Stone* [1951] AC 850 posed a new problem. There a member of a visiting team drove a cricket ball out of the ground onto an unfrequented adjacent public road and it struck and severely injured a lady who happened to be standing in the road. That it might happen that a ball would be driven onto this road could not have been said to be a fantastic or far-fetched possibility: according to the evidence it had happened about six times in 28 years. And it could not have been said to be a far-fetched or fantastic possibility that such a ball would strike someone in the road: people did pass along the road from time to time. So it could not have been said that, on any ordinary meaning of the words, the fact that a ball might strike a person in the road was not foreseeable or reasonably foreseeable—it was plainly foreseeable. But the chance of its happening in the foreseeable future was infinitesimal. A mathematician given the data could have worked out that it was only likely to happen once in so many thousand years. The House of Lords held that the risk was so small that in the circumstances a reasonable man would have been justified in disregarding it and taking no steps to eliminate it.

But it does not follow that, no matter what the circumstances may be, it is justifiable to neglect a risk of such a small magnitude. A reasonable man would only neglect such a risk if he had some valid reason for doing so, e.g., that it would involve considerable expense to eliminate the risk. He would weigh the risk against the difficulty of eliminating it. If the activity which caused the injury to Miss Stone had been an unlawful activity, there can be little doubt but that *Bolton* v *Stone* would have been decided differently. In their Lordships' judgment *Bolton* v *Stone* did not alter the general principle that a person must be regarded as negligent if he does not take steps to eliminate a risk which he knows or ought to know is a real risk and not a mere possibility which would never influence the mind of a reasonable man. What that decision did was to recognise and give effect to the qualification that it is justifiable not to take steps to eliminate a real risk if it is small and if the circumstances are such that a reasonable man, careful of the safety of his neighbour, would think it right to neglect it . . .

In their Lordships' view a properly qualified and alert chief engineer would have realised there was a real risk here and they do not understand Walsh J to deny that. But he appears to have held that if a real risk can properly be described as remote it must then be held to be not reasonably foreseeable. That is a possible interpretation of some of the authorities. But this is still an open question and on principle their Lordships cannot accept this view. If a real risk is one which would occur to the mind of a reasonable man in the position of the defendant's servant and which he would not brush aside as far-fetched, and if the criterion is to be what that reasonable man would have done in the circumstances, then surely he would not neglect such a risk if action to eliminate it presented no difficulty, involved no disadvantage, and required no expense.

SLATTER v BRITISH RAILWAYS BOARD [1966] 2 Lloyd's Rep 395

The plaintiff, an employee of the defendant, was startled by a very loud noise from shunting wagons; he put his hand on a railway line to assist his balance and the hand was severed by a passing railway truck. It was found that the noise was negligently caused and that it could have foreseeably startled someone.

SACHS J, finding for the plaintiff, said: When once one startles somebody, while one cannot foresee the precise way in which they will react or jump or do something as a result of being startled, yet one of the things that is definitely 'on the cards' . . . is that they should jump or [otherwise react] and then one gets to the point that they may be injured.

4.5 Summary

Jones, M., *Textbook on Torts*, 4th edn, Blackstone Press, 1993, p. 135

It is hardly sufficient . . . to say that the test of remoteness of damage is foreseeability because the crucial question is, what is it, precisely, that has to be foreseen? Foreseeability gives the court scope to manipulate the outcome of a particular case by defining what has to be foreseen either broadly or narrowly.

J.G. Fleming, *The Law of Torts*, 8th edn, The Law Book Co. Ltd, 1992, p. 70

The tendency is . . . to define the risk, or rather harm within the scope of the risk, somewhat broadly—insisting on foreseeability not so much of the 'particular' injury as of 'harm of a like general character'—and paying heed neither to the extent nor the precise manner of its occurrence.

Markesinis, B. S., and Deakin, S. F., *Tort Law*, 3rd edn, OUP, 1994, p. 90

This argument, [in relation to the risk approach] however, depends on how risk is formulated. If it is stated in terms of the creation of a 'fire risk' as such, it holds good, but if it is stated in terms of the creation of a 'risk to property', it does not hold good: property is equally at risk whether one does something to set light to it, or to smash it. The word 'risk', therefore is no improvement on 'kind of damage'. Suppose that the defendant carelessly drops a plank into the hold of a ship, Knowing that the plaintiff is working there. The plank narrowly misses the plaintiff, but strikes a spark, which cause a fire, and he is burned. The only foreseeable damage to him was by impact, so the *Wagon Mound* distinction suggests that he should have no remedy for being burned instead of being struck. Would the 'risk' principle endorse, or avoid, such a ridiculous result? If it is said that the risk created by dropping the plank was some kind of injury to the plaintiff, we would be back on *Polemis*, and a similar formulation could equally have applied to *Wagon Mound* itself.

Winfield and Jolowicz on Tort, 14th edn, Sweet & Maxwell 1994, p. 144

Foreseeability is a relative, not an absolute, concept. In *Wagon Mound (No. 1)* the Privy Council accepted and based its reasoning on the trial judge's finding that the defendant did not know and could not reasonably have been expected to know that furnace oil was capable of being set alight when spread on water. In *Wagon Mound (No. 2)* [1967] 1 AC 617 different evidence was presented and in the Privy Council the trial judge's finding to similar effect, not being a primary finding of fact but an inference from other findings, was rejected. It was held that there was a real risk of fire such as would have been appreciated by a properly qualified and alert chief engineer and this, given the fact that there was no justification for discharging oil into Sydney Harbour, was sufficient to fix liability on the defendants. In other words, the mere fact that the damage suffered was unlikely to occur does not relieve the defendant of liability if his conduct was unreasonable—a proposition [difficult to distinguish] from that in *Polemis* itself.

4.6   End of Chapter Assessment Question

David leaves an old paraffin lamp burning in his garden shed, where there is a strong draught. As a result a fire starts, and spreads rapidly. This fire combines with another fire, the source of which is unknown, and the fire produced by this combination threatens Penny's house, which is located a quarter of a mile away. Penny is holding a garden party at the time, and a general panic ensues. Richard, the butler, drops a tray containing rare antique glasses, one of which cuts the arm of Fay, a haemophiliac, who bleeds to death before hospital treatment can be obtained. Penny's house is destroyed in the conflagration.

Advise David, on his liability in tort, if any.

4.7   End of Chapter Assessment Outline Answer

D = David, P = Penny, R = Richard, F = Fay

D has left a paraffin lamp burning in his shed in the presence of a strong draught of air. This creates a fire which spreads rapidly and combines with another fire. The augmented fire destroys P's property and F, one of P's guests, is killed.

In order to assess D's liability it will be necessary to consider first whether the fire in his shed was started **tortiously**. On the facts given there is no clear indication of public or private nuisance, although it is feasible that an 'active' paraffin lamp could, together with the draught, constitute a 'state of affairs'; nor is there anything in the circumstances to suggest that there exists any special use of land sufficient to attract application of the rule analogous to *Rylands* v *Fletcher* for fire: see e.g. *Mason* v *Levy Auto Parts*.

There is no evidence of any intentional/deliberate/reckless behaviour on the part of D, therefore it seems reasonable to conclude that it would be the tort of negligence which would provide an appropriate cause of action for the injured parties.

With regard both to P's claim for damage to property and F's (i.e. her estate's or dependants') claim for death, it would have to be shown that D owed a duty of care to the injured parties on the facts. To this end, the familiar criteria of 'foreseeability'/'proximity'/'just and reasonable' would need to be satisfied. The **general** aspect of *Caparo* v *Dickman* would be relevant at this point.

It would be quite likely that a duty would be owed in the circumstances, especially if e.g., it could be shown by the plaintiffs that the area was prone to fire, say because of unusually hot, dry weather. According to the available evidence the fire 'spreads rapidly'.

The next point to consider is whether D breached the duty of care i.e. was negligent on the facts. Leaving a lamp burning in a shed where there is a strong draught may be thought to be evidence of this. Furthermore, have any appropriate (feasible) steps been taken to prevent the fire from spreading? It has spread for a quarter of a mile: it would presumably take some time for the fire to travel that distance and there would be a duty to abate e.g. *Goldman* v *Hargrave*.

Matters of **causation** are often of importance and D's apparently rapidly spreading fire combined with **another** fire before it threatened P's house. Expert evidence would need to be gathered in order to ascertain the precise position, but the question would arise as to whether D's fire would have spread to P's property on its own or whether it needed to combine with the other fire in order to do so. The 'but for' test would, no doubt, be employed should this issue be raised by D. See, e.g., *Barnett* v *Chelsea Hospital*.

The court would have to calculate the degree of responsibility for the damage caused by the fire according to the degree of blameworthiness of the relevant parties. This could only be done after considering all the evidence; in particular expert opinion would be of crucial importance.

A defendant can be liable for damage provided that his tort is a **substantial** or **material** cause; the tort does not need to be the **sole** cause of the damage. The provisions of the Civil Liability (Contributions) Act 1978 apply in such cases, but on the present facts the origins of the second fire are 'uncertain'. If the combination was **not** necessary, in other words if

D's fire would have spread on its own, **without** augmentation from another source, the 'but for' test would obscure the true picture of events. Where there are several concurrent causes, each of them being sufficient on its own to cause the damage, the 'but for' test would cancel out each cause and thus the court would apply 'common sense' and assess the share of blame as best it could – perhaps on an equal basis. See, e.g., *Knightley* v *Johns*. Again, the provisions of the 1978 Act would apply but again, on the facts, the origins of the second fire are unknown. Therefore, D might be solely responsible in the sense that he could not discover the identity of the other tortfeasor(s) in order to claim contribution.

On the assumption that D's **tortious** behaviour is at least **a** cause of the damage sustained by P and F in the circumstances, it is necessary to consider the role played by R in this case. Is it possible that **he** has been negligent and that his negligence is **the** or **a** cause of the damage? In other words, D should consider whether R's act in dropping the glasses is a *novus actus interveniens* in the circumstances. (In the case of F's damage, this would also raise the possibility of vicarious liability on the part of P.)

It is submitted that R's reaction would, on the facts, be more likely to be regarded as a foreseeable reflex action (see e.g. *Carmarthenshire CC* v *Lewis*) than an act of negligence.

The question of general remoteness of damage also arises on the facts. Would it avail D to argue that the damage suffered by both P and F is not of the 'kind' or 'type' reasonably foreseeable in the circumstances, in terms of *The Wagon Mound*?

Technical evidence is crucial in these matters, but *prima facie* damage by fire (property and personal injury) is the very kind of damage foreseeable in the circumstances. P's house is destroyed and her antique glasses are broken. It is submitted that the special feature of the glasses goes only to **value** not nature and in that sense the 'egg-shell' principle would apply: see *The Arpad*.

According to *Hughes* v *Lord Advocate* the precise **way** in which damage occurs does not have to be foreseeable, and this would strengthen the point made above concerning R's reaction.

As to F's death, the dropping of the glasses by R has already been dealt with above – in two respects viz. the reflex reaction and *Hughes* v *Lord Advocate* – and her haemophilia would come within the terms of the 'egg-shell' principle: see e.g. *Smith* v *Leech Brain*.

It is not known whether the delay in obtaining hospital treatment is the result of any person's or organisation's tortious behaviour, or whether that delay is, in fact, of any causative potency in relation to F's death. Thus, it is not proposed to pursue the matter any further.

This is also true of any possibility of contributory liability (1978 Act) on the part of P – occupiers' liability or liability in ordinary negligence. The question does not supply sufficient information to make any further inquiry worthwhile.

There is, however, one final issue of **potential** importance to consider viz. the question of whether P has, in relation to her damage, performed her obligation to **mitigate** her loss. A plaintiff is expected to take reasonable steps to minimise any loss resulting from the defendant's tort: e.g. *Spartan Steel and Alloys* v *Martin*; *Perry* v *Phillips*. The facts given do not indicate at all whether P did take any such steps (or indeed was **able** to do so). A failure to act when it would have been feasible to do so may also be evidence of contributory negligence, under the terms of the Law Reform (Contributory Negligence) Act 1945, where the defendant can show that the plaintiff has contributed to the damage suffered.

CHAPTER FIVE

NEGLIGENCE: 'PURE' ECONOMIC LOSS/NEGLIGENT MISSTATEMENT

5.1 Introduction

SPARTAN STEEL & ALLOYS LTD v MARTIN & CO. (CONTRACTORS) LTD
[1973] 1 QB 27 (CA)

The defendant negligently drove a power shovel through the cable supplying electricity to the plaintiff's factory, causing a fourteen-hour power cut. The plaintiff claimed under three heads:

(a) damages for the reduced value of metal which had to be removed from a furnace before it solidified and damaged machinery;
(b) the profit which would have been made from that 'melt' had it been completed;
(c) the profit from four other 'melts' which would have been made but for the long power cut.

The Court of Appeal, by a majority, held that only the first two heads were redressable: the third was pure economic loss not flowing from the plaintiff's own physical loss. Lord Denning said this decision was dictated by **policy**; an admittedly arbitrary line had to be drawn somewhere, otherwise liability would rocket out of control. He pointed out that the plaintiff could insure against such a risk, so spreading the cost throughout the community. It would be an unfair burden to place liability on 'one pair of shoulders' in such circumstances.

Edmund Davies LJ (dissenting), admitting that his view did not accord with tradition, said that would have allowed the third head **as well**, since it was a foreseeable and direct consequence of the defendant's negligent act. (Lord Roskill in *Junior Books* (below) gave some support to this view.)

ASWAN ENGINEERING v LUPDINE [1987] 1 All ER 135 (CA)

The plaintiffs were a construction consortium operating in Kuwait and they purchased some waterproofing liquid, 'Lupguard', from the first defendants and this was to be sent to Kuwait. The 'Lupguard' was supplied in plastic pails manufactured by the second defendants, but these pails proved to be incapable of withstanding the heat in Kuwait (they were left outdoors, in direct sunlight for many days) and much of the Lupguard was lost. An action was brought against the first defendants in contract and they joined the second defendants as third parties (there was a contract between the first and second defendants). The first defendants went into liquidation and the plaintiffs sued the second defendants in the tort of negligence.

At first instance it was found that the plaintiffs were entitled to succeed against the first defendants in contract (s. 14 Sale of Goods Act 1979) (although the **first** defendants were not entitled to succeed against the **second** defendants in contract). However, the second defendants did not owe a duty of care in negligence to the plaintiffs, because there was insufficient proximity between the parties.

On appeal it was held that the second defendants were not liable in negligence to the plaintiffs (the first defendants appeal in contract against the second defendants was dismissed) because the damage suffered (i.e. the loss of 'Lupguard') was **not** reasonably foreseeable in the circumstances. Otherwise, according to Lloyd LJ, a duty would be imposed on manufacturers involving liability 'not far short of that of an insurer'.

His Lordship said that in *Muirhead* v *Industrial Tank Specialities Ltd* [1985] 3 All ER 705 the Court of Appeal found as a fact that the defendant manufacturer **knew** that the motors were to be used in pumps which in turn were to be used in fish farms; the objective was to keep lobsters alive. Therefore physical damage to the lobsters (not necessarily death) was likely if the motors failed. Thus, in those circumstances, the damage suffered was of the relevant (i.e. reasonably foreseeable) type . . . 'the scope of the manufacturers duty of care does not extend beyond this point' and it was not necessary to consider the questions of breach of duty and of whether the damage was too remote. However, if these questions had had to be answered, his Lordship would still have been inclined to find in the defendants' favour 'for much the same reasons'. The purchase of the pails was incidental to the purchase of the 'Lupguard' and if the pails **had** been defective and the 'Lupguard' was lost or harmed this **would** have been an example of damage to **other** property of the plaintiffs; an analogy was drawn with a bottle of wine and its cork; the cork is defective and contaminates the wine. Might there not be an action in tort available against the manufacturer? But in the present case the damage suffered, i.e. the physical loss of the 'Lupguard' was not of a reasonable foreseeable type and fell, therefore, 'outside the scope of the defendants' duty of care as a manufacturer'.

The trial judge had said there was insufficient proximity between the parties to establish the relevant duty of care, but according to Lloyd LJ this was merely another way of saying that the damage suffered was not of a reasonably foreseeable type in the circumstances.

His Lordship said one could take an alternative approach and ask whether the first defendants had had a reasonable opportunity of 'intermediate examination'. There **had** been such an opportunity in the present case. It was not intended that the pails be tested to destruction, but it was contemplated that further testing be carried out because the first order from the first defendants to the second defendants was a trial order and the second defendants were entitled to assume that if the first defendants had in mind a special use for the pails further discussions would take place. Thus, the particular use to which the pails were put in the present case was not contemplated (therefore the damage was not reasonably foreseeable).

The plaintiffs further argued that the trial judge had applied the wrong test of proximity, i.e. the *Junior Books Ltd* v *Veitchi* test of very close proximity, instead of the test appropriate to ordinary liability in negligence; he had said that the plaintiffs had relied on the first defendants and not on the second defendants. Lloyd LJ said that he did not accept that criticism. Reliance was an important factor in the *Junior Books* case, said his Lordship, but it could be said that reliance is of some relevance in other manufacturer/consumer contexts—in most of these cases a consumer or user places actual or implicit reliance on the skill and experience of the manufacturer or supplier. [In *Muirhead* (above), Goff LJ considered this aspect of *Junior Books* and the Court of Appeal found that the case involved subject-matter which was not an ordinary commercial product. Lloyd LJ in *Aswan* acknowledged that *Junior Books* appeared to have crossed the line between contract and tort. [*Quaere*: was there a closer proximity and a greater reliance by the appellants in *Junior Books* than in the ordinary run of products liability cases? If so, there may have been some force in the plaintiff's criticisms of the trial judge's approach to proximity in the present case.]

Nicholls LJ considered that the defendants had not committed negligence on the facts, i.e. there was no breach on their part of a duty to take 'reasonable care' because the pails were as fit for their purposed as it was reasonable to expect in the circumstances. The use of the pails in this case (involving long exposure to hot sun) did not come within the scope of the intended use. The test of intention in such cases, said his Lordship, is 'What would a reasonable purchaser understand to be the intended use of the pails?' The answer to that determined the extent of the second defendant's duty of care.

He agreed that, strictly speaking, 'Lupguard' and the pails were different items of property so that the failure of the pails as simple containers caused physical damage to their contents (i.e. the 'Lupguard') through spillage and wastage. However, he thought that this was 'not an attractive proposition' because if that argument was correct certain problems might arise. What would be the legal position of, for example, a manufacturer of plastic bags which were supplied to supermarkets when a bag burst and its contents (shopping goods) fell out and were damaged? Would it not be extending manufacturer's liability under *Donoghue* v *Stevenson* too far to make him liable in such a case? Losses in such instances were likely to be small, but this would not always be the case. According to Nicholls LJ '. . . in the absence of facts giving rise to a very close proximity between manufacturer and user, as in the *Junior Books* case, the manufacturer's duty of care does not give rise to liability in respect of loss of contents'. In such cases perhaps it would be up to the user to satisfy himself that the container was strong enough to hold what he wanted it to hold when used in a way he had in mind.

Fox LJ agreed with Lloyd LJ

5.2   The Decision in *Junior Books* v *Veitchi*

JUNIOR BOOKS LTD v *THE VEITCHI CO. LTD* [1982] 3 All ER 201 (HL)

Establishes the **principle** that it is no longer a sufficient answer to a claim in negligence that the loss is economic in nature and unconnected with physical damage, though because of the very high degree of proximity [**akin to contract**?] between the parties in this case it is difficult to say how much further than that the decision takes us.

The plaintiffs were having a building erected by X and it was necessary to include a special floor for the purpose of taking certain machinery. X contracted with the defendants, who were specialists in the work, for the supply of this floor at the request of the plaintiffs (who had been advised to do this by their architect). Thus, in relation to the plaintiffs the defendants were **subcontractors**.

After the floor was completed it was found to be defective, although no damage to person or property was even imminent let alone caused by this defect. In other words, there was a defect of **quality** alone—the typical situation found in **contract**. The plaintiff's loss consisted of the cost of **repair** or **replacement**.

It was decided in **preliminary** proceedings (no ruling on actual liability was made by the House of Lords) that the defendants probably did owe a duty of care in the **tort** of **negligence** to the plaintiffs; certainly there was a case to argue and the matter was referred back to the court of origin (in Scotland) for resolution of the issue.

You should note that there was no action available in contract against X (the **plaintiffs** had chosen the defendants) and the plaintiff's architect had not been negligent.

5.2.1   CONTRACTUAL RELATIONSHIPS

MUIRHEAD v *INDUSTRIAL TANK SPECIALITIES* [1985] 3 All ER 750 (CA)

The Court of Appeal said that there were special circumstances to be found in *Junior Books* viz. a very close proximity and **reliance** by the plaintiff on the defendant. The court distinguished the present case from *Junior Books*. In *Muirhead* the plaintiffs, as part of their business, wanted to keep live lobsters and purchased from the first defendants a storage tank and a number of pumps. The pump, supplied to the first defendants by the second defendants, proved to be unreliable because the motors which drove them were defective. Consequently the plaintiffs suffered pure financial loss because they could not store the lobsters. The plaintiffs sued successfully the first defendants in **contract** but the defendants proved to be men of straw for they went bankrupt; so the plaintiffs sued the second defendants in **tort**, but without success because their loss was purely financial and arose only under the contract with the first defendants.

Goff LJ, however, thought that the facts of *Junior Books* [construction of a special floor, later found to be defective, for the plaintiff by specialist sub-contractors appointed at the behest of the plaintiff's architects] showed 'the parties had deliberately structured their contractual relationship in order to achieve the result . . . no direct liability inter se'. He thought it 'safest' to regard *Junior Books* as authority for liability on the basis of 'a very close relationship between the parties' on its particular facts.

5.3   Misstatements

5.3.1   LIABILITY IN OTHER SITUATIONS

MISREPRESENTATION ACT 1967

1.   Removal of certain bars to rescission for innocent misrepresentation
Where a person has entered into a contract after a misrepresentation has been to him, and—

(a)   the misrepresentation has become a term of the contract; or

(b)   the contract has been performed;

or both, then, if otherwise he would be entitled to rescind the contract without alleging fraud, he shall be so entitled, subject to the provisions of this Act, notwithstanding the matters mentioned in paragraphs (a) and (b) of this section.

2.   Damages for misrepresentation
(1)   Where a person has entered into a contract after a misrepresentation has been made to him by another party thereto and as a result thereof he has suffered loss, then, if the person making the misrepresentation would be liable to damages in respect thereof had the misrepresentation been made fraudulently, that person shall be so liable notwithstanding that the misrepresentation was not made fraudulently, unless he proves that he had reasonable ground to believe and did believe up to the time the contract was made that the facts represented were true.

(2)   Where a person has entered into a contract after a misrepresentation has been made to him otherwise than fraudulently, and he would be entitled, by reason of the misrepresentation, to rescind the contract, then, if it is claimed, in any proceedings arising out of the contract, that the contract ought to be or has been rescinded, the course or arbitrator may declare the contract subsisting and award damages in lieu of rescission, if of opinion that it would be equitable to do so, having regard to the nature of the misrepresentation and the loss that would be caused by it if the contract were upheld, as well as to the loss that rescission would cause to the other party.

(3)   Damages may be awarded against a person under subsection (2) of this section whether or not he is liable to damages under subsection (1) thereof, but where he is so liable any award under the said subsection (2) shall be taken into account in assessing his liability under the said subsection (1).

3.   Avoidance of provision excluding liability for misrepresentation
[If a contract contains a term which would exclude or restrict—

(a)   any liability to which a party to a contract may be subject by reason of any misrepresentation made by him before the contract was made; or

(b)   any remedy available to another party to the contract by reason of such a misrepresentation,

that term shall be of no effect except in so far as it satisfies the requirement of reasonableness as stated in section 11(1) of the Unfair Contract Terms Act 1977; and it is for those claiming that the term satisfies that requirement to show that it does.]

4.   Amendments of Sale of Goods Act 1893
. . .

5.   Saving for past transactions
Nothing in this Act shall apply in relation to any misrepresentation or contract of sale which is made before the commencement of this Act.

5.3.2 LIABILITY ARISING UNDER *HEDLEY BYRNE*

HEDLEY BYRNE AND CO. LTD v *HELLER AND PARTNERS LTD*
[1963] 2 All ER 575 (HL)

LORD REID: Apart altogether from authority I would think that the law must treat negligent words differently from negligent acts. The law ought so far as possible to reflect the standards of the reasonable man, and that is what *M'Alister* (or *Donoghue)* v *Stevenson* sets out to do. The most obvious difference between negligent words and negligent acts is this. Quite careful people often express definite opinions on social or informal occasions, even when they see that others are likely to be influenced by them; and they often do that without taking that care which they would take if asked for their opinion professionally, or in a business connexion. The appellants agreed that there can be no duty of care on such occasions, and we were referred to American and South African authorities where that is recognised, although their law appears to have gone much further than ours has yet done. But it is at least unusual casually to put into circulation negligently-made articles which are dangerous. A man might give a friend a negligently-prepared bottle of home-made wine and his friend's guests might drink it with dire results; but it is by no means clear that those guests would have no action against the negligent manufacturer. Another obvious difference is that a negligently-made article will only cause one accident, and so it is not very difficult to find the necessary-degree of proximity or neighbourhood between the negligent manufacturer and the person injured. But words can be broadcast with or without the consent or the foresight of the speaker or writer. It would be one thing to say that the speaker owes a duty to a limited class, but it would be going very far to say that he owes a duty to every ultimate 'consumer' who acts on those words to his detriment. It would be no use to say that a speaker or writer owes a duty, but can disclaim responsibility if he wants to. He, like the manufacturer, could make it part of a contract that he is not to be liable for his negligence; but that contract would not protect him in a question with a third party at least if the third party was unaware of it.

So it seems to me that there is good sense behind our present law that in general an innocent but negligent misrepresentation gives no cause of action. There must be something more than the mere misstatement. I therefore turn to the authorities to see what more is required. The most natural requirement would be that expressly or by implication from the circumstances the speaker or writer has undertaken some responsibility, and that appears to me not to conflict with any authority which is binding on this House. Where there is a contract there is no difficulty as regards the contracting parties; the question is whether there is a warranty. The refusal of English law to recognise any *jus quaesitum tertio* causes some difficulties, but they are not relevant here. Then there are cases where a person does not merely make a statement but performs a gratuitous service. I do not intend to examine the cases about that, but at least they show that in some cases that person owes a duty of care apart from any contract, and to that extent they pave the way to holding that there can be a duty of care in making a statement of fact or opinion which is independent of contract . . .

A reasonable man, knowing that he was being trusted or that his skill and judgment were being relied on, would, I think, have three courses open to him. He could keep silent or decline to give the information or advice sought: or he could give an answer with a clear qualification that he accepted no responsibility for it or that it was given without that reflection or inquiry which a careful answer would require: or he could simply answer without any such qualification. If he chooses to adopt the last course he must, I think, be held to have accepted some responsibility for his answer being given carefully, or to have accepted a relationship with the inquirer which requires him to exercise such care as the circumstances require.

If that is right, then if must follow that *Candler v Crane, Christmas & Co.* [1951] 2 KB 164 was wrongly decided. There the plaintiff wanted to see the accounts of a company before deciding to invest in it. The defendants were the company's accountants, and they were told by the company to complete the company's accounts as soon as possible because they were to be shown to the plaintiff who was a potential investor in the company. At the company's request the defendants showed the completed accounts to the plaintiff, discussed them with him, and allowed him to take a copy. The accounts had been carelessly prepared and gave a wholly misleading picture. It was obvious to the defendants that the plaintiff was relying on their skill and judgment and on their having exercised that care which by contract they owed to the company, and I think that any reasonable man in the plaintiff's shoes would have relied on that. This seems to me to be a typical case of agreeing to assume a responsibility; they knew why the plaintiff wanted to see the accounts and why their employers, the company, wanted them to be shown to him, and agreed to show them to him without even a suggestion that he should not rely on them . . .

. . . What the appellants complain of is not negligence in the ordinary sense of carelessness, but rather mis-judgment, in that Mr Heller, while honestly seeking to give a fair assessment, in fact made a statement which gave a false and misleading impression of his customer's credit. It appears that bankers now commonly give references with regard to their customers as part of their business. I do not know how far their customers generally permit them to disclose their affairs, but even with permission, it cannot always be easy for a banker to reconcile his duty to his customer with his desire to give a fairly balanced reply to an inquiry. And inquirers can hardly expect a full and objective statement of opinion of accurate factual information such as skilled men would be expected to give in reply to other kinds of inquiry. So it seems to me to be unusually difficult to determine just what duty beyond a duty to be honest a banker would be held to have undertaken if he gave a reply without an adequate disclaimer of responsibility or other warning . . .

But here the appellants' bank, who were their agents in making the inquiry, began by saying that 'they wanted to know in confidence and without responsibility on our part' that is, on the part of the respondents. So I cannot see how the appellants can now be entitled to disregard that and maintain that the respondents did incur a responsibility to them . . . In the case of a contract it is necessary to exclude liability for negligence, but in this case the question is whether an undertaking to assume a duty to take care can be inferred; and that is a very different matter. Secondly, even in cases of contract general words may be sufficient if there was no other kind of liability to be excluded except liability for negligence: the general rule is that a party is not exempted from liability for negligence 'unless adequate words are used'—*per* Scrutton LJ in *Rutter* v *Palmer*. It being admitted that there was here a duty to give an honest reply, I do not see what further liability there could be to exclude except liability for negligence: there being no contract there was no question of warranty.

I am therefore of opinion that it is clear that the respondents never undertook any duty to exercise care in giving their replies . . .

LORD MORRIS: My lords, it seems to me that if A assumes a responsibility to B to tender him deliberate advice there could be a liability if the advice is negligently given. I say 'could be' because the ordinary courtesies and exchanges of life would become impossible if it were sought to attach legal obligation to every kindly and friendly act. But the principle of the matter would not appear to be in doubt. . . .

My lords, I consider that . . . it should now be regarded as settled that if someone possessed of a special skill undertakes, quite irrespective of contract, to apply that skill for the assistance of another person who relies on such skill, a duty of care will arise. The fact that the service is to be given by means of, or by the instrumentality of, words can make no difference. Furthermore, if, in a sphere in which a person is so placed that others could reasonably rely on his judgment or his skill or on his ability to make careful inquiry, a person takes it on himself to give information or advice to, or allows his information or advice to be passed on to, another person who, as he knows or should know, will place reliance on it, then a duty of care will arise.

I do not propose to examine the facts of particular situations or the facts of recent decided cases in the light of this analysis, but I proceed to apply it to the facts of the case now under review. As I have stated, I approach the case on the footing that the bank knew that what they said would in fact be passed on to some unnamed person who was a customer of National Provincial Bank Ltd. The fact that it was said that 'they', i.e. National Provincial Bank Ltd, 'wanted to know' does not prevent this conclusion. In these circumstances I think that some duty towards the unnamed person, whoever it was, was owed by the bank. There was a duty of honesty. The great question, however, is whether there was a duty of care. The bank need not have answered the inquiry from National Provincial Bank Ltd. It appears, however, that it is a matter of banking convenience or courtesy and presumably of mutual business advantage that inquiries as between banks will be answered. The fact that it is most unlikely that the bank would have answered a direct inquiry from Hedleys does not affect the question as to what the bank must have known as to the use that would be made of any answer that they gave but it cannot be left out of account in considering what it was that the bank undertook to do. It does not seem to me that they undertook before answering an inquiry to expend time or trouble 'in searching records, studying documents, weighing and comparing the favourable and unfavourable features and producing a well-balanced and well-ordered report.' (I quote the words of Pearson LJ.) Nor does it seem to me that the inquiring bank (nor therefore their customer) would expect such a process. . . . There was in the present case no contemplation of receiving anything like a formal and detailed report such as might be given by some concern charged with the duty (probably for reward) of making all proper and relevant inquiries concerning the nature, scope and extent of a company's activities and of obtaining and marshalling all available evidence as to its credit, efficiency, standing and business reputation. There is much to be said, therefore, for the view that if a banker gives a reference in the form of a brief expression of opinion in regard to credit-worthiness he does not accept, and there is not expected from him, any higher duty than that of giving an honest answer. I need not, however, seek to deal with this aspect of the matter which perhaps cannot be covered by any statement of general application, because in my judgment the bank in the present case, by the words which they employed, effectively disclaimed any assumption of a duty of care. They stated that they only responded to the inquiry on the basis that their reply was without responsibility. If the inquirers chose to receive and act upon the reply they cannot disregard the definite terms upon which it was given. They cannot accept a reply given with a stipulation and then reject the stipulation. Furthermore, within accepted principles (as illustrated in *Rutter* v *Palmer*) the words employed were apt to exclude any liability for negligence.

[His Lordship concluded that the appeal should be dismissed.]

LORD DEVLIN: I think, therefore, that there is ample authority to justify your Lordships in saying now that the categories of special relationships which may give rise to a duty to take care in word as well as in deed are not limited to contractual relationships or to relationships of fiduciary duty, but include also relationships which in the words of Lord Shaw in *Nocton* v *Lord Ashburton* [1914] AC 932, 972 are 'equivalent to contract,' that is, where there is an assumption of responsibility in circumstances in which, but for the absence of consideration, there would be a contract. Where there is an express undertaking, an express warranty as distinct from mere representation, there can be little difficulty. The difficulty arises in discerning those cases in which the undertaking is to be implied. In this respect the absence of consideration is not irrelevant. Payment for information or advice is very good evidence that it is being relied upon and that the informer or adviser knows that it is. Where there is no consideration, it will be necessary to exercise greater care in distinguishing between social and professional relationships and between those which are of a contractual character and those which are not. It may often be material to consider whether the adviser is acting purely out of good nature or whether he is getting his reward in some indirect form. The service that a bank performs in giving a reference is not one simply out of a desire to assist commerce. It would discourage the customers of the bank if their deals fell through because the bank had refused to testify to their credit when it was good.

I have had the advantage of reading all the opinions prepared by your Lordships and of studying the terms which your Lordships have framed by way of definition of the sort of relationship which gives rise to a responsibility towards those who act upon information or advice and so creates a duty of care towards them. I do not understand any of your Lordships to hold that it is a responsibility imposed by law upon certain types of persons or in certain sorts of situations. It is a responsibility that is voluntarily accepted or undertaken, either generally where a general relationship, such as that of solicitor and client or banker and customer, is created, or specifically in relation to a particular transaction. In the present case the appellants were not, as in *Woods* v *Martins Bank Ltd* [1959] 1 QB 55, the customers or potential customers of the bank. Responsibility can attach only to the single act, that is, the giving of the reference, and only if the doing of that act implied a voluntary undertaking to assume responsibility. This is a point of great importance because it is, as I understand it, the foundation for the ground on which in the end the House dismisses the appeal. I do not think it possible to formulate with exactitude all the conditions under which the law will in a specific case imply a voluntary undertaking any more than it is possible to formulate those in which the law will imply a contract . . . .

I shall therefore content myself with the proposition that wherever there is a relationship equivalent to contract, there is a duty of care. Such a relationship may be either general or particular. Examples of a general relationship are those of solicitor and client and of banker and customer. For the former *Nocton* v *Lord Ashburton* has long stood as the authority and for the latter there is the decision of Salmon J in *Woods* v *Martins Bank Ltd*, which I respectfully approve. There may well be others yet to be established. Where there is a general relationship of this sort, it is unnecessary to do more than prove its existence and the duty follows. Where, as in the present case, what is relied on is a particular relationship created ad hoc, it will be necessary to examine the particular facts to see whether there is an express or implied undertaking of responsibility.

I regard this proposition as an application of the general conception of proximity. Cases may arise in the future in which a new and wider proposition, quite independent of any notion of contract, will be needed. There may, for example, be cases in which a statement is not supplied for the use of any particular person, any more than in *Donoghue* v *Stevenson* [1932] AC 562, the ginger beer was supplied for consumption by any particular person; and it will then be necessary to return to the general conception of proximity and to see whether there can be evolved from it . . .

Lords Hodson and Pearce were also in favour of dismissing the plaintiff's appeal.

5.3.3   RELIANCE

BRIGGS v GUNNER (1979) 129 NLJ 116

CARNWATH J: [T]he plaintiff, who was a solicitor, sued the defendant, a stockbroker, for negligent misstatement (in the form of advice). The plaintiff had bought shares in a certain company and he claimed that the defendant had held himself out as an expert on these shares and was negligent in advising the plaintiff to buy and not sell. Dealings in the shares were suspended and the plaintiff suffered a considerable loss on his investment. The judge found in favour of the defendant on the ground that the plaintiff had failed to show any negligence in the advice he had received from the defendant. Foster J said: 'In my judgment the *Hedley-Byrne* case [has] not increased the burden on stockbrokers. The Stock Exchange has more than once been described as the market of expectation and if the plaintiff's submission was right no stockbroker would ever have to tender any advice at all . . . a stockbroker has no duty to advise and if he does advise he must do it honestly and to the best of his ability . . . Of course a stockbroker can be negligent if, for instance, he fails to execute an order immediately or gives a client wrong factual information. But in this case the plaintiff only complains of wrong advice. A stockbroker can only give advice to his best ability.' He pointed out that the plaintiff agreed it was his own decision to put all his money into one holding, and had never told the defendant of his general financial position nor that he was borrowing to invest. 'It is a matter of commonsense' not to put 'all one's eggs into one basket'. The plaintiff did tell the defendant that he was looking for long-term capital appreciation but except perhaps in special cases, 'such as a widow with little to invest', there was no duty on the defendant to warn clients to diversify their investments. 'In this case Mr Gunner looked up to Mr Briggs as a solicitor, thought that he came from a rich family and would not have dreamt of questioning his decision . . . A speculator does not rely on any advice given to him. In my judgment there was no breach of any duty by Mr Gunner in watching Mr Briggs put his eggs in one basket and starting to speculate.' There was no doubt that the defendant 'was always optimistic' on the shares but he had no special knowledge of them 'other than the general view of the newspaper reports, the analysts' reports and [the company's own] reports and accounts . . . and the general gossip on the Stock Exchange . . . There can be no doubt that the news of the suspension came as a bombshell to the Market.

'If Mr Briggs really did believe that the figure of £3 to £5 was the actual realisable value of the assets he was alone in so doing . . . Who could believe he could buy for 80 pence something worth £4? I agree that Mr Briggs is naïve, but I fear that he has now got some total blockage over the cause of the folly of his Stock Exchange speculations. But . . . [there is no] negligence on the part of Mr Gunner in the advice which he gave . . . He cannot say that he relied on Mr Gunner's advice as he twice consulted financial editors of well-known newspapers . . .'

Briggs v *Gunner* not only illustrates the difficulties inherent in establishing a duty of care and reliance; it also indicates that a plaintiff may experience considerable problems in convincing the court of the appropriate standard of care which a defendant is expected to observe.

LUXMOORE-MAY v *MESSENGER MAY BAVERSTOCK* [1990] 1 All ER 1067 (CA)

It was held in this case that a provincial art valuer and auctioneer is not negligent merely because he does not notice the potential value of a painting (a 'sleeper') which later sold in London as an original Stubbs. The court found that the valuer's duty is to act with due diligence to give his honest and considered opinion on the sale value of the painting submitted to him.

At first instance the defendants were found liable in negligence to the plaintiffs but the Court of Appeal reversed this decision. Slade LJ said that the nature of the defendants' duty was akin to that of general practitioners and the required standard of skill was not that of the specialist, ie the standard of the provincial auctioneer was to be applied in this case rather than that expected of one of the leading auction houses. Differing and even wrong views could be held without there being a breach of the practitioner's duty. The case should be approached according to the actual circumstances confronting the practitioners at the time 'rather than with the benefit of hindsight'.

An exact science was not involved and it was a matter of opinion and judgment in such cases. '[T]he judgment in the very nature of things may be fallible and may turn out to be wrong.'

The trial judge had demanded too high a standard of skill from the defendants; here the question was one of which many competent valuers and dealers could have held widely differing views. (It has been seen that the issue of reliance was also raised in *Briggs* v *Gunner*.)

WILLIAMS AND ANOTHER v *NATURAL LIFE HEALTH FOODS LTD AND ANOTHER* [1998] 2 All ER 577 (HL)

The House of Lords held that a director or employee of a limited company was not liable under *Hedley Byrne* unless it could be shown **objectively** that the plaintiff **could** reasonably have relied on an assumption of personal responsibility **sufficient** to create a 'special relationship' between the director or employee and the plaintiff. The plaintiffs had taken out a franchise (to run a retail health food shop) from the defendant company and suffered financial loss as a result of negligent advice given by the company in relation to financial projections about the likely future profitability of the shop.

The defendant company having gone into liquidation (it was dissolved in 1993) the plaintiffs had joined Mr Mistlin, the second defendant, who was managing director and principal shareholder in Natural Life Health Foods Ltd. He was now the sole defendant in the action.

Lord Steyn, delivering the judgment of the House of Lords, said that *Henderson* v *Merrett* had decided that the *Hedley Byrne* 'assumption of responsibility' was **not** confined to misstatements; it might apply 'as the extended *Hedley Byrne* principle to any assumption of responsibility for the provision of services'. It was not enough to establish **reliance**, however, to show that there was a special relationship with a **principal** (the defendant company in this case). Where an **agent** (all employee or director of the company in the present case) was sued **personally** there had to be a special relationship between **that** person and the plaintiff. His Lordship said that the 'touchstone of liability' was not the defendant's state of mind. The 'objective' test laid down in *Henderson* required that the main emphasis had to be on things said or done by the **defendant** (or **on his behalf**) in **dealings** with the **plaintiff** – though the 'impact' of this would have to be judged in 'its relevant context'. It was not a case of simple reliance in **fact**; it was a question of whether the plaintiff could **reasonably** have relied on the defendant's personal assumption of responsibility.

The defendant had owned and controlled the company which had held itself out as having the expertise to provide reliable advice to franchisees, and a brochure issued to potential franchisees had made it clear that the expertise came from the defendant's experience in operating his own shop. Those circumstances, however, were not enough to make the defendant personally liable to the plaintiffs.

There had been **no personal dealings** between the **defendant** and the plaintiffs – they had dealt in their pre-contractual negotiations only with **the company**, through Z, an employee of the company. The plaintiffs had not known the defendant and had no material pre-contractual dealings with him.

5.3.4   ASSUMPTION OF RESPONSIBILITY

BANQUE KEYSER ULLMANN SA v SKANDIA (UK) INSURANCE CO. LTD
[1989] 2 All ER 952 (CA) (*WESTGATE INSURANCE* in House of Lords, *below*)

Although voluntary assumption of responsibility is regarded by some judges as a requirement for recovery of damages in every case of pure economic loss (e.g. Dillon LJ in *Simaan General Contracting Co.* v *Pilkington Glass (No. 2)* [1988] 1 All ER 791) it was accepted in the Court of Appeal in *Banque Keyser Ullmann SA* that 'on appropriate facts', 'having regard to the special circumstances and the relationship between the parties' a defendant might be regarded in law (even though not in fact) as having assumed responsibility to the plaintiff. In the present case the Court of Appeal was much impressed by the plaintiff's argument that Lord Keith's opinion, as expressed in *Yuen Kun-Yue* v *Attorney-General for Hong Kong* [1988] AC 175 (PC) was that the existence of a duty of care depends not on voluntary assumption of responsibility, but on a sufficient degree of proximity between the parties; it is the directness and closeness of the relationship between the parties which matters. In this light, the voluntary assumption of responsibility is but one example of a factual situation giving rise to a direct and close relationship.

It was held in *Banque Keyser Ullmann* that an insurer owes a duty of care to disclose to the insured the insured's brokers' dishonesty (known to the insurer) only where the insurer has voluntarily assumed responsibility to disclose and the insured has relied on that assumption of responsibility. (The duty of utmost good faith in the insurance contract cannot be used as a platform to establish a common law duty of care in such circumstances.)

According to Slade LJ it was not necessary in a claim in negligence for economic loss resulting from the act of an independent third party that the manner and means by which the loss was caused or the extent of the loss be reasonably foreseeable. Accordingly, it was enough to show reasonable foresight of the relevant kind of loss. A failure to speak (omission) was involved here, however, and, although in the opinion of the court a mere failure to speak was capable of giving rise to liability for negligent misstatement, there must be a voluntary assumption of responsibility together with reliance on it. In the present case both assumption and reliance were absent. In rare cases, because of special circumstances and the relationship between parties, the law might treat a defendant as having assumed a responsibility to the plaintiff even though there was no evidence of an actual assumption of responsibility (and reliance by the plaintiff); but the defendant insurers did not fit into this category because it was a basic principle of the law of contract that there was no obligation to disclose a material fact during pre-contractual negotiations before entering into an ordinary commercial contract and this prevented a duty of care arising on the part of the insurers. To hold the insurers liable in negligence for their failure to disclose the third party's deception would be contrary to that principle of contract law.

LA BANQUE FINANCIÈRE DE LA CITÉ v WESTGATE INSURANCE CO. LTD
[1990] 2 All ER 947 (HL)

In the *Banque Keyser Ullmann* case the House of Lords, in dismissing the bank's appeal, held (confirming the decision of the Court of Appeal, though on other grounds) as follows:

(a)   There was no duty on the part of an insurer to warn an insured person that the latter's agent had committed a breach of his agent's duty in an earlier transaction, thus the insurer was not responsible for the agent's misconduct towards his principal in subsequent dealings; it followed that the insurers (acting through X) did not owe a duty to tell the banks in the present case that their broker (who was acting through Y) had acted fraudulently with regard to the covering insurance for a loan to U Co.

(b)   In any event, assuming the insurers did owe such a duty, any breach of the duty would have resulted only in loss of full cover—not the actual loss suffered by the banks (i) first due to Z's (who controlled the U Co.) fraud; and (ii) as a result of being unable to claim under the insurance policies because of an exemption clause activated by Z's, rather than Y's fraud; even if the banks had been fully covered in respect of the relevant (credit) insurance policies they could not have claimed under the policies, due to the fraud exclusion clause. It followed that although the cause of the loan to U Co. was Y's fraud it was not the cause of the loss of that loan.

SMITH v ERIC S. BUSH; HARRIS v WYRE FOREST DISTRICT COUNCIL
[1989] 2 All ER 514 (HL)

LORD TEMPLEMAN: In general I am of the opinion that in the absence of a disclaimer of liability the valuer who values a house for the purpose of a mortgage, knowing that the mortgagee will rely and the mortgagor will probably rely on the valuation, knowing that the purchaser mortgagor has in effect paid for the valuation, is under a duty to exercise reasonable skill and care and that duty is owed to both parties to the mortgage for which the valuation is made. Indeed, in both the appeals now under consideration the existence of such a dual duty is tacitly accepted and acknowledged because notices excluding liability for breach of the duty owed to the purchaser were drafted by the mortgagee and imposed on the purchaser. In these circumstances it is necessary to consider the second question which arises in these appeals, namely, whether the disclaimers of liability are notices which fall within the Unfair Contract Terms Act 1977.

In *Harris* v *Wyre Forest DC* the Court of Appeal (Kerr, Nourse LJJ and Caufield J) accepted an argument that the 1977 Act did not apply because the council by their express disclaimer refused to obtain a valuation save on terms that the valuer would not be under any obligation to Mr and Mrs Harris to take reasonable care or exercise reasonable skill. The council did not exclude liability for negligence but excluded negligence so that the valuer and the council never came under a duty of care to Mr and Mrs Harris and could not be guilty of negligence. This construction would not give effect to the manifest intention of the 1977 Act but would emasculate the Act. The construction would provide no control over standard form exclusion clauses which individual members of the public are obliged to accept. A party to a contract or a tortfeasor could opt out of the 1977 Act by declining, in the words of Nourse LJ, to recognise 'their own answerability to the plaintiff' (see [1988] QB 835 at 845). Caulfield J said that the Act 'can only be relevant where there is on the facts a potential liability' (see [1988] QB 835 at 850). But no one intends to commit a tort and therefore any notice which excludes liability is a notice which excludes a potential liability. Kerr LJ sought to confine the Act to 'situations where the existence of a duty of care is not open to doubt' or where there is 'an inescapable duty of care' (see [1988] QB 835 at 853). I can find nothing in the 1977 Act or in the general law to identify or support this distinction. In the result the Court of Appeal held that the Act does not apply to 'negligent misstatements where a disclaimer has prevented a duty of care from coming into existence' (see [1988] QB 835 at 848 per Nourse LJ). My Lords, this confuses the valuer's report with the work which the valuer carries out in order to make his report. The valuer owed a duty to exercise reasonable skill and care in his inspection and valuation. If he had been careful in his work, he would not have made a 'negligent misstatement' in his report.

Section 11(3) of the 1977 Act provides that, in considering whether it is fair and reasonable to allow reliance on a notice which excludes liability in tort, account must be taken of 'all the circumstances obtaining when the liability arose or (but for the notice) would have arisen'. Section 13(1) of the Act prevents the exclusion of any right or remedy and (to that extent) s. 2 also prevents the exclusion of liability 'by reference to . . . notices which exclude . . . the relevant obligation or duty'. Nourse LJ dismissed s. 11(3) as 'peripheral' and made no comment on s. 13(1). In my opinion both these provisions support the view that the 1977 Act requires that all exclusion notices which would in common law provide a defence to an action for negligence must satisfy the requirement of reasonableness.

The answer to the second question involved in these appeals is that the disclaimer of liability made by the council on its own behalf in *Harris's* case and by the Abbey National on behalf of the appellant surveyors in *Smith's* case constitute notices which fall within the 1977 Act and must satisfy the requirement of reasonableness. . . .

LORD GRIFFITHS: . . . Counsel for the council and Mr Lee drew attention to the doubts expressed about the correctness of this decision by Kerr LJ in the course of his judgment in the Court of Appeal, and submitted, on the authority of *Hedley Byrne & Co. Ltd* v *Heller & Partners Ltd* [1964] AC 465, that it was essential to found liability for a negligent misstatement that there had been 'a voluntary assumption of responsibility' on the part of the person giving the advice. I do not accept this submission and I do not think that voluntary assumption of responsibility is a helpful or realistic test for liability. It is true that reference is made in a number of the speeches in the *Hedley Byrne* case to the assumption of responsibility as a test of liability but it must be remembered that those speeches were made in the context of a case in which the central issue was whether a duty of care could arise when there had been an express disclaimer of responsibility for the accuracy of the advice. Obviously, if an adviser expressly assumes responsibility for his advice, a duty of care will arise, but such is extremely unlikely in the ordinary course of events. The House of Lords approved a duty of care being imposed on the facts in *Cann* v *Willson* (1888) 39 ChD 39 and in *Candler* v *Crane, Christmas & Co* [1951] 2 KB 164. But, if the surveyor in *Cann* v *Willson* or the accountant in *Candler* v *Crane, Christmas & Co* had actually been asked if he was voluntarily assuming responsibility for his advice to the mortgagee or the purchaser of the shares, I have little doubt he would have replied: 'Certainly not. My responsibility is limited to the person who employs me.' The phrase 'assumption of responsibility' can only have any real meaning if it is understood as referring to the circumstances in which the law will deem the maker of the statement to have assumed responsibility to the person who acts on the advice.

In *Ministry of Housing and Local Government* v *Sharp* [1970] 2 QB 223 both Lord Denning MR and Salmon LJ rejected the argument that a voluntary assumption of responsibility was the sole criterion for imposing a duty of care for the negligent preparation of a search certificate in the local land charges register.

The essential distinction between the present case and the situation being considered in the *Hedley Byrne* case and in the two earlier cases is that in those cases the advice was being given with the intention of persuading the recipient to act on it. In the present case the purpose of providing the report is to advise the mortgagee but it is given in circumstances in which it is highly probable that the purchaser will in fact act on its contents, although that was not the primary purpose of the report. I have had considerable doubts whether it is wise to increase the scope of duty for negligent advice beyond the person directly intended by the giver of the advice to act on it to those whom he knows may do so. Certainly in the field of the law of mortgagor and mortgagee there is authority that points in the other direction. . . .

. . . I have already given my view that the voluntary assumption of responsibility is unlikely to be a helpful or realistic test in most cases. I therefore return to the question: in what circumstances should the law deem those who give advice to have assumed responsibility to the person who acts on the advice or, in other words, in what circumstances should a duty of care be owed by the adviser to those who act on his advice? I would answer: only if it is foreseeable that, if the advice is negligent, the recipient is likely to suffer damage, that there is a sufficiently proximate relationship between the parties and that it is just and reasonable to impose the liability.

In the case of a surveyor valuing a small house for a building society or local authority, the application of these three criteria leads to the conclusion that he owes a duty of care to the purchaser. If the valuation is negligent and is relied on, damage in the form of economic loss to the purchaser is obviously foreseeable. The necessary proximity arises from the surveyor's knowledge that the overwhelming probability is that the purchaser will rely on his valuation. The evidence was that surveyors knew that approximately 90% of purchasers did so, and the fact that the surveyor only obtains the work because the purchaser is willing to pay his fee. It is just and reasonable that the duty should be imposed, for the advice is given in a professional as opposed to a social context and liability for breach of the duty will be limited both as to its extent and amount. The extent of the liability is limited to the purchaser of the house; I would not extend it to subsequent purchasers. The amount of the liability cannot be very great because it relates to a modest house.

There is no question here of creating a liability of indeterminate amount to an indeterminate class. I would certainly wish to stress that, in cases where the advice has not been given for the specific purpose of the recipient acting on it, it should only be in cases when the adviser knows that there is a high degree of probability that some other identifiable person will act on the advice, that a duty of care should be imposed. It would impose an intolerable burden on those who give advice in a professional or commercial context if they were to owe a duty, not only to those to whom they give advice, but to any other person who might choose to act on it.

Lords Keith and Brandon *agreed*, whilst Lord Jauncey *argued* in favour of dismissing the surveyor's appeal in Smith and allowing the Harris's appeal (the defendant council being vicariously liable for their employee's negligence). The result was a unanimous decision in favour of liability in *both* cases.

ANDERSON (WB) AND SONS LTD v RHODES (LIVERPOOL) LTD [1967] 2 All ER 850

Cairns J extended the duty to 'a statement by a businessman made without formality and without raising any immediate opportunity for investigation'. In this case the defendant was asked by the plaintiff for information on the credit worthiness of X (a potential buyer of potatoes from the plaintiff); he wished to know whether he could give credit to this person. The defendant was acting as a commission agent on the sale of these potatoes and he knew (a) why the plaintiff wanted this information; (b) that the enquiry was important; (c) that the plaintiff would be influenced by the information.

This decision was distinguished by the Privy Council in *Mutual Life and Citizens' Assurance Co. Ltd v Evatt* [1971] AC 793, on the ground that the defendant in *Anderson* had a fiduciary interest in the transaction in which he advised.

YIANNI v EDWIN EVANS AND SONS [1982] QB 438

The judge in this case applied the Wilberforce test to the facts, and held that there was sufficient proximity between the surveyor for a building society, whose report was made to the society, and a mortgagor; he also appeared to extend the scope of reasonable reliance because he said that the evidence showed that most mortgagors did not arrange their own independent survey and therefore the surveyor knew, or ought to have known, that the mortgagor would rely on his report made to the building society. This approach has been criticised as too generous: the mortgagor had not asked the building society for advice and the aim of the survey was to assess the value of the security offered for the loan (see Kerr LJ, in the Court of Appeal in *Harris* v *Wyre Forest DC* (above)). However, the House of Lords appears to have approved the *Yianni* approach in *Smith* v *Bush*, *Harris* v *Wyre Forest DC*. Lord Templeman did say, however, that these were circumstances akin to contract.

5.3.5 A STRICTER TEST

CAPARO INDUSTRIES PLC v DICKMAN [1990] 1 All ER 568 (HL)

LORD BRIDGE: The salient feature of all these cases is that the defendant giving advice or information was fully aware of the nature of the transaction which the plaintiff had in contemplation, knew that the advice or information would be communicated to him directly or indirectly and knew that it was very likely that the plaintiff would rely on that advice or information in deciding whether or not to engage in the transaction in contemplation. In these circumstances the defendant could clearly be expected, subject always to the effect of any disclaimer of responsibility, specifically to anticipate that the plaintiff would rely on the advice or information given by the defendant for the very purpose for which he did in the event rely on it. So also the plaintiff, subject again to the effect of any disclaimer, would in that situation reasonably suppose that he was entitled to rely on the advice or information communicated to him for the very purpose for which he required it. The situation is entirely different where a statement is put into more or less general circulation and may foreseeably be relied on by strangers to maker of the statement for any one of a variety of different purposes which the maker of the statement has no specific reason to anticipate. To hold the maker of the statement to be under a duty of care in respect of the accuracy of the statement to all and sundry for any purpose for which they may choose to rely on it is not only to subject him, in the classic words of Cardozo CJ to 'liability in an indeterminate amount for an indeterminate time to an indeterminate class: see *Ultramares Corporation* v *Touche* (1931) 174 NE 441, 444; it is also to confer on the world at large a quite unwarranted entitlement to appropriate for their own purposes the benefit of the expert knowledge or professional expertise attributed to the maker of the statement. Hence, looking only at the circumstances of these decided cases where a duty of care in respect of negligent statements has been held to exist, I should expect to find that the 'limit or control mechanism . . . imposed upon the liability of a wrongdoer towards those who have suffered economic damage in consequence of his negligence' rested in the necessity to prove, in this category of the tort of negligence, as an essential ingredient of the 'proximity' between the plaintiff and the defendant, that the defendant knew that his statement would be communicated to the plaintiff, either as an individual or as a member of an identifiable class, specifically in connection with a particular transaction or transactions of a particular kind (e.g. in a prospectus inviting investment) and that the plaintiff would be very likely to rely on it for the purpose of deciding whether or not to enter upon that transaction or upon a transaction of that kind. . . .

Some of the speeches in the *Hedley Byrne* case derive a duty of care in relation to negligent statements from a voluntary assumption of responsibility on the part of the maker of the statements. In his speech in *Smith* v *Eric S. Bush* [1990] 1 AC 831, 862, Lord Griffiths emphatically rejected the view that this was the true ground of liability . . .

I do not think that in the context of the present appeal anything turns upon the difference between these two approaches.

These considerations amply justify the conclusion that auditors of a public company's accounts owe no duty of care to members of the public at large who rely upon the accounts in deciding to buy shares in the company. If a duty of care were owed so widely, it is difficult to see any reason why it should not equally extend to all who rely on the accounts in relation to other dealings with a company as lenders or merchants extending credit to the company. A claim that such a duty was owed by auditors to a bank lending to a company was emphatically and convincingly rejected by Millett J in *Al Saudi Banque* v *Clarke Pixley* [1990] Ch 313. The only support for an unlimited duty of care owed by auditors for the accuracy of their accounts to all who may foreseeably rely upon them is to be found in some jurisdictions in the United States of America where there are striking differences in the law in different states. In this jurisdiction I have no doubt that the creation of such an unlimited duty would be a legislative step which it would be for Parliament, not the courts, to take. . . .

The shareholders of a company have a collective interest in the company's proper management and in so far as a negligent failure of the auditor to report accurately on the state of the company's finances deprives the shareholders of the opportunity to exercise their powers in general meeting to call the directors to book and to ensure that errors in management are corrected, the shareholders ought to be entitled to a remedy. But in practice no problem arises in this regard since the interest of the shareholders in the proper management of the company's affairs is indistinguishable from the interest of the company itself and any loss suffered by the shareholders, e.g. by the negligent failure of the auditor to discover and expose a misappropriation of funds by a director of the company, will be recouped by a claim against the auditors in the name of the company, not by individual shareholders.

I find it difficult to visualise a situation arising in the real world in which the individual shareholder could claim to have sustained a loss in respect of his existing shareholding referable to the negligence of the auditor which could not be recouped by the company. But on this part of the case your Lordships were much pressed with the argument that such a loss might occur by a negligent undervaluation of the company's assets in the auditor's report relied on by the individual shareholder in deciding to sell his shares at an undervalue. The argument then runs thus. The shareholder, qua shareholder, is entitled to rely on the auditor's report as the basis of his investment decision to sell his existing shareholding. If he sells at an undervalue he is entitled to recover the loss from the auditor. There can be no distinction in law between the shareholder's investment decision to sell the shares he has or to buy additional shares. It follows, therefore, that the scope of the duty of care owed to him by the auditor extends to cover any loss sustained consequent on the purchase of additional shares in reliance on the auditor's negligent report.

I believe this argument to be fallacious. Assuming without deciding that a claim by a shareholder to recover a loss suffered by selling his shares at an undervalue attributable to an undervaluation of the company's assets in the auditor's report could be sustained at all, it would not be by reason of any reliance by the shareholder on the auditor's report in deciding to sell; the loss would be referable to the depreciatory effect of the report on the market value of the shares before ever the decision of the shareholder to sell was taken. A claim to recoup a loss alleged to flow from the purchase of overvalued shares, on the other hand, can only be sustained on the basis of the purchaser's reliance on the report. The specious equation of 'investment of decisions' to sell or to buy as giving rise to parallel claims thus appears to me to be untenable. Moreover, the loss in the case of the sale would be of a loss of part of the value of the shareholder's existing holding, which, assuming a duty of care owed to individual shareholders, it might sensibly lie within the scope of the auditor's duty to protect. A loss, on the other hand, resulting from the purchase of additional shares would result from a wholly independent transaction having no connection with the existing shareholding.

I believe it is this last distinction which is of critical importance and which demonstrates the unsoundness of the conclusion reached by the majority of the Court of Appeal. It is never sufficient to ask simply whether A owes B a duty of care. It is always necessary to determine the scope of the duty by reference to the kind of damage from which A must take care to save B harmless. 'The question is always whether the defendant was under a duty to avoid or prevent that damage, but the actual nature of the damage suffered is relevant to the existence and extent of any duty to avoid or prevent it;' see *Sutherland Shire Council* v *Heyman*, 60 ALR 1, 48, *per* Brennan J. Assuming for the purpose of the argument that the relationship between the auditor of a company and individual shareholders is of sufficient proximity to give rise to a duty of care, I do not understand how the scope of that duty can possibly extend beyond the protection of any individual shareholder from losses in the value of the shares which he holds. As a purchaser of additional shares in reliance on the auditor's report, he stands in no different position from any other investing member of the public to whom the auditor owes no duty. . . .

Assuming for the purpose of the argument that the relationship between the auditor of a company and individual shareholders is of sufficient proximity to give rise to a duty of care, I do not understand how the scope of that duty can possibly extend beyond the protection of any individual shareholder from losses in the value of the shares which he holds. As a purchaser of additional shares in reliance on the auditor's report, he stands in no different position from any other investing member of the public to whom the auditor owes no duty.

I would allow the appeal and dismiss the cross-appeal.

LORD ROSKILL: My Lords, I confess that, like Lord Griffiths in *Smith* v *Eric S Bush* [1989] 2 All ER 514 at 534, [1989] 2 WLR 790 at 813, I find considerable difficulty in phrases such as 'voluntary assumption of responsibility' unless they are to be explained as meaning no more than the existence of circumstances in which the law will impose a liability on a person making the allegedly negligent statement to the person to whom that statement is made, in which case the phrase does not help to determine in what circumstances the law will impose that liability or, indeed, its scope. The submission that there is a virtually unlimited and unrestricted duty of care in relation to the performance of an auditor's statutory duty to certify a company's accounts, a duty extending to anyone who may use those accounts for any purpose such as investing in the company or lending their company money, seems to me untenable. No doubt it can be said to be foreseeable that those accounts may find their way into the hands of persons who may use them for such purposes or, indeed, other purposes and lose money as a result. But to impose a liability in those circumstances is to hold, contrary to all recent authorities, that foreseeability alone is sufficient, and to ignore the statutory duty which enjoins the preparation of, and certification of, those accounts.

I think that, before the existence and scope of any liability can be determined, it is necessary first to determine for what purposes and in what circumstances the information in question is to be given. If a would-be investor or predator commissions a report which he will use, and which the maker of the report knows he will use, as a basis for his decision whether or not to invest or whether or not to make a bid, it may not be difficult to conclude that, if the report is negligently prepared and as a result a decision is taken in reliance on it and financial losses then follow, a liability will be imposed on the maker of that report. But I venture to echo the caution expressed by my noble and learned friend Lord Oliver that, because different cases may display common features, they are necessarily all cases in which the same consequences regarding liability or the scope of liability will follow. Moreover, there may be cases in which the circumstances in which the report was commissioned justify the inclusion of, and reliance on, a disclaimer such as succeeded in the *Hedley Byrne* case, but by reason of subsequent statutory provisions failed in *Smith* v *Eric S. Bush*.

LORD OLIVER: What can be deduced from the *Hedley Byrne* case, therefore, is that the necessary relationship between the maker of a statement or giver of advice ('the adviser') and the recipient who acts in reliance upon it ('the advisee') may typically be held to exist where (1) the advice is required for a purpose, whether particularly specified or generally described, which is made known, either actually or inferentially, to the adviser at the time when the advice is given; (2) the adviser knows, either actually or inferentially, that his advice will be communicated to the advisee, either specifically or as a member of an ascertainable class, in order that it should be used by the advisee for that purpose; (3) it is known either actually or inferentially, that the advice so communicated is likely to be acted upon by the advisee for that purpose without independent inquiry, and (4) it is so acted upon by the advisee to his detriment. That is not, of course, to suggest that these conditions are either conclusive or exclusive. . . .

In seeking to ascertain whether there should be imposed on the adviser a duty to avoid the occurrence of the kind of damage which the advisee claims to have suffered it is not, I think, sufficient to ask simply whether there existed a 'closeness' between them in the sense that the advisee had a legal entitlement to receive the information upon the basis of which he has acted or in the sense that the information was intended to serve his interest or to protect him. One must, I think, go further and ask, in what capacity was his interest to be served and from what was he intended to be protected? A company's annual accounts are capable of being utilised for a number of purposes and if one thinks about it it is entirely foreseeable that they may be so employed. But many of such purposes have absolutely no connection with the recipient's status or capacity, whether as a shareholder, voting or non-voting, or as a debenture-holder. Before it can be concluded that the duty is imposed to protect the recipient against harm which he suffers by reason of the particular use that he chooses to make of the information which he receives, one must, I think, first ascertain the purpose for which the information is required to be given. Indeed, the paradigmatic *Donoghue* v *Stevenson* case of a manufactured article requires, as an essential ingredient of liability, that the article has been used by the consumer in the manner in which it was intended to be used: see *Grant* v *Australian Knitting Mills Ltd* [1936] AC 85, 104 and *Junior Books Ltd* v *Veitchi Co. Ltd* [1983] 1 AC 520, 549, 552. I entirely follow that if the conclusion is reached that the very purpose of providing the information is to serve as the basis for making investment decisions or giving investment advice, it is not difficult then to conclude also that the duty imposed upon the adviser extends to protecting the recipient against loss occasioned by an unfortunate investment decision which is based on carelessly inaccurate information. . . . I do not believe and I see no grounds for believing that, in enacting the statutory provisions [of the Companies Act 1985], Parliament had in mind the provision of information for the assistance of purchasers of shares or debentures in the market, whether they be already the holders of shares or other securities or persons having no previous proprietary interest in the company. It is unnecessary to decide the point on this appeal, but I can see more force in the contention that one purpose of providing the statutory information might be to enable the recipient to exercise whatever rights he has in relation to his proprietary interest by virtue of which he receives it, by way, for instance, of disposing of that interest. I can, however, see no ground for supposing that the legislature was intending to foster a market for the existing holders of shares or debentures by providing information for the purpose of enabling them to acquire such securities from other holders who might be minded to sell.

For my part, I think that the position as regards the auditor's statutory duty was correctly summarised by O'Connor LJ, in his dissenting judgment when he said, at p. 714:

> The statutory duty owed by auditors to shareholders is, I think, a duty owed to them as a body. I appreciate that it is difficult to see how the over-statement of the accounts can cause damage to the shareholders as a body; it will be the underlying reasons for the over-statement which cause damage, for example fraudulent abstraction of assets by directors or servants, but such loss is recoverable by the company. I am anxious to limit the present case to deciding whether the statutory duty operates to protect the individual shareholder as a potential buyer of further shares. If I am wrong in thinking that under the statute no duty is owed to shareholders as individuals, then I think the duty must be confined to transactions in which the shareholder can only participate because he is a shareholder. The Companies Act 1985 imposes a duty to shareholders as a class and the duty should not extend to an individual save as a member of the class in respect of some class activity. Buying shares in a company is not such an activity.

In my judgment, accordingly, the purpose for which the auditors' certificate is made and published is that of providing those entitled to receive the report with information to enable them to exercise in conjunction those powers which their respective proprietary interests confer upon them and not for the purposes of individual speculation with a view to profit. The same considerations as limit the existence of a duty of care also, in my judgment, limit the scope of the duty and I agree with O'Connor LJ that the duty of care is one owed to the shareholders as a body and not to individual shareholders

To widen the scope of the duty to include loss caused to an individual by reliance on the accounts for a purpose for which they were not supplied and were not intended would be to extend it beyond the limits which are so far deducible from the decisions of this House. It is not, as I think, an extension which either logic requires or policy dictates and I, for my part, am not prepared to follow the majority of the Court of Appeal in making it. In relation to the purchase of shares of other shareholders in a company, whether in the open market or as a result of an offer made to all or a majority of the existing shareholders, I can see no sensible distinction, so far as a duty of care is concerned, between a potential purchaser who is, *vis-à-vis* the company, a total outsider and one who is already the holder of one or more shares. I accordingly agree with what has already fallen from my noble and learned friend Lord Bridge, and I, too, would allow the appeal and dismiss the cross-appeal.

Lord Jauncey delivered a concurring speech, and Lord Ackner agreed with all the speeches.

AL SAUDI BANQUE v *CLARKE PIXLEY* [1989] 3 All ER 361

Millet J held that company auditors do not owe a duty of care to a bank lending money to the company even though it is foreseeable that the bank might request a copy of the accounts. Insufficient proximity existed between the auditors and the bank. The learned judge said: 'In my judgment *Caparo* [i.e. the finding in the Court of Appeal] marks the furthest limit to which the duty of care for negligent misstatement has so far been taken in England, and its reasoning does not encourage any further advance. *Smith* v *Bush* by contrast, suggests a more stringent test to make the requirements for proximity accord more closely with those of the American Restatement or of Denning LJ in his dissenting judgment in *Candler* v *Crane, Christmas & Co.* [1951] 1 All ER 426. These would limit the duty of care in respect not only of the persons to whom it is owed but also of the transactions in which it applies. No such limit was imposed in *Caparo*, and a comparison of Caparo with *Smith* v *Bush* suggests that the tests of proximity may have been too widely stated in *Caparo*, not too narrowly. But even applying the more generous test in *Caparo*, these plaintiffs do not meet it. There was no relationship between them and the defendants. The test of proximity is not satisfied . . .'

MORGAN CRUCIBLE CO. v *HILL SAMUEL BANK LTD* [1991] 1 All ER 148 (CA)

SLADE LJ: The case against the directors was based on the representations made in the defence documents. In *Caparo*, the fatal weakness in the plaintiff's case which negatived the existence of a relationship of proximity was the fact that the relevant statements by the auditors had not been given for the purposes for which the plaintiff had relied on it.

It was at least arguable that this case could be distinguished on its assumed facts, that each of the directors, in making the relevant representations, was aware that Morgan Crucible would rely on them for the purpose of deciding whether to make an increased bid and intended that it should; that was one of the purposes of the defence documents.

It might be that Morgan Crucible at trial would fail to prove the allegation that one of the purposes of the documents was to persuade an offeror to offer the best terms to the shareholders, but that would be a matter of evidence. Although the decision might have wide implications for directors, bankers and accountants, it would not be right by reference to economic considerations to dismiss as unarguable an otherwise arguable case.

The argument related to the possibility of another previously unidentified bidder (a so-called 'white knight'), that the duty of care must be owed either to both original bidder and white knight or neither and that it was the proper conclusion that it was owed to neither would be canvassed at trial. Its correctness was not sufficiently clear to justify the dismissal of Morgan Crucible's claim against the directors. The claim against the directors was not bound to fail at trial.

On the assumed facts, it must be arguable that Hill Samuel, giving advice as experts, owed to Morgan Crucible a duty of care in making representations on profit forecast. The court was not convinced by the submission that a bank could never be held to owe duties to parties with conflicting interests. For the reasons given, Morgan Crucible had an arguable case.

Morgan Crucible's case should therefore be allowed to go to trial where in the context of duty of care, questions of proximity and justice and reasonableness could be considered by reference to the evidence.

JAMES McNAUGHTON PAPER GROUP LTD v *HICKS ANDERSON AND CO.* [1991] 1 All ER 134 (CA)

This case is referred to in **Chapter 5** of the *Learning Text*.

NEILL LJ: In the last 25 years or so since the landmark decision of the House of Lords in *Hedley Byrne & Co. Ltd* v *Heller & Partners Ltd* [1963] 2 All ER 575 consideration has been given in a number of cases in the appellate courts to the circumstances in which a duty of care exists giving rise to liability in negligence where the loss suffered by the plaintiff is a purely economic loss. At the same time the courts have been concerned with the wider problem of trying to isolate and define the essential ingredients of the tort of negligence in all its manifestations.

In the earlier part of this period attempts were made to seek a general principle which, subject to any necessary modification to meet the facts of a particular case, could be applied in all circumstances. This quest for a general principle led finally to the well known passage in the speech of Lord Wilberforce in *Anns* v *Merton London Borough Council* [1977] 2 All ER 492 at 498 . . . In the last ten years, however, there has been a change of direction. In a series of decisions of the Privy Council and of the House of Lords it has been emphasised that no single general principle is able to provide a practical test which can be applied to every situation to determine whether a duty of care is owed and, if so, what is its scope. This series of cases was recently referred to by Lord Bridge in his speech in *Caparo Industries PLC* v *Dickman* [1990] 1 All ER 568 . . . a similar restatement of the present state of the law was given by Lord Goff in *Davis* v *Radcliffe* [1990] 2 All ER 536 at 540 . . .

It therefore seems probable that, at any rate at this stage, the common law in England will develop step by step and in accordance with the views expressed by Brennan J in the High Court of Australia in *Sutherland Shire Council* v *Heyman* (1985) 60 ALR 1 at 43 . . .

It therefore becomes necessary, in the absence of some general principle, to examine each individual case in the light of the concepts of foreseeability, proximity and fairness. The last of these concepts, however, is elusive and may indeed be no more than one of the criteria by which proximity is to be judged. It is perhaps sufficient to underline that in every case the court must not only consider the foreseeability of the damage and whether the relationship between the parties is sufficiently proximate but must also pose and answer the questions: in this situation is it fair, just and reasonable that the law should impose on the defendant a duty of the scope suggested for the benefit of the plaintiff? I turn next to consider what guidance can be obtained from the modern authorities as to how these general concepts are to be applied (in the words of Lord Bridge in *Caparo* 'to determine the essential characteristics of the situation giving rise, independently of any contractual or fiduciary relationship, to a duty of care owed by one party to another to ensure the accuracy of any statement which the one party makes and on which the other party may foreseeably rely to his economic detriment.'

The natural starting point for this search for guidance is of course *Hedley-Byrne*, but I do not propose to make any detailed reference to it for . . . the compelling reasons . . . that Lord Oliver himself in *Caparo* set out . . . the guidance which can be obtained from *Hedley-Byrne*; 'What can be deduced from the *Hedley-Byrne* case, therefore, is that the necessary relationship between the maker of a statement or giver of advice ('the adviser') and the recipient who acts in reliance upon it ('the advisee') may typically be held to exist where (1) the advice is required for a purpose, whether particularly specified or generally described, which is made known, either actually or inferentially, to the adviser at the time when the advice is given; (2) the adviser knows either actually or inferentially, that his advice will be communicated to the advisee, either specifically or as a member of an ascertainable class, in order that it should be used by the advisee for that purpose; (3) it is known either actually or inferentially, that the advice so communicated is likely to be acted upon by the advisee to his detriment. That is not, of course, to suggest that these conditions are either conclusive or exclusive, but merely that the actual decision in the case does not warrant any broader propositions.'

I have considered the four propositions which have been distilled by Lord Oliver from the speeches in *Hedley-Byrne*. I have also considered the more recent authorities and in particular the speeches in the House of Lords in *Smith* v *Eric S Bush* [1989] 2 All ER 514 and in *Caparo*. From this scrutiny it seems to me to be clear: (a) that in contrast to developments in the law in New Zealand, of which the decision in *Scott Group Ltd* v *McFarlane* [1978] 1 NZLR 553 provides an important illustration, in England a restrictive approach is now adopted to any extension of the scope of the duty of care beyond the person directly intended by the maker of the statement to act upon it; and (b) that in deciding whether a duty of care exists in any particular case it is necessary to take all the circumstances into account; but (c) that, notwithstanding (b), it is possible to identify certain matters which are likely to be of importance in most cases in reaching a decision as to whether or not a duty exists . . .

   (a)   The purpose for which the statement was made and on which the claim was based: e.g. Was it made for the express purpose of being communicated to the advisee?
   (b)   The purpose for which the statement was communicated, e.g. for information only?
   (c)   The relationship between the advisor, the advisee, and any relevant third party?
   (d)   The size of any class to which the advisee belonged.
   (e)   The state of knowledge of the adviser (actual and attributed).
   (f)   Reliance by the advisee. Often, it would be useful to look at the matter from the plaintiff's point of view. In business transactions conducted at arm's length it might sometimes be difficult for an advisee to prove that he had been entitled to act on a statement without taking any independent advice or to prove that the adviser had known, actually or inferentially, that he would act without taking such advice . . .

MINORIES FINANCE LTD v ARTHUR YOUNG AND BANK OF ENGLAND; JOHNSON MATTHEY PLC v ARTHUR YOUNG AND BANK OF ENGLAND [1989] 2 All ER 105

Third party proceedings were involved: auditors were being sued in negligence (a) by the organisation which had succeeded a commercial bank (which had become insolvent) and (b) by the parent company of the insolvent bank, and the auditors sought to join the Bank of England in the proceedings. The bank asked the court to strike out the third party notices because they did not owe any duty of care to the failed bank. It was found that it would be 'contrary to commonsense and reason' to suppose that the bank could owe a duty to a commercial bank to 'make good [its] losses [caused by] its own imprudent conduct on the ground that the bank should have discovered and dealt with those shortcomings'. No duty was owed to the partner company as a 'depositor' because money paid by a parent company to a subsidiary (or vice-versa) did not, due to s. 1(5)(d) of the Banking Act 1979, come within the definition of 'deposit' and thus did not come within the scope of the bank's statutory obligations with regard to deposit-taking businesses. Thus, the notices were struck out.

MILLS v WINCHESTER DIOCESAN BOARD OF FINANCE [1989] 2 All ER 317

This was an appeal against striking out orders (pleadings; disclosure of causes of action). In dismissing the appeal it was found that the Charity Commissioners owed no duty of care to potential objects of a charity, in respect of erroneous opinion and advice, on the following grounds:

1.   There existed a statutory right of appeal in respect of such matters (s. 28, Charities Act 1960).
2.   There would be disadvantages in having a negligence action proceeding concurrently with s. 28 proceedings.
3.   There would be a 'negative effect on the general good of charities' were negligence actions available by a wide class of potential objects.
4.   It was doubtful, in any event, whether there was sufficient proximity between the parties.
5.   (Alternatively) taking into account these factors, it would not be 'just and reasonable' to impose a duty of care on the Commissioners in such circumstances. (The judge followed *Jones* v *Department of Employment* and considered, amongst other cases, *Ministry of Housing* v *Sharp* and *Anns* v *Merton*.)

SOUTH AUSTRALIA ASSET MANAGEMENT CORPORATION v YORK MONTAGUE LTD AND OTHERS [1996] 3 All ER 365 (HL) (sub nom. BANQUE BRUXELLES LAMBERT SA v EAGLE STAR INSURANCE CO. LTD)

A valuer of real property negligently overvalued some premises and as a result a lender of money gave a loan on the security of that property. The lender could show that had the valuer performed his task properly, and correctly valued the property, the lender would not have made the loan.

The borrower defaulted and the lender sold the property, but in the meantime the property dropped in value because of the economic recession of the early 1990s. In an action for negligence and breach of contract, the court had to decide whether the claim for damages against the valuer would include the loss due to the fall in the market.

Overturning a unanimous decision of the Court of Appeal, the House of Lords found that the valuer was liable only for that loss which was due to the over-valuation and **not** for that part of the loss which was due to the fall in property prices.

Lord Hoffmann, with whom the rest of the House agreed, drew an analogy with the fictitious example of a mountaineer suing his doctor, where the doctor had negligently certified one of the climber's knees as fit for climbing and the climber suffered injury in a mountaineering accident – in spite of the fact that the accident was not directly connected to the problem with the knee. In his Lordship's opinion, to find the doctor liable for that accident would offend 'common sense, because it makes the doctor responsible for consequences which, though in general terms foreseeable, do not appear to have a sufficient causal connection with the **subject matter of the duty'. (emphasis added)**

Thus, the answer to this conundrum was not to be found in any analysis of causation, but in looking at the **scope of the duty of care**. In each case, a plaintiff must establish that the defendant owes a duty to him and that it **embraces the kind of loss** of which he is complaining.

Within the present context his Lordship drew a distinction between (i) **a duty to provide information** to the plaintiff in order that he could decide on a course of action, and (ii) **a duty to advise** a person as to which course of action he should take.

In (i) the duty would be limited to taking reasonable care to see that the information was accurate, and any negligence would result in liability for the foreseeable consequences of the information being wrong. Where (ii) applied, the defendant's duty would be to take reasonable care in considering all the potential consequences of the course of action, and liability would lie for the foreseeable consequences of the course of action taken by the plaintiff in reliance on that advice.

A valuer would normally come within the first category (though much might depend on the terms of the contract between the parties), i.e. he advises on the value of the property, knowing that this advice is likely to be relied on by the lender in deciding (a) whether to lend and (b) how much to lend. The valuer is not usually asked to **advise** whether to lend; indeed valuers would usually not be equipped to provide advice of that nature.

BANK OF CREDIT AND COMMERCE INTERNATIONAL (OVERSEAS) LTD (IN LIQUIDATION), BCCI HOLDINGS (LUXEMBOURG) SA (IN LIQUIDATION) AND BANK OF CREDIT AND COMMERCE INTERNATIONAL SA (IN LIQUIDATION) v PRICE WATERHOUSE AND OTHERS AND ERNST WHINNEY AND OTHERS, The Times, 4 March 1998 (CA)

The three plaintiffs went into liquidation as the result of the financial collapse of the BCCI banking **group** (of which they were members). The **second** defendants were the auditors of 'Holdings' and 'SA', and the **first** defendants were the auditors of 'Overseas'.

Actions in contract and tort were brought against the defendants by the liquidators for negligently performed audits which failed to detect massive frauds perpetrated on creditors and shareholders of the plaintiff companies, but at this stage of the proceedings the court was concerned only with Overseas' claims against the **second** defendants. Overseas alleged that Ernst Whinney, who were not **its** auditors, owed it a duty of care in negligence in carrying out their duties as auditors of Holdings and SA.

Overseas alleged that the business and operations of Overseas and SA were managed as if they were a business and operations of a **single** bank. At first instance, however, it had been held that the pleadings showed no cause of action by Overseas against Ernst Whinney because Overseas had their **own** auditors (Price Waterhouse) upon whom they relied.

Sir Brian Neill, delivering the judgment of the court, said that the leading cases involving accountants and other professional advisers for economic loss caused to persons **other than their clients** had followed three 'separate but parallel paths', viz.:

1 The 'threefold test' stated by Lord Griffiths in *Smith* v *Eric S. Bush* ([1990] 1 AC 831) and considered in *Caparo Industries plc* v *Dickman* ([1990] 2 AC 605) that raised three essential questions:

(a) Was it reasonably foreseeable that the plaintiff would suffer the kind of damage which occurred?

(b) Was there sufficient proximity between the parties?

(c) Was it just and reasonable that the defendant should owe a duty of care of the scope asserted by the plaintiff?

2 The 'assumption of responsibility' test that was explained in *White* v *Jones* ([1995] 2 AC 207, 268, 273).

3 The adoption of an incremental approach, recognised by Lord Bridge of Harwich in *Caparo* (at p. 618) and which received further support in *Murphy* v *Brentwood District Council* ([1991] 1 AC 398). That approach ensured that developments in the law would take place in measured steps.

The fact that all those approached had been used and approved by the House of Lords in recent years suggested that it could be useful to look at any new set of facts by using each of the three approaches in turn. If the facts were properly analysed and the policy considerations correctly evaluated the several approaches would yield the same result.

The general trend of the authorities made it clear that liability would depend not on intention but on the actual or presumed knowledge of the adviser and on the circumstances of the case.

Here the banking activities of SA and Overseas were conducted as those of a single bank. There were unusual arrangements whereby the accounts of SA and Holdings were audited by Ernst & Whinney whereas the accounts of Overseas, the other principal banking subsidiary, were audited by Price Waterhouse.

The intermingling of the businesses of the two banks supported an argument that Overseas and Price Waterhouse in turn had to rely on Ernst & Whinney.

In cases where parties were dealing at arm's length the court would be slow to extend the orbit of the duty of care to include persons other than the immediate client. There was a barrier which had to be overcome and that barrier would be strengthened if a third party was in receipt of independent advice.

But here the barrier between Ernst & Whinney on the one hand and Overseas and Price Waterhouse on the other hand was a mere shadow. Constant interchange of information had been necessary.

Ernst & Whinney was in effect the supervising firm with responsibilities extending, at least arguably, not only to the boards and regulatory authorities of Holdings and SA but also to the boards and regulatory authorities of Overseas, as well as to Price Waterhouse as Overseas' auditors.

If one applied the threefold test or the assumption of responsibility test to the facts of the case as pleaded, it would be quite wrong to dismiss the claims by Overseas in limine [i.e. **at the 'threshold' stage of proceedings**].

It is important to observe two features of this decision viz. (i) it was an argument on the pleadings only, i.e. as to whether there was a case to argue at **trial** and (ii) the court stressed the **unusual facts** of this case, establishing a special relationship whereby the duty of care owed by professional accountants employed to audit the accounts of a bank might extend to **another** bank which employed its own, independent, auditors.

5.3.6　THREE PARTY RELATIONSHIPS

5.3.6.1　Others

SPRING v GUARDIAN ASSURANCE PLC [1994] 3 All ER 129 (HL)

LORD GOFF: The central issue in this appeal is whether a person who provides a reference in respect of another who was formerly engaged by him as a member of his staff may be liable in damages to that other in respect of economic loss suffered by him by reason of negligence in the preparation of the reference. That issue can, for the sake of convenience, be subdivided into two questions.

(1)   Whether the person who provided the reference *prima facie* owes a duty of care, in contract or tort, to the other in relation to the preparation of the reference.

(2)   If so, whether the existence of such a duty of care will nevertheless be negatived because it would, if recognised, *pro tanto* undermine the policy underlying the defence of qualified privilege in the law of defamation.

. . . an employer who provides a reference in respect of one of his employees to a prospective future employer will ordinarily owe a duty of care to his employee in respect of the preparation of the reference. The employer is possessed of special knowledge, derived from his experience of the employee's character, skill and diligence in the performance of his duties while working for the employer. Moreover, when the employer provides a reference to a third party in respect of his employee, he does so not only for the assistance of the third party, but also, for what it is worth, for the assistance of the employee. Indeed, nowadays it must often be very difficult for an employee to obtain fresh employment without the benefit of a reference from his present or previous employer. It is for this reason that, in ordinary life, it may be the employee, rather than a prospective future employer, who asks the employer to provide the reference; and even where the approach comes from the prospective future employer, it will (apart from special circumstances) be made with either the express or tacit authority of the employee.

The provision of such references is a service regularly provided by employers to their employees; indeed, references are part of the currency of the modern employment market. Furthermore, when such a reference is provided by an employer, it is plain that the employee relies upon him to exercise due skill and care in the preparation of the reference before making it available to the third party. In these circumstances, it seems to me that all the elements requisite for the application of the *Hedley Byrne* principle are present. I need only add that, in the context under consideration, there is no question of the circumstances in which the reference is being provided being, for example, so informal as to negative an assumption of responsibility by the employer.

Where the relationship between the parties is that of employer and employee, the duty of care could be expressed as arising from an implied term of the contract of employment, i.e. that, if a reference is supplied by the employer for the employee, due care and skill will be exercised by him in its preparation. Such a term may be implied despite the absence of any legal obligation on the employer to provide a reference (as I understand to have been accepted by the parties in the present case), and may be expressed to apply even after the employee has left his employment with the employer. But in the present case this adds nothing to the duty of care which arises under the *Hedley Byrne* principle, and so may be applicable as a tortious duty, either where there is no contract between the parties, or concurrently with a contractual duty to the same effect.

I wish however to add that, in considering the duty of care owed by the employer to the employee, although it can and should be expressed in broad terms, nevertheless the central requirement is that reasonable care and skill should be exercised by the employer in ensuring the accuracy of any facts which either (1) are communicated to the recipient of the reference from which he may form an adverse opinion of the employee, or (2) are the basis of an adverse opinion expressed by the employer himself about the employee. I wish further to add that it does not necessarily follow that, because the employer owes such a duty of care to his employee, he also owes a duty of care to the recipient of the reference. The relationship of the employer with the recipient is by no means the same as that with his employee; and whether, in a case such as this, there should be held (as was prima facie held to be so on the facts of the *Hedley Byrne* case itself) a duty of care owed by the maker of the reference to the recipient is a point on which I do not propose to express an opinion, and which may depend on the facts of the particular case before the court . . .

For these reasons, subject to the point on defamation, I am satisfied that the defendants owed a duty of care to the plaintiff in respect of the preparation of the reference . . . It follows that the negligence . . . in the preparation of the reference, as found by the judge, resulted in a breach of that prima facie duty by the defendants . . .

If so, whether such a duty will nevertheless be negatived because it would, if recognised, pro tanto *undermine the policy underlying the defence of qualified privilege in the law of defamation.*

I think it desirable that I should first of all identify the nature of this policy objection. As I understand it, the objection is as follows. First of all, reference is made to the description of the policy underlying the defence of qualified privilege given by Lord Diplock in *Horrocks* v *Lowe* [1974] 1 All ER 662 at 669–670 . . . Second, it is suggested that the policy which underlies the defence of qualified privilege, viz that in the relevant circumstances men should be permitted to communicate frankly and freely with one another about all relevant matters, prevents the recognition of a duty of care owed by the giver of the reference to the subject of the reference . . . it is, I consider, necessary to approach the question as a matter of principle. Since, for the reasons I have given, it is my opinion that in cases such as the present the duty of care arises by reason of an assumption of responsibility by the employer to the employee in respect of the relevant reference, I can see no good reason why the duty to exercise due skill and care which rests upon the employer should be negatived because, if the plaintiff were instead to bring an action for damage to his reputation, he would be met by the defence of qualified privilege which could only be defeated by proof of malice. It is not to be forgotten that the *Hedley Byrne* duty arises where there is a relationship which is, broadly speaking, either contractual or equivalent to contact. In these circumstances, I cannot see that principles of the law of defamation are of any relevance . . .

For these reasons I would allow the appeal; but I would nevertheless remit the matter to the Court of Appeal to consider the issue of the extent to which the damage suffered by the plaintiff was caused by the breach of duty of the defendants.

LORD SLYNN: I do not consider that the existence of either of these two heads of claim, defamation and injurious falsehood, a priori prevents the recognition of a duty of care where, but for the existence of the other two torts, it would be fair, just and reasonable to recognise it in a situation where the giver of a reference has said or written what is untrue and where he has acted unreasonably and carelessly in what he has said . . .

As to the second question it is a relevant circumstance that in many cases an employee will stand no chance of getting another job, let alone a better job, unless he is given a reference. There is at least a moral obligation on the employer to give it. This is not necessarily true when the claim is laid in defamation even if on an occasion of qualified privilege. In the case of an employee or ex-employee the damage is clearly foreseeable if a careless reference is given; there is as obvious a proximity of relationship in this context as can be imagined. The sole question therefore, in my view, is whether balancing all the factors 'the situation should be one in which the court considers it fair, just and reasonable that the law should impose a duty of a given scope upon the one party for the benefit of the other' (*per* Lord Bridge in *Caparo* [1990] 1 All ER 568 at 574).

Hedley Byrne & Co. Ltd v *Heller & Partners Ltd* [1964] AC 465 does not decide the present case, but I find it unacceptable that the person to whom a reference is given about an employee X should be able to sue for negligence if he relies on the statement (and, for example, employs X who proves to be inadequate for the job) as it appears to be assumed that he can; but that X who is refused employment because the recipient relies on a reference negligently given should have no recourse unless he can prove express malice as defined by Lord Diplock in *Horrocks* v *Lowe* [1974] 1 All ER 662 . . .

In my opinion the judge was entitled to find, as he did, that there was here a sufficiently proximate relationship between the companies on whose behalf the reference was given; the damage was clearly foreseeable; and it is fair, just and reasonable in such an employment situation for the law to recognise a duty on the part of the giver of the reference, and the person who within the employer's organisation collates or provides information for the purpose of preparing the reference, to take reasonable care that the information was obtained and passed on with reasonable care. On this aspect of the case I think the judge was right; duty and breach were established.

LORD WOOLF: . . . I find that public policy comes down firmly in favour of not depriving an employee of a remedy to recover the damages to which he would otherwise be entitled as a result of being a victim of a negligent reference.

Under this head there remains to be considered whether it is preferable for the law in this area to be developed by Parliament or by the courts. It is an area of law where previous decisions of the courts have already clearly identified the tests which should be applied in deciding whether the law should be developed. It is also an area where a case-by-case approach is particularly appropriate and so as happened in *Hedley Byrne & Co. Ltd* v *Heller & Partners Ltd* [1963] 2 All ER 575, [1964] AC 465 it appears to me desirable for the courts to provide the remedy which I believe is clearly required.

As I indicated earlier it is possible to approach this appeal as being primarily one involving a contractual issue. This was the preferred approach of Lord Bridge of Harwich in *Scally* v *Southern Health and Social Services Board* [1992] 1 AC 294 in a speech, with which other members of the House agreed, from which I obtained singular assistance. In that case, Lord Bridge stated the obverse of the proposition that I have previously advanced when he said ([1991] 4 All ER 563 at 568, [1992] 1 AC 294 at 303): 'If a duty of the kind in question was not inherent in the contractual relationship, I do not see how it could possibly be derived from the tort of negligence.' In *Scally* it was decided that where a contract of employment negotiated between employers and a representative body contained a particular term conferring on an employee a valuable contingent right to a pension of the benefit of which he could not be expected to be aware unless the term was brought to his attention, there was an implied obligation on the employer to take reasonable steps to publicise that term. Accordingly, when the employer failed to notify the employee of his pension rights, which were therefore lost, he was entitled to recover damages for breach of contract in respect of that loss . . .

As I understand *Scally*, it recognises that, just as in the earlier authorities the courts were prepared to imply by necessary implication a term imposing a duty on an employer to exercise due care for the physical well-being of his employees, so in the appropriate circumstances would the court imply a like duty as to his economic well-being, the duty as to his economic well-being giving rise to an action for damages if it is breached.

Here, it is also possible to specify circumstances which would enable a term to be implied. The circumstances are: (i) the existence of the contract of employment or services; (ii) the fact that the contract relates to an engagement of a class where it is the normal practice to require a reference from a previous employer before employment is offered; (iii) the fact that the employee cannot be expected to enter into that class of employment except on the basis that his employer will, on the request of another prospective employer made not later than a reasonable time after the termination of a former employment, provide a full and frank reference as to the employee.

This being the nature of the engagement, it is necessary to imply a term into the contract that the employer would, during the continuance of the engagement or within a reasonable time thereafter, provide a reference at the request of a prospective employer which was based on facts revealed after making those reasonably careful inquiries which, in the circumstances, a reasonable employer would make.

In this case Mr Spring's employers were in breach of that implied term. Although the person actually writing the reference was not negligent, she delegated the task of ascertaining the facts to others, and as is the case with the employer's duty to exercise reasonable care for the safety of his employee, the employer cannot escape liability by so delegating his responsibility.

It only remains for me to underline what I anticipate is already clear, that is, that the views which I have expressed are confined to the class of case with which I am now dealing. Some of the statements I have made I appreciate could be applied to analogous situations. However, I do not intend to express any view either way as to what will be the position in those analogous situations. I believe that they are better decided when, and if, a particular case comes before the court. This approach can lead to uncertainty which is undesirable. However, that undesirable consequence is in my view preferable to trying to anticipate the position in relation to other situations which are not the subject matter of this appeal.

I would allow this appeal and remit the case to the Court of Appeal so that that court can deal with the question of causation.

LORD KEITH (dissenting): . . . My Lords, if no reasons of policy intervened there might be much to be said for the view that Mr Spring is entitled to succeed in his claim based on negligence, on the basis that it was reasonably foreseeable that damage to him would result if the reference were prepared without reasonable care and it thus incorrectly disparaged him, that there was proximity between him and those who prepared the reference, and that it would be fair, just and reasonable to impose a duty of care on the latter. This would, however, extend the ambit of liability in negligence for pure economic loss. In *Hedley Byrne & Co. Ltd* v *Heller & Partners Ltd* [1964] AC 465 such liability was held to exist in circumstances where a plaintiff has relied to his detriment upon a negligent misstatement by a defendant. In the present case there is no question of reliance by the plaintiff on the carelessly prepared reference. But in any event this is, in my opinion, a case in which the second stage of the test propounded by Lord Wilberforce in *Anns* v *Merton London Borough* . . .

The policy grounds which underlie the defence of qualified privilege in an action for defamation were thus stated by Lord Diplock in *Horrocks* v *Lowe* [1975] AC 135 at 149:

> My Lords, as a general rule, English law gives effect to the ninth Commandment that a man shall not speak evil falsely of his neighbour. It supplies a temporal sanction: if he cannot prove that defamatory matter which he published was true, he is liable in damages to whomsoever he has defamed, except where the publication is oral only, causes no damage and falls outside the categories of slander actionable per se. The public interest that the law should provide an effective means whereby a man can vindicate his reputation against calumny has nevertheless to be accommodated to the competing public interest in permitting men to communicate frankly and freely with one another about matters in respect of which the law recognises that they have a duty to perform or an interest to protect in doing so. What is published in good faith on matters of these kinds is published on a privileged occasion. It is not actionable even though it be defamatory and turns out to be untrue. With some exceptions which are irrelevant to the instant appeal, the privilege is not absolute but qualified. It is lost if the occasion which gives rise to it is misused. For in all cases of qualified privilege there is some special reason of public policy why the law accords immunity from suit—the existence of some public or private duty, whether legal or moral, on the part of the maker of the defamatory statement which justifies his communicating it or of some interest of his own which he is entitled to protect by doing so. If he uses the occasion for some other reason he loses the protection of the privilege.

In my opinion the same grounds of public policy are applicable where the claim is based not on defamation as such but on negligence associated with the making or publication of an untrue statement, where the occasion on which that was done was a privileged one in the sense in which that expression is used in the context of defamation law. If liability in negligence were to follow from a reference prepared without reasonable care, the same adverse consequences would flow as those sought to be guarded against by the defence of qualified privilege. Those asked to give a reference would be inhibited from speaking frankly lest it should be found that they were liable in damages through not taking sufficient care in its preparation. They might well prefer, if under no legal duty to give a reference, to refrain from doing so at all. Any reference given might be bland and unhelpful and information which it would be in the interest of those seeking the reference to receive might be withheld.

As regards the claim for breach of contract, Glidewell LJ giving the judgment of the Court of Appeal, after observing that the trial judge had held that there was no contract between Mr Spring and Guardian Assurance and that it had been argued that he was wrong in this, said ([1993] 2 All ER 273 at 295–296, [1993] ICR 412 at 438–439):

> . . . In our view the judge directed himself entirely correctly that he had to decide whether a term of the kind pleaded was a necessary incident of either contract. He concluded that it was not, and thus that he would not imply such a term. In our view, if the law implied any term in the plaintiff's contract with either Guardian Assurance or Corinium in relation to this matter, such a term would go no further than to require the defendants to comply with their obligations under r. 3.5(2) of the Lautro rules, i.e. to give a reference which made 'full and frank disclosure of all relevant matters which are believed to be true'. With such an obligation the judge of course held that the defendants complied.

I respectfully agree and find it unnecessary to add anything.
Accordingly, I would dismiss the appeal.

Lord Lowry delivered a speech, in which he agreed with Lords Goff, Slynn and Woolf. His Lordship, at p. 153 of the Report, emphasised the importance of the defendants' liability in contract.

Appeal allowed. Case remitted to Court of Appeal for further consideration.

PARKER-TWEEDALE v *DUNBAR BANK PLC (No. 2)* [1990] 2 All ER 588 (CA)

[I]t is established law that a mortgagee owes to his mortgagor a duty to get a proper price for the mortgaged property when he exercises his power of sale in the event of a mortgagor's default. It was held by the Court of Appeal in *Parker-Tweedale* that this duty cannot be extended to a person known by the mortgagee to have a beneficial interest in the property; nor can it be owed to a beneficiary of a trust of which the mortgagor was a trustee and the mortgagee knew this.

Purchas LJ said that the plaintiff who claimed to have a beneficial interest in the property in question relied on the neighbour principle in *Donoghue* v *Stevenson*. The extension of this principle to damages for pecuniary loss established in . . . *Hedley-Byrne* . . . has been the subject of considerable judicial decision in recent years. A tendency . . . in the speeches in . . . *Junior Books* . . . to extend the ambit of this duty has in more recent decisions been restricted. Since . . . *Muirhead* . . . it has been established that there is no general liability in tort for pecuniary loss dissociated from physical damage. Moreover . . . the classic approach by Lord Wilberforce in *Anns* . . . has been questioned particularly with regard to the application of the second part of the test to which the questions of policy applied.

[I]s . . . there in all the circumstances of the case a relationship of proximity established so as to support a duty owed to the person alleging that he has suffered a pecuniary loss by the person whose action is alleged to have caused it . . . ? Where there is a direct contractual relationship the law will be slow to imply a duty greater than that created under the contract even if that contract is silent in a particular aspect: see *Greater Nottingham Co-operative Society Ltd* . . . Even where there is no direct contractual relationship but where there is a contractual context against which the parties came into a relationship short of a direct contractual one, again a duty in tort enlarging the rights enjoyed by the victim of the alleged tort beyond those provided for in the contractual context generally will not be imported: see *Pacific Associates Inc* v *Baxter* [1989] 2 All ER 159.

. . . There is no room for the super-imposition on the duty owed to the mortgagor of a further duty owed by the mortgagee directly to a beneficiary in these circumstances. The beneficiary's rights are against the mortgagor as trustee. [It was pointed out also that the beneficiary could, where the trustee committed some act of misfeasance, take over the trustee's rights and enforce these on behalf of the trust, but not on his own behalf, directly against a third party.] The rights of a beneficiary have already been recognised and protected under the existing equitable principles dealing with the trust and the rights of the beneficiary against the trustees. As Nourse LJ has already said the creation of a duty owed directly by a mortgagee to the beneficiary is both unnecessary and confusing, except where there are wholly exceptional circumstances.

McCULLAGH v LANE FOX AND PARTNERS LTD, *The Times*, 25 January 1994

It was held by Colman J that a seller's estate agent owed a duty of care in the tort of negligence to the purchaser of the property in question, regarding negligent misstatements which the purchaser relied upon in entering into the contract of sale. On the facts, however, his Lordship found that the plaintiff could not establish any loss and accordingly dismissed his action.

In the Court of Appeal (*The Times*, 22 December 1995), however, two judges found that (i) an estate agent who is negligent in stating the size of a property does **not** owe a prospective purchaser a duty of care, provided that the estate agent reasonably believes that the purchaser will not rely on his misstatement because the purchaser intends to obtain an **independent** property survey; and (ii) a duty of care does **not** arise later if the estate agent discovers that the purchaser has decided **not** to commission an independent survey, provided that the estate agent is still unaware of his 'innocent' (albeit negligent) misrepresentation.

Although Hobhouse LJ agreed that no duty of care arose on the facts, his reasoning was somewhat different. In his opinion, a duty of care could have arisen on the estate agent's part, once he became aware of the purchaser's decision to dispense with an independent survey and that he would then rely on the estate agent's misrepresentation – but on the facts of the present case the existence of a **disclaimer** (which satisfied the 'reasonableness' test in the Unfair Contract Terms Act 1977) prevented any such duty of care from arising. The existence of the disclaimer meant that the purchaser was prevented from believing that the estate agent was assuming responsibility for his negligent misstatement. His Lordship reviewed *White* v *Jones* and *Henderson* v *Merrett* and concluded that the principle to be applied is still to be found in *Hedley Byrne*. Under the principle laid down in that case, an **agent** can be as liable as his **principal** for a careless misrepresentation provided that the 'fundamental' elements of **reasonable foreseeability, reliance** and **assumption** of responsibility can be established by the plaintiff.

WHITE v JONES [1995] 1 All ER 691 (HL)

LORD GOFF: It has been recognised on all hands that *Ross* v *Caunters* raises difficulties of a conceptual nature and that, as a result, it is not altogether easy to accommodate the decision within the ordinary principles of the law of obligations.

These conceptual arguments have to be faced; they raise the question of whether the claim properly falls within the law of contract or the law of tort.

The defendants have argued that the claim, if properly analysed, must necessarily have contractual features which cannot ordinarily exist in the case of an ordinary tortious claim.

There is not only the fact that the claim is one for damages for pure economic loss but there is also the need for the defendant solicitor to be entitled to invoke, as against the disappointed beneficiary, any terms of the contract with his client which might limit or exclude liability; the fact that the damages claimed are for the loss of an expectation; and also the fact that the claim in the present case could be said to arise from a pure omission and as such would not, apart from special circumstances, give rise to a claim in tortious negligence.

Faced with points such as those the strict lawyer might well react by saying that the present claim can lie only in contract and is not, therefore, open to a disappointed beneficiary as against the testator's solicitor . . . **in the result** [by extending *Hedley Byrne*] **all the conceptual problems fade innocuously away** [emphasis added].

Finally, there is the objection that if liability is recognised it will be impossible to place any sensible limits to cases in which recovery is allowed.

There have to be boundaries to the availability of the remedy but they will have to be worked out in the future, as practical problems came to light before the courts.

Lord Brown-Wilkinson and Lord Nolan concurred with Lord Goff.

Lord Mustill and Lord Keith however, **dissented**. Their Lordships said they could not reconcile this decision with principle, nor could they regard it as a proper incremental advance of liability. Lord Mustill emphasised the lack of **mutuality** on the present case; mutuality being of the essence of liability arising under *Hedley Byrne*. A special relationship was contemplated in *Hedley Byrne*; this was lacking in *White*.

The elements of request and reliance were absent in the present case, said Lord Mustill. In his Lordship's opinion it followed from this position that the majority ruling in *White*:

[W]as not an application of *Hedley Byrne* by enlargement but the enunciation of something quite different . . .

It is true that the solicitor undertook the task of drawing a will which would be for the advantage of the beneficiaries but he did not draw it for the beneficiaries, he drew it for the testator.

The absence of the cardinal feature in *Hedley Byrne* that the defendants undertook the job for the plaintiffs destroys the possibility of using *Hedley Byrne* as a stepping stone towards the recognition of the cause of action sued upon.

A broad new type of claim might properly be met by a broad new type of rationalisation as happened in *Hedley Byrne* but rationalisation there has to be, and it does not conduce to the orderly development of the law or to the certainty which practical convenience demands if duties are simply conjured up as a matter of positive law to answer the apparent justice of an individual case . . .

The case has been conducted throughout on the basis of a stark choice between a duty of general application or no duty at all and it cannot be right to admit of an intermediate solution which has never been investigated on either the facts or the law.

Weir, T., 'Comment on *White* v *Jones*' (1995) 114 LQR 357

Eleven months elapsed between the hearing of the arguments in *White* v *Jones* and the delivery of their Lordships' speeches, [1995] 2 WLR 187. There was a distinct risk that, despite the substantial sandwich of *Henderson* v *Merrett Syndicates* [1994] 3 WLR 761, we might, like persons too long agog in a food queue, lose our appetite. Now that the speeches have finally been served up, is *White* v *Jones* a Barmecide feast or is there enough to get one's teeth into and chew over?

We may ignore the precise facts. The House did so, except to say that they did not matter. The general, almost abstract question was whether a person deprived of an intended legacy by the negligence of a testator's solicitor could sue the solicitor in tort. Megarry J had answered the question in the affirmative in *Ross* v *Caunters* [1980] Ch 297, but that was under the 13-year reign of Queen *Anns*, now dead. In dismissing the solicitor's appeal, the House did likewise, but only just. Squib or bombshell?

The defendant solicitor's negligent breach of his contract with the testator had caused harm to the plaintiff, the intended beneficiary. This is identical in structure to *Donoghue* v *Stevenson*, where the manufacturer's supply of the defective ginger beer which poisoned Mrs Donoghue was a breach of his contract of sale with Minchella, the restaurateur. Mrs White, however, suffered financial loss only, and not physical harm. *Donoghue* was therefore not in point. Mrs White won all the same, though. One is therefore bound to ask whether this case is not going to do for money what *Donoghue*, also decided by a bare majority, did for health. Time will tell, of course, but a short time may not . . .

Now we may ask whether the actual decision was 'exceptional' or principled. All members of the House were clear that the case was not covered by existing authority. Only *Hedley Byrne & Co. Ltd* v *Heller & Partners Ltd* [1964] AC 465 offered a toe-hold, if that. On this Lord Browne-Wilkinson said: 'although the present case is not directly covered by the decided cases, it is legitimate to extend the law to the limited extent proposed using the incremental approach by way of analogy advocated in *Caparo Industries Plc v Dickman*'. Lord Keith of Kinkel and Lord Mustill were of the contrary opinion, Lord Mustill expressing himself with great eloquence and cogency. He focused on the four distinctive features of *Hedley Byrne* after listing the five respects in which *Henderson* had extended or clarified it. The essence of *Hedley Byrne* he identified as 'mutuality', that the defendant was doing something the plaintiff had asked to be done: 'the undertaking of legal responsibility for careful and diligent performance in the context of a mutual relationship'. That feature was missing in the present case, where the defendant was responding to the testator, not the beneficiary. Lord Goff did not deny this: 'The relevant work . . . cannot be said to have been undertaken for the intended beneficiary. Certainly, again in the absence of special circumstances, there will have been no reliance by the intended beneficiary on the exercise by the solicitor of due care and skill . . .'.

Lord Brown-Wilkinson, on the other hand, thought he could discern in *Hedley Byrne* a principle which covered the present case. He took liability under *Hedley Byrne* to be based on 'a conscious assumption of responsibility for the task rather than a conscious assumption of legal liability to the plaintiff for its careful performance' and said that mutuality, in Lord Mustill's sense, was not required. This last point he sought to support by invoking the fact that trustees are answerable to beneficiaries though they do not act at the beneficiaries' instance. This surprising analogy is not really very persuasive. Nor is this from Lord Nolan:

> If the defendant drives his car on the highway, he implicitly assumes a responsibility towards other road users, and they in turn implicitly rely on him to discharge that responsibility. By taking his car on to the road, he holds himself out as a reasonably careful driver. In the same way, as it seems to me, a professional man or an artisan who undertakes to exercise his skill in a manner which, to his knowledge, may cause loss to others if carelessly performed may thereby implicitly assume a legal responsibility towards them.

It must be said that to see no difference between managing someone else's property and doing some service which might benefit him, or to say that driving and drafting are very much of a muchness, is carrying to rather unreasonable lengths the late twentieth-century horror of discriminating between what ought to be distinguished.

Though Lord Goff and Lord Brown-Wilkinson reached the same conclusion, their approaches are very different. It is as if one of the majority in *Donoghue*, electing to ignore Lord Atkin's general principle, had laid down a rule expressly designed for, and applicable only to, the liability of a producer of food to a consumer poisoned by it. Lord Goff seemed ready to create, to use Lord Mustill's words, 'a specialist pocket of tort law, with a special type of proximity' (a word which appears in none of the majority speeches) 'distinct from the main body of doctrine, sufficient to provide a remedy in the present case.' This is what Nicholls VC did in the court below, with Lord Goff's express approval. Indeed, the decision would be tolerable and innocuous if the only claimants enfranchised by it were disappointed and uninsurable personal legatees and the only defendants mulcted were (insured) negligent solicitors—tolerable, that is, as a matter of 'practical justice', for the way of achieving it is not, as Lord Mustill shows and Lord Keith asserts, reconcilable with principled law.

Lord Browne-Wilkinson, on the other hand, seems to see the outcome as an instance of a general principle, namely that where A embarks on a task (or agrees with B to do so) which, if well done, may benefit a third party financially, he may be liable to that party for not doing it properly. So wide a principle will be impossible to contain, especially as in *Henderson* Lord Goff disallowed the control mechanism of 'fair, just and reasonable': 'It follows that, once the case is identified as falling within the *Hedley Byrne* principle, there should be no need to embark upon any further enquiry whether it is 'fair, just and reasonable' to impose liability for economic loss'—rather a strong thing to say in an opinion which discounted the importance of reliance, and equated not only speech with action but commission with omission (which in the case of speech means silence).

The only hint of possible control is in Lord Browne-Wilkinson's agreement with Lord Mustill that a tortious duty of care may be denied where 'there is a contractual chain of obligations designed by the parties to regulate their dealings'. In *Henderson* the House had admittedly, if unwisely, laid down that a duty in tort always concurs with a contractual duty *inter partes* unless the contract can be taken to have excluded it: now third parties are involved, and there will be extended argument about whether it is the plaintiff's contract or the defendant's, if either, which ousts the general law of tort which is now so pervasive. This seems to be the only way to avoid rehabilitating *Junior Books*, so memorably emasculated by none other than Robert Goff LJ, for it clearly falls within Lord Browne-Wilkinson's principle.

Such cases and very many others hitherto unthinkable will now be brought to court. Solicitors, at any rate in big city firms, can console themselves with the thought that *White* v *Jones* seems set to equal *Anns* in the number of claimants who rely on it to their cost and the solicitors' gain. There was a deluge after Louis XV, too; but he foresaw it and did not do so much to cause it.

PENN v BRISTOL AND WEST BUILDING SOCIETY AND OTHERS, The Times, 19 June 1995

X owned a house jointly with his wife, the plaintiff, and, in collusion with the buyer of the property, forged the conveyance. It was found that this 'sham transaction' did not affect the beneficial joint tenancy of X and the plaintiff. Judge Kolbert, sitting as a Chancery judge in Leeds, held that X's solicitors, who had not taken steps to check whether they had the plaintiff's authority to act, were in breach of a duty of care in negligence owed to the plaintiff.

The judge said:

> Although the wife had never been a client of the solicitors she was reasonably within their contemplation when they received the title deeds, indeed she was necessarily within their contemplation, and her interest as co-owner was sufficiently proximate to the transaction in which they were engaged, concerning as it did her jointly owned home, for the solicitors to owe her a duty of care according to the principles enunciated by the House of Lords in *White* v *Jones* [1995] 2 WLR 187.

GOODWILL v BRITISH PREGNANCY ADVISORY SERVICE [1996] 2 All ER 161 (CA)

The plaintiff knew that her partner had had a vasectomy and did not use any form of contraception, becoming pregnant as a result.

The court found that she had no cause of action in negligence for financial loss against the person who performed the vasectomy. *White* v *Jones* did not apply. That decision, described by Peter Gibson LJ, who delivered the judgment of the court, as belonging to an 'unusual class of cases', produced a special remedy in tort to overcome 'the rank injustice' arising in the circumstances.

His Lordship concluded that the requirements of *Hedley Byrne*, as interpreted in *Caparo*, were not satisfied in the present case i.e. there was no actual or inferential knowledge by the defendants that their advice 'when communicated to the plaintiff by her partner was likely to be acted upon by her without independent inquiry.' It was the *partner* who had been advised, and the plaintiff did not even have an existing sexual relationship with him at the time that the advice was given.

5.3.7 PHYSICAL DAMAGE

CLAY v CRUMP [1964] 1 QB 533 (CA)

The defendant architect was found liable to the plaintiff, on the ordinary *Donoghue* v *Stevenson* neighbour principle, in the following circumstances. The owners of a building engaged demolition contractors to pull down the building and building contractors to erect a new one on the same site. An architect was employed to prepare plans and supervise the work. A wall on the site was also to be demolished but the owners of the building asked the firm of demolition contractors if the wall could be left intact on a temporary basis and they asked the architect for his opinion. He asked the principal of the firm of demolition contractors what he thought. He said he thought the wall was safe and, after visiting the site, he asked his foreman's opinion. He also answered in the affirmative. The architect subsequently visited the site himself. After the demolition contractors left, for the building contractors to start work, the foundations of the wall had been exposed and an expert could, with reasonable care, have seen that the wall was in a dangerous state. Neither the demolition contractors nor the architect that exercised due care and the building contractors merely assumed that the wall had been deliberately left standing and thus gave it only a cursory inspection. It was found that the architect and the demolition contractors knew, or ought to have known, that this assumption would be made in the circumstances. Several days after the building contractors started work the wall collapsed, injuring the plaintiff, an employee of the building contractors. The court found that the architect, the demolition contractors and the building contractors were all liable in negligence to the plaintiff.

Although counsel for the architect based his argument partly on the reasoning in *Candler* v *Crane, Christmas and Co* and *Hedley-Byrne* v *Heller* the court took the familiar proximity approach found in Lord Atkin's neighbour principle in *Donoghue* v *Stevenson*. In other words, the problem was seen in terms of the general neighbour principle rather than the 'special relationship' requirement in *Hedley-Byrne* v *Heller*. [Arguably, this 'special relationship' sets *Hedley-Byrne* apart from *Donoghue* v *Stevenson*.]

DUTTON v BOGNOR REGIS URBAN DISTRICT COUNCIL [1972] 1 QB 373

The **ruling** on the facts in this case was **overturned** by the House of Lords in *Murphy* v *Brentwood DC*. Lord Denning claimed that there was a distinction between 'the several categories of professional men'. The professional man giving advice on financial or property matters, such as accountants, bankers and lawyers, owed a duty only to those who relied on his advice and suffered loss as a result. However, a professional man advising on the safety of buildings, machinery or materials owed a duty to all those who might suffer if his advice were bad. This is so not because the injured persons have relied on him, but because he knew, or ought to have known, that such persons might be injured if his advice were unsound. In *Dutton* a local authority building inspector was held to owe a duty of care to the plaintiff as a professional adviser, even though the plaintiff had not thought of it and had not directly placed reliance on his conduct. [The **statutory context** in such a case may be important.]

SHARPE v AVERY [1938] 4 All ER 85

A member of a party of motor cyclists, who claimed to be familiar with the route of a ride all were undertaking, misled his fellow members on to waste land where a pillion passenger was thrown off a cycle and sustained injuries. Damages were awarded against the representor.

T (A MINOR) v SURREY COUNTY COUNCIL AND OTHERS [1994] 4 All ER 577

SCOTT BAKER JT: The plaintiff claims that the local authority were in breach of statutory duty and that this sounds in damages. The relevant legislation in force at the material time was the Nurseries and Child-Minders Regulations Act 1948 . . .

The way the Act works is that s. 5 gives the local authority a discretion to cancel a registration where circumstances exist that would justify a refusal to register (s. 1(4)). It was clearly the intention of Parliament that only those who are fit to look after children under five should be registered as child-minders. In my judgment, a person cannot be so fit for the purposes of this legislation when there is, as here, an unresolved question about a non-accidental injury . . .

It by no means follows that because the local authority failed to meet its obligations under the Act, an action lies against it for breach of statutory duty. It is a question of the true construction of the Act whether an action lies with a private individual for breach of its provisions . . . The Act was passed for the benefit of the public as a whole and only, in the very broadest sense for the benefit of children under the age of five (the age to which the legislation then related). The Act is similar to some forms of licensing legislation and it is to be noted that only a limited class of children, namely those under five, minded for reward, fall within the catchment of its benefit.

The fact that the Act itself provides no remedy for any breach by the local authority does not of itself give an individual a right to damages . . .

In *Hague* v *Deputy Governor of Parkhurst Prison, Weldon* v *Home Office* [1992] 1 AC 58 at 170 Lord Jauncey said:

. . . I take from these authorities that it must always be a matter for consideration whether the legislature intended that private law rights of action should be conferred upon individuals in respect of breaches of the relevant statutory provision. The fact that a particular provision was intended to protect certain individuals is not of itself sufficient to confer private law rights of action upon them, something more is required to show that the legislation intended such conferment.

I can find nothing in the present Act to indicate such an intention. I detect a considerable reluctance on the part of the courts to impose upon local authorities any liability for breach of statutory duty other than that expressly imposed in the statute. In my judgment the claim for breach of statutory duty fails.

Parliament has entrusted to local authorities a wide measure of power and responsibility over children and it is desirable that they should be left to exercise those powers and responsibilities as far as possible unhindered by the courts. Of course, as was pointed out by Lord Roskill in the *Liverpool* case, and has been many times since, they are not immune from the remedy of judicial review in an appropriate case.

The problem for the court, in the present case, is very different from that in the *Liverpool* case. Here, the question is whether the local authority owed T a duty to take reasonable care in the exercise of its obligations to register and deregister child-minders. If such a duty does exist, the effect is to bring a particular, but limited, category of child under the umbrella of the duty leaving others outside. The local authority's obligations with regard to child-minding only extended at the time to children under five minded for reward.

Whilst it is true that the courts are more ready to find a duty of care owed where the consequence of a breach is personal injury rather than damage to property and still less mere economic loss, to hold that a duty was owed in the present case would be breaking entirely new ground.

It has been argued that the Nurseries and Child-Minders Regulation Act 1948 falls outside the heart of local authority legislation concerning the care of children and I think it does. Therefore it is said that this case falls outside the category of case with which, for example, Ralph Gibson LJ was concerned in *F* v *Wirral Metropolitan BC* [1991] 2 All ER 648 at 676, [1991] Fam 69 at 106, where he could see no sufficient reason for the court to create, or declare, the existence of a new right which had not been recognised before.

The question is whether this opens the door to the creation of liability. What we have here is the local authority required by statute to act as a licensing authority. It is going a long way, without more, to hold a licensing authority liable for the misfeasance of a third party when it negligently grants or refuses to cancel a licence . . .

Mr Swift QC for the plaintiff argues that the present case is very different from the *Bedfordshire CC* case. There, he says the local authority's powers were discretionary. Here they are specifically defined by statute. I note however that in both s. 1(4) and (5) of the 1948 Act the word 'may' rather than 'shall' is used in defining the local authority's obligations.

In my judgment, the issues of breach of statutory duty and common law negligence in respect of the exercise by the local authority of its power under this Act run very much hand in glove. In my judgment, there is no common law duty owed of the nature contended for by the plaintiff and the first strand of the claim fails.

It follows therefore that the plaintiff's claim for negligence fails on all grounds pleaded other than those arising out of the telephone conversation between Mr Bodycomb and Miss D with which I shall now deal . . .

In my judgment, the criteria for founding liability for negligent misstatement are met. Mr Bodycomb was at all times acting as the local authority's nursery and child-minding adviser. He was the only person employed in that capacity for the Ashford area. When he spoke to Miss D on 25 August, he was consulted and speaking as a professional officer with special knowledge and responsibility. He knew, or ought to have known, that what he said would be relied upon. What he said related directly to the safety of the infant plaintiff. There was, in these circumstances, a special relationship of proximity between Mr Bodycomb and the plaintiff. I accept Mr Swift's submission that this case falls four square within the principle laid down in *Hedley Byrne & Co. Ltd* v *Heller & Partners Ltd* [1964] AC 465, but the plaintiff's position is stronger in the present case because he suffered physical injury rather than mere economic loss.

The local authority take one further point. They argue that even if there was a duty of care and a breach of it, such breach was not the cause of the injury to T. Any breach by the local authority, it is contended, was not the effective cause of T's injury. Mr Faulkes went on that it is only in very rare circumstances that a defendant will be held responsible in law for the acts or omissions of a third party. There must, he says, be a very high degree of foreseeability. This type of situation arose in *Al-Kandari* v *JR Brown & Co.* [1988] 1 QB 665. By a father's solicitor's negligence, the father's passport with his two children on it was left with the Kuwait Embassy. The father was able to get possession of it from the embassy, kidnap the children from the mother's care and remove them from the country. They were never returned. Bingham LJ said (1 QB 665 at 677):

> The judge found against the plaintiff on the ground that it was not reasonably foreseeable that Mr Al-Kandari would be given any opportunity to abduct the children. The correct approach is to consider the breach of duty which has been proved and to ask whether an ordinarily competent solicitor in the defendant's position would have foreseen damage of the kind which actually occurred as a not unlikely result of that breach. Such a solicitor would be mindful that this whole arrangement had been made to ensure that Mr Al-Kandari could not use his passport to spirit the children out of the jurisdiction.

In the present case Mr Bodycomb knew that Miss D was considering placing T with Mrs Walton. He knew too, or would have done had he stopped to think about it, that had she known the information that was imparted to him at the two case conferences, she would not have placed T with Mrs Walton. He knew that there was a significant risk to any small baby in Mrs Walton's care. In these circumstances I find the local authority liable in negligence to the plaintiff. There will therefore be judgment for the plaintiff against the local authority and Mrs Walton with damages to be assessed.

Judgment for the plaintiff against the local authority and Mrs Walton.

This decision is also of importance for **Chapter 8** of the *Learning Text*.

5.3.8 GENERAL

MARC RICH AND CO. AG v BISHOP ROCK MARINE CO. LTD 'THE NICHOLAS H' [1995] 3 All ER 307 (HL)

LORD STEYN: In this case the question is whether a classification society owed a duty of care to a third party, the owners of cargo laden on a vessel, arising from the careless performance of a survey of a damaged vessel by the surveyor of the classification society which resulted in the vessel being allowed to sail and subsequently sinking. It is a novel question . . . In other words, on the assumption that the carelessness of the surveyor caused the loss of the cargo the question is whether in law that carelessness amounted to actionable negligence. In short, the question is simply whether in law the classification society owed a duty of care to the owners of the cargo . . .

Counsel for the cargo owners submitted that in cases of physical damage to property in which the plaintiff has a proprietary or possessory interest the only requirement is proof of reasonable foreseeability. For this proposition he relied on observations of Lord Oliver in *Caparo Industries plc* v *Dickman* [1990] 1 All ER 568. Those observations, seen in context, do not support his argument. They merely underline the qualitative difference between cases of direct physical damage and indirect economic loss. The materiality of that distinction is plain. But since the decision in *Home Office* v *Dorset Yacht Co. Ltd* [1970] 2 All ER 294 it has been settled law that the elements of foreseeability and proximity as well as considerations of fairness, justice and reasonableness are relevant to all cases whatever the nature of the harm sustained by the plaintiff . . . It follows that I would reject the first argument of counsel for the cargo owners . . .

It is . . . necessary to examine a number of other factors in order to put the case in its right perspective, and to consider whether some of those factors militate against the recognition of a duty of care . . . Only after an examination of these features will it be possible to address directly the element of proximity and the question whether it is fair, just and reasonable to impose a duty of care.

(a) *Direct physical loss?*

Counsel for the cargo owners argued that the present case involved the infliction of *direct physical loss* . . . In the present case the shipowner was primarily responsible for the vessel sailing in a seaworthy condition. The role of the NKK was a subsidiary one. In my view the carelessness of the NKK surveyor did not involve the direct infliction of physical damage in the relevant sense. That by no means concludes the answer to the general question. But it does introduce the right perspective on one aspect of this case.

(b) *Reliance*

In the present case there was no contact whatever between the cargo owners and the classification society. Moreover . . . it is not even suggested that the cargo owners were aware that NKK had been brought in to survey the vessel . . . The cargo owners simply relied on the owners of the vessel to keep the vessel seaworthy and to look after the cargo . . . In my view this feature is not necessarily decisive but it also contributes to placing the claim in the correct perspective.

(c) *The bill of lading contracts*

The dealings between shipowners and cargo owners are based on a contractual structure, the Hague Rules, and tonnage limitation, on which the insurance of international trade depends . . . Underlying it is the system of double or overlapping insurance of cargo. Cargo owners take out direct insurance in respect of the cargo. Shipowners take out liability risks insurance in respect of breaches of their duties of care in respect of the cargo. The insurance system is structured on the basis that the potential liability of shipowners to cargo owners is limited under the Hague Rules and by virtue of tonnage limitation provisions. And insurance premiums payable by owners obviously reflect such limitations on the shipowners' exposure.

If a duty of care by classification societies to cargo owners is recognised in this case, it must have a substantial impact on international trade . . . the potential exposure of classification societies to claims by cargo owners will be large. That greater exposure is likely to lead to an increase in the cost to classification societies of obtaining appropriate liability risks insurance. Given their role in maritime trade classification societies are likely to seek to pass on the higher cost to owners. Moreover, it is readily predictable that classification societies will require owners to give appropriate indemnities. Ultimately, shipowners will pay.

The result of a recognition of a duty of care in this case will be to enable cargo owners, or rather their insurers, to disturb the balance created by the Hague Rules and Hague-Visby Rules as well as by tonnage limitation provisions, by enabling cargo owners to recover in tort against a peripheral party to the prejudice of the protection of shipowners under the existing system. For these reasons I would hold that the international trade system tends to militate against the recognition of the claim in tort put forward by the cargo owners against the classification society . . .

(e) *The position and role of NKK*

The fact that a defendant acts for the collective welfare is a matter to be taken into consideration when considering whether it is fair, just and reasonable to impose a duty of care: *Hill* v *Chief Constable of West Yorkshire* [1988] 2 All ER 238 and *Elguzouli-Daf* v *Comr of Police of the Metropolis* [1995] 1 All ER 833. Even if such a body has no general immunity from liability in tort, the question may arise whether it owes a duty of care to aggrieved persons, and, if so, in what classes of case, eg only in cases involving the direct infliction of physical harm or on a wider basis . . . Nowadays one would not describe classification societies as carrying on quasi-judicial functions. But it is still the case that . . . they act in the public interest.

The reality is simply that NKK . . . is an independent and non-profit-making entity created and operating for the sole purpose of promoting the collective welfare, namely the safety of lives and ships at sea. In common with other classification societies NKK fulfils a role which in its absence would have to be fulfilled by states. And the question is whether NKK, and other classification sometimes, would be able to carry out their functions as efficiently if they become the ready alternative target of cargo owners, who already have contractual claims against shipowners. In my judgment there must be some apprehension that the classification societies would adopt, to the detriment of their traditional role, a more defensive position.

(f) *Policy factors*

If a duty is held to exist in this case as between the classification society and cargo owners, classification societies would become potential defendants in many cases. An extra layer of insurance would become involved. The settlement process would inevitably become more complicated and expensive. Arbitration proceedings and court proceedings would often involve an additional party. And often similar issues would have to be canvassed in separate proceedings since the classification societies would not be bound by arbitration clauses in the contracts of carriage. If such a duty is recognised, there is a risk that classification societies might be unwilling from time to time to survey the very vessels which most urgently require independent examination. It will also divert men and resources from the prime function of classification societies, namely to save life and ships at sea. These factors are, by themselves, far from decisive. But in an overall assessment of the case they merit consideration.

Is the imposition of a duty of care fair, just and reasonable?

I am willing to assume (without deciding) that there was a sufficient degree of proximity in this case to fulfil that requirement for the existence of a duty of care. The critical question is therefore whether it would be fair, just and reasonable to impose such a duty. For my part I am satisfied that the factors and arguments advanced on behalf of cargo owners are decisively outweighed by the cumulative effect, if a duty is recognised, of the matters discussed in paragraphs (c), (e) and (f), ie the outflanking of the bargain between shipowners and cargo owners; the negative effect on the public role of NKK; and the other considerations of policy. By way of summary, I look at the matter from the point of view of the three parties concerned. I conclude that the recognition of a duty would be unfair, unjust and unreasonable as against the shipowners who would ultimately have to bear the cost of holding classification societies liable, such consequence being at variance with the bargain between shipowners and cargo owners based on an internationally agreed contractual structure. It would also be unfair, unjust and unreasonable towards classification societies, notably because they act for the collective welfare and unlike shipowners they would not have the benefit of any limitation provisions. Looking at the matter from the point of view of cargo owners, the existing system provides them with the protection of the Hague Rules or Hague-Visby Rules. But that protection is limited under such Rules and by tonnage limitation provisions. Under the existing system any shortfall is readily insurable. In my judgment the lesser injustice is done by not recognising a duty of care. It follows that I would reject the primary way in which counsel for the cargo owners put his case . . .

For the reasons already given I would dismiss the appeal.

[The decision of the Court of Appeal was affirmed. Lords Keith, Jauncey and Browne-Wilkinson agreed, but Lord Lloyd dissented.]

LORD LLOYD: . . . The overriding consideration in the present case is that the cargo owners, as we are asked to assume, have suffered physical damage to their cargo, and such damage was caused by Mr Ducat's negligence, for which NKK are responsible on ordinary principles of respondent superior. Since the celebrated formulation of Lord Wilberforce in *Anns* v *Merton London Borough* [1978] AC 728 at 751, a series of important cases in the Court of Appeal and House of Lords have signalled the 'retreat from *Anns*' culminating in the decision of the House in *Murphy* v *Brentwood DC* [1991] 1 AC 398. Almost all these decisions have concerned claims to recover damages for economic loss, unassociated with physical damage or personal injury. The most important exception was *Mobil Oil Hong Kong Ltd* v *Hong Kong United Dockyards Ltd, The Hua Lien* [1991] 1 Lloyd's Rep 309. In that case Lord Brandon of Oakbrook said (at 328);

In their Lordships' view, however, the essential feature of the present case is that the damage sued for is not purely economic loss but ordinary physical damage to property. It follows that the decisions relating to claims for purely economic loss to which their Lordships have referred have no relevance to the present case.

The concept of proximity, and the requirement that it should be fair, just and reasonable to impose a duty of care on the defendant in the particular circumstances of the case, have been developed as a means of containing liability for pure economic loss under the principles stated in *Donoghue* v *Stevenson* [1932] AC 562. At the same time, and by a parallel movement in the opposite direction, the House has in two recent decisions reaffirmed liability for economic loss based on the principle of assumption of responsibility as expounded by the House in *Hedley Byrne & Co. Ltd* v *Heller & Partners Ltd* [1964] AC 465, and going back beyond that decision to *Nocton* v *Lord Ashburton* [1914] AC 932. None of these difficulties arise in the present case. We are not here asked to extend the law of negligence into a new field. We are not even asked to make an incremental advance. All that is required is a straightforward application of *Donoghue* v *Stevenson*. The ground is already marked out by cases such as *Haseldine* v *C A Daw & Son Ltd.* [1941] 2 KB 343, *Clay* v *A J Crump & Sons Ltd* [1964] 1 QB 533, *Voli* v *Inglewood Shire Council* (1963) 110 CLR 74 and *Muirhead* v *Industrial Tank Specialities Ltd* [1986] QB 507. In physical damage cases proximity very often goes without saying. Where the facts cry out for the imposition of a duty of care between the parties, as they do here, it would require an exceptional case to refuse to impose a duty on the ground that it would not be fair, just and reasonable. Otherwise there is a risk that the law of negligence will disintegrate into a series of isolated decisions without any coherent principles at all, and the retreat from *Anns* will turn into a rout. Having given Mr Aikens' arguments my best consideration, I can see no good reason why, on the facts of this case, ordinary well-established principles of the law of negligence should not be allowed to take effect. Accordingly, I would for my part allow the appeal, and restore the order of Hirst J.

BURTON v *ISLINGTON HEALTH AUTHORITY* [1991] 1 All ER 825

POTTS J: Different considerations arise where the loss is caused by physical damage, as Lord Bridge recognised in *Caparo Industries plc* v *Dickman* [1990] 2 AC 605 at 618:

> One of the most important distinctions always to be observed lies in the law's essential approach to the different kinds of damage which one party may have suffered in consequence of the acts or omissions of another. It is one thing to owe a duty of care to avoid causing injury to the person or property of others. It is quite another to avoid causing others to suffer purely economic loss.

In the same case Lord Oliver said ([1990] 2 AC 605 at 632):

> . . . it is now clear from a series of decisions in this House that, at least so far as concerns the law of the United Kingdom, the duty of care in tort depends not solely on the existence of the essential ingredient of the foreseeability of damage to the plaintiff but on its coincidence with a further ingredient to which has been attached the label 'proximity' and which was described by Lord Atkin in the course of his speech in *Donoghue* v *Stevenson* [1932] AC 562 at 581 as 'such close and direct relations that the act complained of directly affects a person whom the person alleged to be bound to take care would know would be directly affected by his careless act.' It must be remembered, however, that Lord Atkin was using these words in the context of loss caused by physical damage where the existence of the nexus between the careless defendant and the injured plaintiff can rarely give rise to any difficulty. To adopt the words of Bingham LJ in the instant case ([1989] QB 653 at 686): 'It is enough that the plaintiff chances to be (out of the whole world) the person with whom the defendant collided or who purchased the offending ginger beer.'

Thus I proceed on the basis that the nature of the duty of care in cases involving physical injury and consequential loss remains as it was before the decisions of the House of Lords in *Carparo Industries plc* v *Dickman* [1990] 2 AC 605 and *Murphy* v *Brentwood DC* [1990] 3 WLR 414. In *Donoghue* v *Stevenson* [1932] AC 562 the foresight of a reasonable man was accepted as a general test as to whether a duty of care existed . . .

NITRIGIN EIREANN TEORANTA v *INCO ALLOYS LTD* [1992] 1 All ER 854

Physical damage (explosion caused by defective furnace pipes) was suffered as a result of the defendants supplying a defective product and the **diligent** plaintiffs **knew** of the defect

(*Murphy* suggests that where a defect is revealed, one cannot wait until damage occurs and then make a claim) **but they had not been able to discover the cause of the defect**. The judge rules that this was not 'knowledge' in *Murphy* terms, therefore they were not 'caught' by that case i.e. they had, **in effect**, no knowledge of the defect. (The plaintiffs had repaired the pipes before the explosion.) According to the judge, May J, even if the plaintiffs had been **negligent** in not knowing the cause of the defect (cracked pipes) they could still claim for physical damage caused to other property by the defective product—though in this case they could be met with the defence of contributory negligence.

It was held that a cause of action in negligence does not accrue when a defect in a chattel (in this case a furnace pipe); occurs if the loss sustained is the pure economic loss in repairing the chattel. However, if the defect subsequently causes physical damage to other property, the loss is not economic loss and a cause of action in negligence then accrues.

MAY J: To establish a claim in negligence based upon *M'Alister (or Donoghue)* v *Stevenson* [1932] AC 562 it is generally necessary to show actual physical injury to persons or damage to property other than the property or thing which is itself the product of the negligence. A plaintiff claiming in negligence cannot normally recover pure economic loss unless there is a special relationship with the defendant amounting to reliance. An example of such a relationship is to be found in *Hedley Byrne & Co. Ltd* v *Heller & Partners Ltd* [1964] AC 465. So much is uncontroversial between the parties to this case, subject to matters which I deal with later in this judgment.

The loss sustained by the owner of a defective chattel which does not cause personal injury or damage to something other than itself is the cost of repairing or replacing the chattel. This is pure economic loss and ordinarily irrecoverable in negligence. Likewise, the owner of a defective building or plant which does not cause personal injury or damage to something other than itself cannot ordinarily recover in negligence the cost of rectifying the defect: see *D & F Estates Ltd* v *Church Comrs for England, Murphy* v *Brentwood DC* and *Dept of the Environment* v *Thomas Bates & Son (New Towns Commission, third party)* [1991] 1 AC 499 at 520 . . .

Mr Harris urges me to find that the relationship between the plaintiffs and the first defendants can be equated with that between the plaintiffs and the defendants in the *Pirelli* case. I am not so persuaded. In the *Pirelli* case, the defendants were a firm of professional consulting engineers engaged to advise and design. Here Mr Harris can glean no more from the pleadings than that the first defendants are alleged to be specialist manufacturers who knew or ought to have known the purpose for which their specialist pipes were needed. In my judgment, that is neither a professional relationship in the sense in which the law treats professional negligence nor a *Hedley Byrne* relationship.

Mr Harris's second lifeline for the purpose of his first argument is *Junior Books Ltd* v *Veitchi Co. Ltd* [1982] 3 All ER 201, [1983] 1 AC 520, a decision of the House of Lords which Mr Harris argues has survived the *D & F Estates* case and *Murphy* v *Brentwood DC*. The *Junior Books* case has not been formally departed from by the House of Lords and Mr Harris points to the same passage in *Murphy's* case in which Lord Keith deals with the *Pirelli* case as expressly acknowledging the survival of the *Junior Books* case . . .

It would be intellectually dishonest in this case to attempt to distinguish the *Junior Books* case and I do not do so. I simply decline to apply it on the basis that it is unique and that it depends on the *Hedley Byrne* doctrine of reliance. I have already held that the relationship in the case before me is not a *Hedley Byrne* relationship.

I accordingly reject Mr Harris's first submission and hold that on the assumed facts the cracking to the pipe in 1983 was damage to the pipe itself constituting a defect of quality resulting in economic loss irrecoverable in negligence. For this reason, a cause of action in negligence did not accrue to the plaintiffs in 1983.

Mr Harris's second argument derives from the law as stated in the passage from Lord Bridge's opinion in *D & F Estates Ltd* v *Church Comrs for England* . . .

Once the defect is discovered, the plaintiff has the means of removing it by replacement or repair and the cost of doing so is irrecoverable economic loss. A latent defect which causes personal injury or damage to property other than the thing itself gives rise to a cause of action but once the defect is no longer latent the law as enunciated by Lord Bridge does not provide a cause of action in negligence. Mr Watson for the plaintiffs argues that there is a distinction between defect and damage and that, whereas the plaintiffs may have known that there was damage in 1983, on the assumed facts they were unaware of the cause of the cracking despite reasonable investigation and accordingly were not aware of the defect. Mr Watson argues that the explosion in 1984 did cause physical damage to property other than the pipe itself, and that this is precisely where a cause of action in negligence does arise and that the cracking in 1983 from a then undiagnosed cause does not, as he put it, quash the cause of action. There is support for this approach in Lord Keith's opinion in *Murphy v Brentwood DC* [1991] 1 AC 398 at 464, where he said:

> But that principle is not apt to bring home liability towards an occupier who knows the full extent of the defect yet continues to occupy the building.

It is argued that on the assumed facts the plaintiffs did not know the full extent of the defect at any time before the explosion.

In my judgment, Mr Harris's argument here fails. The passages relied on suppose that the defect is discovered before any damage is done and that it is repaired or replaced *before any damage is done*. The cost of so doing is then irrecoverable economic loss. But in this case physical damage to other property did occur. The plaintiffs did not diagnose the cause of the cracking and did not sufficiently repair the pipe to avoid the physical damage caused by the explosion. The damage caused by the explosion includes damage of the kind which gives rise to a cause of action in negligence. It may be supposed that, had the plaintiffs diagnosed the cause of the cracking in 1983, they would have dealt with it in a way which would have avoided the explosion. But they did not do so and on the assumed facts this was despite reasonable investigation. In my judgment, the fact of the cracking in 1983 does not turn what was in fact and in truth physical damage to other property into economic loss. It follows that a cause of action accrued to the plaintiffs on 27 June 1984 is not statute-barred.

The question which is begged by this analysis and which needs to be addressed is what the position would be if the plaintiffs ought reasonably to have diagnosed the cause of the cracking in 1983. Would that affect the accrual of a cause of action in negligence? In my judgment it would not. The fact of sufficient physical damage to sustain the plaintiffs' cause of action would remain, but the first defendants could argue on appropriate facts that the plaintiffs' recovery should be reduced or extinguished by the plaintiff's contributory negligence.

In the result therefore I hold that, on the assumed facts and subject to the reservations which I have expressed, the plaintiffs have a cause of action in negligence and that it is not statute-barred.

This decision should be considered also as relevant in the context of **Chapter 7**: *Murphy v Brentwood DC* (*latent* and *patent* defects in premises and chattels).

5.4 Summary

REID v RUSH AND TOMKINS [1989] 2 All ER 228 (CA)

[I]t was held that an employer owes no duty to provide to his employee personal accident insurance covering special risks to the employee whilst he is working abroad; nor is there any duty to advise the employee to obtain for himself such insurance cover where the contract of employment contains no term to that effect. A master's duty in tort could not extend so far. The common law could not devise such a duty which the legislature had not thought fit to impose and it could not be just or reasonable for the court to impose it. A court could not find a duty of care in negligence, although loss to the plaintiff was foreseeable, in a factual situation in which the existence of such a duty had repeatedly been held not to exist (see *The Aliakmon: Leigh & Sillavan Ltd v Aliakmon Shipping Co. Ltd* [1986] AC 785). A master's duty, in the absence of some contractual term, was limited to the protection of the servant against physical harm or disease. A duty in tort could not be imposed to enlarge the duties assumed under the contract of employment (see, e.g. Lord Scarman in *Tai Hing Cotton Mill v Liu Chang Bank* [1986] AC 80).

MAY LJ: I have had the advantage of reading the judgment of Ralph Gibson LJ in draft and I respectfully agree with him that this appeal should be dismissed. As Ralph Gibson LJ has said, the ordinary duty of care owed by a master to his servant arises both in contract and in tort. I agree that it is impossible to imply any term into the plaintiff's contract of service with the defendants in the instant case of which, on the facts alleged in the statement of claim, a breach would entitle the plaintiff to recover by way of damages compensation for the loss he has sustained. This being so, then I also agree that it is not open to us to extend the duty of care owed by the defendants to the plaintiff by imposing a duty in tort which is not contained in any express or implied term of the contract.

Although the point does not arise directly for decision in the instant appeal, however, I would wish to reserve my position on the question whether a duty of care not to cause economic loss may be owed in tort without any assumption of responsibility or reliance, or in the absence of some relationship between the parties which, as Lord Devlin said in *Hedley Byrne & Co. Ltd v Heller & Partners Ltd* [1964] AC 465 at 530, is equivalent to contract. I do not think that so to hold has been necessary for the decision of any of the cases on this topic to which Ralph Gibson LJ has referred. In particular, I do not think that one can establish any positive principle in this regard by way of an argument founded on that which their Lordships did not say in *Yuen Kun-Yeu v A-G of Hong Kong* [1988] AC 175. The state of the law in this particular field is in my respectful opinion by no means satisfactory. This has been because the courts have in recent years sought to widen the scope of the tort of negligence to achieve what has been thought to be a just result in particular cases, without a sufficiently strict adherence to principles. For my part I respectfully adopt the cautionary approach of Lord Bridge in his leading speech in *D & F Estates Ltd v Church Comrs for England* [1989] AC 177 at 201, where he said:

> My Lords, I do not intend to embark on the daunting task of reviewing the wealth of other, mostly later, authority which bears, directly or indirectly, on the question whether the cost of making good defective plaster in the instant case is irrecoverable as economic loss, which seems to me to be the most important question for determination in the present appeal. My abstention may seem pusillanimous, but it stems from a recognition that the authorities, as it seems to me, speak with such an uncertain voice that, no matter how searching the analysis to which they are subject, they yield no clear and conclusive answer. It is more profitable, I believe, to examine the issue in the light of first principles.

Then Lord Bridge referred to the earlier decision in *Junior Books Ltd v Veitchi Co. Ltd* [1983] 1 AC 520. In respect of it he said ([1988] 2 All ER 992 at 1003, [1989] AC 177 at 202):

> The consensus of judicial opinion, with which I concur, seems to be that the decision of the majority is so far dependent on the unique, albeit non-contractual, relationship between the pursuer and the defender in that case and the unique scope of the duty of care owed by the defender to the pursuer arising from that relationship that the decision cannot be regarded as laying down any principle of general application in the law of tort or delict.

Lord Bridge then quoted with approval a passage from the dissenting speech of Lord Brandon in the *Junior Books* case [1983] 1 AC 520 at 549 to the effect that the basic principle stated by Lord Atkin in *Donoghue v Stevenson* [1932] AC 562 was that—

> when a person can or ought to appreciate that a careless act or omission on his part may result in physical injury to other persons or their property, he owes a duty to all such persons to exercise reasonable care to avoid such careless act or omission. It is, however, of fundamental importance to observe that the duty of care laid down in *Donoghue v Stevenson* was based on the existence of a danger of physical injury to persons or their property.

This reservation is not, however, directly material to the decision in the instant appeal, which, as I have said, I agree should be dismissed.

Neill LJ agreed in dismissing the plaintiff's appeal.

This decision is also of importance within the context of **Chapter 8**.

GRAN GELATO LTD v RICHCLIFFE (GROUP) LTD AND OTHERS
[1992] 1 All ER 865 (ChD)

SIR DONALD NICHOLLS V-C: Gran Gelato's claim against Gershon Young depends upon the solicitors themselves owing directly to Gran Gelato a duty to take reasonable care when answering the preliminary inquiries on behalf of their client Richcliff. That Richcliff itself owed such a duty of care is common ground. Indeed, in the light of authorities such as *Esso Petroleum Co. Ltd* v *Mardon* [1976] QB 801 the contrary could not be seriously argued. I was told that the existence of a claim directly against the solicitors may have practical importance in this case because it is questionable whether Richcliff is in a position to satisfy any substantial judgment debt.

The approach now to be adopted by the court when considering issues relating to the existence of a duty of care in the context of negligent misrepresentation is set out in the decision of the House of Lords in *Caparo Industries plc* v *Dickman* [1990] 2 AC 605. For there to be a duty of care there must be a foreseeability of damage and a close and direct relationship which has come to bear the label of 'proximity'. In addition, to adopt the phraseology of Lord Bridge of Harwich, the situation must be one in which the court considers it 'fair, just and reasonable' that the law should impose a duty of a given scope upon the one party for the benefit of the other (see [1990] 1 All ER 568 at 574 [1990] 2 AC 605 at 618).

Here there is no problem about foreseeability or a close and direct relationship. Gershon Young intended, or must be taken to have intended, that Gran Gelato and its solicitors should rely on the accuracy of the answers to the inquiries, and that they should do so in connection with this particular transaction. Gershon Young foresaw, or are to be taken to have foreseen, that Gran Gelato might suffer financial loss if the answers were incorrect. Certainly, in so far as the inquiries related to matters of title, as did inquiry 3(A), Gran Gelato and its solicitors would be relying on Gershon Young to apply their legal expertise as solicitors when answering the inquiries. Thus far, all the indications point towards it being just and reasonable to impose on Gershon Young a duty of care in favour of Gran Gelato. Indeed, all the factors which lead to the conclusion that a duty of care was owed by Richcliff exist also in the case of Gershon Young. The only material difference is that in making the representations Gershon Young were acting not as principals but as agents on behalf of Richcliff. They gave their answers' as Richcliff's solicitors, for and on behalf of Richcliff. Does this make any difference?

By itself, it does not. It is now established that the fact that the person making the representation was acting for a known principal does not necessarily negative the existence of a duty of care owed by him to the representee. The mortgagee's valuer may owe a duty of care to the mortgagor: *Smith* v *Eric S Bush (a firm), Harris* v *Wyre Forest DC* [1990] 1 AC 831. Further, in *Resolute Maritime Inc* v *Nippon Kaiji Kyokai* [1983] 2 All ER 1 at 3–4 Mustill J held that no cause of action in damages lies under the 1967 Act against a negligent agent acting within the scope of his authority. One of the strands in his reasoning was that the 1967 Act does not need to be interpreted as having this effect, because there was no gap here which required to be filled. In such a case the representee can sue the agent at common law, in accordance with *Hedley Byrne* principles (see *Hedley Byrne & Co. Ltd* v *Heller & Partners Ltd* [1964] AC 465).

That was in the context of agents generally. In the particular context of inquiries before contract in a normal conveyancing transaction Morritt J expressed a different view in *Cemp Properties (UK) Ltd* v *Dentsply Research and Development Corp (Denton Hall & Burgin, third party)* [1989] 2 EGLR 205 at 207. He observed that it would be absurd if the solicitor for one party to the transaction owed a duty of care to another party as well as to his own client.

In my view, in normal conveyancing transactions solicitors who are acting for a seller do not in general owe to the would-be buyer a duty of care when answering inquiries before contract or the like. In reaching the conclusion that the law should not generally import a duty of care in such circumstances, three factors have weighed with me. The first lies in the context in which such representations are made. The context is a contract for the sale of an interest in land. The buyer is formally seeking information from the seller about the land and his title to it. The answers given by the solicitor are given on behalf of the seller. The buyer relies upon those answers as answers given on behalf of the seller, although the confidence of the buyer and his solicitors in the reliability of the answers may be increased when they see the answers have been given by a solicitor in the ordinary way. They will expect the seller's solicitor, as a professional acting on behalf of his client, to have got the answers right. I venture to think that in these circumstances one would expect to find that the law provides the buyers with a remedy against the seller if the answers were given without due care. I am far from persuaded that the fair and reasonable reaction to these facts is that there ought also to be a remedy against the other party's solicitor personally.

Secondly, what one finds is that the law does indeed provide the buyer with a remedy against the seller in respect of any misrepresentation in the answers given on his behalf. As already noted, the seller himself owes a duty of care to the buyer. When, as is usual, the answers are given by the seller's solicitor, the seller will be as much liable for any carelessness of his solicitor as he would be for his own personal carelessness. He will be so liable because in the ordinary way the solicitor has implied authority from the seller to answer on his behalf the traditional inquiries before contract made on behalf of the buyer. In providing the answers the solicitor is acting within the scope of his authority. Some of the inquiries will raise questions of fact. Others will raise legal, conveyancing points which the client cannot answer himself. The client leaves all these matters to the solicitor to handle for him, after seeking instructions where appropriate from the client on any particular points on which the client may be expected to have relevant information. Thus, the purchaser to whom incorrect answers are given is not without a remedy even if the fault was that of the seller's solicitor and not the seller himself. Whoever was at fault, the buyer has a remedy for damages at common law against the seller. (This, I interpose, is to be contrasted with a case such as *Smith* v *Eric S Bush (a firm)*. There the mortgagor would have been without remedy if he did not have one against the valuer personally or his employer.)

Thirdly, at the forefront of his submissions, Mr Jackson presented an argument that to impose a duty of care on solicitors would be to expose them to conflicting duties, with one duty owed to their clients, and another different duty owed to the buyer. I am not persuaded that this would be so. The duty to the buyer would be to take reasonable care to see that the answers provided were accurate. That duty would march hand-in-hand with a duty to the same effect owed by the solicitor to his own client. There would be no conflict. Nevertheless, and although I am not impressed by this argument based on conflict, it does seem to me that in the field of negligent misrepresentation caution should be exercised before the law takes the step of concluding, in any particular context, that an agent acting within the scope of his authority on behalf of a known principal himself owes to third parties a duty of care independent of the duty of care he owes to his principal. There will be cases where it is fair, just and reasonable that there should be such a duty. But, in general, in a case where the principal himself owes a duty of care to the third party, the existence of a further duty of care, owed by the agent to the third party, is not necessary for the reasonable protection of the latter. Good reason, therefore, should exist before the law imposes a duty when the agent already owes to his principal a duty which covers the same ground and the principal is responsible to the third party for his agent's shortcomings. I do not think there is good reason for such a duty in normal conveyancing transactions.

I add this. I appreciate that one consequence of this conclusion is that the buyer may be left without an effective remedy if the seller becomes insolvent. I do not think that is sufficient reason for adding onto the solicitor-client relationship a duty owed directly by the solicitor to the non-client in normal conveyancing transactions. That those with whom one deals may become insolvent is an ordinary risk of everyday life . . .

I must emphasise two points. First, there will be special cases where the general rule does not apply and a duty of care will be owed by solicitors to a buyer . . .

Secondly, I must emphasise that nothing I have said detracts in any way from the duties owed by a solicitor to his own client when answering inquiries before contract. Nor does it relieve him from full financial responsibility for any carelessness on his part. If by his carelessness he exposes his principal to a claim by a buyer for negligent misrepresentation, he will be liable to indemnify his client on well-established principles.

Mr Pymont submitted that this was a special case: inquiry 3(A) related to legal rights, the answer was provided by Gershon Young without any disclaimer of liability, there was an express refusal to deduce title, there were practical difficulties in Gran Gelato going direct to Eagle Star to obtain information about the headleases, in correspondence the underlease was said to follow the headleases closely, Gershon Young knew or should have known that Gran Gelato was likely to rely on what Gershon Young said and Gran Gelato paid Gershon Young's bill.

Suffice to say, I cannot see in these features, taken separately or altogether, anything which would make this a special case to which the general rule should not apply. In particular, I cannot think that payment by the buyer of the solicitor's bill as such, as distinct from the bill being met out of the purchase price paid by the buyer to the seller, can determine whether or not the seller's solicitors owe a duty of care to the buyer. My conclusion, therefore, is that Gran Gelato's claim against Gershon Young fails.

Contributory negligence

Richcliff has advanced a defence of contributory negligence. Clearly, this is available as a defence to the claim against Richcliff for damages for breach of the common law duty of care; but is it available to the claim against Richcliff under s. 2(1) of the Misrepresentation Act 1967? In other words, does s. 1 of the Law Reform (Contributory Negligence) Act 1945 apply to a claim by a plaintiff for damages under the 1967 Act . . .

In the present case the conduct of which Gran Gelato complains founds a cause of action both in negligence at common law and under the 1967 Act. As already noted, under the 1967 Act liability is essentially founded on negligence. By parity of reasoning with the conclusion in *Forsikringsaktieselskapet Vesta* v *Butcher* regarding concurrent claims in negligence in tort and contract, the 1945 Act applies in the present case where there are concurrent claims against Richcliff in negligence in tort and under the 1967 Act . . .

GALOO LTD (IN LIQ) AND OTHERS v BRIGHT GRAHAME MURRAY (A FIRM) AND ANOTHER [1995] 1 All ER 16 (CA)

GLIDEWELL LJ: The first plaintiff, Galoo Ltd (Galoo), which is now in liquidation, formerly traded in animal health products. The second plaintiff, Gamine Ltd (Gamine), owned all the shares in Galoo. Both the first and second plaintiffs have changed their names. Galoo was formerly Peter Hand (GB) Ltd, and Gamine was Peter Hand Holdings Ltd.

The defendants, Bright Grahame Murray (BGM), are a firm of chartered accountants. From 1981 until 1991 they were the auditors of the accounts of Galoo, and from 1984 until 1991 of the accounts of Gamine.

In 1987 the third plaintiff, Hillsdown Holdings plc (Hillsdown), purchased 51% of the shares in Gamine from the holders of those shares. Between March 1987 and January 1993 Hillsdown made loans to Galoo and Gamine which amounted in total to over 30m. In May 1991 Hillsdown purchased a further 44.3% of the shares in Gamine.

By a specially indorsed writ issued on 6 October 1992 the plaintiffs claim that the audited accounts of Galoo and Gamine for the years 1985 to 1989 and the draft audited accounts for the year 1990 contained substantial inaccuracies, that in auditing the accounts without discovering or reporting such inaccuracies BGM were negligent and in breach of duties owed in contract and tort to Galoo and Gamine and in tort to Hillsdown, and that as a result the plaintiffs have all suffered loss and damage . . .

The distinction between the set of facts which it was held in *Morgan Crucible* would suffice to establish a duty of care owed by auditors from those facts which it was held in *Caparo* would not have this effect is inevitably a fine one. In my judgment that distinction may be expressed as follows. Mere foreseeability that a potential bidder may rely on the audited accounts does not impose on the auditor a duty of care to the bidder, but if the auditor is expressly made aware that a particular identified bidder will rely on the audited accounts or other statements approved by the auditor, and intends that the bidder should so rely, the auditor will be under a duty of care to the bidder for the breach of which he may be liable . . .

EVANS LJ: I agree entirely with the judgment of Glidewell LJ that both the appeal and the cross-appeal should be dismissed.

With regard to the cross-appeal, I add my express agreement with the passage from the judgment of the learned deputy judge which Glidewell LJ has quoted, in which he stated his reasons for holding that the claim in tort, for losses caused by reliance (as is alleged) upon representations made in or by reference to the completion accounts, at the time of the original purchase, should not be struck out. What he emphasised, rightly in my view, is that this allegation is one which should proceed to trial. It cannot be said as a matter of law at this interlocutory stage that the pleaded facts are necessarily insufficient to give rise to a cause of action. To this extent, the claim may be one which has more in common with the one which was allowed to proceed to trial in *Morgan Crucible Co. plc v Hill Samuel Bank Ltd* [1991] Ch 295 than with the allegation of reliance on audited accounts, prepared by a company statutory auditors and published by them to shareholders, which was struck out in *Caparo Industries plc v Dickman* [1990] 2 AC 605 . . .

It is tempting to distinguish between *Caparo* and *Morgan Crucible* on the basis that in the latter, though not the former case, the identity of a particular purchaser of shares in the company was known to the defendants when they represented that the company's accounts which they had prepared were fair and true. This excludes individual members of the body of existing shareholders to whom the statutory accounts are published (*Caparo*), whilst including an identified take-over bidder, as in *Morgan Crucible*. But there could be intervening situations, for example, where an existing shareholder is known to be a potential purchaser of more shares, with a view to acquiring the whole or a majority of the shares. The identification test would not provide the answer in such a case. No duty of care would be owed to such a person, in my judgment, on those facts alone, because the third of the four propositions listed by Lord Oliver in *Caparo Industries plc v Dickman* [1990] 1 All ER 568 at 589, [1990] 2 AC 605 at 638 already quoted by Glidewell LJ, as it was by Slade LJ in *Morgan Crucible*, would not be satisfied:

> (3) It is known, either actually or inferentially, that the advice so communicated is likely to be acted on by the advisee for that purpose without independent inquiry. . .,

and, vitally, it could not be said that the auditors in such a case 'intended that they should' act upon it, for that purpose ([1991] 1 All ER 148 at 159, [1991] Ch 295 at 320 *per* Slade LJ).

If it is right to confine the duty of care, meaning, to restrict the class of persons who can recover damages if the adviser/represented is negligent, to cases where the defendant is shown not merely to have known that the individual plaintiff would or might rely upon the representation but to have intended that it should be relied upon, by him and for the particular purpose and without intermediate examination, then the resulting analysis comes close to the 'voluntary assumption of responsibility' which has been referred to in many of the authorities but which was discounted as a test of liability in *Smith v Eric S Bush (a firm), Harris v Wyre Forest DC* [1990] 1 AC 831 at 862 *per* Lord Griffiths . . .

Lord Devlin referred in *Hedley Byrne & Co. Ltd v Heller & Partners Ltd* [1964] AC 465 at 530 to 'a relationship . . . equivalent to contract' and it is clear from Lord Griffiths's speech that the contractual analogy cannot serve as a definition of the cases where the duty of care may arise. But if the statement is made to an identifiable person and the maker not only knows that it will or is likely to be acted upon but also intended that it should be acted upon *for a particular purpose*, then these may well exemplify 'circumstances in which the law will deem the maker of the statement to have assumed responsibility' to the person who acts upon it (*per* Lord Griffiths in *Smith's* case). The 'indeterminate class' of persons referred to by Cardozo CJ in *Ultramares Corp v Touche* (1931) 255 NY 170 at 179 is thus reduced to an inter-personal relationship where liability may be imposed, and it would seem unreasonable and even unjust to do so, in my view, if the defendant could not be said to have assumed responsibility towards the plaintiff, not necessarily as an individual, in the circumstances of the case. It is sufficient for present purposes to note that the relationship by definition must be 'voluntary' in the sense that no consideration proceeds from the plaintiff for the defendant's advice.

Nor is it necessary to decide finally whether the facts alleged in the amended statement of claim are sufficient of themselves to establish liability, because that will depend also on the significance of the plaintiffs' right to review the completion accounts, which as already stated in my judgment is an issue fit for trial.

WAITE LJ: I agree that the appeal and the cross-appeal should be dismissed for the reasons given in the judgment of Glidewell LJ.

WALKIN v SOUTH MANCHESTER HEALTH AUTHORITY [1995] 4 All ER 132 (CA)

The plaintiff gave birth to a healthy child after a failed sterilisation operation. Her only claim was for economic loss, in order to circumvent the three-year limitation period for personal injury laid down in the Limitation Act 1980 (the Act imposes a six-year period in respect of economic loss).

It was held that this pleading was in *substance* a claim for personal injury; the breach of duty in negligence that gave rise to personal injury also resulted in economic loss. No amount of special pleading could alter the substance of the claim.

SOMASUNDARUM v M JULIUS MELCHIOR AND CO. [1989] 1 All ER 129 (CA)

It was held that an action for negligence against a barrister or solicitor with regard to the conduct of court proceedings would be struck out if it involved an attack on the court's decision. Immunity from suit with respect to advice given to a client in his plea in criminal proceedings is covered by the immunity covering conduct of litigation; because it is intimately connected with the conduct of the cause in court. This immunity extends to solicitors when acting as advocates—but not where a barrister has also been engaged to advise. (However, any action against the solicitor would probably fail either because—in practice—the solicitor has also been advised by counsel and has not been negligent or, as a matter of causation, counsel's advice breaks any link between the solicitor's advice and the eventual plea.)

MAY LJ: In *Saif Ali* v *Mitchell* (see also *Rondel* v *Worsley*) [The House of Lords] held that a barrister's immunity from suit for negligence was not total but only extended so far as was absolutely necessary in the interests of the administration of justice. It was not confined to what was done in court but extended to pre-trial work

> where the particular work is so intimately connected with the conduct of the cause in court that it can fairly be said to be a preliminary decision affecting the way that cause is to be conducted when it comes to a hearing

The quotation is from the judgement of McCarthy P in *Rees* v *Sinclair* [1974] NZLR 180 at 187 and was approved by the majority of their Lordships' House.

BAKER v KAYE, The Times, 13 December 1996

According to this case, a doctor who carries out a medical examination on behalf of someone's prospective employer owes a duty of care to the person he is examining.

The prospective employee was not the doctor's patient, but the court took the view that the doctor assumed a duty of care to that person because he regarded himself as being under a duty to advise that person to seek medical advice if the examination revealed any illness. That produced a relationship of sufficient legal proximity, and it was 'fair, just and reasonable' to impose a duty of care in the tort of negligence on the doctor. It may be thought that the decisive factor in this decision was the **therapeutic** nature of the responsibility assumed by the doctor towards the prospective employee.

KAPFUNDE v ABBEY NATIONAL PLC AND ANOTHER, The Times, 26 March 1998

The first instance decision in *Baker* v *Kaye* must be considered in the light of the Court of Appeal's decision in *Kapfunde* v *Abbey National plc and another*. The plaintiff had applied for a job with Abbey National and, as part of the process of applying for the post, she had completed a questionnaire giving details of absences from work due to illness. A doctor, employed by the Abbey National as occupational health advisor, advised his employer that the plaintiff's medical history pointed to the likelihood of above-average absenteeism. As a consequence the plaintiff did not get the job.

It was found that the Abbey National could not be vicariously liable for the doctor because he was employed under **a contract for services**, i.e. he was an independent contractor. As to the question of whether the doctor owed a duty of care in negligence to the plaintiff, Kennedy LJ, with whom Millett and Hutchison LJJ agreed, identified the following factors as significant in this case: (i) the lack of any doctor/patient relationship because the doctor never saw Mrs Kapfunde; (ii) the lack of any legal liability on a potential employer to exercise skill and care in processing applications for employment; and (iii) the fact that the claim was only for economic loss, that is, salary and other benefits she would have enjoyed if appointed to the post.

His Lordship said it was accepted between the parties that if the doctor was negligent in his assessment of the plaintiff it was reasonably foreseeable that she might suffer economic loss. Furthermore, it was not disputed that the doctor, should he owe a duty of care, would be expected to conform only to the degree of care expected of 'an ordinary competent occupational health physician'.

The argument in this case centred on the duty of care issue and its attendant concerns of proximity, assumption of responsibility and whether it would be just and reasonable to impose a duty in the circumstances.

Kennedy LJ referred to the decision in *White* v *Jones* which, in his Lordship's opinion, was not confined strictly to its own facts; but it had to be read in the light of *X* v *Bedfordshire CC*. The doctor's position in the present case could be compared with that of the social workers and doctors in *X*, or with that of a doctor conducting an examination for purposes of life insurance, except that the doctor here had made his assessment only on the basis of reading the plaintiff's completed questionnaire. His Lordship, referring to the speech of Lord Browne-Wilkinson in *X*, said that the incremental increase in the categories of negligence made in *White* v *Jones* was only small, viz. sufficient to cover the facts of **that** case, but **not** sufficient to support the imposition of a duty of care in the circumstances of the present case.

There was no special relationship between the parties creating a duty of care. This was a better way of expressing the situation than to say there was insufficient proximity, but 'it amounted to the same thing.'

His Lordship also expressed the opinion that the judge in *Baker* v *Kaye* was wrong in finding that the doctor owed a duty of care to the plaintiff in that case.

COURTS AND LEGAL SERVICES ACT 1990

62. Immunity of advocates from actions in negligence and for breach of contract
A person—
    (a) who is not a barrister; but
    (b) who lawfully provides any legal services in relation to any proceedings,
shall have the same immunity from liability for negligence in respect of his acts or omissions as he would have if he were a barrister lawfully providing those services.

(2) No act or omission on the part of any barrister or other person which is accorded immunity from liability for negligence shall give rise to an action for breach of any contract relating to the provision by him of the legal services in question.

5.5   End of Chapter Assessment Question

Doubledeal set up a tax consultancy service in 1985. The business has thrived. Apart from tax matters Doubledeal has, over the years, given advice to his clients concerning investments. He admits that this policy has helped to expand his business.

Harold goes to Doubledeal in order to consult him about his tax problems. In consequence of the advice given, Harold buys some rare works of art in order to escape inheritance tax. He also asks Doubledeal for his opinion as to the prospects of Unitechnics Ltd, a new company which has been set up to retrain displaced university staff. He invests £40,000 in Unitechnics Ltd, acting on Doubledeal's assurance that the company is in a healthy financial condition.

The conversation then goes on to more mundane matters, but just as Harold is about to leave Doubledeal says: 'By the way, if you have any spare capital in these bad times, Ranchland Ltd (an American-owned real-estate firm operating in Snowdonia) is a good bet'. Two weeks later Harold invests £50,000 in this company.

Some weeks later, Harold learns that he has been wrongly advised concerning his inheritance tax position, and also that Unitechnics Ltd and Ranchland Ltd are just about to go into liquidation, having been in grave financial difficulties for six months. He also receives a bill from Doubledeal: 'For advice re Inheritance Tax'.

Advise Harold on any claim he may have in tort against Doubledeal.

5.6   End of Chapter Assessment Outline Answer

D = Doubledeal and H = Harold

The common law imposes liability in tort upon persons who make statements to others in certain circumstances, i.e. where the statements take the form of misstatements. This is, however, insufficient on its own; a misstatement must have been wrongfully made viz. must either be tainted with fraud, or be made negligently, and only then if there is a duty to take care. The person to whom the misstatement has been made must also have sustained a loss (which may be physical or financial or both) as a result of reliance upon the misstatement.

In the present circumstances there is no apparent evidence of fraud (i.e. the tort of deceit, which requires proof of **intentional** or **reckless** behaviour on the part of the defendant, as in the leading case of *Derry* v *Peek)*, and any liability of D, the purveyor of the information, is more likely to arise in the tort of negligence which is defined in terms of **duty, breach** and **damage**.

The losses sustained by H are of a financial nature (**pure** economic loss in the circumstances – i.e. loss of a financial nature which is **not** the direct consequence of physical injury to the person or to the property). Traditionally, the common law has not given a remedy in negligence to a person who can show only **pure** economic loss, because it is thought undesirable that there should be liability towards an indeterminate number of people, often in respect of an indeterminate amount of money. In *Hedley Byrne* v *Heller*, however, the House of Lords recognised such a claim with regard to negligent misstatement. (An account of the decision should be given at this point; emphasise the notion of the special relationship; the element of reliance; assumption of responsibility; examples of its application in subsequent cases: e.g. *Evatt, Mardon*.)

There is some authority, at first instance, for the proposition that the decision in *Hedley Byrne* is yet merely another application of the Atkinian neighbour principle – see *Yianni* v *Evans*; *JEB Fasteners* v *Bloom*; applying *Dorset Yacht* (*per* Lord Reid) and *Anns* (*per* Lord Wilberforce). According to the views expressed in *Yianni* and the other cases the *Hedley Byrne* requirement of a special relationship is merely another expression of proximity – the greater the degree of foreseeability (likelihood?) of reliance by the plaintiff on the defendant (resulting in loss by the former) the more proximate will be the relationship between the parties. It could be said that this approach by-passed, rather than extended,

Hedley Byrne; the decision being regarded as **illustrative** rather than **definitive** of liability in this area.

More recently, however, this approach has been questioned in the higher courts; see e.g. Lord Brandon in *Aliakmon* (doubt cast on the utility of the Wilberforce test in the context of issues covered by established authority); Lord Keith in *Peabody*, *Yeun Kun Yeu* (a more general criticism of an unqualified application of the Wilberforce test; note also the addition of the **just and reasonable** requirement; *D and F Estates* v *Church Commissioners*, and *Murphy* v *Brentwood DC*. (Add to this the onslaught against *Junior Books* v *Veitchi*, in the context of pure economic loss occurring outside misstatement.)

In the light of these developments it may now be more correct to regard *Hedley Byrne* as having been restored to something approaching its apparently definitive nature; it may now be the case that **extensions** of this decision will be required to cover new situations, albeit subject to the requirements of 'foreseeability'/'proximity'/'just and reasonable' and the dictates of the **incremental** approach to the development of the law.

Caparo plc v *Dickman* is regarded generally as the current leading **interpretative** authority concerning the rule in *Hedley Byrne*, as well as being authority for the **general** incremental approach.

Caparo requires, essentially:

(i)   that the plaintiff is known;

(ii)   that the purpose of the advice, etc., is known;

(iii) that the plaintiff is **likely** to rely on the advice, etc. for the **purpose in mind**.

Reference can also be made here to *Smith* v *Bush*/*Harris* v *Wyre Forest DC*; *Morgan Crucible* v *Hill Samuel*; *James McNaughton Paper Group* v *Hicks, Anderson & Co*; *Henderson* v *Merrett*.

There must, on the facts of each case, be an **assumption of responsibility** by the defendant for his advice, etc.

(i)   **Tax advice**

The *Caparo* criteria appear to be satisfied here.

A **contractual** relationship exists between D and H. There must be sufficient foreseeability/ proximity/reliance/assumption of responsibility/and it must also be just and reasonable to impose a duty of care in the circumstances. Negligent advice? Loss suffered? Actual reliance? It would probably even fall within majority ruling in *Evatt*. Actions in contract and tort may exist side by side for benefit of the same plaintiff.

The possibility of a concurrent action in **contract**, as in *Henderson* v *Merrett*, is not explored in this answer.

(a)   **Unitechnics**

Again, *Caparo* would be satisfied, perhaps, on a *prima facie* basis.

Foreseeability, etc. Business, formal setting? Ordinary, normal course of business was sufficient for minority in *Evatt*. (Consideration/payment/benefit not strictly necessary: see *Hedley Byrne* and more recently, perhaps, *Chaudhry* v *Prabhakar*; though presence of such factor(s) may strengthen a case.) See also *Esso* v *Mardon* and *Howard Marine* v *Ogden*. Here, D has been giving such advice for some years. It also, apparently, helps his business along to supply such information. Previous course of dealing between the parties? (This might be an important factor in the present circumstances.) Does it matter whether information takes form of advice/fact/opinion? No, in principle? See, however *Briggs* v *Gunner*: Yes; considered fact relevant to reasonableness of reliance in cases concerning speculation. However, such a distinction is not drawn generally in the cases.

What **standard of care** is expected in such a case? (Overlap with *Briggs* v *Gunner* point: in that case market of speculation involved and plaintiff himself an experienced investor in stocks and shares; court thought he should have exercised his own judgment and it was therefore unreasonable to rely entirely on defendant especially in relation to information not readily to hand for defendant, whose only duty in circumstances was to be honest.) Of expert? Of experienced professional such as solicitor or accountant? Of someone like bank manager? Must be breach of standard appropriate to the circumstances e.g. *Mardon*. Is D here a professional? Relative position of parties may be important: e.g. two experts. Holding out as having special skill/knowledge (*per Evatt*)? Is H asking for **considered** advice? Seems plaintiff must make it clear that is what he wants – or at least that must be pretty evident from the circumstances. (Assumption of responsibility?)

Unitechnics have been in grave **difficulties** for six months. H discovers this **some weeks later**. Indicates that D, even if he has only to observe standard of non-expert, ought to have been aware of the situation?

Ought H to have realised the situation earlier than he did? Contributory negligence under the Law Reform (Contributory Negligence) Act 1945 may be a relevant consideration.

Cause and effect are necessary, as in all tortious relationships, i.e. is there a causative link between 'advice' and loss? It is essential that H should be in a position to show that there has been 'reliance' and that this 'reliance' is at least a substantial cause of the loss suffered.

(b) Ranchland

Is H likely to rely on D, in accordance with *Caparo?*

Generally, the same considerations apply as above. However, D seems to be giving **volunteered advice**. (Is there a difference between 'advice' and 'opinion' – as in (a) (above)?) On this occasion therefore more difficult to establish liability. *Lambert* v *Lewis*: no liability where information is volunteered by defendant. Is it **volunteered** in present context?

Also, in category of off-the-cuff, social, casual advice? (*Hedley Byrne*). Thus, less reasonable to rely on advice in present circumstances (no assumption of responsibility)?

It is suggested that H be advised as follows:

(a) Tax advice

H will have a cause of action in the tort of negligence under *Hedley Byrne* and *Caparo* against D, provided that H can show the advice was negligently given and that he has suffered actual loss.

(b) Investments

H would, as far as Unitechnics is concerned, appear to have a cause of action in negligence (*Hedley Byrne/Caparo*) against D provided he can establish the points of contention raised above. A cause of action in negligence (*Hedley Byrne/Caparo*) in connection with D's advice on Ranchland would, it is submitted, be more difficult to establish for the reasons stated earlier in this answer.

CHAPTER SIX

NEGLIGENCE: NERVOUS SHOCK/PSYCHIATRIC DAMAGE

6.1 Introduction

6.1.1 GRIEF, SORROW AND ANXIETY

KRALJ AND ANOTHER v McGRATH AND ANOTHER [1986] 1 All ER 54

WOOLF J: This is a case involving a claim for damages by Mr and Mrs Kralj. It is brought against the first defendant, Mr McGrath, who is a consultant obstetrician, and St Teresa's Hospital in Wimbledon. I heard the matter on Tuesday and Wednesday of this week, but in the course of the reply it became apparent that questions of a relatively novel nature in relation to the assessment of damages in a case of this sort arose on the arguments advanced on behalf of the plaintiffs, and in the circumstances I adjourned the matter overnight to give me time to consider those arguments.

It relates to the manner in which Mrs Kralj was treated during her confinement for the birth of twins on 19 March 1980. The first twin, Thomas, was born perfectly satisfactorily and he is now a healthy and happy young five-year-old. Unfortunately the second twin, Daniel, was born in an extremely debilitated state and he died on 16 May 1980.

There are two separate claims put forward in the proceedings. First of all Mrs Kralj puts forward a claim for the very considerable pain and suffering, loss and damage she suffered as a result of the manner in which she was treated during her labour. The second claim is brought under the Law Reform (Miscellaneous Provisions) Act 1934 on behalf of the estate of Daniel. Liability is admitted by both defendants, and so it is only necessary for me to adjudicate on the question of quantum. However, in order to do so it is necessary for me to consider the allegations of negligence which are made because of the way the matter is put forward in relation to the claim for damages on behalf of the plaintiffs and to identify the loss that was suffered by Mrs Kralj . . .

I turn to Mrs Kralj's claim. This falls into different categories. The principal categories (and they can be described in different terms and to some extent overlap and are not exhaustive) are as follows: first, pain and suffering during the period of her labour; second, pain and suffering from her physical complaints after the delivery; third, the consequences of what happened to Daniel; and here there are different heads. First of all there is the nervous shock resulting to Mrs Kralj as a result of being told and seeing what had happened to Daniel, second there is the inconvenience and the distress caused by having to travel back and forth to hospital during the period that Daniel survived, third there is put forward a claim for the grief that Mrs Kralj has naturally undergone as a result of his death, fourth there is the pain and discomfort that Mrs Kralj will go through in respect of the future child who she hopes will be conceived and in connection therewith there is a claim for financial loss . . .

The second matter which raises problems of a general nature arises from the contention of counsel for the plaintiffs that in these circumstances as part of her damages Mrs Kralj is entitled to be compensated for her grief at the loss of Daniel. Counsel accepts that if there had been no other injury to the plaintiff she could not recover damages for the grief she sustained solely due to the loss of Daniel. This concession by counsel is justified, as appears from the speech of Lord Wilberforce in *McLoughlin* v *O'Brian* [1983] AC 410 at 418, a case which was not actually cited to me in argument but which is referred to in a case which was cited to me, namely *Emeh* v *Kensington and Chelsea and Westminster Area Health Authority* [1985] QB 1012. Lord Wilberforce was dealing with the circumstances in which a plaintiff was entitled to recover damages and was not dealing with the question which I am concerned with, which is one of quantum. However, he said:

> While damages cannot, at common law, be awarded for grief and sorrow, a claim for damages for 'nervous shock' caused by negligence can be made without the necessity of showing direct impact or fear of immediate personal injury for oneself.

However, I regard what Lord Wilberforce said as being of general application. The position, as I see it, is as follows. First of all there can be no doubt that Mrs Kralj is entitled to be compensated for the shock she undoubtedly suffered as a result of being told what had happened to Daniel and of seeing him during her visits. Secondly, while damages for grief and suffering for the death of Daniel are not payable in the same way as I indicated when dealing with the question of aggravated damages, if the situation is one where the plaintiff's injuries have on her a more drastic effect than they would otherwise because of the grief which she is sustaining at the same time in relation to the death of a child who died in the circumstances in which Daniel died, that is something which the court can take into account. Again the court is doing no more than compensating the plaintiff for what has happened to her, just as the defendants would have been entitled to have taken into account that the effects were not as great as they would otherwise have been because Daniel proved to be a healthy child, so they must take the consequences which follow if the effect is greater on Mrs Kralj because of the grief that she is undergoing at the same time because of what had happened to Daniel. I emphasise that in considering what is the appropriate figure to award to Mrs Kralj I will look at the consequences to her of what was done to her and not award any damages merely for the fact that, like any other mother, she naturally suffered grief as a result of the death of Daniel . . .

6.2   The Legal Cause of Action

6.2.1   ELEMENTS OF THE CLAIM

S AND ANOTHER v DISTILLERS CO. (BIOCHEMICALS) LTD
J AND OTHERS v DISTILLERS CO. (BIOCHEMICALS) LTD AND OTHERS
[1969] 3 All ER 1412

HINCHCLIFFE J: In these two actions, the plaintiffs claim damages for personal injuries and consequential loss due to the alleged negligence and breach of duty on the part of the defendants, who marketed a drug named thalidomide, which, if taken by a pregnant woman, could and did cause injury to the embryo. These are the first two cases to be heard, and it is to be hoped that the judgment today may conceivably assist in the settlement of the outstanding cases. No question of liability arises. After prolonged negotiations, the court approved a compromise whereby, on the plaintiffs' unreservedly withdrawing all allegations of negligence, the defendants undertook to pay 40 per cent of the damages agreed between the parties or decided by the court. It was decided that these two cases should be tried together for two reasons: (i) D.J. is obviously in the top bracket of deformities, R.S. is in the middle range; and (ii) the J. family in March 1968 had a desperate housing problem and the defendants were good enough to provide £6,500 by way of an interim payment. This was made pursuant to an order of the court. It has been agreed between the parties that the claims of the S. family, that is to say, Mr and Mrs S. and R.S., together with the claim of D.J., should be heard at this trial. As the special damage claim of both Mr and Mrs J. is not agreed and is likely to take some time, the claims of Mr and Mrs J. have been sent over to next term when I shall, of course, give judgment for Mrs J. on her claim for general damage . . .

So far as Mrs S.'s claim is concerned, it is plain that she suffered a grievous shock. For a happily married woman, it is difficult to comprehend any greater shock than seeing your child born misshapen and deformed. The fun and joy of motherhood is partially destroyed. Instead of enjoying and being able to show off the baby to your friends, there is a natural reluctance to do so. This has not been the sort of shock which has worn off like so many cases of shock that come before the courts; this is permanent. Ever since the birth Mrs S. has been depressed, anxious and worried. She is daily reminded of her handicap. There is always a cloud over her happiness. She now has to take drugs prescribed by her doctor and she has a sense of guilt which makes it harder for her to recover, although heaven knows she has nothing to blame herself for. She is entitled to damages for grievous shock, for future travelling expenses quarterly, for special clothes for R.S., together with something for the loss of wages. I award her the sum of £5,000 . . .

ATTIA v *BRITISH GAS PLC* [1987] 3 All ER 455 (CA)

This decision is authority for the proposition that those who suffer shock as a result of fear for their property may recover damages. It was, however, agreed in terms of **remoteness of damage** and NOT in terms of **duty of care**; negligence was **admitted**.

The Court of Appeal considered that it was perfectly feasible to argue that 'nervous shock' (or 'psychiatric damage' as Bingham LJ preferred to describe it) was a reasonably foreseeable result of witnessing damage to one's property. *McLoughlin; Bourhill* v *Young and Jaensch* were considered.

The defendants had a **contract** with the plaintiff to install in her house a central heating system. One day, whilst the work was being carried out, she returned home from a shopping expedition to find the house on fire; her home and its contents suffered severe damage for which the defendants admitted liability in negligence. Liability for the nervous shock she claimed to have sustained as a reaction to this event was denied and the matter became a preliminary issue for resolution by the court before the trial could proceed. The defendants claimed that as a matter of policy nervous shock caused only by damage to property could not be compensated. Further, the plaintiff's shock was not reasonably foreseeable in any event because it was not a direct consequence of the defendants' negligence.

The judge at first instance found for the defendants, but the Court of Appeal said that provided there was 'psychiatric damage' (not merely grief, etc) suffered **as a result** of witnessing the destruction of property, e.g. one's home and possessions, damages could be recovered as long as the psychiatric illness was a reasonably foreseeable consequence of the defendant's negligence. The question of reasonable foreseeability was one of **fact, to be resolved at the trial of the case**.

The facts alleged were **assumed** by the court to be true (for the purposes of this **preliminary** issue); nor was the question of **causation** examined. It was also assumed that the plaintiff was a person of normal disposition or toughness ('**the customary phlegm**'). The court regarded the issue as one of remoteness of damage and, though it was not fantastic or far-fetched (in the light of progressive awareness of mental illness) to suppose that a person might suffer psychiatric illness from shock in the present circumstances, it could be **argued** that the plaintiff's alleged damage was a reasonably foreseeable consequence of the defendants' (admitted) negligence. The court was not prepared to make a 'general a priori ruling', to the effect that such a claim could never be a reasonably foreseeable consequence of someone's negligence, 'on such scanty material' (Dillon LJ).

Woolf LJ said, 'Even assuming that the test is not confined to being one of foreseeability [earlier reference to the divergence of opinion in *McLoughlin and Jaensch* as to the role policy plays in these decisions], I cannot conceive that, if the injury which the plaintiff alleges that she suffered was a foreseeable consequence of the defendant's negligence, there could be any overriding policy reason for preventing her recovering damages . . . she could well have sustained physical injuries as well as the psychiatric injuries of which she complains when she would have been entitled to damages and in my view there can be no reason of policy for distinguishing between the two types of injury.' Bingham LJ agreed that this claim broke new ground, but said it was neither unfair nor inconvenient to move the boundary stone of liability a little further and rule as a matter of principle that nervous shock sustained as a result of damage to property could be reasonably foreseeable. There was no good reason of policy to deny such a claim. The policy argument relied upon by the defendants was 'the familiar floodgates argument'. This could not be 'automatically discounted'. But '[it is not] an argument which can claim a very impressive record of success. All depends on one's judgment of the likely result of a particular extension of the law.' Bingham LJ did not think that a finding for the plaintiff (on the preliminary issue) would 'result in a flood of claims or actions'. The requirements of **reasonable foreseeability of psychiatric damage** would enable the 'good sense of the judge' to ensure 'that the thing stops at the appropriate point'. 'His good sense provides a better, because more flexible, mechanism of control than a necessarily arbitrary rule of law.' (He stressed that since this was not a full trial the court could only decide the broad question of principle of the plaintiff.)

It will be noted that the parties in this case were not strangers to each other and that the court approached the issue only from the point of view of remoteness of damage. It is true that the question of policy was also considered, but it is clear that the claim for nervous shock was allowed to proceed in a 'parasitic' form on the (admitted) duty (and breach) that the defendants owed to the plaintiff in respect of the damage to her home and possessions.

The issue was remitted for trial and the judge awarded the plaintiff £16,409 damages for nervous shock and loss of earnings: *The Guardian*, 11 July 1989.

6.2.2   DUTY OF CARE

BOURHILL v YOUNG [1943] AC 92 (HL)

LORD PORTER: The driver of a car or vehicle is entitled to assume that the ordinary frequenter of the streets has sufficient fortitude to endure such incidents as may from time to time be expected to occur in them, including the noise of a collision and the sight of injury to others, and is not to be considered negligent towards one who does not possess the customary phlegm.

6.2.3   A PERIOD OF EXPANSION?

McLOUGHLIN v O'BRIAN [1982] 2 All ER 298 (HL)

In *McLoughlin* the plaintiff, a wife and mother, was told at home that her husband and children had been seriously hurt in a traffic accident caused by the defendant's negligence. She went to the hospital to be with her family and saw each member in their injured state; she was also told that one of her children was dead. On witnessing this immediate aftermath of the accident she subsequently suffered nervous shock. In response to her claim for damages the judge at first instance held that no duty of care was owed by the defendants to the plaintiff because she was not a reasonably foreseeable victim. The Court of Appeal upheld his judgment, but on a different basis viz. that the shock suffered by the plaintiff was reasonably foreseeable but **public policy** dictated that no duty of care was owed to her. The 'floodgates of litigation' argument, amongst others, was advanced in support of this decision. However, the House of Lords rejected the policy argument and unanimously found in favour of the plaintiff. Liability was extended to the 'immediate aftermath' of an accident. It is instructive to examine the salient features of the speeches in this case. All their Lordships agreed that it was incumbent upon the plaintiff to establish that the shock which in fact she suffered was a reasonably foreseeable result of the defendant's careless driving. Lords Scarman and Bridge found that once causation was established (it must be remembered that the defendants had admitted negligence) this was all that the plaintiff need show and that it was not for the courts to limit, on policy grounds, a right to recover for reasonably foreseeable damage caused by a defendant. Lord Scarman suggested that, apart from special cases, policy was not justiciable (i.e. where common law principle dictated the result, as in the present case) and it was the function of Parliament, not the courts, to set limits on grounds of policy. He thought that the result in the present case **might** be socially undesirable; there was a powerful case for legislation such as that enacted in New South Wales and the Australian Capital Territories.

However, the other judges (Lords Wilberforce, Bridge and Russell) regarded policy as having a much more important role to play in judicial deliberations than that envisaged by the minority; reasonable foreseeability of shock to the plaintiff is a necessary, though not necessarily sufficient, condition of liability and policy may legitimately restrict the range of liability. (It may be noted that Lord Wilberforce did not employ his two-stage test and argued on the basis of a 'logical progression' in the cases, i.e. adopted an approach reminiscent of the incremental approach to be found in the Lord Keith line of cases (see 'Duty of Care' in negligence).) The present case came within the current boundaries of the law.

LORD WILBERFORCE: Although we continue to use the hallowed expression 'nervous shock,' English law, and common understanding, have moved some distance since recognition was given to this symptom as a basis for liability. Whatever is unknown about the mind-body relationship (and the area of ignorance seems to expand with that of knowledge), it is now accepted by medical science that recognisable and severe physical damage to the human body and system may be caused by the impact, through the senses, of external events on the mind. There may thus be produced what is as identifiable an illness as any that may be caused by direct physical impact. It is safe to say that this, in general terms, is understood by the ordinary man or woman who is hypothesised by the courts in situations where claims for negligence are made. Although in the only case which has reached this House (*Bourhill* v *Young* [1943] AC 92) a claim for damages in respect of 'nervous shock' was rejected on its facts, the House gave clear recognition to the legitimacy, in principle, of claims of that character. As the result of that and other cases, assuming that they are accepted as correct, the following position has been reached:

1.   While damages cannot, at common law, be awarded for grief and sorrow, a claim for damages for 'nervous shock' caused by negligence can be made without the necessity of showing direct impact or fear of immediate personal injuries for oneself. The reservation made by Kennedy J in *Dulieu* v *White & Sons* [1901] 2 KB 669, though taken up by Sargant LJ in *Hambrook* v *Stokes Brothers* [1925] 1 KB 141, has not gained acceptance, and although the respondents, in the courts below, reserved their right to revive it, they did not do so in argument. I think that it is now too late to do so. The arguments on this issue were fully and admirably stated by the Supreme Court of California in *Dillon* v *Legg* (1968) 29 ALR 3d 1316.

2.   A plaintiff may recover damages for 'nervous shock' brought on by injury caused not to him—or herself but to a near relative, or by the fear of such injury. So far (subject to 5 below), the cases do not extend beyond the spouse or children of the plaintiff (*Hambrook* v *Stokes Brothers* [1925] 1 KB 141, *Boardman* v *Sanderson* [1964] 1 WLR 1317, *Hinz* v *Berry* [1970] 2 QB 40—including foster children—(where liability was assumed) and see *King* v *Phillips* [1953] 1 QB 429).

3.   Subject to the next paragraph, there is no English case in which a plaintiff has been able to recover nervous shock damages where the injury to the near relative occurred out of sight and earshot of the plaintiff. In *Hambrook* v *Stokes Brothers* an express distinction was made between shock caused by what the mother saw with her own eyes and what she might have been told by bystanders, liability being excluded in the latter case.

4.   An exception from, or I would prefer to call it an extension of, the latter case, has been made where the plaintiff does not see or hear the incident but comes upon its immediate aftermath. In *Boardman* v *Sanderson* the father was within earshot of the accident to his child and likely to come upon the scene: he did so and suffered damage from what he then saw. In *Marshall* v *Lionel Enterprises Inc.* [1972] 2 QR 177, the wife came immediately upon the badly injured body of her husband. And in *Benson* v *Lee* [1972] VR 879, a situation existed with some similarity to the present case. The mother was in her home 100 yards away, and, on communication by a third party, ran out to the scene of the accident and there suffered shock. Your Lordships have to decide whether or not to validate these extensions.

5.   A remedy on account of nervous shock has been given to a man who came upon a serious accident involving numerous people immediately thereafter and acted as a rescuer of those involved (*Chadwick* v *British Railways Board* [1967] 1 WLR 912). 'Shock' was caused neither by fear for himself nor by fear or horror on account of a near relative. The principle of 'rescuer' cases was not challenged by the respondents and ought, in my opinion, to be accepted. But we have to consider whether, and how far, it can be applied to such cases as the present.

Throughout these developments, as can be seen, the courts have proceeded in the traditional manner of the common law from case to case, upon a basis of logical necessity. If a mother, with or without accompanying children, could recover on account of fear for herself, how can she be denied recovery on account of fear for her accompanying children? If a father could recover had he seen his child run over by a backing car, how can he be denied recovery if he is in the immediate vicinity and runs to the child's assistance? If a wife and mother could recover if she had witnessed a serious accident to her husband and children, does she fail because she was a short distance away and immediately rushes to the scene (cf. *Benson* v *Lee*)? I think that unless the law is to draw an arbitrary line at the point of direct sight and sound, these arguments require acceptance of the extension mentioned above under 4 in the interests of justice.

If one continues to follow the process of logical progression, it is hard to see why the present plaintiff also should not succeed. She was not present at the accident, but she came very soon after upon its aftermath. If, from a distance of some 100 yards (cf. *Benson* v *Lee*), she had found her family by the roadside, she would have come within principle 4 above. Can it make any difference that she comes upon them in an ambulance, or, as here, in a nearby hospital, when, as the evidence shows, they were in the same condition, covered with oil and mud, and distraught with pain? If Mr Chadwick can recover when, acting in accordance with normal and irresistible human instinct, and indeed moral compulsion, he goes to the scene of an accident, may not a mother recover if, acting under the same motives, she goes to where her family can be found?

I could agree that a line can be drawn above her case with less hardship than would have been apparent in *Boardman* v *Sanderson* [1964] 1 WLR 1317 and *Hinz* v *Berry* [1970] 2 QB 40, but so to draw it would not appeal to most people's sense of justice. To allow her claim may be, I think it is, upon the margin of what the process of logical progression would allow. But where the facts are strong and exceptional, and, as I think, fairly analogous, her case ought, prima facie, to be assimilated to those which have passed the test.

To argue from one factual situation to another and to decide by analogy is a natural tendency of the human and the legal mind. But the lawyer still has to inquire whether, in so doing, he has crossed some critical line behind which he ought to stop. That is said to be the present case. . . .

We must then consider the policy arguments. In doing so we must bear in mind that cases of 'nervous shock,' and the possibility of claiming damages for it, are not necessarily confined to those arising out of accidents on public roads. To state, therefore, a rule that recoverable damages must be confined to persons on or near the highway is to state not a principle in itself, but only an example of a more general rule that recoverable damages must be confined to those within sight and sound of an event caused by negligence or, at least, to those in close, or very close, proximity to such a situation.

The policy arguments against a wider extension can be stated under four heads.

First, it may be said that such extension may lead to a proliferation of claims, and possibly fraudulent claims, to the establishment of an industry of lawyers and psychiatrists who will formulate a claim for nervous shock damages, including what in America is called the customary miscarriage, for all, or many, road accidents and industrial accidents.

Secondly, it may be claimed that an extension of liability would be unfair to defendants, as imposing damages out of proportion to the negligent conduct complained of. In so far as such defendants are insured, a large additional burden will be placed on insurers, and ultimately upon the class of persons insured—road users or employers.

Thirdly, to extend liability beyond the most direct and plain cases would greatly increase evidentiary difficulties and tend to lengthen litigation.

Fourthly, it may be said—and the Court of Appeal agreed with this—that an extension of the scope of liability ought only to be made by the legislature, after careful research. This is the course which has been taken in New South Wales and the Australian Capital Territory.

The whole argument has been well summed up by Dean Prosser (*Prosser, Torts*, 4th ed. (1971), p. 256):

> The reluctance of the courts to enter this field even where the mental injury is clearly foreseeable, and the frequent mention of the difficulties of proof, the facility of fraud, and the problem of finding a place to stop and draw the line, suggest that here it is the nature of the interest invaded and the type of damage which is the real obstacle.

Since he wrote, the type of damage has, in this country at least, become more familiar and less deterrent to recovery. And some of the arguments are susceptible of answer.

Fraudulent claims can be contained by the courts, who, also, can cope with evidentiary difficulties. The scarcity of cases which have occurred in the past, and the modest sums recovered, give some indication that fears of a flood of litigation may be exaggerated—experience in other fields suggests that such fears usually are. If some increase does occur, that may only reveal the existence of a genuine social need: that legislation has been found necessary in Australia may indicate the same thing.

But, these discounts accepted, there remains, in my opinion, just because 'shock' in its nature is capable of affecting so wide a range of people, a real need for the law to place some limitation upon the extent of admissible claims. It is necessary to consider three elements inherent in any claim: the class of persons whose claims should be recognised; the proximity of such persons to the accident; and the means by which the shock is caused. As regards the class of persons, the possible range is between the closest of family ties—of parent and child, or husband and wife—and the ordinary bystander. Existing law recognises the claims of the first: it denies that of the second, either on the basis that such persons must be assumed to be possessed of fortitude sufficient to enable them to endure the calamities of modern life, or that defendants cannot be expected to compensate the world at large. In my opinion, these positions are justifiable, and since the present case falls within the first class, it is strictly unnecessary to say more. I think, however, that it should follow that other cases involving less close relationships must be very carefully scrutinised. I cannot say that they should never be admitted. The closer the tie (not merely in relationship, but in care) the greater the claim for consideration. The claim, in any case, has to be judged in the light of the other factors, such as proximity to the scene in time and place, and the nature of the accident.

As regards proximity to the accident, it is obvious that this must be close in both time and space. It is, after all, the fact and consequence of the defendant's negligence that must be proved to have caused the 'nervous shock.' Experience has shown that to insist on direct and immediate sight or hearing would be impractical and unjust and that under what may be called the 'aftermath' doctrine one who, from close proximity, comes very soon upon the scene should not be excluded. In my opinion, the result in *Benson* v *Lee* [1972] VR 879 was correct and indeed inescapable. It was based, soundly, upon 'direct perception of some of the events which go to make up the accident as an entire event, and this includes . . . the immediate aftermath . . .' (p. 880). The High Court's majority decision in *Chester* v *Waverley Corporation* (1939) 62 CLR 1, where a child's body was found floating in a trench after a prolonged search, may perhaps be placed on the other side of a recognisable line (Evatt J in a powerful dissent placed it on the same side), but, in addition, I find the conclusion of Lush J to reflect developments in the law.

Finally, and by way of reinforcement of 'aftermath' cases, I would accept, by analogy with 'rescue' situations, that a person of whom it could be said that one could expect nothing else than that he or she would come immediately to the scene—normally a parent or a spouse—could be regarded as being within the scope of foresight and duty. Where there is not immediate presence, account must be taken of the possibility of alterations in the circumstances, for which the defendant should not be responsible.

Subject only to these qualifications, I think that a strict test of proximity by sight or hearing should be applied by the courts.

Lastly, as regards communication, there is no case in which the law has compensated shock brought about by communication by a third party. In *Hambrook* v *Stokes Brothers* [1925] 1 KB 141, indeed, it was said that liability would not arise in such a case and this is surely right. It was so decided in *Abramzik* v *Brenner* (1967) 65 DLR (2d) 651. The shock must come through sight or hearing of the event or of its immediate aftermath. Whether some equivalent of sight or hearing, e.g., through simultaneous television, would suffice may have to be considered.

My Lords, I believe that these indications, imperfectly sketched, and certainly to be applied with common sense to individual situations in their entirety, represent either the existing law, or the existing law with only such circumstantial extension as the common law process may legitimately make. They do not introduce a new principle. Nor do I see any reason why the law should retreat behind the lines already drawn. I find on this appeal that the appellant's case falls within the boundaries of the law so drawn. . . .

LORD EDMUND-DAVIES: My Lords, in the present case two totally different points arising from the speeches of two or your Lordships call for further attention. Both relate to the Court of Appeal's invoking public policy. Unless I have completely misunderstood my noble and learned friend, Lord Bridge of Harwich, he doubts that any regard should have been had to such a consideration and seemingly considers that the Court of Appeal went wrong in paying any attention to it. The sole test of liability, I read him as saying, is the reasonable foreseeability of injury to the plaintiff through nervous shock resulting from the defendants' conceded default. And, such foreseeability having been established to their unanimous satisfaction, it followed that in law no other course was open to the Court of Appeal than to allow this appeal. I have respectfully to say that I cannot accept this approach. It is true that no decision was cited to your Lordships in which the contrary has been held, but that is not to say that reasonable foreseeability is the *only* test of the validity of a claim brought in negligence. If it is surmounted, the defendant would probably be hard put to escape liability.

Lord Wright found it difficult to conceive that any new head of public policy could be discovered (*Fender* v *St John-Mildmay* [1938] AC 1, 41), and, were Lord Halsbury LC sound in denying that any court could invent a new head of policy (*Jansen* v *Driefontein Consolidated Mines Ltd* [1902] AC 484, 491), I should have been in the happy position of accepting the standpoint adopted by my noble and learned friend, Lord Bridge of Harwich. But, as I shall later indicate, the more recent view which has found favour in your Lordships' House is that public policy is not immutable. Accordingly, whilst I would have strongly preferred indicating with clarity where the limit of liability should be drawn in such cases as the present, in my judgment the possibility of a wholly new type of policy being raised renders the attainment of such finality unfortunately unattainable.

As I think, all we can say is that any invocation of public policy calls for the closest scrutiny, and the defendant might well fail to discharge the burden of making it good, as, indeed, happened in *Rondel* v *Worsley* [1969] 1 AC 191. But that is not to say that success for the defendant would be unthinkable, for, in the words of MacDonald J in *Nova Mink Ltd* v *Trans-Canada Airlines* [1951] 2 DLR 241, 256: 'there is always a large element of judicial policy and social expediency involved in the determination of the duty-problem, however it may be obscured by the use of traditional formulae.'

I accordingly hold, as Griffiths LJ [1981] QB 599, 618, did, that 'The test of foreseeability is not a universal touchstone to determine the extent of liability for the consequences of wrongdoing.' Authority for that proposition is both ample in quantity and exalted in status. . . .

I finally turn to consider the following passage in the speech of my noble and learned friend, Lord Scarman:

> Policy considerations will have to be weighed: but the objective of the judges is the formulation of principle. And, if principle inexorably requires a decision which entails a degree of policy risk, the court's function is to adjudicate according to principle, leaving policy curtailment to the judgment of Parliament. . . . If principle leads to results which are thought to be socially unacceptable, Parliament can legislate to draw a line or map out a new path.

And at a later stage my noble and learned friend adds: 'Why then should not the courts draw the line, as the Court of Appeal manfully tried to do in this case? Simply, because the policy issue as to where to draw the line is not justiciable.'

My understanding of these words is that my noble and learned friend shares (though for a different reason) the conclusion of my noble and learned friend, Lord Bridge of Harwich, that, in adverting to public policy, the Court of Appeal here embarked upon a sleeveless errand, for public policy has no relevance to liability at law. In my judgment, the proposition that 'the policy issue . . . is not justiciable' is as novel as it is startling. So novel is it in relation to this appeal that it was never mentioned during the hearing before your Lordships. And it is startling because in my respectful judgment it runs counter to well-established and wholly acceptable law.

I restrict myself to recent decisions of your Lordships' House. In *Rondel* v *Worsley* [1969] 1 AC 191, their Lordships unanimously held that public policy required that a barrister should be immune from an action for negligence in respect of his conduct and management of a case in court and the work preliminary thereto, Lord Reid saying, at p. 228:

Is it in the public interest that barristers and advocates should be protected against such actions? Like so many questions which raise the public interest, a decision one way will cause hardships to individuals while a decision the other way will involve disadvantage to the public interest. . . . So the issue appears to me to be whether the abolition of the rule would probably be attended by such disadvantage to the public interest as to make its retention clearly justifiable.

My Lords, in accordance with such a line of authorities, I hold that public policy issues *are* 'justiciable.' Their invocation calls for close scrutiny, and the conclusion may be that its nature and existence have not been established with the clarity and cogency required before recognition can be granted to any legal doctrine, and before any litigant can properly be deprived of what would otherwise be his manifest legal rights. Or the conclusion may be that adoption of the public policy relied upon would involve the introduction of new legal principles so fundamental that they are best left to the legislature: see, for example, *Launchbury v Morgans* [1973] AC 127, and especially *per* Lord Pearson, at p. 142G. And 'public policy is not immutable' *per* Lord Reid in *Rondel v Worsley* [1969] 1 AC 191, 227. Indeed, Winfield, 'Public Policy in the English Common Law' (1928) 42 Harvard LR 76, described it as '*necessarily* variable,' (p. 93) and wisely added, at pp. 95, 96, 97:

> This variability . . . is a stone in the edifice of the doctrine, and not a missile to be flung at it. Public policy would be almost useless without it. The march of civilisation and the difficulty of ascertaining public policy at any given time make it essential . . . How is public policy evidenced? If it is so variable, if it depends on the welfare of the community at any given time, how are the courts to ascertain it? Some judges have thought this difficulty so great, that they have urged that it would be solved much better by the legislature and have considered it to be the main reason why the courts should leave public policy alone. . . . This admonition is a wise one and judges are not likely to forget it. But the better view seems to be that the difficulty of dicovering what public policy is at any given moment certainly does not absolve the bench from the duty of doing so. The judges are bound to take notice of it and of the changes which it undergoes, and it is immaterial that the question may be one of ethics rather than of law.

In the present case the Court of Appeal did just that, and in my judgment they were right in doing so. But they concluded that public policy required them to dismiss what they clearly regarded as an otherwise irrefragable claim. In so concluding, I respectfully hold that they were wrong, and I would accordingly allow the appeal.

Lords Bridge, Russell, Scarman and Wilberforce also allowed the appeal.

6.2.3.1   The speeches

AUSTRALIAN LAW REFORM

(MISCELLANEOUS PROVISIONS) ORDINANCE 1955 ACT

24.   (1)   The liability of a person in respect of injury caused . . . by act, neglect or default by which another person is killed, injured or put in peril extends to include liability for injury arising wholly or in part from mental or nervous shock sustained by—
   (a)   a parent or the husband or wife of the person so killed, injured or put in peril; or
   (b)   another member of the family of the person so killed, injured or put in peril, where the person was killed, injured or put in peril within the sight or hearing of that other member of the family.

6.2.4   *ALCOCK v CHIEF CONSTABLE OF THE SOUTH YORKSHIRE POLICE* (1991)

6.2.4.1   *Alcock* and beyond

Napier, M. and Wheat, K., *Recovering Damages for Psychiatric Injury,*
Blackstone Press, 1995, pp. 29–30

At present, then, we can say that the limits of event proximity are as stated in *McLoughlin v O'Brian*, with only the most unusual broadcast event meeting the criteria concerned, and the limits of relationship proximity are fluid, subject to evidence. It is interesting to consider the question of evidence and its relation to the decision in *Alcock* v *Chief Constable of the South Yorkshire Police*. It was accepted by the defence that if the plaintiffs established those required degrees of proximity then they would succeed. The courts were asked, therefore, to consider the proximity questions without hearing from the plaintiffs themselves. The sole witness was a psychiatrist highly experienced in treating Falklands War veterans, but no personal testimony was given to the court of any notion of how those spectators felt when they saw the television pictures. It may well be that it would have made no difference, but personal testimony must be of considerable importance when judges are considering whether an experience is sufficiently shocking. Further, no evidence was given about the degree of closeness of the relationships concerned. The decision indicates that there could have been evidence which would have compelled their lordships to acknowledge that a relationship between two brothers may be as close as that which may exist between a parent and child. There is no doubt therefore that much scope has been left to the imaginative and diligent litigator to establish claims of wider proximity.

It is also encouraging to consider the statement of Brennan J in the High Court of Australia in *Sutherland Shire Council* v *Heyman* (1985) 157 CLR 424 at p. 481:

> It is preferable, in my view, that the law should develop novel categories of negligence incrementally and by analogy with established categories, rather than by a massive extension of a prima facie duty of care restrained only by indefinable 'considerations which ought to negative, or to reduce or limit the scope of the duty or the class of person to whom it is owed'.

This was quoted with approval by Lord Bridge in *Caparo Industries plc* v *Dickman* [1990] 2 AC 605 at p. 618 and gives encouragement to the view that the categories of those who can claim for psychiatric injury will extend, albeit slowly or 'incrementally'.

It is tempting to overestimate the impact of the litigation ensuing upon the tragedy that took place at the Hillsborough stadium. That case was primarily about what we will call 'event proximity' under very exceptional circumstances. The very great majority of claims will not ever touch upon that issue and therefore it is vital not to exaggerate the effect of that case. Even when proximity is a worrying and doubtful issue there is no doubting the importance of the individual case and its presentation. The practitioner will have the obstacle course of foreseeability and proximity to negotiate, but, given that policy, however described, is to prevent the opening of those well-known floodgates, then the more individually compelling a case can be, the more likely will be the plaintiff to succeed.

HEVICAN v RUANE [1991] 3 All ER 65

... [A]s a result of the defendant's **admitted** negligent driving of a school minibus, the plaintiff's 'favourite' son was killed; and 'shortly' afterwards the plaintiff was told that the minibus had been involved in an accident. He was taken to a police station where he was told of his son's death and then went to the mortuary where he saw the body.

Afterwards he continued in his employment but after approximately two months he found himself unable to cope and was made redundant.

Medical diagnosis confirmed 'continuing reactive depression'; this prevented him from returning to work. His action for damages for his depression was brought against the estate of the minibus driver.

Mantell J found in the plaintiff's favour—although he was not present at the immediate aftermath of the accident; neither was it foreseeable 'that the nervous shock suffered by the plaintiff would result in continuing psychological illness such as continuing reactive depression'.

It was found that the 'particular injury' need not be contemplated by a defendant ('nervous shock' being foreseeable).

On the issue of **causation**, his Lordship found support for his ruling in the speech of Lord Bridge in *McLoughlin* v *O'Brian* [1982] 2 All ER 298.

RAVENSCROFT v REDERIAKTIEBOLAGET TRANSATLANTIC [1991] 3 All ER 73

... the plaintiff's son was killed in a crushing accident at work. She was called to the hospital by her husband where he told her of their son's death. Imagining the extent of the injuries, her husband would not let her see the body. The family was described as 'very close indeed' and the plaintiff suffered a prolonged grief reaction—a prolonged depressive reaction—which was continuing at the trial. Ward J found for the plaintiff, the defendants having admitted that the son's death was their fault but contending that damages for the plaintiff's nervous shock were not recoverable. Damages were agreed between the parties at £16,500.

The Court of Appeal in *Ravenscroft* v *Rederiaktiebolaget Transatlantic* [1992] 2 All ER 470 **overruled** the decision at first instance in favour of the plaintiff; the decision was inconsistent with the opinions expressed by Lords Ackner, Keith and Oliver in *Alcock* v *Chief Constable of the South Yorkshire Police* (1991).

This decision of the Court of Appeal must cast doubt on the correctness of the ruling in *Hevican* v *Ruane*.

6.2.5 THE PLAINTIFF'S REACTION

PAGE v *SMITH* [1994] 4 All ER 522 (CA)

RALPH GIBSON LJ: In considering whether the plaintiff has established whether the condition of ME, from which he suffered, was made significantly worse for some period of time, or permanently, by the accident of July 1987, it is necessary to have in mind that no doctor claimed to be able to explain how or by what process the experience of the accident could have had that effect. The plaintiff's condition was described as a syndrome, a word which, as I understand it, means a collection of symptoms which tend to occur together and form a characteristic pattern but which may not necessarily be always due to the same cause and which, as Otton J observed, 'makes no unproved aetiological claims'. The authority of a doctor to pronounce upon what may or may not, or will or will not, cause or make worse the symptoms, or render them permanent, comes, as I understand it, from having observed what has happened in the cases of other patients with reference to the appearance of the symptoms and what experience of the patient preceded the appearance, and similarly, with reference to worsening and long continuation of symptoms. It is obviously easier, in such a state of medical knowledge, for a doctor to state what may be or have been the consequence of certain experiences of the patient with reference to the appearance, worsening or continuation of symptoms, than to state with confidence that any particular consequence was in probability the result of any particular experience. And if he is to assess that a particular consequence was in probability caused by a particular experience, as contrasted with that particular consequence possibly having been caused by that experience, it is to be expected that he can point to some body of comparable example observed or reported in clinical experience . . .

The point at which, for my part, the reasoning and conclusion of the judge on the issue of causation appear to be unsatisfactory is in his application of his finding about the degree of severity of the collision to the reasoning and opinions of the doctors . . . It seems to me that the submissions for the defendant must be accepted, namely that there was no clear evidence from any witness to the effect that other cases had been observed or reported in which an accident causing no physical injury, and no more 'nervous shock' than some immediate fright, had caused either the onset or serious or permanent worsening of symptoms of ME. I am unable to accept that the evidence before the court is sufficient to justify a holding that the accident in probability caused or materially contributed to the plaintiff's condition . . .

In order to test whether injury by shock to the plaintiff was so foreseeable, it is necessary, in my judgment, to consider what at trial is shown to have happened to the plaintiff as a result of the defendant's act or omission. It is not enough to ask what was foreseeable by the defendant at the time of his negligent act. If it were sufficient to show, at that time, that he could reasonably foresee physical injury or injury by shock to any person in the vicinity there would have been no problem to be solved in *Bourhill* v *Young* because, as Denning LJ said, the defendant there could reasonably foresee that any person in the vicinity might be injured physically and the physical injury might cause injury by shock. [His Lordship then referred to *Attia* v *British Gas plc* [1987] 3 All ER 455 and continued:] That which happened to the plaintiff as a result of the defendant's careless driving was established at the trial by the findings of primary fact of Otton J. There was no physical injury. There was a 'frightening experience'. There was no evidence that it included fear of his own death or fear for the death of the female passenger of the other driver as the plaintiff's doctors had assumed. Such an experience gives rise by itself to no claim to damages . . .

The fact that this plaintiff was directly involved does not, in my judgment, render irrelevant the question whether injury by nervous shock was reasonably foreseeable as a result of what happened to him in the accident. That fact, of course, makes it much easier for the plaintiff to prove that injury of such a nature was foreseeable. Since the judge did not address the question, it is for this court to decide it upon the basis of the facts found by the judge.

For my part, I have no doubt that such injury was not foreseeable in a person of ordinary fortitude as a result of what happened to the plaintiff in the accident. He suffered no physical injury at all. He suffered such fright and shock as any person may be expected to suffer as a result of a collision of moderate severity with some damage to his car but no injury to him. I have in mind that for this purpose the court should have regard to what may be a reasonably possible result of the collision, even if unlikely. In my judgment it was not foreseeable that the plaintiff should suffer any 'psychiatric damage', or 'psychological injury'. On this ground also I would allow the defendant's appeal and enter judgment for the defendant.

Farquharson and Hoffmann LJJ agreed.

PAGE v *SMITH* [1995] 2 All ER 736 (HL)

LORD BROWNE-WILKINSON: . . . The law has long recognised tangible physical damage to the body of the plaintiff as a head of damage. Medical science has now advanced so far that the process whereby an impact causing direct physical injury to one limb or organ of the body can be demonstrated to have caused consequential physical damage to another limb or organ. Lawyers can readily accept that such consequential, physical damage is the consequence of the original impact. Hence there is a willingness to accept that all such tangible physical damage is foreseeable.

Medical science has also demonstrated that there are other injuries the body can suffer as a consequence of an accident, such injuries not being demonstrably attributable directly to physical injury to the plaintiff. Injuries of this type may take two forms. First, physical illness or injury not brought about by a chain of demonstrable physical events but by mental or emotional stresses, i.e., by a psychiatric route. Examples are a heart attack or a miscarriage produced by shock. In this case, the end product is a physical condition although it has been brought about by a process which is not demonstrably a physical one but lies in the mental or nervous system. The second form is psychiatric illness itself which is brought about by mental or emotional stresses, i.e., by a psychiatric route. Because medical science has so far been less successful in demonstrating the nature of psychiatric illness and the processes whereby it is brought about by the psychiatric route, the courts have been more reluctant to accept the risk of such illness as being foreseeable. But since the decision of this House in *McLoughlin* v *O'Brian* [1982] 2 All ER 298 it has been established that, in certain circumstances, a defendant can be liable for illness or injury, whether psychiatric or physical, produced in a plaintiff by purely psychiatric processes, without any direct physical impact on, or injury to, the limbs or organs of the plaintiff. That case also establishes that such a process is, in certain circumstances, to be treated as foreseeable by a defendant.

It follows that in the present case the fact that the plaintiff suffered no tangible physical injury is irrelevant to the question whether or not he is entitled to recover damages for the recrudescence of his illness. On the judge's findings, the plaintiff suffered injury (the recrudescence of his illness) by the psychiatric route, i.e., by reason of shock exacerbating his condition. The question, therefore, is whether a driver of a car should reasonably foresee that a person involved in an accident may suffer psychiatric injury of some kind (whether or not accompanied by physical injury). I have no doubt that he should. It is not physical injury alone which causes illness or injury: physical or psychiatric illness occurs quite apart from physical injury . . . I am therefore of opinion that any driver of a car should reasonably foresee that, if he drives carelessly, he will be liable to cause injury, either physical or psychiatric or both, to other users of the highway who become involved in an accident. Therefore he owes to such persons a duty of care to avoid such injury. In the present case the defendant could not foresee the exact type of psychiatric damage in fact suffered by the plaintiff who, due to his ME, was 'an eggshell personality'. But that is of no significance since the defendant did owe a duty of care to prevent foreseeable damage, including psychiatric damage. Once such duty of care is established, the defendant must take the plaintiff as he finds him . . . I would therefore allow the appeal and remit the issue of causation (if not agreed) to the Court of Appeal for its determination.

LORD LLOYD: This is the fourth occasion on which the House has been called on to consider 'nervous shock'. On the three previous occasions, *Bourhill* v *Young* [1942] 2 All ER 396, *McLoughlin* v *O'Brian* [1982] 2 All ER 298 and *Alcock* v *Chief Constable of the South Yorkshire Police* [1991] 4 All ER 907, the plaintiffs were, in each case, outside the range of foreseeable physical injury . . . In all these cases the plaintiff was the secondary victim of the defendant's negligence. He or she was in the position of a spectator or bystander. In the present case, by contrast, the plaintiff was a participant. He was himself directly involved in the accident, and well within the range of foreseeable physical injury. He was the primary victim. This is thus the first occasion on which your Lordships have had to decide whether, in such a case, the foreseeability of physical injury is enough to enable the plaintiff to recover damages for nervous shock . . .

If, as in *Malcolm* v *Broadhurst*, the plaintiff had suffered a head injury or a broken leg, or significant bruising, with consequential psychiatric illness, it is very doubtful whether the case would ever have reached the Court of Appeal at all . . . Of course, it would have been necessary to prove that the psychiatric illness was genuine, and that it was caused by the accident. But nobody would have stopped to consider the foreseeability of nervous shock. Nobody would have referred to *Bourhill* v *Young*. We now know that the plaintiff escaped without external injury. Can it be the law that this makes all the difference? Can it be the law that the fortuitous absence of foreseeable physical injury means that a different test has to be applied? Is it to become necessary, in ordinary personal injury claims, where the plaintiff is the primary victim, for the court to concern itself with the different 'kinds' of injury?

Suppose, in the present case, the plaintiff had been accompanied by his wife, just recovering from a depressive illness, and that she had suffered a cracked rib, followed by an onset of psychiatric illness. Clearly, she would have recovered damages, including damages for her illness, since it is conceded that the defendant owed the occupants of the car a duty not to cause physical harm. Why should it be necessary to ask a different question, or apply a different test, in the case of the plaintiff? Why should it make any difference that the physical illness that the plaintiff undoubtedly suffered as a result of the accident operated through the medium of the mind, or of the nervous system, without physical injury? If he had suffered a heart attack, it cannot be doubted that he would have recovered damages for pain and suffering, even though he suffered no broken bones. It would have been no answer that he had a weak heart.

I must say at once that I prefer the simplicity of the judge's approach to what, with respect, seems to be an unnecessary complication introduced by the Court of Appeal. Foreseeability of psychiatric injury remains a crucial ingredient when the plaintiff is the secondary victim, for the very reason that the secondary victim is almost always outside the area of physical impact, and therefore outside the range of foreseeable physical injury. But where the plaintiff is the primary victim of the defendant's negligence, the nervous shock cases, by which I mean the cases following on from *Bourhill* v *Young*, are not in point. Since the defendant was admittedly under a duty of care not to cause the plaintiff foreseeable physical injury, it was unnecessary to ask whether he was under a separate duty of care not to cause foreseeable psychiatric injury . . .

My provisional conclusion, therefore, is that Otton J's approach was correct. The test in every case ought to be whether the defendant can reasonably foresee that his conduct will expose the plaintiff to risk of personal injury. If so, then he comes under a duty of care to that plaintiff. If a working definition of 'personal injury' is needed, it can be found in s. 38(1) of the Limitation Act 1980: ''Personal injuries'' includes any disease and any impairment of a person's physical or mental condition . . .' There are numerous other statutory definitions to the same effect. In the case of a secondary victim, the question will usually turn on whether the foreseeable injury is psychiatric, for the reasons already explained. In the case of a primary victim the question will almost always turn on whether the foreseeable injury is physical. But it is the same test in both cases, with different applications. There is no justification for regarding physical and psychiatric injury as different 'kinds' of injury. Once it is established that the defendant is under a duty of care to avoid causing personal injury to the plaintiff, it matters not whether the injury in fact sustained is physical, psychiatric or both . . . Applying that test in the present case, it was enough to ask whether the defendant should have reasonably foreseen that the plaintiff might suffer physical injury as a result of the defendant's negligence, so as to bring him within the range of the defendant's duty of care. It was unnecessary to ask, as a separate question, whether the defendant should reasonably have foreseen injury by shock; and it is irrelevant that the plaintiff did not, in fact, suffer any external physical injury . . .

In conclusion, the following propositions can be supported. (1) In cases involving nervous shock, it is essential to distinguish between the primary victim and secondary victims. (2) In claims by secondary victims the law insists on certain control mechanisms, in order as a matter of policy to limit the number of potential claimants. Thus, the defendant will not be liable unless psychiatric injury is foreseeable in a person of normal fortitude. These control mechanisms have no place where the plaintiff is the primary victim. (3) In claims by secondary victims, it may be legitimate to use hindsight in order to be able to apply the test of reasonable foreseeability at all. Hindsight, however, has no part to play where the plaintiff is the primary victim. (4) Subject to the above qualifications, the approach in all cases should be the same, namely, whether the defendant can reasonably foresee that his conduct will expose the plaintiff to the risk of personal injury, whether physical or psychiatric. If the answer is yes, then the duty of care is established, even though physical injury does not, in fact, occur. There is no justification for regarding physical and psychiatric injury as different 'kinds of damage'. (5) A defendant who is under a duty of care to the plaintiff, whether as primary or secondary victim, is not liable for damages for nervous shock unless the shock results in some recognised psychiatric illness. It is no answer that the plaintiff was predisposed to psychiatric illness. Nor is it relevant that the illness takes a rare form or is of unusual severity. The defendant must take his victim as he finds him . . .

In the result, I would restore the judgment of Otton J [and] allow the appeal.

LORD KEITH, dissenting, said that in *The Wagon Mound (No 2)* ([1967] 1 AC 617, 636) Lord Reid had stated as a general proposition applicable to cases based on negligence: 'It has now been established . . . that in such cases damages can only be recovered if the injury complained of was not only caused by the alleged negligence but was also an injury of a class or character foreseeable as a possible result of it.'

That general proposition was valid in principle both as regarded persons directly involved in an accident who claimed on the ground of nervous shock and as regarded those who claimed as secondary victims. Reasonable foreseeability being the test, there was no logical ground for distinguishing between the two classes of claimants.

A considerable amount of argument had ranged over the question whether in applying the test of reasonable foreseeability in cases of nervous shock matters fell to be considered prospectively or ex post facto.

In *Bourhill* v *Young* Lord Wright had said: 'It is here, as elsewhere, a question of what the hypothetical reasonable man, viewing from the position, I suppose ex post facto, would say it was proper to foresee.' In *McLoughlin* v *O'Brian* Lord Wilberforce and Lord Bridge of Harwich spoke to similar effect.

His Lordship thought that what those judges had in mind was that it was necessary to look at the circumstances as they actually occurred and consider whether the hypothetical reasonable man, when directing his mind to the act or omission which was called in question, would have foreseen those circumstances, including that some person in the position of the plaintiff might as a result of what happened suffer nervous shock leading to an identifiable illness.

Foreseeability of nervous shock was to be judged in the light of what would be suffered by a person of normal fortitude.

Accordingly, the defendant could be liable only if the hypothetical reasonable man in his position should have foreseen that the plaintiff, regarded as a person of normal fortitude, might suffer nervous shock leading to an identifiable illness. For that purpose the nature of the accident was to be taken into account.

The collision between the two cars was described as one of moderate severity. No one involved sustained any bodily injury whatever.

In his Lordship's opinion a reasonable man in the position of the defendant would not have foreseen that an accident of the nature that he actually brought about might inflict on a person of normal susceptibility such mental trauma as to result in illness.

Lord Ackner agreed with Lords Browne-Wilkinson and Lloyd in allowing the appeal, whilst Lord Jauncey agreed with Lord Keith's dissenting speech.

6.2.6 'PROFESSIONAL' RESCUERS

FROST AND OTHERS v CHIEF CONSTABLE OF THE SOUTH YORKSHIRE POLICE AND OTHERS [1997] 1 All ER 540 (CA)

ROSE LJ: Two grounds for founding liability were argued on appeal: first, breach of a duty of care by the chief constable, arising from the plaintiffs' service as police officers when acting under his direction and control; secondly, breach of a duty owed to them as rescuers . . . I reach the following conclusions as to the principles to be applied.

(i) Since *Bourhill v Young* [1942] 2 All ER 396 it has been recognised that the ambit of persons affected by negligence may extend beyond those actually subject to physical impact, particularly to rescuers . . . (ii) Rescuers are in a special category (see *McLoughlin v O'Brian* [1982] 2 All ER 298 per Lord Wilberforce and *Alcock v Chief Constable of South Yorkshire Police* [1991] 4 All ER 907 per Lord Oliver and Lord Jauncey). (iii) The correctness of *Chadwick v British Transport Commission* [1967] 2 All ER 945 has never been doubted . . . (iv) The ratio of *Chadwick* was that the catastrophe was such as would not normally be seen and it was the horror of the whole experience which caused the plaintiff's injury by shock. (v) *McLoughlin, Page v Smith* [1995] 2 All ER 736 and *McFarlane v EE Caledonia Ltd* [1994] 2 All ER 1 were not rescue cases and *Alcock* was not argued on that basis in the House of Lords. The relevance of the rescue cases in *McLoughlin* was that they were relied on, by way of analogy, to extend the category of persons to whom a duty of care is owed in relation to psychiatric injury. (vi) Lord Lloyd's categorisation of primary and secondary victims in *Page v Smith* did not expressly or by implication have the rescue cases in mind: indeed none of them was cited either in the speeches or in argument. In any event, the present plaintiffs . . . being directly involved, in the course of their employment, in the consequences flowing from their employer's negligence, were primary victims. (vii) In *Alcock* Lord Oliver placed the rescue cases in the first group of nervous shock cases where the plaintiff was involved as a participant, rather than in the second group where the plaintiff was no more than a passive and unwilling witness of injury caused to others. (viii) In the light of (vi) and (vii) Lord Lloyd's requirement in *Page v Smith* for foreseeability of psychiatric injury as a crucial ingredient where the plaintiff is a secondary victim and his statement that foreseeability of injury by shock is not enough in the case of a secondary victim are not presently in point. But his observation that 'There is no justification for regarding physical and psychiatric injury as different "kinds" of injury' is a generally applicable statement of the current law (see, too, per Lord Oliver in *Alcock*). The same comments apply in relation to the speech of Lord Browne-Wilkinson in *Page v Smith*. (ix) If firemen should not be at any disadvantage in relation to compensation for injury (see *Ogwo v Taylor* [1987] 3 All ER 961 per Lord Bridge) there is to my mind no reason why policemen should be at a disadvantage. (x) Whether a particular plaintiff is a rescuer is, in each case, a question of fact to be decided in the light of all the circumstances of the case. Among the factors to be considered, although none is in itself decisive, are the following: the character and extent of the initial incident caused by the tortfeasor; whether that incident has finished or is continuing; whether there is any danger, continuing or otherwise, to the victim or to the plaintiff, the character of the plaintiffs conduct, in itself and in relation to the victim; and how proximate, in time and place, the plaintiff's conduct is to the incident. (xi) . . . Once it is accepted that there is no justification for regarding physical and psychiatric injuries as different kinds of injury, when an employer negligently causes physical injury to one employee, it seems to me to be impossible to contend that he is not equally liable to a fellow employee of normal fortitude working on the same task who sustains psychiatric injury, whether through fear for himself or through witnessing what happens to his fellow workman.

Lord Hope in *Robertson* v *Forth Road Bridge* (1995) 2 March, unreported, a decision of the Court of Session, said 'it is difficult to see why the bystander in the case of a road accident should be denied his claim when a bystander who happens to be an employee but has nothing whatsoever to do with causing the incident is allowed to recover damages for this type of injury'. In my respectful view the answer is that, whereas in cases outwith the master and servant relationship the courts have found it necessary, in identifying those to whom a duty of care is owed, to draw a distinction between primary and secondary victims and to impose limiting criteria to determine those within the second category who can recover, in the master and servant context a duty of care exists by reason of that relationship. The standard of care required in the discharge of that duty and the degree of proximity will of course vary from case to case according among other matters, to the nature of the job and the degree of fortitude to be expected of the employee. So, for example, a rescuer, whether a policeman or layman, may recover against a tortfeasor for physical or psychiatric injury sustained during a rescue. An employee may, depending on the circumstances, recover against his employer for physical or psychiatric injury caused in the course of his employment by the employer's negligence. A mere bystander, whether a policeman or layman, who is not a rescuer and to whom no duty such as that arising from the master and servant relationship is owed by the tortfeasor will not generally recover (*McFarlane*) and will only be able to do so if he is linked by ties of love and affection to a primary victim and otherwise fulfils the criteria for secondary victims enunciated in *McLoughlin, Alcock* and *Page* v *Smith*. (xii) In none of the cases before the House of Lords since *Ogwo* was the plaintiff either a servant of the defendant or a rescuer and although in *McFarlane* the plaintiff was a servant, he was off duty at the time and no claim was made on the basis that his employers owed him a duty of care. This is a crucial matter which explains why some of the present plaintiffs may succeed, whereas the plaintiffs in *Alcock* failed. The distinction is not due to any preference being given by the courts to policemen over laymen. It exists because the court has long recognised a duty of care to guard employees and rescuers against all kinds of injury, whereas, in deciding whether any duty of care exists towards plaintiffs who are not employees, rescuers, or primary victims, the courts have, in recent years, imposed specific criteria in relation to claims for psychiatric injury.

In the light of these principles I turn now to the individual plaintiffs each of whom, it seems to me, can, at least *prima facie*, claim to have sustained shock-induced trauma . . . Sgt Smith was not on duty at the ground . . . It is conceded . . . that she was not a rescuer. She was not at the ground when the negligent loss of control occurred and she was not therefore within the category of those officers to whom, being within the area of risk when the incident occurred, a duty of care was owed by virtue of the master and servant relationship. What she subsequently did was no more than could properly be asked of any police officer in the ordinary carrying out of her duties following a serious incident. In my judgment she is not entitled to recover. Those in the position of DC Hallam were in the gymnasium at the ground when the disaster occurred . . . In my judgment such officers were not rescuers because they were not sufficiently closely involved in the crushing incident or its immediate aftermath. They were, however, at the ground in the course of duty, within the area of risk of physical or psychiatric injury and were thus exposed, by the first defendant's negligence, to excessively horrific events such as were likely to cause psychiatric illness even in a police officer. There was therefore a breach of duty to such persons . . . Insp White . . . was plainly a rescuer participating in the immediate aftermath of the incident and a duty was owed to him both in that capacity and as an employee within the area of risk, which would not be owed to a mere bystander. There was a breach of duty to him. Accordingly. for the reasons given, a duty of care was owed by the first defendant to these plaintiffs apart from Sgt Smith whose appeal I would dismiss. I would allow the appeals of [the other plaintiffs] and, if this is necessary, remit the question of causation in each of these cases for determination by a trial judge.

HENRY LJ: [At] first reading I would have been disposed to find that the police on duty were primary victims because they were participants in the 'accident' – by which I mean the incidents caused by their employer's negligence, and because they were direct victims as their employer owed them a duty of care to protect them from personal injury (psychiatric damage) caused by his negligence. But a close reading of *Page v Smith* [1995] 2 All ER 736 suggests a narrower definition of primary victim . . . I am not sure that the labelling of each plaintiff as a primary or secondary victim really matters, for two reasons. First, *McLoughlin v O'Brian* [1982] 2 All ER 298 makes clear that the relevance of that distinction lies only in whether the proximity or neighbourhood test is (for practical purposes) presumed to be satisfied or must be critically examined. Second, the employer/ employee cases show that even in such cases proximity may be a necessary test and so should be so examined . . . Whatever the language used in simple accident cases, it seems to be me that in circumstances such as this all active participants in the events causing the psychiatric damage should be regarded as primary victims when the defendant is in breach of a pre-existing duty of care to them . . .

It follows that I regard the plaintiffs as having satisfied the proximity test, and that I see no public policy reasons why they should not succeed in their claims. So I differ from the trial judge in that: (1) In my judgment the plaintiffs have (as employees) a good cause of action against the first defendant, and so are, in the American parlance, direct victims. (2) That assists them in establishing that they were primary victims (or if not, participants in the events in Lord Oliver's sense). (3) That it is wrong in fact and in law to regard them as 'bystanders'. It also follows from what I have said and from those conclusions that even if the police officers were secondary victims, the successful plaintiffs can satisfy each of the controls restricting recovery by secondary victims found in Lord Lloyd's propositions. . . .

In conclusion, in addition to my views expressed above, I agree with Rose LJ's twelve propositions, with the following additions or reservations: (vi) Nor did Lord Lloyd have employer/employee cases in mind, nor yet the long drawn-out exposure of those on duty to stress caused by their employer's negligence which foreseeably might cause them psychiatric damage and would make them 'direct victims' in the American use of the phrase, or primary victims here. (xi) I am less critical than him of the decision in *Robertson*, in that it seems to me to be a finding of fact – that they were bystanders – within the scope of the court's discretion on the facts as reported. That is to say, I understand how this could be treated as a *McFarlane* case, but I agree with what is said as to the law. I agree with Rose LJ's conclusions on the individual cases . . .

My emphasis has been on the police officers as direct victims because of the employer/employee relationship. While that duty of care to them is a factor in a case such as this where their employer was negligent, I would expect a duty to be owed to them by any defendant who caused such a disaster as this. Deterrence is part of the public policy behind tort law. Prevention is better than cure, and potential defendants should face up to their safety responsibilities before rather than after an accident. I see no case for any relaxation of the rejection of the fireman's rule in *Ogwo v Taylor*, as the judge seemed to favour. I believe that where a plaintiff is a direct victim because of the duty that either his employer or the tortfeasor owes to him, that that should be the first head of recovery to be considered, because it might be wider and will not (so far as I can foresee) be narrower than any entitlement as a rescuer.

Dealing with the entitlement of a rescuer, it seems to me that public policy favours a wide rather than a narrow definition; to ensure that those brave and unselfish enough to go to the help of their fellow men will be properly compensated if they suffer damage as a result. I agree with what Rose LJ has said as to rescuers.

The dissenting judgment of Judge LJ is omitted.

DUNCAN v BRITISH COAL CORPORATION [1997] 1 All ER 540 (CA)

The plaintiff was a 'pit deputy' (a coal-mine employee, responsible for safety and other matters in the mine) and he tried to resuscitate a miner, for whose safety, etc. he was responsible. This man had been crushed by some machinery and the plaintiff was trying to restart his breathing processes. Duncan's claim for damages for psychiatric injury suffered as a rescuer was rejected by the court because, although he was 'proximate' in terms of **time** to the deceased's injury, he was **not** 'proximate' in **geographical** terms when the accident occurred. The court found that when he arrived at the scene there was no danger either to him or to the deceased, and his first-aid measures came within the **ordinary** scope of his employment; there were no **unusually** distressing factors present in the circumstances.

6.2.7 BYSTANDERS

McFARLANE v *EE CALEDONIA LTD* [1994] 2 All ER 1 (CA)

[I]t was held, overturning the decision of Mrs Justice Smith at first instance, that a worker (the plaintiff) who witnessed the 'Piper Alpha' oil rig disaster from a rescue vessel was not entitled to claim damages for psychiatric injury. He had completed his shift as a painter aboard 'Piper Alpha' and had returned to his quarters on the 'Tharos', which took part in the rescue operations, when the disaster occurred.

Consider the following extracts from the judgment of Stuart Smith LJ, with whom the other judges in the Court of Appeal agreed:

. . . In *Alcock* v *Chief Constable of the South Yorkshire Police* [1991] 4 All ER 907 Lord Oliver identified two categories of those who suffered nervous shock through fear of injury. First, those involved mediately or immediately as a participant in the event who feared injury to themselves and secondly, those who are no more than passive and unwilling witnesses of injury caused to others. In the present case the judge held that the plaintiff was a participant.

There are I think basically three situations in which a plaintiff may be a participant when he sustains psychiatric injury through fear of physical injury to himself. First, where he is in the actual area of danger created by the event, but escapes physical injury by chance or good fortune. Such a person would be one who while actually on the Piper Alpha rig at the time of the fire, escaped physical injury, but might well be in fear of his life or safety.

Secondly, where the plaintiff is not actually in danger, but because of the sudden and unexpected nature of the event he reasonably thinks that he is. [The judge at first instance had found in the plaintiff's favour on **this** basis.] An example of this is *Dulieu* v *White & Sons* [1901] 2 KB 669 . . . A case on the other side of the line is *Bourhill* v *Young* [1942] 2 All ER 396 . . .

Thirdly, the situation may arise where the plaintiff who is not originally within the area of damage comes into it later. In the ordinary way, such a person, who is a volunteer cannot recover, if he has freely and voluntarily entered the area of danger. This is not something that the tortfeasor can reasonably foresee, and the plaintiff may also be met with a defence of *volenti non fit injuria*. However if he comes as a rescuer, he can recover. This is because a tortfeasor who has put A in peril by his negligence must reasonably foresee that B may come to rescue him, even if it involves risking his own safety.

A rescuer [the judge at first instance held that the plaintiff was **not** a rescuer] is entitled to put his own safety at risk, but not that of others, unless they too consent to be part of the rescue. I agree with Mr Hamilton QC that the duty [of the captain of the support vessel] was to ensure the safety of his vessel and those on it. If he acted negligently and in breach of this duty, he and the defendants who employed him would be liable. There is no suggestion of this in this case and no criticism has been made of the handling or operation of the support vessel.

His Lordship said that the foregoing analysis could be tested by 'assuming that the support had no connection with the defendant'.

. . . If the captain had negligently and in breach of his duty taken the vessel into a position of danger where those on board were injured or reasonably feared injury, this would be a *novus actus interveniens* and not something for which the defendants would be liable.

But what is the position if the captain of a rescue vessel takes what seems to be a justified risk, and in doing so his vessel comes into actual danger with the result that it is damaged and personal injury sustained by those on board? In such circumstances the owners of the rig would be liable to an injured plaintiff on the rescue vessel in respect of both physical injury and psychiatric injury resulting from a reasonable fear of personal injury. But in these circumstances the captain, although with hindsight it will be seen that he committed an error of judgment, is not negligent. A reasonable man in the position of the defendants should foresee that if his negligence caused such a catastrophic emergency, those in charge of rescue vessels may not be able to judge to a nicety exactly how near it is safe to bring their vessels. The plaintiff does not come into either of the first two categories, and Mr Hamilton submits that he does not come into the third.

The support vessel was never in actual danger . . . No one [on it] sustained any physical injury, and there is no evidence that anyone other than the plaintiff sustained psychiatric injury. In my judgment it cannot be said that the defendants ought reasonably to have foreseen that the plaintiff or other non-essential personnel on board her would suffer such injury . . . If indeed the plaintiff had felt himself to be in any danger, he could have taken refuge in or behind the helicopter hanger, which was where non-essential personnel were required to muster. The judge thought it was entirely understandable that the plaintiff and other non-essential personnel should wish to see what was happening on the Piper Alpha. I agree with this. What I do not agree with, is that someone who was in truth in fear of his life from spread of the fire and falling debris should not take shelter. Only someone who is rooted to the spot through fear would be unable to do so. The plaintiff never suggested that; he accepted that he had moved about quite freely and could have taken shelter had he wished. Mr Hamilton strongly criticised the judge's finding that the plaintiff was actually in fear for his safety or that such fear was reasonable, even on a subjective basis . . . Mr Hamilton [for the appellant company] also submitted that the plaintiff's failure to seek the protection available to him strongly suggests that he was not genuinely in fear for his safety. As I have already said, I agree with this submission . . .

. . . It is submitted by Mr Wilkinson [for the respondent (plaintiff originally)] that the plaintiff was a rescuer and that even if his injury did not result from fear for his own safety he was entitled to recover because it was due to his experiences in rescuing the survivors. In *Chadwick v British Railways Board* [1967] 2 All ER 945 the plaintiff's deceased husband had gone to the assistance of those involved in the Lewisham train disaster. For twelve hours he gave valuable help at very close quarters to those injured in the carnage. He was entitled to recover damages in respect of the psychoneurotic condition that resulted from his experiences. But the judge held that the plaintiff was not a rescuer even though he was on board the support vessel which went to assist in rescue operations. I agree with the judge's conclusion. The plaintiff was never actively involved in the operation beyond helping to move blankets with a view to preparing the helihanger to receive casualties and encountering and perhaps assisting two walking injured as they arrived on the support vessel. This is no criticism of him, he had no role to play, and there is no reason to doubt that he would have given more help if he could. But since the defendant's liability to a rescuer depends upon his reasonable foreseeability, I do not think that a defendant could reasonably foresee that this very limited degree of involvement could possibly give rise to psychiatric injury . . .

Secondly, it is submitted that the plaintiff was obliged to witness the catastrophe at close range and that it was of such a horrendous nature that even as a bystander the defendants owed him a duty of care. [The judge at first instance expressed no views on this point.] Mr Wilkinson relies on dicta of three of their Lordships in *Alcock's* case . . . Lord Keith said: 'The case of a bystander unconnected with the victims of an accident is difficult. Psychiatric injury to him would not ordinarily, in my view, be within the range of reasonable foreseeability, but could not perhaps be entirely excluded from it if the circumstances of a catastrophe occurring very close to him were particularly horrific'.

Mr Wilkinson submits that it is hardly possible to imagine anything more horrific than the holocaust on the Piper Alpha, especially to the plaintiff who knew that some of his mates were on board. I share Lord Keith's difficulty. The whole basis of the decision in *Alcock's* case is that where the shock is caused by fear of injury to others as opposed to fear of injury to the participant, the test of proximity is not simply reasonable foreseeability. There must be a sufficiently close tie of love and affection between the plaintiff and the victim. To extend the duty to those who have no such connection, is to base the test purely on foreseeability.

It seems to me that there are great practical problems as well. Reactions to horrific events are entirely subjective; who is to say that it is more horrific to see a petrol tanker advancing out of control on a school, when perhaps unknown to the plaintiff none of the children are in the building but are somewhere safe, than to see a child or group of children run over on a pedestrian crossing? There must be few scenes more harrowing than seeing women and children trapped at the window of a blazing building, yet many people gather to witness these calamities.

In my judgment both as a matter of principle and policy the court should not extend the duty to those who are mere bystanders or witnesses of horrific events unless there is a sufficient degree of proximity, which requires both nearness in time and place and a close relationship of love and affection between plaintiff and victim . . .

HEGARTY v EE CALEDONIA LTD [1997] 2 Lloyd's Rep 259 (CA)

The plaintiff was employed as a painter on the Piper Alpha oil rig. He claimed damages for psychiatric injury suffered through witnessing a series of explosions on the rig which killed 167 persons and seriously injured others. At the time of the incident he was on board a support ship which went to help those on the rig. He was present during the rescue operations and claimed to be in danger himself from the fire and explosions, though he claimed **only** for psychiatric damage.

His claim was brought under two heads, viz. (i) for common law negligence; and (ii) for breach of statutory duty under regs. 3, 5 and 32 of the Offshore Installations (Operational Safety Health and Welfare) Regulations 1976 (SI 1976/1019), Mineral Workings (Offshore Installations) Act 1971.

On a **preliminary issue** (this is another **pleadings** case) it was held that the plaintiff was not a primary victim of the disaster, although he suffered a genuine fear of death. While the law will recognise the claim of someone like the pregnant barmaid in *Dulieu* v *White* who sees somebody nearly – but not quite – hitting her, because her fear was a reasonable one in the circumstances, it will **not** accommodate persons who are not directly threatened but genuinely and irrationally believe that they are so threatened. The court followed the reasoning in *McFarlane* v *EE Caledonia Ltd* and *Page* v *Smith*. Thus the claim under (i) was dismissed.

With regard to claim (ii), the Regulations provided that it was the duty of every person, while on or near an offshore installation, not to do anything likely to endanger the safety or health of himself or other persons on or near the installation. On this point, it was said that if the plaintiff came within the Regulations, **strict** liability would be imposed and the plaintiff would not be subject to the control mechanisms imposed on those who merely witnessed disasters. (The action for breach of statutory duty, **if a good one**, would, said Brooke LJ, '. . . with one bound free [the plaintiff] from the control mechanisms imposed on the claims of secondary victims by the House of Lords in *Alcock*.') Their Lordships rejected the plaintiff's claim, however, on the ground that he did not fall within the class of persons the legislation was intended to protect. Under reg. 32 persons who were near the oil rig would only qualify for protection if the breach was **likely** to endanger their health or safety, i.e. that a **likely, not merely foreseeable**, outcome of the breach was that a person in a rescue vessel 100 metres from the rig would suffer impaired mental health.

HUNTER v BRITISH COAL CORPORATION AND CEMENTATION MINING CO. [1998] 2 All ER 97 (CA)

The plaintiff, who was employed by Cementation, was driving a vehicle in the Coal Corporation's mine when he hit a hydrant causing it to leak. He, and a fellow employee of Cementation, X, could not turn off the hydrant; he went in search of a hose to divert the water and while he was away the hydrant exploded, killing X.

The plaintiff, who was 30 metres distant at the time of the accident, heard a message over the tannoy (loudspeaker) system to the effect that someone had been injured and, on his way back, he was told by a colleague that it seemed X had been killed. He went into shock on hearing this news and was prevented from returning to the scene. Thinking he was responsible for X's death, the plaintiff developed a depressive illness and sued the two defendants for psychiatric damage, in negligence and for breach of statutory duty.

At first instance, the judge found both defendants negligent and in breach of statutory duty because at the time of the accident clearances in the roadway were below the prescribed minimum. The plaintiff was found not to have been contributorily negligent.

However, since the plaintiff was neither a 'primary' nor a 'secondary' victim, as defined by Lord Oliver in *Alcock*, liability was not established.

Brooke LJ, with whom Sir John Vinelott concurred, agreed with this finding and the plaintiff's appeal was dismissed. The *Alcock* control mechanisms were applied.

This case is of importance in the context of *Learning Text*, **Chapter 8** (and *Cases and Materials*, **Chapter 8**).

An extract from the **dissenting** judgment of Hobhouse LJ is set out below.

HOBHOUSE LJ: . . . But it appears that there is another recognised category which applies to employees and which potentially covers the plaintiff. This category is recognised and discussed in the speech of Lord Oliver in *Alcock's* case, the judgment of Lord Hope in *Robertson* v *Forth Road Bridge Joint Board, Rough* v *Forth Road Bridge Joint Board* 1996 SLT 263 and the judgment of Henry LJ in *Frost* v *Chief Constable of South Yorkshire* [1997] 1 All ER 540, [1997] 3 WLR 1194. In *Alcock's* case [1991] 4 All ER 907 at 923–924, [1992] 1 AC 310 at 408 Lord Oliver formulated the category as:

> where the negligent act of the defendant has put the plaintiff in the position of being, or of thinking that he is about to be or has been, the involuntary cause of another's death or injury and the illness complained of stems from the shock to the plaintiff of the consciousness of this supposed fact.

This covers the facts of the present case as spoken to by the plaintiff and accepted by the judge. The connecting factor serves to provide a nexus between the plaintiff's injury and the defendants' breach of duty. In the context of the employer/employee relationship, it requires the employer to contemplate that his breaches of duty may involve his employee as an unwilling participant in an accident which may cause injury to others, typically fellow employees. It applies whether or not there is in fact any 'primary' victim. It extends what would otherwise be the scope of the duty of care of the employer towards his employee . . .

In my judgment, the effect of these statements of the law is to identify as the relevant factor the physical participation of the plaintiff in the event which resulted from the employer's breach of duty, which participation caused the plaintiff to believe that he was responsible for his fellow employee's death or injury. If so, the employer is liable for the nervous shock and psychiatric injury caused to the plaintiff as a result of his having participated in the event. It puts the plaintiff into the same class as a 'primary' victim; it puts him and his injury within the scope of the duty of care which the employer owes to him. The test then becomes one of causation; the *Alcock* criteria, or 'control mechanisms' (see *Page* v *Smith* [1995] 2 All ER 736 at 767–768, [1996] AC 155 at 197 per Lord Lloyd), cease to be determinative. Provided that the plaintiff can in the present case prove (as, on the judge's findings, he has proved) the causal relationship between the defendants' breach of duty and his participation in the incident and between that participation and his suffering nervous shock, and provided that he has proved the foreseeability of nervous shock to him as a possible consequence of the breach of duty, the plaintiff has discharged the burden of proof that rests upon him. He is entitled to recover damages for his injury from the defendants. It ceases to be relevant what the actual chain of causation was or whether it was to be foreseen (*Hughes* v *Lord Advocate* [1963] 1 All ER 705, [1963] AC 837 and *Mount Isa Mines Ltd* v *Pusey* (1970) 125 CLR 383): the class or type of injury was foreseeable as a consequence of the breach. The same conclusion is implicit in *Page's* case once it is recognised that the plaintiff's participation is what has brought his injury within the scope of the duty owed to him.

I recognise that there is no previously reported case the facts of which have necessitated the decision of the point raised by the present case. I also recognise that the law could have come to a different conclusion and have decided for policy reasons that the control mechanisms for 'secondary' victims were to be applied in this situation. But that would not in my judgment be a correct reading of the authoritative statement of the law by Lord Oliver in *Alcock's* case nor would it accord with the views of Lord Hope and Henry LJ. I observe that the view of the law I have derived from these authorities is also the view expressed by the Law Commission in its Consultation Paper, *Liability for Psychiatric Illness* (Law Com No. 137) para 5.37:

. . . Lord Oliver's formulation, on the face of it, would allow an involuntary participant to recover even though the shock was not experienced through his or her own unaided senses and even though he or she was not close to the accident in time and space. For example, it would cover the case of a signalman who, by reason of operating his employer's faulty equipment, reasonably believes that he has been instrumental in causing a train to crash (out of sight or hearing) and suffers a shock-induced psychiatric illness as a consequence. We believe that a signalman in that situation probably ought to be able to recover damages as there is no floodgates objection. We therefore do not regard Lord Oliver's formulation to be too wide-ranging . . .

6.2.8   POST-*ALCOCK* DECISIONS IN GENERAL

SION v *HAMPSTEAD HEALTH AUTHORITY* [1994] 5 Med LR 170 (CA)

The plaintiffs son was injured in a traffic accident and admitted to hospital, where he eventually died. In an action brought by the plaintiff for damages for abnormal grief reaction suffered as a result of his son's death, the defendant Health Authority succeeded in its application to have his claim struck out on the basis that he had not suffered sudden 'shock'. The plaintiff, who had alleged negligent treatment of his son, had stayed by the latter's bedside and watched him deteriorate slowly: in effect there had been a 'process' at work upon the plaintiff, from admission into hospital until perceived medical negligence after the inquest. Thus, his son's death was no surprise; rather it was expected.

6.2.9   STATEMENTS

A AND OTHERS v *TAMESIDE AND GLOSSOP HEALTH AUTHORITY AND ANOTHER*, *The Times*, 27 November 1996 (CA)

The Health Authority found that one of its employees (a health worker) was HIV positive and decided to inform a number of patients (114) that there was a very remote risk that they had been infected by the AIDS virus. It did so by sending them letters containing this warning.

It had to be decided whether the Authority was in breach of its duty of care to these patients because it employed this way of communicating the worrying information. At first instance, it had been found that the Authority **was** in breach of its duty, i.e. it had been negligent, because the best method of avoiding the risk of causing psychiatric injury to patients was for an appropriately qualified person (e.g. a GP) to communicate this sensitive information to the patients face to face.

The Court of Appeal allowed the Health Authority's appeal on the basis that the judge had applied the wrong standard of care. The Authority was not bound to employ the best available method of informing the patients and had acted with reasonable care in the circumstances, i.e. it had not breached its duty of care on the facts of the case.

It should be noted that the defendant Health Authority **conceded** that it owed a duty to take care in the circumstances, thus the case is not a strong authority on the existence of a duty in the context of liability for causing psychiatric injury by means of careless words.

In an earlier case, *Allin* v *City and Hackney HA* [1996] 7 Med LR 167, the plaintiff obtained damages for post traumatic stress disorder after being misinformed by the Health Authority that her baby was dead, only to learn six hours later that this was not the case. The Health Authority **accepted** that it owed the plaintiff a duty of care, however, as in *A and Others*.

POWELL v *BOLADY, WEST GLAMORGAN HEALTH AUTHORITY AND OTHERS*, *The Times*, 26 November 1997 (CA)

Mr and Mrs Powell developed post traumatic stress disorder and panic disorder respectively after allegedly discovering that documents had been removed from their son's medical file after his death and different documents substituted. They sued the doctors in their GP's practice for making a false statement which they could have foreseen would cause psychological harm.

The Court of Appeal held, however, that doctors did not owe, in the words of Stuart-Smith LJ, any 'free standing duty of candour' which, if breached, could lay them open to damages claims for personal injury by relatives of patients. His Lordship said that doctors owe a duty of care to their patients, but explaining about a death does not put them into a doctor-patient relationship with relatives.

This decision, on the pleadings, supports the view that doctors have no actionable duty to tell parents the truth about the death of their child. (In this case it was also alleged that the doctors, including a consultant paediatrician employed by the defendant Health Authority, had negligently failed to diagnose the plaintiffs' son's illness, had this illness been treated in time it seems that the boy's life would probably have been saved. It is reported that the Health Authority **admitted** liability for the paediatrician's negligence in this respect, paying £80,000 damages and £20,000 costs.)

6.3 Reform

Law Commission Report No. 249, *Liability for Psychiatric Illness* (1998)

Executive summary

1. This Report (with accompanying Draft Bill) recommends legislative reform designed to remove some unwarranted restrictions that presently apply in relation to liability for negligently inflicted psychiatric illness.

2. Under the present law, the general position[1] is that a person who suffers a reasonably foreseeable recognisable psychiatric illness, as a result of another person's death, injury or imperilment, cannot recover damages for negligence unless he or she can satisfy three main requirements:

(i) that he or she had a close tie of love and affection with the person killed, injured or imperilled;
(ii) that he or she was close to the 'accident' in time and space;
(iii) that he or she directly perceived the 'accident' rather than, for example, hearing about it from a third person.

3. These controls are drawn unnecessarily tightly. The present law produces arbitrary results. Our principal recommendation (which was overwhelmingly supported on consultation) is that the restrictions based on the plaintiffs physical and temporal proximity to the accident and the means by which he or she learned of it should be removed; but that the first control – the need for a close tie of love and affection – should be retained.

4. In addition, we recommend the removal of two further restrictions that appear to apply generally to liability for negligently inflicted psychiatric illness: first, that the illness must be caused by a 'shock' and, secondly, that the illness must not result from the death, injury or imperilment of the defendant him or herself.

5. It is for the Government and Parliament to decide whether to implement by legislation the recommendations in this Report.

---

[1] There are special rules relating to particular classes of plaintiff, for example rescuers.

Negligence (Psychiatric Illness) Bill

ARRANGEMENT OF CLAUSES

New duties of care

Clause
1. Close tie: duty of care.
2. Close tie: duty of care if defendant is victim.
3. Meaning of close tie.

Common law duty of care

4.   Close tie: abolition of common law duty.
5.   Removal of certain restrictions.

General

6.   Commencement.
7.   Extent.
8.   Citation.

(NB: details of the Bill are omitted.)

6.4   End of Chapter Assessment Question

Dahlia takes her daughter, Primrose, to a funfair owned and operated by Nigel. Primrose wants a ride on the big dipper so Dahlia, who does not like high speeds, leaves her in the queue and goes for a ride on the big wheel which is about 80 yards away. While Dahlia is watching from the big wheel, the carriage in which Primrose is riding flies off the rails of the big dipper, due to a loose bolt in the framework, and plummets 60 feet to the ground. Primrose is badly injured, and Dahlia is at first hysterical, and later suffers from recurrent feelings of anxiety, and from insomnia.

Sage, who is also on the big wheel at the time of the accident, is so shocked at what he sees that he later suffers from catastrophic neurosis, and is unable to work for 15 months. Some 10 years earlier Sage had been a voluntary patient at a mental hospital, where he had been treated for a neurotic condition.

Primrose's father, Chrys, sees pictures of the accident on the television news that evening, and is so shocked that he suffers a heart attack.

Discuss any potential liability in tort on the part of Nigel towards Dahlia, Sage and Chrys.

6.5   End of Chapter Assessment Outline Answer

D = Dahlia, P = Primrose, N = Nigel, S = Sage, C = Chrys

N, as owner and operator of the funfair could only be liable in tort on the facts of this problem for some form of inadvertence or strict liability, there being no evidence of any intentional, deliberate or reckless behaviour on his part.

He might owe some special statutory obligation relating to the safety of funfairs (the Health and Safety at Work Executive/Agency have jurisdiction in these matters, for instance) and an action in tort for breach of statutory duty might be available to appropriately injured persons; but no evidence of this is apparent on the face of the problem and consequently cannot be pursued. The question of any statutory **penalties** is obviously outside the terms of our brief in the present context. It is certainly the case that N has a **contractual** relationship with D and S, who are licensees on his funfair, and this fact must mean that the parties are in close proximity. The question might arise indeed, whether action in **contract** is possible: but the terms of the contract are not given and in any event we are to consider only liability in tort. **Concurrent** liability in tort and contract would also have to be considered, but for present purposes it is assumed that a claim in **tort** would be available as an **alternative** to a claim in contract, were an action for breach of contract found to exist.

N would be an 'occupier' of 'premises' and D and S would be 'visitors' thereon for the purposes of liability arising under the Occupiers' Liability Act 1957. This Act imposes a duty upon occupiers to take reasonable care for the safety of their visitors while the latter are using the premises for the purpose(s) for which they have been permitted to enter. 'Safety' includes **physical** safety, but the question of whether it includes safety from psychological injury may be open to debate.

It is proposed, therefore, to consider only the question of whether any liability on N's part could arise in the tort of negligence at common law. Liability for psychiatric damage (or 'nervous shock') inflicted negligently is governed by the rulings of the House of Lords in *McLoughlin* v *O'Brian* and *Alcock* v *Chief Constable of the South Yorkshire Police*.

In *Alcock* their Lordships, applying *McLoughlin*, said that a plaintiff must experience the incident (or its immediate aftermath) leading to the psychiatric injury by **seeing or hearing** it. It is also necessary that the plaintiff should establish a medically recognised psychiatric illness. There are further requirements contained within the '*Alcock* test', and these will emerge later in this opinion.

The respective positions of the putative plaintiffs will now be examined.

D

D actually sees the incident, and is the mother of the victim of the accident, P. *Alcock* is authority for the following requirements:

(a)   a person witnessing an incident allegedly causing psychiatric damage is expected to possess sufficient phlegm and fortitude to experience the ordinary vicissitudes of life without becoming psychologically ill;

(b)   there must be a causative link between witnessing the incident and the mental illness;

(c)   there must be sufficient foreseeability/proximity between the parties;

(d)   there must be a recognised relationship between the victim of the accident and the plaintiff, i.e., there must be a close bond of love and affection between them.

A further point

It may also be necessary, on the authority of *Marc Rich*, to meet the *Caparo* requirement of 'just and reasonable'.

On the facts, it is submitted that D:

(a)   is proximate in terms of time and space;

(b)   would, as P's mother, be **presumed** to have a close bond of love and affection with her child (it would be open to N to rebut this presumption);

(c)   is in the position to surmount the hurdle of 'phlegm and fortitude' because she **is** P's mother (P's **age** might be important) and the incident is likely to be horrific in nature.

D might have a problem with the medical evidence, because N might argue that she is hysterical by nature (it is not clear whether hysteria has been induced by the accident) and that any psychiatric illness is the result of this pre-existing condition – **assuming** that recurrent feelings of anxiety and insomnia would be medically recognised as illness. The basic burden of proof is on D and detailed medical evidence would have to be available in order to form a more definite legal opinion on this point.

In *Brice* v *Brown* the Court of Appeal found that the defendant did not have to take the severely neurotic plaintiff as he found her, but support for the view that the 'egg-shell skull' ('personality' in the present context) principle applies to the **extent** of psychiatric damage can be found in *Malcolm* v *Broadhurst* and *Meah* v *McCreamer*.

S

Much of what has been written concerning D is also relevant here, except

(a)   S is a mere 'bystander', i.e., he has no apparent tie of love and affection to P;

(b)   catastrophic neurosis is a recognised psychiatric illness;

(c)   that S is possibly not a 'sensitive' plaintiff because he may be able to show that his earlier treatment in hospital cured him of his original condition – as in *Chadwick* v *BRB*.

There is *obiter* opinion in *Alcock* that a bystander might qualify as a plaintiff if the incident was of a horrific nature. The Court of Appeal, in *McFarlane* v *EE Caledonian*, however, rejected this approach and ruled that plaintiffs must have a close bond of love and affection with the victim.

On that basis, S is unlikely to succeed – unless the House of Lords ruled otherwise or another Court of Appeal could be persuaded to distinguish the cases.

C

C would qualify under the *Alcock* criterion of 'appropriate relationship' with P, but he would be labouring under great difficulty in relation to the requirement of sight/hearing of the incident. The House of Lords in *Alcock* appeared to rule out the possibility of **any** viewer of ordinary broadcast television succeeding in a claim for damages for psychiatric injury (other than, **perhaps**, a claim against the **broadcaster** where the broadcasting code of ethics was not observed). If an ordinary 'live' broadcast is not recognised as an appropriate form of communicating psychiatric injury, *a fortiori* would the 'television news that evening' not qualify. This may not even be a 'live' transmission of the event; the incident may have occurred hours earlier and have been recorded on film or tape. That possible time lag, in terms of causation, could itself be fatal to C's claim. A heart attack comes within the terms of psychiatric damage: e.g., *Hambrook* v *Stokes Bros.*

A final issue must be addressed viz. the question of N's negligence on the facts. In other words, apart from any argument on 'duty' it would be necessary for the putative plaintiffs to show that N was in **breach** of that duty.

On the present facts it is not readily apparent that the accident is due to N's negligence – though the doctrine of *res ipsa loquitur* might apply. N might attempt to join others in any action – as appropriate i.e., any manufacturer/producer/supplier/erector/installer (the familiar chain of responsibility would emerge e.g., *Lambert* v *Lewis*). Perhaps maintenance engineers/inspectors (if the work was contracted out) would be joined. Any servants of N involved would bring in the possibility of vicarious liability (of N) and the provisions of the Civil Liability (Contributions) Act 1978 would apply as between defendants.

In addition, those third parties (**if any**) could be sued directly in negligence by D, S and C. In the case of manufacturers/producers any liability would fall within the terms of the 'narrow' rule in *Donoghue* v *Stevenson* and the Consumer Protection Act 1987.

This matter, of breach of duty, cannot be explored in detail because of the lack of evidence available, therefore negligence on N's part would have to be assumed.

CHAPTER SEVEN

LIABILITY FOR DANGEROUS PREMISES AND LAND

7.1 Liability Arising in Various Capacities in Negligence

7.1.1 ARCHITECTS AND OTHERS

MURPHY v *BRENTWOOD DISTRICT COUNCIL* [1990] 2 All ER 908 (HL)

LORD KEITH: I see no reason to doubt that the principle of *Donoghue* v *Stevenson* does indeed apply so as to place the builder of premises under a duty to take reasonable care to avoid injury through defects in the premises to the person or property of those whom he should have in contemplation as likely to suffer such injury if care is not taken. But it is against injury through **latent** (emphasis added) defects that the duty exists to guard . . .

In the *Dorset Yacht* case, however, the damage caused was physical . . .

In *Anns* the House of Lords approved, subject to explanation, the decision of the Court of Appeal in *Dutton* v *Bognor Regis UDC* [1972] 1 QB 373 . . . The jump which is here [by Lord Denning in the Dutton case] made from liability under the *Donoghue* v *Stevenson* principle for damage to person or property caused by a latent defect in a carelessly manufactured article to liability for the cost of rectifying a defect in such an article which is ex hypothesi no longer latent is difficult to accept. As Stamp LJ recognised in the same case, there is no liability in tort on a manufacturer towards the purchaser from a retailer of an article which turns out to be useless or valueless through defects due to careless manufacture (see [1972] 1 QB 373 at 414–5). The loss is economic. It is difficult to draw a distinction in principle between an article which is useless or valueless and one which suffers from a defect which would render it dangerous in use but which is discovered by the purchaser in time to avert any possibility of injury. The purchaser may incur expense in putting right the defect, or, more probably, discard the article. In either case the loss is purely economic. Stamp LJ appears to have taken the view that in the case of a house the builder would not be liable to a purchaser where the defect was discovered in time to prevent injury but that a local authority which had failed to discover the defect by careful inspection during the course of construction was so liable. . . . *Batty* v *Metropolitan Property Realization Ltd* [1978] QB 554 was a case where a house which suffered no defects of construction had been built on land subject to the danger of slippage. A landslip carried away part of the garden but there was no danger to the house itself. Due to the prospect, however, that at some future time the house might be completely carried away, it was rendered valueless. There was no possibility of remedial works such as might save the house from being carried away. The Court of Appeal allowed recovery in tort against the builder of damages based on loss of the value of the house. That again was purely economic loss . . . In my opinion it must now be recognised that, although the damage in *Anns* was characterised as physical damage by Lord Wilberforce, it was purely economic loss. In *Sutherland Shire Council* v *Heyman* (1985) 60 ALR 1 at 60–1 where, as observed above, the High Court of Australia declined to follow *Anns* when dealing with a claim against a local authority in respect of a defectively constructed house . . .

It being recognised that the nature of the loss held to be recoverable in *Anns* was pure economic loss, the next point for examination is whether the avoidance of loss of that nature fell within the scope of any duty of care owed to the plaintiffs by the local authority. On the basis of the law as it stood at the time of the decision the answer to that question must be in the negative. The right to recover for pure economic loss, not flowing from physical injury, did not then extend beyond the situation where the loss had been sustained through reliance on negligence misstatements, as in *Hedley Byrne* . . .

On analysis, the nature of the duty held by *Anns* to be incumbent on the local authority went very much further than a duty to take reasonable care to prevent injury to safety or health. The duty held to exist may be formulated as one to take reasonable care to avoid putting a future inhabitant owner of a house in a position in which he is threatened, by reason to a defect in the house, with avoidable physical injury to person or health and is obliged, in order to continue to occupy the house without suffering such injury, to expend money for the purpose of rectifying the defect.`

The existence of a duty of that nature should not, in my opinion, be affirmed without a careful examination of the implications of such affirmation. To start with, if such a duty is incumbent on the local authority, a similar duty must necessarily be incumbent also on the builder of the house. If the builder of the house is to be so subject, there can be no grounds in logic or in principle for not extending liability on like grounds to the manufacturer of a chattel. That would open on an exceedingly wide field of claims, involving the introduction of something in the nature of a transmissible warranty of quality. The purchaser of an article who discovered that it suffered from a dangerous defect before that defect has caused any damage would be entitled to recover from the manufacturer the cost of rectifying the defect, and, presumably, if the article was not capable of economic repair, the amount of loss sustained through discarding it. Then it would be open to question whether there should not also be a right to recovery where the defect renders the article not dangerous but merely useless. The economic loss in either case would be the same. There would also be a problem where the defect causes the destruction of the article itself, without causing any personal injury or damage to other property. A similar problem could arise, if the *Anns* principle is to be treated as confined to real property, where a building collapses when unoccupied.

In America the courts have developed the view that in the case of chattels damage to the chattel itself resulting from careless manufacture does not give a cause of action in negligence or in product liability . . .

In *D & F Estates Ltd* v *Church Commissioners for England* [1989] AC 177 both Lord Bridge and Lord Oliver expressed themselves as having difficulty in reconciling the decision in *Anns* with pre-existing principle and as being uncertain as to the nature and scope of such new principle as it introduced. Lord Bridge suggested that in the case of a complex structure such as a building one element of the structure might be regarded for *Donoghue* v *Stevenson* purposes as distinct from another element, so that damage to one part of the structure caused by a hidden defect in another part might qualify to be treated as damage to 'other property' (see [1989] AC 177 at 206). I think that it would be unrealistic to take this view as regards a building the whole of which had been erected and equipped by the same contractor. In that situation the whole package provided by the contractor would, in my opinion, fall to be regarded as one unit rendered unsound as such by a defect in the particular part. On the other hand, where, for example, the electric wiring had been installed by a sub-contractor and due to a defect caused by lack of care a fire occurred which destroyed the building, it might not be stretching ordinary principles too far to hold the electrical sub-contractor liable for the damage. If in the *East River* case the defective turbine had caused the loss of the ship the manufacturer of it could consistently with normal principles, I would think, properly have been held liable for that loss. But, even if Lord Bridge's theory were to be held acceptable, it would not seem to extend to the founding of liability on a local authority, considering that the purposes of the 1936 Act are concerned with averting danger to health and safety, not danger or damage to property. Further, it would not cover the situation which might arise through discovery, before any damage had occurred, of a defect likely to give rise to damage in the future.

Liability under the *Anns* decision is postulated on the existence of a present or imminent danger to health or safety. But, considering that the loss involved in incurring expenditure to avert the danger is pure economic loss, there would seem to be no logic in confining the remedy to cases where such danger exists. There is likewise no logic in confining it to cases where some damage (perhaps comparatively slight) has been caused to the building, but refusing it where the existence of the danger has come to light in some other way, for example through a structured survey which happens to have been carried out, or where the danger inherent in some particular component or material has been revealed through failure in some other building. Then there is the question whether the remedy is available where the defect is rectified, not in order to avert danger to an inhabitant occupier himself, but in order to enable an occupier, who may be a corporation, to continue to occupy the building through its employees without putting those employees at risk.

In my opinion it is clear that *Anns* did not proceed on any basis of established principle, but introduced a new species of liability governed by a principle indeterminate in character but having the potentiality of covering a wide range of situations, involving chattels as well as real property, in which it had never hitherto been thought that the law of negligence had any proper place.

In my opinion there can be no doubt that *Anns* has for long been widely regarded as an unsatisfactory decision. In relation to the scope of the duty owed by a local authority it proceeded on what must, with due respect to its source, be regarded as a somewhat superficial examination of principle and there has been extreme difficulty, highlighted most recently by the speeches in the *D & F Estates* case, in ascertaining on exactly what basis of principle it did proceed. I think it must now be recognised that it did not proceed on any basis of principle at all, but constituted a remarkable example of judicial legislation. It has engendered a vast spate of litigation, and each of the cases in the field which have reached this House has been distinguished. Others have been distinguished in the Court of Appeal. The result has been to keep the effect of the decision within reasonable bounds, but that has been achieved only by applying strictly the words of Lord Wilberforce and by refusing to accept the logical implications of the decision itself. These logical implications show that the case properly considered has potentiality for collision with long-established principles regarding liability in the tort of negligence for economic loss. There can be no doubt that to depart from the decision would re-establish a degree of certainty in this field of law which it has done a remarkable amount to upset.

So far as policy considerations are concerned, it is no doubt the case that extending the scope of the tort of negligence may tend to inhibit carelessness and improve standards of manufacture and construction. On the other hand, overkill may present its own disadvantages, as we remarked in *Rowling* v *Takaro Properties Ltd* [1988] AC 473 at 502. There may be room for the view that *Anns*-type liability will tend to encourage owners of buildings found to be dangerous to repair rather than run the risk of injury. The owner may, however, and perhaps quite often does, prefer to sell the building at its diminished value, as happened in the present case.

It must, of course, be kept in mind that the decision has stood for some thirteen years. On the other hand, it is not a decision of the type that is to a significant extent taken into account by citizens or indeed local authorities in ordering their affairs. No doubt its existence results in local authorities having to pay increased insurance premiums, but to be relieved of that necessity would be to their advantage, not to their detriment. To overrule it is unlikely to result in significantly increased insurance premiums for householders. It is perhaps of some significance that most litigation involving the decision consists in contests between insurance companies, as is largely the position in the present case. The decision is capable of being regarded as affording a measure of justice, but as against that the impossibility of finding any coherent and logically based doctrine behind it is calculated to put the law of negligence into a state of confusion defying rational analysis. It is also material that *Anns* has the effect of imposing on builders generally a liability going far beyond that which Parliament thought fit to impose on house builders alone by the Defective Premises Act 1972, a statute very material to the policy of the decision but not adverted to in it. There is much to be said for the view that in what is essentially a consumer protection field, as was observed by Lord Bridge in *D & F Estates Ltd* v *Church Commissioners for England* [1989] AC 177 at 207, the precise extent and limits of the liabilities which in the public interest should be imposed on builders and local authorities are best left to the legislature.

My Lords, I would hold that *Anns* was wrongly decided as regards the scope of any private law duty of care resting on local authorities in relation to their future of taking steps to secure compliance with building byelaws or regulations and should be departed from.

227

It follows that *Dutton v Bognor Regis UDC* [1972] 1 QB 373 should be overruled, as should all cases subsequent to *Anns* which were decided in reliance on it.

In the circumstances I do not consider it necessary to deal with the question whether, assuming that the council was under a duty of the scope contended for by the plaintiff, it discharged that duty by acting on the advice of competent consulting engineers.

My Lords, for these reasons I would allow the appeal.

LORD BRIDGE: Since Lord Wilberforce in *Anns* [1978] AC 728 at 760 referred with approval to the dissenting judgment of Laskin J in that case [*Rivtow Marine Ltd* v *Washington Iron Works* (1972) 3 WWR 735 (Canada)], which he described as 'of strong persuasive force', I have read and reread that judgment with the closest attention. I have to say, with all respect, that I find it wholly unconvincing. It depends on the same fallacy as that which vitiates the judgments of Lord Denning MR and Sachs LJ in *Dutton*, in particular, in equating the damage sustained in repairing the chattel to make it safe with the damage which would have been suffered if the latent defect had never been discovered and the chattel had injured somebody in use, the judgment ignores the circumstances that once a chattel is known to be dangerous it is simply unusable. If I buy a secondhand car and find it to be faulty, it can make no difference to the manufacturer's liability in tort whether the fault is in the brakes or in the engine, i.e. whether the car will not stop or will not start. In either case the car is useless until repaired. The manufacturer is no more liable in tort for the cost of the repairs in the one case than in the other.

. . . The reality is that the structural elements in any building form a single indivisible unit of which the different parts are essentially interdependent. To the extent that there is any defect in one part of the structure it must to a greater or lesser degree necessarily affect all other parts of the structure. Therefore any defect in the structure is a defect in the quality of the whole and it is quite artificial, in order to impose a legal liability which the law would not otherwise impose, to treat a defect in an integral structure, so far as it weakens the structure, as a dangerous defect liable to cause damage to 'other property'.

As critical distinction must be drawn here between some part of a complex structure which is said to be a 'danger' only because it does not perform its proper function in sustaining the other parts and some distinct item incorporated in the structure which positively malfunctions so as to inflict positive damage on the structure in which it is incorporated.

Thus, if a defective central heating boiler explodes and damages a house or a defective electrical installation malfunctions and sets the house on fire, I see no reason to doubt that the owner of the house, if he can prove that the damage was due to the negligence of the boiler manufacturer in the one case or the electrical contractor in the other, can recover damages in tort on *Donoghue* v *Stevenson* principles. But the position in law is entirely different where, by reason of the inadequacy of the foundations of the building to support the weight of the superstructure, differential settlement and consequent cracking occurs. Here, once the first cracks appear, the structure as a whole is seen to be defective and the nature of the defect is known. Even if, contrary to my view, the initial damage could be regarded as damage to other property caused by a latent defect, once the defect is known the situation of the building owner is analogous to that of the car owner who discovers that the car has faulty brakes. He may have a house which, until repairs are effected, is unfit for habitation, but subject to the reservation I have expressed with respect to ruinous buildings at or near the boundary of the owners' property, the building no longer represents a source of danger and as it deteriorates will only damage itself.

For these reasons the complex structure theory offers no escape from the conclusion that damage to a house itself which is attributable to a defect in the structure of the house is not recoverable in tort on *Donoghue* v *Stevenson* principles, but represents purely economic loss which is only recoverable in contract or in tort by reason of some special relationship of proximity which imposes on the tortfeasor a duty of care to protect against economic loss.

. . . These may be cogent reasons of social policy for imposing liability on the authority. But the shoulders of a public authority are only 'broad enough to bear the loss' because they are financed by the public at large. It is pre-eminently for the legislature to decide whether these policy reasons should be accepted as sufficient for imposing on the public the burden of providing compensation for private financial losses. If they do so decide, it is not difficult for them to say so.

I would allow the appeal.

LORD OLIVER: In the speech of Lord Bridge and in my own speech in *D & F Estates Ltd* v *Church Commissioners for England* [1989] AC 167 there was canvassed what has been called 'the complex structure theory'. This has been rightly criticised by academic writers, although I confess that I thought that both Lord Bridge and I had made it clear that it was a theory which was not embraced with any enthusiasm but was advanced as the only logically possible explanation of the categorisation of the damage in *Anns* as 'material, physical damage'. Lord Bridge has, in the course of his speech in the present case, amply demonstrated the artificiality of the theory and, for the reasons, which he has given, it must be rejected as a viable explanation of the underlying basis for the decision in *Anns*. However that decision is analysed, therefore, it is in the end inescapable that the only damage for which compensation was to be awarded and which formed the essential foundation of the action was pecuniary loss and nothing more. The injury which the plaintiff suffers in such a case is that his consciousness of the possible injury to his own health or safety or that of others puts him in a position in which, in order to enable him either to go on living in the property or to exploit its financial potentiality without that risk, whether substantial or insubstantial, he has to expend money in making good the defects which have now become patent . . .

The fact is that the categorisation of the damage in *Anns* as 'material, physical damage', whilst, at first sight, lending to the decision some colour of consistency with the principle of *Donoghue* v *Stevenson*, has served to obscure not only the true nature of the claim but, as a result, the nature and scope of the duty on the breach of which the plaintiffs in that case were compelled to reply.

It does not, of course, at all follow as a matter of necessity from the mere fact that the only damage suffered by a plaintiff in an action for the tort of negligence is pecuniary or 'economic' that his claim is bound to fail. It is true that, in an uninterrupted line of cases since 1875, it has consistently been held that a third party cannot successfully sue in tort for the interference with his economic expectation or advantage resulting from injury to the person or property of another person with whom he has or is likely to have a contractual relationship (see *Cattle* v *Stockton Waterworks Co* (1875) LR 10 QB 453, *Simpson & Co* v *Thomson* (1877) 3 App Cas 279, *Sa de Remorquage à Helice* v *Bennetts* [1911] 1 KB 243). That principle was applied more recently by Widgery J in *Weller & Co* v *Foot and Mouth Disease Research Institute* [1966] 1 QB 569 and received its most recent reiteration in the decision of this House in *Leigh & Sillavan Ltd* v *Aliakmon Shipping Co. Ltd, The Aliakmon* [1986] AC 785. But it is far from clear from these decisions that the reason for the plaintiff's failure was simply that the only loss sustained was 'economic'. Rather they seem to have been used either on the remoteness of the damage as a matter of direct causation or, more probably, on the 'floodgates' argument of the impossibility of containing liability within any acceptable bounds if the law were to permit such claims to succeed. The decision of this House in *Morrison Steamship Co. Ltd* v *Greystoke Castle (Cargo Owners)* [1947] AC 265 demonstrates that the mere fact that the primary damage suffered by a plaintiff is pecuniary is no necessary bar to an action in negligence given the proper circumstances (in that case, what was said to be the 'joint venture' interest of shipowners and the owners of cargo carried on board) and if the matter remained in doubt that doubt was conclusively resolved by the decision of this House in *Hedley Byrne & Co. Ltd* v *Heller & Partners Ltd* [1964] AC 465 at 517, where Lord Devlin convincingly demonstrated the illogicality of a distinction between financial loss caused directly and financial loss resulting from physical injury to personal property.

The critical question, as was pointed out in the analysis of Brennan J in his judgment in *Sutherland Shire Council* v *Heyman* (1985) 60 ALR 1, is not the nature of the damage in itself, whether physical or pecuniary, but whether the scope of the duty of care in the circumstances of the case is such as to embrace damage of the kind which the plaintiff claims to have sustained (see *Caparo Industries Plc* v *Dickman* [1990] 2 WLR 358). The essential question which has to be asked in every case, given that damage which is the essential ingredient of the action has occurred, is whether the relationship between the plaintiff and the defendant is such, or, to use the favoured expression, whether it is of sufficient 'proximity', that it imposes on the latter a duty to take care to avoid or prevent that loss which has in fact been sustained. That the requisite degree of proximity may be established in circumstances in which the plaintiff's injury results from his reliance on a statement or advice on which he was entitled to reply and on which it was contemplated that he would be likely to rely is clear from *Hedley Byrne* and subsequent cases, but *Anns* was not such a case and neither is the instant case. It is not, however, necessarily to be assumed that the reliance cases form the only possible category of cases in which a duty to take reasonable care to avoid or prevent pecuniary loss can arise. *Morrison Steamship Co. Ltd* v *Greystoke Castle (Cargo Owners)*, for instance, clearly was not a reliance case. Nor indeed was *Ross* v *Caunters* (a firm) [1980] Ch 297 so far as the disappointed beneficiary was concerned. Another example may be *Ministry of Housing and Local Government* v *Sharp* [1970] 2 QB 223, although this may, on analysis, properly be categorised as a reliance case.

Nor is it self-evident logically where the line is to be drawn. Where, for instance, the defendant's careless conduct results in the interruption of the electricity supply to business premises adjoining the highway, it is not easy to discern the logic in holding that a sufficient relationship of proximity exists between him and a factory owner who has suffered loss because material in the course of manufacture is rendered useless but that none exists between him and the owner of, for instance, an adjoining restaurant who suffers the loss of profit on the meals which he is unable to prepare and sell. In both cases the real loss is pecuniary. The solution to such borderline cases has so far been achieved pragmatically (see *Spartan Steel and Alloys Ltd* v *Martin & Co. (Contractors) Ltd* [1973] 1 QB 27) not by the application of logic but by the perceived necessity as a matter of policy to place some limits, perhaps arbitrary limits, to what would otherwise be an endless, cumulative causative chain bounded only by theoretical foreseeability.

I frankly doubt whether, in searching for such limits, the categorisation of the damage as 'material', 'physical', 'pecuniary' or 'economic' provides a particularly useful contribution. Where it does, I think, serve a useful purpose is in identifying those cases in which it is necessary to search for and find something more than the mere reasonable foreseeability of damage which has occurred as providing the degree of 'proximity' necessary to support the action. In his classical exposition in *Donoghue* v *Stevenson* [1932] AC 562 at 580–581 Lord Atkin was expressing himself in the context of the infliction of direct physical injury resulting from a carelessly created latent defect in a manufactured product. In his analysis of the duty in those circumstances he clearly equated 'proximity' with the reasonable foresight of damage. In the straightforward case of the direct infliction of physical injury by the act of the plaintiff there is, indeed, no need to look beyond the foreseeability by the defendant of the result in order to establish that he is in a 'proximate' relationship with the plaintiff. But, as was pointed out by Lord Diplock in *Home Office* v *Dorset Yacht Co. Ltd* [1970] AC 1004 at 1060, Lord Atkin's test, though a useful guide to characters which will be found to exist in conduct and relationships giving rise to a legal duty of care, is manifestly false if misused as a universal; and Lord Reid, in the course of his speech in the same case, recognised that the statement of principle enshrined in that test necessarily required qualification in cases where the only loss caused by the defendant's conduct was economic. The infliction of physical injury to the person or property of another universally requires to be justified. The causing of economic loss does not. If it is to be categorised as wrongful it is necessary to find some factor beyond the mere occurrence of the loss of the fact that its occurrence could be foreseen. Thus the categorisation of damage as economic serves at least the useful purpose of indication that something more is required and it is one of the unfortunate features of *Anns* that is resulted initially in this essential distinction being lost sight of . . .

There may be very sound social and political reasons for imposing on local authorities the burden of acting, in effect, as insurers that buildings erected in their areas have been properly constructed in accordance with the relevant building regulations. Statute may so provide. It has not done so and I do not, for my part, think that it is right for the courts not simply to expand existing principles but to create at large new principles in order to fulfil a social need in an area of consumer protection which has already been perceived by the legislature but for which, presumably advisedly, it has not thought it necessary to provide.

I would accordingly allow the appeal. It is unnecessary in these circumstances to determine the interesting question of whether, in fact, the defendants in the instant case, who took the only course practically open to them, could be held responsible in law for the negligence of the ex facie competent experts whom they consulted.

Lords Jauncey and McKay were also in favour of allowing the appeal.

This decision is also of importance in the context of **Chapters** 3 and 5 of the *Learning Text*.

DEPARTMENT OF THE ENVIRONMENT v THOMAS BATES AND SON (NEW TOWNS COMMISSION, THIRD PARTY) [1990] 2 All ER 943 (HL)

The court had to consider the liability of a builder in negligence with regard to building repairs and economic loss.

LORD KEITH: The foundation of the plaintiffs' case is *Anns* v *Merton London Borough* [1978] AC 728. That decision was concerned directly only with the liability in negligence of a local authority in respect of its functions in regard to securing compliance with building byelaws and regulations. The position of the builder as regards liability towards a remote purchaser of a building which suffered from defects due to carelessness in construction was touched on very briefly. However, it has since been generally accepted that similar principles govern the liability both of the local authority and of the builder.

It has been held by this House in *Murphy* v *Brentwood DC* [1990] 2 All ER 908 that *Anns* was wrongly decided and should be departed from, by reason of the erroneous views there expressed as to the scope of any duty of care owned to purchasers of houses by local authorities when exercising the powers conferred on them for the purpose of securing compliance with building regulations. The process of reasoning by which the House reached its conclusion necessarily included close examination of the position of the builder who was primarily responsible, through lack of care in the construction process, for the presence of defects in the building. It was the unanimous view that, while the builder would be liable under the principle of *Donoghue* v *Stevenson* [1932] AC 562 in the event of the defect, before it had been discovered, causing physical injury to persons or damage to property other than the building itself, there was no sound basis in principle for holding him liable for the pure economic loss suffered by a purchase who discovered the defect, however such discovery might come about, and who was required to expend money in order to make the building safe and suitable for its intended purpose.

In the present case it is clear that the loss suffered by the plaintiff is pure economic loss. At the time the plaintiffs carried out the remedial work on the concrete pillars the building was not unsafe by reason of the defective construction of these pillars. It did, however, suffer from a defect of quality which made the plaintiff's lease less valuable than it would otherwise have been, in respect that the building could not be loaded up to its design capacity unless any occupier who wished so to load it had incurred the expenditure necessary for the strengthening of the pillars. It was wholly uncertain whether during the currency of their lease the plaintiffs themselves would ever be likely to require to load the building up to its design capacity, but a purchaser from them might well have wanted to do so. Such a purchaser, faced with the need to strengthen the pillars, would obviously have paid less for the lease than if they had been sound. This underlines the purely economic character of the plaintiff's loss. To hold in favour of the plaintiffs would involve a very significant extension of the doctrine of *Anns* so as to cover the situation where there existed no damage to the building and no imminent danger to personal safety or health. If *Anns* was correctly decided, such an extension could reasonably be regarded as entirely logical. The undesirability of such an extension, for the reasons stated in *Murphy* v *Brentwood DC*, formed an important part of the grounds which led to the conclusion that *Anns* was not correctly decided. That conclusion must lead inevitably to the result that the plaintiffs' claim fails.

I would dismiss the appeal.

Lords Brandon, Ackner, Oliver and Jauncey agreed with Lord Keith in dismissing the appeal.

TARGETT v TORFAEN BOROUGH COUNCIL [1992] 3 All ER 27 (CA)

It was held that a landlord who is responsible for the design and construction of a house let by him is under a duty of reasonable care to see that the house is free from defects likely to cause injury to any person whom he ought reasonably to have in contemplation as likely to be affected by such defects. The plaintiff's knowledge of a defect does not, by itself, always negate the duty of care or break the chain of causation. Here the defect was the absence of lighting in the immediate vicinity of two flights of stone steps which gave access to the plaintiff's house. The plaintiff was the tenant of the council. There was also no hand-rail for the lower steps and, before he moved into the house, he complained of the lack of lighting, but nothing had been done. One night the plaintiff fell down the steps and was injured. At first instance the defendants were found liable, but the plaintiff's damages were reduced by 25 per cent for contributory negligence.

The defendants' appeal was dismissed. Russell LJ in applying *Rimmer* v *Liverpool City Council* [1985] QB 1 found that it was still an authority binding on the court and had not been overruled by *Murphy* v *Brentwood DC* [1990] 2 All ER 908 'by implication or otherwise'. (Sir Donald Nicholls VC and Legatt LJ concurred with Russell LJ's judgment.)

RUSSELL LJ: . . . The court was referred to two authorities and I must now turn to them. In *Rimmer* v *Liverpool City Council* [1985] QB 1 the Court of Appeal was concerned with a dwelling house that the local authority had designed and built. The plaintiff became the tenant of the house. He suffered personal injuries when he fell against a pane of glass within the property which, as the county court judge found, was too thin and potentially dangerous. The plaintiff was aware of the thinness of the glass prior to his accident and had complained to the local authority about it. At first instance the judge found in the plaintiff's favour and the local authority appealed. Reliance was placed upon *Cavalier* v *Pope* [1906] AC 428, wherein the House of Lords had decided that, in the absence of a contractual duty to maintain and repair, a landlord was not liable for the dangerous state of an unfurnished house let to a tenant injured by the dangerous conditions. In *Rimmer's* case [1985] QB 1 at 13–14 the judgment of the court was delivered by Stephenson LJ, who said:

> From these authorities we take the law to be that an opportunity for inspection of a dangerous defect, even if successfully taken by A who is injured by it, will not destroy his proximity to B who created the danger, or exonerate B from liability to A, unless A was free to remove or avoid the danger in the sense that it was reasonable to expect him to do so, and unreasonable for him to run the risk of being injured by the danger. It was not reasonable or practical for the plaintiff to leave the flat or to alter the glass panel. He remained in law the council's neighbour, although he had complained that the glass was too thin. We reach our decision without treating *Cavalier* v *Pope* [1906] AC 428 as overruled, for Pope did not design or construct the floor through which Mrs Cavalier fell. He was not a builder-owner, but what may be called a bare landlord, or a landowner as such . . .

For my part I do not read the speeches in *Murphy's* case as supporting Mr Green's propositions. A weekly tenant is in an entirely different position from an owner of a house defectively constructed who discovers the defect thereby rendering it no longer a latent defect . . .

Rimmer's case was not even cited in *Murphy's* case, for in my view it had nothing whatever to do with the problem posed in *Murphy's* case. Likewise I am satisfied that their Lordships did not refer to *Rimmer's* case because it had no relevance.

I am firmly of the opinion that the House of Lords in *Murphy's* case did not overrule *Rimmer's* case by implication or otherwise, and in my view *Rimmer's* case remains an authority binding upon this court.

On the issue of primary liability, therefore, I have come to the conclusion that the recorder's judgment cannot be faulted . . .

SIR DONALD NICHOLLS VC: Before us the appellant's argument was that in *Rimmer's* case, as in the present case, the person injured knew of the dangerous defect which subsequently caused his personal injuries. In *Rimmer's* case the plaintiff considered the glass panel was a danger because it was too thin, and he had complained about this to the defendant local authority. In the present case the plaintiff knew of the lighting position and of the absence of the hand-rail. Accordingly, it was argued, in accordance with the observations of Lord Keith and Lord Bridge, the claim by the plaintiff in *Rimmer's* case, and the claim in the present action, must fail.

I cannot accept this. In *Murphy* v *Brentwood DC* the House of Lords was concerned to consider the principles applicable to a claim to recover the cost of making good a defective product, there a building, which had not yet caused any physical injury to persons or damage to other property. Their Lordships explained why the *Donoghue* v *Stevenson* [1932] AC 562 principle did not embrace such a claim. When the defect was discovered, the goods or building ceased to be dangerous, although they remained defective. The loss sustained by the owner, eg in making good the defect, was economic loss. Thus, their Lordships were concerned with examining the interrelation between the *Donoghue* v *Stevenson* principle and a claim by the owner of goods or a building to recover purely economic loss. That examination did not call for a consideration of whether there were any circumstances in which, under *Donoghue* v *Stevenson*, there might be liability for injuries sustained even though the plaintiff was aware of the existence of the hazard. In *Murphy*'s case a statement of the broad principle was sufficient.

That is the context of the passages relied on in the speeches of Lord Keith and Lord Bridge. Given that context, I cannot read those speeches as an expression of view that in no circumstances can a person recover compensation for personal injuries sustained by using defective goods or a defective building once he has become aware of the existence of the defect. The general principle is, indeed, that such a person cannot recover compensation, because in the ordinary way his knowledge of the existence of the dangerous defect, at any rate in the case of goods, will suffice to enable him to avoid the danger. If he finds there is a decomposed snail in his ginger beer he will not drink it. He does not use underwear which he knows contains a mischievous chemical. Thus in *Grant* v *Australian Knitting Mills Ltd* [1936] AC 85 at 105 Lord Wright said:

> The principle of *Donoghue*'s case can only be applied where the defect is hidden and unknown to the consumer, otherwise the directness of cause and effect is absent: the man who consumes or uses a thing which he knows to be noxious cannot complain in respect of whatever mischief follows, because it follows from his own conscious volition in choosing to incur the risk or certainty of mischance.

But knowledge of the existence of a danger does not always enable a person to avoid the danger. In simple cases it does. In other cases, especially where buildings are concerned, it would be absurdly unrealistic to suggest that a person can always take steps to avoid a danger once he knows of its existence, and that if he does not do so he is the author of his own misfortune. Here, as elsewhere, the law seeks to be realistic. Hence the established principle, referred to by this court in *Rimmer*'s case [1985] QB 1 at 14, that knowledge or opportunity for inspection per se, and without regard to any consequences it may have in the circumstances, cannot be conclusive against the plaintiff. Knowledge, or opportunity for inspection, does not by itself always negate the duty of care or break the chain of causation. Whether it does so depends on all the circumstances. It will only do so when it is reasonable to expect the plaintiff to remove or avoid the danger, and unreasonable for him to run the risk of being injured by the danger.

None of this impinges on the rationale underlying the decision in *Murphy*'s case. The rationale of *Murphy*'s case was that the *Donoghue* v *Stevenson* principle is not designed to compensate for losses arising from defects in quality as such; it is designed to compensate for losses arising from physical injuries to persons or damage to other property flowing from the use of a dangerous product when the user, usually through lack of knowledge of the danger, was unable to take steps to avoid the danger. *Rimmer*'s case is consistent with this. In my view it remains good law.

Legatt LJ delivered a concurring judgment.

Appeal dismissed. Leave to appeal to the House of Lords refused.

LATENT DAMAGE ACT 1986

1. Time limits for negligence actions in respect of latent damage not involving personal injuries
The following sections shall be inserted in the Limitations Act 1980 (referred to below in this Act as the 1980 Act) . . .

2. Provisions consequential on section 1
. . .

3. Accrual of cause of action to successive owners in respect of latent damage to property
  (1) Subject to the following provisions of this section, where—

(a)   a cause of action ('the original cause of action') has accrued to any person in respect of any negligence to which damage to any property in which he has an interest is attributable (in whole or in part); and

(b)   another person acquires an interest in that property after the date on which the original cause of action accrued but before the material facts about the damage have become known to any person who, at the time when he first has knowledge of those facts, has any interest in the property;

a fresh cause of action in respect of that negligence shall accrue to that other person on the date on which he acquires his interest in the property.

(2)   A cause of action accruing to any person by virtue of subsection (1) above—

(a)   shall be treated as if based on breach of a duty of care at common law owed to the person to whom it accrues; and

(b)   shall be treated for the purposes of section 14A of the 1980 Act (special time limit for negligence actions where facts relevant to cause of action are not known at date of accrual) as having accrued on the date on which the original cause of action accrued.

(3)   Section 28 of the 1980 Act (extension of limitation period in case of disability) shall not apply in relation to any such cause of action.

(4)   Subsection (1) above shall not apply in any case where the person acquiring an interest in the damaged property is either—

(a)   a person in whom the original cause of action vests by operation of law; or

(b)   a person in whom the interest in that property vests by virtue of any order made by a court under [the Insolvency Act 1986, s. 145].

(5)   For the purposes of subsection (1)(b) above, the material facts about the damage are such facts about the damage as would lead a reasonable person who has an interest in the damaged property at the time when those facts become known to him to consider it sufficiently serious to justify his instituting proceedings for damages against a defendant who did not dispute liability and was able to satisfy a judgment.

(6)   For the purposes of this section a person's knowledge includes knowledge which he might reasonably have been expected to acquire—

(a)   from facts observable or ascertainable by him; or

(b)   from facts ascertained by him with the help of appropriate expert advice which it is reasonable for him to seek;

but a person shall not be taken by virtue of this subsection to have knowledge of a fact ascertainable by him only with the help of expert advice so long as he has taken all reasonable steps to obtain (and, where appropriate, to act on) that advice.

INVERCARGILL CITY COUNCIL v *HAMLIN* [1996] 1 All ER 756

In *Invercargill City Council* v *Hamlin* [1996] 1 All ER 756, the Privy Council approved a departure by the New Zealand courts from the reasoning in *Murphy*. The New Zealand Court of Appeal, following a line of authority developed in that country in preference to *Murphy*, found a local council liable for the negligence of their building inspector (this was not vicarious liability) who had failed to discover that the foundations of the plaintiff's house did not comply with local by-laws.

The house had been built without adequate foundations and as a result it eventually developed cracks and a number of small defects. Since the builder had by now gone out of business the plaintiff sued the council, and it was found that their building inspector should have known that the foundations were inadequate. A reasonably prudent homeowner would not have discovered the cause of the cracks and defects before they appeared.

The council, relying on *D & F Estates* and *Murphy*, appealed to the Privy Council on two points viz.

(i)   the plaintiff's loss was of a purely economic nature, in respect of which the council owed no duty of care; and

(ii)   with regard to limitation periods, in the case of latent defects a cause of action accrued at the time the tort was committed—in the present case at the time of the inspector's negligence—thus, on the facts, the plaintiff's claim was statute-barred.

It was found by the Privy Council that the New Zealand courts were entitled to follow New Zealand authority in preference to *D & F Estates* and *Murphy*, because the policy behind the law in that country was different. Local councils were regarded as being in control of building work via their by-laws, and purchasers of properties **generally** relied on that control. Thus, the council owed a duty of care in negligence to the plaintiff; *D & F Estates* and *Murphy* should not be followed.

In respect of the limitation point, where latent defects existed in buildings damage caused by those defects to the buildings was economic, and not physical in nature. On the facts, therefore, the plaintiff's cause of action did not start until a reasonably prudent houseowner would have discovered the defect i.e. time did **not** start to run against the plaintiff when the negligence took place or when cracks in the building first appeared. Nevertheless, in a case where the damage became so obvious that a reasonably prudent homeowner would call in an expert the economic loss occurred at that point i.e. that was when the fall in market value of the building took place; in such a case the limitation period would not be postponed. (*Pirelli General Cable Works Ltd* v *Oscar Faber and Partners (a firm)* [1983] 1 All ER 65 (HL) was not followed.)

7.1.2   LANDLORDS

McAULEY v *BRISTOL CITY COUNCIL* [1992] 1 All ER 749 (CA)

[T]he court had to consider the following circumstances. The plaintiff was a joint tenant of the defendants who were obliged by the terms of the contract to maintain the structure and exterior of the property, the tenants undertaking to keep the premises (including the garden) 'in a clean and orderly condition'. Condition 6(c) of the tenancy agreement gave the council's agents and employees access to the premises 'for any purpose which may from time to time be required by the council'. The plaintiff was injured due to the movement of a loose concrete step in the garden and sued the defendants, claiming breach of s. 4(1) of the Defective Premises Act 1972 (which imposes a duty of care in negligence upon landlords). Section 4(4) says that the duty applies [*inter alia*] where a landlord has 'an express or implied right to enter the premises to carry out any description of maintenance or repair of the premises'.

At first instance the court (Bristol County Court) found in favour of the plaintiff and awarded her agreed damages of £4,500. However, the defendants appealed, claiming that Condition 6(c) (above) only conferred the right to enter the house to do repairs; there was no right to carry out repairs to the garden for the purposes of s. 4(1) of the 1992 Act.

The Court of Appeal dismissed the appeal applying *Mint* v *Good* [1950] 2 All ER 1159. Condition 6(c) (above) gave the defendants a right of entry which was not limited to their obligations of repair and maintenance, it conferred a right of entry which was not limited to their obligation of repair and maintenance, it conferred a right 'to enter for any purpose for which from time to time entry might be required by the defendants'—only limited to the achievement of lawful purposes. Thus the provision included the exercise by the defendants of any express or implied right to repair. An implied right to repair did not, said their Lordships, depend on whether permission to enter could be obtained from the tenant or whether such permission had in the past been given, but depended on whether, in the case of an unwilling tenant, the landlord could insist on entry and obtain an injunction to enter and effect repairs if necessary. In order to give 'business efficacy' to this tenancy it might be implied that the landlords had a right to enter and repair any defect in the premises, including the garden, which might expose the tenants or visitors to the risk of injury.

7.2   Liability Arising under the Defective Premises Act 1972

DEFECTIVE PREMISES ACT 1972

1.   Duty to build dwellings properly

(1)   A person taking on work for or in connection with the provision of a dwelling (whether the dwelling is provided by the erection or by the conversion or enlargement of a building) owes a duty—

(a)   if the dwelling is provided to the order of any person, to that person; and

(b)   without prejudice to paragraph (a) above, to every person who acquires an interest (whether legal or equitable) in the dwelling;

to see that the work which he takes on is done in a workmanlike or, as the case may be, professional manner, with proper materials and so that as regards that work the dwelling will be fit for habitation when completed.

(2)   A person who takes on any such work for another on terms that he is to do it in accordance with instructions given by or on behalf of that other shall, to the extent to which he does it properly in accordance with those instructions, be treated for the purposes of this section as discharging the duty imposed on him by subsection (1) above except where he owes a duty to that other to warn him of any defects in the instructions and fails to discharge that duty.

(3)   A person shall not be treated for the purposes of subsection (2) above as having given instructions for the doing of work merely because he has agreed to the work being done in a specified manner, with specified materials or to a specified design.

(4)   A person who—

(a)   in the course of a business which consists of or includes providing or arranging for the provision of dwellings or installations in dwellings; or

(b)   in the exercise of a power of making such provision or arrangements conferred by or by virtue of any enactment;

arranges for another to take on work for or in connection with the provision of a dwelling shall be treated for the purposes of this section as included among the persons who have taken on the work.

(5)   Any cause of action in respect of a breach of the duty imposed by this section shall be deemed, for the purposes of the Limitation Act 1939, the Law Reform (Limitation of Actions, etc.) Act 1954 and the Limitation Act 1963, to have accrued at the time when the dwelling was completed, but if after that time a person who has done work for or in connection with the provision of the dwelling does further work to rectify the work he has already done, any such cause of action in respect of that further work shall be deemed for those purposes to have accrued at the time when the further work was finished.

[*The references in s. 1(5) should now be read as to the Limitation Act 1980. See the Limitation Act, s. 40(2); the Interpretation Act 1978, s. 17(2).*]

2.   Cases excluded from the remedy under section 1

(1)   Where—

(a)   in connection with the provision of a dwelling or its first sale or letting for habitation any rights in respect of defects in the state of the dwelling are conferred by an approved scheme to which this section applies on a person having or acquiring an interest in the dwelling; and

(b)   it is stated in a document of a type approved for the purposes of this section that the requirements as to design or construction imposed by or under the scheme have, or appear to have, been substantially complied with in relation to the dwelling;

no action shall be brought by any person having or acquiring an interest in the dwelling for breach of the duty imposed by section 1 above in relation to the dwelling.

(2)   A scheme to which this section applies—

(a)   may consist of any number of documents and any number of agreements or other transactions between any number of persons; but

(b)   must confer, by virtue of agreements entered into with persons having or acquiring an interest in the dwellings to which the scheme applies, rights on such persons in respect of defects in the state of the dwellings.

(3)   In this section 'approved' means approved by the Secretary of State, and the power of the Secretary of State to approve a scheme or document for the purposes of this section shall be exercisable by order, except that any requirements as to construction or design imposed under a scheme to which this section applies may be approved by him without making any order or, if he thinks fit, by order.

(4)   The Secretary of State—

(a)   may approve a scheme or document for the purposes of this section with or without limiting the duration of his approval; and

(b)   may by order revoke or vary a previous order under this section or, without such an order, revoke or vary a previous approval under this section given otherwise than by order.

(5)　The production of a document purporting to be a copy of an approval given by the Secretary of State otherwise than by order and certified by an officer of the Secretary of State to be a true copy of the approval shall be conclusive evidence of the approval, and without proof of the handwriting or official position of the person purporting to sign the certificate.

(6)　The power to make an order under this section shall be exercisable by statutory instrument which shall be subject to annulment in pursuance of a resolution by either House of Parliament.

(7)　Where an interest in a dwelling is compulsorily acquired—

(a)　no action shall be brought by the acquiring authority for breach of the duty imposed by section 1 above in respect of the dwelling; and

(b)　if any work for or in connection with the provision of the dwelling was done otherwise than in the course of a business by the person in occupation of the dwelling at the time of the compulsory acquisition, the acquiring authority and not that person shall be treated as the person who took on the work and accordingly as owing that duty.

3.　Duty of care with respect to work done on premises not abated by disposal of premises

(1)　Where work of construction, repair, maintenance or demolition or any other work is done on or in relation to premises, any duty of care owed, because of the doing of the work, to persons who might reasonably be expected to be affected by defects in the state of the premises created by the doing of the work shall not be abated by the subsequent disposal of the premises by the person who owed the duty.

(2)　This section does not apply—

(a)　in the case of premises which are let, where the relevant tenancy of the premises commenced, or the relevant tenancy agreement of the premises was entered into, before the commencement of this Act;

(b)　in the case of premises disposed of in any other way, when the disposal of the premises was completed, or a contract for their disposal was entered into, before the commencement of this Act; or

(c)　in either case, where the relevant transaction disposing of the premises is entered into in pursuance of an enforceable option by which the consideration for the disposal was fixed before the commencement of this Act.

4.　Landlord's duty of care in virtue of obligation or right to repair premises demised

(1)　Where premises are let under a tenancy which puts on the landlord an obligation to the tenant for the maintenance or repair of the premises the landlord owes to all persons who might reasonably be expected to be affected by defects in the state of the premises a duty to take such care as is reasonable in all the circumstances to see that they are reasonably safe from personal injury or from damage to their property caused by a relevant defect.

(2)　The said duty is owed if the landlord knows (whether as the result of being notified by the tenant or otherwise) or if he ought in all the circumstances to have known of the relevant defect.

(3)　In this section 'relevant defect' means a defect in the state of the premises existing at or after the material time and arising from, or continuing because of, an act or omission by the landlord which constituted or would if he had had notice of the defect, have constituted a failure by him to carry out his obligation to the tenant for the maintenance or repair of the premises; and for the purposes of the foregoing provision the 'material time' means—

(a)　where the tenancy commenced before this Act, the commencement of this Act; and

(b)　in all other cases, the earliest following times, that is to say—

(i)　the time when the tenancy commences;

(ii)　the time when the tenancy agreement is entered into;

(iii)　the time when possession is taken of the premises in contemplation of the letting.

(4)　Where premises are let under a tenancy which expressly or impliedly gives the landlord the right to enter the premises to carry out any description of maintenance or repair of the premises, then, as from the time when he first is, or by notice or otherwise can put himself, in a position to exercise the right and so long as he is or can put himself in that position, he shall be treated for the purposes of subsections (1) to (3) above (but for no other purpose) as if he were under an obligation to the tenant for that description of maintenance or repair of the premises; but the landlord shall not owe the tenant any duty by virtue of this subsection in respect of any defect in the state of the premises arising from, or continuing because of, a failure to carry out an obligation expressly imposed on the tenant by the tenancy.

(5) For the purposes of this section obligations imposed or rights given by any enactment in virtue of a tenancy shall be treated as imposed or given by the tenancy.

(6) This section applies to a right of occupation given by contract or any enactment and not amounting to a tenancy as if the right were a tenancy, and 'tenancy' and cognate expressions shall be construed accordingly.

5. Application to Crown

This Act shall bind the Crown, but as regards the Crown's liability in tort shall not bind the Crown further than the Crown is made liable in tort by the Crown Proceedings Act 1947.

6. Supplemental

(1) In this Act: 'disposal', in relation to premises, includes a letting, and an assignment or surrender of a tenancy, of the premises and the creation by contract of any other right to occupy the premises, and 'dispose' shall be construed accordingly; 'personal injury' includes any disease and any impairment of a person's physical or mental condition . . .

(2) Any duty imposed by or enforceable by virtue of any provision of this Act is in addition to any duty a person may owe apart from that provision.

(3) Any term of an agreement which purports to exclude or restrict, or has the effect of excluding or restricting, the operation of any of the provisions of this Act, or any liability arising by virtue of any such provision, shall be void.

7.3 Occupiers' Liability to Lawful Visitors

OCCUPIERS' LIABILITY ACT 1957

1. Preliminary

(1) The rules enacted by the two next following sections shall have effect, in place of the rules of the common law, to regulate the duty which an occupier of premises owes to his visitors in respect of dangers due to the state of the premises or to things done or omitted to be done on them.

(2) The rules so enacted shall regulate the nature of the duty imposed by law in consequence of a person's occupation or control of premises and of any invitation or permission he gives (or is to be treated as giving) to another to enter or use the premises, but they shall not alter the rules of the common law as to the persons on whom a duty is so imposed or to whom it is owed; and accordingly for the purpose of the rules so enacted the persons who are to be treated as an occupier and as his visitors are the same (subject to subsection (4) of this section) as the persons who would at common law be treated as an occupier and as his invitees or licensees.

(3) The rules so enacted in relation to an occupier of premises and his visitors shall also apply, in like manner and to the like extent as the principles applicable at common law to an occupier of premises and his invitees or licensees would apply, to regulate—

(a) the obligations of a person occupying or having control over any fixed or moveable structure, including any vessel, vehicle or aircraft; and

(b) the obligations of a person occupying or having control over any premises or structure in respect of damage to property, including the property of persons who are not themselves his visitors.

(4) A person entering any premises in exercise of rights conferred by virtue of an access agreement or order under the National Parks and Access to the Countryside Act 1949, is not, for the purposes of this Act, a visitor of the occupier of those premises.

2. Extent of occupier's ordinary duty

(1)   An occupier of premises owes the same duty, the 'common duty of care', to all his visitors, except in so far as he is free to and does extend, restrict, modify or exclude his duty to any visitor or visitors by agreement or otherwise.

(2)   The common duty of care is a duty to take such care as in all the circumstances of the case is reasonable to see that the visitor will be reasonably safe in using the premises for the purposes for which he is invited or permitted by the occupier to be there.

(3)   The circumstances relevant for the present purposes include the degree of care, and of want of care, which would ordinarily be looked for in such a visitor, so that (for example) in proper cases—

(a)   an occupier must be prepared for children to be less careful than adults; and

(b)   an occupier may expect that a person, in the exercise of his calling, will appreciate and guard against any special risks ordinarily incident to it, so far as the occupier leaves him free to do so.

(4)   In determining whether the occupier of premises has discharged the common duty of care to a visitor, regard is to be had to all the circumstances, so that (for example)—

(a)   where damage is caused to a visitor by a danger of which he had been warned by the occupier, the warning is not to be treated without more as absolving the occupier from liability, unless in all the circumstances it was enough to enable the visitor to be reasonably safe; and

(b)   where damage is caused to a visitor by a danger due to the faulty execution of any work of construction, maintenance or repair by an independent contractor employed by the occupier, the occupier is not to be treated without more as answerable for the danger if in all the circumstance he had acted reasonably in entrusting the work to an independent contractor and had taken such steps (if any) as he reasonably ought in order to satisfy himself that the contractor was competent and that the work had been properly done.

(5)   The common duty of care does not impose on an occupier any obligation to a visitor in respect of risks willingly accepted as his by the visitor (the question whether a risk was so accepted to be decided on the same principles as in other cases in which one person owes a duty of care to another).

(6)   For the purposes of this section, persons who enter premises for any purpose in the exercise of a right conferred by law are to be treated as permitted by the occupier to be there for that purpose, whether they in fact have his permission or not.

3. Effect of contract on occupier's liability to third party

(1)   Where an occupier of premises is bound by contract to permit persons who are strangers to the contract to enter or use the premises, the duty of care which he owes to them as his visitors cannot be restricted or excluded by that contract, but (subject to any provision of the contract to the contrary) shall include the duty to perform his obligations under the contract, whether undertaken for their protection or not, in so far as those obligations go beyond the obligations otherwise involved in that duty.

(2)   A contract shall not by virtue of this section have the effect, unless it expressly so provides, of making an occupier who has taken all reasonable care answerable to strangers to the contract for dangers due to the faulty execution of any work of construction, maintenance or repair or other like operation by persons other than himself, his servants and persons acting under his direction and control.

(3)   In this section, 'stranger to the contract' means a person not for the time being entitled to the benefit of the contract as a party to it or as the successor by assignment or otherwise of a party to it, and accordingly includes a party to the contract who has ceased to be so entitled.

(4)   Where by the terms or conditions governing any tenancy (including a statutory tenancy which does not in law amount to a tenancy) either the landlord or the tenant is bound, though not by contract, to permit persons to enter or use premises of which he is the occupier, this section shall apply as if the tenancy were a contract between the landlord and the tenant.

(5)   This section, in so far as it prevents the common duty of care from being restricted or excluded, applies to contracts entered into and tenancies created before the commencement of the Act, as well as to those entered into or created after its commencement; but, in so far as it enlarges the duty owed by an occupier beyond the common duty of care, it shall have effect only in relation to obligations which are undertaken after the commencement or which are renewed by agreement (whether express or implied) after that commencement.

. . .

5. Implied term in contracts

(1) Where persons enter or use, or bring or send goods to, any premises in exercise of a right conferred by contract with a person occupying or having control of the premises, the duty he owes them in respect of dangers due to the state of the premises or to things done or omitted to be done by them, in so far as the duty depends on a term to be implied in the contract by reason of its conferring that right, shall be the common duty of care.

(2) The foregoing subsection shall apply to fixed and moveable structures as it applies to premises.

(3) This section does not affect the obligations imposed on a person by or by virtue of any contract for the hire of, or for the carriage for reward of persons or goods in, any vehicle, vessel, aircraft or other means of transport, or by virtue of any contract of bailment.

(4) This section does not apply to contracts entered into before the commencement of this Act.

7.3.1 OCCUPIER

HARRIS v BIRKENHEAD CORPORATION [1976] 1 All ER 341 (CA)

In this case the defendant corporation acquired X's house by means of a compulsory purchase order. This statutory procedure gave the corporation an immediate right to enter the premises and this was found by the court sufficient to make the corporation occupier of the house though it had never actually controlled the property. The right to control was enough.

X had let the house to Y, who became the corporation's tenant when the property was compulsorily acquired. Y vacated the premises without informing the corporation and the property became derelict. Children played on the premises and the plaintiff, who was 4 years old, entered as a trespasser and was injured. The corporation was found liable at first instance and the Court of Appeal confirmed this finding.

7.3.2 'LAWFUL VISITOR'

7.3.2.1 Implied permission

FERGUSON v WELSH [1987] 3 All ER 777 (HL)

It was found on an issue relating to the **pleadings** in this case, pleadings that the plaintiff, injured because his employers used an unsafe system for demolishing a building, could not establish liability either under the 1957 Act or under any other branch of law against the owners of the building who had engaged independent contractors to do the demolition work—even where it could be established that the contractor had sub-contracted the job to the plaintiff's employers in disobedience of a prohibition in his contract with the owners. The owners of the building, a local authority, accepted that they were occupiers (with the contractor) but disputed the plaintiff's status as a visitor.

Lord Keith thought there was sufficient evidence to support the argument that (notwithstanding the wrongful sub-contracting of the work) the contractor had ostensible authority from the council to invite the sub-contractors and their employees on to the site. The contractor was put in control of the site for demolition purposes 'and to one who had no knowledge of the council's policy of prohibiting sub-contractors that would indicate that he was entitled to invite whomsoever he pleased on to the site for the purpose of carrying out demolition.' His Lordship said s. 2(4)(b) did not specifically refer to demolition 'but a broad and purposive interpretation might properly lead to the conclusion that demolition was embraced by the word "construction". In certain circumstances it could be inferred that an occupier might be liable 'for something done or omitted to be done on his premises by an independent contractor if he did not take reasonable steps to satisfy himself that the contractor was competent and that the work was being properly done'. Furthermore, there might be 'special circumstances where the occupier knew or had reason to suspect that the contractor was using an unsafe system of work' and the occupier might be expected to take reasonable steps to see that the system was made safe. In the present case there was insufficient evidence to suggest that the council knew or ought to have known that the contractor would ignore the prohibition in his contract or that an unsafe system of work would be adopted.

Lords Brandon and Griffiths agreed.

Lord Oliver agreed, but said if an occupier were to be found liable in such a case he would be liable as a joint tortfeasor.

Lord Goff concurred but said, on the assumption that the plaintiff was a visitor, there was no question 'of the plaintiff's injury arising from a failure by the council to take reasonable care to see that persons in the plaintiff's position would be reasonably safe "in using the premises" for the relevant purposes; for it arose not from his use of the premises but from the manner in which he carried out his work on the premises'. Thus, the 1957 Act did not have anything to do with the present case.

7.3.3   ENTRY BY CONTRACT

SOLE v WJ HALLT LTD [1973] 1 QB 574

The plaintiff was engaged by the defendants, who were building contractors, to carry out work at a house. Whilst working on a staircase without a handrail, he stepped back whilst looking at the ceiling he was installing and was injured when he fell into the staircase well. He claimed damages alleging breach of contract and negligence on the part of the defendants. It was held:

(a)   The defendants were in breach of their common duty of care under s. 2(1) of the Occupiers' Liability Act 1957.

(b)   Since the plaintiff entered the house as a result of a contract with the defendants, s. 5 of the Act imposed on the defendants an implied term of owing the common duty of care to the plaintiff.

(c)   The plaintiff was not confined to claiming under the implied term; he had the option of claiming under s. 2 as a visitor.

(d)   Had his claim only been in contract, his contributory negligence constituting a break in the chain of causation would have been a defence to the claim. But since he had a claim in tort, he was entitled to receive damages reduced in proportion to the extent of his own contributory negligence.

(i)   The court held that the common duty of care imposed by the 1957 Act required the defendant here to provide for his visitor, viz the plaintiff, boards which the plaintiff could use to cover up the open stair well. 'To provide' meant to have boards readily available, 'in a place handy, near the foot or head of the stairs and being obviously available to cover up the well'. Had the defendant supplied boards and subsequently observed that the plaintiff was not using them, then the common duty of care would require the defendant at least to point out that the boards were available for the plaintiff's protection. On the facts, boards had not been provided and there was therefore a breach of the duty owed to the visitor. The judge was satisfied that, had boards been provided, the plaintiff would have used them—so establishing a causal connection between the breach and the damage.

(ii)   In the contract, of the labour-only type, there was no term as to safety provisions. Thus the 1957 Act implied the common duty of care. As there had been a breach of that duty, a breach of contract had also occurred; but the damage was caused by the plaintiff's contributory negligence and not by the breach of contract. Thus the action in contract failed.

On the contractual claim, the judge applied *Quinn* v *Burch Bros* [1966] 2 QB 370 on the question of contributory negligence. In that case, on somewhat similar facts (the defendant, in breach of contract, had not supplied a ladder; the plaintiff used a trestle which slipped, causing him injury) the Court of Appeal held that the plaintiff's negligence, and not the breach of contract, had caused the injury. Salmond LJ said: the defendants realised that if there was a breach of contract on their part to supply the ladder that breach would afford the plaintiff the opportunity of acting negligently, and that he might take it and thereby suffer injury. But it seems to me quite impossible to say that in reality the plaintiff's injury was caused by the breach of contract. The breach of contract merely gave the plaintiff the opportunity to injure himself. Sellers LJ observed that the position would have been very different if the breach of contract had been the supplying of a faulty ladder.

(iii)   It is possible to conclude from *Sole* v *Hallt*, where the duties in both contract and tort were the same, that the Law Reform (Contributory Negligence) Act is not applicable to actions for breach of a contractual duty. If, however, the remarks of Sellers LJ in *Quinn* v *Burch Bros* are taken to indicate that the Act may apply, then *Sole*'s case demonstrates that there may be greater difficulty in establishing a causal connection between the accident and the breach of contract when the latter consists of a complete failure to perform (non-feasance) than when it consists of faulty performance (mis-feasance). In tort actions where contributory negligence is pleaded there is not such a marked concern with questions of causation.

7.3.4 EXCLUSION OF AN OCCUPIER'S LIABILITY UNDER THE 1957 ACT

7.3.4.1 Notice

WHITE v *BLACKMORE* [1972] 3 All ER 158 (CA)

Ashdown v *Samuel Williams* was applied in *White* v *Blackmore* [1972] 2 QB 651. The plaintiff was the widow of White and sued the defendants for negligently causing his death. White was a competitor in 'jalopy' cases of which the defendants were the organisers. He took his wife and child to the races. At the entrance to the field in which the races were being held, and around the track, were exhibited notices which stated: 'Warning to the public. Motor racing is dangerous. It is a condition of admission that all persons having any connection with the promotion and/or organisation and/or conduct of the meeting . . . are absolved from all liabilities arising out of accidents causing damage or personal injury . . . however caused to spectators or ticket-holders'. Since White was a competitor in the races he entered free; his wife and child paid for admission. (It was accepted by both sides in the case that White was not a 'ticket-holder' within the meaning of the notice.) The organisers of the events had arranged the lay-out of the safety-ropes, so that all the ropes, ie the rope around the spectators' enclosure, the pit boundary-rope and the double safety-rope around the track were attached to a single master stake. White left his wife and child in the spectators' enclosure and took part in one race. Afterwards, he joined his family in order to watch the following races, intending to compete again later. He ought to have got under the spectators' rope, but instead he stayed on the track side of the rope, standing next to the master stake. Whilst he was watching a race, the wheel of a competing car caught in the double safety-rope some distance away and all the stakes, including the master stake, were pulled out. He was thrown into the air by the master stake and ropes and later died from his injuries. The trial judge found that the defendants were negligent in tying all the ropes to one stake and were therefore in breach of the common duty of care under s. 2(4)(a) of the 1957 Act. White, however, was one-third to blame for the accident. Since he had clearly seen and understood the notices excluding liability, the defence of *volenti* applied.

On appeal by the wife the Court of Appeal held that *volenti* did not apply where the risk of injury arose not from participation in the dangerous sport but from the organisers' failure to take reasonable precautions for the safety of visitors to the meeting. Since White did not have full knowledge of the risk involved from the faulty lay-out of the ropes, he had not willingly accepted that risk. Nevertheless, their liability was excluded under the 1957 Act, s. 2(1), and this they had done by posting the warning notices, the heading of which . . . 'Warning to the Public' . . . was not to be construed restrictively to exclude competitors.

There was a variance of opinion in the Court of Appeal on the question of exclusion of liability where there is no contractual relationship. Lord Denning, dissented from the above verdict and said '. . . in the absence of contract, the organisers of a sports meeting cannot get out of their responsibilities by putting up warning notices'. The warning notices were not part of a contract, but only warned the visitor of his position at common law. 'Otherwise' in s. 2(1) did not absolve the defendants from liability, as under s. 2(4)(a) of the Act the warning must be sufficient in all the circumstances to enable the visitor to be safe, which was not so in this case. Buckley LJ held, however, that s. 2(4)(a) did not apply here; the notices of exemption, which White must have seen, effectively excluded liability even though no contract had been made between the defendant and White.

7.3.5 DAMAGE

SMITH v *VANGE SCAFFOLDING AND ANOTHER* [1970] 1 All ER 249

The plaintiff was employed by the first defendants, who were independent contractors working on a building site which was occupied by the main contractors, the second defendant. At dusk, the plaintiff was finishing work, and walking to the workmen's hut, when he tripped over a cable which had been left suspended 9 inches above the ground by an employee of the second defendant. The plaintiff was injured. The first defendant had known that the site was excessively untidy but had not complained. Apparently the second defendant had made no effort to keep the site tidy, or to provide safe routes for the workmen.

The plaintiff succeeded in an action against his employers. Their failure to complain was a breach of the duty of care owed by an employer to his employee and was a cause of the accident. He was also successful against the second defendant on two grounds:

(i)   they were vicariously liable for the negligence of their employee in leaving the cable as, in effect, a trip wire; and

(ii)   they were occupiers, and were in breach of their duty under the 1957 Act.

This finding, against the second defendant, is interesting in that, although there was liability both in negligence and under the **Occupiers' Liability Act**, this dual liability was said to arise only where there is, as here, vicarious liability for the former. The 'neighbour' principle cannot be used to create a primary duty when the duty is already fully covered by the Act. (There was also liability for breach of certain statutory regulations.)

7.4   Occupiers' Liability to Entrants other than Visitors coming within the Terms of the 1957 Act

OCCUPIERS' LIABILITY ACT 1984

1.   Duty of occupier to persons other than his visitors

(1)   The rules enacted by this section shall have effect, in place of the rules of the common law, to determine—

(a)   whether any duty is owed by a person as occupier of premises to persons other than his visitors in respect of any risk of their suffering injury on the premises by reason of any danger due to the state of the premises or to things done or omitted to be done on them; and

(b)   if so, what that duty is.

(2)   For the purposes of this section, the persons who are to be treated respectively as an occupier of any premises (which, for those purposes, include any fixed or movable structure) and as his visitors are—

(a)   any person who owes in relation to the premises the duty referred to in section 2 of the Occupiers' Liability Act 1957 (the common duty of care), and

(b)   those who are his visitors for the purposes of that duty.

(3)   An occupier of premises owes a duty to another (not being his visitor) in respect of any such risk as is referred to in subsection (1) above if—

(a)   he is aware of the danger or has reasonable grounds to believe that it exists;

(b)   he knows or has reasonable grounds to believe that the other is in the vicinity of the danger concerned or that he may come into the vicinity of the danger (in either case, whether the other has lawful authority for being in that vicinity or not); and

(c)   the risk is one against which, in all the circumstances of the case, he may reasonably be expected to offer the other some protection.

(4)   Where, by virtue of this section, an occupier of premises owes a duty to another in respect of such a risk, the duty is to take such care as is reasonable in all the circumstances of the case to see that he does not suffer injury on the premises by reason of the danger concerned.

(5)   Any duty owed by virtue of this section in respect of a risk may, in an appropriate case, be discharged by taking such steps as are reasonable in all the circumstances of the case to give warning of the danger concerned or to discourage persons from incurring the risk.

(6)   No duty is owed by virtue of this section to any person in respect of risks willingly accepted as his by that person (the question whether a risk was so accepted to be decided on the same principles as in other cases in which one person owes a duty of care to another).

(7)   No duty is owed by virtue of this section to persons using the highway, and this section does not affect any duty owed to such persons.

(8)   Where a person owes a duty by virtue of this section, he does not, by reason of any breach of the duty, incur any liability in respect of any loss of or damage to property.

(9)   In this section—

'highway' means any part of a highway other than a ferry or waterway;
'injury' means anything resulting in death or personal injury, including any disease and any impairment of physical or mental condition; and
'movable structure' includes any vessel, vehicle or aircraft.

. . .

3.   Application to Crown

Section 1 of this Act shall bind the Crown, but as regards the Crown's liability in tort shall not bind the Crown further than the Crown is made liable in tort by the Crown Proceedings Act 1947.

7.4.1   THE DUTY OF COMMON HUMANITY

PANNETT v *McGUINNESS & CO. LTD* [1972] 3 All ER 137

In *Pannett* v *McGuinness & Co. Ltd* [1972] 3 All ER 137, which was decided after *Herrington's Case*, the Court of Appeal appears to have rejected the distinction between the tests of 'common humanity' and reasonable care. Lord Denning's judgment refers to the necessity of taking such reasonable care as the circumstances of the case demand. Certainly, in the case of trespassing children where there are dangerous circumstances, it seems that the duty of an occupier is to take reasonable care. The facts of this case are as follows. The defendants were contractors working on the demolition of a warehouse which adjoined a park used by children. The work entailed lighting fires in the warehouse to burn rubbish, and three men were appointed to warn children to keep away. The plaintiff, aged five, having previously been warned off before any fires were lit, returned when the men were absent from the site and was injured when he fell into a fire.

It was held that because of the great likelihood of children entering the warehouse and the extra hazard of the fires, common sense and common humanity imposed on the defendants the duty to take all reasonable steps for the safety of children who might trespass on the site. This they had not done and they were liable to the plaintiff.

7.5 End of Chapter Assessment Question

Lax, a students' law society, has organised a dance for its members only at Isadora's, a local nightspot. At the time of the dance the management of Isadora's are in the process of having a new lighting system installed by Flashers Ltd, electrical contractors, and a notice at the entrance to the club reads, 'Beware. Electrical Work in Progress'. Art and Bart, two members of Lax, and Catherine, Bart's 15-year-old girlfriend, turn up for the dance and are admitted on producing tickets which state, 'Valid to Lax members only'. Art is injured when he trips over a trestle left by Flashers in the foyer, which is dimly lit. Bart is injured when a revolving light falls on his head as he is dancing. Catherine goes in search of a toilet through a door marked 'private' and is electrocuted when she feels for a light switch and touches some bare electric wires left by Flashers Ltd.

Discuss the tortious issues, if any, arising in the circumstances.

7.6 End of Chapter Assessment Outline Answer

L = Lax, I = Isadora's, F = Flashers Ltd, A = Art, B = Bart and C = Catherine

A, B and C are all injured on 'premises' i.e. I's 'nightspot', which is presumably a type of nightclub. The law imposes special liability with regard to injuries sustained on premises, and this liability can arise under statute and/or the common law. The liability in question is imposed upon occupiers of those premises, as well as upon other persons.

Occupiers of 'premises' have a duty to take reasonable care for the safety of their 'visitors' under the Occupiers' Liability Act 1957 (the 'common duty of care', which is a duty of care in negligence: s. 2(1)(2)), and a duty to take such care as is reasonable in the circumstances to avoid personal injury to their non-visitors – including trespassers – under the Occupiers' Liability Act 1984 (s. 1(4): a duty wide enough to encompass intentional behaviour as well as negligence). In addition, liability with regard to 'current activities' may arise; but this form of liability, which is not restricted to occupiers *qua* (i.e. **as**) occupiers, is governed by ordinary common law negligence.

The liability of non-occupiers for injuries suffered by **any** entrants on the premises – whether or not those injuries are connected to current activities – will fall to be considered in common law negligence. Independent contractors working on premises would, where appropriate, be liable in this way.

Since the events catalogued in the problem at hand indicate that the sources of danger presented to the entrants are concerned with the actual state of the premises at the time of the injuries, rather than with things done or omitted to be done on the premises, e.g. *Revill* v *Newbery*, the issue of 'current activities' will not be explored in this answer.

On the facts, I is likely to be regarded as having sufficient 'control' (an issue of **fact** in the circumstances of each case: *Wheat* v *Lacon* – because business 'as normal' is apparently being conducted on the 'premises'; see s. 1(3), 1957 Act and s. 1(2) of the 1984 Act) to be in occupation of the nightclub at the relevant time. F may also have sufficient temporary control to qualify as 'occupier', at least in respect of the foyer (the presence of the trestle may suggest this; no information is available regarding the dancing area) but ultimately, as we have seen, this is a question of fact to be determined on the facts of the case. Occupation can be shared, or different persons can be in occupation of different parts of premises: *Wheat* v *Lacon*; *Fisher* v *CHT*.

Thus, on the facts, I and F could, for example, be in joint occupation of the foyer.

It is perhaps unlikely, but not inconceivable, that L might also have enough temporary control to be classed as an occupier. The terms of the arrangement (presumably of a contractual nature) between L and I might have something to say on this matter, but it is not an issue which can be pursued here.

If L is not an occupier it is difficult to see how the society could be liable otherwise than through the contract of admission (L has organised the event and issued tickets); and by that vector a duty of care in negligence at common law may arise (a *Donoghue* v *Stevenson* duty). It is not proposed to examine the issue of **contractual** liability nor the question of **concurrent** liability in contract with L because the tickets allowing entry to I's are for members only. With regard to the possibility of L's liability in **negligence**, however, the facts do not indicate any evidence of negligence on L's part though the issue of L having reponsibility for the negligent organisation/supervision of the event (perhaps together with I) must be left open as an arguable point. (If the society were pursued the technical problem of suing an unincorporated association – which L is likely to be – would have to be borne in mind.)

In view of the uncertainty concerning L's role in the events leading to the injuries suffered, discussion in this opinion is accordingly focused on the potential liability of I and F towards, in the first instance, A and B; C is dealt with separately, in view of the nature of her entry on to the premises.

A and B

Both I and F as 'occupiers' (see s. 1(2), 1957 Act and *Wheat* v *Lacon*) of the 'premises' (I's nightspot) (s. 1(3), 1957 Act) owe the 'common duty of care' (s. 2(1)(2), 1957 Act) to A and B, as their lawful 'visitors' (s. 1(2)(4), 1957 Act). In fact, A and B have entered the premises not merely as invitees/licensees: they have entered, probably, under the terms of an agreement (presumably a contract) between L and I for the use of the premises for the event in question. Thus, s. 3 of the 1957 Act will probably be relevant. (The tickets are likely to be issued in pursuance of an agreement – presumably contractual – between L and its members; A and B are members of L.)

There is no evidence that the agreement provides for a degree of care greater than that laid down in the 1957 Act, therefore it will be assumed that the 'common duty of care' will apply in the circumstances.

The 1957 Act imposes a duty based on proof of **negligence** on the part of the occupier: as Mocatta J put it in *AMF* v *Magnet Bowling*, occupiers are not to be regarded as insurers against all risks. Thus, there must be evidence of negligence on the part of an occupier for liability to arise under the Act. It is for the plaintiff to prove this.

Under the terms of s. 2(4)(a) of the 1957 Act a warning notice **may** exonerate the defendant but only **exceptionally** is a notice on its own (i.e. without any further measure taken in conjunction with the notice) likely to be enough. On the facts, the notice may only warn of the electrical work in progress; it is a moot point whether it adequately warns of a trestle placed in a dimly-lit foyer. Perhaps better lighting would be in order whilst the work is going on. Does the trestle have to be there at the time? It must be said, however, that it is not clear at all on the facts whether the trestle is an obvious danger in the circumstances. Perhaps the provisions of the Law Reform (Contributory Negligence) Act 1945 would apply, providing a partial defence to A's claim.

With regard to the falling light, it is again arguable whether the warning notice gives adequate warning of the relevant danger. Does the notice not refer only to the dangers inherent in electrical installation, such as exposure to bare wires and the like? It may be doubted whether the notice even brings an entrant's attention to the relevant **risk** (*volenti non fit injuria*: s. 2(5), 1957 Act) let alone the nature of the danger in question. It may also be relevant to refer to s. 2(4)(b) of the 1957 Act. An occupier here may seek to discharge his obligation by pointing to the fact that he has employed a reasonably competent contractor (presumably F meets this requirement) to perform the work which causes the injury: e.g. *Haseldine* v *Daw*; *Woodward* v *Mayor of Hastings*.

There is authority for the proposition that a simple task, such as ensuring entrances are clear of obstacles (or at least that visitors are sufficiently aware of such dangers) would attract liability to the occupier/employer in spite of the involvement of an independent contractor (see *Woodward*). The task of guarding against the dangers presented by the trestle could hardly be regarded as an onerous one.

It may be further argued that the accident occurs in the **foyer** (through which all visitors will enter the premises) and I is still running the business, therefore a special, non-delegable duty is owed by I.

The falling light incident may be different – it could be argued that detailed (or even **any**?) supervision by I is unnecessary where a competent contractor is employed to perform the task (*Haseldine*).

With regard to establishing a breach of duty on the facts, the trestle's presence must be due to someone's carelessness – although *res ipsa loquitur* may be employed in case of difficulty. The same is true of the falling light. (This point is also relevant should F be sued in ordinary negligence – below.)

If F does not 'occupy' the foyer and/or the dancing area (a matter of control – above) the company will still owe a duty of care in common law negligence to A and B: *Billings* v *Riden*; *Sharpe* v *Sweeting*.

There may also be vicarious liability on the part of F for the negligence of any identified employees who have caused the injuries to A and B.

C

It is likely that C will be regarded as a trespasser on the premises; in which case the liability of any occupier will be governed by the terms of the Occupiers' Liability Act 1984. C is unlikely to be a member of L, therefore her presence has not been authorised. It could be said that she has gained entry by deception: the management of I are likely to admit all ticket bearers at their 'face value'.

On the other hand, perhaps the management has decided to ignore the (initially) authorised entry (C's age may betray her, for instance) and has in effect 'allowed' her on to the premises by means of some tacit licence. In which case, it could be argued that C becomes a visitor (1957 Act).

The facts indicate, however, that C is a trespasser when she walks through the door marked 'private', after all, she is 15 years of age and should appreciate the meaning of that word. (If she were to be regarded as a visitor under the terms of the 1957 Act, it is submitted that s. 2(3)(a) of that Act would not apply because C could not be regarded as a 'child' – unless perhaps it was known or ought to be known that she could not read or was in some other relevant respect incompetent.)

In any event, the 'conditions of entry' set out in s. 1(3) of the Occupiers' Liability Act 1984 (s. 1(3)(a)(b)(c) should be explained in the form of a summary) would have to be satisfied. The requirement of knowledge, actual or implied of the entrant's presence (or potential presence) – see s. 1(3)(b) – may be difficult for C to satisfy in the circumstances. Furthermore, s. 1(3)(c) says that the risk in question must be of a kind where it is **reasonable** that the occupier should offer the entrant some protection and this matter should be considered in the light of 'all the circumstances of the case'. It may be thought that this requirement would place another difficult obstacle in C's path to recovery of damages.

The 'actual' duty set out in the 1984 Act (s. 1(4)) is to take such care as is reasonable in all the circumstances of the case to see that the entrant is not injured because of the danger in question. Even if C were to reach this stage successfully it is evident that the court is given considerable discretion in framing the occupier's obligation to fit the particular picture.

Otherwise, 'bare' wires do present a pretty obvious danger (albeit behind a door marked 'private') and, assuming argument reached this stage, the employment of independent contractors – implicitly accepted in the 1984 Act as evidence that the occupier has discharged his duty – might not convince the court that I is not liable on the facts.

F should still be considered as potential occupiers in this situation; in this case, similar arguments would be advanced. If F were found not to be occupiers in the particular context, ('bare' wires may indicate work is in progress in this area and therefore there might be sufficient 'control' on F's part) C could still proceed in negligence – even as a trespasser: *Buckland* v *Guildford Gas Co*. Would her presence be reasonably foreseeable in the circumstances? This may be doubtful on the evidence available.

Again, if a servant of F's could be identified, vicarious liability is possible – although reasonable foreseeability of C's presence in relation to the servant's negligence would be in issue.

The provisions of the Civil Liability (Contributions) Act 1978 would apply between the potential defendants, where appropriate.

CHAPTER EIGHT

THE ACTION FOR BREACH OF STATUTORY DUTY AND THE EMPLOYERS' COMMON LAW DUTY OF CARE TO THEIR EMPLOYEES

8.1 The Action for Breach of Statutory Duty

8.1.1 A SPECIAL REMEDY

8.1.1.1 Benefit of a class

CALVELEY v *CHIEF CONSTABLE OF MERSEYSIDE* [1989] 1 All ER 1025

The House of Lords in *Calveley* v *Chief Constable of Merseyside* [1989] 1 All ER 1025 held that a police officer who alleges that disciplinary proceedings against him have been misconducted has no cause of action against his chief constable or the investigating officer in negligence or breach of statutory duty arising out of the Police Act 1964 or the Police (Discipline) Regulations 1977.

LORD BRIDGE: It has not been, nor could be, seriously argued that the duty imposed by s. 49 of the 1964 Act and reg. 6 of the 1977 Regulations to investigate a complaint by a member of the public against a member of a police force was intended to give a cause of action in damages to the member of the police force who is the subject of the complaint if the duty is not performed. Whether the officer conducting the investigation owes a duty of care at common law to the person under investigation is quite a different question. It was, however, submitted that the duty under reg. 7 to give notice to the member subject to investigation as soon as is practicable of the matters alleged against him was intended to give the member a cause of action in damages if not performed. That the duty is imposed for the benefit of the police officer subject to investigation is plain. But it seems to me equally plain that the legislature cannot have contemplated that the object of the duty was to protect the officer from any injury of a kind attracting compensation and cannot therefore have been intended to give him a right to damages for breach of duty. The duty is imposed as a procedural step to protect the position of the officer subject to investigation in relation to any proceedings which may be brought against him. If he is not prejudiced in any such proceedings by failure to perform the duty, he has no ground of complaint. If, as in the case of the plaintiffs . . . the delay in giving notice under reg. 7 coupled with other factors causes irremediable prejudice to the officer in disciplinary proceedings which result in his conviction of an offence against the discipline code, he has his remedy by way of judicial review to quash that conviction and nullify its consequences . . .

8.1.1.2   Public rights and particular damage

Winfield and Jolowicz on Tort, pp. 197–8

The rather battered decision in *Lonrho Ltd* v *Shell Petroleum Co. Ltd (No 2)* also spoke of another exception to the general proposition that the consequences of breach of a statute were prima facie confined to the sanction expressly set forth in the statute. A civil action might lie if the statute created a public right and the plaintiff suffered 'special damage peculiar to himself' from interference with that right. This is rather obscure. It bears some resemblance to the principle upon which an individual can bring a civil action for a public nuisance (one of the cases cited in *Lonrho* being on that tort) but the principal authority relied on concerned not an action for damages but the issue whether a member of the public could, without the assistance of the Attorney-General, seek an injunction to restrain an interference with public rights. However, it was said in *Lonrho* that 'a mere prohibition on members of the public generally from doing what it would otherwise be lawful for them to do is not enough' to create a public right for this purpose. Until this is further elucidated it seems fairly safe to assume that a plaintiff who has failed to show by other means that a criminal statute infringed by the defendant gives him a direct right of action is not very likely to succeed by this route either.

The law on inferring civil actions from statutory duties is not very satisfactory and Lord Denning MR commented with perhaps a little pardonable exaggeration that the legislature 'has left the courts with a guess-work puzzle. The dividing line between the pro-cases and the contra-cases is so blurred and so ill-defined that you might as well toss a coin to decide it.' As Lord du Parcq pointed out the draftsmen of Acts of Parliament are aware of the principles—and lack of principles—applied by the courts to fill the gaps left in legislation, and it can be argued, therefore, that the silence of a statute on the question of civil remedies for its breach is a deliberate invitation to the courts to decide the question for themselves. Certainly it should not be assumed that where the statute is silent this is because its promoters have not adverted to the point—much more likely that it would be politically inconvenient to attempt to answer the question one way or the other. If this is so, then the pretence of seeking for the non-existent intention of Parliament should be abandoned. Not only does it involve an unnecessary fiction, but it may lead to decisions being made on the basis of insignificant details of phraseology instead of matters of substance. If the question whether a person injured by breach of statutory duty is to have a right of action for damages is in truth a question to be decided by the courts, then it should be acknowledged as such and some useful principles of law developed, if that is possible. If it is not, then at least a clear overall presumption might help. At least it can be said that there are numerous decisions on particular statutes so that in many cases it is already settled that a right of action does or does not exist. Even where a right of action has been held to exist, however, it is not enough for the plaintiff simply to prove breach of the statute. There are other elements in the tort which we must now consider. We may, however, note that where the statute creates a criminal offence the victim may choose to seek a compensation order from the criminal court, a procedure which is not dependent upon the establishing of a civil right of action. Though applicable to all criminal offences outside the road traffic field, this mechanism has so far been of limited importance in the type of case considered in this chapter but its role in compensating losses may be expected to increase.

DEAR v *NEWHAM LBC*, *The Times*, 24 February 1988

In *Dear* v *Newham LBC* it was found by the Court of Appeal that a local authority had no obligation to remove items of rubbish from a flat if those items did not fit into a dustbin.

The defendant council had made a bye-law under the Public Health Act 1936 requiring occupiers to put all house refuse in dustbins, and a weekly refuse collection service was operated by the council. However, refuse collectors would remove only refuse which had been put into dustbins and placed in the street.

The plaintiff child suing through her uncle, was injured when she fell from a balcony at her home. The balcony was obstructed by rubbish which the plaintiff's mother had placed there. This rubbish was found in the roof space by the mother when she moved into the flat, and she had made several unsuccessful requests to the council for the removal of this refuse.

At first instance, the council was found to be in breach of their duty under the 1936 Act, to remove refuse and of their duty of care at common law. They were, therefore, liable to the plaintiff.

On appeal, the council claimed that the rubbish was not 'house refuse' within the meaning of s. 72 of the 1936 Act (duty to remove 'house refuse'). According to Slade LJ, this phrase was not defined by Parliament in the Act and the court could not 'insert a definition by a process of judicial legislation'. In the circumstances, said his Lordship, the council's claim was correct: their definition of 'house refuse' accorded with the ordinary use of language and this approach was given strong support by s. 72(3) (1936 Act) which empowered local authorities to provide dustbins and make bye-laws requiring their use.

> Such power would be of limited use if it remained open to a householder to serve a notice requiring the local authority to remove bulky items of rubbish which were not capable of fitting in a dustbin.

It was more likely that the legislature intended such items to be dealt with by s. 74 (which empowers a local authority, at an occupier's request, to 'remove any refuse . . . which they are under no obligation to remove'). Since the council were under no obligation to remove the rubbish in this case, they owed no duty of care to the plaintiff.

RICHARDSON v PITT-STANLEY AND OTHERS [1995] 1 All ER 460 (CA)

RUSSELL LJ: The question raised in this appeal is easily defined but more difficult to resolve. Surprisingly there is no reported decision on the point in this court or elsewhere.

On 1 July 1989 the plaintiff suffered a serious mutilating injury to his hand in an accident that occurred during the course of his employment by Bridge Metals (Basildon) Ltd in their factory at Basildon. It seems that there was a clear breach of s. 14(1) of the Factories Act 1961 which resulted in the injury. In due course the plaintiff obtained judgment against the company with damages to be assessed. Thereafter the company went into liquidation, there being no assets to satisfy any judgment. Furthermore it emerged that the company had not taken out any insurance cover in respect of their liability to their employees injured as was the plaintiff.

By a writ issued on 18 June 1992, indorsed with a statement of claim the plaintiff commenced proceedings against five defendants. The first four were directors of the limited company and the fifth was the company secretary. There was an entirely separate allegation made against the first defendant in his capacity as manager of the company but that does not arise for discussion in this judgment.

Paragraphs 7, 8, 9, 10 and 11 of the statement of claim asserted that all five defendants had committed an offence under s. 5 of the Employer's Liability (Compulsory Insurance) Act 1969 and that consequently the plaintiff had suffered 'loss in an amount equal to the sum which he would have recovered inclusive of damages, interest and costs against the said company had it been properly insured'.

In my judgment the 1969 Act is and was intended to be a statute within the confines of our criminal law. I say this in regard not only to employers but a fortiori in regard to directors. The plaintiff's remedy against the company subsisted at common law and under the 1961 Act. The failure to insure did not deprive the plaintiff of his remedy as such, but rather the enforcement of that remedy by way of the recovery of damages.

In the past, criminal statutes have created civil liability in the field of personal injury litigation but generally the breach of the statute has resulted in direct physical injury to the plaintiff. Not so in this case. The breach of the 1969 statute in this case does no more than involve the plaintiff in economic loss, namely the inability to recover damages. So far as the company is concerned the failure to insure does not provide an effective remedy to the injured workman. He can recover his damages from the assets of the company if there are any; if there are none the absence of insurance does not avail him.

All these considerations, in my judgment, tend to establish that the statute was not intended to create civil liability on the part of the employer. Without the creation of that liability, I cannot believe that directors of a corporate employer could be liable . . .

In my judgment there are a number of distinguishing features between *Monk* v *Warbey* [1935] 1 KB 75 and the instant case. The owner of the motor vehicle, unlike the employer, has no direct liability to the injured party in a road traffic accident occasioned by the negligence of the driver to whom the vehicle has been lent. Secondly, the wording of the s. 143 of the 1972 Act is different to the wording of the 1969 Act. In the former the words used are 'it shall not be lawful' whereas those words do not appear in the 1969 statute. Thirdly, the position of anyone other than the owner of the vehicle is not dealt with by the 1972 Act, and if a director of a company which owns a vehicle has been involved in the failure to insure, the 1972 Act does not create direct criminal responsibility on the part of the director.

In all these circumstances I have come to the conclusion that the judge fell into error in holding that paras 7, 9, 10 and 11 of the statement of claim do disclose a cause of action. I would allow the appeal and restore the order of the master.

STUART-SMITH LJ: . . . In my opinion, there are a number of features about this Act, and ss 1 and 5 in particular, which point against a director who is guilty of an offence under s. 5 being civilly liable.

(1)   Section 1 of the Act does not, in my judgment, impose any civil liability on the employer at the suit of the injured employee. This is because no new liability is created by the section for the benefit of the employee; the liability already exists for breach of the common law duty of care or breach of statutory duty, for example under the Factories Acts; there is therefore no need or purpose in creating any civil liability for failure to insure against these liabilities. Mr Foy submitted that though in practise it would not be used, nevertheless the cause of action against the employer exists. I cannot accept this. It seems to me to be strange that civil liability should be imposed on a director, who consents to, connives at or facilitates by neglect a breach of criminal law by the company of which he is a director, and thus becomes both civilly and criminally liable, when the company itself is not civilly liable.

(2)   Where civil statutory duty is created where the only penalty prescibed is a criminal one, the activity involved is usually declared unlawful per se with a penalty imposed for contravention of that activity, rather than the activity merely being classified as a criminal offence. An example of this is *Monk* v *Warbey* . . .

Although logically it may be thought that there is no difference between declaring an activity to be unlawful and imposing a criminal penalty, and simply imposing a criminal penalty if the activity is proved, I do not see why this should not be regarded as some indication of the intention of Parliament.

In *Rickless's* case it is clear that the decision would have been the other way but for the provisions of European law and the presumption that Parliament must have intended to give effect to those provisions when it enacted the Act in question; though it is right to say that there were other considerations which point against a civil remedy.

(3)   In my opinion, the court will more readily construe a statutory provision so as to provide a civil cause of action where the provision relates to the safety and health of a class of persons rather than where they have merely suffered economic loss. Certainly, the line of authority which has developed into the modern law seems to have stemmed from such cases as *Groves* v *Lord Wimborne* [1898] 2 QB 402, a case under the Factory and Workshop Act 1878, where duties are imposed for the protection of workmen which involve a higher standard of duty than the common law duty of care.

This point clearly cannot be taken too far because *Monk* v *Warbey* itself is a case of protecting the injured claimant against economic loss.

(4)   Very substantial penalties are imposed by the 1969 Act on the employer in default; and similar penalties are imposed on the delinquent director. This is not limited to £1,000, as the deputy judge appears to have thought, but is a maximum of £1,000 per day, which could amount to a very large fine. Moreover, the fact that that is a daily penalty shows that it is to some extent a special penalty, a feature which militates against civil liability. It differs from a fine for a single offence, for example, breach of s. 14 of the Factories Act 1961 for having unfenced machinery.

(5)   At common law a director of a corporate employer to whom the duty of organising employer's liability insurance has been delegated, could not, in my view, be liable in negligence to an employee of the company who suffered economic loss through failure to effect insurance. It seems to me that it would be surprising if Parliament intended to impose an unlimited civil liability on such a director, who may have done no more than overlook the need to renew a policy. Such a person may well have had no personal responsibility for causing the injury, and indeed the employer's liability itself may arise

from the negligence of a fellow employee for which the employer is vicariously liable, but for which none of the directors is personally culpable. As Mr Haycroft points out, this would be a case of piercing the corporate veil with a vengeance.

(6)   Although I am doubtful whether the considerations laid down in *Pepper (Inspector of Taxes)* v *Hart* [1993] AC 593 are satisfied so that the court can derive any real assistance from the Parliamentary debates, what can be said is that in the debate on cl 5 of the Bill, there is no suggestion that any civil liability is imposed on directors (786 HC Official Report (5th series) col 180ff, 11 July 1969) and in the House of Lords (304 HL Official Report (5th series) col 1396, 14 October 1969). Lord Pargiter, who sponsored the Bill in the House, said that 'there is nothing in this Bill . . . to alter the Common Law regarding liability in the relationship between an employer and an employee'.

I do not think this could have been said if it was the intention to impose a wholly new civil liability on the director of a corporate employer.

(7)   The deputy judge considered that the case was indistinguishable from *Monk* v *Warbey*. I do not agree. I have already drawn attention to one distinction in para (2). I agree with Mr Haycroft that there is another. The owner of a motor car who causes or permits another to drive his vehicle puts into the hands of that person a potentially lethal object, which, if it is not driven with proper care, may cause injury to members of the public on the road. There is nothing similar in the action or inaction of a director who commits an offence under s. 5 of this Act.

(8)   Although the words 'facilitate by any neglect' in s. 5 suggest breach of a duty to do something, it is clear to my mind that the duty in question is owed to the company/employer, and not the employee.

Although it may well be that none of these reasons are compelling in themselves, cumulatively in my judgment they point very strongly against the creation of any civil liability on the part of a director who has committed an offence under s. 5.

For these reasons, I would allow the appeal.

SIR JOHN MEGAW (dissenting): In the present case, the plaintiff employee obtained judgment against the corporation employer for damages for breach of the Factories Act duties; but before damages were assessed the employer went into liquidation and there are no assets to satisfy the plaintiff's judgment. The employer had failed to insure. In the circumstances it would be pointless for the plaintiff to seek to sue the employer in a civil court for its failure to insure, even assuming that such proceedings could be brought. But that practical difficulty, as I see it, in no way necessitates the conclusion that the employer was not subject to civil liability for its failure to insure.

The principle, as I understand it to be, is that which was clearly and specifically expressed by Lord Diplock, albeit in a passage of his speech which may have been technically obiter dictum, in *Lonrho Ltd* v *Shell Petroleum Co. Ltd* [1982] AC 173 at 185. The passage has been cited in the judgment of Stuart-Smith LJ. Lord Diplock expressed 'the general rule' to be that 'where an Act creates an obligation, and enforces the performance in a specified manner . . . that performance cannot be enforced in any other manner'. Lord Diplock then goes on to say, however, that—

there are two classes of exception to this general rule. The first is where on the true construction of the Act it is apparent that the obligation . . . was imposed for the benefit or protection of a particular class of individuals, as in the case of the Factories Acts and similar legislation.

In my opinion, that 'first exception' undoubtedly applies in this case. The obligation to insure against bodily injury or disease sustained by employees was imposed by Parliament for one purpose, and one purpose only. The purpose was to give protection to a particular class of individuals, the employees, to eliminate, or, at least, reduce, the risk to an injured employee of finding that he was deprived of his lawful compensation because of the financial position of the employer. I am confident that it was no part of the purpose or intention of Parliament in enacting this legislation to confer a benefit or protection on the employer. It might or might not be in the employer's interest, on its own account, to have insurance against this risk. But that would depend on various factors, such as the relationship of the amount of the premium, as compared with its assessment of the risk. The purpose of Parliament's enactment was the protection of the employees.

Hence the statutory requirement of compulsory insurance comes clearly and specifically within Lord Diplock's 'first exception'. Failure to perform the obligation gives rise to civil liability.

With great respect, I find it difficult to believe that the Parliamentary draftsman would have intended to make provision that there should be no civil right or remedy by using the formula of s. 1 of the 1969 Act, 'shall insure', followed by s. 5, 'shall be guilty of an offence'; as contrasted with the formula of declaring an act or omission to be unlawful and then separately providing a criminal penalty for the breach. Why should such subtle wording be used to indicate that the breach of duty which it contemplates is not actionable when that intention can be expressed in clear and precise words? (See e.g. s.13 of Safety of Sports Grounds Act 1975 and s. 5(1) of Guard Dogs Act 1975.)

It is important to consider the possible consequences of the legislation, if it were to provide for a criminal penalty, but not a civil remedy. An employee, one of the class of individuals for whose protection the duty was imposed, has a claim against the employer which ought to have been, but was not, covered by insurance. The injured employee or his representatives fear that the employer may be in, or heading for, financial difficulties, and discover that there is no insurance. The employee applies to the civil court for an injunction to require the employer to take out a policy forthwith. If there is no civil action, the injunction will be refused for lack of jurisdiction. The employee is left with no remedy. Indeed, his position may be made worse by the legislation, with its provision for a criminal penalty. If the person or body which has the responsibility of initiating criminal proceedings decides to bring those proceedings, they may ultimately result in a conviction and a fine, which may be up to £1,000 a day for the duration of the failure to insure. So, far from being of any benefit to the employee for whose benefit the statutory obligation was intended, the unhappy employee may find that the imposition of the others fine on the employer may have destroyed his last remaining chance of obtaining the compensation due to him.

That, as I see it, points to one excellent reason for the existence and importance of Lord Diplock's 'first exception'. In contrast with cases where the statutory obligation is an entirely general one, owed to the world at large, the fact that the intention of the statutory provision is for the benefit or protection of individuals of a particular, definable, class would make it very surprising if the only remedy for the breach of the duty was one which in no way compensated the individual but which might prevent his being compensated.

The 'first exception' applied with equal force to the liability imposed on the directors etc by the second part of s. 5 of the Act. It is equally imposed for the benefit or protection of the employees. There might be an argument to the contrary, involving what might be described as an exception to the first exception, if the liability imposed on the directors was an absolute liability, as is the liability of the employer itself under the first part of s. 5. But in order that the liability should exist, for the purpose of civil proceedings under the second part of s. 5, it is necessary for the employee to establish that the director in question consented to or connived at the failure to insure, or facilitated that failure by any neglect: in other words, there has to be shown a relevant fault on the part of the individual, other than the mere fact that he has general responsibilities as a director.

For my part, I would dismiss the appeal.

8.1.2   THE STATE OF THE PRE-EXISTING LAW, INCLUDING THE COMMON LAW

WEST WILTSHIRE DISTRICT COUNCIL v GARLAND AND OTHERS (COND AND OTHERS, THIRD PARTIES) [1993] 4 All ER 246

MORRITT J: . . . I will deal first with the issue as to the existence or otherwise of a statutory duty owed by the auditors and enforceable by an action for damages by either the council or the officer. It is not in dispute that if there is such a duty owed to the council then there is a right of contribution within Ord 16, r. 1(1)(a) because of s. 1 of the Civil Liability (Contribution) Act 1978. If such a duty is owed to the officer then it is not disputed that the matter comes within Ord 16, r. 1(1)(c).

This issue depends on the proper construction of the 1982 Act and the answer to the two questions posed by Lord Bridge of Harwich in *Hague* v *Deputy Governor of Parkhurst Prison, Weldon* v *Home Office* [1992] 1 AC 58 at 158–159. They are (1) whether the provision in question is intended to protect the interests of a class of which the council or the officer is a member, and (2) did Parliament intend to confer on the council or the officer a cause of action for a breach of such duty? The first question may be elaborated by considering what was the primary object Parliament intended thereby to achieve: compare *Cutler* v *Wandsworth Stadium Ltd* [1949] AC 398 and *Caparo Industries plc* v *Dickman* [1990] 2 AC 605 at 630 . . .

The object of any audit is to ensure that the money of the body in question has been properly spent and accounted for. If the interest of that body and some other class, for example its members, coincide it may be a question in the case of particular statutes whether the legislation exists for the protection of the body or that class. But where the interest of the body and the class do not overlap the audit requirement must exist primarily for the benefit of the body even though it may also exist for the protection of the class. Thus I do not regard the existence of a statutory duty owed to local government electors as necessarily excluding a duty to the body itself. This is confirmed by a consideration of s. 12(2). This subsection imposes on the bodies specified in it the requirement to have their accounts audited in accordance with the 1982 Act. Many will not have any connection with a class comparable to local government electors so that the statutory duty which is undoubtedly imposed by s. 15 can only be owed to the body in question. It would be odd if the auditor owed a statutory duty to an internal drainage board but not a district council. Accordingly, I answer the first question by holding that Part III in general and s. 15 in particular is intended primarily to protect the local authority.

The second question therefore arises in the case of the council but not of the officers. Did Parliament intend to confer on the local authority a cause of action in damages for breach of such duty? Part III confers a number of rights on a local government elector with corresponding remedies to enable them to be enforced. Thus s. 17 enables him to make objections to the auditor leading to a power to raise the matter in court pursuant to s. 19(4) or s. 29(2) effectively on appeal from the auditor's decision. The result of the exercise of these powers may lead to the recovery of property by the local authority. But the statute does not expressly confer on the local authority any remedy, direct or indirect, for the enforcement of the duty of the auditor. It is true that in appropriate circumstances and subject to the conditions relating to the remedy of judicial review that is a remedy open to the local authority. But it is evident that that remedy affords little or no protection against the consequences of the negligent conduct of a statutory audit.

The auditors contend that nevertheless there is no cause of action. First they rely on s. 30 as indicating that Parliament did not intend that there could be civil proceedings. As is shown by *Bookbinder* v *Tebbit (No. 2)* [1992] 1 WLR 217, s. 30 (1)(a) contemplates that consent may be required from persons other than the bodies referred to in s. 12(2). It is submitted that para (b) would not apply to proceedings between the body and the auditor. Thus, it is said, the limitation of para (c) to criminal proceedings shows that civil proceedings were not in contemplation because such proceedings could not fairly be tried without considering the information obtained by the auditor pursuant to the 1982 Act concerning the body whose accounts were audited. I do not think that this warrants the conclusion that no civil proceedings were contemplated. In civil proceedings between the body and the auditor the body would be bound to give its consent to the disclosure of relevant documents so as to discharge its obligations to give discovery. If the documents relate only to that body there will be no problem. A problem would only arise with documents relating also to some other person whose consent might not be compellable. But I do not see how this point can exclude civil proceedings between the body and the auditor. If, as sometimes happens, the rights of third parties intervene to prevent one party from producing a document it wishes that is no reason for excluding the cause of action altogether.

Then reliance was placed by the auditors on the provisions of ss. 19(4), 20(2), 22(1) and the availability of judicial review. None of the subsections confers any remedy on the council and, as I have already pointed out, the remedy of judicial review is of limited value in righting the wrongs of an inadequate audit. I do not regard any of these provisions as indicative of Parliament's intention not to confer a private law cause of action in damages to enforce the duty.

Third, the auditors relied on the absence of any reported case indicating the existence under the law of England of any such right of action. This is true, though there is authority in Australia which may be distinguishable: see *Frankston and Hastings Shire* v *Cohen* [1960]

ALR 249. No doubt this indicates that I should approach the point with caution, but it cannot be decisive of the point itself.

Fourth, the auditors relied on the statement of Farwell J in *A-G* v *De Winton* [1906] 2 Ch 106 at 119 that the duty of borough auditors was 'of imperfect obligation'. If, it was argued, there is a private law right to bring an action for damages then the obligation is not imperfect. But it was not in issue in that case whether there was any such right and I do not regard the remark as a considered statement even with regard to borough auditors under the legislation then in force, let alone in respect of auditors under the 1982 Act.

Finally, the auditors sought to draw an analogy with others in the field of public law . . .

In conclusion I see nothing in any of these cases to warrant the decision for which the auditors contend. In summary it seems to me that the duty under the statute is owed to the council or other body whose accounts are audited. The statute confers no express right or power on the council or other body to secure the due performance of that duty. The ability of the council to seek judicial review and such powers as it enjoys enabling it to determine whether to re-engage that auditor do not provide an adequate remedy in the case of an audit negligently conducted. The existence of some quasi-judicial functions may in the circumstances justify some modification of the duty but do not warrant the denial of a private law cause of action at all. Accordingly in my judgment the claim, in so far as it is based on breach of a statutory duty owed by the auditor to the council, is not bad in law and is not liable to be struck out on that ground.

In these circumstances the officer's alternative claim to be entitled to sue the auditor for negligence or negligent misrepresentation does arise but the contention that the council is likewise so entitled does not. I can deal with the officer's claim to sue the auditors quite shortly.

This claim has to be approached on the basis that there is no decided case demonstrating that such a cause of action will lie. Thus it is for the officers to establish one. To do so they must demonstrate that there is between them and the auditors a relationship characterised by the law as one of proximity or neighbourhood and that the situation should be one in which the court considers it fair, just and reasonable that the law should impose a duty of a given scope upon the one party for the benefit of the other: see *Caparo Industries plc* v *Dickman* [1990] 2 AC 605 at 617–618. In this case all the breaches of duty except one which are alleged to constitute negligence are the failure to do something but the loss claimed is purely economic in the form of the loss of employment and the benefits that went with it. In the case of the alleged negligent advice there is no allegation of specific inquiries or the voluntary assumption of responsibility. The fact is that the proximity between the officers and the auditors arises solely from the operation of the 1982 Act, but, as I have already held, the purpose of that Act was not to protect the officers. In these circumstances I do not think that it would be fair, just or reasonable that a duty of care should be imposed on the auditors for the benefit of the officers by the common law when Parliament in enacting the 1982 Act chose not to do so. In these circumstances I will order that those parts of the third party notices which rely on (a) any private cause of action at the suit of the officers against the auditors or (b) any cause of action in negligence or for negligent misrepresentation at the suit of the council against the auditors be struck out.

This leaves the auditor's narrow submission in respect of the claim by the council against the auditors for breach of statutory duty. In accordance with my judgment this is capable of being pleaded in a way which discloses a cause of action and is not embarassing. The third party notices do not because they do not recognise that the three auditors were employed at different times so that in some cases the auditor had not been employed when the relevant events took place or had retired. Moreover, the notices do not in a number of respects give the particulars which a pleading should. These defects were recognised by counsel for the officers, who suggested that the appropriate course would be to order the service of third party statements of claim notwithstanding that all parties had hitherto treated the third party notices as third party statements of claim. This seems to me to be a sensible way of dealing with the matter. Thus, having struck out those parts of the third party notices which I have indicated, I will order the service of third party statements of claim and give such other directions as are requisite to enable the remaining issues to be determined.

[The auditors appealed against the refusal of Morritt J to strike out all of the third party notices, and the second and third defendants cross-appealed against the striking out of allegations relating to a common duty to the District Council; they asked for an amendment to the notices to the effect that one of the auditors owed a duty of care at common law to the council *and* its officers when compiling his reports.]

[1995] 2 All ER 17 (CA)

BALCOMBE LJ: . . .

(4)   *Cause of action for breach of duty*
I approach this part of the case bearing in mind the words of Lord Simonds in *Cutler* v *Wandsworth Stadium Ltd* [1949] AC 398 at 407:

> if a statutory duty is prescribed, but no remedy by way of penalty or otherwise for its breach is imposed, it can be assumed that a right of civil action accrues to the person who is damnified by the breach. For, if it were not so, the statute would be but a pious aspiration.

. . . In my judgment, therefore, the judge was wholly correct in his decision on the second issue before him.

(II)   COMMON LAW DUTY OF THE DISTRICT AUDITORS TO THE COUNCIL ENFORCEABLE BY AN ACTION FOR NEGLIGENCE
Fortunately I can treat this issue quite shortly. The judge said that in the circumstances of his decision on issue I . . ., this issue did not arise and it was apparently for this reason that he ordered that those parts of the third party notices which relied on any cause of action in negligence or negligent misrepresentation at the suit of the council against the auditors be struck out.

Because a plaintiff has an action for breach of statutory duty in respect of a negligent performance of the statutory duties it does not follow that he therefore cannot have an action at common law in respect of the same negligence. Thus in *Henderson* v *Merrett Syndicates Ltd* [1994] 3 WLR 761 it was held that there may legitimately be co-existent remedies for negligence in contract and in tort. In my judgment it is equally true that there may be co-existent remedies for negligence in breach of a statutory duty and in tort. Certainly it is not so clear and obvious that the two causes of action cannot co-exist so as to justify striking out on that ground alone the claims sounding in tort as disclosing no cause of action.

Equally, I do not find it necessary to consider the many cases to which we were referred on the substantive question whether there exists a common law duty of care on the part of the district auditors towards the council. It is sufficient to say that, in my judgment, the existence of such a duty enforceable by an action for negligence is clearly arguable and a pleading making such a claim should not be struck out in limine.

(III)   COMMON LAW DUTY OF MR DAY TO THE COUNCIL IN THE PREPARATION, COMPILING, DRAFTING AND ISSUING OF HIS REPORTS
I can see no reason for treating the claims sought to be raised under this head in a manner different to the claims considered under issue II above. At one time I had considered that the making of these reports might be covered by the quasi-judicial exemption of *Everett* v *Griffiths* [1921] 1 AC 631 to which I have referred above. However, while I accept that the decision whether or not to make a report under s. 15(3) is a quasi-judicial function which, in the absence of bad faith, cannot give rise to a liability in damages, once Mr Day had taken the decision to make his reports it is at least arguable that in relation to them he owed to the council a duty of care of the kind considered in *Spring* v *Guardian Assurance plc* [1994] 3 All ER 129, [1994] 3 WLR 354 and *Henderson* v *Merrett Syndicates Ltd.* Accordingly I see no reason why, as a matter of principle, the officers should not be allowed to amend their third party notices and consequent pleadings to raise this issue.

(IV)   COMMON LAW DUTY OF MR DAY TO THE OFFICERS IN THE PREPARATION, COMPILING, DRAFTING AND ISSUING OF HIS REPORTS . . .
I accept that the claim that they now seek to raise does not arise solely from the operation of the 1982 Act, but from the making of the reports by Mr Day under the Act. I accept also that, if the reports had not been made in the exercise of his statutory power, it might well

be arguable that a duty of care existed by Mr Day towards the officers under the principles enunciated by the House of Lords in *Spring* v *Guardian Assurance plc* and *Henderson* v *Merrett Syndicates Ltd*. However, the fact is that these reports were made by Mr Day under s. 15(3), ie because he believed it to be in the public interest that he should do so. Furthermore, para 26 of the code of practice provides: 'The auditor should not be deflected from making a report because its subject matter is critical or unwelcome, if he considers it in the public interest to do so.'

In my judgment it would not, in these circumstances, be fair, just or reasonable that the law should impose a duty upon the district auditor for the benefit of the officers whom he feels that he must, in the public interest, criticise in the report or reports he makes under s. 15(3). The same result can be achieved by saying that in the circumstances in which the reports are made there does not exist between Mr Day and the officers a relationship characterised by the law as one of 'proximity'. Whichever test be adopted, in the last resort it is a question of policy, and I am confident that the provisions of s. 15(3) of the Act and para 6 of the code of practice make it clear that Parliament intended that the district auditor should be free to make his report whenever he considered it to be in the public interest to do so. Short of bad faith he must be free to criticise an officer of the local authority without fear of exposing himself to an action for negligence at the suit of that officer.

Accordingly I would hold that Mr Day owed no common law duty of care to the officers in relation to his reports.

Butler-Sloss and Leggatt agreed in dismissing the appeal and allowing the cross-appeal. The Court of Appeal decided that Morritt J was correct in finding that the *council* had a right of action for breach of statutory duty against the auditors. It was also arguable that the *council* had a *co-existing* action for common law negligence against the auditors (in respect of the same negligence) and to that extent the cross-appeal was allowed. It was also open to the second and third defendants to argue that Day, the auditor, owed a duty of care at common law to the council concerning reports he had decided to make. Day did not, however owe any duty of care to the second and third defendants themselves.

MINISTRY OF HOUSING AND LOCAL GOVERNMENT v SHARP [1970] 1 All ER 1009

The Court of Appeal had to consider s. 17 of the Land Charges Act 1925, the relevant portion of which reads as follows: '(2) The Registrar shall thereupon make the search required and shall issue a certificate setting forth the results thereof. (3) In favour of a purchaser, or an intending purchaser, as against persons interested . . . the certificate . . . shall be conclusive.'

All three judges interpreted the Act after a lengthy detailed consideration of its statutory history. Lord Denning and Salmon LJ considered that a civil action would lie, but Cross LJ thought not. It was said that *if* it is found that a civil action lies it must then be shown that it lies at the instance of the particular plaintiff. The plaintiff succeeds if he can show:

(a)   That he was a member of the class of persons the statute was designed to protect. (The statute in this case was designed to protect the purchaser and also those who registered their charges, for example, the Ministry.)

(b)   The injury suffered is the precise injury that the statute was designed to protect, i.e. the financial loss arising from loss of the benefit of their charge.

(c)   That the statute imposed a duty upon the defendant, which duty has been broken. (It was on this point that the Ministry's action failed in this case.) The majority of the court held that, by implication, the defendant's duty was to search 'diligently', but the plaintiff alleged breach of an absolute duty and so had not attempted to prove any lack of care by the defendant.

(d)   That breach of the duty caused the injury. (Since no breach had been proved the question of causation did not arise in this case.)

CBS SONGS LTD v AMSTRAD ELECTRONICS PLC [1988] AC 1013

The Court of Appeal by a majority refused to grant an injunction to a copyright owner to restrain an incitement to commit an offence of being a party to an infringement of copyright under the Copyright Act 1956 (s. 21(3)). See now the Copyrights Designs and Patents Act 1988 where the owner could not assert a right to a civil action in respect of that infringement.

CBS alleged that, through its advertising campaign for new tape-to-tape recording machines, Amstrad was encouraging the public to break the law of copyright and claimed that where an Act which had been passed for the protection of a class of persons did not create any civil duty a member of that class could still apply for an injunction (as opposed to damages). In such a case the claim was one in equity to enforce the observance of the criminal law.

Nicholls LJ did not accept that such a category of claim existed. CBS was not helped by *Emperor of Austria* v *Day* [1861] 3 de GF & J 216 (Lord Campbell LC in that case said that the court had jurisdiction to protect property from an act threatened which, if completed, would give a right of action, i.e. a cause of action at law).

Counsel for CBS conceded that, since *Lonrho* v *Shell* (2), a plaintiff seeking an injunction to restrain a criminal act had to do more than simply show that the act interfered with his property interest (see Lord Diplock's statement of the general principle and his two exceptions). Nicholls LJ said the present case did not come within the exceptions in *Shell*. CBS relied on the judgment of Oliver LJ in *RCA Corporation* v *Pollard* [1983] Ch 135 in which (after setting out three ways in which a claim by a recording company to have a right to restrain the sale of 'bootlegged' recordings and for damages could have been framed) he said '. . . where there is a breach of a statutory provision for the protection of a class of whom the plaintiff is one and he can show that he is specially damaged by the breach, he may bring proceedings to enforce, not his own civil right of action, but the public duty which has been interfered with or not observed'.

NICHOLLS LJ: That passage does not sustain the burden which [CBS] required it to bear. Oliver LJ could not have been intending to depart from the principles stated in *Lonrho* without any explicit indication that he was doing so.

That an activity attracts criminal liability cannot, by itself, in this field, convert into a cause of action acts which would otherwise not be sufficient for that purpose. Thus the plaintiff's incitement claim could not be legally sustained.

Fox LJ agreed, but Sir Denys Buckley dissented and said that it was not alleged that Amstrad was in breach of a statutory prohibition. He relied on the *Emperor of Austria* case—equitable jurisdiction based on risk of injury to property. That decision, in his Lordship's opinion, arguably (at least) supported the plaintiff's claim for injunctive relief and was not affected by *Lonrho* [or *RCA* v *Pollard* (above) or *Rickless* or *Woolf* v *United Artists Corporation Ltd* (unreported 10 December 1986—CA) (Cases involving statutory prohibitions)].

In the House of Lords [1988] 2 All ER 484 it was held that no duty of care at common law was owed to owners of the copyright. Legislation covered such rights (though its protection might be inadequate) and there had been no breach of the relevant Act. Lord Templeman said: 'The pleading assumes that we are all neighbours now, Pharisees and Samaritans alike, that foreseeability is a reflection of hindsight and that for every mischance in an accident prone world someone solvent must be liable in damages.'

8.2 The Elements of the Cause of Action for Breach of Statutory Duty

8.2.1 THE DEFENDANT MUST HAVE BREACHED THE STATUTE

8.2.1.1 Statute and negligence

AUSTIN ROVER v HM INSPECTOR OF FACTORIES, The Times, **15 August 1989**

[T]he House of Lords had to consider s. 4(2) of the Health and Safety at Work Act 1974 which provides that persons who make non-domestic premises available to those who are not their employees have a duty . . . to take such measures as it is reasonable for a person in his position to take to ensure, so far as is reasonably practicable, that the premises, . . . and any plant or substance . . . provided for use there, is . . . safe and without risks to health.

Their Lordships decided that someone who allows his non-domestic premises to be used as a workplace for persons who are not his employees has a statutory duty (under the 1974 Act) to take reasonable steps to ensure that the premises are safe from any dangers which are reasonable foreseeable in the light of his knowledge of the anticipated use of the premises. He is not required to take steps to avoid unexpected and unknown dangers.

DEXTER v TENBY ELECTRICAL ACCESSORIES LTD,
The Guardian, 22 February 1991 (QBD)

In a criminal prosecution under s. 29(1) of the Factories Act 1961 it was held that the duty placed on the occupier of factory premises by the Factories Act 1961 is to make his premises as safe as is reasonably practicable for all persons who may work there, even if they are not his employees. In this case an electrician employee of independent contractors engaged to repair the occupier's factory roof fell through the roof whilst effecting the repairs and sustained minor injuries. The Health and Safety Executive brought a prosecution under the above provision. The roof was in an unsafe condition and the court held that defendant company, as the occupier of the premises, was in breach of its statutory duty under s. 29(1). The case was remitted to the magistrates for them to continue the hearing.

8.2.2   THE DEFENDANT'S BREACH OF DUTY MUST HAVE CAUSED THE DAMAGE

CUMMINGS (OR McWILLIAMS) v SIR WILLIAM ARROL AND CO. LTD
[1962] 1 All ER 623 (HL)

LORD DEVLIN: My lords, the appellant is the widow of a steel erector who was killed by a fall in the course of his employment by the first respondents. She alleges that the employers were in breach of their duty at common law to the deceased in that they failed to provide him with a safety belt and failed to instruct him to wear it. The courts below have held that the employers were in breach of their duty in failing to provide a safety belt, but that that was not the cause of the deceased's death since he would not have worn it if it had been provided. They have held also that there was no duty on the employers to instruct the deceased to wear it. On this second matter I cannot usefully add anything to the opinions already expressed by your Lordships with which I agree.

On the first matter three points have been taken. First, whether the employers can be heard to say that the deceased would not have worn what they in breach of their duty failed to provide. Secondly, as to the burden of proof: whether it is for the appellant to prove that the deceased would have worn a safety belt if provided or for the employers to prove that he would not. Thirdly, whether, in order to establish as a matter of probability that the deceased either would or would not have worn a safety belt if provided, inferences can be drawn from the deceased's habits and past conduct and from the habits of his fellow employees.

On the first of these matters counsel for the appellant based his case on the proposition that the failure to provide the safety belt was the cause of the defendant's death. In my opinion this proposition is incomplete. There is a missing link. The immediate cause of the deceased's death was the fact that at the time of the fall he was not wearing a safety belt. The cause or reason he was not wearing a safety belt may have been the fact that one was not provided, but the failure to provide operates only through the failure to wear. The correct way of stating the appellant's case is, I think, as follows. The immediate cause of the deceased's death was that at the time of the fall he was not wearing a safety belt: but for the fault of his employers, he would have been wearing a safety belt: therefore the fault of his employers was an effective cause of his death. So stated, it is plain that the reason why the deceased was not wearing a safety belt must be a proper subject for inquiry.

Counsel for the appellant relied on the decision of the Court of Appeal in *Roberts* v *Dorman Long & Co., Ltd.* This also was a case in which the death of a steel erector was caused by his not wearing a safety belt and his employers were in breach of duty in not making one available. The duty relied on was created by reg. 97 of the Building (Safety, Health and Welfare) Regulations 1948, which provided that

. . . there shall be available safety belts . . . which will so far as practicable enable such persons who elect to use them to carry out the work without risk of serious injury.

The court held that it was no answer for the employers in such circumstances to say that if they had made safety belts available, the deceased would not have used them; the fact that they were not available gave him no opportunity of exercising his election. It is clear that this reasoning was based on the words of the regulation: the court held the employers to be guilty of a breach of the regulation but not a breach of their duty at common law. The case does not therefore, in my opinion, assist counsel in his argument against the first respondents; though I shall consider it again when I consider the case against the second respondents which is based on the breach of statutory duty.

The second point raises the question of the burden of proof. The proposition, as I have stated it above, appears to put on the appellant the burden of showing why the deceased was not wearing a safety belt; she must prove her case and it is part of her case that he was not wearing one because of the fault of his employers. But since *ex hypothesi* a prudent employer would provide a belt, it must follow that a prudent employee would wear it when provided. Any inquiry of this sort starts from the presumption that the pursuer or the defendant, as the case may be, has done what is reasonable and prudent; and it is for the opposite party to displace that presumption by pleading and proving negligence or contributory negligence, as the case may be. So if there were no evidence at all to show why the deceased was not wearing a safety belt, it would be proper to conclude that the reason was because the employers had failed to provide one. This question of the burden of proof is frequently important when what is in issue is what a dead workman in fact did. Without his evidence it may be difficult to prove that negligence by the employers was an effective cause of the death: once negligence is proved, the fact that the workman cannot be called to account for his actions often defeats the proof of contributory negligence. But in the present case the question is not what the deceased actually did but what he would have done in circumstances that never arose. Whether the workman is alive or dead, this cannot be proved positively as a matter of fact but can only be inferred as a matter of likelihood or probability. Even when the workman himself is perforce silent, there may be plenty of material, as there is in this case, from which an inference can be drawn one way or the other; and then the question of burden of proof is unimportant.

That brings me to the third of counsel for the appellant's submissions. He submits that what the deceased would have done cannot be proved by inference. It must be proved, he says, by direct evidence, such as a statement by him that he never in any circumstances wore a safety belt. The fact that in the past the deceased never wore a safety belt is not admissible to show that he would not have worn one on the material occasion: such is the argument. There is here, I think with respect, a confusion of thought. The fact that a man under certain conditions on Monday, Tuesday and Wednesday (I take this example from counsel's argument) drove carelessly may be inadmissible to prove the fact that he drove carelessly under the same conditions on Thursday . . . But here the question is not what the deceased did but what he would have done. That is a matter that is incapable of direct proof; it must be a matter of inference. His statement about what he would have done, if he were alive to make it, is only one of the factors which the court would have to take into consideration in its task of arriving at the correct inference. A man's actions in the past may well be a safer guide than his own forecast of his actions in the future.

In my judgment the courts below were right to receive and consider the evidence that the deceased had never used a safety belt in the past when it was available. That is material from which it is permissible to draw the inference that he probably would not have used one if it had been provided on the day of his death. I think also, though with more hesitation, that the courts below were right in considering for what it was worth the evidence of the general practice of steel erectors, though without some evidence of the deceased's own attitude towards safety belts I do not think it would have been worth much.

Undoubtedly a court should be very careful about finding what one may call hypothetical contributory negligence. A defendant, whose negligence has prevented the matter in issue from being put directly to the proof, must expect that a court will be very careful to make sure that it is acting on legitimate inference and not on speculation. But in the present case the evidence, even if it were confined to the deceased's own past acts, is in my opinion conclusive. If he had been injured only by the fall and could have gone into the witness-box, and if he had there sworn that he would have been wearing a safety belt if one had been available that morning, I do not see how he could have been believed.

Viscounts Kilmuit and Simonds, and Lords Morris and Reid were also in favour of dismissing the appeal.

8.2.2.1   The defendant's breach of duty must have caused the damage

ROSS v ASSOCIATED PORTLAND CEMENT MANUFACTURERS LTD
[1964] 2 All ER 452 (HL)

LORD REID: . . . Another typical case of avoiding civil liability was *Ginty* v *Belmont Building Supplies Ltd*. There the plaintiff had been instructed not to work on asbestos roofs without using boards, and he knew that this was the subject of statutory regulations and that this particular roof was unsafe. Boards were available but he did not use them, with the result that he fell through the roof. The terms of the regulation were such that his failure to use the boards constituted offences both by him and by his employers. Pearson J, held that he was not entitled to recover damages. He discussed a number of theories which had been elaborated to explain why damages are not payable in such circumstances, including delegation, an inference from the principle that a person cannot derive advantage from his own wrong, and the need for avoiding circuity of action. He said: 'In my view, the important and fundamental question in a case like this is not whether there was a delegation, but simply the usual question: Whose fault was it?' If the question is put in that way one must remember that fault is not necessarily equivalent in this context to blameworthiness. The question really is whose conduct caused the accident, because it is now well established that a breach of statutory duty does not give rise to civil liability unless there is proved a causal connection between the breach and the plaintiff's injury. With regard to what is to be regarded as a causal connection I may be permitted to repeat by reference my observations in *Stapley* v *Gypsum Mines Ltd*. That approach appears to me to avoid the difficulty which has sometimes been felt in explaining why an employer, put in breach of a statute by the disobedience of his servant, can escape liability to that servant for injuries caused by the breach. If the employer exercised all due diligence, and the breach and resultant injuries were solely caused by the servant's conduct, the employer is liable vicariously for injuries sustained by a third party just as he would be for injuries caused solely by his servant's common law negligence: but he can say to the disobedient servant that his conduct in no way caused or contributed to that servant's injuries . . .

LORD DONOVAN: . . . The respondents say that, even so, the breach must be regarded as playing no part in causing the death of Ross.

   The layman would find such a contention hard to understand; but it is urged to be a right conclusion in law on the following grounds. Ross was an expert or specialist at the job he was asked to do: it was he who assessed its requirements in the shape of proper equipment. The respondents were entitled to rely on him as an expert or specialist for the fulfilment of their statutory obligations. If Ross did not do what he ought to have done, then while the consequent breach of duty becomes vicariously a breach by the respondents, the reality of the matter is that fault was wholly the fault of Ross; and the ensuing accident was his fault alone. The respondents' breach of statutory duty—to use a phrase employed in the case of *Ginty* v *Belmont Building Supplies Ltd*—was simply coterminous with his. In the circumstances they are not liable to pay the appellant damages.

   My Lords, I think that the premises of this contention are unsound. There is no evidence that Ross was an expert or a specialist at repairing safety nets suspended beneath aerial ropeways. He was a steel erector: and no doubt whilst, as such, he was expert at erecting steel structures, and accustomed to work at heights, this is by no means the same thing. There was no evidence that he had done this kind of work before. His mate at the time, one Boughen, another experienced steel erector, certainly had not done so. He was, however, asked this question in cross-examination on behalf of the respondents: 'But it is the sort of job that is well within the range of a person with a steel erector's experience?' To which Boughen anwered 'Yes'. The question is too general and ambiguous for his answer to be of much value. At the most it establishes that some steel erectors will have had experience of 'this sort of job'. It does not establish that the deceased was an expert or a specialist at repairing nets under aerial ropeways, or even that he had ever done it before; and it leaves unanswered the question 'How did the respondents regard him?' They could have answered, but elected to give no evidence. Mr. Brueton on the other hand, an engineer of wide technical experience, gave evidence, which was not contradicted, to the effect that it was very unusual to find a steel-work erector, or even a charge-hand steel-work erector, who had experience of this kind of work.

In my opinion, it was plainly not open on this state of the evidence to draw the conclusion that the deceased man was an expert or a specialist in relation to this particular job: and if that be so the foundation of the argument which imputes the whole fault to him goes.

The respondents go on to say, however, that, having considered how to get to the network he had to repair, the deceased decided on the ladder, rejecting the safe method of a mobile platform. The inference, therefore, is that if the mobile platform had been available he would not have used it. My lords, making all allowances for the disadvantages of having to interpret evidence from a transcript as compared with hearing it, I think that such an inference from it is impossible . . . In my opinion, the evidence does not in the respect now being considered raise even a prima facie case against Ross, but establishes rather that he used the ladder because nothing else at all suitable was provided. If a mobile platform was available, if all that Ross had to do was to ask for one and it would have been provided, then it was for the respondents to call evidence to that effect instead of remaining silent.

The circumstances of this case are essentially different from the circumstances in the case of *Ginty*. There suitable appliances *were* provided by the employer but the man refused or neglected to use them.

Nor is there any parallel between this case and the recent decision of this House in *Cummings (or McWilliams)* v *Sir William Arrol & Co. Ltd* where, on the facts proved, the irresistible inference was that the deceased man would not have used a safety belt even had it been provided. In the present case no inference can be drawn from the evidence that Ross would not have used a mobile platform had it been provided.

In my opinion, the only conclusion open on this part of the case was that the respondents were in breach of their statutory duties, and that such breach was a cause of the death of Ross. I agree that he himself must bear some of the blame, for I think he was negligent in using a ladder which was clearly dangerous. In my opinion, however, the respondents are more to blame: and I agree that two-thirds of the responsibility should be assigned to them . . .

Viscount Simonds, and Lords Guest and Upjohn were also in favour of allowing the appeal.

8.2.3   THE HARM SUFFERED IS WITHIN THE SCOPE OF THE GENERAL CLASS OF RISKS AT WHICH THE STATUTE IS DIRECTED

8.2.3.1   Common law duty

PICKERING v LIVERPOOL DAILY POST AND ECHO NEWSPAPERS PLC, PICKERING v ASSOCIATED NEWSPAPERS HOLDINGS PLC [1991] 2 AC 370 (HL)

LORD BRIDGE: . . . The sole ground on which the plaintiff originally claimed to be entitled to the relief he sought was the prohibition imposed by rule 21(5) of the Mental Health Review Tribunal Rules 1983 which provides:

Except in so far as the tribunal may direct, information about proceedings before the tribunal and the names of any persons concerned in the proceedings shall not be made public.

If this is the correct analysis of the effect of the Rules of 1960 operating in conjunction with section 12(1)(b) of the Act of 1960, I do not believe that the changes effected by the Rules of 1983 can have been intended to bring about any fundamental change in the operation of statutory safeguards protecting the privacy of proceedings before the tribunal. The new

Rules abolish the distinct procedures for informal determinations and formal hearings. Under the Rules of 1983 all proceedings are to be determined after a hearing in accordance with the procedure under Part IV, and rule 21, with one amendment which is for present purposes immaterial, exactly reproduces the provisions of rule 24 of the Rules of 1960. But the circumstance that rule 21(5) now applies to all proceedings before the tribunal does not, in my opinion, attract to it any greater significance than the corresponding rule 24(4) of the Rules of 1960. Its function is still only to ensure that the protection given by the law of contempt to the privacy of the proceedings generally applies to the subject matter of the hearing before the tribunal including the names of any persons concerned except in so far as the tribunal may give a direction to the contrary.

If the Court of Appeal had had their attention drawn to the Rules of 1960, they would not, I think, have regarded rule 21(5) in the Rules of 1983 as having the central significance which they attached to it, either as giving rise to a cause of action in the plaintiff or as giving him a 'sufficient interest' to entitle him to seek an injunction. The question whether the plaintiff, as a patient who had applied to a mental health review tribunal for his discharge, was competent to seek an injunction to restrain a threatened contempt in breach of section 12(1)(b) of the Act of 1960 is a different one to which I will refer later. But this is an appropriate point at which to add some further observations which I feel obliged to make in respectful disagreement with the views expressed in the Court of Appeal with regard to the plaintiff's entitlement to sue. Quite apart from the considerations to which I have drawn attention arising from the Rules of 1960, I should find it impossible to construe rule 21(5) in the Rules of 1983 as giving a cause of action for breach of statutory duty to a patient applying for his discharge to a mental health review tribunal in respect of the unauthorised publication of information about the proceedings on that application. In holding that the rule did give him such a cause of action, Lord Donaldson MR and Glidewell LJ considered that it fell within the principle formulated by Lord Diplock in *Lonrho Ltd* v *Shell Petroleum Co. Ltd (No. 2)* [1982] AC 173, 185:

> where upon the true construction of the Act it is apparent that the obligation or prohibition was imposed for the benefit or protection of a particular class of individuals, as in the case of the Factories Acts and similar legislation.

But in order to fall within the principle which Lord Diplock had in contemplation it must, in my opinion, appear upon the true construction of the legislation in question that the intention was to confer on members of the protected class a cause of action sounding in damages occasioned by the breach. In the well known passage in the speech of Lord Simonds in *Cutler* v *Wandsworth Stadium Ltd* [1949] AC 398, 407–409, in which he discusses the problem of determining whether a statutory obligation imposed on A should be construed as giving a right of action to B, the whole discussion proceeds upon the premise that B will be damnified by A's breach of the obligation. I know of no authority where a statute has been held, in the application of Lord Diplock's principle, to give a cause of action for breach of statutory duty when the nature of the statutory obligation or prohibition was not such that a breach of it would be likely to cause to a member of the class for whose benefit or protection it was imposed either personal injury, injury to property or economic loss. But publication of unauthorised information about proceedings on a patient's application for discharge to a mental health review tribunal, though it may in one sense be adverse to the patient's interest, is incapable of causing him loss or injury of a kind for which the law awards damages. Hence Lord Diplock's principle seems to me to be incapable of application to rule 21(5) . . .

Lords Brandon, Templeman, Goff and Lowry agreed with Lord Bridge in allowing the defendants' appeals and dismissing the plaintiff's cross-appeal.

YOUNG v *CHARLES CHURCH (SOUTHERN) LTD, The Times*, 1 May 1997 (CA)

This case illustrates the point that damages for psychiatric injury may be obtained in a cause of action other than that of negligence, which is governed by the decision in *Alcock*. In *Young* the plaintiff suffered psychiatric illness through seeing a colleague electrocuted in very close physical proximity to himself: indeed, the plaintiff was most fortunate in the circumstances to escape electrocution himself. It was held, in an action for **breach of statutory duty**, that reg. 44(2) of the Construction (General Provisions) Regulations (SI 1961

No. 1580) which embraces 'electrically charged overhead cable or apparatus' provides a cause of action in tort where an employee suffers mental illness.

8.3 Defences

8.3.1 *VOLENTI NON FIT INJURIA*

IMPERIAL CHEMICAL INDUSTRIES LTD v SHATWELL [1964] 2 All ER 999 (HL)

On the issue of *causation* i.e. whether the acts of James Shatwell were a contributing cause of his brother George's injuries the House of Lords decided by a majority that they were.

LORD REID: Applying the principles approved in *Stapley's* case I think that James's conduct did have a causal connection with this accident. It is far from clear that George would have gone on with the test if James had not agreed with him; but, perhaps more important, James did collaborate with him in making the test in a forbidden and unlawful way. His collaboration may not have amounted to much, but it was not negligible. If I had to consider the allocation of fault, I should have difficulty in finding both men equally to blame. If James had been suing in respect of his damage, it would I think be clear that both had contributed to cause the accident, but that the greater part of the fault must be attributed to George . . .

VISCOUNT RADCLIFFE [dissenting]: . . . In my opinion it is fallacious to treat this sort of case as if it had any analogy with such a case as *Admiralty Commissioners* v *S.S. Volute*. The situation there is one in which two persons, each acting independently of the other, have each contributed separately his own wrongful act to a total situation from which damage results. In such a case it is reasonable enough to measure the importance to the whole of the separate contribution of each and to arrive at a conclusion of contributory negligence and of proportionate liability accordingly. But, where the actors are joint actors, the actual contribution made by each is irrelevant to the result, since each was merely taking his agreed or accepted part in achieving the whole. Indeed, though I can see at any rate an argument for making such joint undertakers share equally between them the whole bill for their separate injuries, I can see no argument at all for making each contribute to the other according to the measure of his actual contribution to the common purpose.

This, I suppose, is much the same line of reasoning as was adopted by the Court of Appeal in the *Stapley* case and was treated by this House as being inapplicable to the circumstances of that case . . . But the question is whether what determined *Stapley* need determine this case. I do not think that it need. I cannot say that I find the reasoning of the majority of this House in *Stapley* easy to follow, but the determining point seems to have been their view that once the argument was not accepted that Stapley's death was 'not in any way the result of Dale's negligence', Dale's and his employer's liability must necessarily follow. That conclusion may have been sufficient to dispose of the case before them, but I think that it would be unfortunate if it came to be regarded as authority for any general principle of causation, where joint wrongdoers succeed in inflicting separate injuries on themselves. . . .

LORD PEARCE: Although the law has refused damages to a man who himself breaks a regulation, so that he injures himself, can the man circumvent that difficulty by persuading a colleague to join him in doing the wrongful act? Can the two workmen then each say—'My colleague was negligent along with me; our one joint explosion blew us both up; therefore *his* negligence caused *my* injury and *my* negligence caused *his* injury and our employer must pay damages to each of us accordingly.' It would be illogical and also, I think, against public policy if a workman, intending to commit a breach of regulation or duty, could thus ensure his getting some damages for any resultant accident by luring a fellow-worker to join him in the breach.

Is there some satisfactory answer which would break the chain of the plaintiff's argument, without having unjust repercussions on more meritorious claims?

Apportionment of loss through contributory negligence, which can so often provide a fair result, is of no avail in solving this problem. For if one of the men is held, owing to his greater fault, entitled only to 20 per cent, of his loss, then as a general rule the other must be entitled to 80 per cent of his loss; and the total result would still offend against commonsense.

Must it be said that James caused the accident? That was a question of fact. George suggested the course of action and George's hand created the explosion; but James assented to the course of action and took part in the testing. Had the learned trial judge held that James did not cause George's injury, it would not, I think, have been right to over-rule him. He felt simply bound, however, by the reasoning which led to the decision of fact in *Stapley's* case. He held that the testing was being done by both men together and he regarded the fact that George's hand fired the explosion as merely an incidental factor.

At first sight it may seem odd that when two men mutually assent to do a dangerous act, it should be held that each has partially caused the injuries of the other. One workman owes a duty to another to take care not to injure him, but I doubt, as between equals, whether that duty is greater than or different from the duty of care not to injure some one other than a fellow servant standing within the area of risk from his negligence. Different considerations of course apply, when negligent instructions are given by some one, such as a foreman, who is entitled to give instructions. When two men agree together to take a risk, a jury might well take the simple view that each caused his own injuries. The difficulty of the question is shown by the conflict of opinion in *Stapley's* case between the Court of Appeal and the majority of your lordships' House. In that case it could fairly be argued that the accident could not have happened had Dale gone on working on the roof as he should have done. In the present case, however, we have no knowledge of what would have happened if James had refused. The question of causation is one of fact. But in view of the trial judge's decision and the reasoning which led to the decision in *Stapley's* case, I doubt if it is open to your lordships to take a different view of the facts . . .

The concurring speeches on this point of Lords Hodson and Donovan are omitted. It will be recalled that the House decided unanimously that the defence of *volenti non fit injuria* was available to ICI; therefore the company's appeal was allowed on that point.

8.3.2   CONTRIBUTORY NEGLIGENCE

WESTWOOD v *POST OFFICE* [1973] 3 All ER 184

Technicians went on to the roof of the defendant's building to smoke during working hours, a practice known to and accepted by the management. Usually access to the roof was obtained by a door, but on the day of the accident the men got on to the roof through a window in the lift motor room. While in the lift motor room, the deceased fell through a trapdoor in the floor which collapsed under him.

The trial judge held that the lift room was subject to the provisions of the Offices, Shops and Railway Premises Act 1963, and that the defendants were in breach of their duty because of the defective floor.

The Court of Appeal, reversing this decision, held that:

(a)   The deceased was a trespasser, since there was insufficient evidence to show that the management knew of the use of the lift room to obtain access to the roof.

(b)   The case of *Uddin* v *Associated Portland Cement Manufacturers Ltd* could be distinguished on the ground that the 1963 Act gave protection to 'persons employed to work in office or shop premises', and since the deceased had never been employed to work in the lift motor room, he was not protected.

The effect of this decision was that an employee who went on to a forbidden part of his employer's premises in circumstances making him a trespasser would lose the benefit of any statutory safety provisions and would only have the rights available to a trespasser at common law (see now also Occupiers' Liability Act 1984). It appeared that the protection given to employees under safety legislation by *Uddin's* case had been curtailed. In that case, remember, an employee was held entitled to the protection of the Factories Act even though he 'was on a frolic of his own' and was not acting in the course of his employment.

The decision in *Westwood's* case was reversed by the House of Lords, in a judgment which rejected the view that an employer does not owe a statutory duty to provide safe premises for a trespassing employee. It was found that the lift motor room was a place in office premises as defined by the 1963 Act, or alternatively, premises which must be treated as forming part of office premises, since the activity for the purposes of which the lift motor room existed was that of the telephone exchange. On the trespassing issue, there was no distinction between this case and *Uddin*. The room had not been constructed according to the Act's requirements, that default was the cause of the death and the Act is not restricted to protecting those injured in the course of their employment.

There was a divergence of views of whether Westwood had been contributorily negligent in ignoring the 'keep out' sign on the motor room door, but Lord Kilbrandon, delivering the majority decision, said '. . . the sole act of negligence giving rise to this accident was the respondent's breach of statutory duty. Any fault on the part of the deceased was a fault of disobedience, not a fault of negligence, because he had no reason to foresee that disregard of the order to keep out of the lift motor room would expose him to danger. It would indeed not have done so, had it not been that, unknown to him, the respondents were in breach of their duty to take care for the safety of those employed in the premises'.

HEWETT v ALF BROWN'S TRANSPORT LTD [1991] 1 CR 471

In this case the plaintiff's husband was a lorry driver employed by the defendants and his job entailed contact with lead waste. The plaintiff always banged his overalls against the garden wall or in the sink before washing them. She also banged or wiped his boots. As a result, 'she either inhaled, or came into contact with, lead oxide powder' and was diagnosed as suffering from lead poisoning.

The plaintiff claimed damages for negligence and breach of statutory duty (Control of Lead at Work Regulations 1980) alleging that she was exposed to lead in relation to the conduct of demolition work.

Otton J said that there was a foreseeable risk to families 'from clothing worn by employees exposed to a significant risk of lead poisoning', but that the husband had not been exposed to any risk while removing the waste from the site. Accordingly, the defendants were not in breach of their statutory duty to their employee, the plaintiff's husband, under the 1980 Regulations. Neither were the defendants in breach of their common law duty of care to their employee. It followed that the defendants could not be liable for the plaintiff's injury: '. . . even assuming a duty of care to Mrs Hewitt . . . she had failed to establish any negligence. [T] he degree of exposure of her husband was minimal. So, in a sense, it was to her'.

8.4   An Employer's Liability at Common Law

8.4.1   INTRODUCTION

McDERMID v NASH DREDGING AND RECLAMATION CO. LTD
[1987] 2 All ER 878 (HL)

LORD HAILSHAM: My Lords, this was an action for damages for personal injuries by the plaintiff (appellant) against his employers, the defendants (respondents), as the result of an accident which took place as long ago as 22 June 1975.

The fact that on the date of the hearing of this appeal on 5 May 1987 both the question of liability and the quantum of damages were still open after nearly 12 years for discussion does not shed a very favourable light on our system for dealing with litigation of this type.

The plaintiff was employed as a deckhand by a contract in writing dated 18 June 1975 in connection with dredging work on a fjord at Luleå in Sweden. In the first sentence of this contract it was expressly agreed: 'The employee shall safely comply with the lawful directions of the company's representatives . . .' It must be noted that the defendant employers were a subsidiary (it is believed wholly-owned) of a Dutch company Stevin Baggeren BV (Stevin). The function of the defendants was to provide and pay the British staff engaged in the operation.

At the time of the accident, by direction of the defendants, the plaintiff was working on the deck of a tug (*The Ina*) owned by Stevin and under the command of her Dutch skipper

(Captain Sas) who was an employee of Stevin. The tug was in fact operated turn and turn about by Captain Sas and a British skipper (Captain Clifford) who was an employee of the defendants. At all material times, however, and by direction of the defendants under cl 1 of the contract of service, *The Ina* and the plaintiff were both under the total operational control of Captain Sas and subject to his orders.

The accident may be very simply described. The plaintiff's duty, so far as material, was to tie and untie *The Ina* from a dredger to which she was made fast fore and aft by means in each case of a nylon rope attached to a bollard on the dredger by an eye and to the tug by a number of figure-of-eight loops and two half-hitches. At the time of the accident the plaintiff was under orders to untie with a view to *The Ina* going astern. He safely untied the aft rope and stowed it inboard *The Ina*. He then went forward to untie the forward rope from the dredger. His correct drill, had he completed it, would have been to slacken the rope on *The Ina*'s starboard bollards in order to reduce the tension, to allow the deckhand on the dredger (whom he could clearly see) to take the eye of the rope off the dredger's port bollard, and then haul the rope in and stow it safely inboard *The Ina*, proceed to the wheelhouse and give it a double knock with his hand, in order to signal to Captain Sas that it was safe to move. In the event, after he had loosened the forward rope from *The Ina*'s bollard, and before the deckhand on the dredger had had time to remove the eye of the rope from the bollard on the dredger, Captain Sas, who was at the wheel of *The Ina*, put the engine hard astern. As a result, the rope snaked round the plaintiff's leg, pulled him into the water and caused him injuries which involved the amputation of his leg and damages recently (28 April 1986) assessed at £178,450.05 by Staughton J, to whom the case had been remitted for this purpose by the Court of Appeal.

The plaintiff's claim in the proceedings was based on the allegation inter alia, of a 'non-delegable' duty resting on his employers to take reasonable care to provide a 'safe system of work' (cf *Wilson & Clyde Coal Co. Ltd* v *English* [1938] AC 57). The defendants did not, and could not, dispute the existence of such a duty of care, nor that it was 'non-delegable' in the special sense in which the phrase is used in this connection. This special sense does not involve the proposition that the duty cannot be delegated in the sense that it is incapable of being the subject of delegation, but only that the employer cannot escape liability if the duty has been delegated and then not properly performed. Equally the defendants could not and did not attempt to dispute that it would be a central and crucial feature of any safe system on the instant facts that it would prevent so far as possible the occurrence of such an accident as actually happened, viz injury to the plaintiff as a result of the use of *The Ina*'s engine so as to move *The Ina* before both the ropes were clear of the dredger and stowed safely inboard and the plaintiff was in a position of safety.

Since such a system could easily have been designed and put in operation at the time of the accident in about half a dozen different ways, and since it is quite obvious that such a system would have prevented the accident had it been in operation, and since the duty to provide it was 'non-delegable' in the sense that the defendants cannot escape liability by claiming to have delegated performance of their duty, it is a little difficult to see what possible defence there could ever have been to these proceedings. There was indeed a preposterous suggestion in the defendants' pleading that the plaintiff had caused or contributed to his own misfortune himself. There was never the smallest evidence of this, and, no doubt prudently, the defendants called no evidence, whether by Captain Sas or anyone else, to substantiate it. This frantic attempt to avoid or reduce liability had already died a natural death before the case left the court of trial.

Although the duty of providing a safe system of work was 'non-delegable' in the special sense I have described, it had in fact been delegated on alternate shifts to Captain Sas and Captain Clifford in the circumstances I have described. In both cases the delegation covered, so far as can be ascertained, the whole operation of *The Ina*, the orders to the deckhand, the system of work to be followed, and since the skipper was at the wheel, the operation of the engine. Both Captain Sas and Captain Clifford had designed different systems of work either of which, if followed, would probably have prevented the accident in the instant appeal. The trial judge appeared to think that the system designed by Captain Sas and applicable at the time of the accident to the plaintiff was 'not unsafe'. But this 'system' involved at its crucial stage, i.e. the point of time at which it was necessary to ascertain for certain that both the ropes were inboard and the deckhand safe, a double knock by the deckhand on the wheelhouse, which could not be delivered unless the deckhand were clear of danger. If the proper sequence was observed this would not happen until after the second rope was stowed inboard. The Court of Appeal doubted whether the 'system', if it can be called such, was adequate, and I share this doubt. But it matters not. The accident happened because *The Ina* went full astern before the forward rope was clear of the dredger and with the plaintiff in a position of acute peril. There was no double knock because Captain Sas did not attempt to operate the correct sequence and did in fact operate the engines with the eye of the rope still on the bollard of the dredger. The 'system' was therefore not being operated and was therefore not being 'provided' at all. It matters not whether one says that there was no 'system' in operation at all, or whether one says that the system provided was unsafe, or whether one says that the system in fact provided was not in use at the crucial stage. In any event the defendants had delegated their duty to the plaintiff to Captain Sas, the duty had not been performed, and the defendants must pay for the breach of their 'non-delegable' obligation.

Before your Lordships it was strenuously argued that the fact that Captain Sas operated the engine in such dangerous circumstances was the 'casual' or 'collateral' negligence of an employee of an independent contractor, i.e. Stevin. Since Stevin was itself the holding company of the defendants, the defendants being its wholly-owned subsidiary, I find this morally an unattractive proposition. But the fact was that the plaintiff had delegated their own 'non-delegable' duty to Captain Sas who had charge of the whole operation and his negligence was not 'collateral' or 'casual' but central to the case and in total disregard of the duty owed to the plaintiff to see that the engine was not put in operation at all until it had been ascertained that it was safe to do so. Whether the system as designed by Captain Sas was adequately safe or not, whether it can truthfully be said that there was in any real sense a system at all, or whether there was a system not unsafe but not being operated, the defendants had delegated their own 'non-delegable' duty and it had not been performed.

I do not wish to add anything on the second point in the appeal which related to the attempt to limit the defendants' liability under s. 503 of the Merchant Shipping Act 1894 as amended by s. 3 of the Merchant Shipping (Liability of Shipowners and Others) Act 1958, except to say that I agree with the judgment of the Court of Appeal ([1986] 2 All ER 676 at 686-687, [1986] QB 965 at 980–982), and that the result is a necessary consequence of the correct analysis of the facts which I have endeavoured to give above.

In the event this appeal must be dismissed with costs. In my view it is, and always was, unarguable.

Lords Ackner, Brandon, Bridge and Mackay agreed in dismissing the appeal.

8.4.2 THE PROVISION OF ADEQUATE PLANT, MATERIALS AND PREMISES

EMPLOYER'S LIABILITY (DEFECTIVE EQUIPMENT) ACT 1969

1. Extension of employer's liability for defective equipment.

(1) Where after the commencement of this Act—

(a) an employee suffers personal injury in the course of his employment in consequence of a defect in equipment provided by his employer for the purposes of the employer's business; and

(b) the defect is attributable wholly or partly to the fault of a third party (whether identified or not),

the injury shall be deemed to be also attributable to negligence on the part of the employer (whether or not he is liable in respect of the injury apart from this subsection), but without prejudice to the law relating to contributory negligence and to any remedy by way of contribution or in contract or otherwise which is available to the employer in respect of the injury.

(2) In so far as any agreement purports to exclude or limit any liability of an employer arising under subsection (1) of this section, the agreement shall be void.

(3) In this section—

'business' includes the activities carried on by any public body;

'employee' means a person who is employed by another person under a contract of service or apprenticeship and is so employed for the purposes of a business carried on by that other person, and 'employer' shall be construed accordingly;

'equipment' includes any plant and machinery, vehicle, aircraft and clothing;

'fault' means negligence, breach of statutory duty or other act or omission which gives rise to liability in England and Wales or which is wrongful and gives rise to liability in damages in Scotland; and

'personal injury' includes loss of life, any impairment of a person's physical or mental condition and any disease.

(4)   This section binds the Crown, and persons in the service of the Crown shall accordingly be treated for the purposes of this section as employees of the Crown if they would not be so treated apart from this subsection.

COLTMAN v BIBBY TANKERS LTD ('THE DERBYSHIRE') [1987] 3 All ER 1068 (HL)

In this case the plaintiff claimed that her husband had died as the result of the sinking of the defendant's unseaworthy ship. The House of Lords held that the 91,000 ton ship came within the definition of 'equipment' in the Employer's Liability (Defective Equipment) Act 1969. Their Lordships said that it would not be sensible to find that machinery attached to the ship came within the terms of the Act whilst the vessel's hull did not.

KNOWLES v LIVERPOOL CITY COUNCIL [1993] 4 All ER 321 (HL)

LORD JAUNCEY: My Lords, this appeal related to the construction of s. 1 of the Employers' Liability (Defective Equipment) Act 1969. The facts are simple. The respondent was employed by the appellants as a labourer flagger repairing a pavement in a Liverpool street. While he was manhandling a flagstone into the shovel of a JCB excavator the corner of the flagstone broke off causing the stone to drop with consequent injury to the respondent's finger. The breakage occurred because the manufacturers, who were not the appellants, had failed to cure it properly. This defect could not reasonably have been discovered before the accident . . .

The respondent raised an action against the appellants claiming damages on the ground, inter alia, that they were liable for his injury by virtue of s. 1(1) of the 1969 Act. The recorder of Liverpool upheld the respondent's statutory claim holding that the flagstone was equipment for the purposes of the subsection and was defective. The Court of Appeal took the same view in dismissing the appellants' appeal.

Before the House Mr Braithwaite QC for the appellants sought to draw a distinction between 'plant' on the one hand, which comprehended such things as tools and machinery required for the performance of a particular task, and 'stock-in-trade' on the other, which covered articles produced by the use of plant and machinery. Equipment fell firmly on the side of plant. He argued further that material was to be distinguished from equipment and was therefore excluded from the latter . . .

Given that the 1969 Act was passed to afford to the workmen a remedy which might be denied to him at common law by treating the employer as though he were vicariously liable for the defect in the tool, why should Parliament have restricted the scope of that remedy to tools and plant omitting what Mr Braithwaite described as stock-in-trade but what might more appropriately be described as other articles or material used by the employer in his business? To this question I have been unable to find a logical answer . . .

My Lords, in my view a number of observations of Lord Oliver of Aylmerton who delivered the leading speech in *Coltman* v *Bibby Tankers Ltd* are entirely apposite to this appeal. Lord Oliver, after referring to the purpose of the 1969 Act, expressed the view that if ss. (1) had stood alone and without such assistance as was provided by ss. (3) he would have had no difficulty in concluding that in the context of the 1969 Act a ship was part of the 'equipment' of the business of a ship owner (see [1988] AC 276 at 296). He concluded that the definition in sub-s (3) had been inserted not for the purpose of enlarging the word 'equipment' by including in it articles which would not otherwise fall within it in its ordinary signification but rather for clarification and avoidance of doubt (see [1988] AC 276 at 298). With reference to ss. (3), he said ([1987] 3 All ER 1068 at 1073, [1988] AC 276 at 299):

> The key word in the definition is the word 'any' and it underlines, in my judgment, what I would in any event have supposed to be the case, having regard to the purpose of the Act, that is to say that it should be widely construed so as to embrace every article of whatever kind furnished by the employer for the purposes of his business.

The latter observation, if applicable, is undoubtedly wide enough to cover the flagstone provided by the appellants in the present case.

My Lords, there is nothing in Lord Oliver's speech to suggest that these observations were restricted to cases involving ships or any other particular article. The observations were quite general and I have no doubt that they are just as applicable to this case as they were to the ship in *Coltman* v *Bibby Tankers Ltd*. That being so, the flagstone which broke and injured the respondent was 'equipment' for the purposes of the 1969 Act . . .

Mr Braithwaite referred to the Health and Safety at Work Act 1974 and to various regulations made under that Act and under the Factories Act in which the words 'plant or equipment', 'article', 'material' and 'appliances' were used as demonstrating that where Parliament intended to cover articles or material this was done by the use of specific words. Once again, I do not find that these provisions made for different purposes are of any assistance in construing the 1969 Act.

My Lords, I have no hesitation in concluding that the word 'equipment' in s. 1(1)(a) is habile to cover the flagstone in this appeal. In the first place, the requirement of the subsection is that the equipment is provided 'for the purposes of the employer's business' and not merely for the use of the employee. Thus a piece of defective equipment which causes injury to a workman would fall within the ambit of the subsection even although the workman was neither required to use nor had in fact used it. Whatever the meaning of 'equipment' this would go further than the circumstances in *Davie* v *New Merton Board Mills Ltd* [1959] AC 604, where the defective tool had been provided to the workman for the purposes of his job. In this case, the flagstone had undoubtedly been provided by the appellants for the purposes of their business of repairing and relaying the pavement. In the second place, there can be no logical reason why Parliament having recognised the difficulties facing workmen, as demonstrated by *Davie* v *New Merton Board Mills Ltd*, should have removed those difficulties in part rather than in whole. Indeed, partial removal, as contended for by the appellants, could produce bizarre results. To give one example which I put in argument to counsel, a pump manufacturer buys in tools required for assembling the pumps as well as some components including the bolts for holding together the two parts of the housing. Workman A is tightening a bolt which sheers and injures his eye. Workman B is tightening a similar bolt but his spanner snaps causing him a similar injury. If the appellants are right, workman B could proceed under s. 1(1) of the 1969 Act, but workman A would have no remedy thereunder. My Lords, I cannot believe that Parliament can have intended the Act to produce results such as these. In my view, the only reasonable conclusion is that Parliament intended the 1969 Act to provide a remedy in the situations where an employer had provided for the purpose of his business an article which was defective and caused injury to a workman but where he was for the reasons set out in *Davie* v *New Merton Board Mills Ltd* not in breach of a common law duty of care owed to that workman. In the third place, I consider that the conclusion which I have reached accords with the reasoning of Lord Oliver in *Coltman* v *Bibby Tankers Ltd* [1988] AC 276.

For the foregoing reasons I would dismiss the appeal.

Lords Browne-Wilkinson, Keith, Mustill and Templeman agreed in dismissing the appeal.

8.4.2.1 Plant and premises

SQUARE D LTD v *COOK* [1992] IRLR 34

The plaintiff, who was employed by the defendant on a site in Saudi Arabia, was involved in removing a floor tile in a narrow corridor so that wiring work could be carried out. The removal of the tile resulted in four triangular holes being left in the floor. In attempting to avoid these holes, the plaintiff slipped. This, in turn, resulted in the plaintiff's foot becoming jammed in one of the holes.

The Court of Appeal found that the judge at first instance was wrong in holding that the plaintiff's employers were liable for injuries he received whilst he was working in Saudi Arabia at premises occupied by another organisation.

It was held that there was no negligence on the part of the defendants. They were, apparently, satisfied that the site occupiers and the general contractors working on the site were both reliable companies aware of their obligations with regard to the safety of workers on site. Accordingly, the plaintiff's employers (i.e. the defendants) were under no duty to advise the site occupiers to guard against danger in the present case.

FARQUHARSON LJ: It was casting too high a responsibility on the home-based employers to hold them responsible for the daily events of a site in Saudi Arabia occupied by a third party.

The Court said that the common law duty on employers was to take 'all reasonable steps' to see that their employees were safe in the course of their employment, and this duty '[which] cannot be delegated' extends to a third party's premises on which an employee is directed to work. However, all depends on what is reasonable in the circumstances and various matters must be considered. These include the place of work, the nature of any building on the site, the experience of the employee concerned, the nature of the work involved, the degree of control that the employer can reasonably exercise in the circumstances, and the employer's own knowledge of the defective state of the premises. If several employees are going to work on a foreign site 'or where one or two employees are called upon to work there for a very considerable period of time', it may be that an employer will be expected to inspect the site 'and satisfy himself' that the occupiers of the site (the third party) are aware of their obligations for the safety of persons working there.

8.4.3   THE PROVISION OF A PROPER SYSTEM OF WORKING AND EFFECTIVE SUPERVISION

CHARLTON v FORREST PRINTING INK CO. LTD [1980] IRLR 311

The plaintiff was employed by the defendant to collect wages money. He was instructed to vary his collecting arrangements in order to evade theft but did not do this and was injured in the course of a robbery. It was found by the Court of Appeal that the defendant was not in breach of its employer's duty because it had taken all reasonable steps to minimise the risk of injury involved in the job. Apparently, it was the usual practice of firms of that size in that area to effect their own payroll collection rather than use a security organisation.

WHITE v HOLBROOK PRECISION CASTINGS [1985] IRLR 215 (CA)

The plaintiff was employed as a labourer for 3 months then offered a job as a grinder. Grinders almost always suffer from 'white finger' as a result of vibration. The plaintiff suffered from white finger and had to go back to a less well paid job. He sued his employers for negligence in not providing a safe system of work. In fact there was nothing the employer could do to guard against this problem.

It was held that if a job has risks to health and safety which are not common knowledge but which the employer knows, or ought to know about and against which he cannot guard, he should tell a prospective employee about the risk if it might affect his decision to accept the offer.

PAPE v CUMBRIA COUNTY COUNCIL [1991] IRLR 493

The plaintiff, a cleaner, had to give up work because of acute dermatitis caused by contact with chemical cleansing agents. Finding for the plaintiff, Waite J held that the defendants were in breach of their duty at common law to provide a safe system of work. The defendants had argued that they had discharged their duty by providing gloves and that an employer was not obliged to explain the obvious. However, his Lordship said, 'The dangers of dermatitis or acute eczema from the sustained exposure of unprotected skin to chemical cleansing agents is well known, well enough known to make it the duty of a reasonable employer to appreciate the risks it presents to members of his cleaning staff but at the same time not so well known as to make it obvious to his staff without any necessity for warning or instruction . . . there was a duty on the defendants to warn their cleaners of the dangers of handling chemical cleaning materials with unprotected hands and to instruct them as to the need to wear gloves at all times'.

MULCAHY v MINISTRY OF DEFENCE [1996] 2 All ER 758 (CA)

This case raises the important and novel question of the liability in negligence of the defence authorities for acts committed on the field of battle.

The plaintiff, a regular soldier, was a member of a gunnery, or artillery, crew who was injured in the Gulf War against Iraq in 1991. An artillery gun was fired while the plaintiff was in an unsafe position in relation to it and the blast knocked him down, causing permanent damage to his hearing. He claimed against the Ministry of Defence (1) for vicarious liability with regard to the alleged negligence of the gun commander in ordering the crew to fire the gun while the plaintiff was in the vicinity, and (ii) for personal negligence, as his employer, for failing to maintain a safe system of work.

On appeal from the court at first instance, the Court of Appeal ordered the plaintiff's claim to be struck out because he had no reasonable cause of action to argue at trial.

In general terms, the Crown Proceedings Act 1947 abolished the Crown's previous immunity from actions in contract and tort – but in s. 10 it provided that a serviceman could not sue a fellow serviceman or the Crown for death or bodily harm where this occurred during war service. The Crown Proceedings (Armed Forces) Act 1987, however, abolished this proviso.

Thus, it is only since 1987 that any case law has appeared in this context, and that litigation has not been in connection with 'operations against the enemy'. The Court of Appeal in *Mulcahy* considered this case law and decided that none of the existing authorities was of immediate relevance because they did not deal with this issue of 'operations against the enemy', which was of central importance in the present case.

On the basis that *Burmah Oil (Burmah Trading) Ltd* v *Lord Advocate* [1964] 2 All ER 348 (a famous case involving claims against the Crown for property destroyed by the Crown in wartime) was authority for drawing a line in compensation cases against the state between 'battle damage', which did not attract compensation, and the destruction of property to prevent it from falling into the possession of the enemy, which might be the subject of damages, the court thought it arguable that a claim for compensation could not be made in respect of damage occurring during the course of operations against the enemy.

The court also found some guidance in several cases involving actions in negligence against the police, e.g. *Knightley* v *Johns* [1982] 1 All ER 851 (see *Learning Text* (**4.4.1**)). These were cases in which serving police officers sued their employers, and their Lordships used them to form a judgment in the present case.

Their Lordships concluded that the plaintiff's injury had been sustained in the course of 'operations against the enemy', even though the accident occurred some miles from enemy lines and at a time when a television reporter and crew were visiting the site, and that a claim for compensation could not be made by a serviceman or woman in those circumstances. This view was supported, in their Lordships' opinion, by the distinction drawn in the 'police cases', referred to above, between an operational decision taken by a senior police officer in a case such as *Knightley* v *Johns* and an 'on the spot' decision taken in the course of attempts, for example, to control serious public disorder; in the latter situation a claim for compensation by a police officer would probably not be successful.

The 'police case' on which their Lordships placed most reliance, and which was distinguished on its facts from *Knightley*, was *Hughes* v *National Union of Mineworkers* [1991] 4 All ER 85, where a police officer (the plaintiff) was injured during various incidents of a violent nature which occurred at a coat mine where working miners were being escorted to work during a strike by other miners. The plaintiff claimed that the senior police officer in charge had been negligent in organising his officers at the scene, so exposing him to excessive and avoidable risk of injury.

May J struck out the plaintiffs claim, on the basis that it would be against public policy to impose upon the police a duty of care in respect of the immediate operational control of police forces in circumstances in which public disorder was involved, especially where that disorder involved violence. Furthermore, the plaintiff's injuries had been directly caused by those persons who were creating the public disorder. His Lordship used an argument based on the reasoning in *Hill* v *Chief Constable of West Yorkshire* [1989] AC 53 (see *Learning Text* (**3.5**)).

It is abundantly clear that considerations of public policy outweighed the individual justice of the claim in *Mulcahy*. As Glidewell LJ said, the efficiency of operations will suffer if a duty of care in negligence with regard to the safety of his comrades were to be imposed upon every soldier 'even in the heat of battle'.

A further observation may be in order viz. that it might well be difficult, in practical terms, to fix an **appropriate** standard of care in such circumstances.

WILLIAMS AND OTHERS v BRITISH COAL CORPORATION, The Times, 2 January 1998

In this case Turner J awarded damages to six out of eight former coal miners who had contracted 'crippling' bronchitis and emphysema through contact with coal dust. It was found that the defendant (and the National Coal Board before it) had been negligent in failing to take reasonable measures to minimise the dust which had been found to trigger bronchitis and emphysema. The compensation was **reduced** to take account of the parallel effects of smoking.

Turner J said these cases were only the 'tip of the iceberg' since it was expected that more than 100,000 former miners were expected to submit claims for compensation in the wake of these test cases.

TARRANT v RAMAGE AND OTHERS [1998] 1 Lloyd's Rep 185

Clark J held that the owners of a tug which was operating in the 'Gulf' War zone in 1987 were liable in damages for personal injury suffered by the plaintiff when the tug was struck by a missile. The owners owed a duty of care to the crew to exercise reasonable care for their safety. Accordingly, they ought to have given written instructions to the Master of the tug detailing what they knew of the missiles in use in the area and how best to minimise the risk of the tug being struck.

In **another** case **settled** by a City of London law firm, £100,000 was paid to a former trainee solicitor after she contracted shigella dysentry on a business trip to Ghana. She claimed that her employers had been negligent in failing to give appropriate advice on eating food in Ghana and in not giving sufficient notice of the trip so that she could obtain the necessary inoculations.

8.4.4   NEW TYPES OF DAMAGE

WALKER v NORTHUMBERLAND COUNTY COUNCIL [1995] 1 All ER 737

COLMAN J: There has been little judicial authority on the extent to which an employer owes to his employees a duty not to cause them psychiatric damage by the volume or character of the work which the employees are required to perform. It is clear law that an employer has a duty to provide his employee with a reasonably safe system of work and to take reasonable steps to protect him from risks which are reasonably foreseeable. Whereas the law on the extent of this duty has developed almost exclusively in cases involving physical injury to the employer as distinct from injury to his mental health, there is no logical reason why risk of psychiatric damage should be excluded from the scope of an employer's duty of care or from the co-extensive implied term in the contract of employment. That said, there can be no doubt that the circumstances in which claims based on such damage are likely to arise will often give rise to extremely difficult evidential problems of foreseeability and causation. This is particularly so in the environment of the professions, where the plaintiff may be ambitious and dedicated, determined to succeed in his career in which he knows the work to be demanding, and may have a measure of discretion as to how and when and for how long he works, but where the character or volume of the work given to him eventually drives him to breaking point. Given that the professional work is intrinsically demanding and stressful, at what point is the employer's duty to take protective steps engaged? What assumption is he entitled to make about the employee's resilience, mental toughness and stability of character, given that people of clinically normal personality may have a widely differing ability to absorb stress attributable to their work? . . .

It is reasonably clear from the authorities that once a duty of care has been established the standard of care required for the performance of that duty must be measured against the yardstick of reasonable conduct on the part of a person in the position of that person who owes the duty. The law does not impose upon him the duty of an insurer against all injury or damage caused by him, however unlikely or unexpected and whatever the practical difficulties of guarding against it. It calls for no more than a reasonable response, what is reasonable being measured by the nature of the neighbourhood relationship, the magnitude of the risk of injury which was reasonably foreseeable, the seriousness of the consequence for the person to whom the duty is owed of the risk eventuating, and the cost and practicability of preventing the risk . . .

In *Petch* v *Customs and Excise Comrs* [1993] ICR 789 the plaintiff claimed damages for negligence against the defendants for causing him to have a mental breakdown by the volume and stressful character of the work he was required to do. Dillon LJ approached the issue of breach of duty in these words (at 796–798):

> . . . I take the view, in the light of the general circumstances of this case and the other findings of the judge which I have set out, that, unless senior management in the defendants' department were aware or ought to have been aware that the plaintiff was showing signs of impending breakdown, or were aware or ought to have been aware that his workload carried a real risk that he would have a breakdown, then the defendants were not negligent in failing to avert the breakdown of October 1974.

In the present case, the mental illness and the lasting impairment of his personality which Mr Walker sustained in consequence of the 1987 breakdown was so substantial and damaging that the magnitude of the risk to which he was exposed must be regarded as relatively large.

Moreover, there can, in my judgment, be no doubt on the evidence that by 1985 at the latest it was reasonably foreseeable to Mr Davison, given the information which I have held that he then had, that by reason of stress of work there was in general some risk that Mr Walker might sustain a mental breakdown of some sort in consequence of his work. That said, how great was the reasonably foreseeable risk? Was the risk of incidence of illness so slight as to be in all the circumstances negligible or was it a materially substantial risk? There is no evidence that the council had hitherto encountered mental illness in any other of its area officers or that area officers with heavy workloads or others in middle management in the social services as distinct from fieldworkers were particularly vulnerable to stress-induced mental illness. Accordingly, the question is whether it ought to have been foreseen that Mr Walker was exposed to a risk of mental illness materially higher than that which would ordinarily affect a social services middle manager in his position with a really heavy workload. For if the foreseeable risk were not materially greater than that there would not, as a matter of reasonable conduct, be any basis upon which the council's duty to act arose . . .

I therefore conclude that the council could only have provided Mr Walker with substantial assistance in March 1987 at the expense of some disruption of other social work. It is impossible on the evidence which I have heard to form any clear view on the extent to which work in the Alnwick area would have been disrupted if Mr Anderson or some other team leader had been moved down to Blyth Valley or on the extent to which work at county hall would have been disrupted if Mr Robinson had been seconded to Blyth Valley on a sufficiently available basis, but I infer that the extent of disruption would have been such as to preclude the council from providing at least some services which it would otherwise have been able to provide.

In deciding whether the council was acting reasonably in failing to provide additional staffing to Mr Walker, it is clearly right to take into account and to attach some weight to the fact and extent of that disruption. However, Mr Hawkesworth on behalf of the council contends that because the extent to which the council provided social services to the public in particualr areas was a discretionary or policy decision in respect of the exercise of statutory powers, as distinct from an operational one, if the secondment of additional staff to assist Mr Walker involved withdrawal of services, the council's policy decision not to disrupt its services merely to enable it to support Mr Walker could not amount to a breach of duty of care to Mr Walker. Mr Hawkesworth relies in particular on the developing destinction between policy decisions and operational decisions enunciated by Lord Wilberforce in *Anns* v *Merton London Borough* [1977] 2 All ER 492, [1978] AC 728 and further explored by the Court of Appeal in *Lavis* v *Kent CC* (1992) 90 LGR 416. In other words, Mr Hawkesworth contends, the court is shut out from characterising as unreasonable conduct on the part of a public body which is the consequence of a decision by that body in a policy-making area to carry out its statutory powers in a particular way or to a particular extent . . .

In my judgment, the policy decision/operational decision dichotomy has no more part to play in the context of the duty of care to an employee with whom a statutory body has a contract of employment than would have in the context of any other contract made by such a body. Just as it would be no defence to a claim for non-performance of a contract for the sale of goods that the local authority had resolved as a matter of policy that the use of its scarce resources for the performance of the contract was inexpedient, so it would be no defence to a claim for breach of the implied term in a contract of employment that the employer would exercise reasonable care for the safety of his employee, that its failure to do so was the result of a policy decision on the exercise of its statutory powers. Since the scope of the duty of care owed to an employee to take reasonable steps to provide a safe system of work is co-extensive with the scope of the implied term as to the employee's safety in the contract of employment (*Johnstone* v *Bloomsbury Health Authority* [1992] 2 All ER 293, [1992] QB 333), to introduce a ring fence round policy decisions giving rise to unsafe systems of work for the purposes of claims in tort which was not available to the defendant statutory body in defence to claims in contract would be to implant into employment law a disparity which, in my judgment, would be wholly wrong in principle. Whereas the mutual intention to be imputed to the parties to a contract of employment with a public body could be expected to qualify the employer's duty of safety by requiring the employer to do no more than take reasonable steps to procure the employee's safety at work, it is inconceivable that such mutual intention would require the employer to take only such steps for the employee's safety as political expediency from time to time permitted if the exercise of statutory powers were involved. In the absence of authority to the contrary or of compelling common law principle, there can be no sustainable basis for subjecting the duty of care in tort to such a qualification.

That said, the duty of an employer public body, whether in contract or tort, to provide a safe system of work is, as I have said, a duty only to do what is reasonable, and in many cases it may be necessary to take into account decisions which are within the policy-making area and the reasons for those decisions in order to test whether the body's conduct has been reasonable. In that exercise there can be no basis for treating the public body differently *in principle* from any other commercial employer, although there would have to be taken into account considerations such as budgetary constraints and perhaps lack of flexibility of decision-taking which might not arise with a commercial employer.

Having regard to the reasonably foreseeable size of the risk of repetition of Mr Walker's illness if his duties were not alleviated by effective additional assistance and to the reasonably foreseeable gravity of the mental breakdown which might result if nothing were done, I have come to the conclusion that the standard of care to be expected of a reasonable local authority required that in March 1987 such additional assistance should be provided, if not on a permanent basis, at least until restructuring of the social services had been effected and the workload on Mr Walker thereby permanently reduced. That measure of additional assistance ought to have been provided, notwithstanding that it could be expected to have some disruptive effect on the council's provision of services to the public. When Mr Walker returned from his first illness the council had to decide whether it was prepared to go on employing him in spite of the fact that he had made it sufficiently clear that he must have effective additional help if he was to continue at Blyth Valley. It chose to continue to employ him, but provided no effective help. In so doing it was, in my judgment, acting unreasonably and therefore in breach of its duty of care.

I understand it to be accepted that if there was a breach of duty, damage was caused by that breach. However, in view of the fact that I have decided this case on the second breakdown alone, it is right to add that I am satisfied on the evidence that had the further assistance been provided to Mr Walker, his second breakdown would probably not have occurred.

In the event, there will be judgment for the plaintiff on liability with damages yet to be assessed.

8.4.5 COMPULSORY INSURANCE

EMPLOYERS' LIABILITY (COMPULSORY INSURANCE) ACT 1969

1. Insurance against liability for employees

(1)   Except as otherwise provided by this Act, every employer carrying on any business in Great Britain shall insure, and maintain insurance, under one or more approved policies

with an authorised insurer or insurers against liability for bodily injury or disease sustained by his employees, and arising out of and in the course of their employment in Great Britain in that business, but except in so far as regulations otherwise provide not including injury or disease suffered or contracted outside Great Britain.

(2)   Regulations may provide that the amount for which an employer is required by this Act to insure and maintain insurance shall, either generally or in such cases or classes of case as may be prescribed by the regulations, be limited in such manner as may be so prescribed.

2.   Employees to be covered

(1)   For the purposes of this Act the term 'employee' means an individual who has entered into or works under a contract of service or apprenticeship with an employer whether by way of manual labour, clerical work or otherwise, whether such contract is expressed or implied, oral or in writing.

(2)   This Act shall not require an employer to insure—

(a)   in respect of an employee of whom the employer is the husband, wife, father, mother, grandfather, grandmother, step-father, step-mother, son, daughter, grandson, granddaughter, stepson, stepdaughter, brother, sister, half-brother, half-sister; or

(b)   except as otherwise provided by regulations, in respect of employees not ordinarily in Great Britain.

8.5   Summary

8.5.1   BREACH OF STATUTORY DUTY

'The Interpretation of Statutes': The Law Commission (Law Com. No. 21) and the Scottish Law Commission (Scot. Law Com. No. 11) 1969

(2)   Presumptions
34.   Whatever interpretation might be thought to emerge from the application of the rules [of statutory interpretation] discussed above, the final decision of a court may in fact be greatly influenced by presumptions of intent. Presumptions of intent have been called 'policies of clear statement', i.e., in effect announcements by the courts to the legislature that certain meanings will not be assumed unless stated with special clarity. Legislation is made not only against the background of an existing body of law but also within the framework of a society with particular social and economic values which, it can legitimately be assumed in the absence of evidence to the contrary, the legislature intended to respect. 'Over the years', it has been said, 'the courts have laboured to discern and articulate a great number of principles of social relations. In an almost literal sense these represent a distillation of the experience and wisdom of the society.' A court may, for instance, cut down the generality of certain enactments both in order to harmonise them with the existing law and to give effect to prevailing values—e.g., in restricting the apparently unfettered generality of provisions which entitle the competent authority to grant planning permission or issue site-licences for caravans subject to conditions. Particular presumptions of intention will however be modified or even abandoned with the passage of time, and with the modification of the social values which they embody.
35.   A judge is not effectively bound by the presumptions of intent for the following reasons:

(a)   There is no established order of precedence in the case of conflict between different presumptions.

(b)   The individual presumptions are often of doubtful status, or imprecise scope.

(c)   A court can give a decision on the meaning of a statute which conflicts with a particular presumption without referring to presumptions of intent at all. The possibility for the court to decide in the first plact that the meaning is clear enables it to exclude altogether any operation of a presumption.

(d)   There is no accepted test for resolving a conflict between a presumption of intent, such as the presumption that penal statutes should be construed, restrictively, and giving effect to the purpose of a statute (the 'mischief' of *Heydon's Case*), for example, the purpose of factory legislation to secure safe working conditions.

36.   It has been suggested that the difficulties and uncertainties which arise in regard to presumptions of intent might be avoided by the statutory classification of legislation with appropriate presumptions. We do not think that a general classification of this kind would be practicable. Any comprehensive statutory directives would either have to be so generalised as to afford little guidance to the courts, or so detailed that they would lead to intolerable complexity and rigidity of the law. Our consultations confirm this view.

37.   In rejecting this approach we nevertheless recongnise the force of the arguments, put forward by a number of those whom we have consulted, in favour of laying down statutory presumptions in three difficult areas of interpretation.

The difficulty arises where a statute fails to state whether the criminal liability which it creates is absolute or subject to a requirement of *mens rea* in regard to all or some of its elements. It is true that 'in such cases there has for centuries been a presumption that Parliament did not intend to make criminals of persons who were in no way blameworthy in what they did.' This presumption is very strong in regard to offences which, although statutory in form, have their origins in the common law, but it appears to be much weaker in regard to relatively modern statutory offences providing criminal sanctions within the framework of legislation with a broad social purpose, such as the protection of factory workers or the furtherance of road safety. One way of removing the uncertainty might be to provide a statutory presumption, requiring the courts to import *mens rea* in regard to the prescribed elements of any statutory offence in the absence of express words to the contrary. However, we do not pursue the matter further in this Report. It is being separately investigated by the Law Commission, with the assistance of a Working Party, in connection with their codification of the general principles of English criminal law under Item XVIII of their Second Programme. Subject 11 (Strict Liability) of Published Working Paper No. 17, circulated by the Law Commission on 14 May 1967, is particularly relevant to the problems raised in this paragraph.

38.   The second area in which a statutory presumption might be helpful concerns the determination of civil liability arising from breach of statutory duty. The courts have endeavoured to isolate the factors by reference to which they decide whether civil liability arises, but it is difficult to ascertain from the cases what measure of authority they enjoy and what is the respective weight to be attached to them. In some recent statutes Parliament has expressly excluded in civil action and occasionally it has expressly provided that an obligation imposed by statute is intended to ground a civil action, but in spite of Lord du Parcq's invitation in *Cutler* v *Wandsworth Stadium Ltd* neither of these courses has been generally followed. We recognise that difficulties may still arise in regard to duties imposed by existing legislation; but we think it would be helpful to the courts and the public if they could rely on a statutory presumption in relation to obligations imposed in or authorised by future statutes. We have considered whether the presumption should be in favour of or against a civil action, unless a contrary intention is expressly stated. To avoid any danger of the civil action being restricted in practice by a failure to provide for it in express terms, we recommend that the presumption should take the first form, namely, that the breach of an obligation is intended to be actionable at the suit of any person who by reason of the breach suffers or apprehends damages, unless a contrary intention is expressly stated.

39.   The third area in which we have considered the desirability of a statutory presumption relates to legislation dealing with matters which are subject to international obligations of the United Kingdom (in particular treaties to which the United Kingdom is a party). This question is separately discussed in Section VII of this Report.

8.6   End of Chapter Assessment Question

Chill Hall is a hall of residence at the University of Radical Thinking. Under the Halls of Residence Act 1995, a fictitious statute, it is provided that all premises coming within the term of the Act shall be heated from 1st October to 30th April to a temperature of at least 68°F, except between 11.00 p.m. and 6.00 a.m.

During icy winter weather the hall's boiler stops working. The temperature falls gradually during the evening until it is below freezing point. Paul, a student, suffers from frostbite and pneumonia as a result of exposure to the cold. Wally, the University handyman, is called in by the Warden of Chill Hall to attempt to repair the boiler. He is unable to do so and, in an attempt to heat the building, he drags a heavy oil heater out of a storeroom, injuring his back in the process.

Advise Paul and Wally on any rights of action they may have in the law of tort.

8.7   End of Chapter Assessment Outline Answer

In this problem Paul (P) becomes ill as a result of exposure to the cold, and Wally (W) is injured in a futile attempt to restore some sort of heating to the hall of residence.

There is special legislation in this case which makes provision for the maintenance of an ambient temperature in halls of residence and this legislation may be interpreted as giving a remedy in the law of tort to the injured parties, although *prima facie* it is silent on the matter; furthermore, the tort of negligence would appear to be relevant in the present circumstances since carelessness of some sort could well lie behind the damage suffered by P and W. Both incidents occur on premises, thus the Occupiers' Liability Act 1957 should be considered as a possible source of remedies for the injured parties, both of whom are lawful visitors. Finally, in light of the fact that W is an employee of the University, attention should be given to the issue of employers' liability at common law.

P's claim for compensation will be considered first:

Action for breach of statutory duty

Proceeding on the **assumption** that the Halls of Residence Act 1995 is silent on the matter of a **civil** remedy for compensation in the event of its breach, it will be necessary for P to establish that the conditions laid down in the case law for the common law action for breach of statutory duty are satisfied.

The criteria laid down at common law are as follows:

1.   An obligation must be imposed by the statute on the defendant (e.g. *Harrison* v *NCB*).
2.   The statute must confer a civil right of action on the plaintiff – issues of special remedies/criminal penalties/benefit of a class of persons/public obligations/what, if anything, statute says about its enforcements/state of pre-existing law/alternative remedies available to plaintiff and alternative methods of enforcing the statute are to be considered here. See, e.g., *Knapp* v *Railway Executive*, *Cutler* v *Wandsworth Stadium*, *Phillips* v *Britannia Hygiene Laundry Co.*, *Thornton* v *Kirklees MBC*, *Lonrho Ltd* v *Shell Petroleum Co. Ltd (No. 2)*.
3.   The harm suffered must be within the scope of the general class of risks at which the statute is directed (e.g. *Gorris* v *Scott*).
4.   The defendant must have breached the statute.
5.   The breach must have caused the damage (e.g. *Ginty* v *Belmont Building Supplies Ltd*).

Prima facie P might have an action available for breach of statutory duty, but more information about the statute is needed in order to arrive at a fully considered opinion on the matter.

Occupiers' liability

An action for breach of the common duty of care imposed by the 1957 Act might give P an alternative course of action, though:

1.   Negligence on the part of the University would have to be established, i.e. P would have to establish **breach** of duty, though *res ipsa loquitur* might be available. Furthermore, we cannot be sure on the facts given that the reason for the failure of the boiler is due to the fault of the University. (This argument may also be relevant to the breach of statutory issue – above. In other words, issues of **causation** may be raised by the University.)

2.   Is the damage sustained by P due to the defective state of the premises, or is it the result of an 'activity' carried out thereon? It is submitted that the provision of heating is the province of the **occupier** here and that the matter is not one of a mere 'activity'. The terms of the licence to occupy granted by the University would be of importance on this point.

3.   Is 'illness' as opposed to 'injury' remediable under the 1957 Act? The Act is surely intended to protect the **safety** of the visitor and 'illness' must qualify.

Action in negligence

This alternative cause of action (e.g. *Revill* v *Newbery*) would probably encompass an 'activity' in any case. Assuming negligence could be proved (see above) and that no issue of causation was raised (see above) it would have to be considered whether the University was responsible personally, e.g. for understaffing/employment of incompetent employees (Warden/Wally)/inadequate maintenance of boilers/inadequate back up (a **single** oil heater?) Alternatively, **vicarious** liability for the negligence of the Warden/Wally (duty of care of the employees based on *Donoghue* v *Stevenson*) might be considered.

The University's obligations arising under **contract** (licence to occupy given to P) are not considered. Is this a case where **concurrent** liability in contract and tort exists?

We can now consider W's claim for compensation:

Action for breach of statutory duty

W is unlikely to succeed in an action for breach of statutory duty because he is probably not one of the class intended to be protected by the 1995 statute (*Knapp* v *Railway Executive*). There may well be some other statutory provision(s) relevant in his case, e.g. regulations made under the Health and Safety at Work Act 1974, but the question does not raise such a point – thus the matter should not be taken any further.

Employer's duty (in negligence) at common law

He is more likely to succeed in an action for breach of employer's duty (*Wilson & Clyde Coal Co.* v *English*): unsafe system of work, etc. Could the employers use contributory negligence (under the Law Reform (Contributory Negligence) Act 1945) as a partial defence, e.g. have they provided proper equipment and instructions for moving heavy items? (*Clifford* v *Charles H Challen & Son Ltd*, *Woods* v *Durable Suites Ltd*).

CHAPTER NINE

TRESPASS TORTS

9.1 Trespass to the Person and False Imprisonment

9.1.1 BATTERY

9.1.1.1 Intentionally or negligently

FOWLER v LANNING [1959] 1 All ER 290

FACTS: During a shooting party the plaintiff sustained gunshot wounds. He alleged the defendant was responsible. He issued a writ and served a statement of claims alleging that 'On 19 November 1957, at Vineyard Farm, Corfe Castle, in the County of Dorset, the defendant shot the plaintiff'. He did not plead negligence and the circumstances excluded any suggestion of a deliberate act.

D objected that the statement of claim was bad in law, disclosing no cause of action as neither intention nor negligence was asserted. Thus, a preliminary issue was appealed to the court.

DIPLOCK J:

> The distinction between actions of trespass on the case, and trespass vi et armis should be most carefully and precisely observed, otherwise we shall introduce much confusion and uncertainty . . .

So said De Grey, CJ, in 1773 in *Scott* v *Shepherd* (1773), 3 Wils 403 411. It must gratify the ghosts of generations of special pleaders that today, nearly a century after the passing of the Supreme Court of Judicature Act, 1873, I should be invited to decide whether such a distinction still exists where an unintentional injury to the person of the plaintiff arises directly from an act of the defendant . . .

The point of law is not, however, a mere academic one even at the present stage of the action. The alleged injuries were, I am told, sustained at a shooting party; it is not suggested that the shooting was intentional. The practical issue is whether, if the plaintiff was in fact injured by a shot from a gun fired by the defendant, the onus lies on the plaintiff to prove that the defendant was negligent, in which case, under the modern system of pleading, he must so plead and give particulars of negligence (see R.S.C., Ord. 19, r. 4) or whether it lies on the defendant to prove that the plaintiff's injuries were not caused by the defendant's negligence, in which case the plaintiff's statement of claim is sufficient and discloses a cause of action (see R.S.C., Ord. 19, r. 25). The issue is thus a neat one of onus of proof.

. . . What was the essential difference between the two alternative remedies based on identical facts? It is fashionable today to regard trespass to the person as representing the historic principle that every man acts at his peril and is liable for all the consequences of his acts; negligence as representing the more modern view that a man's freedom of action is subject only to the obligation not to infringe any duty of care which he owes to others (see *per* Lord Macmillan in *Read* v *J Lyons & Co. Ltd* [1946] 2 All ER 471).

But whether this was true of trespass in medieval times—and I respectfully doubt whether it ever was—the strict principle that every man acts at his peril was not applied in the case of trespass to the person even as long ago as 1617. It is true that in that year, in the much-cited case of *Weaver* v *Ward* ((1616), Hob 134), which arose out of a shooting accident during an exercise of trained bands, the Court of King's Bench held that a plea that 'the defendant casualiter et per infortuniam et contra voluntatem suam, in discharging of his piece did hurt and wound the plaintiff' was demurrable. But it would seem that this was because the plea, which was a special plea, was insufficient, because, although it denied intention, it did not negative negligence on the part of the defendant. It is clear from the report that the court was of opinion that the action of trespass to the person would fail if it should appear that the accident was 'inevitable, and that the defendant had committed no negligence to give occasion to the hurt'. This phrase is repeated in many of the later cases. Where it appears, however, it must be read in its historical context and not as if it were being used by judges to whom modern concepts of negligence, contributory negligence, and causation were familiar.

. . . I can summarise the law as I understand it from my examination of the cases as follows:

(1)   Trespass to the person does not lie if the injury to the plaintiff, although the direct consequence of the act of the defendant, was caused unintentionally and without negligence on the defendant's part.

(2)   Trespass to the person on the highway does not differ in this respect from trespass to the person committed in any other place.

(3)   If it were right to say with Blackburn J, in 1865 that negligence is a necessary ingredient of unintentional trespass only where the circumstances are such as to show that the plaintiff had taken on himself the risk of inevitable injury (i.e., injury which is the result of neither intention nor carelessness on the part of the defendant), the plaintiff must today in this crowded world be considered as taking on himself the risk of inevitable injury from any acts of his neighbour which, in the absence of damage to the plaintiff, would not in themselves be unlawful—of which discharging a gun at a shooting party in 1957 or a trained band exercise in 1617 are obvious examples. For Blackburn J . . . was in truth doing no more than stating the converse of the principle referred to by Lord Macmillan in *Read* v *J Lyons & Co. Ltd* [1946] 2 All ER 476, that a man's freedom of action is subject only to the obligation not to infringe any duty of care which he owes to others.

(4)   The onus of proving negligence, where the trespass is not intentional, lies on the plaintiff, whether the action be framed in trespass or in negligence. This has been unquestioned law in highway cases ever since *Holmes* v *Mather* [1875] LR 10 Exch 261, and there is no reason in principle, nor any suggestion in the decided authorities, why it should be any different in other cases. It is, indeed, but an illustration of the rule that he who affirms must prove, which lies at the root of our law of evidence. . . .

If, as I have held, the onus of proof of intention or negligence on the part of the defendant lies on the plaintiff, then, under the modern rules of pleading, he must allege either intention on the part of the defendant, or, if he relies on negligence, he must state the facts which he alleges constitute negligence. Without either of such allegations the bald statement that the defendant shot the plaintiff in unspecified circumstances with an unspecified weapon in my view discloses no cause of action.

Turning next to the alternative of negligent trespass to the person, there is here the bare allegation that on a particular day at a particular place 'the defendant shot the plaintiff'. In what circumstances, indeed with what weapon, from bow and arrow to atomic warhead, is not stated. So bare an allegation is consistent with the defendant's having exercised reasonable care. It may be—I know not—that, had the circumstances been set out with greater particularity, there would have been disclosed facts which themselves shouted negligence, so that the doctrine of res ipsa loquitur would have applied. In such a form the statement of claim might have disclosed a cause of action even although the word 'negligence'. itself had not been used, and the plaintiff in that event would have been limited to relying for proof of negligence on the facts which he had alleged. But I have today to deal with the pleading as it stands. As it stands, it neither alleges negligence in terms nor alleges facts which, if true, would of themselves constitute negligence; nor, if counsel for the plaintiff is right, would he be bound at any time before the trial to disclose to the defendant what facts he relies on as constituting negligence.

I do not see how the plaintiff will be harmed by alleging now the facts on which he ultimately intends to rely. On the contrary, for him to do so, will serve to secure justice between the parties. It offends the underlying purpose of the modern system of pleading that a plaintiff, by calling his grievance 'trespass to the person' instead of 'negligence', should force a defendant to come to trial blindfold; and I am glad to find nothing in the authorities which compels the court in this case to refrain from stripping the bandage from his eyes.

I hold that the statement of claim in its present form discloses no cause of action.

LETANG v *COOPER* [1964] 2 All ER 929 (CA)

FACTS: The plaintiff was sunbathing on a grassed area in the grounds of an hotel. The defendant injured her when he drove his car over her. It was not deliberate but arguably, actionable negligence. The normal limitation period for negligence, nuisance or breach of duty causing personal injury is 3 years (see s. 11, Limitation Act 1980). The limitation period for trespass to the person is 6 years [see s. 2, *ibid*]. The plaintiff missed the 3-year limitation period and brought an action alleging trespass to the person. The trial judge ruled that the defendant's act amounted to trespass. The defendant appealed to the Court of Appeal.

LORD DENNING MR: This argument, as it was developed before us, became a direct invitation to this court to go back to the old forms of action and to decide this case by reference to them. The statute bars *an action on the case*, it is said, after three years, whereas *trespass to the person* is not barred for six years . . . I must say that if we are, at this distance of time, to revive the distinction between trespass and case, we should get into the most utter confusion. The old common lawyers tied themselves in knots over it, and we should find ourselves doing the same. Let me tell you some of their contortions. Under the old law, whenever one man injured another by the *direct* and immediate application of force, the plaintiff could sue the defendant in *trespass* to the person, without alleging negligence (see *Leame* v *Bray* [1803] 3 East 593), whereas if the injury was only consequential, he had to sue in *case*. You will remember the illustration given by Fortescue, J, in *Reynolds* v *Clarke* [1725] 1 Stra 634:

> If a man throws a log into the highway and in that act it hits me, I may maintain trespass because it is an immediate wrong; but if, as it lies there, I tumble over it and receive an injury, I must bring an action upon the case because it is only prejudicial in consequence.

Nowadays, if a man carelessly throws a piece of wood from a house into a roadway, then whether it hits the plaintiff or he tumbles over it the next moment, the action would not be *trespass* or *case*, but simply negligence.

I must decline, therefore, to go back to the old forms of action in order to construe this statute. I know that in the last century Maitland said 'the forms of action we have buried but they still rule us from their graves'. But we have in this century shaken off their trammels. These forms of action have served their day. They did at one time form a guide to substantive rights; but they do so no longer. Lord Atkin told us what to do about them: 'when these ghosts of the past stand in the path of justice, clanking their mediaeval chains, the proper course for the judge is to pass through them undeterred', see *United Australia Ltd* v *Barclays Bank, Ltd* [1940] All ER 20.

The truth is that the distinction between trespass and case is obsolete. We have a different sub-division altogether. Instead of dividing actions for personal injuries into *trespass* (direct damage) or *case* (consequential damage), we divide the causes of action now according as the defendant did the injury intentionally or unintentionally. If one man intentionally applies force directly to another, the plaintiff has a cause of action in assult and battery, or, if you so please to describe it, in trespass to the person. 'The least touching of another in anger is a battery.' If he does not inflict intentionally, but only unintentionally, the plaintiff has no cause of action today in trespass. His only cause of action is in negligence, and then only on proof of want of reasonable care. If the plaintiff cannot prove want of reasonable care, he may have no cause of action at all. Thus, it is not enough nowadays for the plaintiff to plead that 'the defendant shot the plaintiff' (see *Fowler* v *Lanning* [1959] 1 All ER 290). He must also allege that he did it intentionally or negligently. If intentional, it is the tort of assault and battery. If negligent and causing damage, it is the tort of negligence.

The modern law on this subject was well expounded by my brother Diplock, J, in *Fowler v Lanning* with which I fully agree. But I would go this one step further: when the injury is not inflicted intentionally, but negligently, I would say that the only cause of action is negligence and not trespass. If it were trespass, it would be actionable without proof of damage; and that is not the law today.

In my judgment, therefore, the only cause of action in the present case (where the injury was unintentional) is negligence and is barred by reason of the express provision of the statute.

9.1.1.2 Without consent

CHATTERTON v GERSON [1981] 1 All ER 257

FACTS: The plaintiff was suffering chronic and intractable pain as an accidental side-effect of an operation. She was referred to the defendant, an expert in pain-relief, trained in the USA, who recommended a treatment common in the USA but novel in the UK. It did not work, and indeed left the plaintiff considerably worse off. The plaintiff alleged that she had not been given a proper explanation of the risks of the treatment, and, as a result, her consent to the treatment was not 'informed consent'. This meant she had not consented in effect and therefore the treatment amounted to a battery.

BRISTOW J: I have come to the conclusion that on the balance of probability Dr Gerson did give his usual explanation about the intrathecal phenol solution nerve block and its implications of numbness instead of pain plus a possibility of slight muscle weakness, and that Miss Chatterton's recollection is wrong; and on the evidence before me I so find. . . .
The claim
[T]here is no claim that Dr Gerson was negligent either in embarking on treatment of Miss Chatterton's chronic intractable plain by intrathecal phenol solution injection or in the performance of either of the operations which he carried out. The claim against him is put in two ways: (i) that her consent to operation was vitiated by lack of explanation of what the procedure was and what its implications were, so that she gave no real consent and the operation was in law a trespass to her person, that is, a battery; and (ii) that Mr Gerson was under a duty, as part of his obligation to treat his patient with the degree of professional skill and care to be expected of a reasonable skilled practitioner having regard to the state of the art at the time in question, to give Miss Chatterton such an explanation of the nature and implications of the proposed operation that she could come to an informed decision on whether she wanted to have it or would prefer to go on living with the pain which it was intended to relieve; that such explanation as he gave was in breach of that duty; that if he had performed that duty she would have chosen not to have the operation; and that therefore the unhappy consequences resulting from the operation, however wisely recommended and skilfully performed it may have been, are damage to Miss Chatterton which flows from Dr Gerson's breach of duty and for which he is responsible.

10   Trespass to the person and consent
It is clear law that in any context in which consent of the injured party is a defence to what would otherwise be a crime or a civil wrong, the consent must be real. Where, for example, a woman's consent to sexual intercourse is obtained by fraud, her apparent consent is no defence to a charge of rape. It is not difficult to state the principle or to appreciate its good sense. As so often, the problem lies in its application.

No English authority was cited before me of the application of the principle in the context of consent to the interference with bodily integrity by medical or surgical treatment. In *Reibl* v *Hughes* (1978) 21 DLR (2d) 14, which was an action based on negligence by failure to inform the patient of the risk in surgery involving the carotid artery, the Ontario Court of Appeal said that the trial judge was wrong in injecting the issue, Was it a battery? into the case pleaded and presented in negligence. The majority of the court, having referred to the United States cases on what is there called the 'doctrine of informed consent', decided that the action of 'battery' seemed quite inappropriate to cases in which the doctor has acted in good faith, and in the interests of the patient, but in doing so has been negligent in failing to disclose a risk inherent in the recommended treatment. They reversed the finding of the battery. I am told that that decision is now under appeal.

In *Stoffberg* v *Elliot* [1923] CPD 148 Watermeyer J, in his summing up to the jury in an action of assault in this context, directed them that consent to such surgical and medical treatment as the doctors might think necessary is not to be implied simply from the fact of going to hospital. There it was admitted that express consent to the operation should have been obtained but was not, due to oversight.

In my judgment what the court has to do in each case is to look at all the circumstances and say, 'Was there a real consent?' I think justice requires that in order to vitiate the reality of consent there must be a greater failure of communication between doctor and patient than that involved in a breach of duty if the claim is based on negligence. When the claim is based on negligence the plaintiff must prove not only the breach of duty to inform but that had the duty not been broken she would not have chosen to have the operation. Where the claim is based on trespass to the person, once it is shown that the consent is unreal, then what the plaintiff would have decided if she had been given the information which would have prevented vitiation of the reality of her consent is irrelevant.

In my judgment once the patient is informed in broad terms of the nature of the procedure which is intended, and gives her consent, that consent is real, and the cause of the action on which to base a claim for failure to go into risks and implications is negligence, not trespass. Of course, if information is withheld in bad faith, the consent will be vitiated by fraud. Of course, if by some accident, as in a case in the 1940s in the Salford Hundred Court, where a boy was admitted to hospital for tonsilectomy and due to administrative error was circumcised instead, trespass would be the appropriate cause of action against the doctor, though he was as much the victim of the error as the boy. But in my judgment it would be very much against the interests of justice if actions which are really based on a failure by the doctor to perform his dutry adequately to inform were pleaded in trespass.

In this case in my judgment even taking Miss Chatteron's evidence at its face value she was under no illusion as to the general nature of what an intrathecal injection of phenol solution nerve block would be, and in the case of each injection her consent was not unreal. I should add that getting the patient to sign a pro forma expressing consent to undergo the operation 'the effect and nature of which have been explained to me', as was done here in each case, should be a valuable reminder to everyone of the need for explanation and consent. But it would be no defence to an action based on trespass to the person if no explanation had in fact been given. The consent would have been expressed in form only, not in reality.

9.1.1.3 Implied consent: general social contact

WILSON v *PRINGLE* [1986] 2 All ER 440 (CA)

FACTS: The plaintiff and the defendant both aged 13 were pupils at the same school. An incident occurred in which the defendant pulled the plaintiff's bag from his shoulder. The plaintiff fell and suffered serious injury. The plaintiff claimed trespass to the person. The defendant alleged it was 'ordinary horseplay'. The plaintiff sought to enter summary judgment (i.e. asserting that there was no arguable defence). The application came before the Court of Appeal.

CROOM-JOHNSON LJ: The action of trespass to the person, in its sense where there is an assault to or a battery of the plaintiff, is of great antiquity. The court has been referred to a number of authorities in which the ingredients constituting that tort have been discussed and ruled on. In the early days the result of the case sometimes depended on whether a particular issue had been raised in the pleadings. Even if it had been raised, it might not amount to a defence to the action. The technicalities were great. One can detect in the reports the development not only of the action of trespass on the case (leading to the modern action of negligence) but also of the action of trespass to the person itself. . . .

Tuberville v *Savage* (1669) 1 Mod Rep 3 was an action for assault. The defendant clapped his hand on his sword and said to the plaintiff, 'if it were not assizetime, I would not take such language.' The court ruled that there was no threat, and accordingly no assault. This case is authority that there must be not only a deliberate threat (in an assault) or a deliberate touching (in battery) but also hostile behaviour. If the intention is obviously hostile, that will suffice, but it was recognised that there are many circumstances in life where contact with one's fellow men is not only unavoidable but even if deliberate may also be innocent. It was said:

If one strike another upon the hand, or arm, or breast in discourse, it is no assault, there being no *intention* to assault; but if one, intending to assault, strike at another and miss him, this is an assault.

Cole v *Turner* (1704) Holt KB 108 was an action in trespass for assault and battery. Holt CJ ruled that the least touching is a battery if it is done in anger, but that touching without violence or design of harm is no battery, and that violence in a rude and inordinate manner is a battery. Again, the case is authority for the proposition that for a battery there must be either an intention to harm or overt hostility.

It is not possible, even if it were desirable, to ignore the distinction between torts of negligence and torts of trespass strictly so called. This distinction has to be borne in mind in view of a submission made on behalf of the defendant, which would have had the effect of blurring the lines of demarcation between the two causes of action. In a situation (such as the present) in which both causes of action are sought to be raised it is necessary to be as precise as possible in seeing which of the facts giving rise to that situation are appropriate to which cause of action.

The first distinction between the two causes of action where there is personal injury is the element of contact between the plaintiff and defendant, that is a touching of some sort. In the action for negligence the physical contact (where it takes place at all) is normally though by no means always unintended. In the action for trespass, to constitute a battery, it is deliberate. Even so it is not every intended contact which is tortious. Apart from special justifications (such as acting in self-defence) there are many examples in everyday life where an intended contact or touch is not actionable as a trespass. These are not necessarily those (such as shaking hands) where consent is actual or to be implied. They may amount to one of the instances had in mind in *Tuberville* v *Savage* which take place in innocence. A modern instance is the batsman walking up the pavilion steps at Lords after making a century. He receives hearty slaps of congratulation on his back. He may not want them. Some of them may be too heavy for comfort. No one seeks his permission, or can assume he would give it if it were asked. But would an action for trespass to the person lie?

Another ingredient in the tort of trespass to the person is that of hostility. The references to anger sufficing to turn a touch into a battery (*Cole* v *Turner*) and the lack of an intention to assault which prevents a gesture from being an assault are instances of this. If there is hostile intent, that will by itself be cogent evidence of hostility. But the hostility may be demonstrated in other ways.

The defendant in the present case has sought to add to the list of necessary ingredients. He has submitted that before trespass to the person will lie it is not only the touching that must be deliberate but the infliction of injury. The plaintiff's counsel, on the other hand, contends that it is not the injury to the person which must be intentional, but the act of touching or battery which precedes it: as he put it, what must be intentional is the application of force and not the injury. In support of his contention, counsel for the defendant has relied on passages in the judgments in *Fowler* v *Lanning* [1959] 1 All ER 290 and *Letang* v *Cooper* [1964] 2 All ER 929.

In the course of his judgment Diplock J summarised the present law on the onus of proof in four propostions ([1959] 1 All ER 290 at 297). The first is relied on by the present defendant:

(1) Trespass to the person [battery] does not lie if the injury to the plaintiff, although the direct consequence of the act of the defendant, was caused unintentionally and without negligence on the defendant's part.

[His Lordship then considered *Letang* v *Cooper*.]

The judgment of Lord Denning MR was widely phrased, but it was delivered in an action where the only contact between the plaintiff and the defendant was unintentional. It has long been the law that claims arising out of an unintentional trespass must be made in negligence. A careful reading of his judgment shows that he was not adverting to the point now being made by this defendant. Similarly, the first proposition of Diplock J in *Fowler* v *Lanning* was not meant to bear the interpretation now given to it by counsel for the defendant. In our view, the submission made by counsel for the plaintiff is correct. It is the act and not the injury which must be intentional. An intention to injure is not essential to an action for trespass to the person. It is the mere trespass by itself which is the offence.

That does not answer the question, what does entitle an injured plaintiff to sue for the tort of trespass to the person? Reference must be made to one further case: *Williams* v *Humphrey* (12 February 1975, unreported), decided by Talbot J. There the defendant, a boy just under 16, pushed the plaintiff into a swimming pool and caused him physical injury. The judge found the defendant acted negligently and awarded damages. But there was another claim in trespass. Talbot J rejected the submission that the action would not lie unless there was an intent to injure. He held that it was sufficient, if the act was intentional, that there was no justification for it. In the present Ord 14 proceedings the judge relied on that decision.

The reasoning in *Williams* v *Humphrey* is all right as far as it goes, but it does not go far enough. It did not give effect to the reasoning of the older authorities, such as *Tuberville* v *Savage, Cole* v *Turner*, and *Williams* v *Jones* that for there to be either an assault or a battery there must be something in the nature of hostility. It may be evinced by anger, by words or gesture. Sometimes the very act of battery will speak for itself, as where somebody uses a weapon on another.

What, then, turns a friendly touching (which is not actionable) into an unfriendly one (which is)?

We have been referred to two criminal cases. *R* v *Sutton* [1977] 3 All ER 476 was decided in the Court of Appeal, Criminal Division. It was a case concerning alleged indecent assaults on boys who consented in fact although in law they were too young to do so. They were asked to pose for photographs. The only touching of the boys by the appellant was to get them stand in poses. It was touching on the hands, arms, legs or torso but only for the purpose of indicating how he wanted them to pose. It was not hostile or threatening. The court, which was presided over by Lord Widgery CJ, held these were therefore not assaults.

A more recent authority is *Collins* v *Wilcock* [1984] 3 All ER 374. This case was not cited to the judge. It had not been reported at the time of the hearing of the Ord 14 appeal. The facts were that a woman police officer, suspecting that a woman was soliciting contrary to the Street Offences Act 1959, tried to question her. The woman walked away, and was followed by the police officer. The officer took hold of her arm in order to restrain her. The woman scratched the officer's arm. She was arrested, charged with assaulting a police officer in the execution of her duty, and convicted. On appeal by case stated, the appeal was allowed, on the ground that the officer had gone beyond the scope of her duty in detaining the woman in circumstances short of arresting her. The officer had accordingly committed a battery.

The judgment of the Divisional Court was given by Robert Goff LJ. It is necessary to give a long quotation to do full justice to it. He said ([1984] 3 All ER 374 at 377–378):

> The law draws a distinction, in terms more easily understood by philologists than by ordinary citizens, between an assault and a battery. An assault is an act which causes another person to apprehend the infliction of immediate, unlawful, force on his person; a battery is the actual infliction of unlawful force on another person. Both assault and battery are forms of trespass to the person. Another form of trespass to the person is false imprisonment, which is the unlawful imposition of constraint on another's freedom of movement from a particular place. The requisite mental element is of no relevance in the present case. We are here concerned primarily with battery. The fundamental principle, plain and incontestable, is that every person's body is inviolate. It has long been established that any touching of another person, however slight, may amount to a battery. So Holt CJ held in 1704 that 'the least touching of another in anger is a battery.' See *Cole* v *Turner* (1704) Holt KB 108. The breadth of the principle reflects the fundamental nature of the interest so protected; as Blackstone wrote in his Commentaries, 'the law cannot draw the line between different degrees of violence, and therefore totally prohibits the first and lowest stage of it; every man's person being sacred, and no other having a right to meddle with it, in any the slightest manner' (see 3 Bl Com 120). The effect is that everybody is protected not only against physical injury but against any form of physical molestation. But so widely drawn a principle must inevitably be subject to exceptions. For example, children may be subjected to reasonable punishment; people

may be subjected to the lawful exercise of the power of arrest; and reasonable force may be used in self-defence or for the prevention of crime. But, apart from these special instances where the control or constraint is lawful, a broader exception has been created to allow for the exigencies of everyday life. Generally speaking, consent is a defence to battery; and most of the physical contacts of ordinary life are not actionable because they are impliedly consented to by all who move in society and so expose themselves to the risk of bodily contact. So nobody can complain of the jostling which is inevitable from his presence in, for example, a supermarket, an underground station or a busy street; nor can a person who attends a party complain if his hand is seized in friendship, or even if his back is (within reason) slapped (see *Tuberville* v *Savage* (1669) 1 Mod Rep 3).

Although such cases are regarded as examples of implied consent, it is more common nowadays to treat them as falling within a general exception embracing all physical contact which is generally acceptable in the ordinary conduct of daily life. We observe that, although in the past it has sometimes been stated that a battery is only commited where the action is 'angry, or revengeful, or rude, or insolent' (see I Hawk PC c 62, s. 2), we think that nowadays it is more realistic, and indeed more accurate, to state the broad underlying principle, subject to the broad exception. Among such forms of conduct, long held to be acceptable, is touching a person for the purpose of engaging his attention, though of course using no greater degree of physical contact than is reasonably necessary in the circumstances for that purpose. So, for example, it was held by the Court of Common Pleas in 1807 that a touch by a constable's staff on the shoulder of a man who had climbed on a gentleman's railing to gain a better view of a mad ox, the touch being only to engage the man's attention, did not amount to a battery (see *Wiffin* v *Kincard* (1807) 2 Bos & PNR 471, 127 ER 713; for another example, see *Coward* v *Baddeley* (1859) 4 H & N 478, 157 ER 927). But a distinction is drawn between a touch to draw a man's attention, which is generally acceptable, and a physical restraint, which is not. So we find Parke B observing in *Rawlings* v *Till* (1837) 3 M & W 28 at 29, 150 ER 1042, with reference to *Wiffin* v *Kincard*, that 'There the touch was merely to engage a man's attention, not to put a restraint on his person.' Furthermore, persistent touching to gain attention in the face of obvious disregard may transcend the norms of acceptable behaviour, and so be outside the exception. We do not say that more than one touch is never permitted; for example, the lost or distressed may surely be permitted a second touch, or possibly even more, on a reluctant or impervious sleeve or shoulder, as may a person who is acting reasonably in the exercise of a duty. In each case, the test must be whether the physical contact so persisted in has in the circumstances gone beyond generally acceptable standards of conduct; and the answer to that question will depend upon the facts of the particular case.

This rationalisation by Robert Goff LJ draws the so-called 'defences' to an action for trespass to the person (of which consent, self-defence, ejecting a trespasser, exercising parental authority, and statutory authority are some examples) under one umbrella of 'a general exception embracing all physical contact which is generally acceptable in the ordinary conduct of daily life'. It provides a solution to the old problem of what legal rule allows a casualty surgeon to perform an urgent operation on an unconscious patient who is brought into hospital. The patient cannot consent, and there may be no next of kin available to do it for him. Hitherto it has been customary to say in such cases that consent is to be implied for what otherwise be a battery on the unconscious body. It is better to simply say that the surgeon's action is acceptable in the ordinary conduct of everyday life, and not a battery. It will doubtless be convenient to continue to tie the labels of the 'defences' to the facts of any case where they are appropriate. But the rationalisation explains and utilises the expressions of judical opinion which appear in the authorities. It also prevents the approach to the facts, which, with respect to the judge in the present case, causes his judgment to read like a ruling on a demurrer in the days of special pleading.

Nevertheless, it still remains to indicate what is to be proved by a plantiff who brings an action for battery. Robert Goff LJ's judgment is illustrative of the considerations which underlie such an action, but it is not practicable to define a battery as 'physical contact which is not generally acceptable in the ordinary conduct of daily life.'

In our view, the authorities lead one to the conclusion that in a battery there must be an intentional touching or contact in one form or another of the plantiff by the defendant. That touching must be proved to be a hostile touching. That still leaves unanswered the question, when is a touching to be called hostile? Hostility cannot be equated with ill-will or malevolence. It cannot be governed by the obvious intention shown in acts like punching, stabbing or shooting. It cannot be solely governed by an expressed intention, although that may be strong evidence. But the element of hostility, in the sense in which it is now to be considered, must be a question of fact for the tribunal of fact. It may imported from the circumstances. Take the example of the police officer in *Collins* v *Wilcock*. She touched the woman deliberately, but without an intention to do more than restrain her temporarily. Nevertheless, she was acting unlawfully and in that way was acting with hostility. She was acting contrary to the woman's legal right not to be physically restrained. We see no more difficulty in establishing what she intended by means of question and answer, or by inference from the surrounding circumstances, than there is in establishing whether an apparently playful blow was struck in anger. The rules of law governing the legality of arrest may require strict application to the facts of appropriate cases, but in the ordinary give and take of everyday life the tribunal of fact should find no difficulty in answering the question 'was this, or was it not, a battery?' Where the immediate act of touching does not itself demonstrate hostility, the plaintiff should plead the facts which are said to do so.

Although we are all entitled to protection from physical molestation, we live in a crowded world in which people must be considered as taking on themselves some risk of injury (where it occurs) from the acts of others which are not in themselves unlawful. If negligence cannot be proved, it may be that an injured plaintiff who is also unable to prove a battery, will be without redress.

Defences like self-defence, and exercising the right of arrest, are relevant here. Similarly, it may be that allowances must be made, where appropriate, for the idiosyncrasies of individuals or (as was demonstrated in *Walmesley* v *Humenick* [1954] 2 DLR 232) the irresponsibility of childhood and the degree of care and awareness which is to be expected of children.

In our judgment the judge who tried the RSC Ord 14 proceedings took too narrow a view of what has to be proved in order to make out a case of trespass to the person. It will be apparent that there are a number of questions which must be investigated in evidence.

Accordingly we would allow this appeal, and give unconditional leave to defend.

9.1.2 ASSAULT

9.1.2.1 Act

R v *BURSTOW*; *R* v *IRELAND* [1997] 4 All ER 255 (HL)

FACTS: We are mainly concerned with Ireland's case. He had engaged in a series of silent telephone calls to three particular women, who became ill with various psychiatric complaints. He was convicted of assault occasioning actual bodily harm. He appealed, principally on the ground that this activity could not amount, in law, to an assault, because there was not the necessary immediacy of unlawful physical violence.

LORD STEYN: It is easy to understand the terrifying effect of a campaign of telephone calls at night by a silent caller to a woman living on her own. It would be natural for the victim to regard the calls as menacing. What may heighten her fear is that she will not know what the caller may do next. The spectre of the caller arriving at her doorstep bent on inflicting personal violence on her may come to dominate her thinking. After all, as a matter of common sense, what else would she be terrified about? The victim may suffer psychiatric illness such as anxiety neurosis or acute depression. Harassment of women by repeated silent telephone calls, accompanied on occasions by heavy breathing, is apparently a significant social problem. That the criminal law should be able to deal with this problem, and so far as is practicable, afford effective protection to victims is self evident.

From the point of view, however, of the general policy of our law towards the imposition of criminal responsibility, three specific features of the problem must be faced squarely. First, the medium used by the caller is the telephone: arguably it differs qualitatively from a face-to-face offer of violence to a sufficient extent to make a difference. Secondly, ex hypothesi the caller remains silent: arguably a caller may avoid the reach of the criminal law by remaining silent however menacing the context may be. Thirdly, it is arguable that the criminal law does not take into account 'mere' psychiatric illnesses. . . .

R v Ireland: Was there an assault?

It is now necessary to consider whether the making of silent telephone calls causing psychiatric injury is capable of constituting an assault under section 47. The Court of Appeal, as constituted in *Ireland's* case, answered that question in the affirmative. There has been substantial academic criticism of the conclusion and reasoning in *Ireland*: see *Archbold News*, Issue 6, 12 July 1996; *Archbold's Criminal Pleading, Evidence & Practice* (1995), Supplement No. 4 (1996), pp. 345–347; *Smith and Hogan, Criminal Law*, 8th ed., 413; Herring, 'Assault by Telephone' [1997] CLJ 11; 'Assault' [1997] Crim LR 434, 435–436. Counsel's arguments, broadly speaking, challenged the decision in *Ireland* on very similar lines. Having carefully considered the literature and counsel's arguments, I have come to the conclusion that the appeal ought to be dismissed.

The starting point must be that an assault is an ingredient of the offence under section 47. It is necessary to consider the two forms which an assault may take. The first is battery, which involves the unlawful application of force by the defendant upon the victim. Usually, section 47 is used to prosecute in cases of this kind. The second form of assault is an act causing the victim to apprehend an imminent application of force upon her: see *Fagan* v *Metropolitan Police Commissioner* [1969] 1 QB 439, 444D-E. . . .

It is to assault in the form of an act causing the victim to fear an immediate application of force to her that I must turn. Counsel argued that as a matter of law an assault can never be committed by words alone and therefore it cannot be committed by silence. The premise depends on the slenderest authority, namely, an observation by Holroyd J to a jury that 'no words or singing are equivalent to an assault': *Meade's and Belt's* Case (1823) 1 Lew CC 184. The proposition that a gesture may amount to an assault, but that words can never suffice, is unrealistic and indefensible. A thing said is also a thing done. There is no reason why something said should be incapable of causing an apprehension of immediate personal violence, e.g. a man accosting a woman in a dark alley saying 'come with me or I will stab you'. I would, therefore, reject the proposition that an assault can never be committed by words.

That brings me to the critical question whether a silent caller may be guilty of an assault. The answer to this question seems to me to be 'yes, depending on the facts'. It involves questions of fact within the province of the jury. After all, there is no reason why a telephone caller who says to a woman in a menacing way 'I will be at your door in a minute or two' may not be guilty of an assault if he causes his victim to apprehend immediate personal violence. Take now the case of the silent caller. He intends by his silence to cause fear and he is so understood. The victim is assailed by uncertainty about his intentions. Fear may dominate her emotions, and it may be the fear that the caller's arrival at her door may be imminent. She may fear the *possibility* of immediate personal violence. As a matter of law the caller may be guilty of an assault: whether he is or not will depend on the circumstance and in particular on the impact of the caller's potentially menacing call or calls on the victim. Such a prosecution case under section 47 may be fit to leave to the jury. And a trial judge may, depending on the circumstances, put a common sense consideration before jury, namely what, if not the possibility of imminent personal violence, was the victim terrified about? I conclude that an assault may be committed in the particular factual circumstances which I have envisaged. For this reason I reject the submission that as a matter of law a silent telephone caller cannot ever be guilty of an offence under section 47.

9.1.2.2 Immediately

THOMAS v NUM [1985] 2 All ER 1

FACTS: During the miners' strike a large number of strikers attended at pits where there was a small number of strike breakers. The police also attended, and the strike breakers were driven into work and protected by a strong police guard. Nevertheless they were subject to abuse and threatening gestures. The strike breakers sought an injunction to restrain mass picketing. A question arose as to whether the acts of the strikers were unlawful and, if so, on what basis. The case came before SCOTT J:

[His Lordship considered arguments that the picketing was tortious because it breached statutes regulating industrial action.]

[Counsel] submitted that the picketing complained of was tortious under a number of heads. It represented, he said, the tort of assault in that the miners going to work were put in fear of violence. I cannot accept this. Assault is defined in *Clarke and Lindsell on Torts* (15th edn, 1982) para 14/10 as 'an overt act indicating an immediate intention to commit a battery, coupled with the capacity to carry that intention into effect'. The tort of assault is not, in my view, committed, unless the capacity in question is present at the time the overt act is committed. Since the working miners are in vehicles and the pickets are held back from the vehicles, I do not understand how the most violent of threats or gestures could be said to constitute an assault. . . .

The working miners are entitled to use the highway for the purpose of entering and leaving their respective place of work. In the exercise of that right they are at present having to suffer the presence and behaviour of the pickets and demonstrators. The law has long recognised that unreasonable interference with the rights of others is actionable in tort. The law of nuisance is a classic example and was classically described by Lindley MR in *J Lyons & Sons Ltd* v *Wilkins* [1899] 1 Ch 255 at 267. It is, however, not every act of interference with the enjoyment by an individual of his property rights that will be actionable in nuisance. The law must strike a balance between conflicting rights and interests. The point is made in *Clerk and Lindsell* para 23/01:

> A variety of different things may amount to a nuisance in *fact* but whether they are *actionable* as the *tort* of nuisance will depend upon a variety of considerations and a balance of conflicting interests.

Nuisance is strictly concerned with, and may be regarded as confined to, activity which unduly interferes with the use or enjoyment of land or of easements. But there is no reason why the law should not protect on a similar basis the enjoyment of other rights. All citizens have the right to use the public highway. Suppose an individual were persistently to follow another on a public highway, making rude gestures or remarks in order to annoy or vex. If continuance of such conduct were threatened no one can doubt but that a civil court would, at the suit of the victim, restrain by an injunction the continuance of the conduct. The tort might be described as a species of private nuisance, namely unreasonable interference with the victim's rights to use the highway. But the label for the tort does not, in my view, matter.

In the present case, the working miners have the right to use the highway for the purpose of going to work. They are, in my judgment, entitled under the general law to exercise that right without unreasonable harassment by others. Unreasonable harassment of them in their exercise of that right would, in my judgment, be tortious.

A decision whether in this, or in any other similar case, the presence or conduct of pickets represents a tortious interference with the right of those who wish to go to work to do so without harassment must depend on the particular circumstances of the particular case. The balance to which I have earlier referred must be struck between the rights of those going to work and the rights of the pickets.

It was made clear in *Ward Lock & Co. Ltd* v *Operative Printers-Assistants' Society* (1906) 22 TLR 327 that picketing was not, per se, a common law nuisance. The Court of Appeal was in that case considering the question from the point of view of the owner of the premises being picketed. The picketing was peaceful and *per* Vaughan Williams LJ (at 329), 'there was no evidence that the comfort of the plaintiffs or the ordinary enjoyment of the Botolph Printing Works was seriously interfered with by the watching and besetting'. He held, in effect, that there was no common law nuisance being committed.

Similarly, in the present case, the working miners cannot complain of picketing per se or of demonstrations per se. They can only complain of picketing or demonstrations which unreasonably harass them in their entry into and egress from their place of work.

9.1.3 INTERFERENCE WITH LIBERTY

9.1.3.1 Imprisonment

BIRD v *JONES* (1845) 7 QBD 742

FACTS: The defendant had built a grandstand on a bridge, with a view to charging spectators to watch a regatta. The plaintiff wished to walk across the bridge, using the part enclosed by the defendant. The defendant prevented him from going where he intended, but made it clear that he could return to whence he had come. The plaintiff alleged false imprisonment (among other claims).

COLERIDGE J: I am of opinion that there was no imprisonment. To call it so appears to confound partial obstruction and disturbance with total obstruction and detention. A prison may have its boundary large or narrow, visible and tangible, or, though real, still in the conception only; it may itself be moveable or fixed: but a boundary it must have; and that boundary the party imprisoned must be prevented from passing; he must be prevented from leaving that place, within the ambit of where the party imprisoning would confine him, except by prison-breach. Some confusion seems to me to arise from confounding imprisonment of the body with mere want of freedom: it is one part of the definition of freedom to be able to go whithersoever one pleases; but imprisonment is something more than the mere loss of this freedom, it includes the notion of restraint within some limits defined by a will or action exterior to our own.

WILLIAMS J: . . . 'Every confinement of the person' (according to Blackstone (3 Bl. C. 127)) 'is an imprisonment, whether it be in a common prison, or in a private house, or in the stocks, or even by forcibly detaining one in the public street,' which perhaps may seem to imply the application of force more than is really necessary to make an imprisonment. Lord Coke, in his Second Institute (2 Inst. 589), speaks of 'a prison in law' and 'a prison in deed:' so that there may be a constructive, as well as an actual, imprisonment: and, therefore, it may be admitted that personal violence need not be used in order to amount to it. . . . So, if a person should direct a constable to take another in custody, and that person should be told by the constable to go with him, and the orders are obeyed, and they walk together in the direction pointed out by the constable, that is, constructively, an imprisonment, though no actual violence be used. In such cases, however, though little may be said, much is meant and perfectly understood. The party addressed in the manner above supposed feels that he has no option, no more power of going in any but the one direction prescribed to him that if the constable . . . had actually hold of him: no return or deviation from the course prescribed is open to him. And it is that entire restraint upon the will which, I apprehend, constitutes the imprisonment.

9.1.3.2 Justification

ROBINSON v BALMAIN NEW FERRY CO. LTD [1910] AC 295 (PC)

FACTS: The defendant operated a ferry in Sydney Harbour. On one shore was a terminal building, on the other a quay only. All fares were collected by means of turnstiles at the building. Passengers from that shore paid on entry, passengers in the other direction paid on exit. There were notices explaining the arrangement. The plaintiff entered the terminal, paying as he did so. He found there was no ferry for some time and changed his mind. He sought to leave without paying although the notice, which reflected the 'lawful regulations' of the ferry company, stated 'Notice: A fare of one penny must be paid on entering or leaving the wharf. No exception will be made to this rule, whether the passenger has travelled by the ferry or not.' He was refused permission but finally squeezed past the company's officers and went the 'wrong way' through a turnstile. He claimed false imprisonment.

LORD LOREBURN LC: In this case their Lordships entirely agree with the conclusion of the High Court of Australia. There has been considerable difficulty because of the way in which the case seems to have been presented in the Courts of Australia, and particularly in the Supreme Court of New South Wales. There is no note of the summing up of the learned judge who tried the case, and some of the arguments which have been advanced by the learned counsel for the respondents are not consistent with the arguments that were advanced on their behalf in the Australian Courts. But their Lordships think that the relevant facts are all quite beyond dispute, and that some of the facts disputed are quite immaterial.

The plaintiff paid a penny on entering the wharf to stay there till the boat should start and then be taken by the boat to the other side. The defendants were admittedly always ready and willing to carry out their part of this contract. Then the plaintiff changed his mind and wished to go back. The rules as to the exit from the wharf by the turnstile required a penny for any person who went through. This the plaintiff refused to pay, and he was by force prevented from going through the turnstile. He then claimed damages for assault and false imprisonment.

There was no complaint, at all events there was no question left to the jury by the plaintiff's request, of any excessive violence, and in the circumstances admitted it is clear to their Lordships that there was no false imprisonment at all. The plaintiff was merely called upon to leave the wharf in the way in which he contracted to leave it. There is no law requiring the defendants to make the exit from their premises gratuitous to people who come there upon a definite contract which involves their leaving the wharf by another way; and the defendants were entitled to resist a forcible passage through their turnstile.

The question whether the notice which was affixed to these premises was brought home to the knowledge of the plaintiff is immaterial, because the notice itself is immaterial.

When the plaintiff entered the defendants premises there was nothing agreed as to the terms on which he might go back, because neither party contemplated his going back. When he desired to do so the defendants were entitled to impose a reasonable condition before allowing him to pass through their turnstile from a place to which he had gone of his own free will. The payment of a penny was a quite fair condition, and if he did not choose to comply with it the defendants were not bound to let him through. He could proceed on the journey he had contracted for.

Under these circumstances their Lordships consider that, when the defendants at the end of the case submitted that there ought to be a nonsuit, the learned judge ought to have nonsuited the plaintiff. Their Lordships are glad that they can thus arrive, in accordance with law, at this decision, because they regard the plaintiff's conduct as thoroughly unreasonable in this case.

HERD v WEARDALE STEEL COAL & COKE CO. [1915] AC 67 (HL)

FACTS: The plaintiff was a miner at the defendant's pit. During a shift he joined a lightning strike and demanded to be taken to the surface. The defendant's officials refused to do so until the end of the shift (although in fact the plaintiff was allowed up half an hour after the demand and 2 ½ hours before the end of the shift). The plaintiff claimed that the delay in allowing him up amounted to false imprisonment.

VISCOUNT HALDANE LC: My Lords, by the law of this country no man can be restrained of his liberty without authority in law. That is a proposition the maintenance of which is of great importance; but at the same time it is a proposition which must be read in relation to other propositions which are equally important. If a man chooses to go into a dangerous place at the bottom of a quarry or the bottom of a mine, from which by the nature of physical circumstances he cannot escape, it does not follow from the proposition I have enunciated about liberty that he can compel the owner to bring him up out of it. The owner may or may not be under a duty arising from circumstances, on broad grounds the neglect of which may possibly involve him in a criminal charge or a civil liability. It is unnecessary to discuss the conditions and circumstances which might bring about such a result, because they have, in the view I take, nothing to do with false imprisonment.

My Lords, there is another proposition which has to be borne in mind, and that is the application of the maxim *volenti non fit injuria*. If a man gets into an express train and the doors are locked pending its arrival at its destination, he is not entitled, merely because the train has been stopped by signal, to call for the doors to be opened to let him out. He has entered the train on the terms that he is to be conveyed to a certain station without the opportunity of getting out before that, and he must abide by the terms on which he has entered the train. So when a man goes down a mine, from which access to the surface does not exist in the absence of special facilities given on the part of the owner of the mine, he is only entitled to the use of these facilities (subject possibly to the exceptional circumstances to which I have alluded) on the terms on which he has entered. I think it results from what was laid down by the Judicial Committee of the Privy Council in *Robinson v Balmain New Ferry Co.* [1910] AC 295 that that is so. The man had gone in upon the pier knowing that those were the terms and conditions as to exit, and it was not false imprisonment to hold him to conditions which he had accepted. So, my Lords, it is not false imprisonment to hold a man to the conditions he has accepted when he goes down a mine . . .

Now, my Lords, in the present case what happened was this. The usage of the mine—a usage which I think must be taken to have been notified—was that the workman was to be brought up at the end of his shift. In this case the workman refused to work; it may have been for good reasons or it may have been for bad,—I do not think that question concerns us. He said that the work he had been ordered to do was of a kind that was dangerous, and he threw down his tools and claimed to come up to the surface. The manager, or at any rate the person responsible for the control of the cage, said: 'No, you have chosen to come at a time which is not your proper time, and although there is the cage standing empty we will not bring you up in it,' and the workman was in consequence under the necessity of remaining at the bottom of the shaft for about twenty minutes. There was no refusal to bring him up at the ordinary time which was in his bargain; but there was a refusal,—and I am quite ready to assume that the motive of it was to punish him, I will assume it for the sake of argument, for having refused to go on with his work—by refusing to bring him up at the moment when he claimed to come. Did that amount to false imprisonment? In my opinion it did not. No statutory right under the Coal Mines Regulation Act, 1887, avails him, for the reason which I have already spoken of. Nor had he any right in contract. His right in contract was to come up at the end of his shift. Was he then falsely imprisoned? There were facilities, but they were facilities which, in accordance with the conditions that he had accepted by going down, were not available to him until the end of his shift, at any rate as of right.

My Lords, under these circumstances I find it wholly impossible to come to the conclusion that the principle to which I have alluded, and on which the doctrine of false imprisonment is based, has any application to the case. *Volenti non fit injuria*. The man chose to go to the bottom of the mine under these conditions,—conditions which he accepted. He had no right to call upon the employers to make use of special machinery put there at their cost, and involving cost in its working, to bring him to the surface just when he pleased.

My Lords, I am aware that this question is one which will probably give rise to great general interest, but, whatever may be the feeling about questions of this kind, it is still more important that in deciding matters arising out of them strict adherence is maintained to intelligible and well-defined principles of our law so long as they stand part of it. The law of England seems to me, as it stands to-day, to be perfectly defined as regards cases of the kind, and, if it is to be altered, it must be altered by statute. It may obviously be very difficult to make any provision in relation to coal mines which requires that a workman should be entitled to come up at any moment he pleases. The nature of the employment will probably always require reasonable restrictions. But what we are concerned with at the moment is this and this simply: that no conditions existed which enabled the miner in this case to claim the right which he asserted, and that there was nothing which comes within the definition well known in the law of England which amounts to false imprisonment.

R v DEPUTY GOVERNOR OF PARKHURST PRISON, EX PARTE HAGUE; WELDON v HOME OFFICE [1992] 1 AC 58 (HL)

FACTS: H was made subject to a segregation order (i.e. held in solitary confinement) as a disciplinary measure during his prison sentence.

W complained of a strip search and detention. H and W both alleged that their treatment amounted to false imprisonment. The cases proceeded separately, and were then heard together in the House of Lords. Much of the argument and speeches concerned other possible causes of action.

LORD BRIDGE: The Court of Appeal in *Weldon's* case approached the question whether a prisoner serving his sentence can ever sustain a claim for false imprisonment, as they were invited to do by Mr Laws, as a single question which must admit of the same answer irrespective of the identity of the defendant. Ralph Gibson LJ, delivering the leading judgment, with which both Fox and Parker LJJ agreed, said ([1990] 3 All ER 672 at 681):

There is no reason, apparent to me, why the nature of the tort, evolved by the common law for the protection of personal liberty, should be held to be such as to deny its availability to a convicted prisoner whose residual liberty should, in my judgment, be protected so far as the law can properly achieve unless statute requires otherwise. If, however, as [Mr Laws] submits, the tort of false imprisonment is not available to a convicted prisoner against a prison officer, I accept his submission that it could not, for the same reasons, be available to a convicted prisoner against a fellow prisoner.

Ralph Gibson LJ had also delivered the judgment of the Divisional Court in *Hague's* case in which he expressed the view that the segregation of a prisoner would not constitute the tort of false imprisonment if the order for segregation, although not lawfully authorised under r. 43, was given in good faith. Giving the judgment in *Weldon's* case he found it unnecessary to express a final conclusion on this point since, if want of good faith were a necessary ingredient of the tort, he held that it was sufficiently alleged in the pleading against the officers concerned. The pleading, he held, also alleged circumstances capable of amounting to 'intolerable conditions of detention' such as would sustain a claim of false imprisonment on the authority of the decision of the Court of Appeal in *Middleweek* v *Chief Constable of the Merseyside Police* (1985) [1990] 3 All ER 662. It was on these grounds that the Court of Appeal declined to strike out the pleading of false imprisonment in *Weldon's* case.
. . .

In so far as the Court of Appeal's reasoning in these judgments proceeds from the premise urged upon them by Mr Laws that a prisoner's 'right to liberty' is either totally abrogated or partially retained in the form of a 'residual liberty', I think, with all respect, that it is erroneous. To ask at the outset whether a convicted prisoner enjoys in law a 'residual liberty', as if the extent of any citizen's right to liberty were a species of right in rem or a matter of status, is to ask the wrong question. An action for false imprisonment is an action in personam. The tort of false imprisonment has two ingredients: the fact of imprisonment and the absence of lawful authority to justify it. In *Meering* v *Grahame-White Aviation Co. Ltd* (1919) 122 LT 44 at 54 Atkin LJ said that 'any restraint within defined bounds which is a restraint in fact may be an imprisonment'. Thus if A imposes on B a restraint within defined bounds and is sued by B for false imprisonment, the action will succeed or fail according to whether or not A can justify the restraint imposed on B as lawful. A child may be lawfully restrained within defined bounds by his parents or by the schoolmaster to whom the parents have delegated their authority. But if precisely the same restraint is imposed by a stranger without authority, it will be unlawful and will constitute the tort of false imprisonment.
. . . I shall address first what I believe to be the primary and fundamental issue, viz whether any restraint within defined bounds imposed upon a convicted prisoner whilst serving his sentence by the prison governor or by officers acting with the authority of the prison governor and in good faith, but in circumstances where the particular form of restraint is not sanctioned by the Prison Rules, amounts for that reason to the tort of false imprisonment.
The starting point is s. 12(1) of the Prison Act 1952 which provides: 'A prisoner, whether sentenced to imprisonment or committed to prison on remand pending trial or otherwise, may be lawfully confined in any prison.' This provides lawful authority for the restraint of the prisoner within the defined bounds of the prison by the governor of the prison . . . Certainly in the ordinary closed prison the ordinary prisoner will at any time of day or night be in a particular part of the prison, not because that is where he chooses to be, but because that is where the prison regime requires him to be. He will be in his cell, in the part of the prison where he is required to work, in the exercise yard, eating meals, attending education classes or enjoying whatever recreation is permitted, all in the appointed place and at the appointed time and all in accordance with a more or less rigid regime to which he must conform. Thus the concept of the prisoner's 'residual liberty' as a species of freedom of movement within the prison enjoyed as a legal right which the prison authorities cannot lawfully restrain seems to me quite illusory. The prisoner is at all times lawfully restrained within closely defined bounds and if he is kept in a segregated cell, at a time when, if the rules have not been misapplied, he would be in the company of other prisoners in the workshop, at the dinner table or elsewhere, this is not the deprivation of his liberty of movement, which is the essence of the tort of false imprisonment, it is the substitution of one form of restraint for another. . . .

In my opinion, to hold a prisoner entitled to damages for false imprisonment on the ground that he has been subject to a restraint upon his movement which was not in accordance with the Prison Rules would be, in effect, to confer on him under a different legal label a cause of action for breach of statutory duty under the rules. Having reached the conclusion that it was not the intention of the rules to confer such a right, I am satisfied that the right cannot properly be asserted in the alternative guise of a claim to damages for false imprisonment [. . .]

I turn next to the question posed by the example given in the judgment of Parker LJ in *Weldon*'s case [1990] 3 All ER 672 at 686, [1990] 3 WLR 465 at 480, of a prisoner locked in a shed by fellow prisoners . . . The prisoner locked in the shed is certainly restrained within defined bounds and it is *nihil ad rem* that if he were not locked in the shed, he would be locked in his cell or restrained in accordance with the prison regime in some other part of the prison. The restraint in the shed is unlawful because the fellow prisoners acted without the authority of the governor and it is only the governor, who has the legal custody of the prisoner, and persons acting with the authority of the governor who can rely on the provisions of s. 12(1).

This consideration also leads to the conclusion that a prison officer who acts in bad faith by deliberately subjecting a prisoner to a restraint which he knows he has no authority to impose may render himself personally liable to an action for false imprisonment as well as committing the tort of misfeasance in public office. Lacking the authority of the governor, he also lacks the protection of s. 12(1). But if the officer deliberately acts outside the scope of his authority, he cannot render the governor or the Home Office vicariously liable for his tortious conduct. This no doubt explains why Mr Harris did not seek to sustain the decision of the Court of Appeal in his favour on the ground that the plaintiff's pleading should be read as involving an allegation of bad faith.

There remains the question whether an otherwise lawful imprisonment may be rendered unlawful by reason only of the conditions of detention. In *R v Comr of Police of the Metropolis, ex parte Nahar, The Times*, 28 May 1983, two applicants for habeas corpus who had been remanded in custody were held pursuant to the provisions of s. 6 of the Imprisonment (Temporary Provisions) Act 1980 in cells below the Camberwell Green Magistrates' Court which were designed only to enable persons to be held in custody for a few hours at a time and which were obviously deficient in many respects for the purpose of accommodating prisoners for longer periods. They sought their release on the ground that the conditions of their detention rendered it unlawful. The applications were rejected, but Stephen Brown J said in the course of his judgment: 'There must be some minimum standard to render detention lawful. . .' McCullough J said:

> Despite the temporary nature of the detention there contemplated, there must be implied into s. 6 of the 1980 Act some term which relates to the conditions under which a prisoner may lawfully be detained. I say so because it is possible to conceive of hypothetical circumstances in which the conditions of detention were such as would make that detention unlawful. I do not propose to offer any formulation of that term. Were it broken in any particular case I would reject emphatically the suggestion that the matter would not be one for the exercise of the court's jurisdiction to grant the writ of habeas corpus.

These observations were considered by the Court of Appeal in *Middleweek v Chief Constable of the Merseyside Police* [1990] 3 All ER 662. The plaintiff had been awarded damages for false imprisonment by the jury on the basis that his otherwise lawful detention at a police station had been rendered unlawful because it was unreasonable in the circumstances to keep him in a police cell. The defendant successfully appealed, but Ackner LJ, delivering the judgment of the court, said ([1990] 2 All ER 662 at 668):

> We agree with the views expressed by the Divisional Court that it must be possible to conceive of hypothetical cases in which the conditions of detention are so intolerable as to render the detention unlawful and thereby provide a remedy to the prisoner in damages for false imprisonment. . .

I sympathise entirely with the view that the person lawfully held in custody who is subjected to intolerable conditions ought not to be left without a remedy against his custodian, but the proposition that the conditions of detention may render the detention itself unlawful raises formidable difficulties. If the proposition be sound, the corollary must be that when the conditions of detention deteriorate to the point of intolerability, the detainee is entitled immediately to go free. It is impossible, I think, to define with any precision what would amount to intolerable conditions for this purpose. McCullough J understandably and perhaps wisely abstained from any attempt at definition in *Ex parte Nahar*. The examples given by Ackner LJ of a flooded or gas-filled cell are so extreme that they do not, with respect, offer much guidance as to where the line should be drawn. The law is certainly left in a very unsatisfactory state if the legality or otherwise of detaining a person who in law is and remains liable to detention depends on such an imprecise criterion and may vary from time to time as the conditions of his detention change.

The logical solution to the problem, I believe, is that if the conditions of an otherwise lawful detention are truly intolerable, the law ought to be capable of providing a remedy directly related to those conditions without characterising the fact of the detention itself as unlawful. I see no real difficulty in saying that the law can provide such a remedy. Whenever one person is lawfully in the custody of another, the custodian owes a duty of care to the detainee. If the custodian negligently allows, or a fortiori, if he deliberately causes, the detainee to suffer in any way in his health he will be in breach of that duty. But short of anything that could properly be described as a physical injury or an impairment of health, if a person lawfully is kept in conditions which cause him for the time being physical pain or a degree of discomfort which can properly be described as intolerable, I believe that could and should be treated as a breach of the custodian's duty of care for which the law should award damages. For this purpose it is quite unnecessary to attempt any definition of the criterion of intolerability. It would be a question of fact and degree in any case which came before the court to determine whether the conditions to which a detainee had been subjected were such as to warrant an award of damages for the discomfort he had suffered. In principle I believe it is acceptable for the law to provide a remedy on this basis, but that the remedy suggested in the *Nahar* and *Middleweek* cases is not. In practice the problem is perhaps not very likely to arise.

POLICE AND CRIMINAL EVIDENCE ACT 1984

24.   Arrest without warrant for arrestable offences

(4)   Any person may arrest without a warrant—

(a)   anyone who is in the act of committing an arrestable offence;

(b)   anyone whom he has reasonable grounds for suspecting to be committing such an offence.

(5)   Where an arrestable offence has been committed, any person may arrest without a warrant—

(a)   anyone who is guilty of the offence;

(b)   anyone whom he has reasonable grounds for suspecting to be guilty of it.

(6)   Where a constable has reasonable grounds for suspecting that an arrestable offence has been committed, he may arrest without a warrant anyone whom he has reasonable grounds for suspecting to be guilty of the offence.

(7)   A constable may arrest without a warrant—

(a)   anyone who is about to commit an arrestable offence;

(b)   anyone whom he has reasonable grounds for suspecting to be about to commit an arrestable offence.

WALTERS v *W H SMITH* [1911–13] All ER Rep 170

FACTS: The plaintiff was assistant manager of a bookstall owned by the defendant. He was suspected of theft of money and/or stock. A trap was set and a marked book was found in the plaintiff's possession in suspicious circumstances. He was detained and then charged with theft. He was ultimately acquitted. He then brought an action for false imprisonment.

SIR RUFUS ISAACS CJ: During the trial it was contended by the plaintiff that as the defendants admitted that no felony had in fact been committed in respect of the book *Traffic* there was no defence to the claim based upon false imprisonment. The defendants contended that all that they need establish as legal justification for the imprisonment was (i) that an actual felony or felonies had been committed, and (ii) that they had reasonable and probable cause for suspecting the plaintiff of having committed an actual felony or felonies; in other words, it was for the defendants that it was not essential to their defence to prove that the felony for which the plaintiff was arrested had in fact been committed . . . Having regard to the facts proved, I have no doubt that the defendants had reasonable and probable cause for suspecting the plaintiff of having stolen the money or books other than the book *Traffic* when they gave the plaintiff into custody. I further find as a fact that the plaintiff was given into custody for stealing the book *Traffic*, and that although the defendants, when they caused his arrest, were convinced that the man who stole the book was also guilty of the other thefts, they did not cause his arrest for these other thefts, but only for that theft of which they thought they had clear evidence. Doubtless they were influenced to this course by the suspicion, and indeed conviction, in their minds that the plaintiff had committed the other thefts. It induced them to give him into custody for stealing the book, whereas otherwise they might merely have summoned him or, indeed, might not have prosecuted him.

If as a matter of law the defendants must prove that the particular felony for which the plaintiff was imprisoned had in fact been committed, they have failed in their defence, as no felony with regard to *Traffic* had in fact been committed. If as a matter of law the defendants may justify the imprisonment by proof that at the time of the arrest of the plaintiff felonies had been committed other than that for which he had been arrested, and that they had reasonable and probable cause for suspecting the plaintiff of having committed them, they would be entitled to succeed. That is the precise question for decision and one which, so far as I am aware, has never been expressly decided. It was strenuously argued before me by the defendants that in ordering the arrest of the plaintiff they had only caused such an interference with his liberty as was necessary to put matters in train for judicial inquiry, and that the charge subsequently formulated against the plaintiff in the legal proceedings should not be regarded in the claim for false imprisonment. I cannot accept that view, for it became quite clear during the case, and I have found, that the plaintiff was arrested for stealing the book, and I must deal with the case upon that basis. Interference with the liberty of the subject, and especially by a private person, has ever been most jealously guarded by the common law of the land.

At common law a police constable may arrest a person if he has reasonable cause to suspect that a felony has been committed, although it afterwards appears that no felony had been committed, but that is not so when a private person makes or causes the arrest, for, to justify his action, he must prove, among other things, that a felony has actually been committed: see *Beckwith* v *Philby* (1827) 6 B & C 635, *per* Lord Tenterden, CJ. I have come to the conclusion that it is necessary for a private person to prove that the same felony had been committed as that for which the plaintiff had been given into custody . . . In Hale's Pleas of the Crown vol. 2, ch. 10, s. 78, third case, the law is thus stated:

> There is a felony committed, but whether committed by B. or not, non constat, and, therefore, we will suppose that in truth it were not committed by B., but by some person else, yet A. hath probable causes to suspect B. to be the felon, and accordingly doth arrest him; this arrest is lawful and justifiable, and the reason is because if a person should be punished by an action of trespass or false imprisonment for an arrest of a man for felony under these circumstances, malefactors would escape to the common detriment of the people. But to make good such a justification of imprisonment, 1 there must be, in fact, a felony committed by some person, for were there no felony there can be no ground of suspicion. Again, 2 the party (if a private person) that arrests must suspect B. to be the felon. 3 he must have reasonable causes of such suspicion, and these must be alleged and proved.

In quoting as I do that statement of the law by a very distinguished and celebrated Lord Chief Justice I lay particular stress upon his reference to what it is necessary to prove as a justification of imprisonment although the language may be in this connection a little ambiguous. It is under the second head, 'The party (if a private person) that arrests must suspect B. to be the felon.' I take that to mean that the person must suspect B. to be the felon who has committed the felony for which the person has arrested B. . . .

When a person, instead of having recourse to legal proceedings or applying for a judicial warrant for arrest or laying an information or issuing other process well known to the law, gives another into custody, he takes a risk upon himself by which he must abide, and if in the result it turns out that the person arrested was innocent, and that therefore the arrest was wrongful, he cannot plead any lawful excuse unless he can bring himself within the proposition of law which I have enunciated in the judgment. In this case, although the defendants thought, and indeed it appeared that they were justified in thinking, that the plaintiff was the person who had committed the theft, it turned out in fact that they were not. The felony for which they gave the plaintiff into custody had not in fact been committed, and therefore the very basis upon which they must rest any defence of lawful excuse for the wrongful arrest of another fails them in this case. Although I am quite satisfied not only that they acted with perfect bona fides in the matter, but were genuinely convinced after reasonable inquiry that they had in fact discovered the perpetrator of the crime, it now turns out that they were wrong, and it cannot be established that the crime had been committed for which they gave the plaintiff into custody; they have failed in law to justify the arrest and there must therefore in this case be judgment for the plaintiff for the £75 damages which have been awarded with the consequent results.

R v SELF [1992] 3 All ER 476 (CA)

FACTS: The defendant was seen by a store detective to put a bar of chocolate in his pocket and leave the store. A shop assistant and a passerby arrested him, after a chase and struggle. The defendant was acquitted of theft, but convicted of assault with intent to resist arrest (s. 38, Offences against the Person Act 1861). The defendant appealed to the Court of Appeal, Criminal Division.

GARLAND J: . . . This matter comes before the court by leave of the single judge on a point of law. There is one point central to the appeal. It is this. Since the appellant was acquitted of theft neither Mr Frost nor Mr Mole were entitled by virtue of s. 24 of the Police and Criminal Evidence Act 1984 to effect a citizen's arrest. If they were not entitled to do that then this appellant could not be convicted of an assault with intent to resist or prevent the lawful apprehension or detainer of himself, that is to say his arrest.

In order to examine this proposition it is necessary of course to look closely at s. 24 of the Act. But first some mention should be made of the extent to which the learned judge dealt with the matter. Counsel for both the defence and the prosecution have frankly informed us that they did not address their minds to s. 24 and the question of whether or not the two complainants in fact were entitled to arrest the appellant. As a result of that, the learned judge never dealt with the issue, so far as the jury were concerned, by in any way seeking to link count 1, the theft, to counts 2 and 3 should the jury have been minded to acquit the appellant of count 1 before turning to the other counts. All he said was this:

> He [that is one of the two young men] is perfectly entitled to make a citizen's arrest and it is a publicly spirited thing to do whether right or wrong, provided there is reasonable cause to suspect.

It is necessary, as has been said, to turn to the Act. Section 24 deals with powers of arrest without warrant . . .

Although it appears to this court that the resolution of this particular matter is to be achieved by construing the plain words of the Statute, we were referred to authority and in particular to *Walters* v *W H Smith & Son Ltd* [1914] [1911–13] All ER Rep 170 . . .

However, in the judgment of this court, the words of s. 24 do not admit of argument. Subsection (5) makes it abundantly clear that the powers of arrest without a warrant where an arrestable offence has been committed require as a condition precedent an offence committed. If subsequently there is an acquittal of the alleged offence no offence has been committed. The power to arrest is confined to the person guilty of the offence or anyone who the person making the arrest has reasonable grounds for suspecting to be guilty of it. But of course if he is not guilty there can be no valid suspicion, as was pointed out in the passage in *Hale* to which reference has been made.

If it is necessary to go further, one contrasts the words of sub-s. (5) with sub-s. (6), the very much wider powers given to a constable who has reasonable grounds for suspecting that an arrestable offence has been committed. However, it is said on behalf of the Crown that the court should not be assiduous to restrict the citizen's powers of arrest and that, by going back to sub-s. (4) and looking at the words there, 'anyone who is in the act of committing an arrestable offence', perhaps those words can be used to cover the sort of situation that arose in this case where somebody is apparently making good his escape. Having committed the offence of theft, can it be said, asks Mr Sleeman, that the thief is not in substance still committing the offence while running away?

He asks, rhetorically, should the court have to inquire into the exact moment when the ingredients of theft come together—dishonesty, appropriation, intention permanently to deprive—when to analyse the offence carefully may produce absurd results so that in one set of circumstances the offence may be complete and the situation fall within sub-s. (5) and in another be still being committed and fall within sub-s. (4),

The view of this court is that little profit can be had from taking examples and trying to reduce them to absurdity. The words of the statute are clear and applying those words to this case there was no arrestable offence committed. It necessarily follows that the two offences under s. 38 of the Offences against the Person Act could not be committed because there was no power to apprehend or detain the appellant.

9.1.3.3   Knowledge

MURRAY v MINISTRY OF DEFENCE [1988] 2 All ER 521

FACTS: The plaintiff was suspected of collecting funds for the IRA. Her house was raided and searched. Half an hour after the raid began the plaintiff was arrested under emergency powers. The plaintiff alleged false imprisonment, both because (a) she alleged she was initially unlawfully detained without being arrested, and (b) the delay in informing her of the arrest rendered it unlawful. The case ultimately reached the House of Lords, who rejected both arguments. The interest of the case is in the discussion of whether the plaintiff must know she was being detained.

LORD GRIFFITHS (with whom the other members of the Committee agreed): Although on the facts of this case I am sure that the plaintiff was aware of the restraint on her liberty from 7.00 am, I cannot agree with the Court of Appeal that it is an essential element of the tort of false imprisonment that the victim should be aware of the fact of denial of liberty. The Court of Appeal relied on *Herring* v *Boyle* (1834) 1 Cr M & R 377, 149 ER 1126 for this proposition which they preferred to the view of Atkin LJ to the opposite effect in *Meering* v *Grahame-White Aviation Co. Ltd* (1919) 122 LT 44. *Herring* v *Boyle* is an extraordinary decision of the Court of Exchequer: a mother went to fetch her 10 year old son from school on 24 December 1833 to take him home for the Christmas holidays. The headmaster refused to allow her to take her son home because she had not paid the last term's fees, and he kept the boy at school over the holidays. An action for false imprisonment brought on behalf of the boy failed. In giving judgment Bolland B said (1 Cr M & R 377 at 381):

> . . . as far as we know, the boy may have been willing to stay; he does not appear to have been cognizant of any restraint, and there was no evidence of any act whatsoever done by the defendant in his presence. I think that we cannot construe the refusal to the mother in the boy's absence, and without his being cognizant of any restraint, to be an imprisonment of him against his will . . .

I suppose it is possible that there are schoolboys who prefer to stay at school rather than go home for the holidays but it is not an inference that I would draw, and I cannot believe that on the same facts the case would be similarly decided today. In *Meering* v *Grahame-White Aviation Co. Ltd* the plaintiff's employers, who suspected him of theft, sent two of the works police to bring him in for questioning at the company's offices. He was taken to a waiting-room where he said that if he was not told why he was there he would leave. He was told he was wanted for the purpose of making inquiries about things that had been stolen and he was wanted to give evidence; he then agreed to stay. Unknown to the plaintiff, the works police had been instructed not to let him leave the waiting-room until the Metropolitan Police arrived. The works police therefore remained outside the waiting-room and would not have allowed the plaintiff to leave until he was handed over to the Metropolitan Police, who subsequently arrested him. The question for the Court of Appeal was whether on this evidence the plaintiff was falsely imprisoned during the hour he was in the waiting-room, or whether there could be no 'imprisonment' sufficient to found a civil action unless the plaintiff was aware of the restraint on his liberty. Atkin LJ said (122 LT 44 at 53–54):

> It appears to me that a person could be imprisoned without his knowing it. I think a person can be imprisoned while he is asleep, while he is in a state of drunkenness, while he is unconscious, and while he is a lunatic. Those are cases where it seems to me that the person might properly complain if he were imprisoned, though the imprisonment began and ceased while he was in that state. Of course, the damages might be diminished and would be affected by the question whether he was conscious of it or not. . . . If a man can be imprisoned by having the key turned upon him without his knowledge, so he can be imprisoned if, instead of a lock and key or bolts and bars, he is prevented from, in fact, exercising his liberty by guards and warders or policemen. They serve the same purpose. Therefore it appears to me to be a question of fact. It is true that in all cases of imprisonment so far as the law of civil liberty is concerned that 'stone walls do not a prison make' in the sense that they are not the only form of imprisonment, but any restraint within defined bounds which is a restraint in fact may be an imprisonment.

I agree with this passage. In the first place it is not difficult to envisage cases in which harm may result from unlawful imprisonment even though the victim is unaware of it. Dean William L Prosser gave two examples in 'False Imprisonment: Consciousness of Confinement' (1955) 55 Col LR 847, in which he attacked § 42 of the American Law Institute's Restatement of the Law of Torts, which at that time stated the rule that 'there is no liability for intentionally confining another unless the person physically restrained knows of the confinement'. Dean Prosser wrote (at 849):

> Let us consider several illustrations. A locks B, a child two days old, in the vault of a bank. B is, of course, unconscious of the confinement, but the bank vault cannot be opened for two days. In the meantime, B suffers from hunger and thirst, and his health is seriously impaired; or it may be that he even dies. Is this no tort? Or suppose that A abducts B, a wealthy lunatic, and holds him for ransom for a week. B is unaware of his confinement, but vaguely understands that he is in unfamiliar surroundings, and that something is wrong. He undergoes mental suffering affecting his health. At the end of the week, he is discovered by the police and released without ever having known that he has been imprisoned. Has he no action against A? . . . If a child of two is kidnapped, confined, and deprived of the care of its mother for a month, is the kidnapping and the confinement in itself so minor a matter as to call for no redress in tort at all?

The Restatement of the Law of Torts has now been changed and requires that the person confined 'is conscious of the confinement or is harmed by it' (see Restatement of the Law, Second, Torts 2d (1965) § 35, p. 52).

If a person is unaware that he has been falsely imprisoned and has suffered no harm, he can normally expect to recover no more than nominal damages, and it is tempting to redefine the tort in the terms of the present rule in the American Law Institute's Restatement of the Law of Torts. On reflection, however, I would not do so. The law attaches supreme importance to the liberty of the individual and if he suffers a wrongful interference with that liberty it should remain actionable even without proof of special damage.

9.2   Interference with Goods

9.2.1   CONVERSION AND TRESPASS TO GOODS

TORTS (INTERFERENCE WITH GOODS) ACT 1977

1.   Definition of 'wrongful interference with goods'
In this act 'wrongful interference', or 'wrongful interference with goods', means—

  (a)   conversion of goods (also called trover),
  (b)   trespass to goods,
  (c)   negligence so far as it results in damage to goods or to an interest in goods,
  (d)   subject to section 2, any other tort so far as it results in damage to goods or to an
interest in goods.

[and references in this Act (however worded) to proceedings for wrongful interference or
to a claim or right to claim for wrongful interference shall include references to
proceedings by virtue of Part I of the Consumer Protection Act 1987 or Part II of the
Consumer Protection (Northern Ireland) Order 1987 (product liability) in respect of any
damage to goods or to an interest in goods or, as the case may be, to a claim or right to claim
by virtue of that Part in respect of any such damage.]

2. Abolition of detinue

  (1)   Detinue is abolished.
  (2)   An action lies in conversion for loss or destruction of goods which a bailee has
allowed to happen in breach of his duty to his bailor (that is to say it lies in a case which is
not otherwise conversion, but would have been detinue before detinue was abolished).

3. Forms of judgment where goods are detained

  (1)   In proceedings for wrongful interference against a person who is in possession or in
control of the goods relief may be given in accordance with this section, so far as appropriate.
  (2)   The relief is—
  (a)   an order for delivery of the goods, and for payment of any consequential damages, or
  (b)   an order for delivery of the goods, but giving the defendant the alternative of
paying damages by reference to the value of the goods, together in either alternative with
payment of any consequential damages, or
  (c)   damages.
  (3)   Subject to rules of court—
  (a)   relief shall be given under only one of paragraphs (a), (b) and (c) of subsection (2),
  (b)   relief under paragraph (a) of subsection (2) is at the discretion of the court, and
the claimant may choose between the others.
  . . .

5. Extinction of title on satisfaction of claim for damages

  (1)   Where damages for wrongful interference are, or would fall to be, assessed on the
footing that the claimant is being compensated—
  (a)   for the whole of his interest in the goods, or
  (b)   for the whole of his interest in the goods subject to a reduction for contributory
negligence,
payment of the assessed damages (under all heads), or as the case may be settlement of a claim
for damages for the wrong (under all heads), extinguishes the claimant's title to that interest.
  (2)   In subsection (1) the reference to the settlement of the claim includes—
  (a)   where the claim is made in court proceedings, and the defendant has paid a sum
into court to meet the whole claim, the taking of that sum by the claimant, and
  (b)   where the claim is made in court proceedings, and the proceedings are settled or
compromised, the payment of what is due in accordance with the settlement or
compromise, and
  (c)   where the claim is made out of court and is settled or compromised, the payment
of what is due in accordance with the settlement or compromise.
  (3)   It is hereby declared that subsection (1) does not apply where damages are
assessed on the footing that the claimant is being compensated for the whole of his interest
in the goods, but the damages paid are limited to some lesser amount by virtue of any
enactment or rule of law.
  (4)   Where under section 7(3) the claimant accounts over to another person (the 'third
party') so as to compensate (under all heads) the third party for the whole of his interest in
the goods, the third party's title to that interest is extinguished.
  (5)   This section has effect subject to any agreement varying the respective rights of the
parties to the agreement, and where the claim is made in court proceedings has effect
subject to any order of the court.

6. Allowance for improvement of the goods

(1)   If in proceedings for wrongful interference against a person (the 'improver') who has improved the goods, it is shown that the improver acted in the mistaken but honest belief that he had a good title to them, an allowance shall be made for the extent to which, at the time as at which the goods fall to be valued in assessing damages, the value of the goods is attributable to the improvement.

(2)   If, in proceedings for wrongful interference against a person ('the purchaser') who has purported to purchase the goods—

(a)   from the improver, or

(b)   where after such a purported sale the goods passed by a further purported sale on one or more occasions, on any such occasion,

it is shown that the purchaser acted in good faith, an allowance shall be made on the principle set out in subsection (1).

For example, where a person in good faith buys a stolen car from the improver and is sued in conversion by the true owner the damages may be reduced to reflect the improvement, but if the person who bought the stolen car from the improver sues the improver for failure of consideration, and the improver acted in good faith, subsection (3) below will ordinarily make a comparable reduction in the damages he recovers from the improver.

(3)   If in a case within subsection (2) the person purporting to sell the goods acted in good faith, then in proceedings by the purchaser for recovery of the purchase price because of failure of consideration, or in any other proceedings founded on that failure of consideration, an allowance shall, where appropriate, be made on the principle set out in subsection (1).

(4)   This section applies, with the necessary modifications, to a purported bailment or other disposition of goods as it applies to a purported sale of goods.

7. Double liability

(1)   In this section 'double liability' means the double liability of the wrongdoer which can arise—

(a)   where one of two or more rights of action for wrongful interference is founded on a possessory title, or

(b)   where the measure of damages in an action for wrongful interference founded on a proprietary title is or includes the entire value of the goods, although the interest is one or two or more interests in the goods.

(2)   In proceedings to which any two or more claimants are parties, the relief shall be such as to avoid double liability of the wrongdoer as between those claimants.

(3)   On satisfaction, in whole or in part, of any claim for an amount exceeding that recoverable if subsection (2) applied, the claimant is liable to account over to the other person having a right to claim to such extent as will avoid double liability.

(4)   Where, as the result of enforcement of a double liability, any claimant is unjustly enriched to an extent, he shall be liable to reimburse the wrongdoer to that extent.

For example, if a converter of goods pays damages first to a finder of the goods, and then to the true owner, the finder is unjustly enriched unless he accounts over to the true owner under subsection (3); and then the true owner is unjustly enriched and becomes liable to reimburse the converter of the goods.

8. Competing rights to the goods

(1)   The defendant in an action for wrongful interference shall be entitled to show, in accordance with rules of court, that a third party has a better right than the plaintiff as respects all or any part of the interest claimed by the plaintiff, or in right of which he sues, and any rule of law (sometimes called jus tertii) to the contrary is abolished.

(2)   Rules of court relating to proceedings for wrongful interference may—

(a)   require the plaintiff to give particulars of his title,

(b)   require the plaintiff to identify any person who, in his knowledge, has or claims any interest in the goods,

(c)   authorise the defendant to apply for directions as to whether any person should be joined with a view to establishing whether he has a better right than the plaintiff, or has a claim as a result of which the defendant might be doubly liable,

(d)   where a party fails to appear on an application within paragraph (c), or to comply with any direction given by the court on such an application, authorise the court to deprive him of any right of action against the defendant for the wrong either unconditionally, or subject to such terms or conditions as may be specified.

(3)   Subsection (2) is without prejudice to any other power of making rules of court.
. . .

11.   Minor amendments

(1)   Contributory negligence is no defence in proceedings founded on conversion, or on intentional trespass to goods.

(2)   Receipt of goods by way of pledge is conversion if the delivery of the goods is conversion.

(3)   Denial of title is not of itself conversion.

LIMITATION ACT 1980

3.   Time limit in case of successive conversions and extinction of title of owner of converted goods

(1)   Where any cause of action in respect of the conversion of a chattel has accrued to any person and, before he recovers possession of the chattel, a further conversion takes place, no action shall be brought in respect of the further conversion after the expiration of six years from the accrual of the cause of action in respect of the original conversion.

(2)   Where any such cause of action has accrued to any person and the period prescribed for bringing that action has expired and he has not during that period recovered possession of the chattel, the title of that person to the chattel shall be extinguished.

4.   Special time limit in case of theft

(1)   The right of any person from whom a chattel is stolen to bring an action in respect of the theft shall not be subject to the time limits under sections 2 and 3(1) of this Act, but if his title to the chattel is extinguished under section 3(2) of this Act he may not bring an action in respect of a theft preceding the loss of his title, unless the theft in question preceded the conversion from which time began to run for the purposes of section 3(2).

(2)   Subsection (1) above shall apply to any conversion related to the theft of a chattel as it applies to the theft of a chattel; and, except as provided below, every conversion following the theft of a chattel before the person from whom it is stolen recovers possession of it shall be regarded for the purposes of this section as related to the theft.
If anyone purchases the stolen chattel in good faith neither the purchase nor any conversion following it shall be regarded as related to the theft.

(3)   Any cause of action accruing in respect of the theft or any conversion related to the theft of a chattel to any person from whom the chattel is stolen shall be disregarded for the purpose of applying section 3(1) or (2) of this Act to his case.

(4)   Where in any action brought in respect of the conversion of a chattel it is proved that the chattel was stolen from the plaintiff or anyone through whom he claims it shall be presumed that any conversion following the theft is related to the theft unless the contrary is shown.

(5)   In this section 'theft' includes—

(a)   any conduct outside England and Wales which would be theft if committed in England and Wales; and

(b)   obtaining any chattel (in England and Wales or elsewhere) in the circumstances described in section 15(1) of the Theft Act 1968 (obtaining by deception) or by blackmail within the meaning of section 21 of that Act;
and references in this section to a chattel being 'stolen' shall be construed accordingly.

9.2.2 CONVERSION

9.2.2.1   Intentional

HOLLINS v FOWLER [1874–80] All ER Rep 118 (HL)

FACTS: F & Co. were cotton merchants. They instructed their brokers to sell some cotton. B, a cotton broker, offered to buy it. He falsely stated he was acting for S. The brokers agreed on this basis. B then offered the cotton to H & Co., who bought it from him and paid

B. B kept the money. F & Co., who thought they had sold to S, claimed the price from him. At this point the truth started to emerge. F & Co. sued H & Co., who objected that they had already paid. The matter finally reached the House of Lords.

LORD CHELMSFORD: . . . The question upon this appeal is whether the appellants are liable for the conversion of thirteen bales of cotton, the property of the respondents. From the difference of opinion which has existed among the judges, the question may be regarded as one of some difficulty, as it certainly is one of general importance . . .

The question upon the facts is whether the appellants were guilty of a conversion. There can be no doubt that the property and legal right of possession of the cotton remained in the respondents, and Bayley, who had fraudulently obtained possession of it, could not give a title to anyone to whom he transferred the possession, however ignorant the transferee might be of the means by which Bayley acquired it. A great deal of argument was directed to the question of what amounts in law to a conversion. I agree with what was said by Brett, J, in the Court of Exchequer Chamber in this case:

> In all cases where we have to apply legal principles to facts there are found many cases about which there can be no doubt, some being clear for the plaintiff, and some for the defendant; and the difficulties arise in doubtful cases on the border line between the two.

But, to my mind, the proposition which fits this case is that any person who, however innocently, obtains possession of the goods of a person who has been fraudulently deprived of them, and disposes of them, whether for his own benefit or that of any other person, is guilty of a conversion.

The Court of Queen's Bench, in their judgment in this case, thought that it was not distinguishable from *Hardman* v *Booth* (1863) 1 H & C 803. In that case the plaintiffs were worsted manufacturers near Manchester. One of the partners, being in London, called at the place of business of a firm of Gandell & Co., for orders. At that time the firm, which had been long established, and was well known, consisted only of Thomas Gandell, whose son, Edward Gandell, was his clerk, and managed the business. On inquiring for Messrs. Gandell, one of the workmen directed the plaintiff to the counting house, where he saw Edward Gandell, who led him to believe he was one of the firm of Gandell & Co., and under that belief the plaintiffs sent goods to the place of business of Gandell & Co., and invoiced them to Edward Gandell & Co. Edward Gandell who, unknown to the plaintiffs, carried on business with one Todd, pledged the goods with the defendant Booth for advances bona fide made to Gandell and Todd, and the defendant afterwards sold the goods under a power of sale. It was held by the Court of Exchequer that the defendant was liable for a conversion on the ground that there was no contract of sale, inasmuch as the plaintiffs believed they were contracting with Gandell & Co., and not with Edward Gandell personally, and Gandell & Co. never authorised Edward Gandell to contract for them, and, consequently no property passed by the sale, and the defendant, though ignorant of Gandell and Todd's want of title to the goods, was liable in trover for the amount realised by the sale. I agree with the Court of Queen's Bench that *Hardman* v *Booth* is not to be distinguished from the present case.

Lord Cairns LC and Lord Hatherley agreed.

LORD O'HAGAN: The result of your Lordships consideration of this case will, I fear, inflict hardship upon the appellants. They are innocent of any actual wrong doing, but those with whom they are in conflict are as innocent as they, and we can only regard the liability attached to them by the law, without being affected in our judgment by its unpleasant consequences. They appear to me to have been guilty of a conversion in dealing with the respondents' property, and disposing of it to other persons without any right or authority to do so.

9.2.2.2 Forms of conversion

R H WILLIS & SONS v *BRITISH CAR AUCTIONS* [1978] 2 All ER 392 (CA)

FACTS: RHW 'sold' a car on hire-purchase to C. In breach of the hire-purchase agreement (i.e. while the car still belonged to RHW) C sold the car through BCA's auction. (In fact the car did not reach its reserve, but C agreed to accept the amount offered by the highest bidder.) C then became bankrupt. RHW sued BCA in conversion as the buyer at auction and the car had disappeared. The case went to the Court of Appeal.

LORD DENNING MR: The question that arises is the usual one: which of the two innocent persons is to suffer? Is the loss to fall on the motor car dealers? They have been deprived of the £275 due to them on the car. Or on the auctioneers? They sold it believing that Mr Croucher was the true owner. In answering that question in cases such as this, the common law has always acted on the maxim: nemo dat quod non habet. It has protected the property rights of the true owner. It has enforced them strictly as against anyone who deals with the goods inconsistently with the dominion of the true owner. Even though the true owner may have been very negligent and the defendant may have acted in complete innocence, nevertheless the common law held him liable in conversion. Both the 'innocent acquirer' and the 'innocent handler' have been hit hard. That state of the law has often been criticised. It has been proposed that the law should protect a person who buys goods or handles them in good faith without notice of any adverse title, at any rate where the claimant by his own negligence or otherwise has largely contributed to the outcome. Such proposals have however been effectively blocked by the decisions of the House of Lords in the last century of *Hollins v Fowler* [1874–80] All ER Rep 118 and in this century of *Moorgate Mercantile Co. Ltd v Twitchings* [1976] 2 All ER 641, to which I may add the decision of this court in *Central Newbury Car Auctions Ltd v Unity Finance Ltd* [1956] 3 All ER 905.

In some instances the strictness of the law has been mitigated by statute, as for instance, by the protection given to private purchasers by the Hire Purchase Acts. But in other cases the only way in which the innocent acquirers or handlers have been able to protect themselves is by insurance. They insure themselves against their potential liability. This is the usual method nowadays. When men of business or professional men find themselves hit by the law with new and increasing liabilities, they take steps to insure themselves, so that the loss may not fall on one alone, but be spread among many. It is a factor of which we must take account: see *Post Office v Norwich Union Fire Insurance Society Ltd* [1967] 1 All ER 577 at 580 and *Morris v Ford Motor Co. Ltd* [1973] 2 All ER 1084 at 1090.

Sales under the hammer

The position of auctioneers is typical. It is now, I think, well established that if an auctioneer sells goods by knocking down his hammer at an auction and thereafter delivers them to the purchaser—then although he is only an agent—then if the vendor has no title to the goods, both the auctioneer and the purchaser are liable in conversion to the true owner, no matter how innocent the auctioneer may have been in handling the goods or the purchaser in acquiring them: see *Barker v Furlong* [1891] 2 Ch 172 at 181 *per* Romer J and *Consolidated Co. v Curtis & Son* [1892] 1 QB 495. This state of the law has been considered by the Law Reform Committee in 1966 (Law Reform Committee Twelfth Report (Transfer of Title to Chattels) April 1966 (Cmnd 2958)) as to innocent acquirers; and in 1971 (Law Reform Committee Eighteenth Report (Conversion and Detinue) September 1971 (Cmnd 4774)) as to innocent handlers. But Parliament has made no change in it; no doubt it would have done so in the Torts (Interference with Goods) Act 1977 if it had thought fit to do so.

Provisional bids

Such is the position with sales 'under the hammer'. What about sales which follow a 'provisional bid'? I see no difference in principle. In each case the auctioneer is an intermediary who brings the two parties together and gets them to agree on the price. They are bound by the conditions of sale which he has prepared. He retains the goods in his custody. He delivers them to the purchaser on being paid the price. He pays it over to the vendor and deducts his commission. So in principle, I think that on a 'provisional bid' an auctioneer is liable in conversion, just as when he sells under the hammer. There are two decisions, however, which suggest a difference. . . . To my mind those two decisions are a departure from the principles stated by Blackburn J in *Hollins v Fowler* (1875) LR 7 HL 757 at 766, 767. That is the principle which should guide us, especially as it was inferentially accepted by the House of Lords. I cannot help thinking that in those two cases the courts were anxious to protect the auctioneer, as an innocent handler, from the strictness of the law. In doing so they introduced two fine distinctions which are difficult to apply. I do not think we should follow those two cases today, especially when regard is had to the insurance aspect to which I now turn. It is clear that the auctioneers insure against both kinds of sale equally. On every one of the sales, under the hammer or on provisional bids, the auctioneers charge an 'indemnity fee' to the purchaser. He has to pay a premium of £2 on each vehicle purchased. In return for it the auctioneers, British Car Auctions Ltd, through an associate company, the Omega Insurance Co. Ltd, insure the purchaser against any loss he may suffer through any defect in title of the seller. So if the true owner comes along and retakes the goods from the purchaser or makes him pay damages for conversion, the auctioneers (through their associate company) indemnify the purchaser against the loss. The premium thus charged by the auctioneers (through their associate company) is calculated to cover the risk of the seller having no title or a defective title. That risk is the same no matter whether the true owner sues the auctioneer or the purchaser. The auctioneer collects £2 from every purchase to cover that risk. We are told it comes to £200,000 a year. Seeing that they receive these sums, they ought to meet the claims of the true owners out of it. This system is the commercial way of doing justice between the parties. It means that all concerned are protected. The true owner is protected by the strict law of conversion. He can recover against the innocent acquirer and the innocent handler. But those innocents are covered by insurance so that the loss is not borne by any single individual but is spread through the community at large. The insurance factor had a considerable influence on the Law Reform Committee. In view of it they did not recommend any change in the law. So also it may properly have an influence on the courts in deciding issues which come before them.

HOWARD E PERRY & CO. LTD v BRITISH RAILWAYS BOARD [1980] 2 All ER 579

FACTS: BR held some steel belonging to HEP. There was a steelworkers' strike and the railwaymen were taking sympathetic action. HEP requested delivery of their steel and BR refused, as they believed this would inflame their own workforce. HEP sought an order allowing them to enter BR's depot and take the steel away themselves.

SIR ROBERT MEGARRY VC: The main thrust of counsel's contentions was that as a mere refusal in response to a demand was not itself a conversion, though it could be evidence of a conversion (see Clerk and Lindsell on the Law of Torts (p. 678)), and the defendants had at no stage denied the plaintiffs' title to the steel, or attempted to deal with it in any way inconsistent with the plaintiffs' rights, there had been no conversion within the true meaning of that term. There was no conversion, he said, if the reason for the refusal to release the goods was a genuine or reasonable fear, unless this meant that the owner could never have his goods. He accepted that there could be a conversion if the threat induced a withholding of the goods for a long period, measured in months or years, but not if it was merely a matter of days or weeks; and he said that the present case fell into this latter category, though he could not be persuaded to prophesy when the strike of steel workers would end. This contention was based to some extent, I think, on words of Bramwell B in *Hiort v Bott* (1874) LR 9 Exch 86 at 89. The judge there said that a good description of what constituted a conversion was 'where a man does an unauthorized act which deprives another of his property permanently or for an indefinite time'; and I think that counsel interpreted 'indefinite time' as meaning a period which was not only uncertain in length but also of substantial duration.

There seems to me to be considerable force in the observation in Clerk and Lindsell on the Law of Torts (at p 682) that 'It is perhaps impossible to frame a definition which will cover every conceivable case'. What I have to consider here is a case in which the defendants are in effect saying to the plaintiffs: 'We admit that the steel is yours and that you are entitled to possession of it. Yet because we fear that industrial action may be taken against us if we permit you to remove it, we have refused to allow you to collect it for some weeks now, despite your demands, and we will continue to refuse to allow you to collect it until our fears have been removed.' Looking at the matter as one of principle, I would conclude that this is a clear case of conversion. The defendants are denying the plaintiffs most of the rights of ownership, including the right to possession, for a period which plainly is indefinite. It may be short, or it may be long; but it is clearly uncertain. I do not think that a period which will not end until the defendants reach the conclusion that their fears no longer justify the withholding of the steel can very well be called 'definite'. There is a detention of the steel which is consciously adverse to the plaintiffs' rights, and this seems to me to be of the essence of at least one form of conversion. A denial of possession to the plaintiffs does not cease to be a denial by being accompanied by a statement that the plaintiffs are entitled to the possession that is being denied to them.

It seems to me that this view is consistent with the authorities put before me, and also with some others. The cause of action in conversion was stated in the Common Law Procedure Act 1852 as follows: 'That the Defendant converted to his own Use, or wrongfully deprived the Plaintiff of the Use and Possession of the Plaintiff's Goods.' I do not see how it could be said that the defendants are not at the moment wrongfully depriving the plaintiffs of the use and possession of the plaintiffs' goods, unless the defendants' fears of industrial action could be said to prevent their refusal to release the steel from being wrongful. . . .

I have also looked at the Eighteenth Report of the Law Reform Committee (Conversion and Detinue (Cmnd 4774, 1971)), not in order to construe the 1977 Act, but for the statement of the pre-existing law there set out. In para 8, the report states:

> The present position appears to be that conversion will lie in every case in which detinue would lie, save only that detinue lies, but conversion does not lie, against a bailee of goods who in breach of his duty has allowed them to be lost or destroyed.

The report is not, of course, an authority in the sense that a judgment is: but it was signed by four eminent judges (Lord Pearson, Lord Diplock, Buckley and Orr LJJ), and it certainly represented my views when I too signed it. If the report is right on this point, that is the end of the defendants' contention. The report also provides an explanation of the form taken by s. 2 of the 1977 Act.

My conclusion is accordingly that this contention of the defendants fails. For the defendants to withhold the steel from the plaintiffs is a wrongful interference with goods within the 1977 Act unless the reason for the withholding provides a justification. I cannot see that it does. This is no brief withholding made merely in order that the defendants may verify the plaintiffs' title to the steel, or for some other purpose to confirm that the delivery of the steel would be proper. This is a withholding despite the plain right of the plaintiffs to the ownership and possession of the steel, on the ground that the defendants fear unpleasant consequences if they do not deny the plaintiffs what they are entitled to.

9.2.2.3 Separation of possession and ownership

ARMORY v DELAMIRIE [1558–1774] All ER Rep 121

[The full report can be set out—facts, judgment and all. What a change we see today:]

Action of trover for a jewel, tried by Sir John Pratt CJ, at *nisi prius*.
The plaintiff, being a chimney sweeper's boy, found a jewel and took it to the defendant's shop (who was a goldsmith) to know what it was. He delivered it into the hands of the defendant's apprentice who, under pretence of weighing it, took out the stones and called to the master to let him know it came to three halfpence. The master offered the plaintiff that money, which he refused to take and insisted on having the jewel again, whereupon the apprentice gave him back the socket without the stones. In an action of trover against the master,
SIR JOHN PRATT, CJ, ruled the following points:

(i) That the finder of a jewel, though he does not by such finding acquire an absolute property or ownership, yet he has such a property as will enable him to keep it against all but the rightful owner, and consequently may maintain trover.

(ii) That the action will lay against the master who gives a credit to his apprentice and is answerable for his neglect.

(iii) As to the value of the jewel, several of the trade were examined to prove what a jewel of the finest water that would fit the socket would be worth; and Sir John Pratt CJ, directed the jury that, unless the defendant did produce the jewel and show it not to be of the finest water, they should presume the strongest against him and make the value of the best jewels the measure of their damages, which they accordingly did.

9.3 Title Conflicts

9.3.1 THE BASIC PRINCIPLE: *NEMO DAT QUOD NON HABET* (NO ONE CAN TRANSFER A BETTER RIGHT THAN HE HAS)

SALE OF GOODS ACT 1979

21. Sale by person not the owner.

(1) Subject to this Act, where goods are sold by a person who is not their owner, and who does not sell them under the authority or with the consent of the owner, the buyer acquires no better title to the goods than the seller had, unless the owner of the goods is by his conduct precluded from denying the seller's authority to sell.

(2) Nothing in this Act affects—

(a) the provisions of the Factors Acts or any enactment enabling the apparent owner of goods to dispose of them as if he were their true owner;

(b) the validity of any contract of sale under any special common law or statutory power of sale or under the order of a court of competent jurisdiction.

. . .

23. Sale under voidable title.

When the seller of goods has a voidable title to them, but his title has not been avoided at the time of the sale, the buyer acquires a good title to the goods, provided he buys them in good faith and without notice of the seller's defect of title.

24. Seller in possession after sale.

Where a person having sold goods continues or is in possession of the goods, or of the documents of title to the goods, the delivery or transfer by that person, or by a mercantile agent acting for him, of the goods or documents of title under any sale, pledge, or other disposition thereof, to any person receiving the same in good faith and without notice of the previous sale, has the same effect as if the person making the delivery or transfer were expressly authorised by the owner of the goods to make the same.

25. Buyer in possession after sale.

(1) Where a person having bought or agreed to buy goods obtains, with the consent of the seller, possession of the goods or the documents of title to the goods, the delivery or transfer by that person, or by a mercantile agent acting for him, of the goods or documents of title, under any sale, pledge, or other disposition thereof, to any person receiving the same in good faith and without notice of any lien or other right of the original seller in respect of the goods, has the same effect as if the person making the delivery or transfer were a mercantile agent in possession of the goods or documents of title with the consent of the owner.

(2) For the purposes of subsection (1) above—

(a) the buyer under a conditional sale agreement is to be taken not to be a person who has bought or agreed to buy goods, and

(b) 'conditional sale agreement' means an agreement for the sale of goods which is a consumer credit agreement within the meaning of the Consumer Credit Act 1974 under which the purchase price or part of it is payable by instalments, and the property in the goods is to remain in the seller (notwithstanding that the buyer is to be in possession of the goods) until such conditions as to the payment of instalments or otherwise as may be specified in the agreement are fulfilled.

(3) Paragraph 9 of Schedule 1 below applies in relation to a contract under which a person buys or agrees to buy goods and which is made before the appointed day.

(4) In subsection (3) above and paragraph 9 of Schedule 1 below references to the appointed day are to the day appointed for the purposes of those provisions by an order of the Secretary of State made by statutory instrument.

26. Supplementary to sections 24 and 25
In sections 24 and 25 above 'mercantile agent' means a mercantile agent having in the customary course of his business as such agent authority either—
(a) to sell goods, or
(b) to consign goods for the purpose of sale, or
(c) to buy goods, or
(d) to raise money on the security of goods.

9.3.2 PROBLEM AREAS

9.3.2.1 Estoppel: apparent authority and apparent ownership

MERCANTILE CREDIT v HAMBLIN [1964] 3 All ER 592 (CA)

FACTS: Mrs H wanted to borrow money on the security of her car. She approached Mr P, a second hand car dealer of apparent respectability whom she had known for some years. He agreed to assist her and asked her to sign forms which he falsely represented to be for a loan, but which were in fact for a hire-purchase agreement with MC. MC advanced money on the strength of this agreement but Mr P kept it. When MC sought to recover the car under the hire-purchase agreement Mrs H claimed she was not bound by it.

PEARSON LJ: The dispute has arisen between two innocent parties as a result of a fraud committed by another person, Mr Phelan, who was the motor dealer concerned in the transaction. . . .

The defendant only authorised Mr Phelan to make inquiries as to the amount obtainable and to report back to the defendant. Mr Phelan never had actual authority from the defendant to complete the forms or to present them to the plaintiffs. Unless some estoppel operates against the defendant, the presentation of the forms to the plaintiffs was not her act, and she did not make any offer or representation to the plaintiffs. The crucial question is whether as against the plaintiffs the defendant is estopped from denying Mr Phelan's authority to complete the forms and present them on her behalf. Did she give him ostensible authority? Did she hold him out to the plaintiffs as having authority?

First, it is necessary to consider whether as a matter of law there could be any actual or ostensible authority of Mr Phelan as dealer to present the documents on behalf of the defendant as customer to the plaintiffs as the finance company.

In order to clarify this point it will be helpful, I think, to consider what the position would have been if the transaction had gone through according to the arrangement made between the defendant and Mr Phelan. He would have made inquiries of the plaintiffs and ascertained what nett payment they would make for the car and what hire-purchase instalments they would require over what period. He would report the figures to the defendant, and she would agree them and ask him to proceed. He would then with her authority fill in the particulars in the three forms signed by the defendant and in his own supplier's declaration and invoice. Then the documents, containing the defendant's offer to take the car on hire-purchase from the plaintiffs and (on the same piece of paper) Mr Phelan's offer to sell the car to the plaintiffs, would be presented to the plaintiffs and accepted by them. As the plaintiffs would not be able to let the car on hire-purchase to the defendant unless they had become the owners of it and she had ceased to be the owner of it, she would be impliedly consenting to the plaintiffs becoming the owners of the car by purchase from Mr Phelan. Section 21(1) of the Sale of Goods Act, 1893, provides:

> Subject to the provisions of this Act, where goods are sold by a person who is not the owner thereof, and who does not sell them under the authority or with the consent of the owner, the buyer acquires no better title to the goods than the seller had, unless the owner of the goods is by his conduct precluded from denying the seller's authority to sell.

The defendant would by her conduct be precluded from denying Mr Phelan's authority to sell the car to the plaintiffs. Under s. 21(1) there would not be a mere estoppel: the defendant would lose her title and the plaintiffs would acquire the title (*Eastern Distributors Ltd* v *Goldring* [1957] All ER at p. 529).

The forms, duly filled in and presented, would operate primarily as offers, with the defendant saying to the plaintiffs in effect, 'You can buy the car from Mr Phelan, and I will take it on hire-purchase from you'. I think, however, that the completed forms would have also a secondary operation or character. When the forms are read as a whole, and especially when the delivery receipt and confirmation of insurance cover is taken into account, there is probably an implied representation that this is a normal hire-purchase transaction, and that the defendant is not already the owner and is seeking to acquire ownership for the first time by means of the hire-purchase agreement.

Whether the presentation of the documents be regarded as the making of an offer or the making of a representation, the fact remains that there was no actual authority, and the plaintiffs to succeed most show an ostensible authority based on negligence. In order to establish an estoppel by negligence the plaintiffs have to show (i) that the defendant owed to them a duty to be careful, (ii) that in breach of that duty she was negligent, (iii) that her negligence was the proximate or real cause of the plaintiffs being induced to part with the £800 to Mr Phelan.

. . .

In the present case, at the time when the defendant signed the documents in blank, she was not then making a contract but she was contemplating and contingently intending that she would eventually enter into a contract with some persons who would provide her with money on the security of the car. In fact the documents identified those persons as the plaintiffs, but she had not read the documents: consequently she did not have the plaintiffs in contemplation, but did contemplate that there would or might be some such persons with whom she would contract. She intended to make such a contract if and when the conditions were fulfilled, that is to say if and when the amount and terms obtainable were reported to and agreed by her. She signed in blank the documents which would, if the conditions were fulfilled, constitute her offer to be accepted by the providers of the money, whoever they might be. She entrusted the documents to a dealer, who would be able, if so minded, to fill them in and present them to the providers of the money and secure their acceptance. She was arming the dealer with the means to make a contract ostensibly on her behalf. In my judgment there was a sufficient relationship or proximity between the defendant and any persons who might contract to provide her with the money that she was seeking, to impose on her a duty of care with regard to the preparation and custody of the contractual documents. The duty was owing to these persons, whoever they might eventually be found to be. They were in fact the plaintiffs.

The next question is whether the defendant committed any breach of duty, that is to say whether she was negligent. On the peculiar facts of this case I think there should not be a finding of negligence against her. She was well acquainted with Mr Phelan, and he was apparently respectable and solvent and prosperous, and the blank cheque which he gave her would naturally give her confidence that she could rely on his due performance of the arrangement which they had made.

Suppose, however, that she was negligent. There is then the question whether her negligence was the proximate or real cause of the plaintiffs being induced to part with the money. In my judgment the proximate or real cause was the fraud of Mr Phelan. She gave him the means to commit his fraud, but his fraud was not, in the situation as it reasonably appeared to her, a natural or forseeable consequence of what she did, and she should not be held responsible for it. I agree with the learned judge's finding on this point.

It follows that there is no estoppel by negligence, and no ostensible authority or holding out; the alleged hire-purchase agreement was invalid and not binding on the defendant; she has retained her ownership of the car; the plaintiffs' claim fails; and the appeal should be dismissed.

9.3.2.2   Section 2(1) of the Factors Act 1889

FACTORS ACT 1889

1.   Definitions
For the purposes of this Act—

(1) The expression 'mercantile agent' shall mean a mercantile agent having in the customary course of his business as such agent authority either to sell goods or to consign goods for the purpose of sale, or to buy goods, or to raise money on the security of goods:

. . .

2. Powers of mercantile agent with respect to disposition of goods

(1) Where a mercantile agent is, with the consent of the owner, in possession of goods or of the documents of title to goods, any sale, pledge, or other disposition of the goods, made by him when acting in the ordinary course of business of a mercantile agent, shall, subject to the provisions of this Act, be as valid as if he were expressly authorised by the owner of the goods to make the same; provided that the person taking under the disposition acts in good faith, and has not at the time of the disposition notice that the person making the disposition has not authority to make the same.

(2) Where a mercantile agent has, with the consent of the owner, been in possession of goods or of the documents of title to goods, any sale, pledge, or other disposition, which would have been valid if the consent had continued, shall be valid notwithstanding the determination of the consent; provided that the person taking under the disposition has not at the time thereof notice that the consent has been determined.

(3) Where a mercantile agent has obtained possession of any documents of title to goods by reason of his being or having been, with the consent of the owner, in possession of the goods represented thereby, or of any other documents of title to the goods, his possession of the first-mentioned documents shall, for the purposes of this Act, be deemed to be with the consent of the owner.

(4) For the purposes of this Act the consent of the owner shall be presumed in the absence of evidence to the contrary.

9.4 Trespass to Land

9.4.1 A DEFINITION

9.4.1.1 Entering on

KELSEN v *IMPERIAL TOBACCO* [1957] 2 All ER 343

FACTS: The plaintiff was a tobacconist. He occupied a single-storey shop, bounded by a three-storey building upon which the defendant had an advertising hoarding that protruded into the plaintiff's air space. The plaintiff had a trade dispute with the defendant (they wouldn't let him have enough cigarettes during a shortage) and so sought to have the hoarding removed.

McNAIR J: . . . [I come] to the next and, in some ways, most interesting point of the case, namely, whether an invasion of an air space by a sign of this nature gives rise to an action in trespass or whether the rights, if any, of the owner of the air space are limited to complaining of nuisance; for, if his rights are so limited, it is clear on the facts of this case that no nuisance was created, since the presence of this sign in the position which it occupied on the wall of the adjoining premises caused no inconvenience and no interference with the plaintiff's use of his air space. The question of trespass by invasion of the air space has been the subject of considerable controversy. One starts with the decision of Lord Ellenborough in *Pickering* v *Rudd* (1815), 4 Camp 219, where the trespass alleged was that the defendant had broken and entered the plaintiff's close by nailing on the defendant's own house a board which projected several inches from the wall and so far overhung the plaintiff's garden. Lord Ellenborough, in 1815, said (ibid., at p. 220):

I do not think it is a trespass to interfere with the column of air superincumbent on the close. I once had occasion to rule upon the circuit, that a man who, from the outside of a field, discharged a gun into it, so as that the shot must have struck the soil, was guilty of breaking and entering it. A very learned judge, who went the circuit with me, at first doubted the decision, but I believe he afterwards approved of it, and that it met with the general concurrence of those to whom it was mentioned. But I am by no means prepared to say, that firing across a field in vacuo, no part of the contents touching it, amounts to a clausum fregit. Nay, if this board overhanging the plaintiff's garden be a trespass, it would follow that an aeronaut is liable to an action of trespass quare clausum fregit, at the suit of the occupier of every field over which his balloon passes in the course of his voyage. Whether the action may be maintained cannot depend upon the length of time for which the superincumbent air is invaded. If any damage arises from the object which overhangs the close, the remedy is by an action on the case.

Hawkins J, followed that decision and took the same view in *Clifton v Viscount Bury* (1887), 4 TLR 8, where he was dealing with the passage of bullets fired from a musketry range, the bullets passing some seventy-five feet above the surface of the land and not striking the land. He held that that was not trespass, but, if anything, was nuisance.

An early doubt as to the correctness of Lord Ellenborough's statement was expressed by Blackburn J, in *Kenyon v Hart* ((1865), 6 B & S 249 at p. 252), and it seems to me that since that date there has been a consistent line of authority to the contrary. For instance, in *Wandsworth Board of Works v United Telephone Co.* (1884), 13 QBD 904, one of the questions at issue was whether a telephone line running across a street constituted a trespass as against the local authority in whom the street was vested. The main contest in the case was as to the extent of the vesting in the local authority, the conclusion being reached that they did not have vested in them the air space above the street beyond what was necessary for its use as a street; but I think that each of the learned lords justices in that case was quite clear in his conclusion that, if the street and the air space above it had been vested in the local authority, the passage of a telephone line through that air space would have constituted a trespass and not a mere nuisance. I need not elaborate my judgment by citing the passages from the three judgments in that case.

In *Gifford v Dent* [1926] WN 336, Romer J, clearly took the view that a sign which was erected on the wall above the ground floor premises, which had been demised to the plaintiff, and projected some four feet eight inches from the wall constituted a trespass over the plaintiff's air space, that air space being the column of air above the basement which projected out under the pavement. Romer J, said:

> If he was right in the conclusion to which he had come that the plaintiffs were tenants of the forecourt and were accordingly tenants of the space above the forecourt usque ad coelum, it seemed to him that the projection was clearly a trespass upon the property of the plaintiffs.

That decision, I think, has been recognised by the text-book writers, and, in particular, by the late Professor Winfield, as stating the true law. It is not without significance that in the Air Navigation Act, 1920, s. 9(1), which was replaced by s. 40(1) of the Civil Aviation Act, 1949, the legislature found it necessary expressly to negative the action of trespass or nuisance arising from the mere fact of an aeroplane passing through the air above the land. It seems to me clearly to indicate that the legislature were not taking the same view of the matter as Lord Ellenborough in *Pickering v Rudd*, but were taking the view accepted in the later cases, such as *Wandsworth Board of Works v United Telephone Co*, subsequently followed by Romer J, in *Gifford v Dent*. Accordingly, I reach the conclusion that a trespass, and not a mere nuisance, was created by the invasion of the plaintiff's air space by this sign.

LORD BERNSTEIN OF LEIGH v SKYVIEW & GENERAL LTD [1977] 2 All ER 902

FACTS: D's business was aerial photography. They took photographs of houses and offered them to the owners. They had done this in respect of P's house in 1967. He was unhappy that they took the photographs unasked. They did so again in 1974 and P sued, alleging trespass and invasion of privacy.

GRIFFITHS J: I turn now to the law. The plaintiff claims that as owner of the land he is also owner of the air space above the land, or at least has the right to exclude any entry into the air space above his land. He relies on the old Latin maxim, cujus est solum ejus est usque ad coelum et ad inferos, a colourful phrase often on the lips of lawyers since it was first coined by Accursius in Bologna in the 13th century. There are a number of cases in which the maxim has been used by English judges but an examination of those cases shows that they have all been concerned with structures attached to the adjoining land, such as overhanging buildings, signs or telegraph wires, and for their solution it has not been necessary for the judge to cast his eyes towards the heavens; he has been concerned with the rights of the owner in the air space immediately adjacent to the surface of the land.

That an owner has certain rights in the air space above his land is well established by authority. He has the right to lop the branches of trees that may overhang his boundary, although this right seems to be founded in nuisance rather than trespass: see *Lemmon* v *Webb* [1894] 3 Ch 1.

[His Lordship considered *Kelsen* v *Imperial Tobacco Co. Ltd* [1957] 2 All ER 343.]

I do not wish to cast any doubts on the correctness of the decision on its own particular facts. It may be a sound and practical rule to regard any incursion into the air space at a height which may interfere with the ordinary user of the land as a trespass rather than a nuisance. Adjoining owners then know where they stand; they have no right to erect structures overhanging or passing over their neighbours' land and there is no room for argument whether they are thereby causing damage or annoyance to their neighbours about which there may be much room for argument and uncertainty. But wholly different considerations arise when considering the passage of aircraft at a height which in no way affects the user of the land.

There is no direct authority on this question but as long ago as 1815 Lord Ellenborough in *Pickering* v *Rudd* 4 Camp 219 at 221 expressed the view that it would not be a trespass to pass over a man's land in a balloon; and in *Saunders* v *Smith* (1838) 2 Jur 491 at 492 Shadwell V-C said:

> Thus, upon the maxim of law '*Cujus est solum ejus est usque ad coelum,*' an injunction might be granted for cutting timber and severing crops: but, suppose a person should apply to restrain an aerial wrong, as by sailing through the air over a person's freehold in a balloon; this surely would be too contemptible to be taken notice of.

. . .

I can find no support in authority for the view that a landowner's rights in the air space above his property extend to an unlimited height. The problem is to balance the rights of an owner to enjoy the use of his land against the rights of the general public to take advantage of all that science now offers in the use of air space. This balance is in my judgment best struck in our present society by restricting the rights of an owner in the air space above his land to such height as is necessary for the ordinary use and enjoyment of his land and the structures on it, and declaring that above that height he has no greater rights in the air space than any other member of the public.

Applying this test to the facts of this case, I find that the defendants' aircraft did not infringe any rights in the plaintiff's air space, and thus no trespass was committed. It was on any view of the evidence flying many hundreds of feet above the ground and it is not suggested that by its mere presence in the air space it caused any interference with any use to which the plaintiff put or might wish to put his land. The plaintiff's complaint is not that the aircraft interfered with the use of his land but that a photograph was taken from it. There is, however, no law against taking a photograph, and the mere taking of a photograph cannot turn an act which is not a trespass into the plaintiff's air space into one that is a trespass.

I was told by counsel that the plaintiff was particularly anxious that his house should not be photographed from the air lest the photograph should fall into criminal hands as it might prove a valuable aid to a terrorist. This anxiety is readily understandable and must attract sympathy, although I should add that it is not suggested that this was a likely consequence as a result of the defendants' activities. Counsel for the plaintiff, however, conceded that he was unable to cite any principle of law or authority that would entitle the plaintiff to prevent someone taking a photograph of his property for an innocent purpose, provided they did not commit some other tort such as trespass or nuisance in doing so. It is therefore interesting to reflect what a sterile remedy the plaintiff would obtain if he was able to establish that mere infringement of the air space over his land was a trespass. He could prevent the defendants flying over his land to take another photograph, but he could not prevent the defendants taking the virtually identical photograph from the adjoining land provided they took care not to cross his boundary, and were taking it for an innocent as opposed to a criminal purpose.

My finding that no trespass at common law has been established is sufficient to determine this case in the defendants' favour. I should, however, deal with a further defence under the Civil Aviation Act 1949, s. 40(1) of which provides:

No action shall lie in respect of trespass or in respect of nuisance, by reason only of the flight of an aircraft over any property at a height above the ground, which, having regard to wind, weather, and all the circumstances of the case is reasonable, or the ordinary incidents of such flight so long as the provisions of Part II and this Part of this Act and any Order in Council or order made under Part II of this Part of this Act are duly complied with.

It is agreed that all the statutory provisions have been complied with by the defendants, nor is there any suggestion that the aircraft was not flying at a reasonable height; but it is submitted by the plaintiff that the protection given by the subsection is limited to a bare right of passage over land analogous to the limited right of a member of the public to pass over the surface of a highway, and my attention has been drawn to a passage in Shawcross and Beaumont on Air Law 3rd Edn (1966), vol 1, p. 561 in which the editors express this view. I see nothing in the language of the section to invite such a restricted reading which would withdraw from its protection many very beneficial activities carried on from aircraft. For example, we heard during this case that Granada Television, a company of which the plaintiff is chairman, made a series of educational films called 'The Land' for educational purposes. To make the films helicopters flew far and wide over the country and photographed the land below in all its various aspects. Of course they had not obtained the permission of every occupier whose land they photographed—it would have been an impossible task. According to the plaintiff's contention that innocent activity would not be protected even if the helicopters were flying at a reasonable height and complying with all statutory requirements, for they would not be mere birds of passage but making use of the air space for the purpose of aerial photography or survey. As I read the section its protection extends to all flights provided they are at a reasonable height and comply with the statutory requirements. And I adopt this construction the more readily because s. 40(2) imposes on the owner of the aircraft a strict liability to pay damages for any material loss or damage that may be caused by his aircraft.

It is, however, to be observed that the protection given is limited by the words 'by reason only of the flight', so although an owner can found no action in trespass or nuisance if he relies solely on the flight of the aircraft above his property as founding his cause of action, the section will not preclude him from bringing an action if he can point to some activity carried on by or from the aircraft that can properly be considered a trespass or nuisance, or some other tort. For example, the section would give no protection against the deliberate emission of vast quantities of smoke that polluted the atmosphere and seriously interfered with the plaintiff's use and enjoyment of his property; such behaviour remains an actionable nuisance. Nor would I wish this judgment to be understood as deciding that in no circumstances could a successful action be brought against an aerial photographer to restrain his activities. The present action is not founded in nuisance for no court would regard the taking of a single photograph as an actionable nuisance. But if the circumstances were such that a plaintiff was subjected to the harassment of constant surveillance of his house from the air, accompanied by the photographing of his every activity, I am far from saying that the court would not regard such a monstrous invasion of his privacy as an actionable nuisance for which they would give relief. However, that question does not fall for decision in this case and will be decided if and when it arises.

CIVIL AVIATION ACT 1982

76. Liability of aircraft in respect of trespass, nuisance and surface damage

(1)   No action shall lie in respect of trespass or in respect of nuisance, by reason only of the flight of an aircraft over any property at a height above the ground which, having regard to wind, weather and all the circumstances of the case is reasonable, or the ordinary incidents of such flight, so long as the provisions of any Air Navigation Order and of any orders under section 62 above have been duly complied with and there has been no breach of section 81 below.

(2)   Subject to subsection (3) below, where material loss or damage is caused to any person or property on land or water by, or by a person in, or an article, animal or person falling from, an aircraft while in flight, taking off or landing, then unless the loss or damage was caused or contributed to by the negligence of the person by whom it was suffered, damages in respect of the loss or damage shall be recoverable without proof of negligence

or intention or other cause of action, as if the loss or damage had been caused by the wilful act, neglect, or default of the owner of the aircraft.

(3)   Where material loss or damage is caused as aforesaid in circumstances in which—

(a)   damages are recoverable in respect of the said loss or damage by virtue only of subsection (2) above, and

(b)   a legal liability is created in some person other than the owner to pay damages in respect of the said loss or damage,

the owner shall be entitled to be indemnified by that other person against any claim in respect of the said loss or damage.

77.   Nuisance caused by aircraft on aerodromes

(1)   An Air Navigation Order may provide for regulating the conditions under which noise and vibration may be caused by aircraft on aerodromes and may provide that subsection (2) below shall apply to any aerodrome as respects which provision as to noise and vibration caused by aircraft is so made.

(2)   No action shall lie in respect of nuisance by reason only of the noise and vibration caused by aircraft on an aerodrome to which this subsection applies by virtue of an Air Navigation Order, as long as the provisions of any such Order are duly complied with.

9.5 End of Chapter Assessment Question

Yuri, an official of the St Petersburg Heritage Museum, is in a transit lounge at Heathrow airport when he observes in a corner, behind a counter, an icon which he believes to be one missing from his museum. Although there is a notice on the counter stating 'Authorised Personnel Only Beyond This Point' Yuri goes behind the counter to inspect the icon. Close inspection reinforces his belief that the icon is the missing one. He takes possession of it. He is observed by Susan, a security officer, who suspects him of theft and apprehends him. While she is doing so there is a scuffle, Susan suffers a discolated finger and the icon is seriously damaged. Yuri is prosecuted for theft and acquitted.

The Airport Authority retains possession of the icon. The icon is claimed by Carlos, who left it in the lounge. Carlos can prove that he bought the icon at a respectable auction two years ago.

The icon is also claimed by Yuri on behalf of the museum. Yuri can prove that the icon was in the museum collection in 1939, and that it has never been officially disposed of by the museum authorities.

Advise Yuri as to his rights and liabilities in tort arising out of this incident.

9.6 End of Chapter Assessment Outline Answer

There are four separate issues: ownership of the icon, damage to the icon, trespasses to the person arising out of the scuffle and trespass into the restricted area.

If, as seems likely, the icon was stolen (it is immaterial that the theft was abroad: s. 4(5)(a), Limitation Act 1980), the thief will never acquire title by limitation: s. 4, Limitation Act 1980. Carlos bought in good faith and could acquire a title by limitation: s. 4(2), Limitation Act 1980. However the limitation period is six years: s. 2, Limitation Act 1980. It cannot be said whether Carlos has acquired a title without knowing when it was first purchased in good faith. If this was more than six years ago, Carlos will have a good title: s. 3, Limitation Act 1980, as the limitation period runs from the original purchase in good faith and title is extinguished after six years. The museum could still sue the thief, if traced: s. 4(1), Limitation Act 1980. If there was no theft, but some other form of conversion, the time limit will run from the date the museum lost possession to the original converter. The Authority has a possessory title as finders, but this will yield to that of the true owner. If either claimant sues the Authority, as being in actual possession, they can join the other claimant into the action and interplead by disclaiming any interest of their own, leaving the court to resolve the issue between the two claimants: ss. 7-9, Torts (Interference with Goods) Act 1977.

The damage is unlikely to amount to conversion. It was not done by way of assertion of rights of ownership. It would appear to amount to a trespass to the goods, and/or negligence on the part of the person(s) responsible. If Carlos proves to be the true owner he may sue both Yuri and Susan as joint tortfeasors. If the museum is the true owner it may claim against Susan subject to a defence of contributory negligence: s. 1, Law Reform (Contributory Negligence) Act 1945. This will apply only to a claim in negligence: s. 11(1), Torts (Interference with Goods) Act 1977.

Liability in battery will depend on whether Susan is acting lawfully in apprehending Yuri. This is turn depends on whether she was legitimately exercising a power of arrest under s. 24, Police and Criminal Evidence Act 1984. Yuri's behaviour appears to create a reasonable suspicion that he is a thief, and if the offence is still in the process of being committed, Susan does have a power of arrest: s. 24(4)(b) even though it turns out that no offence has been committed. If the offence was complete by the time she intervened, her power only exists if an offence has been committed, and the acquittal negatives this: *Walters* v *WH Smith* (1914), *R* v *Self* (1992). She is therefore acting unlawfully. She would also need to demonstrate that she was exercising the power of arrest, as she has no power simply to detain (cf *Collins* v *Wilcock* (1984)) and doing so properly (cf *Christie* v *Leachinsky* (1947)). If she is acting lawfully Yuri is guilty of battery in resisting arrest, if unlawfully Yuri is prima facie entitled to use reasonable force in self-defence. Conversely, if she is acting lawfully she may use reasonable force herself, if not, her acts are a battery on Yuri. Contributory negligence may also be relevant if it is considered that the party who was technically in the right contributed to the misunderstanding which resulted in violence.

Yuri is a lawful visitor to the lounge, but becomes a trespasser when he enters a prohibited area. Even if it be the case that he does not see or cannot read the notice, his deliberate movement is made at his peril.

CHAPTER TEN

NUISANCE

10.1 Private Nuisance

10.1.1 WHO CAN SUE?

HUNTER AND OTHERS v *CANARY WHARF LTD* [1997] 2 All ER 426 (HL)

FACTS: The facts as set out in Lord Goff's speech.

LORD GOFF OF CHIEVELEY: There are before your Lordships' House appeals in two actions, which raise fundamental questions relating to the law of private nuisance.

In the first action, *Patricia Hunter and others* v *Canary Wharf Ltd*, the appellants (who are the plaintiffs in the action) claim damages in respect of interference with the television reception at their homes. This, they claim, was caused by the construction of the Canary Wharf Tower, which was built on land developed by the defendants. The tower is nearly 250 metres (about 800 feet) high and over 50 metres square. The source of television transmissions in the area is a BBC transmitter at Crystal Palace; and the appellants claim that, because of its size and the metal in its surface (it has stainless steel cladding and metallised windows), it has caused interference with the television signals from Crystal Palace. The appellants all lived at the material time in an area on the Isle of Dogs affected by the interference, which has been called the shadow area. They claim that the interference began in 1989, during the construction of the tower. A relay transmitter was then built to overcome the problem of interference in the shadow area. This came into operation in April 1991, and it is claimed that the aerials at the appellants' homes were adjusted or replaced between July 1991 and April 1992 to achieve satisfactory reception. The appellants claim damages in respect of the interference with their television reception during the intervening period. Their claim was framed in nuisance and in negligence, though their claim in negligence has since been abandoned.

In the second action, *Patricia Hunter and others* v *London Docklands Development Corporation*, the respondents (the plaintiffs in the action) claim damages in respect of damage caused by what they claim to be excessive amounts of dust created by the construction by the appellants of a road 1,800 metres in length, known as the Limehouse Link Road, which was constructed by the appellants between November 1989 and May 1993. The respondents are residents in the affected area, and they advanced their claims in negligence and nuisance and under the Rule in *Rylands* v *Fletcher*, though this last head of claim has been abandoned. . . .

Interference with television signals

I turn first to consider the question whether interference with television signals may give rise to an action in private nuisance. This question was first considered over thirty years ago by Buckley J in *Bridlington Relay Ltd* v *Yorkshire Electricity Board* [1965] Ch 436. That case was concerned not with interference caused by the presence of a building, but with electrical interference caused by the activities of the defendant Electricity Board. Buckley J held that such interference did not constitute a legal nuisance, because it was interference with a purely recreational facility, as opposed to interference with the health or physical comfort or well-being of the plaintiffs. He did not however rule out the possibility that ability to receive television signals free from interference might one day be recognised as 'so important a part of an ordinary householder's enjoyment of his property that such interference should be regarded as a legal nuisance' (see p. 447) . . . That interference with such an amenity might in appropriate circumstances be protected by the law of nuisance has been recognised in Canada, in *Nor-Video Services Ltd* v *Ontario Hydro* (1978) 84 DLR (3d) 221, 231.

However, as I see the present case, there is a more formidable obstacle to this claim. This is that the complaint rests simply upon the presence of the respondents' building on land in the neighbourhood as causing the relevant interference. The gravamen of the appellants' case is that the respondents, by building the Canary Wharf Tower, interfered with the television signals and so caused interference with the reception on the appellants' television sets; though it should not be overlooked that such interference might be caused by a smaller building and moreover that, since it is no defence that the plaintiff came to the nuisance, the same complaint could result from the simple fact of the presence of the building which caused the interference. In this respect the present case is to be distinguished from the *Bridlington Relay* case, in which the problem was caused not just by the presence of a neighbouring building but by electrical interference resulting from the defendant Electricity Board's activities.

As a general rule, a man is entitled to build on his own land, though nowadays this right is inevitably subject to our system of planning controls. Moreover, as a general rule, a man's right to build on his land is not restricted by the fact that the presence of the building may of itself interfere with his neighbour's enjoyment of his land. The building may spoil his neighbour's view (see *Attorney-General* v *Doughty* (1752) 2 Ves Sen 453, and *Fishmongers' Co.* v *East India Co.* (1752) 1 Dick 163); in the absence of an easement, it may restrict the flow of air onto his neighbour's land (*Bland* v *Mosely* (1587) cited in *Aldred's Case* (1610) 9 Co Rep 57b, 58a, and *Chastey* v *Ackland* [1895] 2 Ch 389); and, again in the absence of an easement, it may take away light from his neighbour's windows (*Dalton* v *Angus* (1881) 6 App Cas 740, 794, 795 *per* Lord Selborne LC, 823, *per* Lord Blackburn): nevertheless his neighbour generally cannot complain of the presence of the building, though this may seriously detract from the enjoyment of his land. As Lindley LJ said in *Chastey* v *Ackland* [1895] 2 Ch 389 at p. 402 (a case concerned with interference with the flow of air):

> . . . speaking generally, apart from long enjoyment, or some grant or agreement, no one has a right to prevent his neighbour from building on his own land, although the consequence may be to diminish or alter the flow of air over it on to land adjoining. So to diminish a flow of air is not actionable as a nuisance.

From this it follows that, in the absence of an easement, more is required than the mere presence of a neighbouring building to give rise to an actionable private nuisance. Indeed, for an action in private nuisance to lie in respect of interference with the plaintiff's enjoyment of his land, it will generally arise from something emanating from the defendant's land. Such an emanation may take many forms – noise, dirt, fumes, a noxious smell, vibrations, and suchlike. Occasionally activities on the defendant's land are in themselves so offensive to neighbours as to constitute an actionable nuisance, as in *Thompson-Schwab* v *Costaki* [1956] 1 WLR 335, where the sight of prostitutes and their clients entering and leaving neighbouring premises were held to fall into that category. Such cases must however be relatively rare. In one New Zealand case, *Bank of New Zealand* v *Greenwood* [1984] 1 NZLR 525, the glass roof of a verandah which deflected the sun's rays so that a dazzling glare was thrown on to neighbouring buildings was held, prima facie, to create a nuisance; but it seems that the effect was not merely to reflect the sunlight but to deflect it at such an angle and in such a manner as to cause the dazzling glare, too bright for the human eye to bear, to shine straight into the neighbouring building. One expert witness explained that the verandah glass diffused the light, as if from a multitude of mirrors, into what he described as a high intensity dazzle, which was extremely difficult to look at. On that basis, such a case can be distinguished from one concerned with the mere presence of a building on neighbouring land. At all events the mere fact that a building on the defendant's land gets in the way and so prevents something from reaching the plaintiff's land is generally speaking not enough for this purpose. . . .

Right to sue in private nuisance

I turn next to the question of the right to sue in private nuisance. In the two cases now under appeal before your Lordships' House, one of which relates to interference with television signals and the other to the generation of dust from the construction of a road, the plaintiffs consist in each case of a substantial group of local people. Moreover they are not restricted to householders who have the exclusive right to possess the places where they live, whether as freeholders or tenants, or even as licensees. They include people with whom householders share their homes, for example as wives or husbands or partners, or as children or other relatives. All of these people are claiming damages in private nuisance, by reason of interference with their television viewing or by reason of excessive dust. . . .

The basic position is, in my opinion, most clearly expressed in Professor Newark's classic article on *The Boundaries of Nuisance* in (1949) 65 LQR 480, when he stated (at p. 482) that the essence of nuisance was that 'it was a tort to land. Or to be more accurate it was a tort directed against the plaintiffs enjoyment of rights over land . . . '. The historical origin of the tort lay in the fact that (see p. 481):

Disseisina, transgressio and nocumentum [nuisance] covered the three ways in which a man might be interfered with in his rights over land. Wholly to deprive a man of the opportunity of exercising his rights over land was to disseise him, for which he might have recourse to the assize of novel disseisin. But to trouble a man in the exercise of his rights over land without going so far as to dispossess him was a trespass or a nuisance according to whether the act was done on or off the plaintiff's land.

Later, when distinguishing cases of personal injury, he stated (at pp. 488–489):

In true cases of nuisance the interest of the plaintiff which is invaded is not the interest of bodily security but the interest of liberty to exercise rights over land in the amplest manner. A sulphurous chimney in a residential area is not a nuisance because it makes householders cough and splutter but because it prevents them taking their ease in their gardens. It is for this reason that the plaintiff in an action for nuisance must show some title to realty.

Finally, he proclaimed four theses which should be nailed to the doors of the Law Courts and defended against all comers. The first was that:

The term 'nuisance' is properly applied only to such actionable user of land as interferes with the enjoyment by the plaintiff of rights in land.

There are many authoritative statements which bear out this thesis of Professor Newark. I refer in particular to *Sedleigh-Denfield* v *O'Callaghan* [1940] AC 880, 902–3, *per* Lord Wright; *Read* v *Lyons* [1947] AC 156, 183, *per* Lord Simonds; *Tate & Lyle Ltd* v *Greater London Council* [1983] 2 AC 509, 536–7, *per* Lord Templeman; *Fleming, The Law of Torts*, 8th ed. (1992), p. 416.

Since the tort of nuisance is a tort directed against the plaintiff's enjoyment of his rights over land, an action of private nuisance will usually be brought by the person in actual possession of the land affected, either as the freeholder or tenant of the land in question, or even as a licensee with exclusive possession of the land (see *Newcastle-under-Lyme Corporation* v *Wolstanton Ltd* [1947] Ch 92, 106–8, *per* Evershed J); though a reversioner may sue in respect of a nuisance of a sufficiently permanent character to damage his reversion. . . .

[It] has for many years been regarded as settled law that a person who has no right in the land cannot sue in private nuisance. For this proposition, it is usual to cite the decision of the Court of Appeal in *Malone* v *Laskey* [1907] 2 KB 141. In that case, the manager of a company resided in a house as a licensee of the company which employed him. The plaintiff was the manager's wife who lived with her husband in the house. She was injured when a bracket fell from a wall in the house. She claimed damages from the defendants in nuisance and negligence, her claim in nuisance being founded upon an allegation, accepted by the jury, that the fall of the bracket had been caused by vibrations from an engine operating on the defendants' adjoining premises. The Court of Appeal held that she was unable to succeed in her claim in nuisance. Sir Gorell Barnes P said, at p. 151:

Many cases were cited in the course of the argument in which it had been held that actions for nuisance could be maintained where a person's rights of property had been affected by the nuisance, but no authority was cited, nor in my opinion can any principle of law be formulated, to the effect that a person who has no interest in property, no right of occupation in the proper sense of the term, can maintain an action for a nuisance arising from the vibration caused by the working of an engine in an adjoining house. On that point, therefore, I think that the plaintiff fails, and that she has no cause of action in respect of the alleged nuisance. . . .

The decision in *Malone* v *Laskey* on nuisance has since been followed in many cases, of which notable examples are *Cunard* v *Antifyre Ltd* [1933] 1 KB 551 and *Oldham* v *Lawson (No. 1)* [1976] VR 654. Recently, however, the Court of Appeal departed from this line of authority in *Khorasandjian* v *Bush* [1993] QB 727, a case which I must examine with some care.

The plaintiff, a young girl who at the time of the appeal was 18, had formed a friendship with the defendant, then a man of 28. After a time the friendship broke down and the plaintiff decided that she would have no more to do with the defendant, but the defendant found this impossible to accept. There followed a catalogue of complaints against the defendant, including assaults, threats of violence, and pestering the plaintiff at her parents' home where she lived. As a result of the defendant's threats and abusive behaviour he spent some time in prison. An injunction was granted restraining the defendant from various forms of activity directed at the plaintiff, and this included an order restraining him from 'harassing, pestering or communicating with' the plaintiff. The question before the Court of Appeal was whether the judge had jurisdiction to grant such an injunction, in relation to telephone calls made to the plaintiff at her parents' home. The home was the property of the plaintiff's mother, and it was recognised that her mother could complain of persistent and unwanted telephone calls made to her; but it was submitted that the plaintiff, as a mere licensee in her mother's house, could not invoke the tort of private nuisance to complain of unwanted and harassing telephone calls made to her in her mother's home. The majority of the Court of Appeal (Peter Gibson J dissenting) rejected this submission, relying on the decision of the Appellate Division of the Alberta Supreme Court in *Motherwell* v *Motherwell* (1976) 73 DLR (3d) 62. In that case, the Appellate Division not only recognised that the legal owner of property could obtain an injunction, on the ground of private nuisance, to restrain persistent harassment by unwanted telephone calls to his home, but also that the same remedy was open to his wife who had no interest in the property. In the Court of Appeal Peter Gibson J dissented on the ground that it was wrong in principle that a mere licensee or someone without any interest in, or right to occupy, the relevant land should be able to sue in private nuisance.

It is necessary therefore to consider the basis of the decision in *Motherwell* v *Motherwell* that a wife, who has no interest in the matrimonial home where she lives, is nevertheless able to sue in private nuisance in respect of interference with her enjoyment of that home. The case was concerned with a claim for an injunction against the defendant, who was the daughter of one of the plaintiffs, the other two plaintiffs being her brother and sister-in-law. The main ground of the complaint against the defendant was that, as a result of a paranoid condition from which she suffered which produced in her the conviction that her sister-in-law and her father's housekeeper were inflaming her brother and her father against her, she persistently made a very large number of telephone calls to her brother's and her father's homes, in which she abused her sister-in-law and the housekeeper. The Appellate Division of the Alberta Supreme Court, in a judgment delivered by Clement JA, held that not only could her father and brother, as householders, obtain an injunction against the defendant to restrain this activity as a private nuisance, but so also could her sister-in-law although she had no interest in her husband's property. Clement JA said, at p. 78:

> Here we have a wife harassed in the matrimonial home. She has a status, a right to live there with her husband and children. I find it absurd to say that her occupancy of the matrimonial home is insufficient to found an action in nuisance. In my opinion she is entitled to the same relief as is her husband, the brother.

This conclusion was very largely based on the decision of the Court of Appeal in *Foster* v *Warblington UDC* [1906] 1 KB 648, which Clement JA understood to establish a distinction between 'one who is "merely present"' and 'occupancy of a substantial nature', and that in the latter case the occupier was entitled to sue in private nuisance. However *Foster* does not in my opinion provide authority for the proposition that a person in the position of a mere licensee, such as a wife or husband in her or his spouse's house, is entitled to sue in that action. This misunderstanding must, I fear, undermine the authority of *Motherwell* on this point; and in so far as the decision of the Court of Appeal in *Khorasandjian* v *Bush* is founded upon *Motherwell* it is likewise undermined.

But I must go further. If a plaintiff, such as the daughter of the householder in *Khorasandjian* v *Bush*, is harassed by abusive telephone calls, the gravamen of the complaint lies in the harassment which is just as much an abuse, or indeed an invasion of her privacy, whether she is pestered in this way in her mother's or her husband's house, or she is staying with a friend, or is at her place of work, or even in her car with a mobile phone. In truth, what the Court of Appeal appears to have been doing was to exploit the law of private nuisance in order to create by the back door a tort of harassment which was only partially effective in that it was artificially limited to harassment which takes place in her home. I myself do not consider that this is a satisfactory manner in which to develop the law, especially when, as in the case in question, the step so taken was inconsistent with another decision of the Court of Appeal, viz. *Malone* v *Laskey*, by which the court was bound. In any event, a tort of harassment has now received statutory recognition: see the Protection from Harassment Act 1997. We are therefore no longer troubled with the question whether the common law should be developed to provide such a remedy. For these reasons, I do not consider that any assistance can be derived from *Khorasandjian* v *Bush* by the plaintiffs in the present appeals.

It follows that, on the authorities as they stand, an action in private nuisance will only lie at the suit of a person who has a right to the land affected. Ordinarily, such a person can only sue if he has the right to exclusive possession of the land, such as a freeholder or tenant in possession, or even a licensee with exclusive possession. Exceptionally, however, as *Foster* shows, this category may include a person in actual possession who has no right to be there; and in any event a reversioner can sue in so far as his reversionary interest is affected. But a mere licensee on the land has no right to sue.

The question therefore arises whether your Lordships should be persuaded to depart from established principle, and recognise such a right in others who are no more than mere licensees on the land. At the heart of this question lies a more fundamental question, which relates to the scope of the law of private nuisance. Here I wish to draw attention to the fact that although, in the past, damages for personal injury have been recovered at least in actions of public nuisance, there is now developing a school of thought that the appropriate remedy for such claims as these should lie in our now fully developed law of negligence, and that personal injury claims should be altogether excluded from the domain of nuisance. The most forthright proponent of this approach has been Professor Newark, in his article in (1949) 65 LQR 480 from which I have already quoted. Furthermore, it is now being suggested that claims in respect of physical damage to the land should also be excluded from private nuisance: see, e.g., the article by Conor Gearty on *The Place of Private Nuisance in a Modern Law of Torts* in [1989] CLJ 214. In any event, it is right for present purposes to regard the typical cases of private nuisance as being those concerned with interference with the enjoyment of land and, as such, generally actionable only by a person with a right in the land. Characteristic examples of cases of this kind are those concerned with noise, vibrations, noxious smells and the like. The two appeals with which your Lordships are here concerned arise from actions of this character.

For private nuisances of this kind, the primary remedy is in most cases an injunction, which is sought to bring the nuisance to an end, and in most cases should swiftly achieve that objective. The right to bring such proceedings is, as the law stands, ordinarily vested in the person who has exclusive possession of the land. He or she is the person who will sue, if it is necessary to do so. Moreover he or she can, if thought appropriate, reach an agreement with the person creating the nuisance, either that it may continue for a certain period of time, possibly on the payment of a sum of money, or that it shall cease, again perhaps on certain terms including the time within which the cessation will take place. The former may well occur when an agreement is reached between neighbours about the circumstances in which one of them may carry out major repairs to his house which may affect the other's enjoyment of his property. An agreement of this kind was expressly contemplated by Fletcher Moulton LJ in his judgment in *Malone v Laskey* [1907] 2 KB 141, 153. But the efficacy of arrangements such as these depends upon the existence of an identifiable person with whom the creator of the nuisance can deal for this purpose. If anybody who lived in the relevant property as a home had the right to sue, sensible arrangements such as these might in some cases no longer be practicable.

Moreover, any such departure from the established law on this subject, such as that adopted by the Court of Appeal in the present case, faces the problem of defining the category of persons who would have the right to sue. The Court of Appeal adopted the not easily identifiable category of those who have a 'substantial link' with the land, regarding a person who occupied the premises 'as a home' as having a sufficient link for this purpose. But who is to be included in this category? It was plainly intended to include husbands and wives, or partners, and their children, and even other relatives living with them. But is the category also to include the lodger upstairs, or the au pair girl or resident nurse caring for an invalid who makes her home in the house while she works there? If the latter, it seems strange that the category should not extend to include places where people work as well as places where they live, where nuisances such as noise can be just as unpleasant or distracting. In any event, the extension of the tort in this way would transform it from a tort to land into a tort to the person, in which damages could be recovered in respect of something less serious than personal injury and the criteria for liability were founded not upon negligence but upon striking a balance between the interests of neighbours in the use of their land. This is, in my opinion, not an acceptable way in which to develop the law. . . .

10.1.2   CULPABILITY I: THE MENTAL ELEMENT

10.1.2.1   Liability for acts

CAMBRIDGE WATER CO. v *EASTERN COUNTIES LEATHER* **[1994] 1 All ER 53 (HL)**

FACTS: These appear from Lord Goff's speech.

LORD GOFF OF CHIEVELEY: My Lords, this appeal is concerned with the question whether the appellant company, Eastern Counties Leather plc (ECL), is liable to the respondent company, Cambridge Water Co. (CWC), in damages in respect of damage suffered by reason of the contamination of water available for abstraction at CWC's borehole at Sawston Mill near Cambridge. The contamination was caused by a solvent known as perchloroethene (PCE), used by ECL in the process of degreasing pelts at its tanning works in Sawston, about 1.3 miles away from CWC's borehole, the PCE having seeped into the ground beneath ECL's works and thence having been conveyed in percolating water in the direction of the borehole . . .

ECL was incorporated in 1879, and since that date has continued in uninterrupted business as a manufacturer of fine leather at Sawston. ECL employs about 100 people, all or whom live locally. Its present works are, as the judge found, in general modern and spacious, and admit of a good standard of housekeeping.

The tanning process requires that pelts shall be degreased; and ECL, in common with all other tanneries, has used solvents in that process since the early 1950s. It has used two types of chlorinated solvents—organochlorines known as TCE (trichloroethene) and PCE. Both solvents are cleaning and degreasing agents; and since 1950 PCE has increasingly been in common, widespread and everyday use in dry-cleaning, in general industrial use (e.g. as a machine cleaner or paint-thinner), domestically (e.g. in 'Dab-it-off') and in tanneries. PCE is highly volatile, and so evaporates rapidly in air; but it is not readily soluble in water.

[The] following relevant facts may be selected as being of particular relevance.

(1) The spillage of PCE, and its seepage into the ground beneath the floor of the tannery at ECL's works, occurred during the period which ended in 1976, as a result of regular spillages of small quantities of PCE onto the floor of ECL's tannery.

(2) The escape of dissolved phase PCE, from the pools of neat PCE which collected at or towards the base of the chalk aquifers beneath ECL's works, into the chalk aquifers under the adjoining land and thence in the direction of Sawston Mill, must have begun at some unspecified date well before 1976 and be still continuing to the present day.

(3) As held by the judge, the seepage of the PCE beneath the floor of ECL's works down into the chalk aquifers below was not foreseeable by a reasonable supervisor employed by

ECL, nor was it foreseeable by him that detectable quantities of PCE would be found down-catchment, so that he could not have foreseen, in or before 1976, that the repeated spillages would lead to any environmental hazard or damage. The only foreseeable damage from a spillage of PCE was that somebody might be overcome by fumes from a substantial spillage of PCE on the surface of the ground.

(4)   The water so contaminated at Sawston Mill has never been held to be dangerous to health. But under criteria laid down in the UK Regulations, issued in response to the EEC Directive, the water so contaminated was not 'wholesome' and, since 1985, could not lawfully be supplied in this country as drinking water.

The decision of Ian Kennedy J
The judge dismissed the claims against ECL in nuisance and negligence in the following passage:

> That there should now be an award of damages in respect of the 1991 impact of actions that were not actionable nuisances or negligence when they were committed 15 years before is to my mind not a proposition which the common law would entertain. . . .

The decision of the Court of Appeal: Ballard v *Tomlinson*
There was no appeal by CWC against the judge's conclusion on nuisance and negligence. CWC pursued its appeal to the Court of Appeal relying only on the rule in *Rylands* v *Fletcher*, on which point the judge had decided against it on the ground that the relevant operations of ECL constituted natural use of its land. The Court of Appeal however held ECL to be strictly liable in damages to CWC in respect of the contamination of the percolating water available for extraction by CWC from its borehole at Sawston Mill. This they did on the basis of the decision of the Court of Appeal in *Ballard* v *Tomlinson* (1885) 29 ChD 115.

In that case the plaintiff and the defendant, whose properties were separated only by a highway, each had on his land a well sunk into the chalk aquifer below. The plaintiff had a brewery on his land, for the purpose of which he used water drawn from his well. A printing house was built on the defendant's land, and the defendant constructed a drain from a water closet attached to the printing house, by means of which the sewage from the closet and the refuse from the printing house found their way into the defendant's well. The sewage and refuse which entered the defendant's well polluted the common source of percolating water so that the water which the plaintiff drew from his well was unusable for brewing purposes. The Court of Appeal, reversing the decision of Pearson J (see (1884) 26 Ch D 194), held that the plaintiff was entitled to judgment against the defendant for an injunction and for damages.

The principal argument advanced by the defendant was based on the proposition that the plaintiff had no property in the water percolating beneath his land, and therefore had no cause of action for the pollution of that water. The judgments of the Court of Appeal, which were unreserved, were largely directed to the rejection of that argument. This they did on the basis that the plaintiff had a right to extract water percolating beneath his land, and the defendant had no right to contaminate what the plaintiff was entitled to get. As Brett MR said (29 ChD 115 at 121):

> . . . no one of those who have a right to appropriate [the water] has a right to contaminate that source so as to prevent his neighbour from having the full value of his right of appropriation.

It appears that both Brett MR and Cotton LJ considered that the plaintiff's cause of action arose under the rule in *Rylands* v *Fletcher*, which was the basis upon which the plaintiff's case was advanced in argument. Lindley LJ however treated the case as one of nuisance.

The Court of Appeal treated this decision as determining the present case against ECL. Mann LJ (who delivered the judgment of the court) said (see p 61, ante):

> It was sufficient that the defendant's act caused the contamination. Nor do the judgments contain any warrant for attaching importance to the reasonableness of ECL's inability to foresee that spillages would have the kind of consequence which they did. It does not appear from the report whether Tomlinson either knew or ought to have known

of any risk of damage attendant on his actions, but none of the judges in this court was concerned with his state of actual or imputed knowledge. The situation is one in which negligence plays no part. *Ballard* v *Tomlinson* decided that where the nuisance is an interference with a natural right incident to ownership then the liability is a strict one. The actor acts at his peril in that if his actions result by the operation of ordinary natural processes in an interference with the right then he is liable to compensate for any damage suffered by the owner.

In his judgment in *Ballard* v *Tomlinson* 29 ChD 115 at 124 Cotton LJ spoke of the plaintiff's right to abstract percolating water beneath his land as 'a natural right incident to the ownership of his own land'. In the present context, however, this means no more than that the owner of land can, without a grant, lawfully abstract water which percolates beneath his land, his right to do so being protected by the law of tort, by means of an action for an injunction or for damages for nuisance: see Megarry and Wade *Law of Real Property* (5th edn, 1984) p. 842, and Simpson *History of Land Law* (2nd edn, 1986) pp. 263–264. There is no natural right to percolating water, as there may be no water running in a defined channel; see *Chasemore* v *Richards* (1859) 7 HL Cas 349 at 379 *per* Lord Cranworth, and 49 *Halsbury's Laws* (4th edn) para. 392. In the present case Mann LJ stated that *Ballard* v *Tomlinson* decided that 'where the nuisance is an interference with a natural right incident to ownership then the liability is a strict one'. In my opinion, however, if in this passage Mann LJ intended to say that the defendant was held to be liable for damage which he could not reasonably have foreseen, that conclusion cannot be drawn from the judgments in the case, in which the point did not arise. As I read the judgments, they disclose no more than that, in the circumstances of the case, the defendant was liable to the plaintiff in tort for the contamination of the source of water supplying the plaintiff's well, either on the basis of the rule in *Rylands* v *Fletcher*, or under the law of nuisance, by reason of interference with the plaintiff's use and enjoyment of his land, including his right to extract water percolating beneath his land. It follows that the question whether such a liability may attach in any particular case must depend upon the principles governing liability under one or other of those two heads of the law. To those principles, therefore, I now turn.

Nuisance and the rule in *Rylands* v *Fletcher*

. . . In order to consider the question in the present case in its proper legal context, it is desirable to look at the nature of liability in a case such as the present in relation both to the law of nuisance and the rule in *Rylands* v *Fletcher*, and for that purpose to consider the relationship between the two heads of liability.

I begin with the law of nuisance. Our modern understanding of the nature and scope of the law of nuisance was much enhanced by Professor Newark's seminal article 'The boundaries of nuisance' (1949) 65 LQR 480. The article is avowedly a historical analysis, in that it traces the nature of the tort of nuisance to its origins, and demonstrates how the original view of nuisance as a tort to land (or more accurately, to accommodate interference with servitudes, a tort directed against the plaintiff's enjoyment of rights over land) became distorted as the tort was extended to embrace claims for personal injuries, even where the plaintiff's injury did not occur while using land in his occupation. In Professor Newark's opinion (at p. 487), this development produced adverse effects, viz that liability which should have arisen only under the law of negligence was allowed under the law of nuisance which historically was a tort of strict liability; and that there was a tendency for 'cross-infection to take place, and notions of negligence began to make an appearance in the realm of nuisance proper'. But in addition, Professor Newark considered (at pp. 487–488) it contributed to a misappreciation of the decision in *Rylands* v *Fletcher*:

> This case is generally regarded as an important landmark, indeed a turning point—in the law of tort; but an examination of the judgments shows that those who decided it were quite unconscious of any revolutionary or reactionary principles implicit in the decision. They thought of it as calling for no more than a restatement of settled principles, and Lord Cairns went so far as to describe those principles as 'extremely simple'. And in fact the main principle involved was extremely simple, being no more than the principle that negligence is not an element in the tort of nuisance. It is true that Blackburn J in his great judgment in the Exchequer Chamber never once used the word

'nuisance', but three times he cited the case of fumes escaping from an alkali works—a clear case of nuisance—as an instance of liability, under the rule which he was laying down. Equally it is true that in 1866 there were a number of cases in the reports suggesting that persons who controlled dangerous things were under a strict duty to take care, but as none of these cases had anything to do with nuisance Blackburn J. did not refer to them. But the profession as a whole, whose conceptions of the boundaries of nuisance were now becoming fogged, failed to see in *Rylands* v *Fletcher* a simple case of nuisance. They regarded it as an exceptional case—and the rule in *Rylands* v *Fletcher* as a generalisation of exceptional cases, where liability was to be strict on account of 'the magnitude of danger, coupled with the difficulty of proving negligence' [*Pollock on Torts* (14th edn, 1939) p. 386] rather than on account of the nature of the plaintiff's interest which was invaded. They therefore jumped rashly to two conclusions: firstly, that the rule in *Rylands* v *Fletcher* could be extended beyond the case of neighbouring occupiers; and secondly, that the rule could be used to afford a remedy in cases of personal injury. Both these conclusions were stoutly denied by Lord Macmillan in *Read* v *J. Lyons & Co. Ltd.* ([1946] 2 All ER 471, [1947] AC 156), but it remains to be seen whether the House of Lords will support his opinion when the precise point comes up for decision.

We are not concerned in the present case with the problem of personal injuries, but we are concerned with the scope of liability in nuisance and in *Rylands* v *Fletcher*. In my opinion it is right to take as our starting point the fact that, as Professor Newark considered, *Rylands* v *Fletcher* was indeed not regarded by Blackburn J as a revolutionary decision: see eg his observations in *Ross* v *Fedden* (1872) 26 LT 966 at 968. He believed himself not to be creating new law, but to be stating existing law, on the basis of existing authority; and, as is apparent from his judgment, he was concerned in particular with the situation where the defendant collects things upon his land which are likely to do mischief if they escape, in which event the defendant will be strictly liable for damage resulting from any such escape. It follows that the essential basis of liability was the collection by the defendant of such things upon his land; and the consequence was a strict liability in the event of damage caused by their escape, even if the escape was an isolated event. Seen in its context, there is no reason to suppose that Blackburn J intended to create a liability any more strict than that created by the law of nuisance; but even so he must have intended that, in the circumstances specified by him, there should be liability for damage resulting from an isolated escape.

Of course, although liability for nuisance has generally been regarded as strict, at least in the case of a defendant who has been responsible for the creation of a nuisance, even so that liability has been kept under control by the principle of reasonable user—the principle of give and take as between neighbouring occupiers of land, under which 'those acts necessary for the common and ordinary use and occupation of land and houses may be done, if conveniently done, without subjecting those who do them to an action': see *Bamford* v *Turnley* (1862) 3 B & S 62 at 83, [1861–73] All ER Rep 706 at 712 *per* Bramwell B. The effect is that, if the user is reasonable, the defendant will not be liable for consequent harm to his neighbour's enjoyment of his land; but if the user is not reasonable, the defendant will be liable, even though he may have exercised reasonable care and skill to avoid it. Strikingly, a comparable principle has developed which limits liability under the rule in *Rylands* v *Fletcher*. This is the principle of natural use of the land. I shall have to consider the principle at a later stage in this judgment. The most authoritative statement of the principle is now to be found in the advice of the Privy Council delivered by Lord Moulton in *Rickards* v *Lothian* [1913] AC 263 at 280, when he said of the rule in *Rylands* v *Fletcher*:

It is not every use to which land is put that brings into play that principle. It must be some special use bringing with it increased danger to others, and must not merely be the ordinary use of the land or such a use as is proper for the general benefit of the community.

It is not necessary for me to identify precise differences which may be drawn between this principle, and the principle of reasonable user as applied in the law of nuisance. It is enough for present purposes that I should draw attention to a similarity of function. The effect of this principle is that, where it applies, there will be no liability under the rule in *Rylands* v *Fletcher*; but that where it does not apply, ie where there is a non-natural use, the defendant will be liable for harm caused to the plaintiff by the escape, notwithstanding that he has exercised all reasonable care and skill to prevent the escape from occurring.

Foreseeability of damage in nuisance

It is against this background that it is necessary to consider the question whether foreseeability of harm of the relevant type is an essential element of liability either in nuisance or under the rule in *Rylands* v *Fletcher*. I shall take first the case of nuisance. In the present case, as I have said, this is not strictly speaking a live issue. Even so, I propose briefly to address it, as part of the analysis of the background to the present case.

. . . In the present case, we are not concerned with liability in damages in respect of a nuisance which has arisen through natural causes, or by the act of a person for whose actions the defendant is not responsible, in which cases the applicable principles in nuisance have become closely associated with those applicable in negligence: see *Sedleigh-Denfield* v *O'Callaghan* [1940] 3 All ER 349 and *Goldman* v *Hargrave* [1966] 2 All ER 989. We are concerned with the liability of a person where a nuisance has been created by one for whose actions he is responsible. Here, as I have said, it is still the law that the fact that the defendant has taken all reasonable care will not of itself exonerate him from liability, the relevant control mechanism being found within the principle of reasonable user. But it by no means follows that the defendant should be held liable for damage of a type which he could not reasonably foresee; and the development of the law of negligence in the past sixty years points strongly towards a requirement that such foreseeability should be a prerequisite of liability in damages for nuisance, as it is of liability in negligence. For if a plaintiff is in ordinary circumstances only able to claim damages in respect of personal injuries where he can prove such foreseeability on the part of the defendant, it is difficult to see why, in common justice, he should be in a stronger position to claim damages for interference with the enjoyment of his land where the defendant was unable to foresee such damage. Moreover, this appears to have been the conclusion of the Privy Council in *The Wagon Mound (No 2), Overseas Tankship (UK) Ltd* v *Miller Steamship Co. Pty Ltd* [1967] 1 AC 617. The facts of the case are too well known to require repetition, but they gave rise to a claim for damages arising from a public nuisance caused by a spillage of oil in Sydney Harbour. Lord Reid, who delivered the advice of the Privy Council, considered that, in the class of nuisance which included the case before the Board, foreseeability is an essential element in determining liability. He then continued [1967] 1 AC 617 at 640:

> It could not be right to discriminate between different cases of nuisance so as to make foreseeability a necessary element in determining damages in those cases where it is a necessary element in determining liability, but not in others. So the choice is between it being a necessary element in all cases of nuisance or in none. In their Lordships' judgment the similarities between nuisance and other forms of tort to which *The Wagon Mound (No.1)* [see *Overseas Tankship (UK) Ltd* v *Morts Dock and Engineering Co. Ltd, The Wagon Mound* [1961] AC 388] applies far outweigh any differences, and they must therefore hold that the judgment appealed from is wrong on this branch of the case. It is not sufficient that the injury suffered by the respondents' vessels was the direct result of the nuisance if that injury was in the relevant sense unforeseeable.

It is widely accepted that this conclusion, although not essential to the decision of the particular case, has nevertheless settled the law to the effect that foreseeability of harm is indeed a prerequisite of the recovery of damages in private nuisance, as in the case of public nuisance. I refer in particular to the opinion expressed by Professor Fleming in his book on *Torts* (8th edn, 1992) pp 443–444. It is unnecessary in the present case to consider the precise nature of this principle; but it appears from Lord Reid's statement of the law that he regarded it essentially as one relating to remoteness of damage.

Foreseeability of damage under the rule in Rylands v Fletcher

It is against this background that I turn to the submission advanced by ECL before your Lordships that there is a similar prerequisite of recovery of damages under the rule in *Rylands* v *Fletcher* (1866) LR 1 Exch 265.

I start with the judgment of Blackburn J in *Fletcher* v *Rylands* itself. . . .

Blackburn J spoke of 'anything *likely* to do mischief if it escapes'; and later he spoke of something 'which he *knows* to be mischievous if it gets on to his neighbour's [property]', and the liability to 'answer for the natural and *anticipated* consequences'. Furthermore, time and again he spoke of the strict liability imposed upon the defendant as being that he must keep the thing in at his peril; and, when referring to liability in actions for damage occasioned by animals, he referred (at 282) to the established principle 'that it is quite immaterial whether the escape is by negligence or not'. The general tenor of his statement of principle is therefore that knowledge, or at least foreseeability of the risk, is a prerequisite of the recovery of damages under the principle; but that the principle is one of strict liability in the sense that the defendant may be held liable notwithstanding that he has exercised all due care to prevent the escape from occurring.

There are however early authorities in which foreseeability of damage does not appear to have been regarded as necessary (see e.g. *Humphries* v *Cousins* (1877) 2 CPD 239, [1877–80] All ER Rep 313). Moreover, it was submitted by Mr Ashworth for CWC that the requirement of foreseeability of damage was negatived in two particular cases, the decision of the Court of Appeal in *West* v *Bristol Tramways Co.* [1908] 2 KB 14 and the decision of this House in *Rainham Chemical Works Ltd* v *Belvedere Fish Guano Co. Ltd* [1921] 2 AC 465.

In *West* v *Bristol Tramways Co.* the defendant tramway company was held liable for damage to the plaintiff's plants and shrubs in his nursery garden adjoining a road where the defendant's tramline ran, the damage being caused by fumes from creosoted wooden blocks laid by the defendants between the rails of the tramline. The defendants were so held liable under the rule in *Rylands* v *Fletcher*, notwithstanding that they were exonerated from negligence, having no knowledge of the possibility of such damage; indeed the evidence was that creosoted wood had been in use for several years as wood paving, and no mischief had ever been known to arise from it. The argument that no liability arose in such circumstances under the rule in *Rylands* v *Fletcher* was given short shrift, both in the Divisional Court and in the Court of Appeal. For the Divisional Court, it was enough that the creosote had been found to be dangerous by the jury, Phillimore J holding that creosote was like the wild animals in the old cases. The Court of Appeal did not call upon the plaintiffs, and dismissed the appeal in unreserved judgments. Lord Alverstone CJ relied upon a passage from *Garrett on Nuisances* (2nd edn, 1897) p 129, and rejected a contention by the defendant that, in the case of non-natural use of land, the defendant will not be liable unless the thing introduced onto the land was, to the knowledge of the defendant, likely to escape and cause damage. It was however suggested, both by Lord Alverstone CJ (with whom Gorell Barnes P agreed) and by Farwell LJ that, by analogy with cases concerning liability for animals, the defendant might escape liability if he could show that, according to the common experience of mankind, the thing introduced onto the land had proved not to be dangerous.

The *Rainham Chemicals* case arose out of a catastrophic explosion at a factory involved in the manufacture of high explosive during the First World War, with considerable loss of life and damage to neighbouring property. It was held that the company carrying on the business at the premises was liable for the damage to neighbouring property under the rule in *Rylands* v *Fletcher*; . . . [At trial] it appears to have been admitted that the person in possession of the DNP was liable under the rule in *Rylands* v *Fletcher* for the consequences of the explosion. This was despite the fact that DNP had never been known to explode before and, as Younger LJ pointed out, exactly the same fire and explosion might have occurred if the DNP had been stored at a dyeworks and was not being used in any way in the manufacture of explosives. In the Court of Appeal, Atkin LJ was of the opinion that the fact that the work was known to be dangerous by the contractors and the company was, if relevant, established but it seems clear that no such knowledge could be imputed to either of the two individual defendants.

I feel bound to say that these two cases provide a very fragile base for any firm conclusion that foreseeability of damage has been authoritatively rejected as a prerequisite of the recovery of damages under the rule in *Rylands* v *Fletcher*. Certainly, the point was not considered by this House in the *Rainham Chemicals* case. In my opinion, the matter is open for consideration by your Lordships in the present case, and, despite recent dicta to the contrary (see e.g. *Leakey* v *National Trust for Places of Historic Interest or Natural Beauty* [1980] 1 All ER 17 at 30, [1980] QB 485 at 519 *per* Megaw LJ), should be considered as a matter of principle . . .

. . . The recovery of damages in private nuisance depends on foreseeability by the defendant of the relevant type of damage, it would appear logical to extend the same requirement to liability under the rule in *Rylands* v *Fletcher*.

Even so, the question cannot be considered solely as a matter of history. It can be argued that the rule in *Rylands* v *Fletcher* should not be regarded simply as an extension of the law of nuisance, but should rather be treated as a developing principle of strict liability from which can be derived a general rule of strict liability for damage caused by ultra-hazardous operations, on the basis of which persons conducting such operations may properly be held strictly liable for the extraordinary risk to others involved in such operations. As is pointed out in *Fleming on Torts* (8th edn, 1992) pp. 327–328, this would lead to the practical result that the cost of damage resulting from such operations would have to be absorbed as part of the overheads of the relevant business rather than be borne (where there is no negligence) by the injured person or his insurers, or even by the community at large. Such a development appears to have been taking place in the United States, as can be seen from § 519 of the *Restatement of Torts* (2d) vol 3 (1977). The extent to which it has done so is not altogether clear; and I infer from para 519, and the comment on that paragraph, that the abnormally dangerous activities there referred to are such that their ability to cause harm would be obvious to any reasonable person who carried them on.

I have to say, however, that there are serious obstacles in the way of the development of the rule in *Rylands* v *Fletcher* in this way. First of all, if it was so to develop, it should logically apply to liability to all persons suffering injury by reason of the ultra-hazardous operations; but the decision of this House in *Read* v *J Lyons & Co. Ltd* [1947] AC 156, which establishes that there can be no liability under the rule except in circumstances where the injury has been caused by an escape from land under the control of the defendant, has effectively precluded any such development. Professor Fleming has observed that 'the most damaging effect of the decision in *Read* v *Lyons* is that it prematurely stunted the development of a general theory of strict liability for ultra-hazardous activities' (see *Fleming on Torts* (8th edn, 1992) p. 341). Even so, there is much to be said for the view that the courts should not be proceeding down the path of developing such a general theory. In this connection, I refer in particular to the Report of the Law Commission on *Civil Liability for Dangerous Things and Activities* (Law Com no 32) 1970. In paras 14–16 of the report the Law Commission expressed serious misgivings about the adoption of any test for the application of strict liability involving a general concept of 'especially dangerous' or 'ultra-hazardous' activity, having regard to the uncertainties and practical difficulties of its application. If the Law Commission is unwilling to consider statutory reform on this basis, it must follow that judges should if anything be even more reluctant to proceed down that path.

Like the judge in the present case, I incline to the opinion that, as a general rule, it is more appropriate for strict liability in respect of operations of high risk to be imposed by Parliament, than by the courts. If such liability is imposed by statute, the relevant activities can be identified, and those concerned can know where they stand. Furthermore, statute can where appropriate lay down precise criteria establishing the incidence and scope of such liability.

It is of particular relevance that the present case is concerned with environmental pollution. The protection and preservation of the environment is now perceived as being of crucial importance to the future of mankind; and public bodies, both national and international, are taking significant steps towards the establishment of legislation which will promote the protection of the environment, and make the polluter pay for damage to the environment for which he is responsible—as can be seen from the WHO, EEC and national regulations to which I have previously referred. But it does not follow from these developments that a common law principle, such as the rule in *Rylands* v *Fletcher*, should be developed or rendered more strict to provide for liability in respect of such pollution. On the contrary, given that so much well-informed and carefully structured legislation is now being put in place for this purpose, there is less need for the courts to develop a common law principle to achieve the same end, and indeed it may well be undesirable that they should do so.

Having regard to these considerations, and in particular to the step which this House has already taken in *Read* v *Lyons* to contain the scope of liability under the rule in *Rylands* v *Fletcher*, it appears to me to be appropriate now to take the view that foreseeability of damage of the relevant type should be regarded as a prerequisite of liability in damages under the rule. Such a conclusion can, as I have already stated, be derived from Blackburn J's original statement of the law; and I can see no good reason why this prerequisite should not be recognised under the rule, as it has been in the case of private nuisance. In particular, I do not regard the two authorities cited to your Lordships, *West v Bristol Tramways Co.* [1908] 2 KB 14 and *Rainham Chemical Works Ltd v Belvedere Fish Guano Co. Ltd* [1921] 2 AC 465 as providing any strong pointer towards a contrary conclusion. It would moreover lead to a more coherent body of common law principles if the rule were to be regarded essentially as an extension of the law of nuisance to cases of isolated escapes from land, even though the rule as established is not limited to escapes which are in fact isolated. I wish to point out, however, that in truth the escape of the PCE from ECL's land, in the form of trace elements carried in percolating water, has not been an isolated escape, but a continuing escape resulting from a state of affairs which has come into existence at the base of the chalk aquifer underneath ECL's premises. Classically, this would have been regarded as a case of nuisance; and it would seem strange if, by characterising the case as one falling under the rule in *Rylands* v *Fletcher*, the liability should thereby be rendered more strict in the circumstances of the present case.

The facts of the present case
Turning to the facts of the present case, it is plain that, at the time when the PCE was brought onto ECL's land, and indeed when it was used in the tanning process there, nobody at ECL could reasonably have foreseen the resultant damage which occurred at CWC's borehole at Sawston.

. . . I wish to add that the present case may be regarded as one of what is nowadays called historic pollution, in the sense that the relevant occurrence (the seepage of PCE through the floor of ECL's premises) took place before the relevant legislation came into force; and it appears that, under the current philosophy, it is not envisaged that statutory liability should be imposed for historic pollution (see eg the Council of Europe's Draft Convention on Civil Liability for Damages Resulting from Activities Dangerous to the Environment (Strasbourg, 29 January 1993) article 5.1, and para 48 of the Explanatory Report). If so, it would be strange if liability for such pollution were to arise under a principle of common law.

In the result, since those responsible at ECL could not at the relevant time reasonably have foreseen that the damage in question might occur, the claim of CWC for damages under the rule in *Rylands* v *Fletcher* must fail.

Natural use of land
I turn to the question whether the use by ECL of its land in the present case constituted a natural use, with the result that ECL cannot be held liable under the rule in *Rylands* v *Fletcher*. In view of my conclusion on the issue of foreseeability, I can deal with this point shortly.

The judge held that it was a natural use. He said:

In my judgment, in considering whether the storage of organochlorines as an adjunct to a manufacturing process is a non-natural use of land, I must consider whether that storage created special risks for adjacent occupiers and whether the activity was for the general benefit of the community. It seems to me inevitable that I must consider the magnitude of the storage and the geographical area in which it takes place in answering the question. Sawston is properly described as an industrial village, and the creation of employment is clearly for the benefit of that community. I do not believe that I can enter upon an assessment of the point on a scale of desirability that the manufacture of wash leathers comes, and I content myself with holding that this storage in this place is a natural use of land.

It is a commonplace that this particular exception to liability under the rule has developed and changed over the years. It seems clear that in *Fletcher v Rylands* (1866) LR 1 Ex 265 itself Blackburn J's statement of the law was limited to things which are brought by the defendant onto his land, and so did not apply to things that were naturally upon the land. Furthermore, it is doubtful whether in the House of Lords in the same case Lord Cairns, to whom we owe the expression 'non-natural use' of the land, was intending to expand the concept of natural use beyond that envisaged by Blackburn J. Even so, the law has long since departed from any such simple idea, redolent of a different age; and, at least since the advice of the Privy Council delivered by Lord Moulton in *Rickards* v *Lothian* [1913] AC 263 at 280 natural use has been extended to embrace the ordinary use of land. I ask to be forgiven if I again quote Lord Moulton's statement of the law, which has lain at the heart of the subsequent development of this exception:

> It is not every use to which land is put that brings into play that principle. It must be some special use bringing with it increased danger to others, and must not merely be the ordinary use of the land or such a use as is proper for the general benefit of the community.

Rickards v *Lothian* itself was concerned with a use of a domestic kind, viz the overflow of water from a basin whose runaway had become blocked. But over the years the concept of natural use, in the sense of ordinary use, has been extended to embrace a wide variety of uses, including not only domestic uses but also recreational uses and even some industrial uses.

It is obvious that the expression 'ordinary use of the land' in Lord Moulton's statement of the law is one which is lacking in precision. There are some writers who welcome the flexibility which has thus been introduced into this branch of the law, on the ground that it enables judges to mould and adapt the principle of strict liability to the changing needs of society; whereas others regret the perceived absence of principle in so vague a concept, and fear that the whole idea of strict liability may as a result be undermined. A particular doubt is introduced by Lord Moulton's alternative criterion 'or such a use as is proper for the general benefit of the community'. If these words are understood to refer to a local community, they can be given some content as intended to refer to such matters as, for example, the provision of services; indeed the same idea can, without too much difficulty, be extended to, for example, the provision of services to industrial premises, as in a business park or an industrial estate. But if the words are extended to embrace the wider interests of the local community or the general benefit of the community at large, it is difficult to see how the exception can be kept within reasonable bounds. A notable extension was considered in your Lordships' House in *Read* v *J Lyons & Co. Ltd* [1947] AC 156 at 169–170, 174 *per* Viscount Simon and Lord Macmillan, where it was suggested that, in time of war, the manufacture of explosives might be held to constitute a natural use of land, apparently on the basis that, in a country in which the greater part of the population was involved in the war effort, many otherwise exceptional uses might become 'ordinary' for the duration of the war. It is however unnecessary to consider so wide an extension as that in a case such as the present. Even so, we can see the introduction of another extension in the present case, when the judge invoked the creation of employment as clearly for the benefit of the local community, viz 'the industrial village' at Sawston. I myself, however, do not feel able to accept that the creation of employment as such, even in a small industrial complex, is sufficient of itself to establish a particular use as constituting a natural or ordinary use of land.

Fortunately, I do not think it is necessary for the purposes of the present case to attempt any redefinition of the concept of natural or ordinary use. This is because I am satisfied that the storage of chemicals in substantial quantities, and their use in the manner employed at ECL's premises, cannot fall within the exception. For the purpose of testing the point, let it be assumed that ECL was well aware of the possibility that PCE, if it escaped, could indeed cause damage, for example by contaminating any water with which it became mixed so as to render that water undrinkable by human beings. I cannot think that it would be right in such circumstances to exempt ECL from liability under the rule in *Rylands* v *Fletcher* on the ground that the use was natural or ordinary. The mere fact that the use is common in the tanning industry cannot, in my opinion, be enough to bring the use within the exception, nor the fact that Sawston contains a small industrial community which is worthy of encouragement or support. Indeed I feel bound to say that the storage of substantial quantities of chemicals on industrial premises should be regarded as an almost classic case of non-natural use; and I find it very difficult to think that it should be thought objectionable to impose strict liability for damage caused in the event of their escape. It may well be that, now that it is recognised that foreseeability of harm of the relevant type is a prerequisite of liability in damages under the rule, the courts may feel less pressure to extend the concept of natural use to circumstances such as those in the present case; and in due course it may become easier to control this exception, and to ensure that it has a more recognisable basis of principle. For these reasons, I would not hold that ECL should be exempt from liability on the basis of the exception of natural use.

10.1.2.2 Positive duty to act and liability for omissions

WRINGE v *COHEN* [1939] 4 All ER 241 (CA)

FACTS: The defendant owned a house. The side wall adjoined the plaintiff's shop. The house wall was higher. The house wall was in bad repair. The defendant was liable to repair it, but had not inspected it for two years. The wall collapsed through want of repair and damaged the plaintiff's shop. The plaintiff alleged there was a nuisance arising out of the want of repair. The defendant denied he was at fault.

ATKINSON J: . . . The defendant admitted that he was liable to repair, and had always done the repairs. The judge held that the wall was in a defective condition, and was a nuisance owing to want of repair, and that the defendant was liable to repair . . . He further held that, in those circumstances, there was an absolute duty on the defendant towards the plaintiff to keep his house in such repair that it did not become a nuisance, and awarded the plaintiff £61 17s. 1d. damages, and costs. The defendant had given evidence that the wall was in good repair as far as he knew, but he did not suggest that he had examined it, or even looked at it. A builder gave evidence that 2 years ago the defendant asked him to look at the gable-end, and said that it then looked in a fair state of repair.

It was admitted that there was evidence upon which the judge could find that the defendant had agreed with the tenant to keep the premises in repair, and the appeal was argued on that footing. It was also conceded that there was evidence upon which the judge could properly hold that the wall of the gable-end of the house had, owing to want of repair, become a nuisance—that is, a danger to passers-by and adjoining owners. It is contended for the appellant, however, that these findings do not go far enough to establish his liability for the damage caused by the collapse of the wall. It is said that the defendant is liable only if it is found as a fact that he knew, or ought to have known, of the want of repair, that the judge did not so find, and that we ought to send the case back for a new trial. It is said that the judge was wrong in holding that the obligation to repair was absolute.

In our judgment, if, owing to want of repair, premises upon a highway become dangerous, and, therefore, a nuisance, and a passer-by or adjoining owner suffers damage by their collapse, the occupier, or the owner, if he has undertaken the duty of repair, is answerable, whether or not he knew, or ought to have known, of the danger. The undertaking to repair gives the owner control of the premises, and a right of access thereto for the purpose of maintaining them in a safe condition. On the other hand, if the nuisance is created, not by want of repair, but, for example, by the act of a trespasser, or by a secret and unobservable operation of nature, such as a subsidence under or near the foundations of the premises, neither an occupier nor an owner responsible for repair is answerable, unless with knowledge or means of knowledge he allows the danger to continue. In such a case, he has in no sense caused the nuisance by any act or breach of duty. I think that every case decided in the English courts is consistent with this view.

By common law, it is an indictable offence for an occupier of premises upon a highway to permit them to get into a dangerous condition owing to non-repair. It was not and is not necessary in an indictment to aver knowledge or means of knowledge (see *R* v *Watson* (1703) 2 Ld Raym 856) . . .

Perhaps the most important case for our consideration is *Tarry* v *Ashton* (1876) 1 QBD 314. It is necessary to examine this case with care, and particularly the judgment of Blackburn J... It is a case which, in our view, has been misunderstood in quite a number of later cases. The facts of that case were simple. The plaintiff was walking along the Strand in front of the defendant's house in Nov., 1874, when a large lamp suspended from the front of the house fell upon her and injured her. A man was blowing water out of the gas-pipes. He had placed his ladder against the lamp-bracket. It slipped, and the man fell. The lamp got shaken, and its fastenings broke. In Aug., 1874, the defendant, who had only lately become the tenant of the house, knowing that the lamp and other fittings were of some age, employed an experienced fitter to examine them and put them in thorough repair. After the accident, examination showed that the breakage was caused by the general decay of the connections. The jury found that the defendant was not negligent, and had no knowledge of the want of repair, but that the fitter was negligent . . . At the time of the accident in November, it is clear that the defendant had no knowledge whatever of the defective condition of the lamp. It could not be said, and it was not said, that he ought to have known, as a competent fitter had just been employed to make sure that the lamp was in thorough repair. At no time, even in August, did the defendant know of, or even suspect, disrepair. It was merely that, knowing the lamp was old and might want attention, he took the precaution of employing a fitter to examine it and do whatever might be necessary. In fact, the lamp was in a dangerous condition. It was a nuisance, and the defendant was held liable . . .

He would be responsible to this extent, that as soon as he knew of the danger he would be bound to put the premises in repair or pull them down. So also the occupier would be bound to know that things like this lamp will ultimately get out of order, and, as occupier, there would be a duty cast upon him from time to time to investigate the state of the lamp. If he did investigate, and there were a latent defect which he could not discover, I doubt whether he would be liable; but if he discovers the defect and does not cure it, or if he did not discover what he ought on investigation to have discovered, then I think he would clearly be answerable for the consequences. Now in the present case there is ample evidence that in August the defendant was aware that the lamp might be getting out of repair, and, it being his duty to put it in repair, he employs Chappell to do so. We must assume, I think, that Chappell was a proper person to employ; and I may observe that he was clearly not the defendant's servant, as the jury say, but an independent contractor. But it was the defendant's duty to make the lamp reasonably safe, the contractor failed to do that; and the defendant, having the duty, has trusted the fulfilment of that duty to another who has not done it. Therefore the defendant has not done his duty, and he is liable to the plaintiff for the consequences. It was his duty to have the lamp set right; it was not set right. [*per* Blackburn J].

Why was it 'the defendant's duty to make the lamp safe'? Blackburn J, does not say it was his duty because he was aware that the lamp might be getting out of repair, but merely 'it being his duty to put it in repair.' Surely it was not his duty because he gave his mind to the question of the safety of his premises, and, wishing to ensure that safety, employed a contractor to examine them and do all that might be necessary. He could not be in a worse position than if he had not given the matter a thought, and, therefore, had not had anyone to examine the premises and do what was necessary. The judge must have meant that he was under a duty because, as an occupier, he was bound to keep his premises, including the lamp, from becoming unsafe for want of proper repair. That duty was not performed, and, therefore, he was liable, despite the absence of negligence or knowledge. The judge contrasted the position of a nuisance due to want of repair with that of a nuisance due to a latent defect or an act of trespass. Lush and Quain JJ, rested their judgments on an absolute obligation to prevent one's property from becoming a nuisance. There is no question about that . . .

In *Noble* v *Harrison* [1926] 2 KB 332 a branch of a tree growing on the defendant's land overhanging the highway 30 ft. above the ground broke and fell upon the plaintiff's motor coach. The plaintiff claimed damages, but failed, because the fracture was due to a latent defect which was not discoverable by any reasonably careful inspection, and which was, of course, unknown to the defendant. The claim was based on nuisance. The county court judge had found for the plaintiff. The Divisional Court reversed the decision. Rowlatt J, said, at p. 338:

> The result of [the cases] is that a person is liable for a nuisance constituted by the state of his property: (1) if he causes it; (2) if, by the neglect of some duty, he allowed it to arise; and (3) if, when it has arisen without his own act or default, he omits to remedy it within a reasonable time after he did or ought to have become aware of it.

The judge went on to say, however, that Lush and Quain JJ, had held that there was an absolute duty to keep the lamp in repair, and that Blackburn J, thought that for a latent defect the occupier would not be liable. Adopting that view, confirmed by the principle laid down in *Barker* v *Herbert*, he held that the defect in the branch was clearly latent, and that the defendant was, therefore, not liable, in the absence of knowledge, or means of knowledge.

10.1.2.3 Nuisance arising from natural causes

LEAKEY v *NATIONAL TRUST* [1980] 1 All ER 17 (CA)

FACTS: The defendants owned a rather odd conical hill called Burrow Mump. The geological strata were unstable, and bits of the hill had a tendency to fall off and roll onto the plaintiffs' houses, which were built close to the foot of the hill. The plaintiffs suffered damage as a result and feared further harm. They sought to recover damages from the defendants in nuisance, together with an injunction to restrain future falls (by making the defendants carry out protection work). The defendants alleged that there was no liability in nuisance for harm arising from the natural geology of the land.

The plaintiffs succeeded before O'Connor J and the defendants appealed to the Court of Appeal:

MEGAW LJ: For the defendants in this appeal, the fundamental proposition was formulated by counsel as follows: in English law, neither the owner nor the occupier of land from which, solely as the result of natural causes, natural mineral material encroaches onto, or threatens to encroach onto, adjoining land, causing damage, is under any liability to the adjoining land owner. . . .

. . . [the second proposition], is that, if the first proposition be wrong, so that *Goldman* v *Hargrave* does represent the law of England, nevertheless the liability which is imposed under the *Goldman* v *Hargrave* principle is a liability in negligence and not in nuisance.

Because of the conclusion which I have reached on this main issue, and my reasons for that conclusion, which I do not think differ for the most part in any substantial respect from the reasons expressed in the judgment of O'Connor J, I think that the simplest and most satisfactory method of dealing with the main issue is to start by a brief summary of the facts of, and the decision in, *Goldman* v *Hargrave* [1966] 2 All ER 989.

. . . A redgum tree, 100 feet high, on the defendant's land was struck by lightning and caught fire. The defendant caused the land around the burning tree to be cleared and the tree was then cut down and sawn into sections. So far there could be no complaint that the defendant had done anything which he ought not to have done or left undone anything which he ought to have done, so as in any way to increase the risk which had been caused by this act of natural forces setting fire to the tree. Thereafter the defendant (this was the state of the facts on which the Judicial Committee based their decision) did not do anything which he ought not to have done. He took no positive action which increased the risk of the fire spreading. But he failed to do something which he could have done without any substantial trouble or expense, which would, if done, have eliminated or rendered unlikely the spreading of the fire, that is, to have doused with water the burning or smouldering sections of the tree as they lay on the ground. Instead, the defendant chose to allow or encourage the fire to burn itself out. Foreseeably (again it was the forces of nature and not human action), the weather became even hotter and a strong wind sprang up. The flames from the tree spread rapidly through the defendant's land to the land of neighbours where it did extensive damage to their properties.

The judgment of the Board was delivered by Lord Wilberforce. It was held that the risk of the consequence which in fact happened was foreseeable. This, it is said, 'was not really disputed'. The legal issue was then defined:

> . . . the case is not one where a person has brought a source of danger on to his land, nor one where an occupier has so used his property as to cause a danger to his neighbour. It is one where an occupier, faced with a hazard accidentally arising on his land, fails to act with reasonable prudence so as to remove the hazard. The issue is therefore whether in such a case the occupier is guilty of legal negligence, which involves the issue whether he is under a duty of care, and, if so, what is the scope of that duty.

It is to my mind clear, from this passage and other passages in the judgment, that the duty which is being considered, and which later in the judgment is held to exist, does not involve any distinction of principle between what, in another sphere of the law, used to be known as misfeasance and non-feasance. A failure to act may involve a breach of the duty, though, since the duty which emerges is a duty of reasonable care, the question of misfeasance or non-feasance may have a bearing on the question whether the duty has been broken. It is to my mind clear, also, that no distinction is suggested in, or can properly be inferred from, the judgment as between a hazard accidentally arising on the defendant's land which, on the one hand, gives rise to a risk of damage to a neighbour's property by the encroachment of fire and, on the other hand, gives rise to such a risk by the encroachment of the soil itself, falling from the bank onto the neighbour's land. There is no valid distinction, to my mind, between an encroachment which consists, on the one hand, of the spread of fire from a tree on fire on the land, and, on the other hand, of a slip of soil or rock resulting from the instability of the land itself, in each case, the danger of encroachment, and the actual encroachment, being brought about by the forces of nature.

If any such distinctions as I have referred to in the previous paragraph were sought to be made, I should have thought that their acceptance as being material, as leading to different conclusions of principle in law, would make the law on this topic incoherent, artificial, uncertain and unpredictable. In other words, they would lead to bad law. . . .

I return to the judgment in *Goldman v Hargrave* [1966] 2 All ER 989 at 992. The law of England as it used to be is set out in the following passage:

> . . . it is only in comparatively recent times that the law has recognised an occupier's duty as one of a more positive character than merely to abstain from creating, or adding to, a source of danger or annoyance. It was for long satisfied with the conception of separate or autonomous proprietors, each of which was entitled to exploit his territory in a 'natural' manner and none of whom was obliged to restrain or direct the operations of nature in the interest of avoiding harm to his neighbours.

The judgment of the Board then goes on to review the development of the law which, as the Board held [1966] 2 All ER 989 at 995, had changed the law so that there now exists 'a general duty on occupiers in relation to hazards occurring on their land, whether natural or man-made'.

That change in the law, in its essence and in its timing, corresponds with, and may be viewed as being a part of, the change in the law of tort which achieved its decisive victory in *Donoghue v Stevenson* [1932] AC 562, though it was not until eight years later, in the House of Lords decision in *Sedleigh-Denfield v O'Callaghan*, [1940] 3 All ER 349, that the change as affecting the area with which we are concerned was expressed or recognised in a decision binding on all English courts, and, even then, the full, logical effect of the decision in altering what had hitherto been thought to be the law was not immediately recognised. But *Goldman v Hargrave* has now demonstrated what that effect was in English law.

The *Sedleigh-Denfield* case approved the dissenting judgment of Scrutton LJ in *Job Edwards Ltd v Birmingham Navigations* [1924] 1 KB 341. Thus, as the Judicial Committee recognised in *Goldman v Hargrave*, it was that great judge whose judgment in the *Job Edwards* case 'marked a turning point in the law', eight years before *Donoghue v Stevenson*. In the *Job Edwards* case, Scrutton LJ took the view that the case required to be sent back for a new trial because insufficient facts had been found. But the principle which, differing from Bankes LJ and Astbury J, Scrutton LJ stated was:

> . . . the landowner in possession is liable for a nuisance created by a trespasser, which causes damage to others, if he could, after he knows or ought to have known of it, prevent by reasonable care its spreading.

. . .

After the *Job Edwards* case and before the *Sedleigh-Denfield* case came the judgment of Rowlatt J in the Queen's Bench Divisional Court in *Noble v Harrison* [1926] 2 KB 332 at 338, in which he said:

> . . . a person is liable for a nuisance constituted by the state of his property: (1.) if he causes it; (2.) if by neglect of some duty he allowed it to arise; and (3.) if, when it has arisen without his own act or default, he omits to remedy it within a reasonable time after he did or ought to have become aware of it.

It is head (3) which is relevant for present purposes. If this is the law of England, then *Goldman* v *Hargrave*, correctly represents the law of England in its assertion of 'a general duty on occupiers in relation to hazards occurring on their land, whether natural or man-made'. I shall refer later to a passage in the judgment of Wright J the other member of the court in *Noble* v *Harrison* . . ..

The approval by the House of Lords in the *Sedleigh-Denfield* case of Scrutton LJ's judgment in the *Job Edwards* case meant, at any rate unless it could properly be said that it was a decision inconsistent with an earlier decision of the House of Lords, that it was thereafter the law of England that a duty existed under which the occupier of land might be liable to his neighbour for damage to his neighbour's property as a result of a nuisance spreading from his land to his neighbour's land, even though the existence and the operative effect of the nuisance were not caused by any 'non-natural' use by the defendant of his own land. But the liability was not a strict liability such as that which was postulated by the House of Lords in *Rylands* v *Fletcher* [1868] LR 3 HL 330 as arising where damage was caused to another by an 'unnatural' user of land. The obligation postulated in the *Sedleigh-Denfield* case, in conformity with the development of the law in *Donoghue* v *Stevenson*, was an obligation to use reasonable care. A defendant was not to be liable as a result of a risk of which he neither was aware nor ought, as a reasonable careful landowner, to have been aware. . . .

Rylands v *Fletcher* does not impose strict liability except where there has been some non-natural use of the land. But it does not hold, by way of binding authority, that there can be no duty where there has not been a 'non-natural' use of the land . . .

In *Davey* v *Harrow Corpn* [1958] 1 QB 60 it was held that the encroachment onto a neighbour's land of roots or branches of trees, causing damage, gives the neighbour an action in nuisance; and that no distinction is to be drawn between trees which may have been self-sown and trees which were deliberately planted on the land. Contrast the decision with *Rouse* v *Gravelworks Ltd* [1940] 1 All ER 26. There the defendants had dug out gravel from their land, leaving a large hole adjacent to the boundary with the plaintiff's land. It was held by this court, a two judge court consisting of Slesser and Goddard LJJ, that the plaintiff's claim failed because the damage to his land was caused by 'natural agencies'. It would seem that the decision would have been different if the water which filled the hole left by the excavation of the gravel had been brought in by pumping or perhaps even by percolation emanating from outside the defendants' land and induced by the excavation to flow into that land. If so, I should have thought that few people would regard this as a satisfactory state of the law. It may, perhaps, be arguable that, following *Rylands* v *Fletcher*, there is some special doctrine relating to the rights of landowners to dig out coal or gravel from their land as being a 'natural user'. If there is no such valid distinction, then, in my judgment, the decision in *Rouse* v *Gravelworks Ltd* cannot stand with the decision in *Davey* v *Harrow Corpn*. In that event I have no hesitation in preferring the later decision as stating the law as it now is, subject to the proviso that the duty arising from a nuisance which is not brought about by human agency does not arise unless and until the defendant has, or ought to have had, knowledge of the existence of the defect and the danger thereby created
. . .

It is not without significance that in at least two of the cases in which it has been held that there was no liability for nuisance because of the 'natural user' doctrine it was suggested that the position at least might have been different if the owner or occupier had had knowledge of the existence of the danger: see the decision of the Privy Council in *Rickards* v *Lothian* [1932] 2 Ch 106 at 114, and *Wilkins* v *Leighton* [1932] 2 Ch 106, where Luxmoore J said: 'To make the occupier liable the plaintiff must prove that he had knowledge of the existence of the nuisance.'

Lord Wright in the *Sedleigh-Denfield* case referred to that judgment in *Wilkins* v *Leighton* [1932] 2 Ch 106 with approval, on the basis, as I think is clear from the context, that the defendant in that case did not know of the defect. In other words, it would not have been enough to provide a defence that the user was 'natural' if the defendant had had knowledge of the danger.

. . .

Suppose that we are not bound by *Rylands* v *Fletcher* or any other authority to hold in favour of the defendants where the nuisance arises solely from natural forces; but suppose also that we are not bound by the decision in *Sedleigh-Denfield* or other binding authority to hold that there is a duty on the defendants in a case such as the present. Ought we as a matter of policy to develop the law by holding that there is a duty in a case such as the present?

If, as a result of the working of the forces of nature, there is, poised above my land, or above my house, a boulder or a rotten tree, which is liable to fall at any moment of the day or night, perhaps destroying my house, and perhaps killing or injuring me or members of my family, am I without remedy? (Of course the standard of care required may be much higher where there is risk to life or limb as contrasted with mere risk to property, but can it be said that the duty exists on the one case and not in the other?) Must I, in such a case, if my protests to my neighbour go unheeded, sit and wait and hope that the worst will not befall? If it is said that I have in such circumstances a remedy of going on my neighbour's land to abate the nuisance, that would, or might, be an unsatisfactory remedy. But in any event, if there were such a right of abatement, it would, as counsel for the plaintiffs rightly contended, be because my neighbour owed me a duty. There is, I think, ample authority that, if I have a right to abatement, I have also a remedy in damages if the nuisance remains unabated and causes me damage or personal injury. That is what Scutton LJ said in the *Job Edwards* case with particular reference to *Attorney-General* v *Tod Heatley* [1897] 1 Ch 560. It is dealt with also in the speech of Viscount Maugham in the *Sedleigh-Denfield* case, and in the speech of Lord Atkin.

In the example which I have given above, I believe that few people would regard it as anything other than a grievous blot on the law if the law recognises the existence of no duty on the part of the owner or occupier. But take another example, at the other end of the scale, where it might be thought that there is, potentially, an equally serious injustice the other way. If a stream flows through A's land, A being a small farmer, and there is a known danger that in times of heavy rainfall, because of the configuration of A's land and the nature of the stream's course and flow, there may be an overflow, which will pass beyond A's land and damage the property of A's neighbours: perhaps much wealthier neighbours. It may require expensive works, far beyond A's means, to prevent or even diminish the risk of such flooding. Is A to be liable for all the loss that occurs when the flood comes, if he has not done the impossible and carried out these works at his own expense?

In my judgment, there is, in the scope of the duty as explained in *Goldman* v *Hargrave*, a removal, or at least a powerful amelioration, of the injustice which might otherwise be caused in such a case by the recognition of the duty of care. Because of that limitation on the scope of the duty, I would say that, as a matter of policy, the law ought to recognise such a duty of care.

This leads on to the question of the scope of the duty. This is discussed, and the nature and extent of the duty is explained, in the judgment in *Goldman* v *Hargrave*. The duty is a duty to do that which is reasonable in all the circumstances, and no more than what, if anything, is reasonable, to prevent or minimise the known risk of damage or injury to one's neighbour or to his property. The considerations with which the law is familiar are all to be taken into account in deciding whether there has been a breach of duty, and, if so, what that breach is, and whether it is causative of the damage in respect of which the claim is made. Thus, there will fall to be considered the extent of the risk. What, so far as reasonably can be foreseen, are the chances that anything untoward will happen or that any damage will be caused? What is to be foreseen as to the possible extent of the damage if the risk becomes a reality? Is it practicable to prevent, or to minimise, the happening of any damage? If it is practicable, how simple or how difficult are the measures which could be taken, how much and how lengthy work do they involve, and what is the probable cost of such works? Was there sufficient time for preventive action to have been taken, by persons acting reasonably in relation to the known risk, between the time when it became known to or should have been realised by, the defendant, and the time when the damage occurred? Factors such as these, so far as they apply in a particular case, fall to be weighed in deciding whether the defendant's duty of care requires, or required, him to do anything, and, if so, what. . . .

[As] I understand it, if there be a duty and if its scope is as expounded in *Goldman* v *Hargrave*, the defendants do not now challenge the judgment against them. They say, however, that there is no duty; and one of their arguments for saying that this court, if free to do so, should refrain from holding that such a duty exists is that an essential element of such a duty, if it is to conform with the dictates of justice, is the factor of relative financial resources; but, they say, the introduction of that factor would make the law unworkable . . .

The difficulties which are foreseen, arising out of the passage which I have quoted, include unpredictability of the outcome of litigation, delay in reaching decisions (which in everyone's interests ought to be made promptly) as to protective measures to prevent damage, and the increased complexity, length and expense of litigation, if litigation is necessary. All this, and other disadvantages, would arise, it is suggested, because the parties and their advisers, before they could form a fair and confident view of their respective rights and liabilities, and before they could safely ask the court to decide these matters, whether finally or at an interlocutory hearing, would find it necessary, or at least desirable, to put themselves in a position to ascertain and compare the respective financial resources of the parties. This might involve detailed, embarrassing and prolonged investigation, even before the stage of discovery in an action.

If I thought that that sort of result would be likely to follow, or to follow in a substantial number of proportion of cases where this duty comes in question, I should, at least, hesitate long before accepting that this factor could be regarded as a proper factor in deciding whether the duty had or had not been broken in a particular case. But I do not think that anything of that sort is contemplated by *Goldman* v *Hargrave*.

. . . The defendant's duty is to do that which it is reasonable for him to do. The criteria of reasonableness include, in respect of a duty of this nature, the factor of what the particular man, not the average man, can be expected to do, having regard, amongst other things, where a serious expenditure of money is required to eliminate or reduce the danger, to his means. Just as, where physical effort is required to avert an immediate danger, the defendant's age and physical condition may be relevant in deciding what is reasonable, so also logic and good sense require that, where the expenditure of money is required, the defendant's capacity to find the money is relevant. But this can only be in the way of a broad, and not a detailed, assessment; and, in arriving at a judgment on reasonableness, a similar broad assessment may be relevant in some cases as to the neighbour's capacity to protect himself from damage, whether by way of some form of barrier on his own land or by way of providing funds for expenditure on agreed works on the land of the defendant.

. . . The question of reasonableness of what had been done or offered would fall to be decided on a broad basis, in which, on some occasions, there might be included an element of obvious discrepancy of financial resources. It may be that in some cases the introduction of this factor may give rise to difficulties to litigants and to their advisers and to the courts. But I believe that the difficulties are likely to turn out to be more theoretical than practical. I have not heard or seen anything to suggest that the principle laid down in *British Railways Board* v *Herrington* [1972] AC 877 has given rise to difficulties in trespasser cases. If and when problems do arise, they will have to be solved. I do not think that the existence of such potential difficulties justifies a refusal to accept as a part of the law of England the duty as laid down in *Goldman* v *Hargrave*, including the whole of the exposition as to the scope of the duty. As I have said, no difficulty now arises in this present appeal as regards the application of the *Goldman* v *Hargrave* scope of the duty, once it is held that the duty exists.

10.1.3 CULPABILITY II: UNREASONABLENESS

10.1.3.1 Striking the balance

SEDLEIGH-DENFIELD v *O'CALLAGHAN* [1940] 3 All ER 349 (HL)

FACTS: The defendant was the occupier of a college. The plaintiff owned a neighbouring property. There was originally a ditch, belonging to the defendant, along the boundary. When part of the plaintiff's property was developed part of the ditch was culverted. This was done by the local authority. The defendant's permission was not sought, but the person responsible for maintaining the ditch on the defendant's behalf was aware of the pipe. The mouth of the pipe was not equipped with any guard, and it became blocked. The plaintiff's land was flooded as a result and he claimed against the defendant in nuisance.

On appeal to the House of Lords it was held, *per* Viscount Maughan, in the circumstances the defendant was deemed to have notice of the presence of the culvert and its defective state.

VISCOUNT MAUGHAN: On this view as to the knowledge, or presumed knowledge, of the respondents, the first question is as to their legal position in relation to the appellant.

To put the matter more precisely, were they under a *prima facie* liability as regards the appellant if the ditch overflowed owing to the culvert becoming blocked, with the result that the appellant's land suffered from an overflow of water from the ditch? The appellant contends that the respondents are liable for a private nuisance for which they are responsible. My Lords, I look upon the word nuisance as used in our law as a generic term. It is applied to damage resulting from water, smoke, smell, fumes, gas, noise, heat, electricity, disease, germs, trees, vegetation, and animals, as well as to other matters, and very little thought is sufficient to show that the ways in which damage from these things is caused and may be prevented are widely different. In my opinion, the legal duty of the owner of land towards an adjoining owner may be very different in some of these cases, and may depend on very different considerations. In the present case, we are dealing with the escape of water from an artificial watercourse on the respondents' land . . .

The main defence of the respondents in this case was that the erection of the culvert, with its lack of any proper contrivance for preventing it from becoming blocked with leaves and refuse, was an act of trespass by the Middlesex County Council without the permission or knowledge of the respondents, and that they were, therefore, free from liability. This defence requires careful consideration . . .

The case which was most relied on by the respondents . . . was *Job Edwards Ltd* v *Birmingham Navigations* [1924] 1 KB 341. It was a case where refuse carried over the defendants' embankment and land on to the land of certain mine-owners but without their consent, was found to be on fire. The defendants called on the mine-owners to extinguish it. They declined, but ultimately it was extinguished by the defendants, without prejudice to the legal position. The mine-owners then brought an action for a declaration that they were not liable to pay any part of the cost of putting out the fire, which was a large sum. It was held by Bankes LJ, and Astbury J, that the mine-owners were not liable, since there was no public nuisance and no evidence that they either caused or continued the fire, or were guilty of any negligence in relation to it.

. . . [In] the present case, I am of opinion that the respondents both continued and adopted the nuisance. After the lapse of nearly 3 years, they must be taken to have suffered the nuisance to continue, for they neglected to take the very simple step of placing a grid in the proper place, which would have removed the danger to their neighbour's land. They adopted the nuisance, for they continued during all that time to use the artificial contrivance of the conduit for the purpose of getting rid of water from their property without taking the proper means for rendering it safe. For these reasons, I am of opinion that this appeal should be allowed.

MILLER v *JACKSON* [1977] 3 All ER 338 (CA)

FACTS: The defendants were the committee of a village cricket club. Cricket was played for many years without complaint, as the ground was surrounded by fields. Then one of the fields was developed and the plaintiffs bought a house overlooking the cricket ground. The ground was not very large, and balls were regularly hit into the plaintiffs' garden. Attempts were made to reduce the risk by erecting fencing, but to no avail. Some limited damage had been done to the plaintiffs' property. The plaintiffs brought an action, alleging nuisance and applying for an injunction.

In the Court of Appeal, opinions were divided. Lord Denning considered there was no nuisance.

LORD DENNING: In support of the case, the plaintiff relies on the dictum of Lord Reid in *Bolton* v *Stone* [1951] 1 All ER 1078: 'If cricket cannot be played on a ground without creating a substantial risk, then it should not be played there at all.' I would agree with that saying if the houses or road were there first, and the cricket ground came there second. But I do not agree with Lord Reid's dictum when the cricket ground has been there for 70 years and the houses are newly built at the very edge of it. I recognise that the cricket club are under a duty to use all reasonable care consistently with the playing of the game of cricket, but I do not think the cricket club can be expected to give up the game of cricket altogether.
. . .

It has been often said in nuisance cases that the rule is sic utere tuo ut alienum non laedas. But that is a most misleading maxim. Lord Wright put it in its proper place in *Sedleigh-Denfield* v *O'Callaghan*:

[It] is not only lacking in definiteness but is also inaccurate. An occupier may make in many ways a use of his land which causes damage to the neighbouring landowners, and yet be free from liability . . . a useful test is perhaps what is reasonable according to the ordinary usages of mankind living in society, or, more correctly, in a particular society.

I would, therefore, adopt this test: is the use by the cricket club of this ground for playing cricket a reasonable use of it? To my mind it is a most reasonable use.

. . . It was said, however, that the case of the physician's consulting-room was to the contrary. But that turned on the old law about easements and prescriptions, and so forth. It was in the days when rights of property were in the ascendant and not subject to any limitations except those provided by the law of easements. But nowadays it is a matter of balancing the conflicting interests of the two neighbours. That was made clear by Lord Wright in *Sedleigh-Denfield* v *O'Callaghan*, when he said: 'A balance has to be maintained between the right of the occupier to do what he likes with his own and the right of his neighbour not to be interfered with.' In this case it is our task to balance the right of the cricket club to continue playing cricket on their cricket ground, as against the right of the householder not to be interfered with. On taking the balance, I would give priority to the right of the cricket club to continue playing cricket on the ground, as they have done for the last 70 years. It takes precedence over the right of the newcomer to sit in his garden undisturbed. After all he bought the house four years ago in mid-summer when the cricket season was at its height. He might have guessed that there was a risk that a hit for six might possibly land on his property. If he finds that he does not like it, he ought, when cricket is played, to sit in the other side of the house or in the front garden, or go out: or take advantage of the offers the club have made to him of fitting unbreakable glass, and so forth. Or, if he does not like that, he ought to sell his house and move elsewhere. I expect there are many who would gladly buy it in order to be near the cricket field and open space. At any rate he ought not to be allowed to stop cricket being played on this ground.

This case is new. It should be approached on principles applicable to modern conditions. There is a contest here between the interest of the public at large and the interest of a private individual. The *public* interest lies in protecting the environment by preserving our playing fields in the face of mounting development, and by enabling our youth to enjoy all the benefits of outdoor games, such as cricket and football. The *private* interest lies in securing the privacy of his home and garden without intrusion or interference by anyone. In deciding between these two conflicting interests, it must be remembered that it is not a question of damages. If by a million-to-one chance a cricket ball does go out of the ground and cause damage, the cricket club will pay. There is no difficulty on that score. No, it is a question of an injunction. And in our law you will find it repeatedly affirmed that an injunction is a discretionary remedy. In a new situation like this, we have to think afresh as to how discretion should be exercised. On the one hand, Mrs Miller is a very sensitive lady who has worked herself up into such a state that she exclaimed to the judge: 'I just want to be allowed to live in peace. Have we got to wait until someone is killed before anything can be done?' If she feels like that about it, it is quite plain that, for peace in the future, one or other has to move. Either the cricket club have to move, but goodness knows where. I do not suppose for a moment there is any field in Lintz to which they could move. Or Mrs Miller must move elsewhere. As between their conflicting interests, I am of opinion that the public interest should prevail over the private interest. The cricket club should not be driven out. In my opinion the right exercise of discretion is to refuse an injunction; and, of course, to refuse damages in lieu of an injunction. Likewise as to the claim for past damages. The club were entitled to use this ground for cricket in the accustomed way. It was not a nuisance, nor was it negligence of them so to run it. Nor was the batsman negligent when he hit the ball for six. All were doing simply what they were entitled to do. So if the club had put it to the test, I would have dismissed the claim for damages also. But as the club very fairly say that they are willing to pay for any damage, I am content that there should be an award of £400 to cover any past or future damage.

I would allow the appeal, accordingly.

GEOFFREY LANE LJ saw matters in a different light:

No one has yet suffered any personal injury, although Mrs Craig at least was perhaps lucky to have avoided it. There is no doubt that damage to tiles or windows at the plaintiffs' house is inevitable if cricket goes on. There is little doubt that if the plaintiffs were to stay in their garden whilst matches are in progress they would be in real danger of being hit.

In these circumstances, have the plaintiffs established that the defendants are guilty of nuisance or negligence as alleged? No technical question arises as to the position of the defendants. It is conceded that if the action of the players in striking the ball into the plaintiffs' property is tortious, the defendants are responsible therefor.

Negligence

The evidence of Mr Nevins makes it clear that the risk of injury to property at least was both foreseeable and foreseen. It is obvious that such injury is going to take place so long as cricket is being played on this field. It is the duty of the cricketers so to conduct their operations as not to harm people they can or ought reasonably to foresee may be affected. The defendants' answer to this, as I understand it, is as follows. They have taken every feasible step to prevent injury by erecting as high a fence as is possible having regard to the likely wind forces. They have offered to fit louvred shutters to the plaintiffs' south facing windows to prevent the glass being broken. That argument is fallacious. There is no obligation on the plaintiffs to protect themselves in their own home from the activities of the defendants. Even if there were such an obligation it would be unreasonable to expect them to live behind shutters during the summer weekends and to stay out of their garden . . .

It is true that the risk must be balanced against the measures which are necessary to eliminate it and against what the defendants can do to prevent accidents from happening: *Latimer* v *AEC Ltd* [1953] 2 All ER 449. In that case a sudden storm had caused a factory floor to become flooded and slippery. The defendants did all that could reasonably be expected of them, short of closing the factory, to prevent injury. It was held by the House of Lords that the risk of injury from the slippery floor was not sufficient to require the defendants to shut the factory. Their decision in the words of Lord Oaksey was at the highest 'an error of judgment in circumstances of difficulty and such an error of judgment does not . . . amount to negligence'. In the present case, so far from being one incident of an unprecedented nature about which complaint is being made, this is a series of incidents, or perhaps a continuing failure to prevent incidents from happening, coupled with the certainty that they are going to happen again. The risk of injury to persons and property is so great that on each occasion when a ball comes over the fence and causes damage to the plaintiffs, the defendants are guilty of negligence.

Nuisance

In circumstances such as these it is very difficult and probably unnecessary, except as an interesting intellectual exercise, to define the frontiers between negligence and nuisance: see Lord Wilberforce in *Goldman* v *Hargrave*.

Was there here a use by the defendants of their land involving an unreasonable interference with the plaintiffs' enjoyment of *their* land? There is here in effect no dispute that there has been and is likely to be in the future an interference with the plaintiffs' enjoyment of no 20 Brackenridge. The only question is whether it is unreasonable. It is a truism to say that this is a matter of degree. What that means is this. A balance has to be maintained between on the one hand the rights of the individual to enjoy his house and garden without the threat of damage and on the other hand the rights of the public in general or a neighbour to engage in lawful pastimes. Difficult questions may sometimes arise when the defendants' activities are offensive to the senses, for example by way of noise. Where, as here, the damage or potential damage is physical the answer is more simple. There is, subject to what appears hereafter, no excuse I can see which exonerates the defendants from liability in nuisance for what they have done or from what they threaten to do. It is true no one has yet been physically injured. That is probably due to a great extent to the fact that the householders in Brackenridge desert their gardens whilst cricket is in progress. The danger of injury is obvious and is not slight enough to be disregarded. There is here a real risk of serious injury.

There is, however, one obviously strong point in the defendants' favour. They or their predecessors have been playing cricket on this ground (and no doubt hitting sixes out of it) for 70 years or so. Can someone by building a house on the edge of the field in circumstances where it must have been obvious that balls might be hit over the fence, effectively stop cricket being played? Precedent apart, justice would seem to demand that the plaintiffs should be left to make the most of the site they have elected to occupy with all its obvious advantages and all its equally obvious disadvantages. It is pleasant to have an open space over which to look from your bedroom and sitting room windows, so far as it is possible to see over the concrete wall. Why should you complain of the obvious disadvantages which arise from the particular purpose to which the open space is being put? Put briefly, can the defendants take advantage of the fact that the plaintiffs have put themselves in such a position by coming to occupy a house on the edge of a small cricket field, with the result that what was not a nuisance in the past now becomes a nuisance? If the matter were res integra, I confess I should be inclined to find for the defendants. It does not seem just that a long-established activity, in itself innocuous, should be brought to an end because someone chooses to build a house nearby and so turn an innocent pastime into an actionable nuisance. Unfortunately, however, the question is not open. In *Sturges* v *Bridgman* this very problem arose. The defendant had carried on a confectionary shop with a noisy pestle and mortar for more than 20 years. Although it was noisy, it was far enough away from neighbouring premises not to cause trouble to anyone, until the plaintiff, who was a physician, built a consulting-room on his own land but immediately adjoining the confectionary shop. The noise and vibrations seriously interfered with the consulting-room and became a nuisance to the physician. The defendant contended that he had acquired the right either at common law or under the Prescription Act 1832 by uninterrupted use for more than 20 years to impose the inconvenience. It was held by the Court of Appeal, affirming the judgment of Jessel MR, that use such as this which was, prior to the construction of the consulting room, neither preventable nor actionable, could not found a prescriptive right. That decision involved the assumption, which so far as one can discover has never been questioned, that it is no answer to a claim in nuisance for the defendant to show that the plaintiff brought the trouble on his own head by building or coming to live in a house so close to the defendant's premises that he would inevitably be affected by the defendant's activities, where no one had been affected previously. See also *Bliss* v *Hall* (1838) 7 LJCP 122. It may be that this rule works injustice, it may be that one would decide the matter differently in the absence of authority. But we are bound by the decision in *Sturges* v *Bridgman* and it is not for this court as I see it to alter a rule which has stood for so long.

Injunction
Given that the defendants are guilty of both negligence and nuisance, is it a case where the court should in its discretion give relief, or should the plaintiffs be left to their remedy in damages? There is no doubt that if cricket is played damage will be done to the plaintiffs' tiles or windows or both. There is a not inconsiderable danger that if they or their son or their guests spend any time in the garden during the weekend afternoons in the summer they may be hit by a cricket ball. So long as this situation exists it seems to me that damages cannot be said to provide an adequate form of relief. Indeed, quite apart from the risk of physical injury, I can see no valid reason why the plaintiffs should have to submit to the inevitable breakage of tiles and/or windows, even though the defendants have expressed their willingness to carry out any repairs at no cost to the plaintiffs. I would accordingly uphold the grant of the injunction to restrain the defendants from committing nuisance. However, I would postpone the operation of the injunction for 12 months to enable the defendants to look elsewhere for an alternative pitch.

So far as the plaintiffs are concerned, the effect of such postponement will be that they will have to stay out of their garden until the end of the cricket season but thereafter will be free to use it as they wish.

I have not thought it necessary to embark on any discussion of the possible rights of the defendants arising from matters which were neither pleaded nor argued.

CUMMING-BRUCE LJ agreed with Geoffrey Lane LJ on the law of nuisance, but took a different line on the remedy:

The only problem that arises is whether the learned judge is shown to be wrong in deciding to grant the equitable remedy of an injunction which will necessarily have the effect that the ground which the defendants have used as a cricket ground for 70 years can no longer be used for that purpose. Reeve J correctly directed himself that the principles which apply are those described by Lord Evershed MR in *Pride of Derby and Derbyshire Angling Association Ltd* v *British Celanese Ltd* [1953] 1 All ER 179, and by A L Smith LJ in *Shelfer* v *City of London Electric Lighting Co.* [1895] 1 Ch 287. Did he correctly apply those principles to the facts of the case? There is authority that in considering whether to exercise a judicial discretion to grant an injunction the court is under a duty to consider the interests of the public. So said Lord Romily MR over 100 years ago in *Raphael* v *Thames Valley Railway Co.* (1866) LR 2 Eq 337 but the conflict of interest there was between proprietary private rights and the inconvenience to be suffered by users of a railway: see also *Wood* v *Sutcliffe* (1851) 21 LJCh 253. Courts of equity will not ordinarily and without special necessity interfere by injunction where the injunction will have the effect of very materially injuring the rights of third persons not before the court.

So on the facts of this case a court of equity must seek to strike a fair balance between the right of the plaintiffs to have quiet enjoyment of their house and garden without exposure to cricket balls occasionally falling like thunderbolts from the heavens, and the opportunity of the inhabitants of the village in which they live to continue to enjoy the manly sport which constitutes a summer recreation for adults and young persons, including one would hope and expect the plaintiffs' son. It is a relevant circumstance which a court of equity should take into account that the plaintiffs decided to buy a house which in June 1972 when completion took place was obviously on the boundary of a quite small cricket ground where cricket was played at weekends and sometimes on evenings during the working week. They selected a house with the benefit of the open space beside it. In February, when they first saw it, they did not think about the use of this open space. But before completion they must have realised that it was the village cricket ground, and that balls would sometimes be knocked from the wicket into their garden, or even against the fabric of the house. If they did not realise it, they should have done. As it turns out, the female plaintiff has developed a somewhat obsessive attitude to the proximity of the cricket field and the cricketers who visit her to seek to recover their cricket balls. The evidence discloses a hostility which goes beyond what is reasonable, although as the learned judge found she is reasonable in her fear that if the family use the garden while a match is in progress they will run risk of serious injury if a great hit happens to drive a ball up to the skies and down into their garden. It is reasonable to decide that during matches the family must keep out of the garden. The risk of damage to the house can be dealt with in other ways, and is not such as to fortify significantly the case for an injunction stopping play on this ground.

With all respect, in my view the learned judge did not have regard sufficiently to these considerations. He does not appear to have had regard to the interest of the inhabitants of the village as a whole. Had he done so he would in my view have been led to the conclusion that the plaintiffs having accepted the benefit of the open space marching with their land should accept the restrictions on enjoyment of their garden which they may reasonably think necessary. That is the burden which they have to bear in order that the inhabitants of the village may not be deprived of their facilities for an innocent recreation which they have so long enjoyed on this ground. There are here special circumstances which should inhibit a court of equity from granting the injunction claimed. If I am wrong in that conclusion, I agree with Geoffrey Lane LJ that the injunction should be suspended for one year to enable the defendants to see if they can find another ground.

10.1.3.2 Material considerations

HOLLYWOOD SILVER FOX FARM LTD v *EMMETT* [1936] 1 All ER 825

FACTS: The plaintiff had a silver fox farm. The defendant was a neighbouring farmer, who was in the process of selling part of his farm for development. He considered that a notice on the plaintiff's land advertising his business might deter house buyers. He fell out with the plaintiff when he refused to remove the notice. Silver vixen are very easily disturbed by noise in the breeding season. The defendant arranged for his son to go shooting on the defendant's land near the boundary. The defendant alleged this was to keep down rabbits, but it was proved that it was merely to cause a disturbance. The plaintiff's action in nuisance came before the court.

McNAUGHTEN J: Mr Roche, who put the case for the defendant extremely well, argued that if the defendant had sent his son to shoot at the boundary of his land for the purpose of injuring the plaintiff and that if his conduct was malicious because he wanted to harm the plaintiff, nevertheless he had not committed any actionable wrong. The defendant was entitled to shoot on his own land. He might shoot there to keep down rabbits, or he might shoot for his own pleasure and if it pleased him to annoy his neighbour, although his conduct might be considered unneighbourly, he was entitled at law to do so. In the course of his argument, Mr Roche relied upon the decision of the House of Lords in the case of *Bradford Corpn* v *Pickles* [1895] AC 587. In that case the Corporation of Bradford sought an injunction to restrain the defendant from sinking a shaft on land which belonged to him because, according to their view, his object in sinking the shaft was to draw away water which would otherwise become the property of the Corporation. Pickles was acting maliciously. His sole object in digging was to do harm to the Corporation. The House of Lords decided, once and for all, that in such a case the motive of the defendants is immaterial. In *Allen* v *Flood* [1898] AC 1, Lord Herschell, commenting on *Bradford Corpn* v *Pickles*, said this, at page 124: . . .

It has recently been held in this House, in the case of *Bradford Corpn* v *Pickles*, that acts by the defendant upon his own land were not actionable when they were within his legal rights, even though his motives were to prejudice his neighbour. The language of the noble and learned Lords was distinct. The Lord Chancellor said 'This is not a case where the state of mind of the person doing the act can affect the right. If it was a lawful act, however ill the motive might be, he had a right to do it. If it was an unlawful act, however good the motive might be, he would have no right to do it'. The statement was confined to the class of cases then before the House; but I apprehend that what was said is not applicable only to rights of property, but is equally applicable to the exercise by an individual of his other rights.

In the same case Lord Watson, at page 101, discussing the duck-decoying case of *Keeble* v *Hickeringill* (1706) 11 East 574, said this:

No proprietor has an absolute right to create noises upon his own land, because any right which the law gives him is qualified by the condition that it must not be exercised to the nuisance of his neighbours or of the public. If he violates that condition he commits a legal wrong, and if he does so intentionally, he is guilty of a malicious wrong, in its strict legal sense.

Mr Roche contended that in this case the defendant had committed no nuisance at all in the legal sense of this case and he referred to *Robinson* v *Kilvert* (1889) 41 ChD 88. In that case complaint was made by the appellant that the brown paper which he kept on the ground floor of his premises suffered some damage from heat in the basement below, and it was held by the Court of Appeal that no actionable wrong was being committed by the defendant in that the heating was not of such a character as would interfere with the ordinary use of the rest of the house . . .

It was argued that the keeping of a silver fox farm was not an ordinary use of land in the county of Kent, and what the defendant had done in discharging the bird-scaring cartridges would cause no alarm to the sheep or cattle which are usually to be found on Kentish farms. It was only because Captain Chalmers had brought these highly nervous animals—not natural to this country—that had caused the plaintiffs any loss and if silver foxes were brought to the county of Kent, one could not thereby restrict their neighbours in the matter of shooting. I am not satisfied that there is any substance in that argument. It is a perfectly lawful thing to keep a silver fox farm and I think the fact that the shooting took place intentionally for the purpose of injuring the plaintiffs made it actionable.

The authority for the view that in cases of alleged nuisance by noise, the intention of the person making the noise is not to be disregarded is to be found in the case of *Gaunt* v *Fynney* (1872) 8 Ch App 8. Lord Selborne LC, delivered the judgment of the court, and he was dealing there with the question of nuisances, and he said this, at page 12: 'A nuisance by noise (supposing malice to be out of the question) is emphatically a question of degree.' It has been observed by high authority that Lord Selborne was always extremely careful in the use of language and that parenthetical statement 'supposing malice to be out of the question' clearly indicates what his Lordship thought in the case of alleged nuisance by noise, where the noise was made maliciously. Different considerations would apply to cases where that ingredient was absent. Indeed, the matter is put beyond doubt by the decision of North J, in *Christie* v *Davey* [1893] 1 Ch 316. The plaintiff and the defendant lived side by side in semi–detached houses in Brixton. The plaintiff was a teacher of music and he had a musical family. The result was that throughout clouds of music pervaded his house and were heard in the house of his neighbour. His neighbour did not like music to be heard and after writing rather an unfortunate letter of protest, he took to making noises himself by beating trays and rapping on the wall, and thereupon the music teacher brought an action for an injunction. The action came before North J, and he delivered judgment in favour of the plaintiff and granted an injunction restraining the defendant from permitting any sounds or noises in his house so as to annoy the plaintiff, or the occupiers of his house, and in the course of his judgment he said, at page 326:

> The result is that I think I am bound to interfere for the protection of the plaintiffs. In my opinion the noises which were made in the defendant's house were not of a legitimate kind. They were what, to use the language of Lord Selborne in *Gaunt* v *Fynney* 'ought to be regarded as excessive and unreasonable'. I am satisfied that they were made deliberately and maliciously for the purpose of annoying the plaintiffs. If what has taken place had occurred between two sets of persons, both perfectly innocent, I should have taken an entirely different view of the case. But I am persuaded that what was done by the defendant was done only for the purpose of annoyance, and in my opinion it was not a legitimate use of the defendant's house to use it for the purpose of vexing and annoying his neighbours.

It must be borne in mind that the learned judge could not grant an injunction unless he was satisfied that the nuisance at law had been created because there is no such thing as an equitable nuisance. It is to be observed that the judge was of the opinion that the noises were made intentionally for the purpose of annoying the plaintiff and this was the deciding matter in that case.

10.1.4   WHO IS LIABLE?

10.1.4.1   Landlords

TETLEY v CHITTY [1986] 1 All ER 663

FACTS: The defendant local authority let land to the individual defendant for use as a go-kart track. Noise from this activity disturbed the plaintiff, who claimed that it amounted to a nuisance for which the local authority was liable. The judge found that the level and quality of noise did amount, in fact, to a nuisance.

MCNEILL J: [The plaintiffs' case] was that a landlord, as the council were here, or licensor prior to the granting of the lease, is liable if he authorises a nuisance on his land or grants a lease of his land with a nuisance on it or knowing that a nuisance is going to be caused on it, or for any operation which inevitably will cause a nuisance. Counsel for the council did not dissent from this as a formulation of the appropriate test . . .
  What then is the effect of the authorities? In *White* v *Jameson* (1874) LR 18 Eq 303 the short headnote reads:

> Where the occupier of lands grants a licence to another to do certain acts on the land, and the licensee in doing them commits a nuisance, the occupier may be made a Defendant to a suit to restrain the nuisance.

That was a case in which the landlord had authorised another to burn in his yard, into bricks, clay found in the yard; but the landlord had taken no active part either in erecting the kiln or in burning the bricks.
  Jessel MR, having decided that the burning of the bricks was a nuisance to the plaintiff, held the landlord liable to be sued for the acts complained of. He said (at 305):

> The land on which they were committed was his; and, independently of his having an interest in the profits, the Defendant *Proffitt* did these acts by his license.

It will be noted that in that case it would not seem as if the man Proffitt had any exclusive right in the land and it may be in the light of later authorities that that case, perhaps, goes further than the law as it now stands. In that case the occupier had merely a revocable licence.

Counsel for the second defendants relied on a more recent decision, that of Pennycuick V-C in *Smith* v *Scott* [1973] 1 Ch 314, and on the older decision of *Harris* v *James* [1876] 45 LJQB 545, [1874–80] All ER Rep 1142. Counsel contended that liability could only be established if the nuisance were committed with the landlord's express or implied authority. It is, he said, insufficient to show merely a likely consequence: a plaintiff to succeed must show a necessary consequence. Here the necessary consequence that nuisance would be caused to each of the plaintiffs has not, he said, been established.

In *Harris* v *James* 45 LJQB 545 at 546, [1874–80] All ER Rep 1142 at 1143 Blackburn J pointed out:

> There can be no doubt that where a person authorises and requires another to commit a nuisance he is liable for that nuisance, and if the authority be given in the shape of a lease he is not the less liable . . . I do not think when a person demises property he is to be taken to authorise all that the occupier may do . . . In the present case, as I understand the averments, the field was let for the very purpose and object of being worked as a lime quarry and for erecting lime kilns and burning lime. When, then, it is stated as a fact that the injury complained of arose from the natural and necessary consequence of carrying out this object, and as the result of lime getting and lime burning, then I think we must say that the landlord authorised the lime burning and the nuisance arising from it as being the necessary consequence of letting the field in the manner and with the objects described.

. . . In *Smith* v *Scott* [1973] 1 Ch 314 Pennycuick V-C had to deal with a somewhat unusual factual situation. The plaintiff was the owner of a dwelling house in a street where other houses in which were being acquired by the local authority for housing homeless families. The local authority put into the house next to the plaintiff's house a family known by the corporation to be likely to cause a nuisance though on terms expressly prohibiting the committing of a nuisance. Well, it will be no surprise to see that after the tenants went in they so damaged the plaintiff's premises and caused such a noise that he had to leave and go and live elsewhere. The case was framed in three ways: in nuisance, in the rule in *Rylands* v *Fletcher* [1868] LR 3 HL 330 and in negligence. I do not deal with Pennycuick V-C's rulings on the second and third of those, as they have no relevance to the present case. But he did hold, dismissing the action, that the corporation were not liable, as landlords, for a nuisance committed by their tenants for they had neither expressly nor impliedly authorised the nuisance:

> I must then consider the law applicable to the foregoing conclusions of fact. Apart from the allegation of improper motive, counsel for Mr Smith based his case on three propositions of law, namely, (1) the corporation in placing the Scotts in no 25 with knowledge that they were likely to cause a nuisance to their neighbours themselves committed the wrongful act of nuisance . . . [(2) and (3) I need not read.] I will consider those propositions in the same order. (1) It is established beyond question that the person to be sued in nuisance is the occupier of the property from which the nuisance emanates. In general, a landlord is not liable for nuisance committed by his tenant, but to this rule there is, so far as now in point, one recognised exception, namely, that the landlord is liable if he has authorised his tenant to commit the nuisance: see *Harris* v *James* (1876) 45 LJQB 545. But this exception has, in the reported cases, been rigidly confined to circumstances in which the nuisance has either been expressly authorised or is certain to result from the purposes for which the property is let . . .
>   I have used the word 'certain', but 'certainty' is obviously a very difficult matter to establish. It may be that, as one of the textbooks suggests, the proper test in this connection is 'virtual certainty' which is another way of saying a very high degree of probability, but the authorities are not, I venture to think, altogether satisfactory in this respect. Whatever the precise test may be, it would, I think, be impossible to apply the exception to the present case. The exception is squarely based in the reported cases on express or implied authority—see in particular the judgment of Blackburn J in *Harris* v *James*. The exception is not based on cause and probable result, apart from express or implied authority. In the present case, the corporation let no 25 to the Scotts as a

dwelling-house on conditions of tenancy which expressly prohibited the committing of a nuisance, and, notwithstanding that the corporation knew the Scotts were likely to cause a nuisance, I do not think it is legitimate to say that the corporation impliedly authorised the nuisance.

His Lordship went on to hold that the noise nuisance was a necessary consequence of the land being used as authorised by the council.

10.1.5 DEFENCES

10.1.5.1 Statutory authority

ALLEN v *GULF OIL REFINING LTD* [1981] 1 All ER 353 (HL)

FACTS: Gulf were authorised by a specific Act of Parliament to construct and operate an oil refinery together with ancillary works such as railway connections and sidings. The plaintiff, a nearby resident, complained that the operation of the refinery amounted to a nuisance. On a preliminary point the judge accepted Gulf's argument that they had statutory authority for their actions and that this was a defence. The Court of Appeal took the opposite view and Gulf appealed to the House of Lords.

LORD WILBERFORCE: We are here in the well-charted field of statutory authority. It is now well settled that where Parliament by express direction or by necessary implication has authorised the construction and use of an undertaking or works, that carries with it an authority to do what is authorised with immunity from any action based on nuisance. The right of action is taken away (see *Hammersmith and City Railway Co.* v *Brand* (1869) LR 4 HL 171 at 215 [1861–73] All ER Rep 60 at 72 *per* Lord Cairns). To this there is made the qualification, or condition, that the statutory powers are exercised without 'negligence', that word here being used in a special sense so as to require the undertaker, as a condition of obtaining immunity from action, to carry out the work and conduct the operation with all reasonable regard and care for the interests of other persons (see *Geddis* v *Proprietors of the Bann Reservoir* (1878) 3 App Cas 430 at 455 *per* Lord Blackburn). It is within the same principle that immunity from action is withheld where the terms of the statute are permissive only, in which case the powers conferred must be exercised in strict conformity with private rights (see *Metropolitan Asylum District Managers* v *Hill* (1881) 6 App Cas 193, [1881–5] All ER Rep 536).

What then is the scope of the statutory authority conferred in this case? The Act was a private Act, promoted by the appellants, no doubt mainly in their own commercial interests. In order to establish their projected refinery with its ancillary facilities (jetties, railway lines etc), and to acquire the necessary land, they had to seek the assistance of Parliament. And so they necessarily had to satisfy Parliament that the powers they were seeking were in the interest of the public to whom Parliament is responsible. . . .

My Lords, all of this shows most clearly that Parliament considered it in the public interest that a *refinery*, not merely the works (jetties etc), should be constructed, and constructed on lands at Llanstadwell to be compulsorily acquired . . . I cannot but regard this as an authority, whether it should be called express or by necessary implication may be a matter of preference, but an authority to construct and operate a *refinery* on the lands to be acquired, a refinery moreover which should be commensurate with the facilities for unloading offered by the jetties (for large tankers), with the size of the lands to be acquired, and with the discharging facilities to be provided by the railway lines. I emphasise the words *a refinery* by way of distinction from *the refinery* because no authority was given or sought except in the indefinite forms. But that there was authority to construct and operate *a refinery* seems to me indisputable.

The respondent's contention against this is a curious one. She points to the sections (mainly s. 15) dealing with works; these specify in great detail what is to be carried out, in the way of construction of jetties and of railway lines. Here, she says, is plain statutory authority of the kind conferred in the well-known cases concerned with railways. By contrast there is no authority to construct or operate a refinery, not even by implication. There is nothing but power to acquire lands. The construction of the refinery is left entirely to the promoters; there is no specification of the size or nature of the refinery, they have 'carte blanche' and therefore the intention must be that they must construct it with regard to private rights. The case is similar, she says, to that of *Metropolitan Asylum District Managers* v *Hill*. This argument has remarkable consequences. It follows that if the respondent, or any other person, can establish a nuisance, he or she is entitled (subject only to a precarious appeal to Lord Cairn's Act (the Chancery Amendment Act 1858)) to an injunction. This may make it impossible for the refinery to be operated; that in turn would leave the appellants as the owners and occupiers of a large area of land which they have compulsorily acquired under the authority of the Gulf Oil Refining Act 1965 for the purpose of a refinery, and which, in accordance with well-known principles, they could not use for any other purpose. Such consequences must be accepted if they clearly flow from the terms of the Act.

But I must say that I find the construction which would give rise to this result to be not only far from clear but a most artificial reading of the enactment. It is true, and at one time I was impressed by the point, that, by contrast with the detailed specification given to the 'works', by description, plans, levels etc, the Act conspicuously does not define or specify the refinery even in general terms, and this might appear to support an argument that this was left altogether outside the Parliamentary authority. But I think that it was answered by the case in this House of *Manchester Corpn* v *Farnworth* [1930] AC 171. In that case the statutory authority was simply, in general terms, for the erection of a generating station, without specification, but nevertheless it was held that, subject to the 'negligence' exception, the usual rule applied (see particularly *per* Viscount Dunedin [1930] AC 171 at 183. There could be 'no action for nuisance caused by the making or doing of that thing [ie the thing authorised] if the nuisance is the inevitable result of the making or doing so authorised'. That, in my opinion, describes the situation in the present case. It is true that the 1965 Act does not, as did the relevant Act considered in the *Manchester Corpn* case (the Manchester Corporation Act 1914 (4 & 5 Geo 5 c cxlvi)), confer express authority to use or operate any refinery which might be installed on the site, but the preamble refers to 'refinement', ie operation of the refinery, and authority to construct must in this case carry authority to refine. The two cases are entirely parallel.

If I am right on this point, the position as regards the action would be as follows. The respondent alleges a nuisance, by smell, noise, vibration etc. The facts regarding these matters are for her to prove. It is then for the appellants to show, if they can, that it was impossible to construct and operate a refinery on the site, conforming with Parliament's intention, without creating the nuisance alleged, or at least a nuisance. Involved in this issue would be the point discussed by Cumming-Bruce LJ in the Court of Appeal, that the establishment of an oil refinery etc was bound to involve some alteration to the environment and so of the standard of amenity and comfort which neighbouring occupiers might expect. To the extent that the environment has been changed from that of a peaceful unpolluted countryside to an industrial complex (as to which different standards apply: see *Sturges* v *Bridgman* (1879) 11 ChD 852). Parliament must be taken to have authorised it. So far, I venture to think, the matter is not open to doubt. But in my opinion the statutory authority extends beyond merely authorising a change in the environment and an alteration of standard. It confers immunity against proceedings for any nuisance which can be shown (the burden of so showing being on the appellants) to be the inevitable result of erecting a refinery on the site, not, I repeat, the existing refinery, but any refinery, however carefully and with however great a regard for the interest of adjoining occupiers it is sited, constructed and operated. To the extent and only to the extent that the actual nuisance (if any) caused by the actual refinery and its operation exceeds that for which immunity is conferred, the plaintiff has a remedy.

For myself I would respond in this sense to the question asked, rather than in the purely negative sense favoured by the Court of Appeal, and to that extent I would allow the appeal.

10.2 Public Nuisance

A-G v PYA QUARRIES LTD [1957] 1 All ER 894 (CA)

FACTS: Quarry operations affected neighbours by producing vibration (which caused personal discomfort, but not physical damage to property) and also dust. The Attorney General commenced relator proceedings (actually conducted by the County & District

Councils) alleging a public nuisance and seeking an injunction. The defendants disputed that the matters complained of constituted a *public* nuisance. Oliver J granted the injunction and the defendants appealed to the Court of Appeal.

ROMER LJ: Counsel for the defendants, in challenging the injunction which the learned judge granted in relation to vibration and dust, based his criticisms of the judgment on the following general grounds. He first submitted that the judge approached the matter as though it was a private, and not a public, nuisance which was in issue; and that he applied tests and followed lines of inquiry which are apt and relevant in cases of private nuisance, but which are to some extent irrelevant, and are certainly indecisive, where a public nuisance is alleged. Counsel's second submission (which is to some extent associated with the first) was that the learned judge paid insufficient attention to the expert evidence which was called before him. The third criticism of the judgment is that the learned judge failed to address his mind to the position as it existed at the date of the writ, but primarily founded his decision to grant the injunctions now complained of on incidents which had occurred between the writ and the trial.

Before considering these contentions in any detail it would, I think, be convenient to consider the nature of a public nuisance as distinct from nuisances which are customarily described as 'private'. . . .

In *Stephen's Digest of The Criminal Law* (9th Edn.) p. 179, it is stated that

> A common nuisance is an act not warranted by law or an omission to discharge a legal duty, which act or omission obstructs or causes inconvenience or damage to the public in the exercise of rights common to all His Majesty's subjects.

The following definition of nuisance appears in 3 Blackstone's Commentaries (ch. 13, p. 262):

> Nuisance, *nocumentum*, or annoyance, signifies any thing that works hurt, inconvenience, or damage. And nuisances are of two kinds: *public* and *common* nuisances, which affect the public, and are an annoyance to *all* the king's subjects; for which reason we must refer them to the class of public wrongs, or crimes and misdemeanours; and *private* nuisances, which are the objects of our present consideration, and may be defined as anything done to the hurt or annoyance of the lands, tenements or hereditaments of another.

This passage from Blackstone is cited in *Pearce & Meston's Law Of Nuisances*, p. 1, and the learned authors point out that 'anything that works hurt, inconvenience or damage' is too broad as including many things which are not nuisances, being damna sine injuria.

Finally, in a form of indictment for a public nuisance by smells given in 3 *Chitty on Criminal Law* (2nd Edn.), pp. 652–654, the relevant allegation is that the air

> was corrupted and rendered wholly insalubrious to the great damage and common nuisance of all the liege subjects of our said Lord the King, not only there inhabiting and residing, but also going, returning, and passing through the said streets and highways, and against the peace, etc.

It is difficult to ascertain with any precision from these citations how widely spread the effect of a nuisance must be for it to qualify as a public nuisance and to become the subject of a criminal prosecution or of a relator action by the Attorney-General. It is obvious, notwithstanding Blackstone's definition, that it is not a prerequisite of a public nuisance that all of Her Majesty's subjects should be affected by it; for otherwise no public nuisance could ever be established at all.

I do not propose to attempt a more precise definition of a public nuisance than those which emerge from the text-books and authorities to which I have referred. It is, however, clear, in my opinion, that any nuisance is 'public' which materially affects the reasonable comfort and convenience of life of a class of Her Majesty's subjects. The sphere of the nuisance may be described generally as 'the neighbourhood'; but the question whether the local community within that sphere comprises a sufficient number of persons to constitute a class of the public is a question of fact in every case. It is not necessary, in my judgment, to prove that every member of the class has been injuriously affected; it is sufficient to show that a representative cross-section of the class has been so affected for an injunction to issue . . .

DENNING, LJ: I entirely agree with the judgment of Romer LJ, and have little to add. Counsel for the defendants raised at the outset this question: What is the difference between a public nuisance and a private nuisance? He is right to raise it because it affects his clients greatly. The order against them restrains them from committing a public nuisance, not a private one. The classic statement of the difference is that a public nuisance affects Her Majesty's subjects generally, whereas a private nuisance only affects particular individuals. But this does not help much. The question: when do a number of individuals become Her Majesty's subjects generally? is as difficult to answer as the question: when does a group of people become a crowd? Everyone has his own views. Even the answer 'Two's company, three's a crowd' will not command the assent of those present unless they first agree on 'which two'. So here I decline to answer the question how many people are necessary to make up Her Majesty's subjects generally. I prefer to look to the reason of the thing and to say that a public nuisance is a nuisance which is so widespread in its range or so indiscriminate in its effect that it would not be reasonable to expect one person to take proceedings on his own responsibility to put a stop to it, but that it should be taken on the responsibility of the community at large. Take the blocking up of a public highway or the non-repair of it: it may be a footpath very little used except by one or two householders; nevertheless the obstruction affects everyone indiscriminately who may wish to walk along it. Take next a landowner who collects pestilential rubbish near a village or permits gypsies with filthy habits to encamp on the edge of a residential neighbourhood. The householders nearest to it suffer the most, but everyone in the neighbourhood suffers too. In such cases the Attorney-General can take proceedings for an injunction to restrain the nuisance: and when he does so he acts in defence of the public right, not for any sectional interest. When, however, the nuisance is so concentrated that only two or three property owners are affected by it, such as the three attorneys in Clifford's Inn, then they ought to take proceedings on their own account to stop it and not expect the community to do it for them: see *R* v *Lloyd* (1802), 4 Esp. 200 . . .

The defendants, however, have now taken such good remedial measures that objectionable incidents take place only rarely and then by accident. So far as stones are concerned, the injunction is absolute: but so far as dust and vibration are concerned it is dependent on it being a nuisance 'to Her Majesty's subjects', that is, a public nuisance. The question then arises whether every rare incident is a public nuisance. Suppose six months went by without any excessive vibration and then there was by some mischance a violent explosion on an isolated occasion terrifying many people. Would that be a public nuisance? Would it subject the defendants to proceedings for contempt? I should have thought that it might, but the punishment would be measured according to the degree to which the defendants were at fault. I quite agree that a private nuisance always involves some degree of repetition or continuance. An isolated act which is over and done with, once and for all, may give rise to an action for negligence or an action under the rule in *Rylands* v *Fletcher*, ((1868) LR 3 HL 330) but not an action for nuisance. A good example is an explosion in a factory which breaks windows for miles around. It gives rise to an action under *Rylands* v *Fletcher*, but no other action if there was no negligence: see *Read* v *J Lyons & Co. Ltd* ([1946] 2 All ER 471). But an isolated act may amount to a public nuisance if it is done in such circumstances that the public right to condemn it should be vindicated. I referred to some authorities on this point in *Southport Corpn* v *Esso Petroleum Co. Ltd* ([1954] 2 All ER 561 at p. 571). In the present case, in view of the long history of stones, vibrations and dust, I should think it incumbent on the defendants to see that nothing of the kind happens again such as to be injurious to the neighbourhood at large, even on an isolated occasion.

10.2.1 PRIVATE ACTIONS

HALSEY v ESSO PETROLEUM [1961] 2 All ER 145

FACTS: Esso operated an oil distribution depot in an industrial area which adjoined a residential area. The distribution process involved heating certain grades of oil to keep them liquid. The plant operated day and night. There were two oil-fired boilers which emitted smuts. These damaged clothes on the plaintiff's washing line and the paintwork of his car (which he parked in the street outside his house). There was a pungent and nauseating smell of oil, serious enough to annoy an ordinary person but not actually harmful to health. There was vibration from the boilerhouse and noise from the road tankers throughout the night. The plaintiff alleged nuisance.

VEALE J: I have been referred to a very large number of authorities, but seems to me that, save on one point to which I will refer later, there can be little dispute as to the law which has to be applied to the facts. As long ago as 1865, in *St Helen's Smelting Co.* v *Tipping* (1865) 11 HL Cas 642 Lord Westbury, LC, said:

. . . in matters of this description it appears to me that it is a very desirable thing to mark the difference between an action brought for a nuisance upon the ground that the alleged nuisance produces material injury to the property, and an action brought for a nuisance on the ground that the thing alleged to be a nuisance is productive of sensible personal discomfort. With regard to the latter, namely, the personal inconvenience and interference with one's enjoyment, one's quiet, one's personal freedom, anything that discomposes or injuriously affects the senses or the nerves, whether that may or may not be denominated a nuisance, must undoubtedly depend greatly on the circumstances of the place where the thing complained of actually occurs. If a man lives in a town, it is necessary that he should subject himself to the consequences of those operations of trade which may be carried on in his immediate locality, which are actually necessary for trade and commerce, and also for the enjoyment of property, and for the benefit of the inhabitants of the town and of the public at large. If a man lives in a street where there are numerous shops, and a shop is opened next door to him, which is carried on in a fair and reasonable way, he has no ground for complaint, because to himself individually there may arise much discomfort from the trade carried on in that shop. But when an occupation is carried on by one person in the neighbourhood of another, and the result of that trade, or occupation, or business, is a material injury to property, then there unquestionably arises a very different consideration. I think, my Lords, that in a case of that description, the submission which is required from persons living in society to that amount of discomfort which may be necessary for the legitimate and free exercise of the trade of their neighbours, would not apply to circumstances the immediate result of which is sensible injury to the value of the property.

In this case smell and noise come into one category, actual deposits in the way of harmful smuts and oily drops come into the other. I bear in mind the observations of Lord Loreburn, LC, in *Polsue & Alfieri, Ltd* v *Rushmer* [1907] AC at p. 123. Lord Loreburn, LC said:

The law of nuisance undoubtedly is elastic, as was stated by Lord Halsbury in the case of *Colls* v *Home & Colonial Stores, Ltd* [1904] AC 179 at p. 185. He said: 'What may be called the uncertainty of the test may also be described as its elasticity. A dweller in towns cannot expect to have as pure air, as free from smoke, smell, and noise as if he lived in the country, and distant from other dwellings, and yet an excess of smoke, smell, and noise may give a cause of action, but in each of such cases it becomes a question of degree, and the question is in each case whether it amounts to a nuisance which will give a right of action'. This is a question of fact . . .

One useful approach to the considerations to be taken into account in a case of alleged nuisance by noise is to be found in the judgment of Luxmoore, J, in *Vanderpant* v *Mayfair Hotel Co., Ltd* [1929] All ER Rep at p. 380. Luxmoore, J, said:

Apart from any right which may have been acquired against him by contract, grant or prescription, every person is entitled as against his neighbour to the comfortable and healthy enjoyment of the premises occupied by him, and in deciding whether, in any particular case, his right has been interfered with and a nuisance thereby caused, it is necessary to determine whether the act complained of is an inconvenience materially interfering with the ordinary physical comfort of human existence, not merely according to elegant or dainty modes and habits of living, but according to plain and sober and simple notions obtaining among English people: see *Walter v Selfe* (1851) 4 D G & Sm 315 at p. 322 and the remarks of Knight Bruce, V-C. It is also necessary to take into account the circumstances and character of the locality in which the complainant is living. The making or causing of such a noise as materially interferes with the comfort of a neighbour, when judged by the standard to which I have just referred, constitutes an actionable nuisance, and it is no answer to say that the best known measures have been taken to reduce or prevent the noise complained of, or that the cause of the nuisance is the exercise of a business or trade in a reasonable and proper manner. Again, the question of the existence of a nuisance is one of degree and depends on the circumstances of the case.

So far as the present case is concerned, liability for nuisance by harmful deposits could be established by proving damage by the deposits to the property in question, provided, of course, that the injury was not merely trivial. Negligence is not an ingredient of the cause of action, and the character of the neighbourhood is not a matter to be taken into consideration. On the other hand nuisance by smell or noise is something to which no absolute standard can be applied. It is always a question of degree whether the interference with comfort or convenience is sufficiently serious to constitute a nuisance. The character of the neighbourhood is very relevant and all the relevant circumstances have to be taken into account. What might be a nuisance in one area is by no means necessarily so in another. In an urban area, everyone must put up with a certain amount of discomfort and annoyance from the activities of neighbours, and the law must strike a fair and reasonable balance between the right of the plaintiff on the one hand to the undisturbed enjoyment of his property, and the right of the defendant on the other hand to use his property for his own lawful enjoyment. That is how I approach this case.

. . .

Nuisance is commonly regarded as a tort in respect of land. In *Read v J Lyons & Co., Ltd* [1946] 2 All ER 471 at p. 482, Lord Simonds said '. . . only he has a lawful claim who has suffered an invasion of some proprietary or other interest in land'. In this connexion the allegation of damage to the plaintiff's motor car calls for special consideration, since the allegation is that when the offending smuts from the defendants' chimney alighted on it, the motor car was not actually on land in the plaintiff's occupation, but was on the public highway outside his door. Whether or not a claim in respect of private nuisance lies for damage to the motor car in these circumstances, in my judgment such damage is covered by the doctrine in *Rylands v Fletcher* (1865) LR 3 HL 330. If it be the fact that harmful sulphuric acid or harmful sulphate escaped from the defendants' premises and damaged the motor car in the public highway, I am bound by the decision of the Court of Appeal in *Charing Cross Electricity Supply Co. v Hydraulic Power Co.* [1914] 3 KB 772 and *Miles v Forest Rock Granite Co. (Leicestershire), Ltd* [1918] 34 TLR 500 in neither of which cases was the plaintiff in occupation of land. This doctrine of *Rylands v Fletcher*, whether or not it is strictly based on nuisance, applies to the sulphuric acid or sulphate in smuts or oily drops wherever they alight: on washing hung out to dry, as well as on to a motor car in the street. In my judgment the plaintiff is also right in saying that if the motor car was damaged in this way while on the public highway, it is a public nuisance in respect of which he has suffered special damage . . .

It is said by the defendants that since the public highway is for the use of everyone, the plaintiff cannot complain if all that the defendants do is to make use of their right to use the public highway. I agree, if that is all that the defendants have done. If a person makes an unreasonable use of the public highway, for instance, by parking stationary vehicles on it, a member of the public who suffers special damage has a cause of action against him for public nuisance. Similarly, in my view, if a person makes an unreasonable use of the public highway by concentrating in one small area of the highway vehicles in motion and a member of the public suffers special damage, he is equally entitled to complain, although in most cases concentration of moving as opposed to stationary vehicles will be more likely to be reasonable. This is a question of reasonable user . . .

In the particular circumstances of this case I do not think that it matters very much whether one regards the alleged nuisance by vehicular noise as a private or a public nuisance. The history as a cause of action for a private nuisance is set out by Lord Wright in *Sedleigh-Denfield* v *O'Callaghan* [1940] 3 All ER at p. 364. The ground of responsibility is the possession and control of the land from which the nuisance proceeds, though Lord Wright refers to 'possibly certain anomalous exceptions.' Public nuisance, on the other hand, can, as Denning, LJ, said in the Court of Appeal in *Southport Corpn* v *Esso Petroleum Co., Ltd* [1954] 2 All ER 561 at p. 571 cover a multitude of sins, great and small. In this latter case Devlin, J, said:

It is clear that to give a cause of action for private nuisance the matter complained of must affect the property of the plaintiffs. But I know of no principle that it must emanate from land belonging to the defendant. Counsel for the defendants cited *Cunard* v *Antifyre, Ltd* [1932] All ER Rep 560 and I think that the statement of the principle is put there as clearly and concisely as it can be. Talbot, J, said 'Private nuisances, at least in the vast majority of cases, are interferences for a substantial length of time by owners or occupiers of property with the use or enjoyment of neighbouring property; and it would manifestly be inconvenient and unreasonable if the right to complain of such interference extended beyond the occupier, or (in case of injury to the reversion) the owner, of such neighbouring property.' It is clear from this statement of principle that the nuisance must affect the property of the plaintiff, and it is true that in the vast majority of cases it is likely to emanate from the neighbouring property of the defendant. But no statement of principle has been cited to me to show that the latter is a prerequisite to a cause of action, and I can see no reason why, if land or water belonging to the public or waste land is misused by the defendant, or if the defendant as a licensee or trespasser misuses someone else's land, he should not be liable for a nuisance in the same way as an adjoining occupier would be.

. . .

In the present case the offending noise is partly in the depot before and as the vehicles emerge into the highway, and as they re-enter, and partly in the short stretch of highway immediately outside the entrance and exit to the depot, which is also immediately outside the plaintiff's house. There is no element of obstruction of or danger on and to the highway as such. The noise is an interference with the enjoyment by the plaintiff of his house. It is not an interference with the rights of the plaintiff or his visitors as members of the public to use the highway. The fact is that the defendants concentrate at their premises a number of particularly heavy and noisy vehicles. They send them out at night, making a very loud noise as they go, and they direct them to return, and the vehicles make a further very loud noise as they come back.

The noise outside and inside the plaintiff's house is, in my judgment, attributable to the defendants' mode of operation of their depot, and the principles of law to be applied seem to me to be the same as those in respect of alleged nuisance by noise of the plant itself. Applying those principles which involve consideration of the whole of the relevant circumstances, I hold that the defendants are also guilty of nuisance in this respect, but only during the night shift. I do not think that any proper comparison can be made with noisy undertakings like railways, which are carried on under statutory authority, nor, in my judgment, can Rainville Road, Fulham, properly be compared with the Great North Road . . . If I treat this part of the case as public nuisance, as counsel for the plaintiff argued in the alternative, I ask myself: Is it reasonable to concentrate outside the plaintiff's house during the night, not on odd occasions, but every night, and not once a night, but at irregular intervals during the night and early hours of the morning, particularly noisy vehicles, sometimes in convoy, the noise of one of which is approximately 83 decibels? I bear in mind the importance of the defendants' business. I also, I hope, bear in mind all the circumstances, including the circumstance that a man is entitled to sleep during the night in his own house. I have no hesitation in saying that the plaintiff has satisfied me that the defendants' use of their tankers in all the circumstances is unreasonable. On this view they are liable as for a public nuisance, since it is conceded that noise can be special damage if it affects the plaintiff more than the ordinary member of the public. On this alternative view also the defendants are liable, since I find that the plaintiff has indeed suffered a special damage which is substantial and not transient or fleeting.

10.2.2   PARTICULAR DAMAGE

10.2.2.1   Loss of trade

TATE & LYLE INDUSTRIES LTD v *GREATER LONDON COUNCIL*
[1983] 1 All ER 1159 (HL)

FACTS: The plaintiffs had a plant on the banks of the Thames with private jetties to allow sugar to be shipped to and from the plant. The defendants constructed two ferry terminals nearby. These caused siltation of the approaches to the plaintiffs' jetties which only remained usable as a result of additional dredging works. If the defendants had considered this, they could have adopted alternative designs for the terminals, which would have reduced siltation by 75 per cent. The plaintiffs alleged negligence, breach of duty and nuisance, namely the obstruction of the right of navigation. The defendants alleged, *inter alia*, that they had statutory authority for the terminals.

LORD TEMPLEMAN:
Public nuisance
The Thames is a navigable river over which the public have the right of navigation, that is to say a right to pass and re-pass over the whole width and depth of water in the River Thames and the incidental right of loading and unloading. The public right of navigation was expressly preserved by s. 210 of the Port of London (Consolidation) Act 1920 whereby—

(1)   Subject to the provisions of this Act it shall be lawful for all persons whether for pleasure or profit to go and be, pass and re-pass in vessels over or upon any and every part of the Thames through which Thames water flows . . .

The construction of the ferry terminals interfered with the public right of navigation over the Thames between the main shipping channel and Tate & Lyle's jetties by causing siltation on the bed and foreshore of the river and siltation in the channel and berth dredged by Tate & Lyle. This interference with the public right of navigation caused particular damage to Tate & Lyle because vessels of the requisite dimensions were unable to pass and repass over the bed and foreshore between the main channel and the refined sugar jetty and vessels of the required dimensions were unable to pass and repass over the channel dredged by Tate & Lyle between the main shipping channel and the raw sugar jetty and could not be accommodated in the berth dredged by Tate & Lyle adjacent to the raw sugar jetty.

An individual who suffers damage resulting from a public nuisance is, as a general rule, entitled to maintain an action. In the present case the GLC and the PLA assert that in constructing the ferry terminals the GLC were acting in pursuance of statutory authority contained in the London County Council (Improvements) Act 1962 and the Port of London (Consolidation) Act 1920, and the combined effect of those two Acts was to authorise the interference with the public right of navigation which was in fact caused by the construction of the ferry terminals. There was therefore no public nuisance and Tate & Lyle have no cause of action in respect of any public nuisance.

In the alternative, it is argued, Tate & Lyle's damages based on public nuisance must be limited to damages suffered in connection with the refined sugar jetty. The plans of the GLC for the ferry terminals were approved in 1964. The licences to Tate & Lyle granted by the PLA to construct the raw sugar jetty and to dredge the channel and berth required for the raw sugar jetty were not granted until 1965. Tate & Lyle, it is submitted, have no right of action in respect of the raw sugar jetty which was constructed after the plans for the ferry terminals were approved and contemporaneously with the construction of the ferry terminals.

Statutory authority
The GLC plead that if they were guilty of creating a public nuisance they are nevertheless excused because they were authorised by the London County Council (Improvements) Act 1962 to carry out the operations of which complaint is made. They were authorised by

statute to construct the terminals in accordance with a design approved by the PLA and not otherwise.

The defence of statutory authority to an action for nuisance was summarised in the speech of Lord Wilberforce in *Allen* v *Gulf Oil Refining Ltd* [1981] 1 All ER 353 . . .

In the present case Parliament authorised the terminals and thereby granted immunity from the consequences of the terminals provided that the GLC paid 'all reasonable regard and care for the interests' of public navigation and for the interests of Tate & Lyle liable to suffer particular damage from any interference with the right of public navigation . . .

The Court of Appeal held that there was 'no duty on the GLC to consider anyone else's interest in siltation' because s. 50 of the 1962 Act contemplated that the PLA could inspect the design of the terminals and could nullify the effects of any siltation at the expense of the GLC. At the same time the Court of Appeal held that there was no duty on the PLA to ensure that the design of the terminals produced the minimum siltation, and no duty to nullify the effects of siltation. Thus the statute conferred immunity from unnecessary siltation in causing unnecessary adverse effects on third parties such as Tate & Lyle. I decline to construe s. 50 of the 1962 Act so as to relieve the GLC from any elementary duty to cause no more harm than was necessary . . .

Measure of damages

The cost of the additional dredging required to remedy the siltation caused by the terminals was £540,000. The judge found that an alternative design could, and should, have been adopted and that 'if such a design had been adopted it would have resulted . . . in only one-quarter of the accretion' caused by the design which was in fact selected. One-quarter of the cost of the additional dredging was the inevitable consequence of the exercise by the GLC of its statutory power to construct the terminals; one-quarter of the additional dredging costs is therefore not recoverable by Tate & Lyle.

On behalf of Tate & Lyle it was urged that the terminals as constructed created an unauthorised interference with the right of public navigation, and that the GLC are responsible for all the consequences of that interference, and not only for three-quarters of the cost of the additional dredging. I cannot accept that argument. To maintain the public right of navigation, Tate & Lyle would have been bound to carry out some additional dredging in any event, and their damages are the cost of dredging which would have been avoided if the terminals had been designed to avoid siltation as much as possible. Tate & Lyle claim that if the design of the terminals had only caused one-quarter of the siltation which in fact occurred, then the PLA might have undertaken the additional dredging and recovered the cost from the GLC. This is speculation and the fact is that the GLC adamantly maintained that the terminals were not responsible for any siltation.

In these circumstances I am of the opinion that Tate & Lyle are entitled to recover from the GLC the sum of £405,000 representing three-quarters of the additional dredging caused by the terminals.

10.3 Harassment

10.3.1 REMEDIES FOR HARASSMENT

10.3.1.1 *Wilkinson* v *Downton*

WILKINSON v *DOWNTON* [1897] 2 QB 57

FACTS: The defendant wished to play a practical joke on the plaintiff. He 'falsely and maliciously' represented to her that her husband had been seriously injured and was in danger. As a result the plaintiff laid out money for a cab to fetch her husband home, and also suffered serious illness brought on by the shock. The action was tried before Wright J and a jury.

WRIGHT J: The real question is as to the £100, the greatest part of which is given as compensation for the female plaintiff's illness and suffering. It was argued for her that she is entitled to recover this as being damage caused by fraud, and, therefore, within the doctrine established by *Pasley* v *Freeman* (1789) 3 Term Rep 51 and *Langridge* v *Levy* (1837)

2 M & W 519. I am not sure that this would not be an extension of that doctrine, the real ground of which appears to be that a person who makes a false statement, intending it to be acted on, must make good the damage naturally resulting from its being acted on. Here is no *injuria* of that kind. I think, however, that the verdict may be supported on another ground. The defendant has, as I assume for the moment, wilfully done an act calculated to cause physical harm to the female plaintiff, i.e., to infringe her legal right to personal safety, and has thereby in fact caused physical harm to her. That proposition, without more, appears to me to state a good cause of action, there being no justification alleged for the act. This wilful *injuria* is in law malicious, although no malicious purpose to cause the harm which was caused, nor any motive of spite, is imputed to the defendant.

It remains to consider whether the assumptions involved in the proposition are made out. One question is whether the defendant's act was so plainly calculated to produce some effect of the kind which was produced, that an intention to produce it ought to be imputed to the defendant regard being had to the fact that the effect was produced on a person proved to be in an ordinary state of health and mind. I think that it was. It is difficult to imagine that such a statement, made suddenly and with apparent seriousness, could fail to produce grave effects under the circumstances upon any but an exceptionally indifferent person, and therefore an intention to produce such an effect must be imputed, and it is no answer in law to say that more harm was done than was anticipated, for that is commonly the case with all wrongs. The other question is whether the effect was, to use the ordinary phrase, too remote to be in law regarded as a consequence for which the defendant is answerable. Apart from authority I should give the same answer, and on the same grounds, as to the last question, and say that it was not too remote. Whether, as the majority of the Lords thought in *Lynch* v *Knight* (1861) 9 HL Cas 577, the criterion is in asking what would be the natural effect on reasonable persons, or whether, as Lord Wensleydale thought, the possible infirmities of human nature ought to be recognised, it seems to me that the connection between the cause and the effect is sufficiently close and complete.

JANVIER v *SWEENEY* [1919] 2 KB 316 (CA)

FACTS: The defendant, a private detective, was instructed to obtain some letters. The plaintiff was a servant in the house where the letters were kept. She was engaged to an enemy alien interned on the Isle of Man. In order to intimidate the plaintiff into handing over the letters, the defendant told her he was a police inspector and wished to speak to her as she had been 'corresponding with a German spy'. This caused the plaintiff to become ill with 'shock, neurasthenia and shingles'. The action came before the Court of Appeal.

BANKES LJ: It is no longer contended that this was not a wrongful act which would amount to an actionable wrong if damage which the law recognises can be shown to have flowed directly from that act. But counsel for the defendant, Barker, contended that no action would lie for words followed by such damage as the plaintiff alleges here. In order to sustain that contention it would be necessary to overrule *Wilkinson* v *Downton*. In my opinion, that judgment was right. It has been approved in subsequent cases. It did not create any new rule of law, though it may be said to have extended existing principles over an area wider than that which they had been recognised as covering, because the court there accepted the view that the damage there relied on was not in the circumstances too remote in the eye of the law. . . .

Wilkinson v *Downton* was subsequently considered in *Dulieu* v *White & Sons*. I wish to refer to two passages from the judgment of Phillimore J. He said ([1901] 2 KB at p. 682):

> I think there may be cases in which A. owes a duty to B. not to inflict a mental shock on him or her, and that in such a case, if A. does inflict such a shock upon B.—as by terrifying B.—and physical damage thereby ensues, B. may have an action for the physical damage, though the medium through which it has been inflicted is the mind.

> [The] principles and cases seem to establish that terror wrongfully induced and inducing physical mischief gives a cause of action . . . Once get the duty and the physical damage following on the breach of duty, and I hold that the fact of one link in the chain of causation being mental only makes no difference.

I adopt those passages which seem to me to state the law accurately. If the law so stated applies to this case it follows that the plaintiff is entitled to succeed.

10.3.2   STATUTORY HARASSMENT

10.3.2.1   Protection from Harassment Act 1997

PROTECTION FROM HARASSMENT ACT 1997

1.   Prohibition of harassment

(1)   A person must not pursue a course of conduct—

(a)   which amounts to harassment of another, and

(b)   which he knows or ought to know amounts to harassment of the other.

(2)   For the purposes of this section, the person whose course of conduct is in question ought to know that it amounts to harassment of another if a reasonable person in possession of the same information would think the course of conduct amounted to harassment of the other.

(3)   Subsection (1) does not apply to a course of conduct if the person who pursued it shows—

(a)   that it was pursued for the purpose of preventing or detecting crime,

(b)   that it was pursued under any enactment or rule of law or to comply with any condition or requirement imposed by any person under any enactment, or

(c)   that in the particular circumstances the pursuit of the course of conduct was reasonable.

3.   Civil remedy

(1)   An actual or apprehended breach of section 1 may be the subject of a claim in civil proceedings by the person who is or may be the victim of the course of conduct in question.

(2)   On such a claim, damages may be awarded for (among other things) any anxiety caused by the harassment and any financial loss resulting from the harassment.

. . .

7.   Interpretation of this group of sections

(1)   This section applies for the interpretation of sections 1 to 5.

(2)   References to harassing a person include alarming the person or causing the person distress.

(3)   A 'course of conduct' must involve conduct on at least two occasions.

(4)   'Conduct' includes speech.

FAMILY LAW ACT 1996

42.   Non-molestation orders

(1)   In this Part a 'non-molestation order' means an order containing either or both of the following provisions—

(a)   provision prohibiting a person ('the respondent') from molesting another person who is associated with the respondent;

(b)   provision prohibiting the respondent from molesting a relevant child.

(2)   The court may make a non-molestation order—

(a)   if an application for the order has been made (whether in other family proceedings or without any other family proceedings being instituted) by a person who is associated with the respondent; or

(b)   if in any family proceedings to which the respondent is a party the court considers that the order should be made for the benefit of any other party to the proceedings or any relevant child even though no such application has been made.

. . .

(5)   In deciding whether to exercise its powers under this section and, if so, in what manner, the court shall have regard to all the circumstances including the need to secure the health, safety and well-being—

(a)   of the applicant or, in a case falling within subsection (2)(b), the person for whose benefit the order would be made; and

(b)   of any relevant child.

(6)   A non-molestation order may be expressed so as to refer to molestation in general, to particular acts of molestation, or to both.

. . .

HOUSING ACT 1996

152.   Power to grant injunctions against anti-social behaviour

(1)   The High Court or a county court may, on an application by a local authority, grant an injunction prohibiting a person from—

(a)   engaging in or threatening to engage in conduct causing or likely to cause a nuisance or annoyance to a person residing in, visiting or otherwise engaging in a lawful activity in residential premises to which this section applies or in the locality of such premises,

(b)   using or threatening to use residential premises to which this section applies for immoral or illegal purposes, or

(c)   entering residential premises to which this section applies or being found in the locality of any such premises.

(2)   This section applies to residential premises of the following descriptions—

(a)   dwelling-houses held under secure or introductory tenancies from the local authority;

(b)   accommodation provided by that authority under Part VII of this Act or Part III of the Housing Act 1985 (homelessness).

(3)   The court shall not grant an injunction under this section unless it is of the opinion that—

(a)   the respondent has used or threatened to use violence against any person of a description mentioned in subsection (1)(a), and

(b)   there is a significant risk of harm to that person or a person of a similar description if the injunction is not granted.

(4)   An injunction under this section may—

(a)   in the case of an injunction under subsection (1)(a) or (b), relate to particular acts or to conduct, or types of conduct, in general or to both, and

(b)   in the case of an injunction under subsection (1)(c), relate to particular premises or a particular locality;

and may be made for a specified period or until varied or discharged.

. . .

CRIME AND DISORDER ACT 1998

1.   Anti-social behaviour orders

(1)   An application for an order under this section may be made by a relevant authority if it appears to the authority that the following conditions are fulfilled with respect to any person aged 10 or over, namely—

(a)   that the person has acted in an anti-social manner, that is to say, in a manner that caused or was likely to cause harassment, alarm or distress to one or more persons not of the same household as himself; and

(b)   that such an order is necessary to protect persons in the local government area in which the harassment, alarm or distress was caused or was likely to be caused from further anti-social acts by him;

and in this section 'relevant authority' means the council for the local government area or any chief officer of police any part of whose police area lies within that area.

. . .

(4)   If, on such an application, it is proved that the conditions mentioned in subsection (1) above are fulfilled, the magistrates' court may make an order under this section (an 'anti-social behaviour order') which prohibits the defendant from doing anything described in the order.

. . .

(6)   The prohibitions that may be imposed by an anti-social behaviour order are those necessary for the purpose of protecting persons in the local government area from further anti-social acts by the defendant.

10.4   End of Chapter Assessment Question

Harvey is the owner of a small-holding on which he has established a riding school. He has two immediate neighbours, Oenone, an elocution teacher and Sonya, a taxi-driver. Harvey has a contract to provide weekly riding lessons to the 400 pupils of St Trinian's, a local girls' school. Oenone complains that on the days when the junior girls are receiving lessons, there is so much disturbance and disruption from their chattering, screaming and shouting that she and her own pupils cannot hear themselves think.

Every summer Harvey holds two or three large charity gymkhanas. Sonya complains that on these occasions the approach roads to her house are so congested by parked cars, horseboxes and other vehicles attracted by the gymkhana that she cannot get her taxi out, and she has lost business as a result.

Advise Harvey as to his liability to Oenone and Sonya.

10.5   End of Chapter Assessment Outline Answer

The first issue is Oenone's complaint of noise nuisance. It appears that her property alone is affected. Assuming she is the owner or tenant she has standing to sue: *Malone* v *Lasky* (1907). The complaint is of interference rather than damage so account must be taken of the nature of the area and the level of amenity to be expected there; *St Helen's Smelting* v *Tipping* (1865), *Sturges* v *Bridgman* (1879).

The presence of the girls on a regular basis clearly constitutes a state of affairs. The essential question is whether the degree of noise disturbance is unacceptable in its context; c.f. *Sedleigh-Denfield* v *O'Callaghan* (1940) and *Miller* v *Jackson* (1977). This is a matter of weighing and assessing the intensity of the interference, its utility and appropriateness and any other relevant factors. Here it can be argued on the one hand that a rural area should be tranquil, but on the other hand a business of this kind is appropriate to the area. There is no suggestion of malice: *Christie* v *Davey* (1893), but the nature of Oenone's profession, which would seem to demand a high level of quiet, may mean that she is to be seen as oversensitive: *Robinson* v *Kilvert* (1889). This will however be immaterial if the disturbance would affect a person of normal sensitivity: *Mackinnon Industries* v *Walker* (1951). The result will be the same if Oenone has got herself so worked up as a result of the disturbance that she has convinced herself that it is worse than it really is (c.f. *Miller* v *Jackson*).

If the noise is found to be a nuisance then an injunction may issue. Harvey may have to cease teaching these pupils or reorganise their tuition to remove the excessive noise. Alternatively there may be a limitation on times when he can make a noise so Oenone can teach round these times (c.f. *Kennaway* v *Thompson* (1981)).

It again seems clear that Harvey has attracted the visitors to the gymkhanas. Obstructing a highway is a classic example of public nuisance. It is an interference with a public right, namely the right of free passage, and it is clearly more than incidental or transitory. The local authority will no doubt be concerned and may well seek to remove the threat of obstruction. They may do this in various ways, including orders under the Road Traffic Regulation Acts, but may also seek an injunction under s. 221, Local Government Act 1972. There is however a derivative right of action available to any person who suffers particular damage over and above the interference to which all are subjected. Exceptionally this will include economic loss of the kind sustained by Sonya and she will be able to recover damages: *Rose* v *Miles* (1815). Sonya could also consider commencing relator proceedings if the local authority are unwilling to intervene. If successful these will result in an injunction restraining the nuisance (if necessary banning the gymkhanas altogether).

CHAPTER ELEVEN

HAZARDOUS ACTIVITIES

11.1 How the 'Hazardous Activities' Rule Developed

11.1.1 THE CASE OF *RYLANDS* v *FLETCHER* ITSELF

RYLANDS v *FLETCHER* [1861–73] All ER Rep 1 (HL)

FACTS: The defendants constructed a reservoir for the purposes of their textile mill. They employed a competent contractor. The plaintiff owned a colliery, the workings of which connected to disused mine workings linked to shafts on the reservoir site. The contractors were aware of the shafts, but neither knew nor suspected the existence of the underground workings. They did not use proper care to ensure that the lining of the reservoir was adequate to prevent water flooding into the shafts. Flooding did take place, and the plaintiff had to abandon his mine. It was held that, in the absence of any reason to suspect that there was any connection with the plaintiff's workings, the defendants owed him no duty of care.

The majority of the Court of Exchequer considered that there was no liability. The case went on appeal to the Court of Exchequer Chamber.

BLACKBURN J: It appears from the statement in the Case, that the plaintiff was damaged by his property being flooded by water which, without any fault on his part, broke out of a reservoir constructed on the defendant's land by the defendant's orders and maintained by the defendants. It appears from the statement in the Case, that the coal under the defendant's land had, at some remote period, been worked out, but that this was unknown at the time when the defendants gave directions to erect the reservoir, and the water in the reservoir would not have escaped from the defendant's land, and no mischief would have been done to the plaintiff, but for this latent defect in the defendant's subsoil. It further appears from the Case that the defendants selected competent engineers and contractors to make the reservoir, and themselves personally continued in total ignorance of what we have called the latent defect in the subsoil, but that the persons employed by them, in the course of the work, became aware of the existence of ancient shafts filled up with soil, though they did not know or suspect that they were shafts communicating with old workings. It is found that the defendants personally were free from all blame, but that, in fact, proper care and skill was not used by the persons employed by them to provide for the sufficiency of the reservoir with reference to these shafts. The consequence was, that the reservoir, when filled with water, burst into the shafts, the water flowed down through them into the old workings, and thence into the plaintiff's mine, and there did the mischief. The plaintiff, though free from all blame on his part, must bear the loss, unless he can establish that it was the consequence of some default for which the defendants are responsible.

The question of law, therefore arises: What is the liability which the law casts upon a person who, like the defendants, lawfully brings on his land something which, though harmless while it remains there, will naturally do mischief if it escape out of his land? It is agreed on all hands that he must take care to keep in that which he has brought on the land, and keep it there in order that it may not escape and damage his neighbour's, but the question arises whether the duty which the law casts upon him under such circumstances is an absolute duty to keep it in at his peril, or is, as the majority of the Court of Exchequer have thought, merely a duty to take all reasonable and prudent precautions in order to keep it in, but no more. If the first be the law, the person who has brought on his land and kept there something dangerous, and failed to keep it in, is responsible for all the natural consequences of its escape. If the second be the limit of his duty, he would not be answerable except on proof of negligence, and consequently would not be answerable for escape arising from any latent defect which ordinary prudence and skill could not detect. Supposing the second to be the correct view of the law, a further question arises subsidiary to the first, namely, whether the defendants are not so far identified with the contractors whom they employed as to be responsible for the consequences of their want of skill in making the reservoir in fact insufficient with reference to the old shafts, of the existence of which they were aware, though they had not ascertained where the shafts went to.

We think that the true rule of law is that the person who, for his own purposes, brings on his land, and collects and keeps there anything likely to do mischief if it escapes, must keep it in at his peril, and, if he does not do so, he is prima facie answerable for all the damage which is the natural consequence of its escape. He can excuse himself by showing that the escape was owing to the plaintiff's default, or, perhaps, that the escape was the consequence of vis major, or the act of God; but, as nothing of this sort exists here, it is unnecessary to inquire what excuse would be sufficient. The general rule, as above stated, seems on principle just. The person whose grass or corn is eaten down by the escaped cattle of his neighbour, or whose mine is flooded by the water from his neighbour's reservoir, or whose celler is invaded by the filth of his neighbour's privy, or whose habitation is made unhealthy by the fumes and noisome vapours of his neighbour's alkali works, is damnified without any fault of his own; and it seems but reasonable and just that the neighbour who has brought something on his own property which was not naturally there, harmless to others so long as it is confined to his own property, but which he knows will be mischievous if it gets on his neighbour's, should be obliged to make good the damage which ensues if he does not succeed in confining it to his own property. But for his act in bringing it there no mischief could have accrued, and it seems but just that he should at his peril keep it there, so that no mischief may accrue, or answer for the natural and anticipated consequences. On authority this, we think, is established to be the law, whether the thing so brought be beasts or water, or filth or stenches.

The case that has most commonly occurred, and which is most frequently to be found in the books, is as to the obligation of the owner of cattle which he has brought on his land to prevent their escaping and doing mischief. The law as to them seems to be perfectly settled from early times; the owner must keep them in at his peril, or he will be answerable for the natural consequences of their escape, that is, with regard to tame beasts, for the grass they eat and trample upon, although nor for any injury to the person of others, for our ancestors have settled that it is not the general nature of horses to kick or bulls to gore, but if the owner knows that the beast has a vicious propensity to attack man he will be answerable for that too. As early as 1480 (*Anon.* (1480) YB 20 Edw 4 fo 10, pl 10), Brian, CJ, lays down the doctrine in terms very much resembling those used by Lord Holt in *Tenant* v *Goldwin* (1704) 1 Salk 21, 360, which will be referred to later. It was trespass with cattle. Plea: that the plaintiff's land adjoined a place where the defendant had common; that the cattle strayed from the common, and the defendant drove them back as soon as he could. It was held a bad plea. Brian, CJ, says:

> It behoves him to use his common so that it shall do no hurt to another man, and if the land in which he has common be not inclosed, it behoves him to keep the beasts in the common, and out of the land of any other.

He adds, when it was proposed to amend by pleading that they were driven out of the common by dogs,

> that although that might give a right of action against the master of the dogs, it was no defence to the action of trespass by the person on whose land the cattle went. . . .

As has been already said, there does not appear to be any difference in principle between the extent of the duty cast on him who brings cattle on his land to keep them in, and the extent of the duty imposed on him who brings on his land water, filth or stenches, or any other thing which will, if it escapes, naturally do damage, to prevent their escaping and injuring his neighbour. *Tenant* v *Goldwin* is an express authority that the duty is the same, and is to keep them in at his peril . . .

> The reason he gave for his judgment was because it was the defendant's wall, and the defendant's filth, and he was bound of common right to keep his wall so as his filth might not damnify his neighbour, and that it was a trespass on his neighbour, as if his beasts should escape, or one should make a great heap on the border of his ground, and it should tumble and roll down upon his neighbour's . . . he must repair the wall of his house of office, for he whose dirt it is must keep it, that it may not trespass.

. . .

No case has been found in which the question of the liability for noxious vapours escaping from a man's works by inevitable accident has been discussed, but the following case will illustrate it. Some years ago several actions were brought against the occupiers of some alkali works at Liverpool for the damage alleged to be caused by the chlorine fumes of their works. The defendants proved that they had, at great expense, erected a contrivance by which the fumes of chlorine were condensed, and sold as muriatic acid, and they called a great body of scientific evidence to prove that this apparatus was so perfect that no fumes possibly could escape from the defendant's chimneys. On this evidence it was pressed upon the juries that the plaintiff's damage must have been due to some of the numerous other chimneys in the neighbourhood. The juries, however, being satisfied that the mischief was occasioned by chlorine, drew the conclusion that it had escaped from the defendant's works somehow, and in each case found for the plaintiff. No attempt was made to disturb these verdicts on the ground that the defendants had taken every precaution which prudence or skill could suggest to keep those fumes in, and that they could not be responsible unless negligence were shown, yet if the law be as laid down by the majority of the Court of Exchequer it would have been a very obvious defence. If it had been raised, the answer would probably have been that the uniform course of pleading in actions for such nuisances is to say that the defendant caused the noisome vapours to arise on his premises and suffered them to come on the plaintiff's without stating that there was any want of care or skill on the defendant's part; and that *Tenant* v *Goldwin* showed that this was founded on the general rule of law that he whose stuff it is must keep it so that it may not trespass. There is no difference in this respect between chlorine and water; both will, if they escape, do damage, the one by scorching and the other by drowning, and he who brings them on his land must at his peril see that they do not escape and do that mischief . . . But it was further said by Martin, B, that when damage is done to personal property, or even to the person by collision, either upon land or at sea, there must be negligence in the party doing the damage to render him legally responsible. This is no doubt true, and this is not confined to cases of collision, for there are many cases in which proof of negligence is essential, as, for instance, where an unruly horse gets on the footpath of a public street and kills a passenger: *Hammack* v *White* (1862) 11 CBNS 588, or where a person in a dock is struck by the falling of a bale of cotton which the defendant's servants are lowering: *Scott* v *London Dock Co.* (1865) 34 LJ Ex 220. Many other similar cases may be found. But we think those cases distinguishable from the present. Traffic on the highways, whether by land or sea, cannot be conducted without exposing those whose persons or property are near it to some inevitable risk; and, that being so, those who go on the highway, or have their property adjacent to it, may well be held to do so subject to their taking upon themselves the risk of injury from that inevitable danger, and persons who, by the licence of the owners, pass near to warehouses where goods are being raised or lowered, certainly do so subject to the inevitable risk of accident. In neither case, therefore, can they recover without proof of want of care or skill occasioning the accident; and it is believed that all the cases in which inevitable accident has been held an excuse for what prima facie was a trespass can be explained on the same principle, namely, that the circumstances were such as to show that the plaintiff had taken the risk upon himself. But there is no ground for saying that the plaintiff here took upon himself any risk arising from the uses to which the defendants should choose to apply their land. He neither knew what there might be, nor could he in any way control the defendants, or hinder their building what reservoirs they liked, and storing up in them what water they pleased, so long as the defendants succeeded in preventing the water which they there brought from interfering with the plaintiff's property.

The view which we take of the first point renders it unnecessary to consider whether the defendants would or would not be responsible for the want of care and skill in the persons employed by them. We are of opinion that the plaintiff is entitled to recover, but as we have not heard any argument as to the amount, we are not able to give judgment for what damages. The parties probably will empower their counsel to agree on the amount of damages; should they differ on the principle the case may be mentioned again.

The defendants appealed to the House of Lords.

LORD CAIRNS LC: The principles on which this case must be determined appear to me to be extremely simple. The defendants, treating them as the owners or occupiers of the close on which the reservoir was constructed, might lawfully have used that close for any purpose for which it might, in the ordinary course of the enjoyment of the land, be used, and if, in what I may term the natural user of that land, there had been any accumulation of water, either on the surface or underground, and if by the operation of the laws of nature that accumulation of water had passed off into the close occupied by the plaintiff, the plaintiff could not have complained that that result had taken place. If he had desired to guard himself against it, it would have lain on him to have done so by leaving or by interposing some barrier between his close and the close of the defendants in order to have prevented that operation of the laws of nature.

As an illustration of that principle, I may refer to a case which was cited in the argument before your Lordships, *Smith* v *Kenrick* (1849) 7 CB 515 in the Court of Common Pleas. On the other hand, if the defendants, not stopping at the natural use of their close, had desired to use it for any purpose which I may term a non-natural use, for the purpose of introducing into the close that which, in its natural condition, was not in or upon it—for the purpose of introducing water, either above or below ground, in quantities and in a manner not the result of any work or operation on or under the land, and if in consequence of their doing so, or in consequence of any imperfection in the mode of their doing so, the water came to escape and to pass off into the close of the plaintiff, then it appears to me that that which the defendants were doing they were doing at their own peril; and if in the course of their doing it the evil arose to which I have referred—the evil, namely, of the escape of the water, and its passing away to the close of the plaintiff and injuring the plaintiff—then for the consequence of that, in my opinion, the defendants would be liable. As *Smith* v *Kenrick* is an illustration of the first principle to which I have referred, so also the second principle to which I have referred is well illustrated by another case in the same court, *Baird* v *Williamson* (1863) 15 CBNS 376 which was also cited in the argument at the Bar.

These simple principles, if they are well founded, as it appears to me they are, really dispose of this case. The same result is arrived at on the principles referred to by Blackburn, J., in his judgment in the Court of Exchequer Chamber, where he states the opinion of that court as to the law in these words . . . [see above].

In that opinion, I must say; I entirely concur. Therefore, I have to move your Lordships that the judgment of the Court of Exchequer Chamber be affirmed, and that present appeal be dismissed with costs.

LORD CRANWORTH: I concur with my noble and learned friend in thinking that the rule of law was correctly stated by Blackburn, J, in delivering the opinion of the Exchequer Chamber. If a person brings or accumulates on his land anything which, if it should escape, may cause damage to his neighbour, he does so at his peril. If it does escape and cause damage, he is responsible, however careful he may have been, and whatever precautions he may have taken to prevent the damage. In considering whether a defendant is liable to a plaintiff for damage which the plaintiff may have sustained, the question in general is, not whether the defendant has acted with due care and caution, but whether his acts have occasioned the damage. This is all well explained in the old case of *Lambert and Olliot* v *Bessey* (1680) T Raym 421, 467. The doctrine is founded on good sense, for when one person in managing his own affairs causes, however innocently, damage to another, it is obviously only just that he should be the party to suffer. He is bound sic uti suo ut non laedat alienum. This is the principle of law applicable to cases like the present, and I do not discover in the authorities which were cited anything conflicting with it. . . .

Applying these principles of these decisions to the case now before the House, I come without hesitation to the conclusion that the judgment of the Exchequer Chamber was right. The plaintiff had a right to work his coal through the lands of Mr Whitehead and up to the old workings. If water naturally rising in the defendant's land . . . had by percolation found its way down to the plaintiff's mine through the old workings and so had impeded his operations, that would not have afforded him any ground of complaint. Even if all the old workings had been made by the defendants they would have done no more than they were entitled to do, for, according to the principle acted on in *Smith v Kenrick*, the person working the mine under the close in which the reservoir was made had a right to win and carry away all the coal without leaving any wall or barrier against Whitehead's land. But that is not the real state of the case. The defendants, in order to effect an object of their own, brought on to their land, or on to land which for this purpose may be treated as being theirs, a large accumulated mass of water, and stored it up in a reservoir. The consequence of this was damage to the plaintiff, and for that damage, however skilfully and carefully the accumulation was made, the defendants, according to the principles and authorities to which I have adverted, were certainly responsible. I concur, therefore, with my noble and learned friend in thinking that the judgment below must be affirmed, and that there must be judgment for the defendant in error.

11.1.2 THE CURRENT RULES

11.1.2.1 Non-natural user

RICKARDS v *LOTHIAN* [1911–13] All ER Rep 71 (PC)

FACTS: The defendant was the landlord of a building in multiple occupation. He provided a wash basin on an upper floor. This was left running, with the plughole blocked, by a malicious third party. The plaintiff was a tenant who suffered damage to his property from the resulting flood. He brought a claim alleging negligence and breach of the rule in *Rylands v Fletcher*. The case proceeded from the Australian Courts to the Privy Council. The Board concluded that there was ample evidence to support findings that there was no negligence, either in design or in operation of the basin by the caretaker.

LORD MOULTON: The principal contention, however, on behalf of the plaintiff was based on the doctrine customarily associated with *Rylands v Fletcher*. It was contended that it was the defendant's duty to prevent an overflow from the lavatory basin, however caused, and that he was liable in damages for not having so done, whether the overflow was due to any negligent act on his part, or to the malicious act of a third person. The legal principle which underlies the decision in *Rylands v Fletcher* was well known in English law from a very early period, but it was explained and formulated in a strikingly clear and authoritative manner in that case, and therefore, is usually referred to by that name. It is nothing other than an application of the old maxim *sic utere tuo ut alienum non læs* . . . So far as is necessary for the present case the law on the point is thus laid down by Blackburn J (LR 1 Exch at pp. 279, 280) . . .

It will be seen that Blackburn J, with characteristic carefulness, indicates that exceptions to the general rule may arise where the escape is in consequence of vis major, or the act of God, but declines to deal further with that question because it was unnecessary for the decision of the case then before him.

A few years later the question of law thus left undecided in *Rylands v Fletcher* came up for decision in a case arising out of somewhat similar circumstances. The defendant in *Nicholls v Marsland* (1876) LR 2 ExD 1, had formed on her land certain ornamental pools which contained large quantities of water. A sudden and unprecedented rainfall occurred, giving rise to a flood of such magnitude that the jury found that it could not reasonably have been anticipated. This flood caused the lakes to burst their dams, and the plaintiff's adjoining lands were flooded. The jury found that there was no negligence in the construction or maintenance of the lakes. But they also found that if such a flood could have been anticipated, the dams might have been so constructed that the flooding would have been prevented. Upon these findings the judge at the trial directed a verdict for the plaintiff, but gave leave to move to enter a verdict for the defendant. On the argument of the rule the Court of Exchequer directed the verdict to be entered for the defendant, and on appeal to the Court of Appeal that judgment was unanimously affirmed. The judgment of the Court of Appeal (Cockburn CJ, James and Mellish LJJ, Baggallay JA, and Archibald J) was read by Mellish LJ. After pointing out that the facts of the case rendered it necessary to decide the point left undecided in *Rylands* v *Fletcher* he proceeds to lay down the law thereupon in the following language:

> ... the ordinary rule of law is that when the law creates a duty and the party is disabled from performing it without any default of his own, by the act of God, or the King's enemies, the law will excuse him; but when a party by his own contract creates a duty, he is bound to make it good notwithstanding any accident by inevitable necessity. We can see no good reason why that rule should not be applied to the case before us. The duty of keeping the water in and preventing its escape is a duty imposed by the law, and not one created by contract. If, indeed, the making a reservoir was a wrongful act in itself, it might be right to hold that a person could not escape from the consequences of his own wrongful act. But it seems to us absurd to hold that the making or the keeping a reservoir is a wrongful act in itself. The wrongful act is not the making or keeping the reservoir, but the allowing or causing the water to escape. If, indeed, the damages were occasioned by the act of the party without more—as where a man accumulates water on his own land, but, owing to the peculiar nature or condition of the soil, the water escapes and does damage to his neighbour—the case of *Rylands* v *Fletcher* establishes that he must be held liable. The accumulation of water in a reservoir is not in itself wrongful; but the making it and suffering water to escape, if damage ensue, constitute a wrong. But the present case is distinguished from that of *Rylands* v *Fletcher* in this, that it is not the act of the defendant in keeping this reservoir, an act in itself lawful, which alone leads to the escape of the water, and so renders wrongful that which but for such escape would have been lawful. It is the supervening vis major of the water caused by the flood, which, superadded to the water in the reservoir (which of itself would have been innocuous), causes the disaster. A defendant, cannot, in our opinion, be properly said to have caused or allowed the water to escape, if the act of God or the Queen's enemies was the real cause of its escaping without any fault on the part of the defendant. If a reservoir was destroyed by an earthquake, or the Queen's enemies destroyed it in conducting some warlike operation, it would be contrary to all reason and justice to hold the owner of the reservoir liable for any damage which might be done by the escape of the water. We are of opinion, therefore, that the defendant was entitled to excuse herself by proving that the water escaped through the act of God.

Their Lordships are of opinion that all that is there laid down as to a case where the escape is due to vis major or the King's enemies applies equally to a case where it is due to the malicious act of a third person, if, indeed, that case is not actually included in the above phrase. To follow the language of the judgment just recited—a defendant cannot in their Lordships' opinion be properly said to have caused or allowed the water to escape if the malicious act of a third person was the real cause of its escaping without any fault on the part of the defendant. It is remarkable that the very point involved in the present case was expressly dealt with by Bramwell B, in delivering the judgment of the Court of Exchequer in the same case. He says (LR 10 Exch. at pp. 259, 260):

> What has the defendant done wrong? What right of the plaintiff has she infringed? She has done nothing wrong, she has infringed no right. It is not the defendant who let loose the water and sent it to destroy the bridges. She did indeed store it, and store it in such quantities that if it was let loose it would do as it did, mischief. But suppose that a stranger let it loose, would the defendant be liable? If so, then if a mischievous boy bored a hole in a cistern in any London house, and the water did mischief to a neighbour, the occupier of the house would be liable. That cannot be. Then why is the defendant liable if some agent over which she has no control lets the water out? ... I admit that it is not a question of negligence. A man may use all care to keep the water in ... but would be liable if through any defect, though latent, the water escaped ... But here the act is that of an agent he cannot control.

Following the language of this judgment their Lordships are of opinion that no better example could be given of an agent which the defendant cannot control than that of a third party surreptitiously and by a malicious act causing the overflow ...

Their Lordships agree with the law as laid down in the judgments above cited, and are of opinion that a defendant is not liable on the principle of *Rylands* v *Fletcher* for damage caused by the wrongful acts of third persons.

But there is another ground upon which their Lordships are of opinion that the present case does not come within the principle laid down in *Rylands* v *Fletcher*. It is not every use to which land is put that brings into play that principle. It must be some special use bringing with it increased danger to others and must not merely be the ordinary use of the and or such a use as is proper for the general benefit of the community. To use the language of Lord Robertson in *Eastern and South African Telegraph Co.* v *Cape Town Tramways Cos.* [1902] AC at p. 393, the principle of *Rylands* v *Fletcher* 'subjects to a high liability the owner who uses his property for purposes other than those which are natural.' This more fully expressed by Wright J, in his judgment in *Blake* v *Woolf* [1898] 2 QB 426. In that case the plaintiff was the occupier of the lower floors of the defendant's house, the upper floors being occupied by the defendant himself. A leak occurred in the cistern at the top of the house which, without any negligence on the part of the defendant, caused the plaintiff's premises to be flooded. In giving judgment for the defendant, Wright J, says:

> The general rule, as laid down in *Rylands* v *Fletcher* is that prima facie a person occupying land has an absolute right not to have his premises invaded by injurious matter, such as large quantities of water which his neighbour keeps upon his land. That general rule is, however, qualified by some exceptions, one of which is that, where a person is using his land in the ordinary way and damage happens to the adjoining property without any default or negligence on his part, no liability attaches to him. The bringing of water on to such premises as these and the maintaining a cistern in the usual way seems to me to be an ordinary and reasonable user of such premises as these were; and, therefore, if the water escapes without any negligence or default on the part of the person bringing the water in and owning the cistern, I do not think that he is liable for any damage that may ensue.

Their Lordships are in entire sympathy with these views. The provision of a proper supply of water to the various parts of a house is not only reasonable, but has become, in accordance with modern sanitary views, an almost necessary feature of town life. It is recognised as being so desirable in the interests of the community that in some form or other it is usually made obligatory in civilised countries. Such a supply cannot be installed without causing some concurrent danger of leakage or overflow. It could be unreasonable for the law to regard those who instal or maintain such a system of supply as doing so at their own peril, with an absolute liability for any damage resulting from its presence even when there has been no negligence. It would be still more unreasonable if, as the respondent contends, such liability were to be held to extend to the consequences of malicious acts on the part of third persons. In such matters as the domestic supply of water or gas, it is essential that the mode of supply should be such as to permit ready access for the purpose of use, and hence it is impossible to guard against wilful mischief. Taps may be turned on, ball cocks fastened open, supply pipes cut, and waste pipes blocked. Against such acts no precaution can prevail. It would be wholly unreasonable to hold an occupier responsible for the consequences of such acts which he is powerless to prevent, when the provision of the supply is not only a reasonable act on his part but probably a duty. Such a doctrine would, for example, make a householder liable for the consequences of an explosion caused by a burglar breaking into his house during the night and leaving a gas tap open. There is, in their Lordships' opinion, no support either in reason or authority for any such view of the liability of a landlord or occupier. In having on his premises such means of supply he is only using those premises in an ordinary and proper manner, and, although he is bound to exercise all reasonable care, he is not responsible for damage not due to his own default, whether that damage be caused by inevitable accident or the wrongful acts of third persons. On these grounds their Lordships are of opinion that the direction of the learned judge at the trial to the effect that

> if the plugging up were a deliberately mischievous act by some outsider unless it were instigated by the defendant himself, the defendant would not be responsible.

was correct in law, and that, upon the finding of the jury that the plugging up was the malicious act of some person, the judge ought to have directed the judgment to be entered for the defendant. The appeal must, therefore, be allowed and judgment entered for the defendant in the action with costs in all the courts, and the plaintiff must pay the costs of this appeal, and their Lordships will humbly advise His Majesty accordingly.

11.1.2.2   Escape

READ v J LYONS & CO. LTD [1946] 2 All ER 471 (HL)

FACTS: The plaintiff, a munitions inspector, was injured by an explosion in the factory where she worked. She did not allege negligence but relied on the fact that munitions making was a hazardous activity carrying strict liability. Cassels J found for her on this basis, but was reversed by the Court of Appeal. The plaintiff appealed to the House of Lords.

VISCOUNT SIMON LC: I agree that the action fails. The appellant was a person present in the factory in pursuance of a public duty . . . and was, consequently, in the same position as an invitee. The respondents were managers of the factory as agents for the Ministry of Supply and had the same responsibility to an invitee as an ordinary occupier in control of the premises. The duties of an occupier of premises to an invitee have been analysed in many reported cases, but in none of them, I think, is there any hint of the proposition necessary to support the claim of the appellant in this case. The fact that the work that was being carried on was of a kind which requires special care is a reason why the standard of care should be high, but it is no reason for saying that the occupier is liable for resulting damage to an invitee without any proof of negligence at all.

Blackburn J, in delivering the judgment of the Court of Exchequer Chamber in *Fletcher* v *Rylands* LR 1 Exch. 265, at p. 279, laid down the proposition that:

> . . . the person who, for his own purposes brings on his lands and collects and keeps there, anything likely to do mischief if it escapes, must keep it in at his peril, and, if he does not do so, is *prima facie* answerable for all the damage which is the natural consequence of its escape.

It has not always been sufficiently observed that in the House of Lords, when the appeal from *Fletcher* v *Rylands* was dismissed and Blackburn J's pronouncement was expressly approved, Lord Cairns, LC, emphasised another condition which must be satisfied before liability attaches without proof of negligence. This is that the use to which the defendant is putting his land is a 'non-natural' use. Blackburn J, had made a parenthetic reference to this sort of test when he said:

> . . . it seems but reasonable and just that the neighbour, who has brought something on his own property, *which was not naturally there*, harmless to others so long as it is confined to his own property, but which he knows to be mischievous if it gets on his neighbour's, should be obliged to make good the damage which ensues if he does not succeed in confining it to his own property.

I confess to finding this test of 'non-natural' user (or of bringing on the land what was not 'naturally there', which is not the same test) difficult to apply. Blackburn J, in the sentence immediately following that which I have last quoted, treats cattle-trespass as an example of his generalisation. The pasturing of cattle must be one of the most ordinary uses of land, and strict liability for damage done by cattle enclosed on one man's land if they escape thence into the land of another is one of the most ancient propositions of our law. It is, in fact, a case of pure trespass to property, and thus constitutes a wrong without any question of negligence: see *per* Lord Coleridge CJ, in *Ellis* v *Loftus Iron Co.* (LR 10 CP 10, at p. 12). The circumstances in *Fletcher* v *Rylands* did not constitute a case of trespass because the damage was consequential, not direct. It is to be noted that all the counts in the declaration in that case set out allegations of negligence (see LR 1 Ex. 265), but in the House of Lords Lord Cairns LC, begins his opinion by explaining that ultimately the case was treated as determining the rights of the parties independently of any question of negligence.

The classic judgment of Blackburn J, besides deciding the issue before the court and laying down the principle of duty between neighbouring occupiers of land on which the decision was based, sought to group under a single and wider proposition other instances in which liability is independent of negligence, such, for example, as liability for the bite of a defendant's monkey. There are instances, no doubt, in our law in which liability for damage may be established apart from proof of negligence, but it appears to me logically unnecessary and historically incorrect to refer to all these instances as deduced from one common principle. The conditions under which such a liability arises are not necessarily the same in each class of case. Lindley LJ, issued a valuable warning in *Green* v *Chelsea Waterworks Co.* 70 LT 547, at p. 549, when he said of *Rylands* v *Fletcher* that that decision:

> . . . is not to be extended beyond the legitimate principle on which the House of Lords decided it. If it were extended as far as strict logic might require, it would be a very oppressive decision.

It seems better, therefore, when a plaintiff relies on *Rylands* v *Fletcher* to take the conditions declared by this House to be essential for liability in that case and to ascertain whether these conditions exist in the actual case.

Now, the strict liability recognised by this House to exist in *Rylands* v *Fletcher* is conditioned by two elements which I may call the condition of 'escape' from the land of something likely to do mischief if it escapes, and the condition of 'non-natural use' of the land. This second condition has in some later cases, which did not reach this House, been otherwise expressed, e.g. as 'exceptional' user, when such user is not regarded as 'natural' and at the same time is likely to produce mischief if there is an 'escape' . . . It is not necessary to analyse this second condition on the present occasion, for in the case now before us the first essential condition of 'escape' does not seem to me to be present at all. 'Escape,' for the purposes of applying the proposition of *Rylands* v *Fletcher* means escape from a place which the defendant has occupation of, or control over, to a place which is outside his occupation or control. Blackburn J, several times refers to the defendant's duty as being the duty of 'keeping a thing in' at the defendant's peril and by 'keeping in' he means, not preventing an explosive substance from exploding, but preventing a thing which may inflict mischief from escaping from the area which the defendant occupies or controls. In two well-known cases the same principle of strict liability for escape was applied to defendants who held a franchise to lay pipes under a highway and to conduct water (or gas) under pressure through them: *Charing Cross Electric Co.* v *Hydraulic Power Co.* [1913] 3 KB 772; *Northwestern Utilities, Ltd* v *London Guarantee, etc., Co.* [1936] AC 108.

In *Howard* v *Furness Houlder Argentine Lines, Ltd* [1936] All ER 781 Lewis J, had before him a case of injury caused by an escape of steam on board a ship where the plaintiff was working. The judge was, I think, right in refusing to apply the doctrine of *Rylands* v *Fletcher* on the ground that the injuries were caused on the premises of the defendants. Apart altogether from the judge's doubt (which I share) whether the owners of the steamship by generating steam therein are making a non-natural use of their steamship, the other condition on which the proposition in *Rylands* v *Fletcher* depends was not present, any more than it is in the case with which we have now to deal. Here there is no escape of the relevant kind at all and the appellant's action fails on that ground.

In these circumstances it becomes unnecessary to consider other objections that have been raised, such as the question whether the doctrine of *Rylands* v *Fletcher* applies where the claim is for damages for personal injury as distinguished from damages to property. It may be noted, in passing, that Blackburn J, himself when referring to the doctrine of *Rylands* v *Fletcher* in the later case of *Cattle* v *Stockton Waterworks* (1875) LR 10 QB 453 leaves this undealt with. He treats damages under the *Rylands* v *Fletcher* principle as covering damages to property, such as workmen's clothes or tools, but says nothing about liability for personal injuries.

11.1.3 THE STATUS OF THE TORT

NUCLEAR INSTALLATIONS ACT 1965

7. Duty of licensee of licensed site

(1) Where a nuclear site licence has been granted in respect of any site, it shall be the duty of the licensee to secure that—

(a) no such occurrence involving nuclear matter as is mentioned in subsection (2) of this section causes injury to any person or damage to any property of any person other than the licensee, being injury or damage arising out of or resulting from the radioactive properties, or a combination of those and any toxic, explosive or other hazardous properties, of that nuclear matter; and

(b)   no ionising radiations emitted during the period of the licensee's responsibility—

(i)   from anything caused or suffered by the licensee to be on the site which is not nuclear matter; or

(ii)   from any waste discharged (in whatever form) on or from the site,

cause injury to any person or damage to any property of any person other than the licensee.

(2)   The occurrences referred to in subsection (1)(a) of this section are—

(a)   any occurrence on the licensed site during the period of the licensee's responsibility, being an occurrence involving nuclear matter;

(b)   any occurrence elsewhere than on the licensed site involving nuclear matter which is not excepted matter and which at the time of the occurrence—

(i)   is in the course of carriage on behalf of the licensee as licensee of that site; or

(ii)   is in the course of carriage to that site with the agreement of the licensee from a place outside the relevant territories; and

(iii)   in either case, is not on any other relevant site in the United Kingdom;

(c)   any occurrence elsewhere than on the licensed site involving nuclear matter which is not excepted matter and which—

(i)   having been on the licensed site at any time during the period of the licensee's responsibility; or

(ii)   having been in the course of carriage on behalf of the licensee as licensee of that site,

has not subsequently been on any relevant site, or in the course of any relevant carriage, or (except in the course of relevant carriage) within the territorial limits of a country which is not a relevant territory.

(3)   In determining the liability by virtue of subsection (1) of this section in respect of any occurrence of the licensee of a licensed site, any property which at the time of the occurrence is on that site, being—

(a)   a nuclear installation; or

(b)   other property which is on that site—

(i)   for the purpose of use in connection with the operation, or the cessation of the operation, by the licensee of a nuclear installation which is or has been on that site; or

(ii)   for the purpose of the construction of a nuclear installation on that site, shall, notwithstanding that it is the property of some other person, be deemed to be the property of the licensee.

12.   Right to compensation by virtue of ss. 7 to 10

(1)   Where any injury or damage has been caused in breach of a duty imposed by section 7, 8, 9 or 10 of this Act—

(a)   subject to sections 13(1), (3) and (4), 15 and 17(1) of this Act, compensation in respect of that injury or damage shall be payable in accordance with section 16 of this Act wherever the injury or damage was incurred;

(b)   subject to subsections (3) and (4) of this section and to section 21(2) of this Act, no other liability shall be incurred by any person in respect of that injury or damage.

(2)   Subject to subsection (3) of this section, any injury or damage which, though not caused in breach of such a duty as aforesaid, is not reasonably separable from injury or damage so caused shall be deemed for the purposes of subsection (1) of this section to have been so caused.

(3)   Where any injury or damage is caused partly in breach of such a duty as aforesaid and partly by an emission of ionising radiations which does not constitute such a breach, subsection (2) of this section shall not affect any liability of any person in respect of that emission apart from this Act, but a claimant shall not be entitled to recover compensation in respect of the same injury or damage both under this Act and otherwise than under this Act.

13.   Exclusion, extension or reduction of compensation in certain cases

(1)   Subject to subsections (2) and (5) of this section, compensation shall not be payable under this Act in respect of injury or damage caused by a breach of a duty imposed by section 7, 8, 9 or 10 thereof if the injury or damage—

(a)   was caused by such an occurrence as is mentioned in section 7(2)(b) or (c) or 10(2)(b) of this Act which is shown to have taken place wholly within the territorial limits of one, and one only, of the relevant territories other than the United Kingdom; or

(b)   was incurred within the territorial limits of a country which is not a relevant territory.

(2)   In the case of a breach of a duty imposed by section 7, 8 or 9 of this Act, subsection (1)(b) of this section shall not apply to injury or damage incurred by, or by persons or property on, a ship or aircraft registered in the United Kingdom.

(4)   The duty imposed by section 7, 8, 9, 10 or 11 of this Act—

(a)   shall not impose any liability on the person subject to that duty with respect to injury or damage caused by an occurrence which constitutes a breach of that duty if the occurrence, or the causing thereby of the injury or damage, is attributable to hostile action in the course of any armed conflict, including any armed conflict within the United Kingdom; but

(b)   shall impose such a liability where the occurrence, or the causing thereby of the injury or damage, is attributable to a natural disaster, notwithstanding that the disaster is of such an exceptional character that it could not reasonably have been foreseen.

(6)   The amount of compensation payable to or in respect of any person under this Act in respect of any injury or damage caused in breach of a duty imposed by section 7, 8, 9 or 10 of this Act may be reduced by reason of the fault of that person if, but only if, and to the extent that, the causing of that injury or damage is attributable to any act of that person committed with the intention of causing harm to any person or property or with reckless disregard for the consequences of his act.

11.2   Fire

11.2.1   THE GENERAL NEGLIGENCE BASED ACTION

11.2.1.1   Meaning of 'accidental'

MUSGROVE v *PANDELIS* [1918–19] All ER Rep 589

FACTS: The defendant's servant, Coumis, while starting the defendant's car managed to ignite the petrol in the carburettor (not an uncommon fault in cars at that time). He should have turned off the tap allowing petrol to flow from the tank to the carburettor. The fire would then have quickly burnt itself out harmlessly. The servant failed to do this, and the fire then spread to the plaintiff's adjoining premises.

BANKS LJ: The plaintiff alleges that the fire was caused by Coumis's negligence. The negligence finally relied on was that he did not at once turn off the petrol tap and so stop the further flow of petrol into the carburettor. If that had been done, the fire would have exhausted itself without doing any damage. The defendant's main defence, apart from disputing the negligence, was based on s. 86 of the Fires Prevention (Metropolis) Act, 1774, and the argument has been chiefly directed to the construction of that section. Lush J, came to the conclusion that the section did not apply at all; and I agree. He also held that, if that view was not correct, the fire which caused the damage had not an accidental beginning within the meaning of the Act. And there also I agree.

Section 86 of the Act was passed to take the place of a section in almost the same words of the Act of 6 Anne, c. 31, s. 6. In order to see what alteration these statutes effected, it is material to consider the state of the law before the earlier statute was passed. A man was liable at common law for damage done by fire originating on his own property (i) for the mere escape of the fire; (ii) if the fire was caused by the negligence of himself or his servants, or by his own wilful act; (iii) upon the principle of *Rylands* v *Fletcher*. This principle was not then known by that name, because *Rylands* v *Fletcher* was not then decided; but it was an existing principle of the common law. The alteration which those statutes effected was to give protection in cases falling under the first heading of liability mentioned above. It is thus stated by Lord Denman CJ, in *Filliter* v *Phippard* (1847) 11 QB 347:

The ancient law, or rather custom of England, appears to have been, that a person in whose house a fire originated, which afterwards spread to his neighbour's property and destroyed it, must make good the loss.

That was the principle of the common law to which the statutes were directed. They altered the law so as to exclude the liability of a 'person in whose house, chamber, stable, barn, or other building, or on whose estate any fire shall . . . accidentally begin.' It is plain that the statutes did not touch the other heads of liability at common law. The second head is not within the protection; that was decided by *Filliter* v *Phippard* where it held that the Act of Geo. 3 did not apply to a fire which was caused either deliberately or negligently. Why, if that is the law as to the second head of liability, should it be otherwise as to the third head, the liability on the principle of *Rylands* v *Fletcher*? If that liability existed, there is no reason why the statute should alter it and yet leave untouched the liability for fire caused by negligence or design. That the principle of *Rylands* v *Fletcher* existed long before that case was decided is plain. In *Vaughan* v *Menlove* (1837) 3 Bing NC 468 Tindal CJ, says: 'There is a rule of law which says you must so enjoy your own property as not to injure that of another.' . . . *Rylands* v *Fletcher* is merely an illustration of that old principle, and in my opinion Lush J, was right in saying that this case, if it falls within that principle, is not within the protection of the statute. The question then is whether this motor car, with its petrol tank full or partially filled with petrol, was a dangerous thing to bring into the garage within the principle of *Rylands* v *Fletcher*. Counsel for the defendant says a motor car is not a dangerous thing unless it is in such a condition that an accident is to be apprehended. But the expectation of danger is not the basis of the principle of *Rylands* v *Fletcher*. A thing may be dangerous although the danger is unexpected. I agree with Lush J, that this motor car was dangerous within that principle. The defendant brought it, or caused it to be brought, upon his premises, and he is responsible for the fire which resulted, and is not within the protection of the statute. The other point is the meaning of the fire to which the statute refers when it speaks of a person in whose house, chamber, stable, &c., 'any fire shall . . . accidentally begin.' The section is dealing with a fire which occasions damage, and it is in reference to that fire that it says no action shall be maintained nor shall any recompense be made by such person for any damage suffered or occasioned thereby. No more can be said as matter of law than that the fire contemplated by the Act is the fire which causes the damage, and so it is necessary in each case to consider what that fire was in view of the facts of the particular case. In this case it is impossible to say that the spark which ignited the petrol, though no doubt it was the original cause of the fire, was the fire which caused the damage. As well might it be said that a housemaid lighting a match makes a fire which, becoming ignited from the grate, ultimately consumes the house. In this case the fire which caused the damage began when the flaming petrol acquired such volume as to become a source of danger. So long as the fire was merely the ignition of a small amount of petrol, which if left to itself would have burnt itself out in the carburettor, it was like the housemaid's match; but when it became a raging fire supplied from the petrol tank so that it spread to parts of the car and from them to the property, this was the fire which caused the damage. It did not accidentally begin. It was the direct consequence of Coumis's negligence in not turning off the petrol tap. This was the view of Lush J, and I agree with him.

The defendant's counsel contended that negligence ought not to be imputed to Coumis; that he was placed in a difficult position, and cannot be blamed for not having taken the best possible course on the first possible opportunity. That is a point of much weight which was properly pressed upon the court below and in this court; but it was open to Lush J, to take the view that the real cause of the disaster was the meddling with a motor car by a man who had no more than an elementary knowledge of its construction, and did not recognise that in the circumstances the only thing to do was to turn off the tap. Whether the damage was caused by Coumis's negligence, for which the defendant is responsible, or by the defendant's own negligence in employing a man with so little knowledge, in either case the judgment must stand and the appeal must be dismissed.

SOCHACKI v *SAS* [1947] 1 All ER 344

FACTS: The plaintiff was a lodger in the defendant's house. He had a fire in the grate and, one day, a fire started in his room and spread to the rest of the house, causing considerable damage. The plaintiff commenced an action for a debt owing him and the defendants counterclaimed for damages arising from the fire. There was no evidence the plaintiff was negligent in having or looking after the fire in the grate.

LORD GODDARD CJ: The question which I have to determine is whether or not the plaintiff is responsible for damage caused by the fire in the absence of any evidence of negligence. In my opinion, he is not. I do not think the doctrine in *Rylands* v *Fletcher* applies to a case of this sort. He was using his room in the ordinary, natural way in which the room could be used. It is not the case of a fire starting on one owner's premises and spreading to the premises of an adjoining owner. If a fire is negligently or improperly started by a person on his land, as, for instance, lighting a bonfire which spreads, he may be liable, not merely to an adjoining owner who suffers damage, but to any other person who suffers damage. If I happen to be on somebody else's land at a time when a fire spreads to that land and my motor car or property is destroyed, I have just as much right against the person who improperly allows the fire to escape from his land as the owner of the land on which I happen to be. I do not doubt that for a moment, but here the fire was being used by a man in a fireplace in his own room. There was an ordinary, natural, proper, everyday use of a fireplace in his room. The fireplace was there to be used. The plaintiff was using it with the assent of the defendants. There is no necessity for him to show that the defendants said in so many words: 'You may have a fire.' They licensed him to be the occupier of a room at a time when it was natural and proper for a man to have a fire. If a person goes into lodgings where the landlady provides a fireplace, and he uses it for a fire in a proper way, the landlady, in my opinion, has no claim against that person if a fire happens to take place in his room unless there is negligence on his part. The consequence of holding otherwise would certainly be remarkable, because it seems to me that, if I gave effect to counsel's argument, it would follow that, if a man living in a house lit a fire in his room, and, owing to the construction of the fireplace or some defect in a fire-brick, a fire took place, he would be responsible, because, it is said, if one lights the fire, one is responsible for keeping the fire in. I do not think that is the law. If a person living in a house does no more than light a fire in a fireplace, and through some unhappy accident a fire occurs, he is certainly not liable under *Rylands* v *Fletcher*, a very hard-worked case, which the House of Lords said recently should not be extended. Therefore, in the absence of evidence of negligence, there is no ground for holding the plaintiff liable on the counterclaim.

Counsel for the defendants argued that I am bound to apply the doctrine of *res ipsa loquitur*, but I do not think this is a case of *res ipsa loquitur*. Everybody knows fires occur through accidents which happen without negligence on anybody's part. There is nothing here to show that the plaintiff left any improper fire in his room, any larger fire than usual, a fire which was too large for the grate, or anything like that. There was a fire burning in his room. He left his room for two or three hours. I do not consider that the doctrine of *res ipsa loquitur* could possibly apply to a case such as this. I come to the conclusion here that there is no evidence of negligence against the plaintiff in this case, and without evidence of negligence there is no liability on the plaintiff for the fire.

11.2.2 THE LATEST WORD ON FIRE

MASON v LEVY AUTO PARTS OF ENGLAND LTD [1967] 2 All ER 62

FACTS: A wholly unexplained fire broke out in the defendant's yard, where they stored a variety of items, many flammable, such as paint and oil. The fire spread to the plaintiff's adjoining hedge. The defendants successfully pleaded the defence under s. 86, Fires Prevention (Metropolis) Act 1774, but the plaintiff also relied on *Rylands* v *Fletcher*.

MACKENNA J: Has the plaintiff proved that the defendants were negligent, which is his second point? Or has he brought the case within *Rylands* v *Fletcher* or any similar principle of liability, which is his third point? In his particulars the plaintiff charges the defendants with providing no adequate means of detecting or extinguishing fire. I do not think that either of these charges was proved. The defendants were under no duty to maintain a constant look-out for fire, and this fire was in any case detected at an early stage by the defendant's workmen. The appliances recommended by the fire brigade had been provided, and if it proved impossible to control or extinguish the fire by these means that is not the fault of the defendants for failing to provide more or better equipment. Such appliances are, anyhow, intended only as first-aid. That they were ineffective to control or extinguish this fire is not proof of any culpable failure to provide more adequate equipment. Then it is said that the crates were so closely stacked 'that there was no reasonable access between them for fire-fighting purposes'. This was true of some parts of the yard, but I have no reason to suppose that if it had been otherwise this fire would have been controlled. As I see it, the plaintiff's real case against the defendants is in the allegation that they 'so used their land by cluttering it with combustible material closely packed that the plaintiff's land was endangered'. This, like the plaintiff's other allegations, is put against the defendants in alternative ways, including negligence, nuisance, allowing a dangerous thing, namely fire, to escape from their land, and as a failure so to use their land as not to harm the plaintiff.

I shall consider it under the two last of these heads, beginning, as one must, with *Musgrove* v *Pandelis* in the Court of Appeal, whose facts are too well known to be re-told: in that case Bankes LJ, reasoned thus: (a) there were at common law three separate heads of liability for damage done by fire originating on a man's property, (i) for the mere escape of the fire; (ii) if the fire was caused by the negligence of himself or his servants, or by his own wilful act; (iii) on the principle of *Rylands* v *Fletcher*. (b) *Filliter* v *Phippard* (1847) 11 QB 347 decided that the statute did not cover the second case. (c) Bankes LJ, asked: 'Why, if that is the law as to the second head of liability, should it be otherwise as to the third head, the liability on the principle of *Rylands* v *Fletcher*?' The answer, I would have said with respect, is obvious enough. There were not three heads of liability at common law but only one. A person from whose land a fire escaped was held liable to his neighbour unless he could prove that it had started or spread by the act of a stranger or of God. *Filliter's* case had given a special meaning to the words 'accidental fire' used in the statute, holding that they did not include fires due to negligence, but covered only cases of 'a fire produced by mere chance, or incapable of being traced to any cause.' But it does not follow, because that meaning may be given to 'accidental,' that the statute does not cover cases of the *Rylands* v *Fletcher* kind where the occupier is held liable for the escape though no fault is proved against him. In such cases the fire may be 'produced by mere chance' or may be 'incapable of being traced to any cause.' Bankes LJ was making a distinction unknown to the common law, between 'the mere escape of fire' (which was his first head) and its escape under *Rylands* v *Fletcher* conditions (which was his third), and was imputing an intention to the legislature of exempting from liability in the former case and not in the latter. In holding that an exemption given to accidental fires, 'any law, usage, or custom to the contrary notwithstanding,' does not include fires for which liability might be imposed upon the principle of *Rylands* v *Fletcher*, the Court of Appeal went very far. But it is my duty to follow them unless *Musgrove's* case has been overruled, or unless its principle does not apply to the facts proved here.

Musgrove's case has not been overruled; that is certain. . . .

What then, is the principle? As Romer LJ in *Collingwood's* case pointed out ([1936] 3 All ER 200), it cannot be exactly that of *Rylands* v *Fletcher*. A defendant is not held liable under *Rylands* v *Fletcher* unless two conditions are satisfied: (i) that he has brought something on to his land likely to do mischief if it escapes, which has in fact escaped, and (ii) that those things happened in the course of some non-natural user of the land. But in *Musgrove's* case the car had not escaped from the land, neither had the petrol in its tank. The principle must be, Romer LJ said, the wider one on which *Rylands* v *Fletcher* itself was based, 'sic utere tuo . . .'

If, for the rule in *Musgrove's* case to apply, there need be no escape of anything brought on to the defendant's land, what must be proved against him? There is, it seems to me, a choice of alternatives. The first would require the plaintiff to prove (1) that the defendant had brought something on to his land likely to do mischief if it escaped; (2) that he had done so in the course of a non-natural user of the land; and (3) that the thing had ignited and that the fire had spread. The second would be to hold the defendant liable if (1) he brought on to his land things likely to catch fire, and kept them there in such conditions that if they did ignite the fire would be likely to spread to the plaintiffs land; (2) he did so in the course of some non-natural use; and (3) the things ignited and the fire spread. The second test is, I think, the more reasonable one. To make the likelihood of damage if the thing escapes a criterion of liability, when the thing has not in fact escaped but has caught fire, would not be very sensible.

11.3 End of Chapter Assessment Question

What torts, if any, have been committed in the following cases:

(a) Damian has bought an old rubbish tip to use as a lorry park. Methane from the tip builds up in the basement of Enid's bungalow, which explodes, injuring Enid and her mother, Gertrude, who is visiting her.

(b) Hamlet establishes a hostel for wayward children. In November the children scour the neighbourhood for timber and remove gates and fences belonging to various neighbours. On Guy Fawkes Night the resultant bonfire causes such dense smoke that the nearby motorway is closed for an hour. On 7 November the fire, which has been left to burn itself out, is revived by a strong wind and burns down the neighbouring bus shelter

11.4 End of Chapter Assessment Outline Answer

(a) Damian may potentially be liable in negligence, private nuisance or the rule in *Rylands* v *Fletcher*. His predecessor (X), who operated the tip may also be liable. Much will depend on what Damian and X knew, or ought to have known about the state of the tip and the state of knowledge about the behaviour of methane in landfill sites. This is a recognised hazard today as a result of explosions and other problems at various sites, but was not recognised as a problem until the mid 1980s. Prior to this it was assumed that any methane produced percolated to the surface and dispersed.

If Enid can establish any of the causes of action she will be able to recover for the damage to her property and for her personal injuries. Both are foreseeable types of harm for negligence and in nuisance. The weight of opinion is that damages can be recovered for personal injuries in *Rylands* v *Fletcher*: *Hale* v *Jennings Bros* (1938), *Perry* v *Kendricks Transport* (1956), but there are dicta to the contrary in *Read* v *Lyons* (1947). Gertrude cannot sue in nuisance as she is a non-occupier: *Malone* v *Lasky* (1907). She probably cannot sue under *Rylands* v *Fletcher*, as the dicta in *Weller* v *Foot & Mouth Disease Research Institute* (1966) limiting claims to occupiers must be preferred to those in *Perry* v *Kendricks Transport* and *Shiffman* v *Order of St John* (1936) in the light of the reassimilation of the rule to nuisance in *Cambridge Water* v *Eastern Counties Leather* (1994). She would therefore need to prove negligence, i.e., that Damian (and/or X) foresaw or ought to have foreseen a build-up, escape and explosion. This foresight need not be precise but there must be a real rather than a fanciful risk: *Hughes* v *Lord Advocate* (1963). She must also establish a duty of care: *Caparo* v *Dickman* (1989).

In view of the decision in *Cambridge Water* it will be preferable to rely on *Rylands* v *Fletcher* rather than private nuisance in some other form if the elements of negligence are not all present. Use of land as a rubbish tip is likely to be regarded as non-natural under the more relaxed interpretation of that term in *Cambridge Water*. There has been an accumulation and a dangerous escape. The key issue will be whether harm of this kind was foreseeable. The advantage to Enid is that the original activities need not be negligent. In *Cambridge Water* the House of Lords declined to consider liability on the basis of current knowledge. The crucial question the defendant should have asked himself at the time is 'Do my activities (in designing, operating or capping off the tip) even if done carefully create a risk of methane migration to adjoining property resulting in explosion?'

(b) The first question is whether the depredations of the children entail liability for Hamlet. The establishment of a disruptive activity on premises may be a private nuisance: *Thompson-Schwab* v *Costaki* (1956). Hamlet appears to be actively operating this activity, rather than merely permitting them to occupy the premises so cannot avoid liability on the basis of *Smith* v *Scott* (1973). It was held in *A-G* v *Corke* (1933) that permitting an encampment of transients who then 'escaped' and committed anti-social acts was within the rule in *Rylands* v *Fletcher*, but this seems dubious as the specific acts result from the free will of the actors and has not been followed in New Zealand: *Matheson* v *Northcote College* (1975). The individual children are of course liable in conversion and or trespass to goods, but Hamlet will not be jointly liable unless they were acting on his instructions.

The smoke from the fire would appear to constitute a public nuisance. It certainly interferes with the public right to use the motorway. It is not suggested that the smoke itself is toxic, so *Rylands* v *Fletcher* does not seem appropriate. The later spread of the fire may be actionable both on the basis of the common law liability for fire and the quasi *Rylands* v *Fletcher* liability as set out in *Mason* v *Levy Auto Parts of England* (1967). The original fire was started intentionally. Unless it is argued that the flare-up is to be treated as a separate fire (c.f. *Musgrove* v *Pandelis* (1919) and *Sochacki* v *Sas* (1947)) which is itself accidental the defence to the common law claim under s. 86 of the Fires Prevention (Metropolis) Act 1774 will not apply. For the *Rylands* v *Fletcher* liability, there has clearly been an accumulation of flammable material and the fire has spread. The only question is whether this amounts to a non-natural user. This will be a question of fact and degree. An ordinary domestic scale bonfire is plainly natural; a major event with imported materials on a large scale may well be non-natural.

CHAPTER TWELVE

DEFAMATION

12.1 General Considerations

DEFAMATION ACT 1952

2. Slander affecting official, professional or business reputation
In an action for slander in respect of words calculated to disparage the plaintiff in an office, profession, calling, trade or business held or carried on by him at the time of the publication, it shall not be necessary to allege or prove special damage, whether or not the words are spoken of the plaintiff in the way of his office, profession, calling, trade or business.

3. Slander of title, etc
(1) In an action for slander of title, slander of goods or other malicious falsehood, it shall not be necessary to allege or prove special damage—

(a) if the words upon which the action is founded are calculated to cause pecuniary damage to the plaintiff and are published in writing or other permanent form; or

(b) if the said words are calculated to cause pecuniary damage to the plaintiff in respect of any office, profession, calling, trade or business held or carried on by him at the time of the publication.

(2) Section one of this Act shall apply for the purposes of this section as it applies for the purposes of the law of libel and slander.

5. Justification
In an action for libel or slander in respect of words containing two or more distinct charges against the plaintiff, a defence of justification shall not fail by reason only that the truth of every charge is not proved if the words not proved to be true do not materially injure the plaintiff's reputation having regard to the truth of the remaining charges.

6. Fair comment
In an action for libel or slander in respect of words consisting partly of allegations of fact and partly of expression of opinion, a defence of fair comment shall not fail by reason only that the truth of every allegation or fact is not proved if the expression of opinion is fair comment having regard to such of the facts alleged or referred to in the words complained of as are proved.
. . .

10. Limitation on privilege at elections
A defamatory statement published by or on behalf of a candidate in any election to local government authority or to Parliament shall not be deemed to be published on a privileged occasion on the ground that it is material to a question in issue in the election, whether or not the person by whom it is published is qualified to vote at the election.

11. Agreements for indemnity
An agreement for indemnifying any person against civil liability for libel in respect of the publication of any matter shall not be unlawful unless at the time of the publication that

person knows that the matter is defamatory, and does not reasonably believe that there is a good defence to any action brought upon it.

DEFAMATION ACT 1996

1.   Responsibility for publication

(1)   In defamation proceedings a person has a defence if he shows that—

(a)   he was not the author, editor or publisher of the statement complained of,

(b)   he took reasonable care in relation to its publication, and

(c)   he did not know, and had no reason to believe, that what he did caused or contributed to the publication of a defamatory statement.

(2)   For this purpose 'author', 'editor' and 'publisher' have the following meanings, which are further explained in subsection (3)—

'author' means the originator of the statement, but does not include a person who did not intend that his statement be published at all;

'editor' means a person having editorial or equivalent responsibility for the content of the statement or the decision to publish it; and

'publisher' means a commercial publisher, that is, a person whose business is issuing material to the public, or a section of the public, who issues material containing the statement in the course of that business.

(3)   A person shall not be considered the author, editor or publisher of a statement if he is only involved—

(a)   in printing, producing, distributing or selling printed material containing the statement;

(b)   in processing, making copies of, distributing, exhibiting or selling a film or sound recording (as defined in Part I of the Copyright, Designs and Patents Act 1988) containing the statement;

(c)   in processing, making copies of, distributing or selling any electronic medium in or on which the statement is recorded, or in operating any equipment by means of which the statement is retrieved, copied or distributed;

(d)   as the broadcaster of a live programme containing the statement in circumstances in which he has no effective control over the maker of the statement;

(e)   as the operator of or provider of access to a communications system by means of which the statement is transmitted, or made available, by a person over whom he has no effective control.

In a case not within paragraphs (a) to (e) the court may have regard to those provisions by way of analogy in deciding whether a person is to be considered the author, editor or publisher of a statement.

(4)   Employees or agents of an author, editor or publisher are in the same position as their employer or principal to the extent that they are responsible for the content of the statement or the decision to publish it.

(5)   In determining for the purposes of this section whether a person took reasonable care, or had reason to believe that what he did caused or contributed to the publication of a defamatory statement, regard shall be had to—

(a)   the extent of his responsibility for the content of the statement or the decision to publish it,

(b)   the nature or circumstances of the publication, and

(c)   the previous conduct or character of the author, editor or publisher.

(6)   This section does not apply to any cause of action which arose before the section came into force.

2.   Offer to make amends

(1)   A person who has published a statement alleged to be defamatory of another may offer to make amends under this section.

(2)   The offer may be in relation to the statement generally or in relation to a specific defamatory meaning which the person making the offer accepts that the statement conveys ('a qualified offer').

(3)   An offer to make amends—

(a)   must be in writing,

(b) must be expressed to be an offer to make amends under section 2 of the Defamation Act 1996, and

(c) must state whether it is a qualified offer and, if so, set out the defamatory meaning in relation to which it is made.

(4) An offer to make amends under this section is an offer—

(a) to make a suitable correction of the statement complained of and a sufficient apology to the aggrieved party,

(b) to publish the correction and apology in a manner that is reasonable and practicable in the circumstances, and

(c) to pay the aggrieved party such compensation (if any), and such costs, as may be agreed or determined to be payable.

The fact that the offer is accompanied by an offer to take specific steps does not affect the fact that an offer to make amends under this section is an offer to do all the things mentioned in paragraphs (a) to (c).

(5) An offer to make amends under this section may not be made by a person after serving a defence in defamation proceedings brought against him by the aggrieved party in respect of the publication in question.

(6) An offer to make amends under this section may be withdrawn before it is accepted; and a renewal of an offer which has been withdrawn shall be treated as a new offer.

3. Accepting an offer to make amends

(1) If an offer to make amends under section 2 is accepted by the aggrieved party, the following provisions apply.

(2) The party accepting the offer may not bring or continue defamation proceedings in respect of the publication concerned against the person making the offer, but he is entitled to enforce the offer to make amends, as follows.

(3) If the parties agree on the steps to be taken in fulfilment of the offer, the aggrieved party may apply to the court for an order that the other party fulfil his offer by taking the steps agreed.

(4) If the parties do not agree on the steps to be taken by way of correction, apology and publication, the party who made the offer may take such steps as he thinks appropriate, and may in particular—

(a) make the correction and apology by a statement in open court in terms approved by the court, and

(b) give an undertaking to the court as to the manner of their publication.

(5) If the parties do not agree on the amount to be paid by way of compensation, it shall be determined by the court on the same principles as damages in defamation proceedings.

The court shall take account of any steps taken in fulfilment of the offer and (so far not agreed between the parties) of the suitability of the correction, the sufficiency of the apology and whether the manner of their publication was reasonable in the circumstances, and may reduce or increase the amount of compensation accordingly.

(6) If the parties do not agree on the amount to be paid by way of costs, it shall be determined by the court on the same principles as costs awarded in court proceedings.

(7) The acceptance of an offer by one person to make amends does not affect any cause of action against another person in respect of the same publication, subject as follows.

(8) In England and Wales or Northern Ireland, for the purposes of the Civil Liability (Contribution) Act 1978—

(a) the amount of compensation paid under the offer shall be treated as paid in bona fide settlement or compromise of the claim; and

(b) where another person is liable in respect of the same damage (whether jointly or otherwise), the person whose offer to make amends was accepted is not required to pay by virtue of any contribution under section 1 of that Act a greater amount than the amount of the compensation payable in pursuance of the offer.

(9) In Scotland—

(a) subsection (2) of section 3 of the Law Reform (Miscellaneous Provisions) (Scotland) Act 1940 (right of one joint wrongdoer as respects another to recover contribution towards damages) applies in relation to compensation paid under an offer to make amends as it applies in relation to damages in an action to which that section applies; and

(b) where another person is liable in respect of the same damage (whether jointly or otherwise), the person whose offer to make amends was accepted is not required to pay by virtue of any contribution under section 3(2) of that Act a greater amount than the amount of compensation payable in pursuance of the offer.

(10)   Proceedings under this section shall be heard and determined without a jury.

4.   Failure to accept offer to make amends

(1)   If an offer to make amends under section 2, duly made and not withdrawn, is not accepted by the aggrieved party, the following provisions apply.

(2)   The fact that the offer was made is a defence (subject to subsection (3)) to defamation proceedings in respect of the publication in question by that party against the person making the offer.

A qualified offer is only a defence in respect of the meaning to which the offer related.

(3)   There is no such defence if the person by whom the offer was made knew or had reason to believe that the statement complained of—

(a)   referred to the aggrieved party or was likely to be understood as referring to him, and

(b)   was both false and defamatory of that party;

but it shall be presumed until the contrary is shown that he did not know and had no reason to believe that was the case.

(4)   The person who made the offer need not rely on it by way of defence, but if he does he may not rely on any other defence.

If the offer was a qualified offer, this applies only in respect of the meaning to which the offer related.

(5)   The offer may be relied on in mitigation of damages whether or not it was relied on as a defence.

. . .

7.   Ruling on the meaning of a statement

In defamation proceedings the court shall not be asked to rule whether a statement is arguably capable, as opposed to capable, of bearing a particular meaning or meanings attributed to it.

. . .

15.   Reports, &c. protected by qualified privilege

(1)   The publication of any report or other statement mentioned in Schedule 1 to this Act is privileged unless the publication is shown to be made with malice, subject as follows.

(2)   In defamation proceedings in respect of the publication of a report or other statement mentioned in Part II of that Schedule, there is no defence under this section if the plaintiff shows that the defendant—

(a)   was requested by him to publish in a suitable manner a reasonable letter or statement by way of explanation or contradiction, and

(b)   refused or neglected to do so.

For this purpose 'in a suitable manner' means in the same manner as the publication complained of or in a manner that is adequate and reasonable in the circumstances.

(3)   This section does not apply to the publication to the public, or a section of the public, of matter which is not of public concern and the publication of which is not for the public benefit.

(4)   Nothing in this section shall be construed—

(a)   as protecting the publication of matter the publication of which is prohibited by law, or

(b)   as limiting or abridging any privilege subsisting apart from this section.

17.   Interpretation

(1)   In this Act—

'publication' and 'publish', in relation to a statement, have the meaning they have for the purposes of the law of defamation generally, but 'publisher' is specially defined for the purposes of section 1;

'statement' means words, pictures, visual images, gestures or any other method of signifying meaning; and

'statutory provision' means—

(a) a provision contained in an Act or in subordinate legislation within the meaning of the Interpretation Act 1978, or

(b) a statutory provision within the meaning given by section 1(f) of the Interpretation Act (Northern Ireland) 1954.

12.2 Reference to the Plaintiff

12.2.1 INDIRECT REFERENCE

KNUPFFER v LONDON EXPRESS NEWSPAPERS **[1944] 1 All ER 495 (HL)**

FACTS: The defendant published a newspaper article describing the activities of a political group of Russian exiles called Mlado Russ (Young Russia). The group had a large membership abroad but only 24 members in the UK. The article referred to the organisation in general, not to the UK branch or any individual. The words used would have been defamatory if used of a named person. The plaintiff was the active head of the UK branch. He produced witnesses who testified that they understood the article as referring to him.

The case ultimately went to the House of Lords.

VISCOUNT SIMON LC: My Lords, it is an essential element of the cause of action for defamation that the words complained of should be published 'of the plaintiff.' If the words are not so published, the plaintiff is not defamed and cannot have any right to ask that the defendant should be held responsible to him in respect of them. In the case now before us the trial judge, Stable J, decided that the words of the libel did refer to the plaintiff. The Court of Appeal, consisting of MacKinnon and Goddard, LJ, decided that the words could not be regarded as referring to the plaintiff, and consequently allowed the appeal and dismissed the action. This is the issue which we now have to decide.

The defendants printed and published in their newspaper on July 1, 1941, the words following, which are set out in the statement of claim:

But the quislings on whom Hitler flatters himself he can build a pro-German movement within the Soviet Union are an emigre group called Mlado Russ or Young Russia.

They are a minute body professing a pure Fascist ideology who have long sought a suitable fuehrer—I know with what success. Established in France and the United States they claim to have secret agents able to enter or leave the Soviet Union at will.

Hitler intends to nominate a puppet fuehrer from their ranks to replace the Soviet national leaders of the Kremlin, and establish a reactionary totalitarian serf state on the German and Italian model.

The proposed line of operation is the seducing of Red Army officers from their allegiance to their country and with their aid destroying trade unions, co-operatives, collective farms, and the Soviet Parliamentary system with a ruthless massacre of all the present leaders, great and small, of the Russian people.

The vast majority of Russian emigrés repudiate these people, but Hitler is accustomed to find instruments among the despised dregs of every community. He intends Ukrainian pogroms as a starting point for general anarchy in Russia.

In these words there is no specific mention of the plaintiff from beginning to end, and the only countries in which it is stated that this group of emigrés is established are France and the United States. Evidence was given at the trial that the plaintiff had joined the Young Russia Party in 1928, that in 1935 he became assistant representative of the Young Russia Movement in Great Britain, and that in 1938 he was appointed representative of the Movement in Great Britain and head of the British branch of the Movement. The headquarters of the Movement were in Paris until June, 1940, when they were removed to America.

These facts standing alone, however, do not justify the conclusion that the words complained of are capable of being read as a defamation of the plaintiff. The words make allegations of a defamatory character about a body of persons—some thousands in number—who belong to a society whose members are to be found in many countries. . . .

Where the plaintiff is not named, the test which decides whether the words used refer to him is the question whether the words are such as would reasonably lead persons acquainted with the plaintiff to believe that he was the person referred to. There are cases in which the language used in reference to a limited class may be reasonably understood to refer to every member of the class, in which case every member may have a cause of action. A good example is *Browne* v *Thomson & Co.* (1912) SC 359, where a newspaper article stated that in Queenstown instructions were issued 'by the Roman Catholic religious authorities that all Protestant shop assistants were to be discharged', and where 7 pursuers who averred that they were the sole persons who exercised religious authority in name and on behalf of the Roman Catholic Church in Queenstown were held entitled to sue for libel as being individually defamed. Lord President Dunedin in that case said, at p. 363:

> I think it is quite evident that if a certain set of people are accused of having done something, and if such accusation is libellous, it is possible for the individuals in that set of people to show that they have been damnified, and it is right that they should have an opportunity of recovering damages as individuals.

In the present case, however, the appellant rejected the view that every member of the Young Russia Group could bring his own action on the words complained of, and relied on his own prominence or representative character in the Movement as establishing that the words referred to himself. There is, however, nothing in the words which refers to one member of the group rather than another. *Le Fanu* v *Malcolmson* (1848) 11 HL Cas 637 was, it is true, a decision of this House in which Lord Cottenham LC, and Lord Campbell held that the verdict of a jury awarding damages to the owners of a factory in the county of Waterford against the proprietor of a newspaper published in that county could be upheld, notwithstanding that the letter-press in the course of denouncing the alleged cruelty with which factory operatives were treated did not specifically refer to the plaintiff's factory. It appears, however, that in that case there were circumstances, such as the location of the factory, which enabled the jurors to identify the plaintiff's factory as the factory pointed at, and the Lord Chancellor observed at p. 664:

> If a party can publish a libel so framed as to describe individuals though not naming them, and not specifically describing them by any express form of words, but still so describing them that it is known who they are, as the jurors have found it to be here, and if those who must be acquainted with the circumstances connected with the party described may also come to the same conclusion, and may have no doubt that the writer of the libel intended to mean those individuals, it would be opening a very wide door to defamation, if parties suffering all the inconvenience of being libelled were not permitted to have that protection which the law affords.

It will be observed that *Le Fanu* v *Malcolmson* was a case where there were facts pointing to the particular factory which was meant to be referred to, though the article spoke in more general terms of a factory in Waterford. In the present case the statement complained of is not made concerning a particular individual, whether named or unnamed, but concerning a group of people spread over several countries and including considerable numbers. No facts were proved in evidence which could identify the plaintiff as the person individually referred to. Witnesses called for the appellant were asked the carefully framed question, 'To whom did your mind go when you read that article?' and they not unnaturally replied by pointing to the appellant himself. But that is because they happened to know the appellant as the leading member of the society in this country, and not because there is anything in the article itself which ought to suggest even to his friends that he is referred to as an individual.

There are two questions involved in the attempt to identify the appellant as the person defamed. The first question is a question of law—can the article, having regard to its language, be regarded as capable of referring to the appellant? The second question is a question of fact, namely, does the article in fact lead reasonable people, who know the appellant, to the conclusion that it does refer to him? Unless the first question can be answered in favour of the appellant, the second question does not arise, and where the trial judge went wrong was in treating evidence to support the identification in fact as governing the matter, when the first question is necessarily, as a matter of law, to be answered in the negative.

I move that this appeal be dismissed.

LORD ATKIN . . . I add a few words, however, for I wish to emphasise the point that the judgments in the Court of Appeal appear to over-elaborate the law of libel as applicable to this case. I venture to think that it is a mistake to lay down a rule as to libel on a class, and then qualify it with exceptions. The only relevant rule is that in order to be actionable the defamatory words must be understood to be published of and concerning the plaintiff. It is irrelevant that the words are published of two or more persons if they are proved to be published of him: and it is irrelevant that the two or more persons are called by some generic or class name.

There can be no law that a defamatory statement made of a firm, or trustees, or the tenants of a particular building is not actionable, if the words would reasonably be understood as published or each member of the firm or each trustee or each tenant. The reason why a libel published of a large or indeterminate number of persons described by some general name generally fails to be actionable is the difficulty of establishing that the plaintiff was in fact included in the defamatory statement: for the habit of making unfounded generalisations is ingrained in ill-educated or vulgar minds: or the words are occasionally intended to be a facetious exaggeration. Even in such cases words may be used which enable the plaintiff to prove that the words complained of were intended to be published of each member of the group, or at any rate of himself. Too much attention has been paid, I venture to think, in the textbooks and elsewhere to the decision of Willes J in 1858, in *Eastwood* v *Holmes* (1858) 1 F & F 347. It is a *nisi prius* decision in which the judge non-suited the plaintiff both because he thought there was no evidence that the words were published of the plaintiff and for other reasons, and so far as the first ground is concerned, it appears to me on the facts to be of doubtful correctness. His words, 'It only reflects on a class of persons,' are irrelevant unless they mean it does not reflect on the plaintiff: and his instance 'All lawyers are thieves' is an excellent instance of the vulgar generalisations to which I referred. It will be as well for the future for lawyers to concentrate on the question whether the words were published of the plaintiff rather than on the question whether they were spoken of a class. I agree that in the present case the words complained of are apparently an unfounded generalisation conveying imputations of disgraceful conduct, but not such as could reasonably be understood to be spoken of the plaintiff . . .

12.2.2   MISTAKEN IDENTITY

12.2.2.1   Accidental confusion

HULTON v *JONES* [1908–10] All ER 29 (CA)

FACTS: The defendant published an account of goings on at Dieppe. It was written as fact, although it seems to have been meant as fiction and contained references to one Artemus Jones, apparently a pillar of respectability in Peckham, in Dieppe with his mistress. The plaintiff, a barrister named Artemus Jones, with no connections to either Peckham or Dieppe, alleged defamation. The defendants denied any deliberate reference (although he had written for one of their journals previously, and the name may have lodged in the sub-conscious of the present writer). The plaintiff produced witnesses who stated they took the piece as fact and as referring to the plaintiff. The question of whether a confusion of this kind was actionable went to the House of Lords.

In the Court of Appeal Farwell LJ gave a judgment which was specifically endorsed by Lord Atkinson and Lord Gorell.

FARWELL LJ: The defendants contend that the verdict and judgment in this case cannot stand because it was proved that neither the writer of the libellous article nor any person in the defendants' employment, under whose notice it came before it was published, knew or had even heard of the existence of the plaintiff, and that it, therefore, necessarily follows that the defendants cannot have intended the libellous words to apply to the plaintiff.

The question for us is whether this contention is right. The old declaration in an action for libel still accurately states the issues that have to be proved, viz., that the defendants falsely and maliciously printed and published of the plaintiff . . . It is hardly necessary to say that actual malice is not necessary; malice in law is sufficient, and that is shown by the falsity and defamatory nature of the words as soon as it has been proved that they were written of the plaintiff. But the plaintiff has to prove (i) the publication, and (ii) that it is of the plaintiff; and then he has to prove the libellous nature of the words—i.e., the innuendo. It is contended that the libel cannot be published of the plaintiff if it be proved that his existence was unknown to the defendant. A plaintiff need not, of course, be named in the libel; it is sufficient if he be sufficiently described, and for this purpose recourse may be had to the innuendo. As Lord Campbell says in *Le Fanu* v *Malcomson* ((1848) 1 HL Cas at pp. 668, 669):

> It comes round to the old rule, that you cannot by an innuendo extend the natural meaning of the words which are spoken or written, but by the innuendo you may point out the particular individual to whom the words apply.

The first step is to prove that the words published, whether by name, nickname, or description, are such as reasonably to lead persons acquainted with the plaintiff to believe that he is the person to whom the libel refers; the next step is to prove that that is the true intent and meaning of the words used. That is what I understand to be meant by Lord Cottenham in *Le Fanu* v *Malcomson* . . .

It is, however, argued that when Lord Cottenham says, 'the writer of the libel intended to mean these individuals,' he was referring to the intention in the writer's mind as distinct from the intention expressed in the words that he had used as explained by the relevant surrounding circumstances.

In my opinion, this is not so, and I may remark that it was not the contention of the appellant's counsel in that case; he opened his case by asserting (ibid. at p. 646) that it was necessary to show 'that the libel on the record should point to the plaintiffs', etc. The rule is well settled that the true intention of the writer of any document, whether it be contract, will, or libel, is that which is apparent from the natural and ordinary interpretation of the written words; and this, when applied to the description of an individual, means the interpretation that would be reasonably put upon those words by persons who knew the plaintiff and the circumstances . . . It has been held that a mistake in the statement is no defence. . . .

In the present case they jury have found that the libellous article described an actual scene at Dieppe, and that 'Artemus Jones' mentioned therein described an actual person and not a mere type. If the defendants had proved in the present case not only that the writer of the article did not know of the plaintiff's existence, but also that there was an Artemus Jones other than the plaintiff, who was present at Dieppe in the company alleged, then the circumstances with reference to which the words 'Artemus Jones' were used would show that the plaintiff was not the person intended; but the writer of the libel has chosen to state as a fact that Artemus Jones was present in order (as he says) to avoid the banality of using 'A. B'. or a blank. He has, therefore, for his own purposes chosen to assert a fact of a person bearing the very unusual name of Artemus Jones recklessly, and caring not whether there was such a person or not or what the consequences might be to him. An action for defamation differs from other actions in tort, such, for instance, as trespass, in that it is of the essence of defamation that the plaintiff should be aimed at or intended by the defendant. The man who throws a squib into a crowd, not intending to hit anyone, is liable for the consequences of his act whatever his intentions may have been, because the two elements necessary to constitute such a tort—viz., a wrongful act by the defendant and actual damage to the plaintiff—are both present. But it is not enough for a plaintiff in libel to show that the defendant has made a libellous statement and that the plaintiff's friends and acquaintances understood it to be written of him; he must also show that the defendant printed and published it of him, for if the defendant can prove that it was written truly of another person the plaintiff would fail.

. . . In my opinion, the defendant intends the natural meaning of his own words in describing the plaintiff as much as in the innuendo. The inquiry is not: What did the defendant mean in his own breast? but: What do the words mean having regard to the surrounding circumstances? . . .

It is quite possible that a defendant might know two persons of the same name, and might use words equally applicable to both and describe each so that he appeared to his own circle of friends and acquaintances to be the person attacked, and might really intend to strike at both; it would certainly be somewhat shocking if such a man could successfully defend an action by one, Artemus Jones, by swearing (and truly swearing) that he meant the other, and then defeat the second action by swearing (and truly swearing) that he meant the first. If a man chooses to make statements of fact about persons whom he names, as in this case, I see no reason why he should not be liable to everyone whom he injures who can convince a jury that he is reasonably intended by the words used.

I am, therefore, of opinion that the defendant cannot complain of Channell J's summing up. I do not think that he intended to rule anything more than that the alleged actual, as distinguished from the expressed, intention of the defendant was under the circumstances of this particular case immaterial. I do not understand him to have withdrawn from the jury the question whether the plaintiff was the person of whom the libel was published, which was, in my opinion, a question for them to decide, but to have ruled that the fact that anyone of the plaintiff's name was unknown to the writer or anyone in the defendant's office through whose hands the libels passed was not a conclusive defence requiring him to stop the case—and in this he was, in my opinion, right. The ignorance was of course a material fact, both in considering the question of the true intent of the defendants, and also in considering the damages, but I think that these were before the jury. . . .

The defendants appealed to the House of Lords. . . .

LORD LOREBURN, LC: I think that this appeal must be dismissed. A question in regard to the law of libel has been raised which does not seem to me to be entitled to the support of your Lordships. Libel is a tortious act. What does the tort consist in? It consists in using language which others knowing the circumstances would reasonably think to be defamatory of the person complaining of and injured by it. A person charged with libel cannot defend himself by showing that he intended in his own breast not to defame the plaintiff. He has none the less imputed something disgraceful, and has none the less injured the plaintiff. A man may publish a libel in good faith believing it to be true, and it may be found by the jury that he acted in good faith believing it to be true, and reasonably believing it to be true, but that in fact the statement was false. Under those circumstances he has no defence to the action.

It was suggested that there was a misdirection by the learned judge in the present case. I see none. He laid down the law in his summing-up as follows:

> The real point upon which your verdict must turn is: Ought or ought not sensible and reasonable people reading this article to think that it was a mere imaginary person such as I have said—Tom Jones, Mr Pecksniff as a humbug, Mr Stiggins, or any name of that sort which one reads of in literature used as a type? If you think that any reasonable person would think that, it is not actionable at all. If, on the other hand, you do not think that, but think that people would suppose it to mean some real person—those who did not know the plaintiff, of course, would not know who the real person was, but those who did know of the existence of the plaintiff would think that it was the plaintiff—then the action is maintainable, subject to such damages as you think under all the circumstances are fair and right to give to the plaintiff.

I see no objection in law to that passage. The damages are certainly heavy, but I think that your Lordships ought to remember two things. The first is that the jury were entitled to think, in the absence of proof satisfactory to them—and they were the judges of it—that some ingredient of recklessness entered into the publication and the writing of this article, especially as the respondent had been employed on this very newspaper, and his name was well known in the paper and also in the district in which the paper circulated. In the second place, the jury were entitled to say: 'This kind of article is a kind of article to be condemned.'

There is no tribunal more fitted or more competent to decide in regard to publications—especially publications in the newspaper press—whether they bear a stamp and character which ought to enlist sympathy and to secure protection. If they think that the licence is not fairly used, and that the tone and the style of the article and the libel in question is one that is reprehensible and ought to be checked, it is for the jury to say so; and for my part, although I think that the damages are certainly high in this case, I am not prepared to advise your Lordships to interfere, especially as the Court of Appeal have not thought it right to interfere, with the verdict which is now seeking confirmation.

NEWSTEAD v *LONDON EXPRESS NEWSPAPERS* [1939] 4 All ER 319

FACTS: A newspaper report referred to the conviction for bigamy of 'Harold Newstead, thirty-year-old Camberwell man'. This was true of one Harold Newstead (a barman) but not of the plaintiff, a hairdresser who fitted the description. He brought an action in libel. The jury found in his favour (damages one farthing), and the defendant appealed:

SIR WILFRED GREENE MR: . . . After giving careful consideration to the matter, I am unable to hold that the fact that defamatory words are true of A makes it as a matter of law impossible for them to be defamatory of B, which was in substance the main argument on behalf of the appellants. At first sight, this looks as though it would lead to great hardship, but the hardships are in practice not so serious as might appear, at any rate in the case of statements which are ex facie defamatory. Persons who make statements of this character may not unreasonably be expected, when describing the person of whom they are made, to identify that person so closely as to make it very unlikely that a judge would hold them to be reasonably capable of referring to someone else, or that a jury would hold that they did so refer. This is particularly so in the case of statements which purport to deal with actual facts. If there is a risk of coincidence, it ought, I think, in reason to be borne, not by the innocent party to whom the words are held to refer, but by the party who puts them into circulation. In matters of fiction, there is no doubt more room for hardship. Even in the case of matters of fact it is no doubt possible to construct imaginary facts which would lead to hardship. There may also be hardship if words, not on their faces defamatory, are true of A but are reasonably understood by some as referring to B, and, as applied to B, are defamatory. Such cases, however, must be rare. The law as I understand it is well settled, and can be altered only by legislation. The appeal must be dismissed with costs.

12.2.3   NATURAL MEANING AND INNUENDO

12.2.3.1   Inferences

LEWIS v *DAILY TELEGRAPH* [1963] 2 All ER 151

FACTS: The defendant newspapers each published articles to the effect that the police were investigating the affairs of a company of which the plaintiff was chairman. He claimed that the articles meant, by innuendo, that he was guilty of, or suspected of fraud. The defendants admitted that the natural meaning was defamatory, but pleaded justification. They argued that there was no good reason to adopt the innuendo.

LORD REID: The essence of the controversy between the parties is that the appellants maintain that those passages are capable of meaning that they were guilty of fraud. The respondents deny this: they admit that the paragraphs are libellous but maintain that the juries ought to have been directed that they are not capable of the meaning which the appellants attribute to them. The learned judge directed the juries in such a way as to leave it open to them to accept the appellants' contention and it is obvious from the amounts of damages awarded that the juries must have done this.

The gist of the two paragraphs is that the police, the City Fraud Squad, were inquiring into the appellants' affairs. There is no doubt that in actions for libel the question is what the words would convey to the ordinary man: it is not one of construction in the legal sense. The ordinary man does not live in an ivory tower and he is not inhibited by a knowledge of the rules of construction. So he can and does read between the lines in the light of his general knowledge and experience of wordly affairs. . .

What the ordinary man would infer without special knowledge has generally been called the natural and ordinary meaning of the words. But that expression is rather misleading in that it conceals the fact that there are two elements in it. Sometimes it is not necessary to go beyond the words themselves as where the plaintiff has been called a thief or a murderer. But more often the sting is not so much in the words themselves as in what the ordinary man will infer from them and that is also regarded as part of their natural and ordinary meaning. Here there would be nothing libellous in saying that an inquiry into the appellants' affairs was proceeding: the inquiry might be by a statistician or other expert. The sting is in inferences drawn from the fact that it is the fraud squad which is making the inquiry. What those inferences should be is ultimately a question for the jury but the trial judge has an important duty to perform.

Generally the controversy is whether the words are capable of having a libellous meaning at all and undoubtedly it is the judge's duty to rule on that. I shall have to deal later with the test which he must apply. Here the controversy is in a different form. The respondents admit that their words were libellous, although I am still in some doubt as to what is the admitted libellous meaning. But they sought and seek a ruling that these words are not capable of having the particular meaning which the appellants attribute to them. I think that they are entitled to such a ruling and that the test must be the same as that applied in deciding whether words are capable of having any libellous meaning. I say that because it appears that when a particular meaning has been pleaded either as a 'true' or a 'false' innuendo it has not been doubted that the judge must rule on the innuendo. And the case surely cannot be different where a part of the natural and ordinary meaning is, and where it is not, expressly pleaded. The leading case is *Capital and Counties Bank* v *George Henty & Sons* (1882), 7 App. Cas. 741 at p. 745. In that case Lord Selborne LC, said:

> The test according to the authorities is whether, under the circumstances in which the writing was published, reasonable men to whom the publication was made would be likely to understand it in a libellous sense.
>
> What is the sense in which any ordinary reasonable man would understand the words of this communication so as to expose the plaintiff to hatred or contempt or ridicule.
>
> It is not enough to say that by some person or another the words might be understood in a defamatory sense.

These statements of the law appear to have been generally accepted and I would not attempt to restate the general principle.

In this case it is, I think, sufficient to put the test in this way. Ordinary men and women have different temperaments and outlooks. Some are unusually suspicious and some are unusually naïve. One must try to envisage people between these two extremes and see what is the most damaging meaning that they would put on the words in question. So let me suppose a number of ordinary people discussing one of these paragraphs which they had read in the newspaper. No doubt one of them might say—'Oh, if the fraud squad are after these people you can take it they are guilty.' But I would expect the others to turn on him, if he did say that, with such remarks as—'Be fair. This is not a police state. No doubt their affairs are in a mess or the police would not be interested. But that could be because Lewis or the cashier has been very stupid or careless. We really must not jump to conclusions. The police are fair and know their job and we shall know soon enough if there is anything in it. Wait till we see if they charge him. I wouldn't trust him until this is cleared up, but it is another thing to condemn him unheard.'

What the ordinary man, not avid for scandal, would read into the words complained of must be a matter of impression. I can only say that I do not think that he would infer guilt of fraud merely because an inquiry is on foot. And if that is so then it is the duty of the trial judge to direct the jury that it is for them to determine the meaning of the paragraph but that they must not hold it to impute guilt of fraud because as a matter of law the paragraph is not capable of having that meaning. So there was here, in my opinion, misdirection of the two juries sufficiently serious to require that there must be new trials.

Before leaving this part of the case I must notice an argument to the effect that you can only justify a libel that the plaintiffs have so conducted their affairs as to give rise to suspicion of fraud, or as to give rise to an inquiry whether there has been fraud, by proving that they have acted fraudulently. Then it is said that, if that is so, there can be no difference between an allegation of suspicious conduct and an allegation of guilt. To my mind there is a great difference between saying that a man has behaved in a suspicious manner and saying that he is guilty of an offence and I am not convinced that you can only justify the former statement by proving guilt. I can well understand that if you say there is a rumour that X is guilty you can only justify by proving that he is guilty because repeating someone else's libellous statement is just as bad as making the statement directly. But I do not think that it is necessary to reach a decision on this matter of justification in order to decide that these paragraphs can mean suspicion but cannot be held to infer guilt.

LORD HODSON: It is in conjunction with secondary meanings that much of the difficulty surrounding the law of libel exists. These secondary meanings are covered by the word 'innuendo' which signifies pointing out what and who is meant by the words complained of. Who is meant raises no problem here but what is meant is of necessity divided into two parts much discussed in this case. Libels are of infinite variety and the literal meaning of the words even of such simple phrases as 'X is a thief' does not carry one very far for they may have been spoken in play or other circumstances showing that they could not be taken by reasonable persons as imputing an accusation of theft. Conversely to say that a man is a good advertiser only becomes capable of a defamatory meaning if coupled with proof, for example, that he was a professional man whose reputation would suffer if such were believed of him.

The first subdivision of the innuendo has lately been called the false innuendo as it is no more than an elaboration or embroidering of the words used without proof of extraneous facts. The true innuendo is that which depends on extraneous facts which the plaintiff has to prove in order to give the words the secondary meaning of which he complains.

. . . The defendants, having admitted that the words are defamatory in their ordinary meaning, have always maintained that their ordinary meaning does not go so far as to include actual guilt of fraud. They have sought to justify by proving that an inquiry was in fact held, not by proving actual suspicion of fraud. . . . After listening to many days of argument I am myself satisfied that the words cannot reasonably be understood to impute guilt. Suspicion no doubt can be inferred from the fact of the inquiry being held, if such was the case, but to take the further step and infer guilt is in my view wholly unreasonable. This is to draw an inference from an inference and to take two substantial steps at the same time.

The distinction between suspicion and guilt is illustrated by the case of *Simmons* v *Mitchell* (1880), 6 App Cas 156 which decided that spoken words which convey a mere suspicion that the plaintiff has committed a crime punishable by imprisonment will not support an action without proof of special damage. It has been argued before your lordships that suspicion cannot be justified without proof of actual guilt on the analogy of the rumour cases such as *Watkins* v *Hall* (1868), LR 3 QB 396. Rumour and suspicion do, however, essentially differ from one another. To say that something is rumoured to be the fact is, if the words are defamatory, a republication of the libel. One cannot defend an action for libel by saying that one has been told the libel by someone else, for this might be only to make the libel worse. The principle, as stated by Blackburn J, in *Watkins* v *Hall* (1868), LR 3 QB at p. 401, is that a party is not the less entitled to recover damages from a court of law for injurious matter published concerning him because another person previously published it. It is wholly different with suspicion. It may be defamatory to say that someone is suspected of an offence, but it does not carry with it that that person has committed the offence for this must surely offend against the ideas of justice, which reasonable persons are supposed to entertain. If one repeats a rumour one adds one's own authority to it, and implies that it is well founded, that is to say, that it is true. It is otherwise when one says or implies that a person is under suspicion of guilt. This does not imply that he is in fact guilty, but only that there are reasonable grounds for suspicion, which is a different matter.

Having reached the conclusion that the innuendo should not have been left to the jury as a separate issue and that the natural and ordinary meaning of the words does not convey actual guilt of fraud, I agree with the Court of Appeal that there must be a new trial, for the learned judge left the question to the jury 'Did they find for plaintiffs or defendants?' without a direction that the words were incapable of the extreme meaning which I have rejected.

The responsibility of the judge to exclude a particular meaning which the plaintiff seeks to ascribe to words in their natural or ordinary meaning is, I think, clearly established by the decision of this House in *Capital and Counties Bank* v *George Henty & Sons*. Henty & Sons had sent out a circular to a number of their customers giving notice that they would not receive in payment cheques drawn on any of the vouchers of the bank. There was no evidence to support the innuendo that the words imputed insolvency to the bank, and it was held that in their natural and ordinary meaning the words were not libellous. Lord Blackburn said:

[The] prosecutor or plaintiff must also satisfy a jury that the words are such and so published as to convey *the* libellous imputation. If the defendant can get either the court or the jury to be in his favour he succeeds. The prosecutor, or plaintiff, cannot succeed unless he gets both the court and the jury to decide for him.

12.2.3.2 True (or legal) innuendo

MORGAN v *ODHAMS PRESS LTD* [1971] 2 All ER 1156 (HL)

FACTS: The defendant published an article about the alleged kidnapping of a witness in a greyhound doping case. It was alleged she had been held captive at a house in Finchley. The plaintiff was not named in the article. The witness had stayed at his house around the time of the alleged kidnapping (although some distance from Finchley) and witnesses said they connected him to the story as a result.

The question of whether the story could be understood as referring to the plaintiff was referred to the House of Lords.

LORD REID: It must often happen that a defamatory statement published at large does not identify any particular person and that an ordinary member of the public who reads it in its context cannot tell who is referred to. But readers with special knowledge can and do read it as referring to a particular person. A number of matters are not in dispute in this case. It does not matter whether the publisher intended to refer to the plaintiff or not. It does not even matter whether he knew of the plaintiff's existence. And it does not matter that he did not know or could not have known the facts which caused the readers with special knowledge to connect the statement with the plaintiff. Indeed the damage done to the plaintiff by the publication may be of a kind which the publisher could not have foreseen. That may be out of line with the ordinary rule limiting damage for which a tortfeasor is liable, but that point does not arise in this case.

On the other hand when people come and say that they thought that the plaintiff was referred to by a statement which does not identify anyone there must be some protection for a defendant who is thus taken unawares. It is now well settled that the plaintiff must give sufficient particulars of the special facts on which he or his witnesses rely. But that in itself may not be enough. It may be plain and obvious that no sensible person could, by reason of knowing these facts, jump to the conclusion that the defamatory words refer to the plaintiff. Then RSC Ord. 18, r. 19 can be used to stop the case from going to trial. Otherwise the case goes to trial.

The next protection for the defendant is that at the end of the plaintiff's case the judge may be called on to rule whether the words complained of are capable of referring to the plaintiff in light of the special facts or knowledge proved in evidence. The main question in this case is: how is he to make that decision? It is often said that because a question is for the judge to answer it must be a question of law. I have more than once stated my view that the meaning of words is not a question of law in the true sense, even in other departments of the law where a much stricter test of the meaning of words is adopted than in the law of libel. It is simply a question which our law reserves for the judge. . . .

Some people may think that the law has gone too far in holding that the publisher of a defamatory statement which identifies no one is liable if knowledge of special facts which the publisher could not know causes sensible people to think that the statement applies to someone the publisher had never heard of. That may be arguable: I express no opinion about it, farther than to say that in deciding the question one would require to have in mind not only the innocent publisher but also the person who wishes to injure the reputation of the plaintiff but tries to avoid liability by disguising his libel so that it conveys nothing to the ordinary reader but causes those with special knowledge to infer that it is aimed at the plaintiff.

If this new limitation is intended to distinguish between an innocent publisher and a publisher who has the plaintiff in mind it fails in its object. It would still leave the publishers of matter not ex facie defamatory in its nature liable in at least three cases; where he uses what he thinks is a fancy name (*E Hulton & Co.* v *Jones* [1910] AC 20), where the plaintiff happens to have the same name as the person to whom he intends to refer (*Newstead* v *London Express Newspaper Ltd* [1940] 1 KB 377) and where he happens to put in something which could be regarded by those with special knowledge as a pointer or peg although he never intended it to point to the plaintiff. I can see no substantial distinction between that case and the case where those with special knowledge are caused to infer that there is a reference to the plaintiff by the narration of facts and circumstances which coupled with that special knowledge do indicate the plaintiff . . . There was no peg or pointer in *Cassidy v Daily Mirror Newspapers Ltd* [1929] 2 KB 331 or in *Hough v London Express Newspaper Ltd* [1940] 2 KB 507. . . . I see nothing wrong with these decisions. They do, however, show that the court recognises that rather far-fetched inferences may be made by sensible readers. I therefore reject the argument that the plaintiff must fail because the defendants article contained no pointer or peg for his identification. . . .

One other matter I must mention at this stage. One of the witnesses thought that the article referred to the plaintiff but completely disbelieved it; he thought it was rubbish. It was argued that he must be left out of account because no tort is committed by making a defamatory statement about X to a person who utterly disbelieves it. That is plainly wrong. It is true that X's reputation is not diminished but the person defamed suffers annoyance or worse when he learns that a defamatory statement has been published about him. There may be no clear authority that publishing a defamatory statement is a tort whether it is believed or disbelieved. But very often there is no authority for an obvious proposition: no one has had the hardihood to dispute it. . . .

12.2.3.3 False innuendo

ALLSOP v CHURCH OF ENGLAND NEWSPAPERS [1972] 2 All ER 26

FACTS: The plaintiff was a broadcast journalist, and complained that the following passage in an article in the defendants' newspaper was defamatory of him:

> On account of the television debate in Church Assembly next week I have tried to see a bit more television recently. That's how I had to put up with 25 minutes of discussion in '24 Hours' last Thursday night, about a man Kenneth Allsop described as a 'black magician.' It reflected Allsop's pre-occupation with the bent, like his week on Danish pornography recently—a programme which, by the way, the Danish Embassy plainly did not regard as a balanced presentation. One sometimes wonders if the BBC are right to have a man like Allsop, for all his brilliance, in such an influential position in television. In fairness to him, I must add that the black magician bit was extended because of a film break-down during a feature on a factory where there is a worker-ownership. Mr. Allsop repeated this the following evening and it was a jolly good programme. I mentioned his pre-occupation with the bent, and a further illustration of that was a few weeks ago when he was flashing black and white nudes on the screen with a 'roving reporter' presentation. The whole question of the treatment of the violence and sex and obscenity on the screen needs much more in depth study. The USA National Commission on the Causes and Prevention of Violence reported in September on violence in television programmes. It emphatically states that television is a contributory factor to violence in society. It presses the importance of an external check on them and this is something which our BBC needs more urgently than almost anything else. ITV does as well of course, but there is more control over it already through its contract. The BBC charter at present puts them outside the reach of the Director of Public Prosecutions. Only Parliament has the power to deal with this and should do it soon. No public service should have the autonomy some BBC officials claim.

The defence was fair comment on a matter of public interest. The defendants applied for an order that the plaintiff supply particulars of all innuendoes or indirect meanings relied on. Swanwick J refused this order, but the Court of Appeal granted it.

LORD DENNING MR: Counsel for the plaintiff says that the law is settled. A plaintiff, he says, is not bound to plead or give any particulars of any innuendo unless he wishes to rely on what is called a 'legal' innuendo or a 'true' innuendo, that is to say, when he wishes to rely on some meaning other than the ordinary meaning. In that case he has to give the particulars required by RSC Ord 82, r. 3(1), which states that:

Where in an action for libel or slander the plaintiff alleges that the words or matters complained of were used in a defamatory sense other than their ordinary meaning, he must give particulars of the facts and matters on which he relies in support of such sense.

That rule was passed in 1949. It does not apply in a case like the present, where the plaintiff is only complaining of the ordinary meaning. Counsel for the plaintiff says that as a result of that rule, since 1949 when a plaintiff is relying on the ordinary meaning, he has never been required to set out any innuendo or indirect meaning which he says the words bear. I cannot accept counsel's submission. I do not think that the law is settled in his favour. On the contrary, the House of Lords in *Lewis* v *Daily Telegraph Ltd* [1964] AC 234 expressly left it open. Two of their Lordships made it clear that, even when a plaintiff was only relying on the ordinary meaning, it was at the least highly desirable that he should state the meanings which he said the words bore. They left open the point whether it was necessary or not. Lord Devlin said:

... I am satisfied that the pleading of an innuendo in every case where the defamatory meaning is not quite explicit is at the least highly desirable ...

and then:

I understand your lordships all to be of the opinion that the pleading of the ordinary or popular innuendo is permissible, but do not intend that the House should rule on whether it is necessary. I agree that the point does not arise directly in this case, and, therefore, I, too shall reserve my judgment on it. But I make the comment that, if it is not necessary, it is nevertheless a form of pleading universally used from the earliest times until 1949, and I can see nothing in the new rule that should alter so well established a practice.

Lord Hodson said:

It is desirable that he should do so, for, where there is no true innuendo, the judge should define the limits of the natural and ordinary meaning of the libel and leave to the jury only those meanings which he rules are capable of being defamatory.

Since that case, the same view was well expressed by Salmon LJ in *Slim* v *Daily Telegraph Ltd* [1968] 1 All ER 497 at 512.

After all, there may be many opinions as to what inference words bear. It would be unfair to expect the defendant to guess which meaning or meanings the plaintiff intends to attribute to them. He might guess wrong, and thus not only waste a great deal of time and money in raising a defence of justification or fair comment which would prove to be wholly irrelevant at the trial but he might also come to court wholly unprepared to meet the actual case sought to be made against him.

Those are the views of experienced practitioners both at the Bar and on the Bench, to which I would add my own. It is very desirable to have the plaintiff set forth what he says is the defamatory meaning borne by the words. The reasons are: in the first place, so that the defendant should know the case which he has to meet and to decide whether to plead justification or fair comment, or to apologise: and, in the second place, so that the trial can be properly conducted. Counsel for the plaintiff agrees that at the trial the plaintiff's counsel will suggest to the jury the meanings which he says the words bear. The judge will have to rule then and there whether the words are reasonably capable of those meanings. It is much better for those meanings to be set down beforehand, so that everybody should know where they stand and, in particular, the judge should be able to give his ruling as to the meanings. ...

All this satisfies me that in most cases it is not only desirable, but also necessary, for the plaintiff to set out in his pleading the meaning which he says the words bear. At any rate, he should do so when there are two or more ordinary meanings which the words bear. The only exception is when there is only one ordinary meaning which is clear and explicit.

In this case we have the words 'pre-occupation with the bent.' What does the word 'bent' mean in this context? It is not used in any of the ordinary meanings attributed to it. If you look at a dictionary you will not get any help. The word 'bent' is there given in the sense of a person having a 'bent' towards science or literature. That is not the meaning here. It is sometimes used as 'bent' meaning curved or crooked, like a 'bent' stick. That is not the meaning here. Another meaning given by the dictionary to 'bent' is a name given to grass of a reedy habit. That does not fit either. No dictionary meaning fits into this sentence. 'Bent' is used here as a piece of slang. It has no precise meaning. It has no meaning which is commonly understood. It may have acquired a particular meaning among some group or other of persons. But, if so, what is it? It may mean only something unusual, something out of the ordinary, or out of line—which would not be defamatory. It may mean something crooked or perverted in a sexual sense, or in a financial sense, or it may be an even worse sense—which would be defamatory. I do not know what meaning a jury would attribute to it. Each of them might have a different view.

Seeing that the words may be grossly defamatory, or only slightly defamatory, or not defamatory at all, I am clearly of opinion that the plaintiff should give particulars saying what is the meaning, or meanings, which he says that the words bear. That is only fair to the defendants so that they should be able to know what to do. They may wish to plead fair comment or to apologise; or, if it is grossly defamatory, they may still want to apologise even more humbly. At any rate, they ought to be able to know the case which is going to be put against them. I agree that the matter is one of some considerable importance, but I think that in many cases—and this is one—it is necessary for a plaintiff to plead an innuendo in a libel action when he relies on the natural and ordinary meaning. I would, therefore, order particulars in this case.

12.3 Publication

12.3.1 INNOCENT DISSEMINATION

GOLDSMITH v *SPERRINGS LTD* [1977] 2 All ER 566 (CA)

FACTS: The defendants were distributors of *Private Eye*. The plaintiff, a prosperous business man, was attacked in three consecutive issues of *Private Eye*. He commenced proceedings for libel against the magazine and its distributors—including wholesalers such as the defendants. His object appeared to be to impede the circulation of *Private Eye*, since any distributor who undertook not to handle it had proceedings against him discontinued.

The defendants sought to have the proceedings stayed as an abuse of the process of the court, alleging that the object of impeding distribution was collateral to the proper purpose of the action.

The Court of Appeal (Lord Denning MR dissenting) refused the stay.

SCARMAN LJ: I dissent from Lord Denning MR with diffidence and very great respect; but at the end of the day, notwithstanding the persuasive eloquence of counsel for the defendants, I take a different view of the facts from that which Lord Denning MR has taken. As I see it, this appeal (for it is really one appeal, though there are several appellants, each of whom appeals in his own separate action) turns on a question of fact. The history of the matter is complex, but the question can be shortly put and answered. If the plaintiff's purpose in initiating or pursuing his actions against the secondary distributors be to destroy *Private Eye*, i.e. to use his wealth so as to suppress it, he is abusing the process of the court. Neither wealth nor power entitles a man to censor the press. If, however, his purpose be to vindicate and protect his reputation, the use of all remedies afforded him by the law for that purpose cannot be an abuse of the court's process. It is never easy to determine a man's purpose. Ordinarily this task of judgment is tackled only after trial. In the instant case, we are being asked to pass judgment on the plaintiff's purpose on a preliminary application, the effect of which, if successful, will prevent him bringing to trial actions in each of which (it was admitted in argument) he is pleading a cause of action recognised by the law. It is right therefore, that to obtain before trial the summary arrest of a plaintiff's proceedings as an abuse of the process of the court the task of satisfying the court that a stay should be imposed is, and should be seen to be, a heavy one: see *Shackleton v Swift* [1913] 2 KB 304 at 311, 312. Unless the court is satisfied, a stay is a denial of justice by the court—a situation totally intolerable.

In the instant proceedings the defendants have to show that the plaintiff has an ulterior motive, seeks a collateral advantage for himself beyond what the law offers, is reaching out 'to effect an object not within the scope of the process': *Grainger* v *Hill* (1838) 4 Bing NC 212 at 221 *per* Tindal CJ. In a phrase, the plaintiff's purpose has to be shown to be not that which the law by granting a remedy offers to fulfil, but one which the law does not recognise as a legitimate use of the remedy sought: see *Re Majory* [1955] 2 All ER 65 at 78, *per* Evershed MR. It was, no doubt, with these considerations in mind that at the outset of his argument for the plaintiff counsel submitted that the defendants cannot get their case off the ground unless they can satisfy the court that his client's purpose in starting or continuing his actions against the 'secondary' distributors was to stifle the future publication of *Private Eye* by depriving it of its commercial outlets. The judge was not satisfied this was the plaintiff's purpose. Neither am I. The plaintiff has asserted on his oath that it was not his purpose to shut off the channels of distribution of *Private Eye*, that he sued the distributors merely as participators in the publication of what he regarded as very grave and damaging libels. In his affidavit he described negotiations into which he entered between 26th April and 11th May 1976 with 'the principal defendants', i.e the publishers, editor, and main distributors of the magazine, for the settlement of all pending litigation between them. He put forward terms of settlement which would in no way impede or obstruct the future publication of Private Eye and, according to his sworn word, it was understood by all who took part in the discussion that, if there was a settlement, he would not pursue the remaining actions against the secondary distributors.

The settlement went off because amongst the terms proposed by the plaintiff was one designed to protect his solicitor from being libelled, a term which the Private Eye negotiators found unacceptable. No application has been made in these proceedings to cross-examine the plaintiff. He has not been confronted with the challenge direct. Instead, he has to meet a case based on adverse inference said to arise from surrounding circumstances. It is this circumstantial case which has, as I understand his judgment, impressed Lord Denning MR. Insofar as Lord Denning MR is saying that the plaintiff's purpose must be objectively ascertained, i.e. by reference to what a reasonable man placed in his situation would have in mind when initiating or pursuing the actions, I respectfully agree with him. But he does appear to me to attach critical importance to two matters, which, in my judgment, do not bear out his conclusion. First, he observes, truly enough, that the law offers to a defamed plaintiff no more than damages and an injunction to prevent publication of the libel or similar libels. He concludes that a plaintiff who seeks, or by way of settlement is pleased to take, more than these two remedies is abusing the process of the court. The logic is superficially attractive; but the conclusion is suspect. Men go to law to redress a grievance. They may not know or understand the limits of the remedies provided by law—though no one suggests that the plaintiff's advisers could be said to suffer from ignorance of the law. But equally a man, while pursuing the remedies offered by law, may negotiate, to secure by agreement with the parties sued, terms more favourable than, or different from, what he would get in the absence of agreement. Such a negotiation, undertaken by properly advised parties, each of whom may have a legitimate interest in avoiding litigation and may be prepared to concede more than the law requires of them to achieve that end, does not necessarily mean that the plaintiff by his litigation is reaching out to secure a collateral advantage. In the context of libel, he may reasonably see in settlement a more effective way of protecting his reputation than by action; and, whether he pursues his litigation to judgment or settles it, he may in either case be seeking no more than the way he thinks best in the circumstances to protect his reputation. Since that is the object of the law of libel (see Gatley on Libel and Slander 7th Edn (1974), para 1) it would, in my judgment, need strong evidence that the plaintiff was in fact seeking something beyond the protection and vindication of his reputation before the court could stay his action as an abuse of process.

Secondly, Lord Denning MR relies strongly on his view as to the nature and availability of the cause of action against a secondary distributor of libellous matter. He may, or may not, be right in his view of the law. Before Stocker J it was conceded that the plaintiff has a cause of action against the distributors; and it was not argued before us to the contrary. Be that as it may, Gatley on Libel and Slander 7th Edn (1974), paras 237–242 assumes that there is a cause of action, subject to the defence of innocent dissemination. In such circumstances how can Lord Denning MR's researches provide any clue to the purpose of the plaintiff? He must be judged on the view of the law honestly and reasonably entertained by his advisers and not yet challenged by his opponents, namely that the cause of action exists subject to certain defences the burden of proving which is on the defendant.

. . .

[The] plaintiff cannot be said to have been unreasonable in believing that he was the victim of a virulent and damaging campaign of calumny in the columns of *Private Eye*. It was understandable that he should think it necessary for the protection of his reputation that he should proceed not only against *Private Eye* but against its distributors; and the law afforded him a remedy. It is understandable that he should have thought it prudent to act against responsible businessmen who would be likely to heed the law as well as against the principal defendants whose respect for the libel laws might reasonably seem suspect to him and whose finances might well prove unable to meet the damages likely to be awarded him if he should succeed. One does not ask whether what he alleges to have been his appreciation of the situation was correct; but whether in the circumstances it was reasonable and credible. In my judgment, it was.

My second comment is on the ringing submission,—it is still echoing down the corridors of my mind, made by counsel at the very outset of his argument for the defendants. He submitted that to dismiss the appeal would be to imperil the freedom of the press. He warned the court that this was, in his words, 'the most important case on the freedom of the press to come before the courts for a very long time'.

A submission of such gravity coming from a leader of counsel for the defendants' distinction is not to be lightly brushed aside. Nevertheless, it is, in my judgment, based on a confusion of thought. If the true issue be, as on the authorities it must be, what was (and is) the purpose of the plaintiff in pursuing the rights given him by law against the secondary distributors, the plaintiff is not putting the press in peril. If his purpose be illegitimate, his actions will be stayed. If it is not, he is exercising rights given him by law. If, therefore, there be in these proceedings a threat to press freedom, the threat comes not from the plaintiff but from the law itself, in that it provides a cause of action against distributors as well as publishers. That is a matter for Parliament, not the courts. So long as the cause of action exists, it may be invoked unless it can be shown that it is being used to secure a collateral advantage. If the effect of the law is to diminish freedom of the press, Parliament will have to decide where the balance is to be struck between freedom and the protection of the defamed citizen. Some, no doubt, will argue against any restraint being imposed on distributors of newspapers. Some may even wish to go so far as to call for a legal obligation to be imposed on all newsagents and others engaged in the business of newspaper distribution to provide an outlet for all newspapers and periodicals, whatever they publish. Others, however, will argue that the existing law provides in the action against a secondary distributor a valuable additional remedy for an individual who is defamed by a scurrilous or financially dubious publication. We do not have to consider these questions.

My third, and final, comment on the argument to which we have listened is that decision in this appeal is not helped by reference to the wealth of the plaintiff. Wealth may well have afforded him the chance of invoking the law to protect his reputation in a way in which—alas!—a poorer man could not. If so, the inference is simply that this branch of the law is not, as it should be, available to poor men.

12.4 Defences

12.4.1 PRIVILEGE

12.4.1.1 Qualified privilege

ADAM v *WARD* [1916–17] All ER Rep 157 (HL)

FACTS: The plaintiff was a former army officer, turned MP. He had a long standing grievance about the circumstances in which he, and other officers, had been removed from their posts in a cavalry regiment and transferred to a staff post on half pay.

He made imputations against a senior officer in the House of Commons, and this resulted in an open letter from the Army Council to that officer in which it was stated that the allegations made by the plaintiff were without foundation. The plaintiff sued on this letter. The defendant admitted it was, in context, defamatory of the plaintiff (by implicitly stating that he had pursued false and vindictive complaints) but claimed qualified privilege.

The jury found that the publication of the open letter was not privileged and the defendant appealed. The Court of Appeal ruled that the occasion was privileged and the plaintiff appealed to the House of Lords, which dismissed his appeal.

LORD ATKINSON: It was not disputed in this case on either side that a privileged occasion is, in reference to qualified privilege, an occasion where the person who makes a communication has an interest or a duty, legal, social, or moral, to make it to the person to whom it is made, and the person to whom it is so made has a corresponding interest or duty to receive it. This reciprocity is essential. Nor is it disputed that a privileged communication, a phrase often used loosely to describe a privileged occasion, and vice versa, is a communication made upon an occasion which rebuts the prima facie presumption of malice arising from a statement prejudicial to the character of the plaintiff, and puts the latter on proof that there was malice in fact . . . Nor that the question whether the occasion is a privileged occasion or not is, if the facts be not in dispute, or if in dispute have been found by the jury, a question of law to be decided by the judge at the trial. Nor yet that a person making a communication on a privileged occasion has not, in the first instance and as a condition of immunity, to prove affirmatively that he honestly believes the statement made to be true, his *bona fides* being in such a case always presumed. All these matters were not questioned. They could not be questioned. Nor was it suggested that, while on the question of malice the *bona fide* belief of the defendant that he was under a moral or social duty to make the communication is relevant and important, the existence in fact of this duty or interest, not merely the defendant's belief in its existence, is the thing which is relevant to the question whether the occasion was or was not privileged: *per* Lindley LJ, in *Stuart v Bell* [1891] 2 QB at p. 349.

It was, however, strenuously contended on the part of the appellant, as I understood, that the language used in a communication made on a privileged occasion must, if it is to be protected, merely be such as is reasonably necessary to enable the party making it to protect the interest or discharge the duty upon which the qualified privileges is founded. It has long been established by unquestioned and unquestionable authority, I think, that this is not the law . . . [The] authorities, in my view, clearly establish that a person making a communication on a privileged occasion is not restricted to the use of such language merely as is reasonably necessary to protect the interest or discharge the duty which is the foundation of his privilege; but that, on the contrary, he will be protected, even though his language should be violent or excessively strong, if, having regard to all the circumstances of the case, he might have honestly and on reasonable grounds believed that what he wrote or said was true and necessary for the purpose of his vindication, though in fact it was not so. . . .

The law of privilege is well settled. Malice is a necessary element in an action for libel, but from the mere publication of defamatory matter malice is implied, unless the publication were on what is called a privileged occasion. If the communication were made in pursuance of a duty or on a matter in which there was a common interest in the party making and the party receiving it, the occasion is said to be privileged. This privilege is only qualified, and may be rebutted by proof of express malice. It is for the judge, and the judge alone, to determine as a matter of law whether the occasion is privileged, unless the circumstances attending it are in dispute, in which case the facts necessary to raise the question of law should be found by the jury. It is further for the judge to decide whether there is any evidence of express malice fit to be left to the jury—that is, whether there is any evidence on which a reasonable man could find malice. Such malice may be inferred either from the terms of the communication itself, as if the language be unnecessarily strong, or from any facts which show that the defendant in publishing the libel was actuated by spite or some indirect motive. The privilege extends only to a communication upon the subject with respect to which privilege exists, and it does not extend to a communication upon any other extraneous matter which the defendant may have made at the same time. The introduction of such extraneous matter may afford evidence of malice which will take away protection on the subject to which privilege attaches. The communication on the extraneous matter is not made upon a privileged occasion at all, inasmuch as the existence of privilege on one matter gives no protection to irrelevant libels introduced into the same communication.

That the occasion of this letter was privileged seems to me to be clear beyond all controversy. Major Adam had made a violent attack upon the character of Major-General Scobell, who appealed to the Army Council for inquiry. It was the duty of the Army Council to inquiry into the truth of this charge and to make the result of that inquiry known as widely as possible. It is said that there was unnecessary publicity given to their findings, but it must be remembered that Major Adam's speech in the House of Commons had been extensively reported, as he obviously intended it should be when he made his attack upon Major-General Scobell, and the Army Council did no more than their duty in giving a wide publicity to their finding that the charge was unfounded. It had been said that their observations as to the plaintiff, Major Adam, were not relevant to their vindication of Major-General Scobell, and that privilege does not extend to this portion of the letter. These observations appear to me to be directly relevant. The plaintiff did not mention in his speech in the House of Commons that he was himself interested in the matter, and anyone who heard or read his speech would have been left under the impression that he was a perfectly disinterested person who had taken up the case of a brother officer. The vindication by the Army Council of Major-General Scobell would have been incomplete if the true relation of Major Adam to these proceedings had been left out. The two passages especially impugned were—first, the statement that the plaintiff was one of the officers who had been removed from the regiment, and second, the following instance:

> Further, as showing the absence of hostile bias, the Army Council note that in the case of Major Adam, who in 1906 was called upon to retire from the service in consequence of adverse reports, which were duly communicated to him, you intervened on his behalf and urged the council to give him another chance in an extra-regimental appointment. In the result it was decided to give Major Adam this chance.

So far from being alien to the investigation of the charge made by the plaintiff against Major-General Scobell both these passages appear to me to be directly relevant to it. It was essential to show that Major-General Scobell had been actuated by a friendly feeling towards the plaintiff, and it was as incidental to this that the fact that the plaintiff had been called on to retire should be introduced. The privilege extended to the whole letter, and there is nothing either in the letter itself or in the surrounding circumstances to supply any evidence of express malice. I agree with the Court of Appeal in thinking that the judge ought to have ruled that the occasion was privileged.

12.4.1.2   Malice

HORROCKS v LOWE [1974] 1 All ER 662 (HL)

FACTS: The plaintiff was a Conservative member of Bolton Corporation and the defendant a Labour member. A dispute arose over the refusal by the plaintiff's company to release a restrictive covenant over land owned by the Corporation.

The defendant made a speech at a council meeting (admittedly an occasion of qualified privilege) attacking the plaintiff in very heated terms. Some of what he said was untrue. The judge ruled he had spoken honestly, and without personal spite, but was so driven by his concern to expose the plaintiff's supposed misdeeds that his state of mind was one of 'gross and unreasoning prejudice' from which express malice could be inferred. The Court of Appeal allowed the defendant's appeal and the House of Lords dismissed the plaintiff's further appeal.

LORD DIPLOCK: Stirling J found expressly that Mr Lowe 'believed and still believes that everything he said was true and justifiable.' He also found, however, that owing to Mr Lowe's anxiety to have Mr Horrocks removed from the Management and Finance Committee his state of mind was one of 'gross and unreasoning prejudice'—a phrase borrowed from the judgment of Lord Esher MR in *Royal Aquarium & Summer & Winter Garden Society v Parkinson* [1892] 1 QB 431. That case he regarded as—

authority for the proposition that such an attitude [of mind] if proved, is evidence from which a jury could properly infer malice even if honest belief in the words used exists.

Paragraph 770 of the current edition of Gatley on Libel and Slander, the only book to which he was referred in Manchester, appears to support this view.

It will become necessary to examine in more detail some of the judge's other findings as to Mr Lowe's conduct and attitude of mind; but the finding that Mr Lowe believed that everything he said was true and justifiable lies at the root of this appeal.

The business of the Bolton borough council was conducted by its members on party political lines. Mr Horrocks was a member of the Conservative caucus which at the relevant time was in a majority. Mr Lowe was a member of the Labour caucus. Both were members of the important Management and Finance Committee of the council. Mr Horrocks was also chairman and majority shareholder in Land Development and Building Ltd, a property company engaged in dealing in and developing property within the borough. In 1961 this company had sold to the Bolton corporation some land in Bishops Road subject to a restrictive covenant against building on it. Later the company sold building plots on some of the remainder of the land assuring the purchasers of these plots that nothing would be built on the land that had been conveyed to the corporation. Unfortunately, this restrictive covenant was overlooked by the officials of the corporation when a 99 year lease of part of the land subject to it was later granted to the Conservative club for the erection of a club house. Building work had proceeded nearly to roof-height when, in August 1969, the company's solicitors drew the attention of the corporation and the club to the restrictive covenant and demanded that the building be removed.

The matter was dealt with at meetings of the Management and Finance Committee of which the chairman was a Conservative, Alderman Telford. Mr Lowe was present, but Mr Horrocks, because of his personal interest, absented himself, when the matter was discussed. No solution to the difficulty could be found and ultimately the corporation accepted the liability to find another site for the Conservative club and to pay them very substantial compensation for their wasted expenditure. A statement to this effect was to be made at the meeting of the borough council of 5th November 1969 by Alderman Telford.

Mr Lowe and other members of the Labour caucus took the view that because of his personal interest in the development of land in Bolton Mr Horrocks ought not to be a member of the Management and Finance Committee. He had expressed this view at the meeting of that committee on 27th October 1969 but was powerless to obtain acceptance of it by the committee because of the Conservative majority on the committee and in the council itself. He gave notice that he intended to raise the matter again at the council meeting on 5th November on the occasion of the statement by Alderman Telford about the Bishops Road site. This he did and what he said at that meeting of the council is the slander in respect of which this action has been brought. It consisted in large part of a recital of what he understood to be the facts about the Bishops Road affair. It was hard hitting criticism of Mr Horrocks's conduct. The sting of it was in the words quoted by Stirling J:

I don't know how to describe his attitude whether it was brinkmanship, megalomania or childish petulance ... I suggest that he has misled the town, the Leader of the party and his political and club colleagues some of whom are his business associates. I therefore request that he be removed from the Committee to some other where his undoubted talents can be used to the advantage of the Corporation.

My Lords, as a general rule, English law gives effect to the ninth Commandment that a man shall not speak evil falsely of his neighbour. It supplies a temporal sanction: if he cannot prove that defamatory matter which he published was true, he is liable in damages to whomsoever he has defamed, except where the publication is oral only, causes no damage and falls outside the categories of slander actionable per se. The public interest that the law should provide an effective means whereby a man can vindicate his reputation against calumny, has nevertheless to be accommodated to the competing public interest in permitting men to communicate frankly and freely with one another about matters with respect to which the law recognises that they have a duty to perform or an interest to protect in doing so. What is published in good faith on matters of these kinds is published on a privileged occasion. It is not actionable even though it be defamatory and turns out to be untrue. With some exceptions which are irrelevant to the instant appeal, the privilege is not absolute but qualified. It is lost if the occasion which gives rise to it is misused. For in all cases of qualified privilege there is some special reason of public policy why the law accords immunity from suit—the existence of some public or private duty, whether legal or moral, on the part of the maker of the defamatory statement which justifies his communicating it or of some interest of his own which he is entitled to protect by doing so. If he uses the occasion for some other reason he loses the protection of the privilege.

So, the motive with which the defendant on a privileged occasion made a statement defamatory of the plaintiff becomes crucial. The protection might, however, be illusory if the onus lay on him to prove that he was actuated solely by a sense of the relevant duty or a desire to protect the relevant interest. So he is entitled to be protected by the privilege unless some other dominant and improper motive on his part is proved. 'Express malice' is the term of art descriptive of such a motive. Broadly speaking, it means malice in the popular sense of a desire to injure the person who is defamed and this is generally the motive which the plaintiff sets out to prove. But to destroy the privilege the desire to injure must be the dominant motive for the defamatory publication; knowledge that it will have that effect is not enough if the defendant is nevertheless acting in accordance with a sense of duty or in bona fide protection of his own legitimate interests.

The motive with which a person published defamatory matter can only be inferred from what he did or said or knew. If it be proved that he did not believe that what he published was true this is generally conclusive evidence of express malice, for no sense of duty or desire to protect his own legitimate interests can justify a man in telling deliberate and injurious falsehoods about another, save in the exceptional case where a person may be under a duty to pass on, without endorsing, defamatory reports made by some other person.

Apart from those exceptional cases, what is required on the part of the defamer to entitle him to the protection of the privilege is positive belief in the truth of what he published or, as it is generally though tautologously termed, 'honest belief.' If he publishes untrue defamatory matter recklessly, without considering or caring whether it be true or not, he is in this, as in other branches of the law, treated as if he knew it to be false. But indifference to the truth of what he publishes is not to be equated with carelessness, impulsiveness or irrationality in arriving at a positive belief that it is true. The freedom of speech protected by the law of qualified privilege may be availed by all sorts and conditions of men. In affording to them immunity from suit if they have acted in good faith in compliance with a legal or moral duty or in protection of a legitimate interest the law must take them as it finds them. In ordinary life it is rare indeed for people to form their beliefs by a process of logical deduction from facts ascertained by a rigorous search for all available evidence and a judicious assessment of its probative value. In greater or in less degree according to their temperaments, their training, their intelligence, they are swayed by prejudice, rely on intuition instead of reasoning, leap to conclusions on inadequate evidence and fail to recognise the cogency of material which might cast doubt on the validity of the conclusions they reach. But despite the imperfection of the mental process by which the belief is arrived at it may still be 'honest', i.e. a positive belief that the conclusions they have reached are true. The law demands no more.

Even a positive belief in the truth of what is published on a privileged occassion. . . [may not suffice], the commonest case is where the dominant motive which actuates the defendant is not a desire to perform the relevant duty or to protect the relevant interest, but to give vent to his personal spite or ill-will towards the person he defames. If this be proved, then even positive belief in the truth of what is published will not enable the defamer to avail himself of the protection of the privilege to which he would otherwise have been entitled. There may be instances of improper motives which destroy the privilege apart from personal spite. A defendant's dominant motive may have been to obtain some private advantage unconnected with the duty or the interest which constitutes the reason for the privilege. If so, he loses the benefit of the privilege despite his positive belief that what he said or wrote was true.

Judges and juries should, however, be very slow to draw the inference that a defendant was so far actuated by improper motives as to deprive him of the protection of the privilege unless they are satisfied that he did not believe that what he said or wrote was true or that he was indifferent to its truth or falsity. The motives with which human beings act are mixed. They find it difficult to hate the sin but love the sinner. Qualified privilege would be illusory, and the public interest that it is meant to serve defeated, if the protection which it affords were lost merely because a person, although acting in compliance with a duty or in protection of a legitimate interest, disliked the person whom he defamed or was indignant at what he believed to be that person's conduct and welcomed the opportunity of exposing it. It is only where his desire to comply with the relevant duty or to protect the relevant interest plays no significant part in his motives for publishing what he believes to be true that 'express malice' can properly be found.

There may be evidence of the defendant's conduct on occasions other than that protected by the privilege which justify the inference that on the privileged occasion too his dominant motive in publishing what he did was personal spite or some other improper motive, even although he believed it to be true. But where, as in the instant case, conduct extraneous to the privileged occasion itself is not relied on, and the only evidence of improper motive is the content of the defamatory matter itself or the steps taken by the defendant to verify its accuracy, there is only one exception to the rule that in order to succeed the plaintiff must show affirmatively that the defendant did not believe it to be true or was indifferent to its truth of falsity. Juries should be instructed and judges should remind themselves that this burden of affirmative proof is not one that is lightly satisfied....

My Lords, what is said by members of a local council at meetings of the council or of any of its committees is spoken on a privileged occasion. The reason for the privilege is that those who represent the local government electors should be able to speak freely and frankly, boldly and bluntly, on any matter which they believe affects the interests or welfare of the inhabitants. They may be swayed by strong political prejudice, they may be obstinate and pig-headed, stupid and obtuse; but they were chosen by the electors to speak their minds on matters of local concern and so long as they do so honestly they run no risk of liability for defamation of those who are the subjects of their criticism.

In the instant case Mr Lowe's speech at the meeting of the Bolton borough council was on matters which were undoubtedly of local concern. With one minor exception the only facts relied on as evidence from which express malice was to be inferred had reference to the contents of the speech itself, the circumstances in which the meeting of the council was held and the material relating to the subject-matter of Mr Lowe's speech which was within his actual knowledge or available to him on enquiry. The one exception was his failure to apologise to Mr Horrocks when asked to do so two days later. A refusal to apologise is at best but tenuous evidence of malice, for it is consistent with a continuing belief in the truth of what he said. Stirling J found it to be so in the case of Mr Lowe.

So the judge was left with no other material on which to found an inference of malice except the contents of the speech itself, the circumstances in which it was made and, of course, Mr Lowe's own evidence in the witness box. Where such is the case the test of malice is very simple. It was laid down by Lord Esher himself, as Brett LJ, in *Clark* v *Molyneux* (1877) 3 QBD 237. It is: has it been proved that the defendant did not honestly believe that what he said was true, i.e. was he either aware that it was not true or indifferent to its truth or falsity? In *Royal Aquarium & Summer & Winter Garden Society* v *Parkinson* Lord Esher MR applied the self-same test. In the passage cited by Stirling J he was doing no more than disposing of a suggestion made in the course of the argument that reckless disregard of whether what was stated was true or false did not constitute malice unless it were due to personal spite directed against the individual defamed. All Lord Esher MR was saying was that such indifference to the truth or falsity of what was stated constituted malice even though it resulted from prejudice with regard to the subject-matter of the statement rather than with regard to the particular person defamed. But however gross, however unreasoning the prejudice it does not destroy the privilege unless it has this result. If what it does is to cause the defendant honestly to believe what a more rational or impractical person would reject or doubt he does not thereby lose the protection of the privilege.

12.4.2 FAIR COMMENT

12.4.2.1 Comment on true facts

KEMSLEY v *FOOT* [1952] 1 All ER 501 (HL)

FACTS: The plaintiff was the proprietor of a group of newspapers. The defendant, Michael Foot, used the words 'Lower than Kemsley' as the title of an article actually attacking a different newspaper and its editor. The defendant alleged that the words were defamatory of him. The defendant pleaded fair comment, although he had not stated anything about the Kemsley newspapers.

The matter finally reached the House of Lords. The speeches largely concerned the specific pleadings which were being attacked as improper or irrelevant.

LORD PORTER: [It] is not, in my view, necessary to set out the particulars in detail. It is enough to say that they contain excerpts from the appellant's newspaper . . . Paragraph 3 is, perhaps, as good an example as can be adduced of the matters relied on. It begins as follows:

> The [appellant] in exercise of such control as aforesaid [i.e., general editorial control] caused or permitted to be published, as items of news, matter which did not correspond with the facts or was so coloured with comment as not to give an accurate representation of the news it purported to report, and headlines which distorted the news reported thereunder.

So far as I can discover no allegation of conscious lying is asserted in terms. The comment on these matters is said to be criticism of the way in which the appellant's newspapers are conducted, and to assert that that conduct is of a low character, [and] that the respondents are entitled to criticise that conduct . . . The appellant for his part, maintains that the right of comment is dependent on the existence in the words alleged to be libellous of a statement of some fact or facts on which comment is made so that those reading the comment may be able to judge for themsleves whether it is justified or not. It is not, as I understand, contended that the words contained in that article are fact and not comment. Rather it is alleged that they are comment with no facts to support it. The question for your Lordships' decision is, therefore, whether a plea of fair comment is only permissible where the comment is accompanied by a statement of facts on which the comment is made, and to determine the particularity with which the facts must be stated.

Before one comes to consider the general question it is, I think, desirable to determine what the language of the alleged libel can be held to assert. It may, in my opinion, be construed as containing an inference that the Kemsley Press is of a low and undesirable quality and that Lord Kemsley is responsible for its tone. Indeed, as I understand the defence and such particulars as have been delivered, an imputation no less severe has been accepted by the respondents as being a true interpretation of the words used. Although the article complained of uses the phrase 'Lower than Kemsley,' that language is accompanied by an attack on Lord Beaverbrook's papers, and it is at least arguable that the attack is on the Kemsley Press and not on Lord Kemsley's personal character save in so far as it is exhibited in the Press for which he is responsible. Nevertheless, libel must reflect on a person and Lord Kemsley is held up as worthy of attack on the ground that he is a newspaper proprietor who prostitutes his position by conducting his newspapers or permitting them to be conducted in an undesirable way. In this sense the criticism does not differ from that which takes place when what is called literary criticism comes in question. In such case the attack is not on the personal character of the person libelled, it is on him as responsible for certain productions, e.g., an article in the Press, a book, a musical composition, or an artistic work. Later I shall have to come back to the truth and accuracy of this analogy, but I have thought it right to set out the basis of literary criticism at this point, because a distinction is sought to be drawn and, indeed, in some of the decided cases has been drawn, between literary criticism and a personal attack on the character of an individual.

If an author writes a play or a book or a composer composes a musical work, he is submitting that work to the public and, thereby, inviting comment. Not all the public will see or read or hear it, but the work is public in the same sense as a case in the law courts is said to be heard in public. Obviously not all those who wish to attend a trial can do so, but in so far as there is room for them in the court all are entitled to do so, and the subject-matter on which comment can be made is indicated to the world at large. The same observation is true of a newspaper. Whether the criticism is confined to a particular issue or deals with the way in which it is, in general, conducted, the subject-matter on which criticism has been made has been submitted to the public, though by no means all those to whom the alleged libel has been published will have seen or are likely to see the various issues. Accordingly, its contents and conduct are open to comment on the ground that the public have at least the opportunity of ascertaining for themselves the subject-matter on which the comment is founded. I am assuming that the reference is to a known journal. For the present purpose it is not necessary to consider how far criticism without facts on which to base it is subject to the same observation in the case of an obscure publication. A further ground for the distinction sought to be drawn between an attack on an individual and criticism of a literary work appears to suggest that comment on the literary production must be confined to criticism of it as literature. This is not so. A literary work can be criticised for its treatment of life and morals as freely as it can for bad writing, e.g., it can be criticised as having an immoral tendency. The fairness of the criticism does not depend on the fact that it is confined to form or literary content.

The question, therefore, in all cases is whether there is a sufficient substratum of fact stated or indicated in the words which are the subject-matter of the action, and I find my view well expressed in the remarks contained in *Odgers on Libel and Slander* (5th ed., 1911) at p. 203:

> Sometimes, however, it is difficult to distinguish an allegation of fact from an expression of opinion. It often depends on what is stated in the rest of the article. If the defendant accurately states what some public man has really done, and then asserts that 'such conduct is disgraceful,' this is merely the expression of his opinion, his comment on the plaintiff's conduct. So, if without setting it out, he identifies the conduct on which he comments by a clear reference. In either case, the defendant enables his readers to judge for themselves how far his opinion is well founded; and, therefore, what would otherwise have been an allegation of fact becomes merely a comment. But if he asserts that the plaintiff has been guilty of disgraceful conduct, and does not state what that conduct was, this is an allegation of fact for which there is no defence but privilege or truth. The same considerations apply where a defendant has drawn from certain facts an inference derogatory to the plaintiff. If he states the bare inference without the facts on which it is based, such inference will be treated as an allegation of fact. But if he sets out the facts correctly, and then gives his inference, stating it as his inference from those facts, such inference will, as a rule, be deemed a comment. But even in this case the writer must be careful to state the inference as an inference, and not to assert it as a new and independent fact; otherwise, his inference will become something more than a comment, and he may be driven to justify it as an allegation of fact.

But the question whether an inference is a bare inference in this sense must depend on all the circumstances. Indeed, it was ultimately admitted on behalf of the appellant that the facts necessary to justify comment might be implied from the terms of the impugned article, and, therefore, the inquiry ceases to be: Can the defendant point to definite assertions of fact in the alleged libel on which the comment is made? and becomes: Is there subject-matter indicated with sufficient clarity to justify comment being made?, and whether the comment actually made is such as an honest though prejudiced man might make.

Is there, then, in this case sufficient subject-matter on which to make comment. In an article which is concerned with what has been described as 'the Beaverbrook Press' and which is violently critical of Lord Beaverbrook's newspapers, it is, I think, a reasonable construction of the words 'Lower than Kemsley' that the allegation which is made is that the conduct of the Kemsley Press was similar to, but not quite so bad as, that of the Press controlled by Lord Beaverbrook, i.e., it is possibly dishonest, but in any case low. The exact meaning, however, is not, in my opinion, for your Lordships, but for the jury. All I desire to say is that there is subject-matter and it is at least arguable that the words directly complained of imply as fact that Lord Kemsley is in control of a number of known newspapers and that the conduct of those newspapers is in question. Had the contention that all the facts justifying the comment must appear in the article been maintainable, the appeal must have succeeded. But the appellant's representatives did not feel able to, and, I think, could not, support so wide a contention. The facts, they admitted, might be implied and the respondents' answer to their contention is: 'We have pointed to your Press. It is widely read. Your readers will, and the public generally can, know at what our criticism is directed. It is not bare comment. It is comment on a well-known matter, much better known, indeed, than a newly printed book or a once performed play.' . . . In the present case, for instance, the substratum of fact on which comment is based is that Lord Kemsley is the active proprietor of and responsible for the Kemsley Press. The criticism is that that Press is a low one. As I hold, any facts sufficient to justify that statement would entitle the respondents to succeed on a plea of fair comment. Twenty facts might be given in the particulars and only one justified, yet if that one fact was sufficient to support the comment so as to make it fair, a failure to prove the other nineteen would not of necessity defeat the respondents' plea. The protection of the plaintiff in such a case would, in my opinion, be, as it often is in cases of the like kind, the effect which an allegation of a number of facts which cannot be substantiated would have on the minds of a jury who would be unlikely to believe that the comment was made on the one fact or was honestly founded on it, and, accordingly, would find it unfair. It is true that Kennedy J, in *Joynt* v *Cycle Trade Publishing Co.* ([1904] 2 KB 292) says that a comment cannot be fair which is built on facts which are not truly stated, and in the same case in the Court of Appeal (*ibid.*, 298) Vaughan Williams LJ, quotes the language of Crompton J, in *Campbell* v *Spottiswoode* (32 LJQB 200):

> If he [the critic] . . . imputes to the person whom he is criticising base and sordid motives which are not warranted by the facts, I cannot think for a moment that because he bona fide believes that he is publishing what is true, that is any defence in point of law.

But in each of these cases the court was dealing with the lack of any basis of fact sufficient to warrant the comment made and, in any case, what is fair or unfair comment and what amounts to an imputation of base and sordid motives are matters for the jury and not a subject for your Lordships' decision. In reaching the conclusion which I have stated I am not conscious of being at variance with the authorities, or, at any rate, with cases decided in this country.

The main support for the appellant's argument is founded on the observations of Fletcher Moulton LJ in *Hunt* v *Star Newspaper Co., Ltd* ([1908] 2 KB 319). The observations relied on are:

> The law as to fair comment, so far as is material to the present case, stands as follows: In the first place, comment in order to be justifiable as fair comment must appear as comment and must not be so mixed up with the facts that the reader cannot distinguish between what is report and what is comment: see *Andrews* v *Chapman*. The justice of this rule is obvious. If the facts are stated separately and the comment appears as an inference drawn from those facts, any injustice that it might do will be to some extent negatived by the reader seeing the grounds upon which the unfavourable inference is based. But if fact and comment be intermingled so that it is not reasonably clear what portion purports to be inference, he will naturally suppose that the injurious statements are based on adequate grounds known to the writer though not necessarily set out by him. In the one case the insufficiency of the facts to support the inference will lead fairminded men to reject the inference. In the other case it merely points to the existence of extrinsic facts which the writer considers to warrant the language he uses . . . In the next place, in order to give room for the plea of fair comment the facts must be truly stated. If the facts upon which the comment purports to be made do not exist the foundation of the plea fails.

LORD OAKSEY: My Lords, I agree. The forms in which a comment on a matter of public importance may be framed are almost infinitely various, and, in my opinion, it is unnecessary that all the facts on which the comment is based should be stated in the libel in order to admit the defence of fair comment. It is not, in my opinion, a matter of importance that the reader should be able to see exactly the grounds of the comment. It is sufficient if the subject which, *ex hypothesi*, is of public importance is sufficiently and not incorrectly or untruthfully stated. A comment based on facts untruly stated cannot be fair. What is meant in cases in which it has been said that comment to be fair must be on facts truly stated is, I think, that the facts, so far as they are stated in the libel, must not be untruly stated. In the present case the word which indicates the subject is 'Kemsley' and it must be read in its context and in that context it must, I think, mean the newspapers controlled by

Lord Kemsley. That is the subject-matter of the comment. The comment is that those newspapers are nearly as low as Lord Beaverbrook's newspapers, about which many defamatory statements are made in the alleged libel. It is not, in my opinion, a statement of fact that a newspaper is low. It is a comment. It may be a statement of fact to say that a man is fraudulent for there is a legal sanction for fraud, but there is no legal sanction for publishing low newspapers. I think, therefore, that the words 'lower than' are words of comment and that the particulars were alleged for the purpose of supporting the comment, and, if it is proved to the satisfaction of the jury that an honest man might have made such a comment on Lord Kemsley's newspapers, the defence of fair comment will have been established. It is one thing to publish a defamatory statement of fact, it is quite another to allege a defamatory statement of fact in a pleading in order to show that a published comment was fair. A defendant who has made a defamatory comment on a matter of public importance must be entitled to adduce any relevant evidence to show that the comment was fair, and, in order to do so, must be entitled to allege and attempt to prove facts which he contends justify the comment. Whether the facts alleged are satisfactorily proved or not it will still be for the jury to say whether they consider that the comment in the circumstances proved might have been made by an honest man. I am, therefore, of opinion that the order of the Court of Appeal was right and this appeal should be dismissed.

12.5 End of Chapter Assessment Questions

(1) *The News of the People* recently carried the following story headlined, 'Wife of Acrobat Sues Other Women':

> Mrs Rita Kyte, ex-trapeze artist wife of world-famous acrobat Jasper Kyte is suing her husband for divorce citing two women as co-respondents. The first is well known; she is a historian of circuses who has been researching into the history of Big Tops, and was to be seen with Mr Kyte during and outside working hours in the last two months.
>
> The other is Eleanor Rigby, a 38-year-old spinster from Neasden with a passion for fairs and circuses.

Annabelle Lee, famed for studies of popular entertainment in the 19th and 20th centuries, issues a writ alleging libel. She says that she did do research into Big Tops and that she was to be seen in the company of many circus employees, including Kyte, but that there was never any affair between them.

Eleanor Rigby (the 'real' one) issues a libel writ, as does another lady of the same name.

Advise the paper.

(Note: When the Family Law Act 1996 is in force, adultery will no longer be a component of a divorce petition.)

(2) During a debate in the House of Commons on the subject of education, questions were raised, by the way of example, about the running of a comprehensive school at Eatanswill by the headmaster, Mr Micawber. The speeches of several members showed considerable bias, and some of the charges against Mr Micawber were clearly defamatory and also (no doubt unintentionally) untrue. Next day the *Eatanswill Chronicle*, a local newspaper, published a detailed précis of this part of the debate and also a 'Parliamentary sketch' giving a reporter's impressions of these speeches and referring to the fuller précis. The reporter honestly believed in the truth of what he wrote, but his personal acquaintance with Mr Micawber led him to show unreasonable prejudice against those speakers who had supported the headmaster.

Advise Mr Micawber as to his prospects of a successful action for damages against Wardle & Co. Ltd, the proprietors of the newspaper.

12.6 End of Chapter Assessment Outline Answers

1. Will the plaintiffs establish a prima facie case? They must prove publication of defamatory words which relate to them.
   Publication is not in issue and any defamation will be libel, but reference and defamatory meaning will be in issue.

Reference:

Annabelle Lee (AL)

This is not a direct reference, but seems to be a clear enough indirect reference, certainly to students of the subject. It is individual, not a class: *Knupffer* v *London Express Newspapers* (1944). Although the identity is strictly a matter of inference from other facts and thus an innuendo, it is a simple one: *Morgan* v *Odhams Press* (1971).

Eleanor Rigby (the intended one)

No problem: express and detailed reference.

Eleanor Rigby (the namesake)

It is possible to publish a story, referring to X1 but understood to refer accidentally also to X2: *Newstead* v *London Express Newspapers* (1940). Usually the circumstantial detail will be enough to exclude the accidental victim. It is possible to offer amends under s. 2, Defamation Act 1996. It is unusual for proceedings to be brought as damages tend to be nominal, and most accidental victims actually settle for a correction or explanation. There is no other defence open, as she was not intended to be referred to; cf *Hulton* v *Jones* (1910) As the paper are the publishers, they cannot rely on s. 1 of the Defamation Act 1996 (accidental defamation).

Defamatory meaning:

If it is true that proceedings have been issued, and the two women are named as respondents, although this part of the report is prima facie defamatory (indicating that they are immoral as being accused of adultery) it can be justified. The question is therefore how much further the report goes in terms of supporting information and inference: *Lewis* v *Daily Telegraph* (1964). It seems that judges, who determine what meanings words are capable of bearing, will not readily read a statement that a matter is under investigation, or that a charge has been made as carrying an implication of guilt unless there is a further peg on which to hang this. In relation to AL the statements about seeing Kite outside office hours may be a false innuendo, comparable to the euphemism 'just good friends' and therefore actionable in themselves. This can be cross-referred to the main statement. It will be for the jury to ascertain what meaning the words actually bear and whether there is a libel.

The most obvious defence is justification. If the judges confine the meaning to the narrow 'these women are charged in divorce proceedings with adultery' this may well succeed. If an improper association can be proved, it will succeed even if the meaning is accepted as being wider. AL's admission that she was an associate of Kyte does not amount to justification. It fails to meet the real sting in the innuendo. No question of privilege (this is not a report of court proceedings) or fair comment (the statements are wholly factual) arises.

(Note: Adultery is no longer directly relevant to divorce proceedings: Family Law Act 1996.)

2. There is here no doubt about either publication (for which Wardle & Co. are fully responsible), reference to Mr Micawber, who is identified by name or the defamatory nature of the statements, which is specified in the question. There is thus a prima facie case. The crucial question is whether Wardle & Co. have a defence. Justification appears to be irrelevant, as the defamatory remarks are stated not to be true.

The actual proceedings in the House are of course subject to absolute privilege. This does not extend to reports of the proceedings, but these have qualified privilege at common law: *Wason* v *Walter* (1868). This will cover the report described in the question as a précis. There is nothing to suggest that this is anything other than fair and accurate, and it is contemporaneous. It does not appear to be inspired by malice.

The 'Sketch' may in part also qualify as a privileged fair and accurate report, but it seems that it is, at least substantially, comment on the debate. It will or may be necessary to unravel which is which. It is sufficient that it is comment on privileged facts. The matter is fairly obviously one of public interest. It is sufficient if the facts relied on are referred to: *Kemsley* v *Foot* (1952). The real nub of the defence will be whether the comment is fair. The main test is whether it was malicious in the sense that no fair minded man could hold the views expressed. In *Horrocks* v *Lowe* (1975) which is regarded as applying to malice in relation to fair comment as well as qualified privilege the House of Lords gave very considerable latitude to the expression of honest sentiments, even though prejudiced to a great degree. It would seem from the case that honest belief will nearly always result in a ruling by judges of fair comment, although the issue is initially one for the jury. This is one area where the judges appear to lean in favour of free speech. In these circumstances, unless the passages complained of are quite egregiously offensive and obviously motivated by personal spite as opposed to a difference of political or other attitudes, it is likely that the defence of fair comment will succeed.

CHAPTER THIRTEEN

PRODUCT LIABILITY

13.1 Tortious Remedies: Common Law

13.1.1 INTRODUCTION

DONOGHUE v *STEVENSON* [1932] AC 562 (HL)

FACTS: The pursuer claimed that, having drunk part of a bottle of ginger-beer bought for her by a friend, she poured the rest out of the opaque bottle, and a decomposed snail floated out. She became violently ill, and claimed damages against the manufacturers who, relying on a series of decided cases, denied that they owed any legal duty. The House of Lords decided, by a bare majority that such a duty existed.

LORD ATKIN: The sole question for determination in this case is legal: Do the averments made by the pursuer in her pleading, if true, disclose a cause of action? I need not re-state the particular facts. The question is whether the manufacturer of an article of drink sold by him to a distributor in circumstances which prevent the distributor or the ultimate purchaser or consumer from discovering by inspection any defect is under any legal duty to the ultimate purchaser or consumer to take reasonable care that the article is free from defect likely to cause injury to health. I do not think a more important problem has occupied your Lordships in your judicial capacity, important both because of its bearing on public health and because of the practical test which it applies to the system of law under which it arises. We are solely concerned with the question whether as a matter of law in the circumstances alleged the defender owed any duty to the pursuer to take care. . . .

It is remarkable how difficult it is to find in the English authorities statements of general application defining the relations between parties that give rise to the duty. The courts are concerned with the particular relations which come before them in actual litigation, and it is sufficient to say whether the duty exists in those circumstances. The result is that the courts have been engaged upon an elaborate classification of duties as they exist in respect of property, whether real or personal, with further divisions as to ownership, occupation or control, and distinctions based on the particular relations of the one side or the other, whether manufacturer, salesman or landlord, customer, tenant, stranger, and so on. In this way it can be ascertained at any time whether the law recognises a duty, but only where the case can be referred to some particular species which has been examined and classified. And yet the duty which is common to all the cases where liability is established must logically be based upon some element common to the cases where it is found to exist. To seek a complete logical definition of the general principle is probably to go beyond the function of the judge, for, the more general the definition, the more likely it is to omit essentials or introduce non-essentials. The attempt was made by Lord Esher in *Heaven* v *Pender* (1883) 11 QBD 503 in a definition to which I will later refer. As framed it was demonstrably too wide, though it appears to me, if properly limited, to be capable of affording a valuable practical guide.

At present I content myself with pointing out that in English law there must be and is some general conception of relations giving rise to a duty of care, of which the particular cases found in the books are but instances. The liability for negligence, whether you style it such or treat it as in other systems as a species of 'culpa,' is no doubt based upon a general public sentiment of moral wrongdoing for which the offender must pay. But acts or omissions which any moral code would censure cannot in a practical world be treated so as to give a right to every person injured by them to demand relief. In this way rules of law arise which limit the range of complainants and the extent of their remedy. The rule that you are to love your neighbour becomes in law: You must not injure your neighbour, and the lawyers' question: Who is my neighbour? receives a restricted reply. You must take reasonable care to avoid acts or omissions which you can reasonably foresee would be likely to injure your neighbour. Who then, in law, is my neighbour? The answer seems to be persons who are so closely and directly affected by my act that I ought reasonably to have them in contemplation as being so affected when I am directing my mind to the acts or omissions which are called in question. This appears to me to be the doctrine of *Heaven* v *Pender* as laid down by Lord Esher when it is limited by the notion of proximity introduced by Lord Esher himself and A L Smith LJ, in *Le Lievre and another* v *Gould* [1893] 1 QB 491. Lord Esher MR, says [1893] 1 QB at p. 497:

> That case established that, under certain circumstances, one man may owe a duty to another, even though there is no contract between them. If one man is near to another, or is near to the property of another, a duty lies upon him not to do that which may cause a personal injury to that other, or may injure his property.

So A L Smith LJ, says [1893] 1 QB at p. 504:

> The decision of *Heaven* v *Pender* was founded upon the principle that a duty to take due care did arise when the person or property of one was in such proximity to the person or property of another that, if due care was not taken damage might be done by the one to the other.

I think that this sufficiently states the truth if proximity be not confined to mere physical proximity, but be used, as I think it was intended, to extend to such close and direct relations that the act complained of directly affects a person whom the person alleged to be bound to take care would know would be directly affected by his careless act. That this is the sense in which nearness or 'proximity' was intended by Lord Esher is obvious from his own illustration in *Heaven* v *Pender* (11 QBD at p. 510) of the application of his doctrine to the sale of goods.

> This [i.e., the rule he has just formulated] includes the case of goods, &c., supplied to be used immediately by a particular person or persons, or one of a class of persons, where it would be obvious to the person supplying, if he thought, that the goods would in all probability be used at once by such persons before a reasonable opportunity for discovering any defect which might exist, and where the thing supplied would be of such a nature that a neglect of ordinary care or skill as to its condition or the manner of supplying it would probably cause danger to the person or property of the person for whose use it was supplied, and who was about to use it. It would exclude a case in which the goods are supplied under circumstances in which it would be a chance by whom they would be used, or whether they would be used or not, or whether they would be used before there would probably be means of observing any defect, or where the goods would be of such a nature that a want of care or skill as to their condition or the manner of supplying them would not probably produce danger of injury to person or property.

I draw particular attention to the fact that Lord Esher emphasises the necessity of goods having to be 'used immediately' and 'used at once before a reasonable opportunity of inspection'. This is obviously to exclude the possibility of goods having their condition altered by a lapse of time, and to call attention to the proximate relationship, which may be too remote where inspection even by the person using, certainly by an intermediate person, may reasonably be interposed. With this necessary qualification of proximate relationship, as explained in *Le Lievre and another* v *Gould*, I think the judgment of Lord Esher expresses the law of England. Without the qualification, I think that the majority of the court in *Heaven* v *Pender* was justified in thinking that the principle was expressed in too general terms. There will, no doubt, arise cases where it will be difficult to determine whether the contemplated relationship is so close that the duty arises. But in the class of now before the court I cannot conceive any difficulty to arise. A manufacturer puts up article of food in a container which he knows will be opened by the actual consumer. There can be no inspection by any purchaser and no reasonable preliminary inspection by the consumer. Negligently in the course of preparation he allows the contents to be mixed with poison. It is said that the law of England and Scotland is that the poisoned consumer has no remedy against the negligent manufacturer. If this were the result of the authorities, I should consider the result a grave defect in the law and so contrary to principle that I should hesitate long before following any decision to that effect which had not the authority of this House. I would point out that in the assumed state of the authorities not only would the consumer have no remedy against the manufacturer, he would have none against anyone else, for in the circumstances alleged there would be no evidence of negligence against anyone other than the manufacturer, and except in the case of a consumer who was also a purchaser no contract and no warranty of fitness, and in the case of the purchase of a specific article under its patent or trade name, which might well be the case in the purchase of some articles of food or drink, no warranty protecting even the purchaser-consumer. There are other instances than of articles of food and drink where goods are sold intended to be used immediately by the consumer, such as many forms of goods sold for cleaning purposes, when the same liability must exist. The doctrine supported by the decision below would not only deny a remedy to the consumer who was injured by consuming bottled beer or chocolates poisoned by the negligence of the manufacturer, but also to the user of what should be a harmless proprietary medicine, an ointment, a soap, a cleaning fluid or cleaning powder. I confine myself to articles of common household use, where everyone, including the manufacturer, knows that the articles will be used by persons other than the actual ultimate purchaser—namely, by members of his family and his servants, and, in some cases, his guests. I do not think so ill of our jurisprudence as to suppose that its principles are so remote from the ordinary needs of civilised society and the ordinary claims which it makes upon its members as to deny a legal remedy where there is so obviously a social wrong.

It will be found, I think, on examination, that there is no case in which the circumstances have been such as I have just suggested where the liability has been negatived. There are numerous cases where the relations were much more remote where the duty has been held not to exist. There are also dicta in such cases which go further than was necessary for the determination of the particular issues, which have caused the difficulty experienced by the courts below. I venture to say that in the branch of the law which deals with civil wrongs, dependent in England, at any rate, entirely upon the application by judges of general principles also formulated by judges, it is of particular importance to guard against the danger of stating propositions of law in wider terms than is necessary, lest essential factors be omitted in the wider survey and the inherent adaptability of English law be unduly restricted. For this reason it is very necessary, in considering reported cases in the law of torts, that the actual decision alone should carry authority, proper weight, of course, being given to the dicta of the judges.

In my opinion, several decided cases support the view that in such a case as the present the manufacturer owes a duty to the consumer to be careful. A direct authority is *George* v *Skivington* (1869) ER 5 Exch 1. That was a decision on a demurrer to a declaration which averred that the defendant professed to sell a hairwash made by himself and that the plaintiff, Joseph George, bought a bottle to be used by his wife, the plaintiff Emma George, as the defendant then knew, and that the defendant had so negligently conducted himself in preparing and selling the hairwash that it was unfit for use, whereby the female plaintiff was injured. Kelly CB said that there was no question of warranty, but whether the chemist was liable in an action on the case for unskilfulness and negligence in the manufacture of it:

Unquestionably there was such a duty towards the purchaser, and it extends, in my judgment, to the person for whose use the vendor knew the compound was purchased.

A very recent case, which has the authority of this House, is *Chapman (or Oliver)* v *Saddler & Co.* [1929] AC 584. In that case a firm of stevedores employed to unload a cargo of maize in bags provided the rope slings by which the cargo was raised to the ship's deck by their own men using the ship's tackle and was then transported to the dock side by the shore porters, of whom the plaintiff was one. The porters relied on examination by the stevedores and had themselves no opportunity of examination. In these circumstances this House, reversing the decision of the First Division, held that there was a duty owed by the stevedore company to the porters to see that the slings were fit for use, and restored the judgment of the Lord Ordinary, Lord Morison, in favour of the pursuer.

It now becomes necessary to consider the cases which have been referred to in the courts below as laying down the proposition that no duty to take care is owed to the consumer in such a case as this. . . .

Winterbottom v *Wright* (1842) 10 M & W 109 was a case decided on a demurrer. The plaintiff had demurred to two of the pleas as to which there was no decision by the court, but on the hearing of the plaintiff's demurrer the court, in accordance with the practice of the day, were entitled to consider the whole record, including the declaration, and, owing to the conclusion that this declaration disclosed no cause of action, gave judgment for the defendant: see *Sutton's Personal Actions at Common Law*, p. 113. The advantage of the procedure is that we are in a position to know the precise issue at law which arose for determination. The declaration was in case and alleged that the defendant had contracted with the Postmaster-General to provide the mail coach to convey mails from Hartford to Holyhead and to keep the mails in safe condition, that Atkinson and others, with notice of the said contract, had contracted with the Postmaster-General to convey the road mail coach from Hartford to Holyhead, and that the plaintiff, relying on the said first contact, hired himself to Atkinson to drive the mail coach, but that the defendant so negligently conducted himself and so utterly disregarded his aforesaid contract that, the defendant having the means of knowing and well knowing all the aforesaid premises, the mail coach, being in a dangerous condition owing to certain latent defects and to no other cause, gave way, whereby the plaintiff was thrown from his seat and injured. It is to be observed that no negligence apart from breach of contract was alleged—in other words, no duty was alleged other than the duty arising out of the contract. It is not stated that the defendant knew or ought to have known of the latent defect. The argument of the defendant was that on the fact of the declaration the wrong arose merely out of the breach of a contract, and that only a party to the contract could sue. The Court of Exchequer adopted that view, as clearly appears from the judgments of Alderson and Rolfe BB. There are dicta by Lord Abinger which are too wide as to an action of negligence being confined to cases of breach of a public duty. The actual decision appears to have been manifestly right, no duty to the plaintiff arose out of the contract, and the duty of the defendant under the contract with the Postmaster-General to put the coach in good repair would not have involved such direct relations with the servant of the person whom the Postmaster-General employed to drive the coach as would give rise to a duty of care owed to such servant.

We now come to *Longmeid* v *Holliday* (1851) 6 Exch 761, the dicta in which have had considerable effect in subsequent decisions. In that case the declaration in case alleged that the plaintiff, Frederick Longmeid, had bought from the defendant, the maker and seller of 'the Holliday lamp,' a lamp to be used by himself and his wife Eliza in the plaintiffs' shop; that the defendant induced the sale by the false and fraudulent warranty that the lamp was reasonably fit for the purpose; and that the plaintiff Eliza, confiding in the said warranty, lighted the lamp, which exploded, whereby she was injured. The jury found all the facts for the plaintiffs except the allegation of fraud; they were not satisfied that the defendant knew of the defects. The plaintiff Frederick had already recovered damages on the contract of sale for breach of the implied warranty of fitness. The declaration made no averment of negligence. Verdict was entered at the trial by Martin B for the plaintiff, but with liberty to the defendant to move to enter the verdict for him. A rule having been obtained, plaintiff's counsel sought to support the verdict on the ground that this was an action, not for a breach of duty arising solely from contract, but for an injury resulting from conduct amounting to fraud.

Parke B who delivered the judgment of the court, held that, fraud having been negatived, the action could not be maintained on that ground. He then went on to discuss cases in which a third person not a party to a contract may sue for damages sustained if it is broken. After dealing with the negligence of a surgeon or of a carrier, or of a firm in breach of contract committing a nuisance on a highway, he deals with the case where anyone delivers to another without notice an instrument in its nature dangerous or under particular circumstances, as a loaded gun, and refers to *Dixon* v *Bell*, though what this case has to do with contract is difficult to see. He then goes on:

But it would be going much too far to say that so much care is required in the ordinary intercourse of life between one individual and another that, if a machine not in its nature dangerous—a carriage, for instance—but which might become so by a latent defect entirely unknown, although discoverable by the exercise of ordinary care, should be lent or given by one person, even by the person who manufactured it, to another, the former should be answerable to the latter for a subsequent damage accruing by the use of it.

It is worth noticing how guarded this dictum is. The case put is a machine, such as a carriage, not in its nature dangerous, which might become dangerous by a latent defect entirely unknown. Then there is the saving 'although discoverable by the exercise of ordinary care,' discoverable by whom it is not said; it may include the person to whom the innocent machine is 'lent or given'. Then the dictum is confined to machines 'lent or given' (a later sentence makes it clear that a distinction is intended between these words and 'delivered to the purchaser under the contract of sale'), and the manufacturer is introduced for the first time—'even by the person who manufactured it.' I do not for a moment believe that Parke B had in his mind such a case as a loaf negligently mixed by the baker with poison which poisoned a purchaser's family. He is, in my opinion, confining his remarks primarily to cases where a person is seeking to rely upon a duty of care which arises out of a contract with a third party, and has never even discussed the case of a manufacturer negligently causing an article to be dangerous and selling it in that condition whether with immediate or mediate effect upon the consumer. It is noteworthy that he refers to 'letting or giving' chattels, operations known to the law, where the special relations thereby created have a particular bearing on the existence or non-existence of a duty to take care.

Next in this chain of authority come *George v Skivington* and *Heaven v Pender*, which I have already discussed. The next case is *Earl v Lubbock* [1905] 1 KB 253. The plaintiff sued in the county court for personal injuries due to the negligence of the defendant. The plaintiff was a driver in the employ of a firm who owned vans. The defendant, a master wheelwright, had contracted with the firm to keep their vans in good and substantial repair. The allegation of negligence was that the defendant's servant had negligently failed to inspect and repair a defective wheel, and had negligently repaired the wheel. The learned county court judge had held that the defendant owed no duty to the plaintiff, and the Divisional Court (Lord Alverstone CJ, Wills and Kennedy JJ) and the Court of Appeal agreed with him. Collins MR said that the case was concluded by *Winterbottom v Wright*. In other words, he must have treated the duty as alleged to arise only from a breach of contract, for, as has been pointed out, that was the only allegation in *Winterbottom v Wright*, negligence, apart from contract, being neither averred nor proved. It is true that he cites with approval the dicta of Lord Abinger in the case, but obviously I think his approval must be limited to those dicta so far as they related to the particular facts before the Court of Appeal, and to cases where, as Lord Abinger says, the law permits a contract to be turned into a tort. Stirling LJ it is true, said that to succeed the plaintiff must bring his case within the proposition of the majority in *Heaven v Pender*, that any one who, without due warning, supplies to others for use an instrument which to his knowledge is in such a condition as to cause danger is liable for injury. I venture to think that the lord justice was mistakenly treating a proposition which applies one test of a duty as though it afforded the only criterion. Mathew LJ appears to me to put the case on its proper footing when he says:

> The argument of counsel for plaintiff was that the defendant's servants had been negligent in the performance of the contract with the owners of the van, and that it followed as a matter of law that anyone in their employment . . . had a cause of action against the defendant. It is impossible to accept such a wide proposition, and, indeed, it is difficult to see how, if it were the law, trade could be carried on.

I entirely agree. I have no doubt that in that case the plaintiff failed to show that the repairer owed any duty to him. The question of law in that case seems very different from that raised in the present case. . . .

The nature of the thing may very well call for different degrees of care, and the person dealing with it may well contemplate persons as being within the sphere of his duty to take care who would not be sufficiently proximate with less dangerous goods, so that not only the degree of care but the range of persons to whom a duty is owed may be extended. But they all illustrate the general principle. In *Dominion Natural Gas Co. Ltd* v *Collins* [1909] AC 640 the appellants had installed a gas apparatus and were supplying natural gas on the premises of a railway company. They had installed a regulator to control the pressure and their men negligently made an escape valve discharge into the building instead of into the open air. The railway workmen—the plaintiffs—were injured by an explosion in the premises. The defendants were held liable. Lord Dunedin, in giving the judgment of the Judicial Committee, consisting of himself, Lord Macnaghten, Lord Collins, and Sir Arthur Wilson, after stating that there was no relation of contract between the plaintiffs and the defendants, proceeded ([1909] AC at p. 646):

> There may be, however, in the case of anyone performing an operation, or setting up and installing a machine, a relationship of duty. What that duty is will vary according to the subject-matter of the things involved. It has, however, again and again been held that in the case of articles dangerous in themselves, such as loaded firearms, poisons, explosives, and other things ejusdem generis, there is a peculiar duty to take precaution imposed upon those who send forth or install such articles when it is necessarily the case that other parties will come within their proximity.

This, with respect, exactly sums up the position. The duty may exist independently of contract. Whether it exists or not depends upon the subject-matter involved, but clearly in the class of things enumerated there is a special duty to take precautions. This is the very opposite of creating a special category in which alone the duty exists. I may add, though it obviously would make no difference in the creation of a duty, that the installation of an apparatus to be used for gas perhaps more closely resembles the manufacture of a gun than a dealing with a loaded gun. In both cases the actual work is innocuous; it is only when the gun is loaded or the apparatus charged with gas that the danger arises.

It is always a satisfaction to an English lawyer to be able to test his application of fundamental principles of the common law by the development of the same doctrines by the lawyers of the courts of the United States. In that country I find that the law appears to be well established in the sense which I have indicated. The mouse had emerged from the ginger-beer bottle in the United State before it appeared in Scotland, but there it brought a liability upon the manufacturer. I must not in this long judgment do more than refer to the illuminating judgment of Cardozo J in *McPherson* v *Buick Motor Co.* (1916) 217 NY 382, in the New York Court of Appeals, in which he states the principles of the law as I should desire to state them and reviews the authorities in States other than his own. Whether the principle which he affirms would apply to the particular facts of that case in this country would be a question for consideration if the case arose. It might be that the course of business, by giving opportunities of examination to the immediate purchaser or otherwise, prevented the relation between manufacturer and the user of the car from being so close as to create a duty. But the American decision would undoubtedly lead to a decision in favour of the pursuer in the present case.

If your Lordships accept the view that the appellant's pleading discloses a relevant cause of action, you will be affirming the proposition that by Scots and English law alike a manufacturer of products which he sells in such a form as to show that he intends them to reach the ultimate consumer in the form in which they left him, with no reasonable possibility of intermediate examination, and with the knowledge that the absence of reasonable care in the preparation or putting up of the products will result in injury to the consumer's life or property, owes a duty to the consumer to take that reasonable care.

It is a proposition that I venture to say no one in Scotland or England who was not a lawyer would for one moment doubt. It will be an advantage to make it clear that the law in this matter, as in most others, is in accordance with sound common sense. I think that this appeal should be allowed.

13.1.2   PROVING NEGLIGENCE

MASON v *WILLIAMS & WILLIAMS LTD AND THOMAS TURTON & SONS LTD*
[1955] 1 All ER 808

FACTS: The plaintiff was injured at work when a metal splinter flew off a cold chisel he was using. He sued the first defendants, his employers, for negligence in respect of the issue and use of the tool, and also the second defendants, the manufacturers, for supplying a dangerously defective item. The evidence showed that the head of the chisel was dangerously hard, the result of a manufacturing defect.

FINNEMORE J: I appreciate that I am faced with another problem, as was indicated in the case of M'Alister (or Donoghue) v Stevenson that res ipsa loquitur does not apply and that the court has to be satisfied, and therefore the plaintiff has got to prove, that there was negligence on the part of the manufacturers. Of course that cannot be proved normally by saying that on such and such a date such and such a workman did this, that or the other. I think that when you have eliminated anything happening in this case at the employers' factory, whither, as is undisputed, this chisel came direct from the manufacturers—and when it came from the manufacturers the head was too hard, and that undue hardness could have been produced only while it was being manufactured by them, and could have been produced by someone there either carelessly or deliberately to make a harder and more durable head—that is really as far as any plaintiff can be expected to take his case. What the plaintiff says here is:—'This is your chisel, you made it and I used it as you made it, in the condition in which you made it, in the way you intended me to use it, and you never relied on any intermediate examination; therefore I have discharged the onus of proof by saying that this trouble must have happened through some act in the manufacture of this chisel in your factory, and that was either careless or deliberate, and in either event it was a breach of duty towards me, a person whom you contemplated would use this article which you made, in the way you intended it to be used.' He is entitled to succeed against the manufacturers.

13.2   Statutory Liability

CONSUMER PROTECTION ACT 1987

1.   Purpose and construction of Part I

(1)   This Part shall have effect for the purpose of making such provision as is necessary in order to comply with the product liability Directive and shall be construed accordingly.

(2)   In this Part, except in so far as the context otherwise requires—

'agricultural produce' means any produce of the soil, of stock-farming or of fisheries;

'dependant' and 'relative' have the same meaning as they have in, respectively, the Fatal Accidents Act 1976 and the Damages (Scotland) Act 1976;

'producer', in relation to a product, means—

(a)   the person who manufactured it;

(b)   in the case of a substance which has not been manufactured but has been won or abstracted, the person who won or abstracted it;

(c)   in the case of a product which has not been manufactured, won or abstracted but essential characteristics of which are attributable to an industrial or other process having been carried out (for example, in relation to agricultural produce), the person who carried out that process;

'product' means any goods or electricity and (subject to subsection (3) below) includes a product which is comprised in another product, whether by virtue of being a component part or raw material or otherwise; and

'the product liability Directive' means the Directive of the Council of the European Communities, dated 25th July 1985, (No. 85/374/EEC) on the approximation of the laws, regulations and administrative provisions of the member States concerning liability for defective products.

(3)   For the purposes of this Part a person who supplies any product in which products are comprised, whether by virtue of being component parts or raw materials or otherwise, shall not be treated by reason only of his supply of that product as supplying any of the products so comprised.

2.   Liability for defective products

(1)   Subject to the following provisions of this Part, where any damage is caused wholly or partly by a defect in a product, every person to whom subsection (2) below applies shall be liable for the damage.

(2)   This subsection applies to—

(a)   the producer of the product;

(b)   any person who, by putting his name on the product or using a trade mark or other distinguishing mark in relation to the product, has held himself out to be the producer of the product;

(c)   any person who has imported the product into a member State from a place outside the member States in order, in the course of any business of his, to supply it to another.

(3)   Subject as aforesaid, where any damage is caused wholly or partly by a defect in a product, any person who supplied the product (whether to the person who suffered the damage, to the producer of any product in which the product in question is comprised or to any other person) shall be liable for the damage if—

(a)   the person who suffered the damage requests the supplier to identify one or more of the persons (whether still in existence or not) to whom subsection (2) above applies in relation to the product;

(b)   that request is made within a reasonable period after the damage occurs and at a time when it is not reasonably practicable for the person making the request to identify all those persons; and

(c)   the supplier fails, within a reasonable period after receiving the request, either to comply with the request or to identify the person who supplied the product to him.

(4)   Neither subsection (2) nor subsection (3) above shall apply to a person in respect of any defect in any game or agricultural produce if the only supply of the game or produce by that person to another was at a time when it had not undergone an industrial process.

(5)   Where two or more persons are liable by virtue of this Part for the same damage, their liability shall be joint and several.

(6)   This section shall be without prejudice to any liability arising otherwise than by virtue of this Part.

3.   Meaning of 'defect'

(1)   Subject to the following provisions of this section, there is a defect in a product for the purposes of this Part if the safety of the product is not such as persons generally are entitled to expect; and for those purposes 'safety', in relation to a product, shall include safety with respect to products comprised in that product and safety in the context of risks of damage to property, as well as in the context of risks of death or personal injury.

(2)   In determining for the purposes of subsection (1) above what persons generally are entitled to expect in relation to a product all the circumstances shall be taken into account, including—

(a)   the manner in which, and purposes for which, the product has been marketed, its get-up, the use of any mark in relation to the product and any instructions for, or warnings with respect to, doing or refraining from doing anything with or in relation to the product;

(b)   what might reasonably be expected to be done with or in relation to the product; and

(c)   the time when the product was supplied by its producer to another;
and nothing in this section shall require a defect to be inferred from the fact alone that the safety of a product which is supplied after that time is greater than the safety of the product in question.

4.   Defences

(1)   In any civil proceedings by virtue of this Part against any person ('the person proceeded against') in respect of a defect in a product it shall be a defence for him to show—

(a)   that the defect is attributable to compliance with any requirement imposed by or under any enactment or with any Community obligation; or

(b)   that the person proceeded against did not at any time supply the product to another; or

(c)   that the following conditions are satisfied, that is to say—

(i)   that the only supply of the product to another by the person proceeded against was otherwise than in the course of a business of that person's; and

(ii)   that section 2(2) above does not apply to that person or applies to him by virtue only of things done otherwise than with a view to profit; or

(d)   that the defect did not exist in the product at the relevant time; or

(e)   that the state of scientific and technical knowledge at the relevant time was not such that a producer of products of the same description as the product in question might be expected to have discovered the defect if it had existed in his products while they were under his control; or

(f)   that the defect—

(i)   constituted a defect in a product ('the subsequent product') in which the product in question had been comprised; and

(ii)   was wholly attributable to the design of the subsequent product or to compliance by the producer of the product in question with instructions given by the producer of the subsequent product.

(2)   In this section 'the relevant time', in relation to electricity, means the time at which it was generated, being a time before it was transmitted or distributed, and in relation to any other product, means—

(a)   if the person proceeded against is a person to whom subsection (2) of section 2 above applies in relation to the product, the time when he supplied the product to another;

(b)   if that subsection does not apply to that person in relation to the product, the time when the product was last supplied by a person to whom that subsection does apply in relation to the product.

5.   Damage giving rise to liability

(1)   Subject to the following provisions of this section, in this Part 'damage' means death or personal injury or any loss of or damage to any property (including land).

(2)   A person shall not be liable under section 2 above in respect of any defect in a product for the loss of or any damage to the product itself or for the loss of or any damage to the whole or any part of any product which has been supplied with the product in question comprised in it.

(3)   A person shall not be liable under section 2 above for any loss of or damage to any property which, at the time it is lost or damaged, is not—

(a)   of a description of property ordinarily intended for private use, occupation or consumption; and

(b)   intended by the persons suffering the loss or damage mainly for his own private use, occupation or consumption.

(4)   No damages shall be awarded to any person by virtue of this Part in respect of any loss of or damage to any property if the amount which would fall to be so awarded to that person, apart from this subsection and any liability for interest, does not exceed £275.

(5)   In determining for the purposes of this Part who has suffered any loss of or damage to property and when any such loss or damage occurred, the loss or damage shall be regarded as having occurred at the earliest time at which a person with an interest in the property had knowledge of the material facts about the loss or damage.

(6)   For the purposes of subsection (5) above the material facts about any loss of or damage to any property are such facts about the loss or damage as would lead a reasonable person with an interest in the property to consider the loss or damage sufficiently serious to justify his instituting proceedings for damages against a defendant who did not dispute liability and was able to satisfy a judgment.

(7)   For the purposes of subsection (5) above a person's knowledge includes knowledge which he might reasonably have been expected to acquire—

(a)   from facts observable or ascertainable by him; or

(b)   from facts ascertainable by him with the help of appropriate expert advice which it is reasonable for him to seek;

but a person shall not be taken by virtue of this subsection to have knowledge of a fact ascertainable by him only with the help of expert advice unless he has failed to take all reasonable steps to obtain (and, where appropriate, to act on) that advice.

6.   Application of certain enactments etc

(1)   Any damage for which a person is liable under section 2 above shall be deemed to have been caused—

(a)   for the purposes of the Fatal Accidents Act 1976, by that person's wrongful act, neglect or default; . . .

(2) Where—

(a) a person's death is caused wholly or partly by a defect in a product, or a person dies after suffering damage which has been so caused;

(b) a request such as mentioned in paragraph (a) of subsection (3) of section 2 above is made to a supplier of the product by that person's personal representatives or, in the case of a person whose death is caused wholly or partly by the defect, by any dependant or relative of that person; and

(c) the conditions specified in paragraphs (b) and (c) of that subsection are satisfied in relation to that request,

this Part shall have effect for the purposes of the Law Reform (Miscellaneous Provisions) Act 1934, the Fatal Accidents Act 1976 and the Damages (Scotland) Act 1976 as if liability of the supplier to that person under that subsection did not depend on that person having requested the supplier to identify certain persons or on the said conditions having been satisfied in relation to a request made by that person.

(3) Section 1 of the Congenital Disabilities (Civil Liability) Act 1976 shall have effect for the purposes of this Part as if—

(a) a person were answerable to a child in respect of an occurrence caused wholly or partly by a defect in a product if he is or has been liable under section 2 above in respect of any effect of the occurrence on a parent of the child, or would be so liable if the occurrence caused a parent of the child to suffer damage;

(b) the provisions of this Part relating to liability under section 2 above applied in relation to liability by virtue of paragraph (a) above under the said section 1; and

(c) subsection (6) of the said section 1 (exclusion of liability) were omitted.

(4) Where any damage is caused partly by a defect in a product and partly by the fault of the person suffering the damage, the Law Reform (Contributory Negligence) Act 1945 and section 5 of the Fatal Accidents Act 1976 (contributory negligence) shall have effect as if the defect were the fault of every person liable by virtue of this Part for the damage caused by the defect.

(5) In subsection (4) above 'fault' has the same meaning as in the said Act of 1945.

(6) Schedule 1 to this Act shall have effect for the purpose of amending the Limitation Act 1980 and the Prescription and Limitation (Scotland) Act 1973 in their application in relation to the bringing of actions by virtue of this Part.

(7) It is hereby declared that liability by virtue of this Part is to be treated as liability in tort for the purposes of any enactment conferring jurisdiction on any court with respect to any matter.

(8) Nothing in this Part shall prejudice the operation of section 12 of the Nuclear Installations Act 1965 (rights to compensation for certain breaches of duties confined to rights under that Act).

7. Prohibition on exclusions from liability

The liability of a person by virtue of this Part to a person who has suffered damage caused wholly or partly by a defect in a product, or to a dependant or relative of such a person, shall not be limited or excluded by any contract term, by any notice or by any other provision.

COUNCIL DIRECTIVE
of 25 July 1985
**on the approximation of the laws, regulations and administrative provisions
of the Member States concerning liability for defective products**
(85/374/EEC:L 210/29)

THE COUNCIL OF THE EUROPEAN COMMUNITIES,
Having regard to the Treaty establishing the European Economic Community, and in particular Article 100 thereof,

Having regard to the proposal from the Commission,

Having regard to the opinion of the European Parliament,

Having regard to the opinion of the Economic and Social Committee,

Whereas approximation of the laws of the Member States concerning the liability of the producer for damage caused by the defectiveness of his products is necessary because the existing divergences may distort competition and affect the movement of goods within the common market and entail a differing degree of protection of the consumer against damage caused by a defective product to his health or property;

Whereas liability without fault on the part of the producer is the sole means of adequately solving the problem, peculiar to our age of increasing technicality, of a fair apportionment of the risks inherent in modern technological production;

Whereas liability without fault should apply only to movables which have been industrially produced; whereas, as a result, it is appropriate to exclude liability for agricultural products and game, except where they have undergone a processing of an industrial nature which could cause a defect in these products; whereas the liability provided for in this Directive should also apply to movables which are used in the construction of immovables or are installed in immovables;

Whereas protection of the consumer requires that all producers involved in the production process should be made liable, in so far as their finished product, component part or any raw material supplied by them was defective; whereas, for the same reason, liability should extend to importers of products into the Community and to persons who present themselves as producers by affixing their name, trade mark or other distinguishing feature or who supply a product the producer of which cannot be identified;

Whereas, in situations where several persons are liable for the same damage, the protection of the consumer requires that the injured person should be able to claim full compensation for the damage from any one of them;

Whereas, to protect the physical well-being and property of the consumer, the defectiveness of the product should be determined by reference not to its fitness for use but to the lack of the safety which the public at large is entitled to expect; whereas the safety is assessed by excluding any misuse of the product not reasonable under the circumstances;

Whereas a fair apportionment of risk between the injured person and the producer implies that the producer should be able to free himself from liability if he furnishes proof as to the existence of certain exonerating circumstances;

Whereas the protection of the consumer requires that the liability of the producer remains unaffected by acts or omissions of other persons having contributed to cause the damage; whereas, however, the contributory negligence of the injured person may be taken into account to reduce or disallow such liability;

Whereas the protection of the consumer requires compensation for death and personal injury as well as compensation for damage to property; whereas the latter should nevertheless be limited to goods for private use or consumption and be subject to a deduction of a lower threshold of a fixed amount in order to avoid litigation in an excessive number of cases; whereas this Directive should not prejudice compensation for pain and suffering and other non-material damages payable, where appropriate, under the law applicable to the case;

Whereas a uniform period of limitation for the bringing of action for compensation is in the interests both of the injured person and of the producer;

Whereas products age in the course of time, higher safety standards are developed and the state of science and technology progresses; whereas, therefore, it would not be reasonable to make the producer liable for an unlimited period for the defectiveness of his product; whereas therefore, liability should expire after a reasonable length of time, without prejudice to claims pending at law;

Whereas, to achieve effective protection of consumers, no contractual derogation should be permitted as regards the liability of the producer in relation to the injured person;

Whereas under the legal systems of the Member States an injured party may have a claim for damages based on grounds of contractual liability or on grounds of non-contractual liability other than that provided for in this Directive; in so far as these provisions also serve to attain the objective of effective protection of consumers, they should remain unaffected by this Directive; whereas, in so far as effective protection of consumers in the sector of pharmaceutical products is already also attained in a Member State under a special liability system, claims based on this system should similarly remain possible;

Whereas, to the extent that liability for nuclear injury or damage is already covered in all Member States by adequate special rules, it has been possible to exclude damage of this type from the scope of this Directive;

Whereas, since the exclusion of primary agricultural products and game from the scope of this Directive may be felt, in certain Member States, in view of what is expected for the protection of consumers, to restrict unduly such protection, it should be possible for a Member State to extend liability to such products;

Whereas, for similar reasons, the possibility offered to a producer to free himself from liability if he proves that the state of scientific and technical knowledge at the time when he put the product into circulation was not such as to enable the existence of a defect to be discovered may be felt in certain Member States to restrict unduly the protection of the consumer; whereas it should therefore be possible for a Member State to maintain in its legislation or to provide by new legislation that this exonerating circumstance is not admitted; whereas, in the case of new legislation, making use of this derogation should, however, be subject to a Community stand-still procedure, in order to raise, if possible, the level of protection in a uniform manner throughout the Community;

Whereas, taking into account the legal traditions in most of the Member States, it is inappropriate to set any financial ceiling on the producer's liability without fault; whereas, in so far as there are, however, differing traditions, it seems possible to admit that a Member State may derogate from the principle of unlimited liability by providing a limit for the total liability of the producer for damage resulting from a death or personal injury and caused by identical items with the same defect, provided that this limit is established at a level sufficiently high to guarantee adequate protection of the consumer and the correct functioning of the common market;

Whereas the harmonisation resulting from this cannot be total at the present stage, but opens the way towards greater harmonisation; whereas it is therefore necessary that the Council receive at regular intervals, reports from the Commission on the application of this Directive, accompanied, as the case may be, by appropriate proposals;

Whereas it is particularly important in this respect that a re-examination be carried out of those parts of the Directive relating to the derogations open to the Member States, at the expiry of a period of sufficient length to gather practical experience on the effects of these derogations on the protection of consumers and on the functioning of the common market,

HAS ADOPTED THIS DIRECTIVE:

Article 1. The producer shall be liable for damage caused by a defect in his product.

Article 2. For the purpose of this Directive 'product' means all movables, with the exception of primary agricultural products and game, even though incorporated into another movable or into an immovable. 'Primary agricultural products' means the products of the soil, of stock-farming and of fisheries, excluding products which have undergone initial processing. 'Product' includes electricity.

Article 3. 1. 'Producer' means the manufacturer of a finished product, the producer of any raw material or the manufacturer of a component part and any person who, by putting his name, trade mark or other distinguishing feature on the product presents himself as its producer.

Without prejudice to the liability of the producer, any person who imports into the Community a product for sale, hire or any form of distribution in the course of his business shall be deemed to be a producer within the meaning of this Directive and shall be responsible as a producer.

3. Where the producer of the product cannot be identified, each supplier of the product shall be treated as its producer unless he informs the injured person, within a reasonable time, of the identity of the producer or of the person who supplied him with the product. The same shall apply, in the case of an imported product, if this product does not indicate the identity of the importer referred to in paragraph 2, even if the name of the producer is indicated.

Article 4. The injured person shall be required to prove the damage, the defect and the causal relationship between defect and damage.

Article 5. Where, as a result of the provisions of this Directive, two or more persons are liable for the same damage, they shall be liable jointly and severally, without prejudice to the provisions of national law concerning the rights of contribution or recourse.

Article 6. 1. A product is defective when it does not provide the safety which a person is entitled to expect, taking all circumstances into account, including:

(a)   the presentation of the product;

(b)   the use to which it could reasonably be expected that the product would be put;

(c)   the time when the product was put into circulation.

2.   A product shall not be considered defective for the sole reason that a better product is subsequently put into circulation.

Article 7.   The producer shall not be liable as a result of this Directive if he proves:

(a)   that he did not put the product into circulation; or

(b)   that, having regard to the circumstances, it is probable that the defect which caused the damage did not exist at the time when the product was put into circulation by him or that this defect came into being afterwards; or

(c)   that the product was neither manufactured by him for sale or any form of distribution for economic purpose nor manufactured or distributed by him in the course of his business; or

(d)   that the defect is due to compliance of the product with mandatory regulations issued by the public authorities; or

(e)   that the state of scientific and technical knowledge at the time when he put the product into circulation was not such as to enable the existence of the defect to be discovered; or

(f)   in the case of a manufacturer of a component, that the defect is attributable to the design of the product in which the component has been fitted or to the instructions given by the manufacturer of the product.

Article 8.   1.   Without prejudice to the provisions of national law concerning the right of contribution or recourse, the liability of the producer shall not be reduced when the damage is caused both by a defect in product and by the act or omission of a third party.

2.   The liability of the producer may be reduced or disallowed when, having regard to all the circumstances, the damage is caused both by a defect in the product and by the fault of the injured person or any person for whom the injured person is responsible.

Article 9.   For the purpose of Article 1, 'damage' means:

(a)   damage caused by death or by personal injuries;

(b)   damage to, or destruction of, any item of property other than the defective product itself, with a lower threshold of 500 ECU, provided that the item of property:

(i)   is of a type ordinarily intended for private use or consumption, and

(ii)   was used by the injured person mainly for his own private use or consumption.

This Article shall be without prejudice to national provisions relating to non-material damage.

Article 10   1.   Member States shall provide in their legislation that a limitation period of three years shall apply to proceedings for the recovery of damages as provided for in this Directive. The limitation period shall begin to run from the day on which the plaintiff became aware, or should reasonably have become aware, of the damage, the defect and the identity of the producer.

2.   The laws of Member States regulating suspension or interruption of the limitation period shall not be affected by this Directive.

Article 11.   Member States shall provide in their legislation that the rights conferred upon the injured person pursuant to this Directive shall be extinguished upon the expiry of a period of 10 years from the date on which the producer put into circulation the actual product which caused the damage, unless the injured person has in the meantime instituted proceedings against the producer.

Article 12.   The liability of the producer arising from this Directive may not, in relation to the injured person, be limited or excluded by a provision limiting his liability or exempting him from liability.

Article 13.   This Directive shall not affect any rights which an injured person may have according to the rules of the law of contractual or non-contractual liability or a special liability system existing at the moment when this Directive is notified.

Article 14.   This Directive shall not apply to injury or damage arising from nuclear accidents and covered by international conventions ratified by the Member States.

Article 15.   1.   Each Member State may:

(a)   by way of derogation from Article 2, provide in its legislation that within the meaning of Article 1 of this Directive 'product' also means primary agricultural products and game;

(b)   by way of derogation from Article 7(e), maintain or, subject to the procedure set out in paragraph 2 of this Article, provide in this legislation that the producer shall be liable even if he proves that the state of scientific and technical knowledge at the time when he put the product into circulation was not such as to enable the existence of a defect to be discovered.

2. A Member State wishing to introduce the measure specified in paragraph 1(b) shall communicate the text of the proposed measure to the Commission. The Commission shall inform the other Member States thereof.

The Member State concerned shall hold the proposed measure in abeyance for nine months after the Commission is informed and provided that in the meantime the Commission has not submitted to the Council a proposal amending this Directive on the relevant matter. However, if within three months of receiving the said information, the Commission does not advise the Member State concerned that it intends submitting such a proposal to the Council, the Member State may take the proposed measure immediately.

If the Commission does submit to the Council such a proposal amending this Directive within the aforementioned nine months, the Member State concerned shall hold the proposed measure in abeyance for a further period of 18 months from the date on which the proposal is submitted.

3. Ten years after the date of notification of this Directive, the Commission shall submit to the Council a report on the effect that rulings by the courts as to the application of Article 7(e) and of paragraph 1(b) of this Article have on consumer protection and the functioning of the common market. In the light of this report the Council, acting on a proposal from the Commission and pursuant to the terms of Article 100 of the Treaty, shall decide whether to repeal Article 7(e).

Article 16. 1. Any Member State may provide that a producer's total liability for damage resulting from a death or personal injury and caused by identical items with the same defect shall be limited to an amount which may not be less than 70 million ECU.

2. Ten years after the date of notification of this Directive, the Commission shall submit to the Council a report on the effect on consumer protection and the functioning of the common market of the implementation of the financial limit on liability by those Member States which have used the option provided for in paragraph 1. In the light of this report the Council, acting on a proposal from the Commission and pursuant to the terms of Article 100 of the Treaty, shall decide whether to repeal paragraph 1.

Article 17. This Directive shall not apply to products put into circulation before the date on which the provisions referred to in Article 19 enter into force.

13.3 End of Chapter Assessment Questions

(1)   Latifa buys a fish tank from Allpets Pet Stores. It is fitted with a heater, which came separately packed and labelled as the Allpets Allstar Tankkosy. In fact it was manufactured in China and imported to Finland (in January 1995) by Finchin Impex A/S. Latifa is impressed with the heater and buys a second one for another tank which she has owned for some time. The English instructions simply refer to the need to use a 3 amp fused plug. There are additional instructions, in Finnish and Chinese only, which state that the heater has a dual level transformer which should be set to H for connection to a 230v supply as in the UK and to L for connection to a 110v supply.

After the heaters have been in use for a month there is an explosion because they have been set at L. The two tanks, the valuable fish in them and an antique oriental carpet are destroyed and Latifa's cleaner sustains serious personal injury.

Advise on liability.

Would it affect your advice if Latifa's main source of income was selling fish she had bred?

(2)   Norman recently bought a 'Flamegrill' barbecue set from his local branch of Wyoming Homecare. It incorporated an accessory described as 'The latest miracle of Japanese electronic wizardry: a fully automated, foolproof infrared temperature sensor'. The instructions state that if the sensor is touched against any item of food, a light will flash if the food is fully cooked through. The sensor is preprogrammed to recognise most common barbecued foods, including beef, chicken and pork.

Norman organises a barbecue to raise funds for the village church steeple appeal. The ticket price includes refreshments. Many of the guests, and Norman himself, suffer food poisoning which is diagnosed as resulting from the consumption of marinaded pork spare ribs, which Norman purchased from Bob, the local butcher. These were affected by trichinella. This is commonly present in raw pork, but is killed by adequate heating. The sensor was used on all the ribs and indicated that they were fully cooked.

Most of the guests bought their own tickets. The exceptions were Cynthia, the vicar, who was admitted free, and Ann and Ben who turned up without tickets. Just before leaving, Ann wrote out a cheque for the cost of two tickets.

Considerable development work has been done on this form of sensor. This indicates that it does perform as indicated above. Some three months before this particular barbecue was manufactured, a research paper was delivered to a seminar at Hamburger University, in which it was demonstrated that inaccurate readings could be obtained in respect of 'bone-in' meat, especially pork.

Consider the liability of:

(a)   Norman;
(b)   Any other potential defendant.

13.4 End of Chapter Assessment Outline Answers

1.   There are two plaintiffs, Latifa in respect of the property damage, and the cleaner in respect of personal injuries. Latifa has a choice of remedies; she may claim against Allpets for breach of contract, or alternatively against the manufacturer or Finchin on the basis of common law manufacturer's/distributor's liability, or under the CPA 1987 against Finchin as an importer into the EC and Allpets as 'own branders'; both are deemed to be producers for the purposes of liability: s. 2(2), CPA 1987. The cleaner is restricted to the tortious remedies as she is not in privity of contract: *Priest* v *Last* (1903).

The contractual remedy will be for breach of the implied condition of satisfactory quality: s. 14(2), SGA 1979. This is non-excludable where Latifa deals as consumer: s. 6(2)(a), UCTA 1977. Latifa will recover for the value of the goods and consequential loss which is reasonably contemplatable: *Parsons* v *Uttley Ingham* (1978). This will however not extend to any emotional distress. If she were a professional breeder, her loss would include loss of profits. The implied term could in theory be excluded (there is nothing to suggest any attempt to do so) provided this satisfies the requirement of reasonableness: s. 6(3) UCTA, 1977.

The common law tortious liability is a duty of care. It will be necessary to show want of due care. The standard imposed by the courts can be very high (e.g. *Grant* v *Australian Knitting Mills* (1936)), but not every defect will be ascribed to negligence: *Daniels* v *White and Tarbard* (1938). If the manufacturer shows that proper instructions were given to the distributor to adjust the voltage controls they may escape liability on the basis that the goods were to be subject to intermediate modification or inspection, although if this is so, failure by Finchin (or Allpets) may render them liable: *Kubach* v *Hollands* (1937). If successful the cleaner will recover damages for personal injuries (including loss of earnings) on the usual basis, while Latifa can recover for the reasonably foreseeable consequential loss caused by the defective heaters, but not for their value. It was suggested in *Parsons* v *Uttley Ingham* that the measure of damages for physical harm should be the same in contract and tort and in practice, although the test of remoteness of damage is differently worded, it will in practice result in the same award (subject to the exclusion of the defective item itself in tort).

The CPA 1987 remedy may be the preferable one. The plaintiff need only prove relevant harm caused by a defective product supplied by the producer. A product is defective if its safety, in relation to harm to persons and/or property is not such as persons generally are entitled to expect: s. 3(1), CPA 1987. It is immaterial that the heaters are potentially safe if they are actually set to the wrong voltage. The defect may lie in the instructions, which are clearly inadequate for use in England: s. 3(2)(a).

The cleaner appears to have no difficulty in claiming for her personal injuries in the usual way. No defence is suggested by the facts given.

Latifa can in principle make a claim if her loss exceeds the threshold of £275. She can in any event claim in respect of the carpet. She cannot claim in respect of the defective products themselves: s. 5(2). Under the 1987 Act she cannot claim against Allpets for damage to the tank which she bought with the heater fitted, as this is a 'product which has been supplied with the [defective] product . . . comprised in it: s. 5(2). She may be able to claim for the tank against Finchin if they only supplied this component. The Act does not appear at this point to transpose the Directive accurately. The Directive only excludes claims in respect of the defective product itself: Article 9(b). As the Act is expressly intended to implement the Directive, a court should interpret it in conformity with the Directive, either pursuant to *Pickstone* v *Freemans* (1989) or *Marleasing* (1992). In the last resort Latifa may have a claim against the UK government for failure to implement the Directive: *Francovich* (1993), *Faccini-Dori* v *Recreb* (1994), *Factortame III* (1996). If the fish are simply pets, she should recover for them and for the second tank. If she is a commercial breeder she will not recover for either tank or the fish. For property damage to be within the Act it must be of a kind ordinarily intended for private use and actually so used: s. 5(3) CPA 1987.

2. Norman has a contract with most of the guests (there is none with Cynthia, and in principle Ann has a contract while Ben doesn't. However in *Lockett* v *A M Charles Ltd* (1938) it was held that the contract for a restaurant meal was made by two married diners jointly, although only one paid). However this is not made in the course of a business, and so there are no implied terms. N certainly owes his guests a duty of care, both in selecting the meat and in preparing it, although this will be the standard of the competent amateur, rather than that of a professional restaurateur: *Wells* v *Cooper* (1958). It is however far from clear that he has breached the duty of care. He has sourced his chops from an apparently reputable source and cooked them in accordance with the manufacturer's directions on a state of the art barbecue.

It is therefore necessary to consider whether the CPA 1987 applies. It may apply to the chops and/or to the barbecue. Norman and Bob have both 'produced' the chops. The original pig carcases from which the chops came were at that stage agricultural produce. Each has applied processes to them which are responsible for their essential characteristics (marinading and cooking). It is not clear who butchered the carcases. Bob will be liable under the Act only if the chops had undergone an industrial process prior to his supply of them: s. 2(4), CPA 1987. This will be the case if they were processed in a large commercial abattoir, but not if all processing has been done by Bob on a small artisanal scale. The Directive refers to 'initial' processing: Article 2, although one of the recitals in the preamble refers to industrial processing. If there is a discrepancy this will be resolved as indicated in answer 1. Norman may also argue that the goods had not been processed prior to his supply, but may also have a specific defence. His supply is not in the course of a business, and if the raising of funds for the church steeple appeal does not amount to something done 'with a view to profit' he will be outside the ambit of the Act: s. 4(1)(c), CPA 1987.

The barbecue is clearly a product. It appears to be of Japanese manufacture. The manufacturer may be liable in negligence under *Donoghue* v *Stevenson* (1932) principles if negligence can be shown, although this appears to be a design fault rather than a manufacturing fault. High standards are exacted in relation to manufacturing faults *(Grant* v *Australian Knitting Mills* (1936)), but design faults are more difficult to establish (e.g. *Roe* v *Minister of Health* (1954)). The importer into the EC will however be liable as producer under the CPA 1987. There seems no doubt that the barbecue is defective: it produces poisonous food! There may however be a defence available under s. 4(1)(e), the 'state of the art' defence. The research does appear to indicate that the device is effective and free from defect. Under the Act the question is whether the state of scientific and technical knowledge was such that a producer of products of this description might have been expected to find the defect. This clearly suggests a variable test, with producers of technically or scientifically advanced products expected to have a higher level of knowledge and research input than manufacturers of less sophisticated products. Again this appears to diverge from the Directive, where the standard appears to be absolute and to refer to the state of scientific and technical knowledge full stop: Article 7(e). Here the distinction may be significant, as the defect was known to science, although it is not clear whether the manufacturer ought to have been aware of this research paper. If there is a discrepancy it will be resolved as already indicated.

CHAPTER FOURTEEN

ANIMALS

14.1 Introduction

14.1.1 STRICT LIABILITY

ANIMALS ACT 1971

1. New provisions as to strict liability for damage done by animals

(1) The provisions of sections 2 to 5 of this Act replace—

(a) the rules of the common law imposing a strict liability in tort for damage done by an animal on the ground that the animal is regarded as ferae naturae or that its vicious or mischievous propensities are known or presumed to be known;

(b) subsections (1) and (2) of section 1 of the Dogs Act 1906 as amended by the Dogs (Amendment) Act 1928 (injury to cattle or poultry); and

(c) the rules of the common law imposing a liability for cattle trespass.

(2) Expressions used in those sections shall be interpreted in accordance with the provisions of section 6 (as well as those of section 11) of this Act.

2. Liability for damage done by dangerous animals

(1) Where any damage is caused by an animal which belongs to a dangerous species, any person who is a keeper of the animal is liable for the damage, except as otherwise provided by this Act.

(2) Where damage is caused by an animal which does not belong to a dangerous species, a keeper of the animal is liable for the damage, except as otherwise provided by this Act, if—

(a) the damage is of a kind which the animal, unless restrained, was likely to cause or which, if caused by the animal, was likely to be severe; and

(b) the likelihood of the damage or of its being severe was due to characteristics of the animal which are not normally found in animals of the same species or are not normally so found except at particular times or in particular circumstances; and

(c) those characteristics were known to that keeper or were at any time known to a person who at that time had charge of the animal as that keeper's servant or, where that keeper is the head of a household, were known to another keeper of the animal who is a member of that household and under the age of sixteen.

3. Liability for injury done by dogs to livestock

Where a dog causes damage by killing or injuring livestock, any person who is a keeper of the dog is liable for the damage, except as otherwise provided by this Act.

4. Liability for damage and expenses due to trespassing livestock

(1) Where livestock belonging to any person strays on to land in the ownership or occupation of another and—

(a) damage is done by the livestock to the land or to any property on it which is in the ownership or possession of the other person; or

(b) any expenses are reasonably incurred by that other person in keeping the livestock while it cannot be restored to the person to whom it belongs or while it is detained in pursuance of section 7 of this Act, or in ascertaining to whom it belongs; the person to whom the livestock belongs is liable for the damage or expenses, except as otherwise provided by this Act.

(2)   For the purposes of this section any livestock belongs to the person in whose possession it is.

5.   Exceptions from liability under sections 2 to 4

(1)   A person is not liable under sections 2 to 4 of this Act for any damage which is due wholly to the fault of the person suffering it.

(2)   A person is not liable under section 2 of this Act for any damage suffered by a person who has voluntarily accepted the risk thereof.

(3)   A person is not liable under section 2 of this Act for any damage caused by an animal kept on any premises or structure to a person trespassing there, if it is proved either—

(a)   that the animal was not kept there for the protection of persons or property; or

(b)   (if the animal was kept there for the protection of persons or property) that keeping it there for that purpose was not unreasonable.

(4)   A person is not liable under section 3 of this Act if the livestock was killed or injured on land on to which it had strayed and either the dog belonged to the occupier or its presence on the land was authorised by the occupier.

(5)   A person is not liable under section 4 of this Act where the livestock strayed from a highway and its presence there was a lawful use of the highway.

(6)   In determining whether any liability for damage under section 4 of this Act is excluded by subsection (1) of this section the damage shall not be treated as due to the fault of the person suffering it by reason only that he could have prevented it by fencing; but a person is not liable under that section where it is proved that the straying of the livestock on to the land would not have occurred but for a breach by any other person, being a person having an interest in the land, of a duty to fence.

6.   Interpretation of certain expressions used in sections 2 to 5

(1)   The following provisions apply to the interpretation of sections 2 to 5 of this Act.

(2)   A dangerous species is a species—

(a)   which is not commonly domesticated in the British Islands; and

(b)   whose fully grown animals normally have such characteristics that they are likely, unless restrained, to cause severe damage or that any damage they may cause is likely to be severe.

(3)   Subject to subsection (4) of this section, a person is a keeper of an animal if—

(a)   he owns the animal or has it in his possession; or

(b)   he is the head of a household of which a member under the age of sixteen owns the animal or has it in his possession;

and if at any time an animal ceases to be owned by or to be in the possession of a person, any person who immediately before that time was a keeper thereof by virtue of the preceding provisions of this subsection continues to be a keeper of the animal until another person becomes a keeper thereof by virtue of those provisions.

(4)   Where an animal is taken into and kept in possession for the purpose of preventing it from causing damage or of restoring it to its owner, a person is not a keeper of it by virtue only of that possession.

(5)   Where a person employed as a servant by a keeper of an animal incurs a risk incidental to his employment he shall not be treated as accepting it voluntarily.

7.   Detention and sale of trespassing livestock

(1)   The right to seize and detain any animal by way of distress damage feasant is hereby abolished.

(2)   Where any livestock strays on to any land and is not then under the control of any person the occupier of the land may detain it, subject to subsection (3) of this section, unless ordered to return it by a court.

(3)   Where any livestock is detained in pursuance of this section the right to detain it ceases—

(a)   at the end of a period of forty-eight hours, unless within that period notice of the detention has been given to the officer in charge of a police station and also, if the person detaining the livestock knows to whom it belongs, to that person; or

(b)   when such amount is tendered to the person detaining the livestock as is sufficient to satisfy any claim he may have under section 4 of this Act in respect of the livestock; or

(c)   if he has no such claim, when the livestock is claimed by a person entitled to its possession.

(4)   Where livestock has been detained in pursuance of this section for a period of not less than fourteen days the person detaining it may sell it at a market or by public auction, unless proceedings are then pending for the return of the livestock or for any claim under section 4 of this Act in respect of it.

(5)   Where any livestock is sold in the exercise of the right conferred by this section and the proceeds of the sale, less the costs thereof and any costs incurred in connection with it, exceed the amount of any claim under section 4 of this Act which the vendor had in respect of the livestock, the excess shall be recoverable from him by the person who would be entitled to the possession of the livestock but for the sale.

(6)   A person detaining any livestock in pursuance of this section is liable for any damage caused to it by a failure to treat it with reasonable care and supply it with adequate food and water while it is so detained.

(7)   References in this section to a claim under section 4 of this Act in respect of any livestock do not include any claim under that section for damage done by or expenses incurred in respect of the livestock before the straying in connection with which it is detained under this section.

8.   Duty to take care to prevent damage from animals straying on to the highway

(1)   So much of the rules of the common law relating to liability for negligence as excludes or restricts the duty which a person might owe to others to take such care as is reasonable to see that damage is not caused by animals straying on to a highway is hereby abolished.

(2)   Where damage is caused by animals straying from unfenced land to a highway a person who placed them on the land shall not be regarded as having committed a breach of the duty to take care by reason only of placing them there if—

(a)   the land is common land, or is land situated in an area where fencing is not customary, or is a town or village green; and

(b)   he had a right to place the animals on that land.

9.   Killing of or injury to dogs worrying livestock

(1)   In any civil proceedings against a person (in this section referred to as the defendant) for killing or causing injury to a dog it shall be a defence to prove—

(a)   that the defendant acted for the protection of any livestock and was a person entitled to act for the protection of that livestock; and

(b)   that within forty-eight hours of the killing or injury notice thereof was given by the defendant to the officer in charge of a police station.

(2)   For the purposes of this section a person is entitled to act for the protection of any livestock if, and only if—

(a)   the livestock or the land on which it is belongs to him or to any person under whose express or implied authority he is acting; and

(b)   the circumstances are not such that liability for killing or causing injury to the livestock would be excluded by section 5(4) of this Act.

(3)   Subject to subsection (4) of this section, a person killing or causing injury to a dog shall be deemed for the purposes of this section to act for the protection of any livestock if, and only if, either—

(a)   the dog is worrying or is about to worry the livestock and there are no other reasonable means of ending or preventing the worrying; or

(b)   the dog has been worrying livestock, has not left the vicinity and is not under the control of any person and there are no practicable means of ascertaining to whom it belongs.

(4)   For the purposes of this section the condition stated in either of the paragraphs of the preceding subsection shall be deemed to have been satisfied if the defendant believed that it was satisfied and had reasonable ground for that belief.

(5)   For the purposes of this section—
    (a)   an animal belongs to any person if he owns it or has it in his possession; and
    (b)   land belongs to any person if he is the occupier thereof.

10.   Application of certain enactments to liability under sections 2 to 4
For the purposes of [the Fatal Accidents Act 1976], the Law Reform (Contributory
Negligence) Act 1945 and [the Limitation Act 1980] any damage for which a person is liable
under sections 2 to 4 of this Act shall be treated as due to his fault.

11. General interpretation
In this Act—

'common land' and 'town or village green' have the same meanings as in the Commons
Regulation Act 1965;
'damage' includes the death of, or injury to, any person (including any disease and any
impairment of physical or mental condition);
'fault' has the same meaning as in the Law Reform (Contributory Negligence) Act 1945;
'fencing' includes the construction of any obstacle designed to prevent animals from
straying;
'livestock' means cattle, horses, asses, mules, hinnies, sheep, pigs, goats and poultry, and
also deer not in the wild state and, in section 3 and 9 also, while in captivity, pheasants,
partridges and grouse;
'poultry' means the domestic varieties of the following, that is to say, fowls, turkeys,
geese, ducks, guinea-fowls, pigeons, peacocks and quails; and
'species' includes sub-species and variety.

14.2   Dangerous Animals

WALLACE v NEWTON [1982] 2 All ER 106

FACTS: The plaintiff, a groom, was injured by a horse. The horse (Lord Justice) was
known to be nervous and unpredictable in temperament. The plaintiff claimed that this
was a characteristic not normally found in horses.

PARK J: Under s. 2(2)(a) of the Animals Act 1971 the plaintiff has to establish first that the
damage which she suffered was of a kind which Lord Justice was likely to cause, and on
this part of the case there is no dispute. Under s. 2(2)(b) the plaintiff has to establish that
the likelihood of the damage was due to characteristics of Lord Justice which were not
normally found in horses. The question is whether the words 'characteristics which are not
normally found in horses' have to be interpreted as meaning that Lord Justice must be
shown to have had a vicious tendency to injure people by attacking them or whether the
words have to be given their ordinary natural meaning, that is that Lord Justice had
characteristics of a kind not usually found in horses. If the plaintiff has to establish that her
injuries were due to Lord Justice's vicious tendency to injure people, then her claim would
fail. He was not, as the plaintiff herself agreed, a vicious horse or a dangerous horse in the
way in which the defendant understood that word. On the other hand, if she has to
establish that her injuries were due to a characteristic of Lord Justice which was unusual
in a horse, then she would establish this limb of her case. I think this is the meaning to be
given to the words in s. 2(2)(b).

On the evidence I am satisfied that, certainly during the period that the plaintiff had Lord
Justice in her charge, the horse was unpredictable and unreliable in his behaviour, and in
that way he was, as the plaintiff said, dangerous. The injury to her arm was due to this
characteristic, which is not normally found in a horse. So, in my judgment, the plaintiff has
established the second limb of her case.

Under s. 2(2)(c) the plaintiff has to prove that these characteristics were known to
the defendant, as Lord Justice's keeper, or at any time known to a person who at that time
had charge of Lord Justice as the defendant's servant. I have no doubt at all that Tom Read
well knew about Lord Justice's unpredictability and unreliability and because of that

knowledge he very properly warned the plaintiff about the horse. The defendant says that she knew nothing of the incident a week before the plaintiff's accident and of the consequent change of procedure. I am sure that her evidence is honest, but she is, and has been since her husband's death in 1969, a very busy, active woman. She has a large farm, she has stables, she has horses of all kinds and many outside interests, particularly in the world of ponies and horses. The events with which this case is concerned happened over four years ago. Lord Justice was first put on the market for sale about three years ago and was eventually sold in 1979. I think the defendant has completely forgotten all that happened to the plaintiff in 1977. Indeed she has had no need to remember the plaintiff's troubles. I got the impression they made little mark on her mind at the time, and I very much doubt if she has thought about them since. To me it is inconceivable that Tom Read did not tell her everything about Lord Justice and in particular about the incident which occurred a week before the accident. I think that the defendant at the material time knew as much about the horse as Tom Read.

For these reasons I am satisfied that the defendant is liable to the plaintiff under the provisions of s. 2(2) of the Act. Having come to that conclusion, it is not necessary for me to make any finding, nor do I make any finding, on the alternative ground that the plaintiff's injuries were caused by negligence on the part of the defendant, her servants or agents.

CURTIS v BETTS [1990] 1 All ER 769

FACTS: The plaintiff (a ten year old boy) was bitten by a large dog (a bull mastiff) belonging to his neighbours. Prior to this the plaintiff had been on friendly terms with the dog. The bite occurred when the plaintiff approached the dog as it was being loaded into its owner's Land Rover. The dog regarded the car as part of its territory and was apt to defend it. The plaintiff asserted strict liability on the basis of Animals Act 1971, s. 2(2).

SLADE J: The plaintiff's claim was pleaded on three alternative bases, namely (1) that Max was an animal belonging to a dangerous species, (2) that Mr Rolfe Betts was guilty of negligence at common law and (3) that both defendants were strictly liable under s. 2(2) of the Animals Act 1971. The first contention was not pursued at the trial. The second disappeared on the judge's findings that the dog had not escaped from the back of the defendant's Land Rover and run across the road before attacking Lee, and that there was no failure properly to control the dog. . . .

Dogs do not belong to a 'dangerous species' within the definition of that phrase contained in s. 6(2) of the 1971 Act. The keeper of an animal not belonging to a dangerous species will be liable for damage caused by it, provided that the plaintiff can show that each of the three requirements (which I will call respectively 'requirements (a), (b) and (c)') is satisfied.

Lord Denning MR in *Cummings* v *Granger* [1977] 1 All ER 104 at 108 described s. 2(2) as 'very cumbrously worded' and giving rise to 'several difficulties'. I agree. Particularly in view of the somewhat tortuous wording of the subsection, I think it desirable to consider each of the three requirements separately and in turn.

Requirement (a)

The kind of damage in the present case was personal injury. The judge, rightly, did not find that this damage was 'of a kind which [Max] unless restrained was likely to cause'. Indeed, he made it plain that in general Max was a docile and lazy dog. However, he found that Max's action 'in jumping up and biting a child on the side of the face was likely to cause severe damage'. By this route he found that the personal injury caused to Lee was of a kind 'which, if caused by the animal, was likely to be severe', so that the second head of requirement (a) was satisfied.

Counsel for the defendants submitted that the judge's approach to requirement (a) was erroneous. In this context he referred us to and relied on a passage in North *The Modern Law of Animals* (1972) p 56 where it is said:

This second type of damage envisaged by s. 2(2)(a) is one that must prove to be rare in practice. For there to be liability on this basis, an animal must have caused damage in circumstances where it was unlikely that an animal of that species would cause the kind of damage in question but the animal had such abnormal characteristics that it was likely that, if it did cause damage, the damage would be severe.

He pointed out that there was no evidence or finding that Max had *abnormal* characteristics (that is to say abnormal in the case of bull mastiffs as a breed) such as rendered it likely that, if he did damage, the damage would be severe.

I agree with the latter point, but, with respect to Professor North, am unable to agree with the approach to the construction of requirement (a) suggested by him, for two reasons. First, while I accept that requirements (b) and (c) have to be read in conjunction with the preceding requirement (a), I see no necessity or justification for reading words into requirement (a) itself through a process of implication effected by reference to the succeeding requirements. The broad purpose of requirement (a), as I read it, is to subject the keeper of a non-dangerous animal to liability for the damage caused by it in any circumstances where the damage is of a kind which the particular animal in question, unless restrained, was likely to cause or which, if caused by that animal, was likely to be severe, provided that the plaintiff can also satisfy the additional requirements (b) and (c). While conceivably the reference to the likelihood of severity of damage may give rise to questions of degree on particular facts, I would not, for my part, ordinarily anticipate difficulty in applying requirement (a) in practice.

Second, Professor North's work (including p 56) was drawn to the attention of this court in argument in *Cummings* v *Granger*. Nevertheless, Lord Denning MR, with whose judgment Bridge LJ expressly agreed, himself adopted the simple approach to the construction of the second limb of requirement (a) which, with respect, seems to me the right one. In the context of requirement (a) he did not find it necessary to consider whether the dog in question had characteristics not normal to Alsatians. He said [1976] 1 All ER 104 at 108:

Section 2(2)(a): this animal was a dog of the Alsatian breed. If it did bite anyone, the damage was 'likely to be severe'.

So too in the present case. Max was a dog of the bull mastiff breed. If he did bite anyone, the damage was likely to be severe. For this simple reason the judge was, in my judgment, right to hold that requirement (a) was satisfied.

Requirement (b)

The construction and application of requirement (b) give rise to rather greater difficulties. In particular, on a first reading I was puzzled by the legislature's use of the phrase 'the likelihood of the damage or of its being severe', instead of the simple phrase 'the damage', especially since the subsequent phrase 'due to' at first sight appeared to me to bear the simple meaning 'caused by'. However, another, broader, meaning is also given to the word 'due' by the *Shorter Oxford Dictionary* (3rd edn), namely 'To be ascribed or attributed'. If one reads the phrase 'due to' as bearing the broader sense of 'attributable to' I think that this particular difficulty disappears.

Just as in my view requirement (a) in any given case falls to be considered having regard to the particular facts of that case, so too in my view, in the consideration of requirement (b) the existence or non-existence of the relevant likelihood has to be determined having regard to the particular facts. If, therefore, the plaintiff is relying on the second limb of requirement (b) he will have to show that *on the particular facts* the likelihood of the damage or of its being severe was attributable to characteristics of the animal not normally found except at particular times or in particular circumstances corresponding with the particular facts of the case.

The broad purpose of requirement (b), as I read it, is to ensure that even in a case falling within requirement (a) the defendant, subject to one exception, will still escape liability if, on the particular facts, the likelihood of damage was attributable to potentially dangerous characteristics of the animal which are normally found in animals of the same species. The one exception is this. The mere fact that a particular animal shared its potentially dangerous characteristics with other animals of the same species will not preclude satisfaction of requirement (b) if on the particular facts the likelihood of damage was attributable to characteristics normally found in animals of the same species at times or in circumstances corresponding with those in which the damage actually occurred. In *Cummings v Granger* [1977] 1 All ER 104 at 110 Ormrod LJ gave the examples of 'a bitch with pups or an Alsatian dog running loose in a yard which it regards as its territory when a stranger enters into it'. If, in his example, the damage is caused by a bitch accompanying her pups or an Alsatian dog defending its territory requirement (b) will be satisfied.

It was, I think, common ground before us that, in concluding that requirement (b) was satisfied, the judge based his conclusion exclusively on the second limb of that requirement, ie he found that the likelihood of the severe damage being caused by Max was—'due to characteristics of the animal which are not normally found in animals of the same species . . . except at particular times or in particular circumstances.' This conclusion gives rise to two questions: (1) what were the relevant characteristics of Max? and (2) in the particular circumstances, was the likelihood of the damage due (ie attributable) to those characteristics?

As to question (1), the judge concluded that bull mastiffs have a tendency to react fiercely at particular times and in particular circumstances, namely when defending the boundaries of what they regard as their own territory. In my judgment there was evidence before him amply sufficient to entitle him to make that finding. The defendants' expert witness, Mrs Hand, in her written report described mastiffs as tending to be 'a natural protector of their own environment', though she added that 'they are not looking for trouble'. Another witness called by the defendants, Mr Athol Hill, gave evidence that he was interested in dogs, particularly bull mastiffs, and that he had sold Max, who was one of a litter of ten, when he was a little over eight weeks old. He accepted in cross-examination that it is fair comment to suggest that they are territorial animals. When questioned by the court he said that they 'tended to defend their own territory' . . .

[The] judge was, in my opinion, entitled to find that Max had characteristics which are not normally found in bull mastiffs, except at particular times or in particular circumstances, namely the tendency to react fiercely when defending what they regarded as their own territory.

However, to establish requirement (b) the plaintiff still had to establish that the likelihood of damage was, on the particular facts, due to these characteristics. The judge concluded that this had been established, but, with respect, his reasons for this conclusion might perhaps have been stated with greater clarity. He said:

> . . . it is also pointed out that like all dogs they tend very much to protect their territory and it may be that Max thought that Lee was invading his territory as his territory might include the rear of the Land Rover.

I cannot believe that in this particular context the judge was using the phrase 'which expression may have included the rear of the Land Rover' merely to refer to a hypothetical possibility. I think that in its context his use of this phrase must have been intended as a way of saying, in shorthand, that Max did regard the rear of the Land Rover as part of his territory. I proceed on the basis that the judge made this inference. Whether he was entitled to do so is another question, to which I now turn. . . .

Counsel for the defendants told us that the suggestion that Max regarded his territory as including the rear of the Land Rover was made for the first time by counsel for the plaintiff in his closing speech. He submitted that it was unsupported by the evidence. At most, in his submission, the plaintiff's evidence showed that the dog tended to behave in a frightening and aggressive manner when guarding his own territory such as the playground. The judge, in his submission, failed to have sufficient regard to the different circumstances pertaining at the time of the attack on the plaintiff, and in particular the facts that (i) the attack occurred on the public highway, (ii) the dog was then held on a lead by Mr Rolfe Betts, (iii) Lee was (as the judge found) well known to and particularly friendly with the dog, (iv) prior to the attack (as the judge found) Lee called out the dog's name and approached him on his bicycle and (v) there was no evidence that before the attack the dog was excited, barking, snarling or baring his teeth. It is difficult for this court to derive the full flavour of Mrs Hand's evidence from the brief notes of her evidence before us, but in my judgment, this evidence cannot have precluded the judge from reaching the conclusion which he did reach. As counsel for the defendants accepted, it is common knowledge and experience that many dogs regard the car in which they are customarily transported as their own territory, at least when they are inside it. The Land Rover was the vehicle in which Max was transported three times a week to the neighbouring park for the purpose of exercise. Counsel for the defendants stressed the fact that when this accident occurred the dog was not yet actually inside the Land Rover. Nevertheless, at the relevant time Max had emerged from the gate leading from the school yard and was standing just by the open boot of the vehicle, waiting to be lifted into it.

In my judgment, in the light of all the evidence and of his own common knowledge and experience, it was open to the judge, albeit without expert evidence to support his conclusion, to infer that Max regarded his territory as including the rear of the Land Rover. I do not think that he was obliged to accept as conclusive the evidence of Mrs Hand apparently dismissing as irrelevant the aggressive behaviour of the dog when inside the playground at the school gates. Though I do not attach too much weight to this point, I observe that Mrs Hand herself in her report had referred to mastiffs being natural protectors of 'their own environment'. It must be a question of fact and degree what their environment includes.

It follows that, in my judgment, there are no sufficient grounds for interfering with the judge's conclusion that the likelihood of the damage being severe was on the facts due to the relevant characteristics of the dog. Requirement (b) is thus satisfied. But were those characteristics known to the defendants?

Requirement (c)

I can deal with this point shortly. In this context I refer to two particular passages in the judgment. The judge said:

> I was impressed with the care taken by the Betts brothers in getting the dogs into the Land Rover. It was almost a military operation in the way that the two dogs were taken on leads one held by each brother held in close and the tail gate of the Land Rover lowered with great care. Apparently Max although he weighed almost ten stone had to be lifted almost bodily into the Land Rover. It may be a mis-reading of the situation, but it seemed to me that the brothers kept the strictest control over the dogs as soon as they got out of the school yards into the public highway. It is true that they are very large dogs who might cause trouble if they wandered, but I think it is fair to raise a question mark over the whole proceedings and ask why was so much care taken in respect of these two dogs if in fact the brothers did not fear, suspect or perhaps foresee that something untoward might happen if the dogs were loose . . . It is true that the appropriate evidence in each case must be peculiar to that case, but it is significant in the present case that there is ample evidence of Max and Nellie both jumping up at the gate when people passed by both growling and snarling. Indeed, it is quite clear that certain more timid ladies tended to pass on the other side of the road to avoid coming too close to the dogs. It is clear on her own evidence that Mrs Betts herself knew of these events at the back gate, even though she says she had never observed them herself. It is clear from the way that Mr Betts and his brother got the two dogs into the car that they were particularly careful that the dogs did not escape. I am therefore satisfied on the balance of probabilities that the defendants knew of the tendency of these dogs to be what one may term fierce, when protecting the boundaries of what they considered their territory, which expression may have included the rear of the Land Rover.

In this court counsel for the defendants accepted that, in the light of the judge's findings, this court must proceed on the basis that (contrary to their own evidence) the defendants knew at least that the two dogs had the habit of jumping up at the school gate in the playground and growling and snarling at passers-by. This concession was, in my opinion, a realistic one, having regard to all the evidence. In my judgment, it follows that the defendants must be taken to have known of Max's relevant characteristics, namely his tendency to react fiercely when defending what he regarded as his own territory. In my judgment, therefore, the remaining requirement (c), is satisfied and liability on the part of the defendants is established.

14.3 End of Chapter Assessment Question

Sheba is a cat. She is normally placid, but dislikes being injected. She then struggles, scratches and bites with surprising ferocity. Her owner, Mary, knows about this. She asks her new boyfriend, John, to take Sheba to the vet for her annual injections. Sheba lets fly at the vet and manages to scratch his eye, causing serious injuries.

Advise Mary.

14.4 End of Chapter Assessment Outline Answer

Cats are not a dangerous species, as they are commonly domesticated in the UK: Animals Act 1971, s. 6(2). However, Mary, as the keeper of the cat is liable for the injury to the vet if the requirements of s. 2(2) of the Act are satisfied. John is unlikely to be liable as he does not appear to become a keeper simply by taking charge of the cat for a temporary purpose. In any event he would be able to avoid liability on the basis that he was not aware of the peculiar characteristics of this particular cat: s. 2(2)(c).

So far as Mary is concerned, she does know this, and it is immaterial that she has asked an innocent third party to look after the cat at the material time. It will be a matter of argument whether this characteristic is commonly found in cats, whether or not only at particular times: s. 2(2)(b). If cats do normally scratch and fight when injected (and some certainly do!) but do not normally do so otherwise, the requirement is satisfied: *Curtis* v *Betts* (1990). If this is established, the first limb of the section is also likely to be established, at least on the basis that the cat was likely to scratch if not restrained, even though it was not likely that serious harm would result: s. 2(2)(a).

The only defence available to Mary would be that the vet took the risk upon himself, as an expert: s. 5(2).

CHAPTER FIFTEEN

REMEDIES

15.1 Damages

15.1.1 COMPENSATORY DAMAGES

15.1.1.1 Land and buildings

DODD PROPERTIES LTD v *CANTERBURY CITY COUNCIL* [1980] 1 All ER 928

FACTS: The defendants' pile driving operations in connection with construction works caused serious structural damage to the plaintiffs' building. The defendants denied liability until shortly before trial and *quantum* remained in dispute. As a result, the plaintiffs had not carried out repairs at the earliest feasible date as this would have put them under financial pressure and there was no assurance of recovery from the defendants. They claimed the (much greater) cost of doing works after the hearing. The judge awarded only the cost at the earlier date on the ground that the plaintiffs' financial situation was an irrelevant extrinsic circumstance. The plaintiffs appealed to the Court of Appeal.

MEGAW LJ: The general principle, referred to in many authorities, has recently been recognised by Lord Wilberforce in *Miliangos* v *George Frank (Textiles) Ltd* [1975] 3 All ER 801 at 813, namely that 'as a general rule in English law damages for tort or for breach of contract are assessed as at the date of the breach'. But in the very passage in which this 'general rule' is there stated, it is stressed that it is not a universal rule. That it is subject to many exceptions and qualifications is clear. Cantley J in the present case rightly recognised that that was so, in the passage from his judgment which I have recently read.

Indeed, where, as in the present case, there is serious structural damage to a building, it would be patently absurd, and contrary to the general principle on which damages fall to be assessed, that a plaintiff, in a time of rising prices, should be limited to recovery on the basis of the prices of repair at the time of the wrongdoing, on the facts here, being two years, at least, before the time when, acting with all reasonable speed, he could first have been able to put the repairs in hand. Once that is accepted, as it must be, little of practical reality remains in postulating that, in a tort such as this, the 'general rule' is applicable. The damages are not required by English law to be assessed as at the date of breach.

The true rule is that, where there is a material difference between the cost of repair at the date of the wrongful act and the cost of repair when the repairs can, having regard to all the relevant circumstances, first reasonably be undertaken, it is the latter time by reference to which the cost of repairs is to be taken in assessing the damages. That rule conforms with the broad and fundamental principle as to damages, as stated in Lord Blackburn's speech in *Livingstone* v *Rawyards Coal Co.* [1880] 5 App Cas 25 where he said that the measure of damages is—

that sum of money which will put the party who has been injured, or who has suffered, in the same position as he would have been in if he had not sustained the wrong for which he is now getting his compensation or reparation.

In any case of doubt, it is desirable that the judge, having decided provisionally as to the amount of damages, should, before finally deciding, consider whether the amount conforms with the requirement of Lord Blackburn's fundamental principle. If it appears not to conform, the judge should examine the question again to see whether the particular case falls within one of the exceptions of which Lord Blackburn gave examples, or whether he is obliged by some binding authority to arrive at a result which is inconsistent with the fundamental principle. I propose to carry out that exercise later in this judgment.

The judge has held, in a passage which I have already read, that as a commercial decision, judged exclusively from the plaintiffs' point of view, it was reasonable to postpone incurring the expense of the repairs up to, for so I understand what the judge says, the time when the action had been heard and liability decided, resulting in a judgment which, when complied with, would have put the plaintiffs in funds. The reasons why that deferment of repairs was reasonable from the plaintiffs' point of view included the fact, not that they were 'impecunious' (meaning poverty-stricken or unable to raise the necessary money) but that the provision of the money for repairs would have involved for them a measure of 'financial stringency'. Other reasons, consistent with commercial good sense, why the repairs should be deferred include those mentioned in evidence by a director of the plaintiff companies, whose evidence was accepted by the judge as truthful and reliable. If there had been no money problem, he said, he would still not have spent money on the building before he was sure of recovering the cost from the defendants. It would not have made commercial sense to spend this money on a property which would not produce corresponding additional income. So long as there was a dispute, either as to liability or amount of compensation, he would have done no more than to keep the building weatherproof and 'in working order'.

If that was, as the judge held, reasonable from the point of view of the plaintiffs as being grounds for deferring the carrying out of repairs, and if the time at which the cost of the repairs falls to be completed in order to ascertain the amount of damages is the time when it has become reasonable to do the repairs, why did the judge reject 1978, for which the plaintiffs contended, and accept 1970 for which the defendants contended?

There are, as I see it, two possible answers to that question. The first answer is that what is reasonable has to be looked at from the point of view of both parties and a balance struck. The judge's findings of reasonableness of the deferment from the point of view of the plaintiffs does not, therefore, conclude the matter. But I do not think that that was the answer intended to be given by Cantley J. He nowhere refers to the question in any such form and there is no indication of any attempt by him to strike a balance. If a balance had to be struck, surely it would be right, even in a climate of indulgence to contract-breakers or tortfeasors, that the scales should move heavily in the favour of the innocent party as against the wrongdoer, in any comparison of respective disadvantages or unfairness? . . .

The second possible answer is that which I believe to have influenced the judge. He thought that the decision in the *Liesbosch* case precluded him from taking into account, in considering the reasonableness of the deferment of repairs, any part of the deferment which was caused by 'financial stringency'.

The *Liesbosch* case has been the subject of much debate and much speculation, and a considerable measure of disagreement, as to its ratio decidendi and the scope of its application, particularly in the light of later House of Lords decisions . . . I do not think that, on any fair view of the ratio decidendi of the *Liesbosch* case, it applies to the issue with which we are concerned. Amongst other reasons, there are these two. First, it was not 'financial stringency', let alone 'impecuniousness' as in the *Liesbosch* case, which on any fair view, on the judge's findings, was the cause, or even, I think, an effective cause, of the decision to postpone repairs. The 'financial stringency' which would have been created by carrying out the repairs was merely one factor among a number of factors which together produced the result that commercial good sense pointed towards deferment of the repairs. The second reason which I would mention is that, once it is accepted that the plaintiffs were not in any breach of any duty owed by them to the defendants in failing to carry out repairs earlier than the time when it was reasonable for the repairs to be put in hand, this becomes, for all practical purposes, if not in theory, equated with a plaintiff's ordinary duty to mitigate his damages. Lord Wright in his speech in the *Liesbosch* case accepted Lord Collin's dictum in *Clippens Oil Co. Ltd* v *Edinburgh and District Water Trustees* [1907] AC 291: '. . . in my opinion the wrong-doer must take his victim talem qualem, and if the position of the latter is aggravated because he is without the means of mitigating it, so much the worse for the wrongdoer . . .' I agree with the observations of Oliver J in *Radford* v *De Froberville* [1978] 1 All ER 33 as to the relationship between the duty to mitigate and the measure, or amount, of damages in relation to a question such as the question with which we are here concerned. A plaintiff who is under a duty to mitigate is not obliged, in order to reduce the damages, to do that which he cannot afford to do, particularly where, as here, the plaintiff's 'financial stringency', so far as it was relevant at all, arose, as a matter of common sense, if not as a matter of law, solely as a consequence of the defendant's wrongdoing.

My provisional answer to the question raised in the first issue would thus be that the damages in this case are to be assessed by reference to the 1978 cost of repairs.

15.1.1.2 Chattels

LIESBOSCH DREDGER v *SS EDISON* [1933] All ER Rep 144 (HL)

FACTS: The plaintiff's dredger was sunk by the defendants' ship. The defendants admitted liability. The dredger was in use on a dredging contract. The plaintiffs could not afford to buy a replacement, although replacements were available. They hired a dredger for 14 months instead and then purchased it with the co-operation of the harbour board for whom they were working. There was also a six-month delay in making the hired dredger available. The defendants disputed liability for the hire charges and loss of profit due to delay awarded by the registrar and affirmed by Langton J, but disallowed in the Court of Appeal. The plaintiffs appealed to the House of Lords.

LORD WRIGHT: The substantial issue is what in such a case as the present is the true measure of damage. It is not questioned that when a vessel is lost by collision due to the sole negligence of the wrong-doing vessel the owners of the former vessel are entitled to what is called restitutio in integrum, which means that they should recover such a sum as will replace them so far as can be done by compensation in money, in the same position as if the loss had not been inflicted on them, subject to the rules of law as to remoteness of damage. The respondents contend that all that is recoverable as damages is the true value to the owners of the lost vessel, as at the time and place of loss. Before considering what is involved in this contention, I think it desirable to examine the claim made by the appellants, which found favour with the registrar and Langton J, and which in effect is that all their circumstances, in particular their want of means, must be taken into account, and hence the damages must be based on their actual loss, provided only that, as the registrar and the judge have found, they acted reasonably in the unfortunate predicament in which they were placed, even though but for their financial embarrassment they could have replaced the *Liesbosch* at a moderate price and with comparatively short delay.

In my judgment, the appellants are not entitled to recover damages on this basis. The respondents' tortious act involved the physical loss of the dredger; that loss must somehow be reduced to terms of money. But the appellants' actual loss in so far as it was due to their impecuniosity arose from that impecuniosity as a separate and concurrent cause, extraneous to and distinct in character from the tort; the impecuniosity was not traceable to the respondents' acts, and, in my opinion, was outside the legal purview of the consequences of these acts. The law cannot take account of everything that follows a wrongful act; it regards some subsequent matters as outside the scope of its selection, because 'it were infinite to trace the cause of causes,' or consequences of consequences. Thus, the loss of a ship by collision due to the other vessel's sole fault may force the shipowner into bankruptcy, and that, again, may involve his family in suffering, loss of education, or opportunities, in life, but no such loss could be recovered from the wrongdoer. In the varied web of affairs the law must abstract some consequences as relevant, not, perhaps, on grounds of pure logic but simply for practical reasons. In the present case, if the appellants' financial embarrassment is to be regarded as a consequence of the respondents' tort, I think it is too remote, but I prefer to regard it as an independent cause, though its operative effect was conditioned by the loss of the dredger.

The question of remoteness of damage has been considered in many authorities and from many aspects, but no case has been cited to your Lordships which would justify the appellants' claim. . . .

Polemis v *Furness, Withy & Co.* [1921] 3 KB 560, a case in the tort of negligence, was cited as illustrating the wide scope possible in damages for tort. That case, however, was concerned with the immediate physical consequences of the negligent act, and not with the co-operation of an extraneous matter such as the plaintiffs' want of means. I think, therefore, that it is not material further to consider that case here. Nor is the appellants' financial disability to be compared with that physical delicacy or weakness which may aggravate the damage in the case of personal injuries, or with the possibility that the injured man in such a case may be either a poor labourer or a highly paid professional man. The former class of circumstances goes to the extent of actual physical damage, and the latter consideration goes to interference with profit-earning capacity; whereas the appellants' want of means was, as already stated, extrinsic.

I agree with the conclusion of the Court of Appeal that the registrar and Langton J, proceeded on a wrong basis, and that the damages must be assessed as if the appellants had been able to go into the market and buy a dredger to replace the *Liesbosch*. On that basis it is necessary to decide between the conflicting views put forward, on the one hand, by the respondents, that all that is recoverable is the market price of the dredger, together with cost of transport to Patras, and interest, and, on the other hand, by the appellants, that they are also entitled to damages in addition for loss during the period of inevitable delay before the substituted dredger could arrive and start work at Patras . . . The true rule seems to be that the measure of damages in such cases is the value of the ship to her owner as a going concern at the time and place of the loss. In assessing that value regard must naturally be had to her pending engagements, either profitable or unprofitable. The rule, however, obviously requires some care in its application; the figure of damages is to represent the capitalised value of the vessel as a profit-earning machine, not in the abstract, but in view of the actual circumstances . . . Many, varied and complex are the types of vessels and the modes of employment in which their owners may use them. Hence the difficulties constantly felt in defining rules as to the measure of damages. I think it impossible to lay down any universal formula. A ship of war, a supply ship, a lightship, a dredger employed by a public authority, a passenger liner, a trawler, a cable ship, a tug boat (to take a few instances), all may raise quite different questions before their true value can be ascertained. The question here under consideration is again different; the *Liesbosch* was not under charter nor intended to be chartered, but, in fact, was being employed by the owners in the normal course of their business as civil engineers, as an essential part of the plant which they were using in performance of their contract at Patras. Just as, in the other cases considered, what must be ascertained is the real value to the owner as part of his working plant and ignoring remote considerations at the time of loss; if it were possible without delay to replace a comparable dredger exactly as and where the *Liesbosch* was at the market price, the appellants would have suffered no damage save the cost of doing so—that is, in such an assumed case the market price, the position being analogous to that of the loss of goods for which there is a presently available market. But that is in this case a merely fanciful idea. Apart from any consideration of the appellants' lack of means, some substantial period was necessary to procure at Patras a substituted dredger. Hence, I think, the appellants cannot be restored to their position before the accident unless they are compensated, if I may apply the words of Lord Herschell in *The Greta Holme* ([1897] AC at p. 605): 'In respect of the delay and prejudice caused to them in carrying out the works entrusted to them.' He adds: 'It is true these damages cannot be measured by any scale.' Lord Herschell was there dealing with damages in the case of a dredger which was out of use during repairs, but in the present case I do not think the court is any the more entitled to refuse, on the ground that there is difficulty in calculation, to consider as an element in the value of the dredger to the appellants the delay and prejudice in which its loss involved them; nor is it enough to take the market value—that is, the purchase price (say, in Holland), even increased by the cost of transport—and add to that 5 per cent. interest as an arbitrary measure . . . From these principles it follows that the value of the *Liesbosch* to the appellants, capitalised as at the date of the loss, must be assessed by taking into account: (i) the market price of a comparable dredger in substitution; (ii) costs of adaptation, transport, insurance, &c., to Patras; (iii) compensation for disturbance and loss in carrying out their contract over the period of delay between the loss of the *Liesbosch* and the time at which the substituted dredger could reasonably have been available for use in Patras, including in that loss such items as overhead charges, expenses of staff and equipment, and so forth, thrown away, but neglecting any special loss due to the appellants' financial position. On the capitalised sum so assessed interest will run from the date of the loss.

MATTOCKS v MANN [1993] RTR 13 (CA)

FACTS: The plaintiff's car was damaged by the defendant, who admitted liability. The plaintiff needed transport, but could not pay for the repairs until the claim was settled. In the meantime she hired a series of cars. The defendant disputed his liability for the hire charges on the basis that these arose from the plaintiff's impecuniosity. The master disallowed part of the hire charges and the plaintiff appealed to the Court of Appeal. One of the periods for which hire charges were disputed was that between completion of the repairs and release of the plaintiff's car, which only occurred when the defendant put her in funds.

BELDAM LJ: This is another case in which we were pressed with what is sometimes termed as 'the principle of *The Liesbosch case*' [1933] AC 449, HL(E) in that the plaintiff's inability herself to provide the resources to pay for the repairs was the effective cause of her having to hire a car from 6 June until the repairers finally released the car on 29 October. The passage in Lord Wright's judgment, at p 460, has been often quoted, but less often quoted is the passage in his judgment in *Monarch Steamship Co.* v *Karlshamns* [1949] AC 196, 223–224, in which he himself explained the limited nature of the decision in the *Liesbosch* case. Furthermore the law has not stood still since 1933 and does not simply apply principles whatever the circumstances in which the question arises. It has to take account of the particular circumstances of each case; and, as the law has developed, as Kerr LJ said in the case of *Perry* v *Sydney Phillips & Son* [1981] 1 WLR 1297 the principle of *The Liesbosch* has been subjected to what he termed 'considerable attenuation.'

A similar argument to that advanced in this case was advanced in *Bolton* v *Price* (unreported) Court of Appeal (Civil Division) Transcript No 1159 of 1989 in which I gave the judgment of the court. I there said that at the present day it is generally accepted that, in what Lord Wright termed 'the varied web of affairs' that follows a sequence of events after an accident of this kind, it is only in an exceptional case that it is possible or correct to isolate impecuniosity, as it is sometimes called, or the plaintiff's inability to pay for the cost of repairs from his own resources as a separate cause and as terminating the consequences of a defendant's wrong. It seems to me necessary today to consider whether, having regard to all the circumstances of the case and the resources available to a plaintiff, resources known by the defendant or her representatives to be of a kind that will not be able to provide for repairs themselves, in all the circumstances the plaintiff has acted reasonably and with commercial prudence. We were also pressed, as the court had been in *Bolton* v *Price* with a decision of this court in *Ramwade Ltd* v *W J Emson & Co. Ltd* [1987] RTR 72. That was a claim made by plaintiffs against insurance brokers who had failed to carry out their instructions to obtain comprehensive insurance cover for their lorry. The lorry was damaged beyond repair. The plaintiffs claimed from their brokers not only the sum which would have been payable to them to enable them to replace the vehicle but also the cost of hiring an alternative vehicle from the time when it was contended they would have been paid had they been comprehensively insured until the trial of the action. The court in that case held that the hire charges were not a consequence of the broker's failure to provide comprehensive cover. There were several reasons for this. First, hire charges would not have been recoverable under the terms of the comprehensive policy, so that at first sight to include such charges in damages was not necessary to put the plaintiffs in the position in which they would have been if the defendant brokers had complied with their instructions. In short, the damages for hire charges were too remote, or, if put in terms of contractual damages, they were not reasonably within the contemplation of the parties at the time the agreement was made. In that case the court felt able to isolate the plaintiffs' lack of resources as the real and substantial cause of the separate claim for damages for the cost of hiring an alternative vehicle. Additionally, the court said, the plaintiffs' claim could in the circumstances of the case really be regarded as a claim for non-payment of damages which was not permissible, any such claim being limited to interest.

Mr Anthony says that in this case, as opposed to *Bolton* v *Price* where the car had actually been finally repaired, it is possible to isolate the plaintiff's inability to provide the resources as the sole intervening cause of the continuing cost of hiring a vehicle. I disagree. In these days when everybody looks to one or other of the insurers of vehicles involved in an accident, it is clearly contemplated that where the cost of repairs are of the substantial kind involved in this case, the source of payment of that cost will be the insurers. Looking here at the whole history of events, one cannot isolate the plaintiff's inability to meet the cost of those repairs and say that that brought an end to the period for which it was reasonable that the second defendant's insurers should be liable. On the contrary, they had instructed their engineer to negotiate the proper cost with the garage; they had told the plaintiff through her representative that she could give instructions for repairs to go ahead; that there was no question between them of liability, and that they were indemnifying the defendant. It was agreed between them at that time that the repairs would be paid for by the defendant's insurers, and, in reliance upon that, the plaintiff gave her instructions and awaited the return of her vehicle, which could only be returned to her when the repairers had received the money. That money was not forthcoming, and it seems to me in those circumstances that to suggest there was either an entirely separate cause of the remaining hire charges or that the plaintiff ought to bear that cost because she had failed to mitigate her damage is unsupportable in the social conditions which obtain today.

15.1.2 PERSONAL INJURIES

15.1.2.1 General damages

HOUSECROFT v BURNETT [1986] 1 All ER 332 (CA)

FACTS: This was a case where the plaintiff suffered injuries of maximum severity at the hands of the defendant. Liability was admitted. The court was invited to look afresh at the basis of award in such cases, and did so.

O'CONNOR LJ: The injuries sustained by the plaintiff resulted in tetraplegia. Three complaints are made about the assessment of damages. (1) The judge awarded £80,000 for pain, suffering and loss of amenity. Although this is the largest award to a tetraplegic under this head so far recorded, it is attacked on the ground that if the inflation factor is applied to comparable awards in the late 1960s and early 1970s a six-figure award is demonstrated . . .

Before I consider the grounds for attacking the assessment of damages, I think it desirable to set out in tabular form just how the total award was made up:

1.	Pain suffering and loss of amenity	£80,000
2.	Loss of expectation of life	£1,250
3.	Future motoring expenses, ie provision for outdoor mobility.	
	Agreed at	£14,000
4.	A miscellany of future expenses: holidays, heat, services of a gardener.	
	Agreed at £1,050 pa. Judge applied multiplier of 13	£13,650
5.	Provision of therapeutic equipment, telephone, future medical	
	expenses. Agreed at	£12,000
6.	Future physiotherapy. Agreed at	£600
7.	Alterations to house. Agreed at	£20,000
8.	Special damage. Agreed at	£7,000
9.	Past care	£10,000
10.	Future care	£108,550
11.	Future loss of earnings	£56,000
		£323,050

I turn now to the challenge to the award of £80,000 for pain, suffering and loss of amenity. The principles governing the amount of such awards and the function of this court in relation thereto are set out by Lord Diplock in his speech in *Wright v British Rlys Board* [1983] 2 AC 773:

My Lords, claims for damages in respect of personal injuries constitute a high proportion of civil actions that are started in the courts in this country. If all of them proceeded to trial the administration of civil justice would break down; what prevents this is that a high proportion of them are settled before they reach the expensive and time-consuming stage of trial, and an even higher proportion of claims, particularly the less serious ones, are settled before the stage is reached of issuing and serving a writ. This is only possible if there is some reasonable degree of predictability about the sum of money that would be likely to be recovered if the action proceeded to trial and the plaintiff succeeded in establishing liability. The principal characteristic of actions for personal injuries that militate against predictability as to the sum recoverable are, first, that the English legal system requires that any judgment for tort damages, not being a continuing tort, shall be for one lump sum to compensate for all loss sustained by the plaintiff in consequence of the defendant's tortious act whether such loss be economic or non-economic, and whether it has been sustained during the period prior to the judgment or is expected to be sustained thereafter. The second characteristic is that non-economic loss constitutes a major item in the damages. Such loss is not susceptible of *measurement* in money. Any figure at which the assessor of damages arrives cannot be other than artificial and, if the aim is that justice meted out to all litigants should be even-handed instead of depending on idiosyncrasies of the assessor, whether jury or judge, the figure must be 'basically a conventional figure derived from experience and from awards in comparable cases' . . .

The need for a judge in assessing damages for non-economic loss to have regard to awards in comparable cases has led to progressive general increases in the level of awards, particularly for serious injuries. These have been intended to reflect, though admittedly imperfectly, the general increase in the level of salaries and wages and, more particularly since inflation became rampant, the decrease in the real value of money due to this cause. It is with the increase in the nominal amount of awards in 'the money of the day' (to borrow the apt phrase used by Barwick CJ in *O'Brien* v *McKean* (1968) 118 CLR 540 at 545) due to inflation that your Lordships are primarily concerned in the instant case. That increase in awards has taken place irregularly by fits and starts rather than following the actual shape of the rising curve of inflation; and there have been periods, particularly between 1973 and 1979, when it lagged significantly behind the decrease in real value of the money of the day. This was pointed out in *Walker* v *John McLean & Sons Ltd* [1979] 1 WLR 760 at 765, where the Court of Appeal reaffirmed the rule of practice that damages for non-economic loss are to be assessed by reference to the value of money at the date of the trial and not at some other and lower sum calculated by reference to an earlier and higher value of the pound . . .

My Lords, given the inescapably artificial and conventional nature of the assessment of damages for non-economic loss in personal injury actions and of treating such assessment as a debt bearing interest from the date of service of the writ, it is an important function of the Court of Appeal to lay down guidelines both as to the quantum of damages appropriate to compensate for various types of commonly occurring injuries and as to the rates of 'interest' from time to time appropriate to be given in respect of non-economic loss and of the various kinds of economic loss. The purpose of such guidelines is that they should be simple and easy to apply though broad enough to permit allowances to be made for special features of individual cases which make the deprivation caused to the particular plaintiff by the non-economic loss greater or less than the general run of cases involving injuries of the same kind. Guidelines laid down by an appellate court are addressed directly to judges who try personal injury actions; but confidence that trial judges will apply them means that all those who are engaged in settling out of court the many thousands of claims that never reach the stage of litigation at all or, if they do, do not proceed as far as trial will know very broadly speaking what the claim is likely to be worth if 100% liability is established. As regards assessment of damages for non-economic loss in personal injury cases, the Court of Appeal creates the guidelines as to the appropriate conventional figure by increasing or reducing awards of damages made by judges in individual cases for various common kinds of injuries. Thus, so-called 'brackets' are established, broad enough to make allowance for circumstances which make the deprivation suffered by an individual plaintiff in consequence of the particular kind of injury greater or less than in the general run of cases, yet clear enough to reduce the unpredictability of what is likely to be the most important factor in arriving at settlement of claims. 'Brackets' may call for alteration not only to take account of inflation, for which they ought automatically to be raised, but also, it may be, to take account of advances in medical science which may make particular kinds of injuries less disabling or advances in medical knowledge which may disclose hitherto unsuspected long-term effects of some kinds of injuries or industrial diseases . . .

The task of updating awards to compensate for the fall in the value of money is not, and cannot be, a precise art. The bracket which emerges from decisions of this court must have a spread, because this court does not interfere with an award under this head unless it is manifestly too high or too low or it can be shown that the judge has erred in principle in relation to some element that goes to make up the award. The human condition is so infinitely variable that it is impossible to set a tariff, but some injuries are more susceptible to some uniformity in compensation than others. One such is an injury which results in tetraplegia for in the nature of things the variables are more or less limited to age, awareness, pain and expectation of life.

This concept of updating the level of awards presupposes a datum for comparison. Here is the first difficulty. Section 22 of the Administration of Justice Act 1968, which made the award of interest on damages in personal injuries cases compulsory, came into force on 1 January 1970 and *Jefford* v *Gee* [1970] 2 QB 130, which laid down the guidelines on how this was to be done, was decided in this court later that year. The old division of damages into general and special was not appropriate when questions of interest came to be considered. Future loss and future expense had to be isolated; and this led to the proliferation of heads of damage; the table which I have set out is a good example of the pattern which has developed.

Before 1970 it is only occasionally that one can get a figure for pain, suffering and loss of amenity separated from the award of general damages. When the award is separated it will be found that it includes sometimes expressly, and certainly by implication, matters which are separately assessed today. I must give some examples of this: I will start with *Fowler* v *Grace* (1970) 114 SJ 193, referred to in Kemp and Kemp *The Quantum of Damages* vol 2, para 1–151. A woman, aged 28 with two children, was injured and was a tetraplegic. In 1969 she was awarded £39,450, broken down as follows:

1.	Pain, suffering and loss of amenity	£25,000
2.	Future nursing care	£9,600
3.	Adaptation of house	£3,000
4.	Special damage	£1,350
5.	Loss of expectation of life	£500
		£39,450

In addition, her husband, who was joined as a plaintiff, was awarded £7,600 for future care of his wife. Today this would be added to the £39,450 as the Court of Appeal recognised in dismissing an appeal against the amount of the award in February 1970. Compare the heads of damage with those in the table in the present case. It will be seen that item 1 in *Fowler* v *Grace* is to be compared with items 1, 3, 4, 5 and 6 in the present case, so that we compare £25,000 not with £80,000 but with £120,250 . . .

For at least the last ten years when a claim by a tetraplegic has come to trial, counsel for the plaintiff has presented the judge with a list of awards multiplied by the appropriate inflation factor taken from the table in Kemp and Kemp *The Quantum of Damages*. The resulting figures appear to show that the going rate in use by the judges is too low, and the judge is invited to be bold and take a leap upwards. This submission was made to me in *Chambers* v *Karia*, to Taylor J in *Brown* v *Merton Sutton and Wandsworth Area Health Authority* [1982] 1 All ER 650, and to the trial judge and in turn to us in the present case. Counsel for the plaintiff duly produced his table. I have come to the conclusion that this exercise has served its purpose, and that the time has come to make a fresh start. The 1969 to 1979 awards do not offer a true comparison for the reasons I have given when examining *Fowler* v *Grace*. The 1973 to 1978 awards were too low, as was recognised in *Walker* v *John McLean & Sons Ltd*. The more recent awards are a better guide because they are net of sums assessed separately which in fact compensate for loss of amenity in part. The cases show that this case is a typical middle-of-the-road case of tetraplegia. These are cases where the injured person is not in physical pain, is fully aware of the disability, has an expectation of life of 25 years or more, powers of speech, sight and hearing are present, and needs help with bodily functions. The factors which operate to make the case one for awarding more than average are physical pain and any diminution in the powers of speech, sight or hearing. The factors which operate to make the case one for awarding less than average are lack of awareness of the condition and a reduction in expectation of life. These factors often cancel each other to a greater or lesser extent, especially where there is severe brain damage . . .

So I come to the present case, which has to be valued in July 1983. The judge dealt with the injuries in his judgment . . .

The plaintiff sustained (a) a head injury, though not of very severe consequence, (b) a fracture dislocation of the fifth cervical vertebra with damage to the spinal cord and (c) fracture of the right shoulder-blade and two ribs. There was no damage to the brain. She now has permanent paralysis of all four limbs. She has some use of her arms but not of her hands, nor of her legs. She has no sensation in the legs or private parts. She is almost completely tetraplegic. . . . She is, therefore, in permanent need of constant and regular care, nursing and attention. She is relatively free from pain and discomfort and can use her arms to a very limited degree. For example, by reason of a fixed extension to this powerless hand, she is able to press an electric typewriter keyboard one letter painfully time after time individually. Her mental anguish is incalculable and her case ought to be regarded as one of the most grievous in this category because she was of such a degree of intellect, high promise and awareness of burgeoning womanhood that the permanent and perpetual recognition of her stricken condition and all that has been snatched from her is something that merits compensation to the highest scale of accepted figures by way of damages in this type of catastrophic injury.' . . .

Kilner Brown J, in making his assessment said:

The only way that I can approach this is to say that I take by way of comparison the top awards so far and edge up just a little, though were it left to me alone without the guidance I would increase the award of £80,000 which I think is right, by a very large amount indeed.

While understanding and sharing the judge's sympathy for the plaintiff, I do not think that the case is other than an average example of cases of tetraplegia. I think that the award under this head was too much. I think that £70,000 would have been an adequate assessment. It is important to remember that the award under this head in cases of catastrophic injury invariably forms part of a much larger total award. I am conscious that we are considering this case some 20 months after judgment and, as I have said, I think the time has come for a fresh start. I have come to the conclusion that as a guideline in April 1985 a figure of £75,000 should be used for an average case of tetraplegia. When the factors to which I have referred earlier in this judgment are taken into consideration, there will be cases where an award of very much less will be appropriate, but I would not expect there to be many cases calling for much increase on what has to be a conventional sum. For these reasons the submission that the award of £80,000 is too little fails.

MOELIKER v A REYROLLE & CO. LTD [1977] 1 All ER 9 (CA)

FACTS: The plaintiff successfully claimed damages for an industrial injury. His hand was injured and this affected, *inter alia*, his ability to enjoy his main hobby, sea fishing, as his hand became very painful in cold weather. One of the disputed issues on *quantum* of damage was the allowance for this loss of amenity. The trial judge awarded £2,250 for loss of most of the thumb and forefinger of the left (non-dominant) hand and resulting numbness, tenderness and minor cosmetic disability.

BROWNE LJ: This was, of course, a far less serious injury than many which the courts have to consider, but as hand injuries go it was a nasty one, even for a right-handed man. The most serious physical features are probably the weakness of the pinch-grip and the pain and numbness in the hand in cold weather. He has been deprived for half the year of his favourite (indeed, apparently, his only) recreation. He will have to live with the discomforts and disabilities resulting from this accident (even though they are not of very great severity) for perhaps 30 years. On the whole, I have come to the conclusion that £2,250 under this head is too low, and I would increase it to £3,000.

LIM POH CHOO v *CAMDEN & ISLINGTON AHA* **[1979] 2 All ER 910 (HL)**

FACTS: The plaintiff, a doctor with a promising career, was severely injured by medical negligence. She suffered brain damage which left her only intermittently sentient and with no real appreciation of her condition. The case was complicated by changes in her care arrangements between trial and appeal, and between levels of appeal. One issue considered was the level of award for pain, suffering and loss of amenity.

LORD SCARMAN:
The questions of principle
It will be convenient to take these questions in the order in which I have listed the appellants' main submission.
(A)   *The total of damages (£254,765)*
   The submission that the total of the award was excessive was one of the broadest generality. Whether or not he can establish duplication or overlap or any other error in calculating the separate items of the award, counsel for the appellants submitted that an award of damages, being a 'jury question', must be fair to both sides, and that in a case such as the present a judge should bear in mind (a) comparable cases, (b) the effect of high awards on the level of insurance premiums or, if, as here, the taxpayer foots the bill, on the taxpayer, (c) the availability of care for the victim under the national health service and (d) public policy. Such generalities as that damages must be treated as a jury question and kept in line with public policy I do not find helpful. Their very breadth merely contributes to uncertainty and inconsistency in an area of the law, the history if not the present practice of which is notorious for both vices. Invoking the memory of the days when juries assessed damages for personal injuries does no more than remind us that the modern practice of reasoned awards by judges is a substantial advance on the inscrutable awards of juries. Of course, awards must be fair. But this means no more than that they must be a proper compensation for the injury suffered and the loss sustained. Nor in this case do I find helpful a comparison of one total award with another. In so far as an award consists of 'conventional' items, e.g. for pain and suffering, comparability with other awards is certainly of value in keeping the law consistent. But pecuniary loss depends on circumstances; and, where (as in the present case) such loss predominates, comparison with total awards in other cases does not help, and may be misleading.
   The two specific matters counsel for the appellants mentioned, the burden on the public (through premiums or taxes) and the availability of national health service care, prove on examination to be for the legislator, not the judge. As to the first, the principle of the law is that compensation should as nearly as possible put the party who has suffered in the same position as he would have been in if he had not sustained the wrong (*per* Lord Blackburn in *Livingstone* v *Rawyards Coal Co.* (1880) 5 App Cas 25 at 39). There is no room here for considering the consequences of a high award on the wrongdoer or those who finance him. And, if there were room for any such consideration, on what principle, or by what criterion, is the judge to determine the extent to which he is to diminish on this ground the compensation payable?
   The second matter, though introduced by counsel for the appellants as part of his general submissions on the total award, is really one, as he recognised, which falls to be considered in assessing the cost of future care. It is convenient, however, to deal with it at this stage. Section 2(4) of the Law Reform (Personal Injuries) Act 1948 provides that in an action for damages for personal injuries there shall be disregarded, in determining the reasonableness of any expenses, the possibility of avoiding those expenses or part of them by taking advantage of facilities available in the national health service. In *Harris* v *Brights Asphalt Contractors Ltd* [1973] 1 QB 617 at 635 Slade J said of the subsection:

I think all [it] means is that, when an injured plaintiff in fact incurs expenses which are reasonable, that expenditure is not to be impeached on the ground that, if he had taken advantage of the facilities available under the National Health Service Act 1946, those reasonable expenses might have been avoided. I do not understand section 2(4) to enact that a plaintiff shall be deemed to be entitled to recover expenses which in fact he will never incur.

In *Cunningham* v *Harrison* [1973] QB 942 the Court of Appeal expressed the same view, Lawton LJ saying that a defendant can, notwithstanding the statute, submit that the plaintiff will probably not incur such expenses because he will be unable to obtain outside the national health service the domestic and nursing help which he requires.

I agree with Slade J and the Court of Appeal. It has not been suggested that expenses so far incurred in the care and treatment of Dr Lim have been unreasonable. They are, therefore, protected by the subsection. But it is open to serious question whether for the rest of her life it will continue to be possible to obtain for Dr Lim, outside the national health service, the domestic and nursing help she will require. However, Lord Denning MR and Lawton LJ both of whom were parties to the decision in *Cunningham* v *Harrison*, have proceeded in the instant case on the basis, which the trial judge must also have accepted, that it will be possible and that the expense of doing so is reasonable. In the absence of any evidence to the contrary, I am not prepared to take a different view, though I recognise the force of the case developed in the Pearson report (Cmnd 7054–1, paras 340–342) for legislation repealing the subsection.

The attack, therefore, on the total of damages awarded as being excessive, merely by reason of its size, fails. If the appellants are to succeed, they must show that one or more of the component items of the award are wrong.

(B) *The award for pain and suffering and loss of amenities*

Counsel for the appellants recognised, at the outset of his argument, that, if *Wise* v *Kaye* [1962] QB 638 and *H West & Son Ltd* v *Shephard* [1964] AC 326 were correctly decided, his first submission (that the sum awarded should be comparable with the small conventional awards in fatal cases for loss of expectation of life) must fail.

My Lords, I think it would be wrong now to reverse by judicial decision the two rules which were laid down by the majority of the House in *H West & Son Ltd* v *Shephard*, namely (1) that the fact of unconsciousness does not eliminate the actuality of the deprivation of the ordinary experiences and amenities of life (see the formulation used by Lord Morris of Borth-y-Gest) and (2) that, if damages are awarded on a correct basis, it is of no concern to the court to consider any question as to the use that will thereafter be made of the money awarded. The effect of the two cases (*Wise* v *Kaye* being specifically approved in *H West & Son Ltd* v *Shephard* [1964] AC 326) is twofold. First, they draw a clear distinction between damages for pain and suffering and damages for loss of amenities. The former depend on the plaintiff's personal awareness of pain, her capacity for suffering. But the latter are awarded for the fact of deprivation, a substantial loss, whether the plaintiff is aware of it or not. Secondly, they establish that the award in *Benham* v *Gambling* [1941] AC 157 (assessment in fatal cases of damages for loss of expectation of life) is not to be compared with, and has no application to, damages to be awarded to a living plaintiff for loss of amenities. . . .

I do not underrate the formidable logic and good sense of the minority opinions expressed in *Wise* v *Kaye* and *H West & Son Ltd* v *Shephard*. The quality of the minority opinions was, however, matched by the equally formidable logic and good sense of the majority opinions. The question on which opinions differed was, in truth, as old and as obstinate as the philosopher's stone itself. A decision having been taken by this House in 1963 (the year *H West & Son Ltd* v *Shephard* was decided), its reversal would cause widespread injustice, unless it were to be part and parcel of a comprehensive reform of the law. For since 1962 settlements have proceeded on the basis that the rule adopted in *Wise* v *Kaye* was correct: and judges have had to assess damages on the same basis in contested cases. We are in the area of 'conventional' awards for non-pecuniary loss, where comparability matters. Justice requires that such awards continue to be consistent with the general level accepted by the judges. If the law is to be changed by the reversal of *H West & Son Ltd* v *Shephard*, it should be done not judicially but legislatively within the context of a comprehensive enactment dealing with all aspects of damages for personal injury. . . .

(C)   *Loss of earnings, and duplication (overlap)*

The appellants' submission is brief and simple. In para 8 of their case it was put in three short sentences:

> The Plaintiff ought not to have been awarded damages for loss of earnings as well as for loss of amenities and cost of care. The sum awarded for cost of care exceeded her estimated loss of earnings and *covered all her needs*. The additional award of damages for loss of earnings was duplicatory.

As developed in argument, the submission was a twofold one. First, it was submitted that in catastrophic cases 'loss of earnings' does not reflect a real loss. Secondly, if damages are recoverable for loss of earnings, duplication with other heads of damage is to be avoided. The law must, therefore, ensure that no more is recovered for loss of earnings than what the plaintiff, if not injured, would have saved, or reserved for the support of his, or her, dependants. Since there was no evidence to suggest that Dr Lim would have accumulated any surplus income after meeting her working and living expenses, the trial judge's award for loss of earnings was wholly wrong.

The first submission is contrary to an established line of authority which, beginning with *Phillips* v *London and South Western Railway Co.* [1879] 5 CPD 280, has recently received the seal of this House's approval in *Pickett* v *British Rail Engineering Ltd* [1980] AC 136. It is also contrary to the principle of the common law that a genuine deprivation (be it pecuniary or non-pecuniary in character) is a proper subject of compensation. The principle was recognised both in *Phillips's* case [1879] 5 CPD 280 at 292; [1874–80] All ER Rep 1176 at 1181, *per* Brett LJ, where the loss was pecuniary, and in *H West & Son Ltd* v *Shephard* [1964] AC 326 at 349, *per* Lord Morris of Borth-y-Gest, where the loss was non-pecuniary.

The second submission is more formidable. Undoubtedly, the courts must be vigilant to avoid not only duplication of damages but the award of a surplus exceeding a true compensation for the plaintiff's deprivation or loss.

The separate items, which together constitute a total award of damages, are interrelated. They are the parts of a whole, which must be fair and reasonable. 'At the end', as Lord Denning MR said in *Taylor* v *Bristol Omnibus Co. Ltd* [1975] 1 WLR 1054 at 1057, 'the judges should look at the total figure in the round, so as to be able to cure any overlapping or other source of error'. In most cases the risk of overlap is not great, nor, where it occurs, is it substantial. Living expenses continue, or progressively increase, for most plaintiffs after injury as they would have done if there had been no injury. But where, as in *Pickett's* case, the plaintiff claims damages for the earnings of his 'lost years', or, as in the present case, the claim is in respect of a lifetime's earnings lost because, though she will live, she cannot earn her living, a real risk arises that the plaintiff may recover, not merely compensation for loss, which is the entitlement given by law, but a surplus greater than could have been achieved if there had been no death or incapacity. Two deductions, therefore, fall to be made from the damages to be awarded. First, as the cases have always recognised, the expenses of earning the income which has been lost. Counsel for the respondent conceded this much. Secondly, the plaintiff's living expenses. This is necessarily a hypothetical figure in the case of a 'lost years' claim, since the plaintiff does not survive to earn the money; and, since there is no cost of care claim (the plaintiff being assumed to be dead), it falls to be deducted from the loss of earnings award. But where, as in the present case, the expectancy of life is not shortened but incapacity exists, there will be a cost of care claim as well as a loss of earnings claim. How should living expenses be assessed and deducted in such a case? One approach, analogous to the method necessarily adopted in 'lost years' cases, would be to attempt an assessment of how much the plaintiff would have spent and on what, always a most speculative exercise. How, for instance, could anyone tell how Dr Lim would have ordered her standard of living, had she been able to pursue her career? Another approach is, however, available in the case of a living plaintiff. In *Shearman* v *Folland* [1950] 2 KB 43, the Court of Appeal deducted what has been described as the 'domestic element' from the cost of care. Inevitably, a surviving plaintiff has to meet her living expenses. This approach, being on the basis of a future actuality (subject to the uncertainties of life), is far less hypothetical than the former (which, faute de mieux, has to be adopted in 'lost years' cases). It is a simpler, more realistic, calculation and accords more closely with the general principle of the law that the courts in assessing compensation for loss are not concerned either with how the plaintiff would have used the moneys lost or how she (or he) will use the compensation received.

In the present case, my Lords, it is perfectly possible to estimate the domestic element in Dr Lim's cost of care. The estimated figure must, therefore, be deducted in the assessment of her damages for the cost of her care. In the result, Dr Lim will recover in respect of her future loss a capital sum which, after all proper discounts, will represent her loss of earnings, net after allowing for working expenses, and her cost of care, net after deducting the domestic element. A capital sum so assessed will compensate for a genuine loss and for a genuine item of additional expenditure, both of which arise from the injury she has sustained. It will not contain any element of duplication or go beyond compensation into surplus.

15.1.2.2 Pecuniary loss

HUNT v SEVERS [1994] 2 All ER 385 (HL)

FACTS: The plaintiff was injured in a road accident for which the defendant, her fiance — later her husband — admitted liability. Her injuries amounted to 'in terms of complications the worst paraplegic case [the doctors in the case] had ever come across'. The issue in dispute was whether she could recover for the cost of services actually rendered to her by the defendant. The amount was substantial: £17,000 for care to date and £60,000 for future care out of a total award of just over £600,000. There was no dispute that such an award would be proper in the case of any other voluntary carer.

LORD BRIDGE: The starting point for any inquiry into the measure of damages which an injured plaintiff is entitled to recover is the recognition that damages in the tort of negligence are purely compensatory. He should recover from the tortfeasor no more and no less than he has lost. Difficult questions may arise when the plaintiff's injuries attract benefits from third parties. According to their nature these may or may not be taken into account as reducing the tortfeasor's liability. The two well-established categories of receipt which are to be ignored in assessing damages are the fruits of insurance which the plaintiff himself has provided against the contingency causing his injuries (which may or may not lead to a claim by the insurer as subrogated to the rights of the plaintiff) and the fruits of the benevolence of third parties motivated by sympathy for the plaintiff's misfortune. The policy considerations which underlie these two apparent exceptions to the rule against double recovery are, I think, well understood: see, for example *Parry v Cleaver* [1970] AC 1 at 14 and *Hussain v New Taplow Paper Mills Ltd* [1988] AC 514 at 528. But I find it difficult to see what considerations of public policy can justify a requirement that the tortfeasor himself should compensate the plaintiff twice over for the self same loss. If the loss in question is a direct pecuniary loss (e.g. loss of wages) *Hussain's* case is clear authority that the defendant employer, as the tortfeasor who makes good the loss either voluntarily or contractually, thereby mitigates his liability in damages pro tanto. The Court of Appeal, in the judgment appealed from, readily accepted a number of examples advanced in argument for the defendant as showing that a tortfeasor may mitigate his liability by making good in kind the physical damage which his tort has caused to the plaintiff's property. In a wide-ranging argument before your Lordships, where many hypothetical examples were examined of gratuitous services rendered by a tortfeasor to an injured plaintiff in satisfaction of a need occasioned by his tort, Mr McGregor QC for the plaintiff was constrained to accept as a general rule that the tortfeasor, having provided those services, cannot also be held liable to the plaintiff in damages for their value. But he submitted that where the tortfeasor is a relative or close friend of the plaintiff and gratuitously provides services of an intimate personal or domestic character, he is required by law, as a narrow exception to the general rule, also to pay the plaintiff the value of those services.

The law with respect to the services of a third party who provides voluntary care for a tortiously injured plaintiff has developed somewhat erratically in England. The voluntary carer has no cause of action of his own against the tortfeasor. The justice of allowing the injured plaintiff to recover the value of the services so that he may recompense the voluntary carer has been generally recognised, but there has been difficulty in articulating a consistent juridical principle to justify this result.

In *Roach* v *Yates* [1938] 1 KB 256 the injured plaintiff needed to be cared for day and night and his wife and sister-in-law both gave up their employment to provide that care for him and together lost wages of £3 a week. A claim for the value of their services at £3 a week was included in the special damages claimed and a similar claim made as an element in general damages related to future loss. The services were given voluntarily but the plaintiff was held entitled to recover in respect of them. Referring to the nursing services required by the plaintiff, Greer LJ said:

> ... he can get those services, and perhaps get them better, only from the attendance being given to him by his wife and his sister-in-law, but, quite naturally, he would feel that he ought to compensate them for what they have lost by giving up the work at which they were earning the sum of £3. I think that Mr Beyfus was right in saying that we must take into account, at any rate, for the period during which he may now be expected to live, the sum of £3 a week as the minimum expense which this unfortunate man would have to incur in retaining the services of his wife and his sister-in-law ...

In *Cunningham* v *Harrison* [1973] QB 942 and *Donnelly* v *Joyce* [1974] QB 454 judgments were delivered by different divisions of the Court of Appeal on successive days. In *Cunningham* the wife of a severely disabled plaintiff, who had initially looked after him, had died before the trial. Lord Denning MR said;

> Before dealing with [the claim for future nursing expenses] I would like to consider what the position would have been if the wife had not died and had continued to look after her husband, as she had been doing. The plaintiff's advisers seem to have thought that a husband could not claim for the nursing services rendered by a wife unless the husband was legally bound to pay her for them. So, on their advice on 11th July 1972 an agreement was signed whereby the husband agreed to pay his wife £2,000 per annum in respect of her nursing services. We were told that such advice is often given by counsel in such cases as these when advising on evidence. I know the reason why such advice is given. It is because it has been said in some cases that a plaintiff can only recover for services rendered to him when he was legally liable to pay for them: see for instance *Kirkham* v *Boughey* [1958] 2 QB 338 at 342 and *Janney* v *Gentry* (1966) 110 SJ 408. But, I think that view is much too narrow. It seems to me that when a husband is grievously injured—and is entitled to damages—then it is only right and just that, if his wife renders services to him, instead of a nurse, he should recover compensation for the value of the services that his wife has rendered. It should not be necessary to draw up a legal agreement for them. On recovering such an amount, the husband should hold it on trust for her and pay it over to her. She cannot herself sue the wrongdoer ... but she has rendered services necessitated by the wrongdoing, and should be compensated for it. If she had given up paid work to look after him, he would clearly have been entitled to recover on her behalf, because the family income would have dropped by so much: see *Wattson* v *Port of London Authority* [1969] 1 Lloyd's Rep 95 at 102 *per* Megaw J. Even though she had not been doing paid work but only domestic duties in the house, nevertheless all extra attendance on him certainly calls for compensation.

In *Donnelly* v *Joyce*, the injured plaintiff was a boy of six. His mother gave up her work for a period to provide necessary care for him and the disputed item in his claim related to the mother's loss of wages. The judgment of the court delivered by Megaw LJ contains a lengthy review of the authorities, but the key passage relied on by the trial judge and the Court of Appeal in the instant case reads [1974] QB 454 at 461–462:

> We do not agree with the proposition, inherent in counsel for the defendant's submission, that the plaintiff's claim, in circumstances such as the present, is properly to be regarded as being, to use his phrase, 'in relation to someone else's loss', merely because someone else has provided to, or for the benefit of, the plaintiff—the injured person—the money, or the services to be valued as money, to provide for needs of the plaintiff directly caused by the defendant's wrongdoing. The loss *is* the plaintiff's loss. The question from what source the plaintiff's needs have been met, the question who has paid the money or given the services, the question whether or not the plaintiff is or is not under a legal or moral liability to repay, are, so far as the defendant and his liability are

concerned, all irrelevant. The plaintiff's loss, to take this present case, is not the expenditure of money to buy the special boots or to pay for the nursing attention. His loss is the existence of the need for those special boots or for those nursing services, the value of which for purposes of damages—for the purpose of the ascertainment of the amount of his loss—is the proper and reasonable cost of supplying those needs. That, in our judgment, is the key to the problem. So far as the defendant is concerned, the loss is not someone else's loss. It is the plaintiff's loss. Hence it does not matter, so far as the defendant's liability to the plaintiff is concerned, whether the needs have been supplied by the plaintiff out of his own pocket or by a charitable contribution to him from some other person whom we shall call 'the provider'; it does not matter, for that purpose, whether the plaintiff has a legal liability, absolute or conditional, to repay to the provider what he has received, because of the general law or because of some private agreement between himself and the provider; it does not matter whether he has a moral obligation, however ascertained or defined, so to do. The question of legal liability to reimburse the provider may be very relevant to the question of the legal right of the provider to recover from the plaintiff. That may depend on the nature of the liability imposed by the general law or the particular agreement. But it is not a matter which affects the right of the plaintiff against the wrongdoer.

With respect, I do not find this reasoning convincing. I accept that the basis of a plaintiff's claim for damages may consist in his need for services but I cannot accept that the question from what source that need has been met is irrelevant. If an injured plaintiff is treated in hospital as a private patient he is entitled to recover the cost of that treatment. But if he receives free treatment under the National Health Service, his need has been met without cost to him and he cannot claim the cost of the treatment from the tortfeasor. So it cannot, I think, be right to say that in all cases the plaintiff's loss is 'for the purpose of damages . . . the proper and reasonable cost of supplying [his] needs'. . . .

By concentrating on the plaintiff's need and the plaintiff's loss as the basis of an award in respect of voluntary care received by the plaintiff, the reasoning in *Donnelly* v *Joyce* diverts attention from the award's central objective of compensating the voluntary carer. Once this is recognised it becomes evident that there can be no ground in public policy or otherwise for requiring the tortfeasor to pay to the plaintiff, in respect of the services which he himself has rendered, a sum of money which the plaintiff must then repay to him. The case for the plaintiff was argued in the Court of Appeal without reference to the circumstance that the defendant's liability was covered by insurance. But before your Lordships Mr McGregor, recognising the difficulty of formulating any principle of public policy which could justify recovery against the tortfeasor who has to pay out of his own pocket, advanced the bold proposition that such a policy could be founded on the liability of insurers to meet the claim. Exploration of the implications of this proposition in argument revealed the many difficulties which it encounters. But I do not think it necessary to examine these in detail. The short answer, in my judgment, to Mr McGregor's contention is that its acceptance would represent a novel and radical departure in the law of a kind which only the legislature may properly effect. At common law the circumstance that a defendant is contractually indemnified by a third party against a particular legal liability can have no relevance whatever to the measure of that liability.

15.1.2.3 Social security and other benefits

PARRY v *CLEAVER* [1969] 1 All ER 555 (HL)

FACTS: The plaintiff was a police constable injured at work by the defendant's negligence. He was obliged to take medical retirement and received a pension from a contributory occupational scheme. The issue in dispute was whether this pension should be taken into account in assessing his loss of earnings until retirement. The case ultimately reached the House of Lords.

LORD REID: My Lords, the facts of this case are of a pattern becoming increasingly common. The appellant was in pensionable employment. By the negligent driving of the respondent he was disabled from continuing in that employment. So he received a disablement pension. How are damages for his financial loss to be assessed? In particular how is the disablement pension to be dealt with? The authorities are not consistent with each other, so I find it necessary to begin by considering general principles.

Two questions can arise. First, what did the appellant lose as a result of the accident? What are the sums which he would have received but for the accident but which by reason of the accident he can no longer get? And secondly, what are the sums which he did in fact receive as a result of the accident but which he would not have received if there had been no accident? And then the question arises whether the latter sums must be deducted from the former in assessing the damages.

British Transport Commission v *Gourley* [1956] AC 185 did two things. With regard to the first question it made clear, if it had not been clear before, that it is a universal rule that the plaintiff cannot recover more than he has lost. And, more important, it established the principle that in this chapter of the law we must have regard to realities rather than technicalities. The plaintiff would have had to pay tax in respect of the income which he would have received but for the accident. So what he really lost was what would have remained to him after payment of tax. From a technical point of view income tax and surtax were probably too remote. Apart from PAYE, tax is not payable out of income, its amount depends on a calculation which includes many other factors besides earnings, and standard rate of tax varies from year to year. So a good many lawyers disapproved of the decision of this House. But this House preferred realities to '*res inter alios*' and 'remoteness'.

But *Gourley's* case had nothing whatever to do with the second question. It did not arise. None of the noble and learned Lords who took part gave it more than a passing reference, and I am satisfied that none of them intended to go out of their way to pronounce on it. Before *Gourley's* case it was well established that there was no universal rule with regard to sums which came to the plaintiff as a result of the accident but which would not have come to him but for the accident. In two large classes of case such sums were disregarded—the proceeds of insurance and sums coming to him by reason of benevolence. If *Gourley's* case had any bearing on this matter it must have impinged on these classes. But no one suggests that it had any effect as regards sums coming to the plaintiff by reason of benevolence, and I see no reason why it should have made any difference as regards insurance.

I cannot accept the view that disregarding these types of receipt is anomalous. In dealing with damages under Lord Campbell's Act (i.e., the Fatal Accidents Act 1846) such receipts were not disregarded until the law was altered by recent legislation. There, there was a universal rule. Here, there never was. The common law has treated this matter as one depending on justice, reasonableness and public policy.

So I must enquire what are the real reasons, disregarding technicalities, why these two classes of receipts are not brought into account. I take first the case of benevolence. I do not use the word 'charity' because, rightly or wrongly, many people object to it . . .

It would be revolting to the ordinary man's sense of justice, and therefore contrary to public policy, that the sufferer should have his damages reduced so that he would gain nothing from the benevolence of his friends or relations or of the public at large, and that the only gainer would be the wrongdoer. We do not have to decide in this case whether these considerations also apply to public benevolence in the shape of various un-covenanted benefits from the welfare state, but it may be thought that Parliament did not intend them to be for the benefit of the wrongdoer.

As regards moneys coming to the plaintiff under a contract of insurance, I think that the real and substantial reason for disregarding them is that the plaintiff has bought them and that it would be unjust and unreasonable to hold that the money which he prudently spent on premiums and the benefit from it should enure to the benefit of the tortfeasor. Here again I think that the explanation that this is too remote is artificial and unreal. Why should the plaintiff be left worse off than if he had never insured? In that case he would have got the benefit of the premium money; if he had not spent it he would have had it in his possession at the time of the accident grossed up at compound interest. I need not quote from the well-known case of *Bradburn* v *Great Western Ry Co.* (1874) LR 10 Exch 1 but I may refer to an old Scottish case, *Forgie* v *Henderson* (1818) 1 Murr 413 where the pursuer was assaulted by the defender. During part of his resulting illness he received an allowance from a friendly society, and Lord Chief Commissioner Adam said in charging the jury (1818) 1 Murr at p. 118:

I do not think you can deduct the allowance from the Society, as that is of the nature of an insurance, and is a return of money paid.

And I would also refer to the judgment of Asquith, LJ in *Shearman v Folland* where he said [1950] 2 KB 43 at p. 46:

If the wrongdoer were entitled to set-off what the plaintiff was entitled to recoup or had recouped under his policy, he would, in effect, be depriving the plaintiff of all benefit from the premiums paid by the latter and appropriating that benefit to himself.

Then I ask—why should it make any difference that he insured by arrangement with his employer rather than with an insurance company? In the course of the argument the distinction came down to be as narrow as this: if the employer says nothing or merely advises the man to insure and he does so, then the insurance money will not be deductible; but if the employer makes it a term of the contract of employment that he shall insure himself and he does so, then the insurance money will be deductible. There must be something wrong with an argument which drives us to so unreasonable a conclusion.

It is said to make all the difference that both the future wages of which he has been deprived by the fault of the defendant, and the benefit which has accrued by reason of his disablement come from the same source or arise out of the same contract. This seems to be founded on an idea of remoteness which is, I think, misconceived. Remoteness from the defendant's point of view is a familiar conception in connection with damages. He pays damages for loss of a kind which he might have foreseen but not for loss of a kind which was not foreseeable by him. But here we are not dealing with that kind of remoteness. No one has ever suggested that the defendant gets the benefit of receipts by the plaintiff after his accident if they are of a kind which he could have foreseen, but not if they are of a kind which he could not have foreseen, or vice versa. That the plaintiff may, in consequence of the defendant's fault, receive benefit from benevolence or insurance is no more or no less foreseeable or remote than that he may get a benefit from a pension to be paid by his employer. If remoteness has any relevance here it is quite a different kind of remoteness—the connection or absence of connection between the source of the benefit and the source of the wages. But what has that got to do with the defendant? It is rational to make the extent of the defendant's liability depend on remoteness from his point of view—on what he knew or could or should have foreseen. But it is, to my mind, an irrational technicality to make that depend on the remoteness or closeness of relationship between the plaintiff's source of loss and source of gain. Surely the distinction between receipts which must be brought into account and those which must not must depend not on their source but on their intrinsic nature . . .

What, then, is the nature of a contributory pension? Is it in reality a form of insurance or is it something quite different? Take a simple case where a man and his employer agree that he shall have a wage of £20 per week to take home (leaving out of account PAYE, insurance stamps and other modern forms of taxation) and that between them they will put aside £4 per week . . . It is generally recognised that pensionable employment is more valuable to a man than the mere amount of his weekly wage. It is more valuable because by reason of the terms of his employment money is being regularly set aside to swell his ultimate pension rights whether on retirement or on disablement. His earnings are greater than his weekly wage. His employer is willing to pay £24 per week to obtain his services, and it seems to me that he ought to be regarded as having earned that sum per week. The products of the sums paid into the pension fund are in fact delayed remuneration for his current work. That is why pensions are regarded as earned income.

But the man does not get back in the end the accumulated sums paid into the fund on his behalf. This is a form of insurance. Like every other kind of insurance what he gets back depends on how things turn out. He may never be off duty and may die before retiring age leaving no dependants. Then he gets nothing back. Or he may by getting a retirement or disablement pension get much more back than has been paid in on his behalf. I can see no relevant difference between this and any other form of insurance. So, if insurance benefits are not deductible in assessing damages and remoteness is out of the way, why should his pension be deductible?

Then it is said that instead of getting a pension he may get sick pay for a time during his disablement—perhaps his whole wage. That would not be deductible, so why should a pension be different? But a man's wage for a particular week is not related to the amount of work which he does during that week. Wages for the period of a man's holiday do not differ in kind from wages paid to him during the rest of the year. And neither does sick pay; it is still wages. So during the period when he receives sick pay he has lost nothing. We never reach the second question of how to treat sums of a different kind which he would never have received but for his accident.

A pension is intrinsically of a different kind from wages. If one confines one's attention to the period immediately after the disablement it is easy to say that but for the accident he would have got £x, now he gets £y, so his loss is £x—£y. But the true situation is that wages are a reward for contemporaneous work but that a pension is the fruit, through insurance, of all the money which was set aside in the past in respect of his past work. They are different in kind.

. . . The Fatal Accidents Act 1959, provides in s. 2 (1):

In assessing damages in respect of a person's death in any action under the Fatal Accidents Act, 1846, or under the Carriage by Air Act, 1932, there shall not be taken into account any insurance money, benefit, pension or gratuity which has been or will or may be paid as a result of the death.

Subsection (2) defines benefit as meaning benefit under the National Insurances Acts, and payment by a friendly society or trade union.

If public policy, as now interpreted by Parliament, requires all pensions to be disregarded in actions under the Fatal Accidents Acts, I find it impossible to see how it can be proper to bring pensions into account in common law actions. Plaintiffs were formerly worse off under Lord Campbell's Act and I can think of no reason why the position should now be reversed so as to make them worse off at common law. In my judgment, a decision that pensions should not be brought into account in assessing damages at common law is consistent with general principles, with the preponderating weight of authority, and with public policy as enacted by Parliament and I would therefore so decide.

SMOKER v LONDON FIRE & CIVIL DEFENCE AUTHORITY [1991] 2 AC 502 (HL)

FACTS: In each case the plaintiffs were disabled in accidents at work for which the defendant employer was liable. Each received a contributory occupational disability pension. In each case the employers were also contributors. The disputed issue was whether the employers could treat the pensions as reducing the claim for loss of earnings. Again, the case reached the House of Lords.

LORD TEMPLEMAN: The question raised by these appeals is not devoid of authority from several common law countries. In *Bradburn* v *Great Western Rly Co.* (1874) LR 10 Exch 1, [1874–80] All ER Rep 195 it was held in an action for injuries caused by the defendant's negligence that the sum received by the plaintiff on an accident insurance policy could not be taken into account in reduction of damages. Bramwell B said:

The jury have found that the plaintiff has sustained damages through the defendants' negligence to the amount of 217*l*. but it is said that because the plaintiff has received 31*l*. from the office in which he insured himself against accidents, therefore the damages do not amount to 217*l*. One is dismayed at this proposition.

In the same case Pigott B said:

The plaintiff is entitled to recover the damages caused to him by the negligence of the defendants, and there is no reason or justice in setting off what the plaintiff has entitled himself to under a contract with third persons, by which he has bargained for the payment of a sum of money in the event of an accident happening to him. He does not receive that sum of money because of the accident, but because he has made a contract providing for the contingency; an accident must occur to entitle him to it, but it is not the accident, but his contract, which is the cause of his receiving it.

The reason for the decision in *Bradburn* v *Great Western Rly Co.* was said by Asquith LJ in *Shearman* v *Folland* [1950] 2 KB 43 at 46 to be as follows:

If the wrongdoer were entitled to set-off what the plaintiff was entitled to recoup or had recouped under his policy, he would, in effect, be depriving the plaintiff of all benefit from the premiums paid by the latter, and appropriating that benefit to himself.

In *Payne* v *Railway Executive* [1952] 1 KB 26 a sailor injured in a railway accident as a result of negligence on the part of the defendant received a disability pension from the Royal Navy. The Court of Appeal declined to allow the defendant to set off the amount of the pension against the damages payable by the defendant. Cohen LJ cited with approval the statement by the trial judge, Sellers J:

The plaintiff has become entitled to the pension by reason of his naval service, it being one of the benefits such service affords. The pension would have been paid if the accident had been without any negligence on the part of the railway company. It was argued for the plaintiff that a pension must be disregarded in making the assessment just as insurance is to be disregarded, and that as a matter of principle a wrongdoer should not get the benefit of the fortuitous circumstance that the plaintiff was serving in the Royal Navy at the time and had consequently received a pension. I agree with that contention. Just as the wrongdoer cannot appropriate to himself the benefit of the premiums paid by the injured party to cover accident risks, so he cannot, I think, appropriate the benefits accruing from the injured party's service which similarly entitles him to those benefits.

In *British Transport Commission* v *Gourley* [1956] AC 185 this House held that in awarding damages for loss of earnings actual and prospective the court must allow deduction for the income tax and surtax which the plaintiff would have had to pay on his earnings. Earl Jowitt said:

The broad general principle which should govern the assessment of damages in cases such as this is that the tribunal should award the injured party such a sum of money as will put him in the same position as he would have been in if he had not sustained the injuries . . . The principle can . . . afford some guidance to the tribunal in assessing compensation for the financial loss resulting from an accident, and in such cases it has been referred to as 'the dominant rule of law' . . . There are, no doubt, instances to be found in the books of exceptional cases in which this dominant rule does not apply, as, for instance, in cases of insurance, or cases calling for exemplary or punitive damages, or in certain cases dealing with the loss of use of a chattel.

[His Lordship then referred to other cases including *Parry* v *Cleaver* and continued:]

In the present case counsel for the appellants sought to distinguish the decision of this House in *Parry* v *Cleaver* [1969] 1 All ER 555, [1970] AC 1 on the ground that the appellants are in the triple position of employers, tortfeasors and insurers. In my opinion this makes no difference to the principle that the plaintiff has bought his pension, which is, in the words of Lord Reid, 'the fruit, through insurance, of all the money which was set aside in the past in respect of his past work'. The fruit cannot be appropriated by the tortfeasor.

The appellants claim that there has been a change of circumstance in that it can be shown that *Parry* v *Cleaver* introduced uncertainty in the law and that since 1970 there has been a clear trend at common law against double recovery. But *Parry* v *Cleaver* established clearly that pension benefits are not deductible and that double recovery is not involved. The cases on which the appellants rely are mainly those in which the courts have decided that payments which correspond to wages must be taken into account when assessing loss of wages. Thus unemployment benefit (*Nabi* v *British Leyland* [1980] 1 All ER 667, [1980] 1 WLR 529), family income supplement (*Gaskill* v *Preston* [1981] 3 All ER 427), supplement-ary benefit (*Lincoln* v *Hayman* [1982] 2 All ER 819, [1982] 1 WLR 488), payments under job release schemes and student maintenance grants are statutory wages which reduce the loss of contractual wages resulting from the tort. In *Hussain v New Taplow Paper Mills Ltd* [1988] AC 514 at 530 the plaintiff was entitled to receive full-scale pay over 13 weeks and thereafter half his pre-accident earnings, and the House held that these payments were deductible because, in the words of Lord Bridge of Harwich:

> . . . it has always been assumed as axiomatic that an employee who receives under the terms of his contract of employment either the whole or part of his salary or wages during a period when he is incapacitated for work cannot claim damages for a loss which he has not sustained . . .

The appellants also relied on the decision of this House in *Wilson v National Coal Board* 1981 (SC) (HL) 9 that a redundancy payment must in certain circumstances be brought into account against damages for tort. In that case an injured miner received a redundancy payment for early dismissal but claimed damages for loss of earnings on the footing that he would have continued to be employed until he retired at the age of 62. In the Court of Session in that case the Lord President (Emslie) said (at 15):

> The pursuer simply cannot be allowed to profit by adopting two quite inconsistent postures, on the one hand that of the man who has lost his employment with the defenders wholly or mainly as the result of the closure of Littlemill Colliery, and, on the other hand, having been compensated for that actual loss of employment, that of the man who has not lost his employment with the defenders, and who but for the accident would have continued to work for them for the rest of his working life.

I can find nothing in the authorities which casts doubt over the effect or logic of this House in *Parry v Cleaver*.

The appellants relied on s. 22 of the Social Security Act 1989 and Sch 4 to that Act. These provisions direct that social security benefits shall not be deducted in the assessment of damages for tort but that the tortfeasor shall repay to the state out of the damages thus assessed the amount of the social security benefits provided by the state for the benefit of the victim. These provisions, far from assisting the appellants, only demonstrate that Parliament is quite capable of legislating in this field but has not legislated to reduce the damages payable by the tortfeasor.

HUSSAIN v NEW TAPLOW PAPER MILLS LTD [1988] AC 514 (HL)

FACTS: The plaintiff was injured at work. His employers were held two thirds to blame and damages awarded accordingly. They claimed to be entitled to set against the damages for loss of earnings contractual sick pay funded by insurance taken out by them and at their cost. The issue reached the House of Lords.

LORD BRIDGE: The dispute relates exclusively to sums payable [under] the defendants' permanent health insurance scheme (the scheme) . . . The liability to provide the benefits is that of the defendants alone. But the defendants' insurance policy with NEL effectively indemnifies them against this liability. The defendants' contracts with their employees and their policy of insurance with NEL are to this extent linked that NEL may require evidence of the employee's good health before the defendants may accept the employee for membership of the scheme. But once accepted the employee, if he leaves the defendants and takes other employment, may in certain circumstances have the option of taking out a new and individual public health insurance policy for himself with NEL on defined terms and without medical evidence. It is contended for the plaintiff, and I am content to assume, that the combined effect of the contract of employment and the defendants' insurance policy is that when an employee who is in receipt of benefit under the scheme ceases for any reason to be employed by the defendants he continues to be entitled to the equivalent benefit directly from NEL . . . What happened in the plaintiff's case was that the defendants treated him more generously than their contractual obligations required. They paid him at the full rate of his pre-accident earnings for 15 months following the accident and thereafter until trial at half the rate of his pre-accident earnings. Since the trial they have paid and will continue to pay him, in addition to his earnings as a weighbridge attendant, half the difference between those earnings and his pre-accident earnings. No claim is made for any loss of earnings for the first 13 weeks after the accident when the plaintiff was receiving his full wage as sick pay, nor in respect of the amount representing half his pre-accident earnings which for the following year the defendants continued to pay him on an ex gratia basis. But it is claimed that the plaintiff is entitled to recover as special damages from the end of 13 weeks after the accident half his loss of earnings for the following year representing the amount of lost earnings recouped to him under the scheme and his full loss of earnings thereafter until trial, disregarding the scheme payments. Similarly, he claims that his future loss must be calculated on the difference between his earning capacity as a machine operator and a weighbridge attendant without regard to the payments due under the scheme. I need not go into the detail of the figures. They are not in dispute. On the basis of full liability, the damages assessed by the trial judge included sums referrable to the disputed loss of earnings and loss of earning capacity amounting to £35,321.82. Two-thirds of this amount, £23,547.45, was, therefore, the sum included in the judge's award which the Court of Appeal deducted as excessive and which the plaintiff now claims to have restored . . .

[His Lordship then referred to *Parry* v *Cleaver* and the principles regulating double recovery, and continued:]

There are, however, a variety of borderline situations where a plaintiff may receive money which, but for the wrong done to him by the defendant, he would not have received and where there may be no obvious answer to the question whether the rule against double recovery or some principle derived by analogy from one of the two classic exceptions to that rule should prevail. Some of these problems have been resolved by legislation, sometimes in the form of a compromise solution providing that a proportion only of certain statutory benefits is to be taken into account when assessing damages. But where there is no statute applicable the common law must solve the problem unaided and the possibility of a compromise solution is not available . . .

Counsel for the plaintiff seeks to apply by analogy a principle said to be established by *Parry* v *Cleaver* in support of the argument that all payments to an employee enjoying the benefit of the defendants' permanent health insurance scheme are effectively in the nature of the fruits of insurance accruing to the benefit of the employee in consideration of the contributions he has made by his work for the defendants prior to incapacity. Much emphasis was laid on the long-term nature of the scheme payments to which the plaintiff has become entitled and it was submitted that they are strictly comparable to a disability pension. Both these arguments fall to the ground, as it seems to me, in the light of the concession rightly made at an early stage that the nature of payments under the scheme is unaffected by the duration of the incapacity which determines the period for which payments will continue to be made. The question whether the scheme payments are or are not deductible in assessing damages for loss of earnings must be answered in the same way whether, after the first 13 weeks of incapacity, the payments fall to be made for a few weeks or for the rest of an employee's working life. Looking at the payments made under the scheme by the defendants in the first weeks after the expiry of the period of 13 weeks of continuous incapacity, they seem to me indistinguishable in character from the sick pay which the employee receives during the first 13 weeks. They are payable under a term of the employee's contract by the defendants to the employee qua employee as a partial substitute for earnings and are the very antithesis of a pension, which is payable only after employment ceases. The fact that the defendants happen to have insured their liability to meet these contractual commitments as they arise cannot affect the issue in any way.

In this jurisdiction there is no authority directly in point, perhaps because it has always been assumed as axiomatic that an employee who receives under the terms of his contract of employment either the whole or part of his salary or wages during a period when he is incapacitated for work cannot claim damages for a loss which he has not sustained . . .

The same or a closely analogous principle has been applied here and in Australia to the deduction from lost earnings of unemployment benefit in assessing damages. In *Parsons* v *BNM Laboratories Ltd* [1964] 1 QB 95 at 130–131, Harman LJ said:

Unemployment insurance is a sum receivable by contract made by the employed man and his employer each of whom contributes to the state on the footing that if and when the servant is unemployed the state will make good part of his earnings to him. I do not think that such a payment is truly analogous to insurance moneys, as in the leading case of *Bradburn* v *Great Western Rly Co.* (1874) LR 10 Exch 1, where there was a purely voluntary contract made by the plaintiff. This is a contribution which he is bound to make with the very object of mitigating the damage which inability to work will do him. It is just as if his employer continued to pay part of his wages. The loss he suffers is pro tanto diminished and therefore cannot be charged against the wrongdoer.

This decision was later affirmed by this House in *Westwood* v *Secretary of State for Employment* [1985] AC 20 at 43, where I observed in the course of a speech with which the other members of the Appellate Committee agreed that 'the whole purpose of the compulsory scheme which makes unemployment benefit available to all those who lose their employment is to provide the unemployed man with a substitute for earnings'. And the same conclusion was reached by the High Court of Australia in *Redding* v *Lee* (1983) 47 ALR 241. In the judgment of Mason and Dawson JJ which expresses the conclusions of the majority on this point, it is said (at 261):

As we indicated earlier, the central question in this appeal is whether the unemployment benefits can be said to be a substitute or partial substitute for wages, justifying the same treatment as wages in terms of assessment of damages.

Having answered the question affirmatively, the judgment concluded that unemployment benefit was deductible

. . .

From the point of view of justice, reasonableness and public policy the case seems to me far removed from the principle underlying the insurance cases stemming from *Bradburn* v *Great Western Rly Co.* LR 10 Exch 1. It positively offends my sense of justice that a plaintiff, who has certainly paid no insurance premiums as such, should receive full wages during a period of incapacity to work from two different sources, his employer and the tortfeasor. It would seem to me still more unjust and anomalous where, as here, the employer and the tortfeasor are one and the same. I would accordingly dismiss the appeal.

15.1.2.4 Provisional damages

WILLSON v *MoD* [1991] 1 All ER 638

FACTS: The plaintiff injured his ankle at work. His employers admitted liability. The plaintiff had a continuing disability, and further degeneration and arthritis were predicted. The plaintiff sought provisional damages to cover these eventualities.

SCOTT BAKER J: In this particular case Mr Langstaff argues that there are three events which, if they occur, should occasion a further award. These events are as follows: (i) that the plaintiff develops arthritis to the extent that surgery is required; (ii) that he develops arthritis to the extent that he changes his employment; (iii) that he suffers further injury in the nature of further damage to the ankle or elsewhere.

The section which provides for provisional damages awards to be made is s. 32A of the Supreme Court Act 1981. It provides as follows:

(1) This section applies to an action for damages for personal injuries in which there is proved or admitted to be a chance that at some definite or indefinite time in the future the injured person will, as a result of the act or omission which gave rise to the cause of action, develop some serious disease or suffer some serious deterioration in his physical or mental condition.

(2) Subject to subsection (4) below, as regards any action for damages to which this section applies in which a judgment is given in the High Court, provision may be made by rules of court for enabling the court, in such circumstances as may be prescribed, to award the injured person—(a) damages assessed on the assumption that the injured person will not develop the disease or suffer the deterioration in his condition; and (b) further damages at a future date if he develops the disease or suffers the deterioration.

Rules of court were made as envisaged by the section and they are to be found at RSC Ord 37, r. 8. It is not necessary for me to describe the rule or rules in detail. I simply refer to one matter and that is that by use of the word 'may' in r. 8(1) the court has a discretion whether or not to make an award of provisional damages when the criteria set out in s. 32A are met.

In this case there are really three questions that have to be considered. One is whether it is proved that there is a chance, the second is whether it is proved that there is a chance of some serious deterioration in the plaintiff's physical condition, and the third is, if the plaintiff succeeds in passing over both those hurdles, whether the court should exercise its discretion in his favour in the circumstances of the case. It seems to me appropriate to consider each of the three events postulated by Mr Langstaff separately.

A chance, it will be appreciated, is not defined in s. 32A. This has been considered in a number of previous cases. It seems to me that the legislature has used a wide word here and used it deliberately. I think Mr Nixon is right when he points out that it can cover a wide range between, on the one hand, something that is de minimis and, on the other hand, something that is a probability. In my view, to qualify as a chance it must be measurable rather than fanciful. There is certainly, in my judgment, in this case a chance of osteoarthritis developing and a chance of the plaintiff suffering further traumatic injury. I think that there is a chance that he will develop arthritis to the extent that he requires surgery. I think that there is a chance that he will develop arthritis to the extent that he has to change his employment and I think there is a chance that he will suffer further injury in the nature of further damage to his ankle or elsewhere. However slim those chances may be, I think that they are measurable within the meaning of this section. I bear in mind of course the medical evidence and, in particular, the helpful summary of the medical reports that counsel have put before me in the shape of a one-page document.

The second question turns on the words 'serious deterioration in his physical condition'. It is clear that, as drafted, the word 'serious' appears to qualify the words 'deterioration in his physical condition'. There is a question of how 'serious' should be interpreted in the light of this section. On one view, 'serious' could cover a wide range of circumstances from something not far beyond the trivial at the bottom end of the scale to something approaching the catastrophic at the top end of the scale.

In my judgment, what is envisaged here is something beyond ordinary deterioration. Whether deterioration is serious in any particular case seems to me to be a question of fact depending on the circumstances of that case, including the effect of the deterioration upon the plaintiff. For example, where a plaintiff suffers a hand injury and there is a deterioration it may be a matter of great gravity for a concert pianist but a matter of rather less importance for somebody else. Insofar as it is material—and I do not think much turns on it in this case—I favour the wider interpretation of 'serious deterioration' as advanced on the plaintiff's behalf.

I now turn in a little more detail to look at the three events that are envisaged in the present case and to consider whether, if they occur, they can be described as a serious deterioration. First of all, the development of arthritis to the extent that surgery is required. Osteoarthritis is a progressive condition. It is very common in cases where damage is suffered to an articular surface. I am not satisfied that it is established that deterioration to the point of surgery being required falls within the definition of serious deterioration in the circumstances of this case. It seems to me to be simply an aspect of a progression of this particular disease.

Secondly, development of arthritis to the extent that he changes employment. Again, it seems to me very much the same approach can be applied as with regard to the requirement of surgery and I do not think that deterioration triggering a change of employment can properly be described as serious within the meaning of the section.

Thirdly, that the plaintiff suffers a further injury in the nature of further damage to the ankle or elsewhere. It is important to refer back to the medical evidence. I refer in particular to Mr Jefferiss's report of 23 January 1988:

> This ankle will, however, be more liable to a severe injury of the inversion type, which might cause a greater degree of disruption of the ligamentous tissues than if his current degree of ligamentous insufficiency did not exist.

There is evidence that from time to time, because of the instability of his left ankle, the plaintiff is prone to falling over. He told me in evidence that some two and a half months ago he fell over when carrying a new cash register into the stores and that on a number of previous occasions when moving things around the general stores he fell over because of instability of the ankle. Obviously he avoids such things as walking over rough ground where the risk of falling over is likely to be great but he cannot eliminate the risk altogether and it seems to me likely that on occasions in the future his ankle will give way and he will fall over.

What is going to happen in such circumstances? According to Mr Jefferiss, he is more liable to a severe injury of the inversion type. So far, he has not suffered such an injury. There is, in my view, a chance that he may suffer such an injury in the future but it seems to me to be entirely speculative as to the nature and gravity of any injury that he may suffer. So there are, in a sense, two possibilities: (i) the possibility that he falls over and (ii) the possibility that, if he does, he suffers a further injury.

I am not satisfied that it is established that there is a chance of serious deterioration because it seems to me there is no real evidence as to what may happen if he does fall over. Serious injury, in my view, is not to be equated with serious deterioration in his physical condition.

It is also argued by Mr Langstaff that the injury may not occur to the ankle but, for example, because of the instability of the ankle, he may fall over and damage his arm. This, it seems to me, is becoming more remote. There is clearly a chance of this happening, however remote, but I am not satisfied that there is a chance of serious deterioration being caused as a result of this. I am, however, satisfied (see *Hughes* v *Cheshire* CC (2 March 1989, unreported)) that an injury elsewhere caused in such circumstances would at least be capable of coming within the section. I am not, however, satisfied that it is established that there is a chance of *serious*—and I emphasise that word—deterioration in this case. That is not a matter that I have found entirely easy. . . .

The question then arises as to which cases are appropriate for a provisional damages award and which are not. I deal with this because, although I formed the view that there was no serious deterioration envisaged, that was not a matter that I found entirely easy and indeed there are some matters that may more properly be dealt with under the heading of 'discretion' rather than taking into account the circumstances of the case in looking at whether or not the section was complied with.

The general rule in English law is that damages are assessed on a once-and-for-all basis. Section 32A of the 1981 Act creates a valuable statutory exception. In my judgment, the section envisages a clear and severable risk rather than a continuing deterioration, as is the typical osteoarthritic picture.

In my judgment, many disabilities follow a developing pattern in which the precise results cannot be foreseen. Within a general band this or that may or may not occur. Such are not the cases for provisional damages. The courts have to do their best to make an award in the light of a broad medical prognosis.

In my judgment, there should be some clear-cut event which, if it occurs, triggers an entitlement to further compensation.

Argument was addressed to the question of whether or not the discretion should be exercised. No doubt the courts will work out over a period of time the various factors that it may be relevant to take into account in the exercise of such a discretion. In my judgment, the important factors in this case are, first, to look and see whether, in respect of any of the three events outlined by Mr Langstaff, there can truly be said to be a clear-cut identifiable threshold. In my judgment, there cannot.

I also take into account the degree of risk and the consequences of the risk. They do not seem to me to be such as to place this case in the category where there is a great demand that there ought to be only a provisional damages award.

In a sense, this point leads into the third aspect that I regard as particularly relevant to the exercise of this discretion, and that is weighing up the possibility of doing justice by a once-and-for-all assessment against the possibility of doing better justice by reserving the plaintiff's right to return.

It seems to me that the case falls within the general run of cases where there are uncertainties as to the future. Nobody can look into a crystal ball and see precisely how the plaintiff's ankle will develop, but I think that the uncertainties are such that they can all properly be taken into account in making a once-and-for-all assessment of damages today. My conclusion therefore is that this is not an appropriate case in which to exercise discretion in favour of a provisional damages order.

15.1.3   AGGRAVATED AND EXEMPLARY DAMAGES

15.1.3.1   The present law

BROOME v CASSELL [1972] AC 1027 (HL)

FACTS: The defendants published a book which was seriously defamatory of the plaintiff by depicting the plaintiff as being in gross dereliction of duty while commanding a wartime arctic convoy. One publisher had rejected the book as defamatory, but the book as published expressly advertised the allegations against the plaintiff. The plaintiff claimed exemplary damages on the basis that publication in this manner was calculated to make a profit from the defamation. The Court of Appeal dismissed appeals against awards of exemplary damages. The defendants further appealed to a seven member committee of the House of Lords, as the appeal involved reconsideration of the law stated in *Rookes* v *Barnard* [1964] 1 All ER 367. Part of the case turned on the extent to which the Court of Appeal could reinterpret or decline to follow House of Lords decisions.

So far as the basis of exemplary damages was concerned, the majority endorsed, with clarification, what was said in *Rookes* v *Barnard*.

LORD HAILSHAM OF MARYLEBONE LC:
The law before Rookes v Barnard
   Whatever else may be said, the Court of Appeal's judgment is based on one assumption which is plainly incorrect. This assumption is, to quote its most characteristic expression on the lips of Lord Denning MR: 'Prior to *Rookes* v *Barnard*, the law as to exemplary damages was settled.' In point of fact, it was nothing of the kind. Lord Denning MR went on immediately to quote from Mayne and MacGregor on Damages the following passage:

> Such damages are variously called punitive damages, vindictive damages, exemplary damages, and even retributory damages. They can apply only where the conduct of the defendant merits punishment, which is only considered to be so when his conduct is wanton, as when it discloses fraud, malice, violence, cruelty, insolence, or the like, or, as it is sometimes put, where he acts in contumelious disregard of the plaintiff's rights . . . Such damages are recognised to be recoverable in appropriate cases in defamation . . .

If Lord Denning MR had gone on to quote from a subsequent passage of the same edition he would have read the following passage, inconsistent with his construction of the foregoing, under the heading 'A Double Rationale' which should, I hope, have disabused him of the idea that the law of punitive damages was in fact settled prior to *Rookes* v *Barnard*. The passage is as follows:

> 3.   A Double Rationale
> Through all these various cases, however, runs another thread, giving a very different explanation of the position. *For indeed it cannot be said that English law has committed itself finally and fully to exemplary damages, and many of the above cases point to the rationale not of punishment of the defendant but of extra compensation for the plaintiff for the injury to his feelings and dignity. This is, of course, not exemplary damages at all. It is another head of non-pecuniary loss to the plaintiff.*
> [The italics are mine.]

Indeed, in the well-known American textbook on the law of damages by the late Professor Charles T McCormick, published in 1935 by the West Publishing Co. of Minnesota, occurs the following passage to the same effect:

> In England, where exemplary damages had their origin, it is still not entirely clear whether the accepted theory is that they are a distinct and strictly punitive element of the recovery, or they are merely a swollen or 'aggravated' allowance of compensatory damages permitted in cases of outrage. It is only in America that the cases have clearly separated exemplary from compensatory damages, and it is only here that the doctrine, thus definitely isolated, has been attacked and criticised.

More characteristic than either of these passages and more illustrative of the confusion which reigned before *Rookes* v *Barnard* [1964] AC 1129 is the paragraph on the subject in Lord Simonds's edition of Halsbury's Laws of England (3rd Edn) 223, para 391:

> *Exemplary damages*. Where the wounded feeling and injured pride of a plaintiff, or the misconduct of a defendant, may be taken into consideration, the principle of *restitutio in integrum* no longer applies. Damages are then awarded not merely to recompense the plaintiff for the loss he has sustained by reason of the defendant's wrongful act, but to punish the defendant in an exemplary manner, and vindicate the distinction between a wilful and an innocent wrongdoer. Such damages are said to be 'at large', and, further, have been called exemplary, vindictive, penal, punitive, aggravated, or retributory.

This passage clearly shows the extraordinary confusion of terminology reflecting differences in thinking and principle which existed up to 1964. Apart from anything else, 'aggravated' damages, classed as compensatory by Mayne and MacGregor, and by Professor McCormick, are assimilated to exemplary or punitive damages as such, as is the phrase damages 'at large'—an expression so indefinite in its connotation that counsel for the appellants in argument felt able to include within it (as this passage suggests inappropriately) even the general damages for pain and suffering in a personal injuries case. Clearly, before *Rookes* v *Barnard*, the thinking and the terminology alike called aloud for further investigation and exposition, and, since in such cases it is the classic function of this House to make such reviews, I cannot accept the simplistic doctrine of the Court of Appeal [1971] 2 All ER 187 either that there was no need to make it, or that the only thing to restore clarity is to go back to the state of the law as it was in 1963. In passing, I may say that I do not attach so much importance as did the Court of Appeal to the circumstances that the two categories mentioned by Lord Devlin had never been discussed in argument by counsel. The cases and textbooks on exemplary damages had been exhaustively read, and when this House undertakes a careful review of the law it is not to be described as acting per incuriam or ultra vires if it identifies and expounds principles not previously apparent to the counsel who addressed it or to the judges and textbook writers whose divergent or confusing expressions led to the necessity for the investigation. Of course, in a sense, it would be easy enough to direct a jury under the old law if one simply said to them that any conduct of which they chose on rational grounds to disapprove would give rise to an award of exemplary damages and that any sum they chose to think appropriate as the penalty would be acceptable. But no one in recent years has ever thought this, although it is noteworthy that as recently as 1891 the author of Sedgwick's 'A Treatise on the Measure of Damages' was writing 8th Edn, pp 502 et seq:

> Until comparatively recent times juries were as arbitrary judges of the amount of damages as of the facts . . . Even as late as the time of Lord Mansfield it was possible for counsel to state the law to be that 'The Court cannot measure the ground on which the jury find damages that may be thought large; *they may find upon facts within their own knowledge*' . . . *The doctrine of exemplary damages is thus seen to have originated in a survival in this limited class of cases of the old arbitrary power of the jury*. [The italics are mine.]

Clearly modern juries must be given adequate professional guidance and the object of Lord Devlin's opinion in *Rookes* v *Barnard* [1964] AC 1129 was to enable them to have it. Speaking for myself, and whatever view I formed of the categories, I would find it impossible to return to the chaos which is euphemistically referred to by Phillimore LJ as 'the law as it was before *Rookes* v *Barnard*'.

Before I examine the actual decision in *Rookes* v *Barnard* I would now propose to make two sets of observations of a general character. The first relates to the context in which damages must be awarded, the second to the terminology to be used in particular classes of case.

The Subjective Element in Damages

Of all the various remedies available at common law, damages are the remedy of most general application at the present day, and they remain the prime remedy in actions for breach of contract and tort. They have been defined as 'the pecuniary compensation, obtainable by success in an action, for a wrong which is either a tort or a breach of contract'. They must normally be expressed in a single sum to take account of all the factors applicable to each cause of action and must of course be, expressed in English currency. *Mayne and McGregor on Damages*, 12th Edn, para 1.

In almost all actions for breach of contract, and in many actions for tort, the principle of restitutio in integrum is an adequate and fairly easy guide to the estimation of damage, because the damage suffered can be estimated by relation to some material loss. It is true that where loss includes a pre-estimate of future losses, or an estimate of past losses which cannot in the nature of things be exactly computed, some subjective element must enter in. But the estimate is in things commensurable with one another, and convertible at least in principle to the English currency in which all sums of damages must ultimately be expressed.

In many torts, however, the subjective element is more difficult. The pain and suffering endured, and the future loss of amenity, in a personal injuries case are not in the nature of things convertible into legal tender . . . Nor, so far as I can judge, is there any purely rational test by which a judge can calculate what sum, greater or smaller, is appropriate. What is surprising is not that there is difference of opinion about such matters, but that in most cases professional opinion gravitates so closely to a conventional scale. Nevertheless, in all actions in which damages, purely compensatory in character, are awarded for suffering, from the purely pecuniary point of view the plaintiff may be better off. The principle of restitutio in integrum, which compels the use of money as its sole instrument for restoring the status quo, necessarily involves a factor larger than any pecuniary loss.

In actions of defamation and in any other actions where damages for loss of reputation are involved, the principle of restitutio in integrum has necessarily an even more highly subjective element. Such actions involve a money award which may put the plaintiff in a purely financial sense in a much stronger position than he was before the wrong. Not merely can he recover the estimated sum of his past and future losses, but, in case the libel, driven underground, emerges from its lurking place at some future date, he must be able to point to a sum awarded by a jury sufficient to convince a bystander of the baselessness of the charge. As Windeyer J well said in *Uren v John Fairfax & Sons Pty Ltd* (1967) 117 CLR 118 at 150:

> It seems to me that, properly speaking, a man defamed does not get compensation *for* his damaged reputation. He gets damages *because* he was injured in his reputation, that is simply because he was publicly defamed. For this reason, compensation by damages operates in two ways—as a vindication of the plaintiff to the public, and as consolation to him for a wrong done. Compensation is here a solatium rather than a monetary recompense for harm measurable in money.

This is why it is not necessarily fair to compare awards of damages in this field with damages for personal injuries. Quite obviously, the award must include factors for injury to the feelings, the anxiety and uncertainty undergone in the litigation, the absence of apology, or the reaffirmation of the truth of the matters complained of, or the malice of the defendant. The bad conduct of the plaintiff himself may also enter into the matter, where he has provoked the libel, or where perhaps he has libelled the defendant in reply. What is awarded is thus a figure which cannot be arrived at by any purely objective computation. This is what is meant when the damages in defamation are described as being 'at large'. In a sense, too, these damages are of their nature punitive or exemplary in the loose sense in which the terms were used before 1964, because they inflict an added burden on the defendant proportionate to his conduct, just as they can be reduced if the defendant has behaved well—as for instance by a handsome apology—or the plaintiff badly, as for instance by provoking the defendant, or defaming him in return. In all such cases it must be appropriate to say with Lord Esher MR in *Praed v Graham* (1889) 24 QBD at 55:

> . . . in actions of libel . . . the jury in assessing damages are entitled to look at the whole conduct of the defendant [I would personally add 'and of the plaintiff'] from the time the libel was published down to the time they give their verdict. They may consider what his conduct has been before action, after action, and in court during the trial.

It is this too which explains the almost indiscriminate use of 'at large', 'aggravated' 'exemplary', and 'punitive' before *Rookes* v *Barnard* [1964] AC 1129. To quote again from Professor McCormick's work, it was originally only in America that the distinction between 'aggravated' damages (which take into account the defendant's bad conduct for compensating the plaintiff's injured feelings) and 'punitive' or 'exemplary' damage was really drawn. My own view is that no English case, and perhaps even in no statute, where the word 'exemplary' or 'punitive' or 'aggravated' occurs before 1964 can one be absolutely sure that there is no element of confusion between the two elements in damages. It was not until Lord Devlin's speech in *Rookes* v *Barnard* that the expressions 'aggravated' on the one hand and 'punitive' or 'exemplary' on the other acquired separate and mutually exclusive meanings as terms of art in English law.

The next point to notice is that it has always been a principle in English law that the award of damages when awarded must be a single lump sum in respect of each separate cause of action. Of course, where part of the damage can be precisely calculated, it is possible to isolate part of it in the same cause of action. It is also possible and desirable to isolate different sums of damages receivable in respect of different torts, as was done here in respect of the proof copies. But I must say I view with some distrust the arbitrary subdivision of different elements of general damages for the same tort, as was done in *Loudon* v *Ryder* [1953] 2 QB 202, and even, subject to what I say later, what was expressly approved by Lord Devlin in *Rookes* v *Barnard* for the laudable purpose of avoiding a new trial. In cases where the award of general damages contains a subjective element, I do not believe it is desirable or even possible simply to add separate sums together for different parts of the subjective element, especially where, as was done by agreement in this case, the subjective element relates under different heads to the same factor, in this case the bad conduct of the defendant. I would think with Lord Atkin in *Ley* v *Hamilton* (1935) 153 LT 384 at 386:

> The 'punitive' element is not something which is *or can* [the italics are mine] be added to some known factor which is non-punitive.

or in the words of Windeyer J in *Uren* v *John Fairfax & Sons Pty Ltd*:

> The variety of the matters which, it has been held, may be considered in assessing damages for defamation must in many cases mean that the amount of a verdict is the product of a mixture of *inextricable* considerations. [The italics again are mine.]

In other words the whole process of assessing damages where they are 'at large' is essentially a matter of impression and not addition. When exemplary damages are involved, and even though, in theory at least, it may be possible to winnow out the purely punitive element, the dangers of double counting by a jury or a judge are so great that, even to avoid a new trial, I would have thought the dangers usually outweighed the advantages. Indeed, although it must be wholly illegitimate to speculate in such a matter, the thought crossed my mind more than once during the hearing that it may even have happened in this case.

Terminology

This brings me to the question of terminology. It has been more than once pointed out the language of damages is more than usually confused. For instance, the term 'special damage' is used in more than one sense to denominate actual past losses precisely calculated (as in a personal injuries action), or 'material damage actually suffered' as in describing the factor necessary to give rise to the cause of action in cases, including cases of slander, actionable only on proof of 'special damage'. If it is not too deeply embedded in our legal language, I would like to see 'special damage' dropped as a term of art in its latter sense and some phrase like 'material loss' substituted. But a similar ambiguity occurs in actions of defamation, the expressions 'at large', 'punitive', 'aggravated', 'retributory', 'vindictive' and 'exemplary' having been used in, as I have pointed out, inextricable confusion. In awarding 'aggravated' damages the natural indignation of the court at the injury inflicted on the plaintiff is a perfectly legitimate motive in making a generous rather than a more moderate award to provide an adequate solatium. But that is because the injury to the plaintiff is actually greater and as the result of the conduct exciting the indignation demands a more generous solatium . . .

As between 'punitive' or 'exemplary', one should, I would suppose, choose one to the exclusion of the other, since it is never wise to use two quite interchangeable terms to denote the same thing. Speaking for myself, I prefer 'exemplary', not because 'punitive' is necessarily inaccurate, but 'exemplary' better expresses the policy of the law as expressed in the cases. It is intended to teach the defendant and others that 'tort does not pay' by demonstrating what consequences the law inflicts rather than simply to make the defendant suffer an extra penalty for what he has done, although that does, of course, precisely describe its effect.

The expression 'at large' should be used in general to cover all cases where awards of damages may include elements for loss of reputation, injured feelings, bad or good conduct by either party, or punishment, and where in consequence no precise limit can be set in extent. It would be convenient if, as the appellants' counsel did at the hearing, it could be extended to include damages for pain and suffering or loss of amenity. Lord Devlin uses the term in this sense in *Rookes* v *Barnard*, when he defines the phrase as meaning all cases where 'the award is not limited to the pecuniary loss that can be specifically proved'. But I suspect that he was there guilty of a neologism. If I am wrong, it is a convenient use and should be repeated . . .

Where Solatium is Enough

The true explanation of *Rookes* v *Barnard* is to be found in the fact that, where damages for loss of reputation are concerned, or where a simple outrage to the individual or to property is concerned, aggravated damages in the sense I have explained can, and should in every case lying outside the categories, take care of the exemplary element, and the jury should neither be encouraged nor allowed to look beyond as generous a solatium as is required for the injuria simply in order to give effect to feelings of indignation. It is not that the exemplary element is excluded in such cases. It is precisely because in the nature of things it is, and should be, included in every such case that the jury should neither be encouraged nor allowed to look for it outside the solatium and then to add to the sum awarded another sum by way of penalty additional to the solatium. To do so would be to inflict a double penalty for the same offence.

The surprising thing about *Rookes* v *Barnard* is not that Lord Devlin restricted the award of exemplary damages viewed as an addition to or substitution for damages by way of solatium to the three so-called categories, but that he allowed the three so-called categories to exist by way of exception to the general rule. That he did this is due at least in part to the fact that he felt himself bound by authority to do so, but partly also because he thought that there were cases where, over and above the figure awarded for loss of reputation, for injured feelings, for outraged morality, and to enable a plaintiff to protect himself against future calumny or outrage of a similar kind, an additional sum was needed to vindicate the strength of the law and act as a supplement to its strictly penal provisions . . .

The Meaning of the Categories

As regards the meaning of the particular categories, I have come to the conclusion that what Lord Devlin said was never intended to be treated as if his words were verbally inspired, and much of the criticism of them which has succeeded reports of the case has been based on interpretations which are false to the whole context and unduly literal even when taken in isolation from it.

The only category exhaustively discussed before us was the second, since the first could obviously have no application to the instant case. But I desire to say of the first that I would be surprised if it included only servants of the government in the strict sense of the word. It would, in my view, obviously apply to the police, despite *A-G for New South Wales* v *Perpetual Trustee Co. Ltd* [1955] AC 457, and almost as certainly to local and other officials exercising improperly rights of search or arrest without warrant, and it may be that in the future it will be held to include other abuses of power without warrant by persons purporting to exercise legal authority. What it will not include is the simple bully, not because the bully ought not to be punished in damages, for he manifestly ought, but because an adequate award of compensatory damages by way of solatium will necessarily have punished him. I am not prepared to say without further consideration that a private individual misusing legal powers of private prosecution or arrest as in *Leith* v *Pope* [1779] 2 Wm Bl 1327, where the defendant had the plaintiff arrested and tried on a capital charge, might not at some future date be assimilated into the first category. I am not prepared to make an exhaustive list of the emanations of government which might or might not be included. But I see no reason to extend it beyond this field, to simple outrage, malice or contumelious behaviour. In such cases a properly directed jury will not find it necessary to differentiate between what the plaintiff ought to receive and the defendant ought to pay, since the former will always include the latter to the extent necessary to vindicate the strength of the law.

When one comes to the second category we reach a field which was more exhaustively discussed in the case before us. It soon became apparent that a broad rather than a narrow interpretation of Lord Devlin's words was absolutely essential, and that attempts to narrow the second category by a quotation out of context of one sentence from the passage wherein it is defined simply will not do.

It [i.e. the motive of making a profit] is a factor also that is taken into account in damages for libel; one man should not be allowed to sell another man's reputation for profit. Where a defendant with a cynical disregard for a plaintiff's rights has calculated that the money to be made out of his wrongdoing will probably exceed the damages at risk, it is necessary for the law to show that it cannot be broken with impunity. *This category is not confined to moneymaking in the strict sense. It extends to cases in which the defendant is seeking to gain at the expense of the plaintiff some object,—perhaps some property which he covets,—which either he could not obtain at all or not obtain except at a price greater than he wants to put down. Exemplary damages can properly be awarded whenever it is necessary to teach a wrongdoer that tort does not pay.* [The italics are mine.]

Even a casual reading of the above passage shows that the sentence:

Where a defendant with a cynical disregard for a plaintiff's rights has calculated that the money to be made out of his wrongdoing will probably exceed the damages at risk, it is necessary for the law to show that it cannot be broken with impunity.

is not intended to be exhaustive but illustrative, and is not intended to be limited to the kind of mathematical calculations to be found on a balance sheet. The sentence must be read in its context. The context occurs immediately after the sentence ending: 'one man should not be allowed to sell another man's reputation for profit', where the word 'calculation' does not occur. The context also includes the final sentence: 'Exemplary damages can properly be awarded whenever it is necessary to teach a wrongdoer that tort does not pay.' The whole passage must be read sensibly as a whole, together with the authorities on which it is based.

It is true, of course, as was well pointed out by Widgery J in *Manson* v *Associated Newspapers Ltd* [1965] 2 All ER 954 at 960, that the mere fact that a tort, and particularly a libel, is committed in the course of a business carried on for profit is not sufficient to bring a case within the second category. Nearly all newspapers, and most books, are published for profit. What is necessary in addition is (i) knowledge that what is proposed to be done is against the law or a reckless disregard whether what is proposed to be done is illegal or legal, and (ii) a decision to carry on doing it because the prospects of material advantage outweigh the prospects of material loss. It is not necessary that the defendant calculates that the plaintiff's damages if he sues to judgment will be smaller than the defendant's profit. This is simply one example of the principle. The defendant may calculate that the plaintiff will not sue at all because he has not the money (I suppose the plaintiff in a contested libel action like the present must be prepared nowadays to put at least £30,000 at some risk), or because he may be physically or otherwise intimidated. What is necessary is that the tortious act must be done with guilty knowledge for the motive that the chances of economic advantage outweigh the chances of economic, or perhaps physical, penalty.

At this stage one must examine some of the counter-arguments which found favour in the Court of Appeal. How, it may be asked, about the late Mr Rachman, who is alleged to have used hired bullies to intimidate statutory tenants by violence or threats of violence into giving vacant possession of their residences and so placing a valuable asset in the hands of the landlord? My answer must be that if this is not a cynical calculation of profit and cold-blooded disregard of a plaintiff's rights, I do not know what is. It is also argued that the second category does not take care of the case of a man who pursues a potential plaintiff to ruin out of sheer hatred and malice. The answer is that it does not do so because this is already taken care of in the full compensation or solatium for the injuria involved in which the jury can give full rein to their feeling of legitimate indignation without going outside the bounds of compensatory damages in the sense in which I have explained the phrase, that is, damages of sufficient size to enable the plaintiff to point to the size of the award to indicate the baselessness of the false charge, and damages for the outrage inflicted in exact proportion as it was unprovoked, unatoned for, or malicious. I would have thought the second category was ample to cover any form of injury committed within the scope of those torts for which aggravated and exemplary damages may be awarded where the motive was material advantage.

15.2 Injunctions

15.2.1 WHERE INJUNCTIONS ARE LIKELY TO BE USEFUL

PRIDE OF DERBY & DERBYSHIRE ANGLING ASSOCIATION v BRITISH CELANESE
[1953] Ch 149 (CA)

FACTS: The plaintiffs owned fishing rights on the River Derwent. The defendants' factory and sewage works discharged effluent into the river which seriously polluted it, killing the fish. The plaintiffs sought an injunction to restrain the nuisance by pollution. Harman J granted the injunction together with an enquiry as to damages. The Corporation and the Water Board appealed to the Court of Appeal. British Celanese, who were found to be the most serious polluters, did not.

SIR RAYMOND EVERSHED MR: The secondary argument of the corporation was that if the plaintiffs had a cause of action, the judge ought not to have granted an injunction, but should have left them to their remedy in damages. . . .

I can deal more briefly with the question of the appropriate remedy . . . I venture to think that the fallacy which underlies this part of the corporation's argument is based on the statement made on their part that an injunction is purely discretionary—if by that is meant that, in a case where a person's rights, such as the plaintiffs' rights, are being damaged and there is a threat of continuing damage, the question whether an injunction will be granted is determined by the court on the balance of convenience on one side or the other. In my judgment, that is not a correct statement of the position. It is, I think, well settled that, if A. proves that his proprietary rights are being wrongfully interfered with by B., and that B. intends to continue his wrong, then A. is prima facie entitled to an injunction, and he will be deprived of that remedy only if special circumstances exist, including the circumstance that damages are an adequate remedy for the wrong that he has suffered. In the present case, it is quite plain that damages would be a wholly inadequate remedy for the plaintiff association. The general rule which I have stated applies, in my opinion, to local authorities as well as to other citizens. Equally, of course, the court will not impose on a local authority, or on anyone else, an obligation to do something which is impossible, or which cannot be enforced, or which is unlawful. Therefore, the practice is adopted in the case of local authorities of granting injunctions, and then suspending their operation for a time, long or short. . . .

What, after all, are the alternatives? It is suggested by counsel for the corporation that the plaintiffs should be left to bring a series of actions for damages. In every such action the plaintiffs would have again to prove their case, for the corporation could put them to such proof by a mere traverse of the facts alleged. The result would, obviously, be a vast expenditure of costs, a matter on which, I understand, the corporation are themselves particularly tender. I think that much the same result would follow if the plaintiffs were merely given liberty to apply for an injunction, for they would then, presumably, have to establish as a matter of fact that some circumstances had arisen which then justified the granting of an injunction which had not been granted at the time of the trial. Nor, in my judgment, would the matter be materially affected even if the corporation were to give some kind of undertaking to get on with the work when it was possible or convenient to do so in the ordinary way. It appears to me that, the corporation having been proved to be wrongdoers (and not disputing that they are wrongdoers), the onus should be on them, if they want a further suspension, to satisfy the court that justice requires that a further suspension should be granted. If the corporation show that they are unable to do more than they are doing, or that they cannot get any licences under reg. 56A, then I have no doubt that a further suspension will be granted until such time as this urgent matter can be put in hand. Finally, the objection that the injunction is permanent in form seems to me to be entirely unsubstantial. In any event, there is, at the end of the order, liberty to apply, and, when all the matters of which the plaintiffs complain have been put right, the court will, no doubt, be ready to hear any application which the corporation might be minded to make to discharge the injunction. As a matter, therefore, of jurisdiction and general principle, I see no ground whatever why the injunction which was granted should not be granted. Still less do I see any ground on which this court could be invited to interfere with the discretion exercised by the learned judge.

KENNAWAY v THOMPSON [1980] 3 All ER 329 (CA)

FACTS: The plaintiff, who lived some 400 yards from the defendant's lake, complained that there was a noise nuisance from motor boat racing on that lake. The use of the lake dated back to the 1960s. The plaintiff built her house in 1969. Subsequently the frequency and intensity of use of the lake by noisier boats increased substantially. The defendant conceded that there was a nuisance. The trial judge awarded £1,000 damages for nuisance to date, but declined to grant an injunction, on the basis that this would deprive a large number of watersports enthusiasts of their pleasure. Instead he awarded £15,000 damages under Lord Cairns' Act.

The plaintiff appealed against the refusal to grant an injunction.

LAWTON LJ: Counsel for the plaintiff has submitted that the judge misdirected himself. What he did, it was said, was to allow the club to buy itself the right to cause a substantial and intolerable nuisance. It was no justification to say that this was for the benefit of that section of the public which was interested in motor boat racing. Once the plaintiff had proved that the club had caused a nuisance which interfered in a substantial and intolerable way with the use and enjoyment of her house she was entitled to have it stopped by injunction.

Counsel for the defendant submitted that this court should not interfere with the exercise of the judge's discretion. He was entitled to take into account the effect which an injunction would have on the club and on those members of the public who enjoyed watching or taking part in motor boat racing.

Counsel for the plaintiff based his submissions primarily on the decision of this court in *Shelfer v City of London Electric Lighting Co.* [1895] 1 Ch 287. The opening paragraph of the headnote, which correctly summarises the judgment, is as follows:

> *Lord Cairns' Act* (21 and 22 Vict. c. 27), in conferring upon Courts of Equity a jurisdiction to award damages instead of an injunction, has not altered the settled principles upon which those Courts interfered by way of injunction; and in cases of continuing actionable nuisance the jurisdiction so conferred ought only to be exercised under very exceptional circumstances.

In the judgment, in a much-quoted passage, Lindley LJ said:

> . . . ever since *Lord Cairns' Act* was passed the Court of Chancery has repudiated the notion that the Legislature intended to turn that Court into a tribunal for legalising wrongful acts; or in other words, the Court has always protested against the notion that it ought to allow a wrong to continue simply because the wrongdoer is able and willing to pay for the injury he may inflict. Neither has the circumstance that the wrongdoer is in some sense a public benefactor (e.g., a gas or water company or a sewer authority) ever been considered a sufficient reason for refusing to protect by injunction an individual whose rights are being persistently infringed.

A L Smith LJ, in his judgment, set out what he called a good working rule for the award of damages in substitution for an injunction. His working rule does not apply in this case. The injury to the plaintiff's legal rights is not small; it is not capable of being estimated in terms of money save in the way the judge tried to make an estimate, namely by fixing a figure for the diminution of the value of the plaintiff's house because of the prospect of a continuing nuisance; and the figure he fixed could not be described as small. The principles enunciated in *Shelfer's* case, which is binding on us, have been applied time and time again during the past 85 years. The only case which raises a doubt about the application of the *Shelfer* principles to all cases is *Miller* v *Jackson* [1977] QB 966, a decision of this court. The majority, Geoffrey Lane and Cumming-Bruce LJJ, Lord Denning MR dissenting, adjudged that the activities of an old-established cricket club which had been going for over seventy years, had been a nuisance to the plaintiffs by reason of cricket balls landing in their garden. The question then was whether the plaintiffs should be granted an injunction. Geoffrey Lane LJ was of the opinion that one should be granted. Lord Denning MR and Cumming-Bruce LJ thought otherwise. Lord Denning MR said that the public interest should prevail over the private interest. Cumming-Bruce LJ stated that a factor to be taken into account when exercising the judicial discretion whether to grant an injunction was that the plaintiffs had bought their house knowing that it was next to the cricket ground. He thought that there were special circumstances which should inhibit a court of equity from granting the injunction claimed. The statement of Lord Denning MR that the public interest should prevail over the private interest runs counter to the principles enunciated in *Shelfer's* case and does not accord with the reason of Cumming-Bruce LJ for refusing an injunction. We are of the opinion that there is nothing in *Miller* v *Jackson*, binding on us, which qualifies what was decided in *Shelfer*. Any decisions before *Shelfer's* case (and there were some at first instance as counsel for the defendants pointed out) which give support for the proposition that the public interest should prevail over the private interest must be read subject to the decision in *Shelfer's* case.

It follows that the plaintiff was entitled to an injunction and that the judge misdirected himself in law in adjudging that the appropriate remedy for her was an award of damages under Lord Cairns's Act. But she was only entitled to an injunction restraining the club from activities which caused a nuisance, and not all of their activities did. As the judge pointed out, and counsel for the plaintiff accepted in this court, an injunction in general terms would be unworkable.

Our task has been to decide on a form of order which will protect the plaintiff from the noise which the judge found to be intolerable but which will not stop the club from organising activities about which she cannot reasonably complain.

When she decided to build a house alongside Mallam Water she knew that some motor boat racing and water skiing was done on the club's water and she thought that the noise which such activities created was tolerable. She cannot now complain about that kind of noise provided it does not increase in volume by reason of any increase in activities. The intolerable noise is mostly caused by the large boats; it is these which attract the public interest.

Now nearly all of us living in these islands have to put up with a certain amount of annoyance from our neighbours. Those living in towns may be irritated by their neighbours' noisy radios or incompetent playing of musical instruments; and they in turn may be inconvenienced by the noise caused by our guests slamming car doors and chattering after a late party. Even in the country the lowing of a sick cow or the early morning crowing of a farmyard cock may interfere with sleep and comfort. Intervention by injunction is only justified when the irritating noise causes inconvenience beyond what other occupiers in the neighbourhood can be expected to bear. The question is whether the neighbour is using his property reasonably, having regard to the fact that he has a neighbour. The neighbour who is complaining must remember, too, that the other man can use his property in a reasonable way and there must be a measure of 'give and take, live and let live'.

Understandably the plaintiff finds intolerable the kind of noise which she has had to suffer for such long periods in the past; but if she knew that she would only have to put up with such noise on a few occasions between the end of March and the beginning of November each year, and she also knew when those occasions were likely to occur, she could make arrangements to be out of her house at the material times. We can see no reason, however, why she should have to absent herself from her house for many days so as to enable the club members and others to make noises which are a nuisance. We consider it probable that those who are interested in motor boat racing are attracted by the international and national events, which tend to have the larger and noisier boats. Justice will be done, we think, if the club is allowed to have, each racing season, one international event extending over three days, the first day being given over to practice and the second and third to racing. In addition there can be two national events, each of two days but separated from the international event and from each other by at least four weeks. Finally there can be three club events, each of one day, separated from the international and national events and each other by three weeks. Any international or national event not held can be replaced by a club event of one day. No boats creating a noise of more than 75 decibels are to be used on the club's water at any time other than when there are events as specified in this judgment. If events are held at weekends, as they probably will be, six weekends, covering a total of ten days, will be available for motor boat racing on the club's water. Water skiing, if too many boats are used, can cause a nuisance by noise. The club is not to allow more than six motor boats to be used for water skiing at any one time. An injunction will be granted to restrain motor boat racing, water skiing and the use of boats creating a noise of more than 75 decibels on the club's water save to the extent and in the circumstances indicated.

15.2.2 INTERLOCUTORY INJUNCTIONS

AMERICAN CYANAMID v *ETHICON* [1975] AC 396 (HL)

FACTS: The plaintiffs alleged that the defendants were infringing their patent in relation to dissolving surgical sutures, and applied for an interlocutory injunction to restrain the defendants from marketing the allegedly infringing product pending trial. The case raised questions as to the tests to be applied in such cases generally, and was finally determined by the House of Lords.

LORD DIPLOCK: My Lords, when an application for an interlocutory injunction to restrain a defendant from doing acts alleged to be in violation of the plaintiff's legal right is made on contested facts, the decision whether or not to grant an interlocutory injunction has to be taken at a time when ex hypothesi the existence of the right or the violation of it, or both, is uncertain and will remain uncertain until final judgment is given in the action. It was to mitigate the risk of injustice to the plaintiff during the period before that uncertainty could be resolved that the practice arose of granting him relief by way of interlocutory injunction; but since the middle of the 19th century this has been made subject to his undertaking to pay damages to the defendant for any loss sustained by reason of the injunction if it should be held at the trial that the plaintiff had not been entitled to restrain the defendant from doing what he was threatening to do. The object of the interlocutory injunction is to protect the plaintiff against injury by violation of his right for which he could not be adequately compensated in damages recoverable in the action if the uncertainty were resolved in his favour at the trial; but the plaintiff's need for such protection must be weighed against the corresponding need of the defendant to be protected against injury resulting from his having been prevented from exercising his own legal rights for which he could not be adequately compensated under the plaintiff's undertaking in damages if the uncertainty were resolved in the defendant's favour at the trial. The court must weigh one need against another and determine where 'the balance of convenience' lies.

In those cases where the legal rights of the parties depend on facts that are in dispute between them, the evidence available to the court at the hearing of the application for an interlocutory injunction is incomplete. It is given on affidavit and has not been tested by oral cross-examination. The purpose sought to be achieved by giving to the court discretion to grant such injunctions would be stultified if the discretion were clogged by a technical rule forbidding its exercise if on that incomplete untested evidence the court evaluated the chances of the plaintiff's ultimate success in the action at 50 per cent or less, but permitting its exercise if the court evaluated his chances at more than 50 per cent.

The notion that it is incumbent on the court to undertake what is in effect a preliminary trial of the action on evidential material different from that on which the actual trial will be conducted, is, I think, of comparatively recent origin, though it can be supported by references in earlier cases to the need to show 'a probability that the plaintiff is entitled to relief' (*Preston* v *Luck* (1884) 27 ChD 497 *per* Cotton LJ) or 'a strong prima facie case that the right which he seeks to protect in fact exists' (*Smith* v *Grigg Ltd* [1924] 1 KB 655 *per* Atkin LJ). These are to be contrasted with expressions in other cases indicating a much less onerous criterion, such as the need to show that there is 'certainly a case to be tried' (*Jones* v *Pacaya Rubber and Produce Co. Ltd* [1911] 1 KB 445 *per* Buckley LJ) which corresponds more closely with what judges generally treated as sufficient to justify their considering the balance of convenience on applications for interlocutory injunctions, at any rate up to the time when I became a member of your Lordships' House.

An attempt had been made to reconcile these apparently differing approaches to the exercise of the discretion by holding that the need to show a probability or a strong prima facie case applied only to the establishment by the plaintiff of his right, and that the lesser burden of showing an arguable case to be tried applied to the alleged violation of that right by the defendant (*Donmar Productions Ltd* v *Bart* [1967] 2 All ER 338 *per* Ungoed Thomas J *Harman Pictures NV* v *Osborne* [1967] 2 All ER 324 *per* Goff J).

Your Lordships should in my view take this opportunity of declaring that there is no such rule. The use of such expressions as 'a probability', 'a prima facie case', or 'a strong prima facie case' in the context of the exercise of a discretionary power to grant an interlocutory injunction leads to confusion as to the object sought to be achieved by this form of temporary relief. The court no doubt must be satisfied that the claim is not frivolous or vexatious; in other words, that there is a serious question to be tried.

It is no part of the court's function at this stage of the litigation to try to resolve conflicts of evidence on affidavit as to facts on which the claims of either party may ultimately depend nor to decide difficult questions of law which call for detailed argument and mature considerations. These are matters to be dealt with at the trial. One of the reasons for the introduction of the practice of requiring an undertaking as to damages on the grant of an interlocutory injunction was that 'it aided the court in doing that which was its great object, viz abstaining from expressing any opinion upon the merits of the case until the hearing' (*Wakefield* v *Duke of Buccleuch* (1865) 12 LT 628). So unless the material available to the court at the hearing of the application for an interlocutory injunction fails to disclose that the plaintiff has any real prospect of succeeding in his claim for a permanent injunction at the trial, the court should go on to consider whether the balance of convenience lies in favour of granting or refusing the interlocutory relief that is sought.

As to that, the governing principle is that the court should first consider whether if the plaintiff were to succeed at the trial in establishing his right to a permanent injunction he would be adequately compensated by an award of damages for the loss he would have sustained as a result of the defendant's continuing to do what was sought to be enjoined between the time of the application and the time of the trial. If damages in the measure recoverable at common law would be adequate remedy and the defendant would be in a financial position to pay them, no interlocutory injunction should normally be granted, however strong the plaintiff's claim appeared to be at that stage. If, on the other hand, damages would not provide an adequate remedy for the plaintiff in the event of his succeeding at the trial, the court should then consider whether, on the contrary hypothesis that the defendant were to succeed at the trial in establishing his right to do that which was sought to be enjoined, he would be adequately compensated under the plaintiff's undertakings as to damages for the loss he would have sustained by being prevented from doing so between the time of the application and the time of the trial. If damages in the measure recoverable under such an undertaking would be an adequate remedy and the plaintiff would be in a financial position to pay them, there would be no reason on this ground to refuse an interlocutory injunction.

It is where there is doubt as to the adequacy of the respective remedies in damages available to either party or to both, that the question of balance of convenience arises. It would be unwise to attempt even to list all the various matters which may need to be taken into consideration in deciding where the balance lies, let alone to suggest the relative weight to be attached to them. These will vary from case to case.

Where other factors appear to be evenly balanced it is a counsel of prudence to take such measures as are calculated to preserve the status quo. If the defendant is enjoined temporarily from doing something that he has not done before, the only effect of the interlocutory injunction in the event of his succeeding at the trial is to postpone the date at which he is able to embark on a course of action which he has not previously found it necessary to undertake; whereas to interrupt him in the conduct of an established enterprise would cause much greater inconvenience to him since he would have to start again to establish it in the event of his succeeding at the trial.

Save in the simplest cases, the decision to grant or to refuse an interlocutory injunction will cause to whichever party is unsuccessful on the application some disadvantages which his ultimate success at the trial may show he ought to have been spared and the disadvantages may be such that the recovery of damages to which he would then be entitled either in the action or under the plaintiff's undertaking would not be sufficient to compensate him fully for all of them. The extent to which the disadvantages to each party would be incapable of being compensated in damages in the event of his succeeding at the trial is always a significant factor in assessing where the balance of convenience lies; and if the extent of the uncompensatable disadvantage to each party would not differ widely, it may not be improper to take into account in tipping the balance the relative strength of each party's case as revealed by the affidavit evidence adduced on the hearing of the application. This, however, should be done only where it is apparent on the facts disclosed by evidence as to which there is no credible dispute that the strength of one party's case is disproportionate to that of the other party. The court is not justified in embarking on anything resembling a trial of the action on conflicting affidavits in order to evaluate the strength of either party's case.

I would reiterate that, in addition to those to which I have referred, there may be many other special factors to be taken into consideration in the particular circumstances of individual cases.

15.2.3   UNDERTAKINGS AS TO DAMAGES

OXY ELECTRIC LTD v *ZAINUDDIN* [1990] 2 All ER 902

FACTS: The defendants proposed to build a mosque on an industrial estate. The plaintiffs, whose plant was on the estate, alleged that this was in breach of a restrictive covenant. Not wishing to run the risks associated with a cross-undertaking in damages the plaintiffs claimed only a permanent injunction. The defendants, anxious to avoid the costs of delay, applied to have the action struck out unless the plaintiffs applied for an interlocutory injunction.

HOFFMANN J: The present position is, therefore, that the defendants are not subject to any order restraining them from proceeding with the development, but, until the plaintiff's entitlement to a permanent injunction has been decided at the trial and any subsequent appeal, the defendants are at risk that they may be stopped. The trial has been fixed for 15 October this year. The defendants say that this state of uncertainty is causing them continuing loss and unless they take the risk of pressing ahead they will have to incur additional expense in suspending the building contract. The delay itself is also likely to inflate the costs. There is, as things now stand, no way in which the defendants could be compensated for this loss if they are successful at the trial. The mere bringing of unsuccessful legal proceedings which causes the defendants loss does not give rise to any cause of action unless the plaintiff was malicious.

The defendants therefore now apply to have the claim for a permanent injunction struck out unless the plaintiff is willing to apply for an interlocutory injunction and to support its cross-undertaking with adequate security. What in effect the defendants are therefore saying is that the plaintiff should not be allowed to proceed unless it agrees now that in the event of failure it will compensate the defendants for any loss they had suffered as if the proceedings had been malicious.

The application is based on a recent decision of Sir Nicolas Browne-Wilkinson V-C in *Blue Town Investments Ltd* v *Higgs & Hill plc* [1990] 2 All ER 897, [1990] 1 WLR 696, and counsel for the defendants acknowledged that until he read that decision the idea of making this application had not occurred to the defendants' advisers. In the *Blue Town* case the plaintiff had been complaining of a development which it said would interfere with its rights of light. Sir Nicolas Browne-Wilkinson V-C found on the affidavit evidence that in correspondence in March 1989 the defendants had offered either to modify their development so as to avoid such interference or to pay the plaintiff compensation for the loss of light. The plaintiff had chosen the latter alternative and the assessment of the compensation had been referred to the parties' surveyors. It appears, however, that the plaintiff was unwilling to accept the figure on which they agreed and in September, six months later and three months after work had commenced, it issued a writ claiming a permanent injunction. The Vice-Chancellor said that there had been acquiescence which made it 'almost inconceivable' that the plaintiff would obtain a final injunction at the trial. He described its chances as 'minimal' and said that its case was 'thin'. But the Vice-Chancellor was unwilling to strike out the claim to an injunction either under RSC Ord 18, r. 19 or under the inherent jurisdiction simply on the ground that it was vexatious and bound to fail. The burden, he said, on a person seeking to strike out a claim was a heavy one. Such orders should be made only in the clearest and most obvious cases and, despite the comments which I have quoted on the plaintiff's chances, he felt that this burden had not been satisfied. What the Vice-Chancellor did do was to give the plaintiff the option of maintaining its claim if it was willing to apply for an interlocutory injunction and to give the appropriate cross-undertaking in damages. It is not entirely clear from the report whether the defendants were willing to concede that an interlocutory injunction should be granted, and in view of the Vice-Chancellor's comments on acquiescence and delay it would seem that they might have had some grounds for opposing one, but I think it must be assumed that the Vice-Chancellor thought that there was a realistic prospect that the plaintiff could satisfy the conditions which he laid down for maintaining their claim to an injunction.

Counsel for the defendants submits that I should take a similar course here and strike out the claim to an injunction unless the plaintiff is willing to apply for an interlocutory injunction. In this case, however, counsel has made it clear that he does not concede that such an injunction should be granted.

Counsel for the plaintiff submits that the Vice-Chancellor had no jurisdiction to do what he did in the *Blue Town* case and that I should not follow his decision. Either the claim to an injunction should have been struck out as unarguable, frivolous and vexatious, or it should not have been struck out at all. The right to maintain it should not have to be purchased by a cross-undertaking in damages given in connection with an interlocutory injunction which the plaintiff does not want. Counsel for the plaintiff drew attention to the strong public policy against denying a citizen the right to bring a bona fide claim before the court in the ordinary way. This policy is reflected in the reluctance of the court to strike out a claim summarily, either under Ord 18, r. 19 or the inherent jurisdiction. It is equally reflected in the rule that in the absence of malice there is no cause of action at common law for damage caused by threats of litigation or the existence of the litigation itself. Accordingly, counsel for the plaintiff submitted that there was no jurisdiction to impose conditions on the right of a litigant to prosecute his claim.

It seems to me, with all respect to Sir Nicolas Browne-Wilkinson V-C, that there is a great deal of force in what counsel for the plaintiff has said. Counsel for the defendants conceded that a court would have no jurisdiction to require an impecunious plaintiff to give security for the defendant's costs as a condition of allowing him to proceed with an unpromising but nevertheless arguable claim. If the claim cannot be struck out under Ord 18, r. 19 or the inherent jurisdiction, in accordance with established principles, it must be allowed to proceed in the ordinary way. I cannot, for myself, see any difference in principle between the imposition of a condition designed to protect a defendant against loss caused through wasted legal expense and a condition designed to protect him against loss caused by uncertainty created by the existence of the claim.

In the *Blue Town* case Sir Nicolas Browne-Wilkinson V-C drew a parallel with the jurisdiction which had been exercised by Templeman J in *Clearbrook Property Holdings Ltd v Verrier* [1973] 3 All ER 614, [1974] 1 WLR 243 to vacate a caution or land charge but to entertain an application by the cautioner for an interlocutory injunction which would also prevent the defendant from dealing with the property but, unlike the caution or land charge, would involve the giving of a cross-undertaking in damages. It seems to me, however, that the vacation of a caution or land charge, which is a legal interference with the landowner's freedom to deal with his property, is a very different matter from denying a plaintiff the right to make a claim in a court of justice. The mere existence of the claim to an injunction constitutes no interference with the defendant's liberty. The uncertainty which it creates is no more than a necessary consequence of the existence of a claim which has not yet been adjudicated. If the defendants are confident of their case, they are free to ignore the claim at their own risk, but I cannot see that the *Clearbrook* case provides me with jurisdiction for transferring that risk to the plaintiff.

I am also puzzled about the exercise of the jurisdiction in practice. Sir Nicolas Browne-Wilkinson V-C regarded the plaintiff's claim as bordering on vexatious because the defendant had a virtually unanswerable defence of acquiescence or delay. Yet he seems to have regarded the case as suitable for the grant of an interlocutory injunction. This is a reversal of the normal attitude of the court. And what happens when, as here, the plaintiff is impecunious and can offer no credible cross-undertakings? Is a poor plaintiff struck out when a rich plaintiff's claim would survive?

For those reasons I must express respectful doubt as to the existence of the jurisdiction asserted by Sir Nicolas Browne-Wilkinson V-C in the *Blue Town* case, but it is unnecessary for me formally to dissent from it, because in my judgment there is a substantial difference between that case and this. It was clearly critical to the exercise of the Vice-Chancellor's discretion that the facts before him came as close to constituting an abuse of process as one could without actually crossing the line. In this case, I certainly do not think that the plaintiff's chances of obtaining an injunction could be described as minimal or almost inconceivable. It is not necessary for me to go into the facts, but sufficient for me to say that I think that the plaintiff has a seriously arguable case.

Counsel for the defendants submitted that this was a plain case in which, even if the covenant was being infringed, the court would refuse an injunction and award instead a modest sum of damages under the Chancery Amendment Act 1858 (Lord Cairns's Act). He said that all the criteria mentioned by A L Smith LJ in the well-known passage in his judgment in *Shelfer* v *City of London Electric Lighting Co., Meux's Brewery Co.* v *City of London Electric Lighting Co.* [1895] 1 Ch 287 at 322–323, [1891–4] All ER Rep 838 at 848 were satisfied: the injury to the plaintiff's rights was small, the damage was capable of being estimated in money, a small money payment would be adequate compensation and the grant of an injunction would be oppressive. . . .

[T]he authorities on Lord Cairns's Act, and in particular the judgment in *Shelfer*'s case, to which I have already referred, make it clear that the jurisdiction to refuse an injunction and grant damages instead ought to be exercised only in what Lindley LJ described as 'very exceptional circumstances'. He said ([1895] 1 Ch 287 at 315–316, [1891–4] All ER Rep 838 at 844):

. . . the Court has always protested against the notion that it ought to allow a wrong to continue simply because the wrongdoer is able and willing to pay for the injury he may inflict. Neither has the circumstance that the wrongdoer is in some sense a public benefactor (e.g., a gas or water company or a sewer authority) ever been considered as sufficient reason for refusing to protect by injunction an individual whose rights are being persistently infringed. Expropriation, even for a money consideration, is only justifiable when Parliament has sanctioned it.

Again, it seems to me, therefore, that . . . it must be seriously arguable that the circumstances of this case cannot be brought within the narrow conditions for the jurisdiction under Lord Cairns's Act.

15.3   End of Chapter Assessment Questions

1.   Penny, a sole practitioner solicitor and Alf, her husband, who does not work but looks after their two small children are injured in a car crash. This is entirely the fault of the other driver, Dan.

Penny is unable to work for twelve months. Her net profits after tax for the last three years averaged £50,000. She has received state benefits totalling £10,000. She suffered multiple injuries including a fractured pelvis. She will not be able to have any more children, although she and Alf were hoping to have a family of six. One of her arms has suffered very serious soft tissue damage and may have to be amputated at some time in the future.

Alf is in a coma for two weeks. He then recovers consciousness. He is totally paralysed and helpless. After a further six weeks he dies.

Penny's mother looks after Penny and the children until Penny is able to return to work. Penny then employs a nanny and housekeeper at a total cost of £20,000 per annum.

Advise Dan of the basis on which he will be liable in damages.

You have been given some figures to assist you in working out the likely award under some of the heads of damage, but you will only be able to indicate others in outline.

2.   Charon operates a number of speedboats on the River Styx. Pluto, who has lived near the river for 30 years and Persephone, who has just moved to the area, both complain about noise. This is mainly when the boats are starting out and when engines are being tested. There is a large fence on Charon's land to deaden the sound, but this has fallen into disrepair. Charon offers to provide double glazing for both the complainants. Pluto rejects the offer out of hand, Persephone provisionally agrees, but later changes her mind. Both Pluto and Persephone apply for a final injunction preventing Charon operating speedboats at all, or in the alternative requiring him to repair and keep in repair the fence. Charon is in the process of erecting a large boathouse.

Advise Charon.

15.4   End of Chapter Assessment Outline Answers

1.   Penny is entitled to damages for her own injuries. Normally this will be a lump sum. It is made up of:

- Pain, suffering and loss of amenity: figures awarded for similar injuries will be updated. The distress at not having further children can be included in the global figure. Exceptionally, a provisional award may be made on the assumption that she does not lose her arm. If it does have to be amputated, a further award can be made to cover this: s. 32A, Supreme Court Act 1981.

- Loss of earnings: the pre-accident figures will be used as a basis. Penny may be able to recover more if she can show that her earnings were on a rising trend. She can also recover for any loss during the period when she is re-establishing her practice. The DSS will recoup the benefits paid.

- Cost of care: her mother is entitled to a reasonable amount for the work done: *Cunningham* v *Harrison* (1973).

Alf's estate may claim on his behalf for damages for pain and suffering between the accident and the death, including distress at loss of expectation of life, if relevant: s. 1, Law Reform (Miscellaneous Provisions) Act 1934.

Penny is entitled to the conventional award for bereavement: s. 1A, Fatal Accidents Act 1976.

There will be a Fatal Accidents Act claim (s. 1). Although Penny and the children were not financially dependent on Alf, the children were dependent on him as a carer: *Berry* v

Humm & Co (1915). However the valuation of those services is likely to fall far short of the commercial cost of a nanny and housekeeper: *Spittle* v *Bunney* (1988); the cost was taken as the net wage of a full-time nanny, discounted to allow for the fact that the children would in time need less looking after. Some allowance is made for the quality of care provided by a natural carer (cf *Spittle* v *Bunney*).

2.   The first issue is whether any of Charon's activities actually constitute an actionable nuisance, and if so which. Any claim for an injunction can only relate to these aspects of his activities: *Kennaway* v *Thompson* (1981).

If Charon's activities have not altered in their scope, Pluto will not be able to claim. His cause of action arose when the nuisance first affected him: *Sturges* v *Bridgman* (1879) and will now be statute barred: s. 2, Limitation Act 1980. If, on the other hand they have increased so as to become a nuisance, by reason of greater intensity, louder engines etc. this will be actionable: cf *Kennaway* v *Thompson*. Persephone is not precluded from pursuing a claim by virtue of the fact that she has moved to the nuisance, but this will be a factor which the court will take into account when assessing whether Persephone will be granted an injunction: *Miller* v *Jackson* (1977).

Normally there is nothing to prevent a plaintiff seeking only a final injunction. This will not stop Charon's operations until the full hearing. If the negative injunction sought is granted Charon will not need the boathouse. It will no doubt be prudent to deter completing it until the case has been heard and this may increase the costs. This is however simply the consequence of the uncertainties of litigation and Charon cannot insist on an interlocutory injunction being applied for, with the associated cross-undertaking as to damages: *Oxy Electric* v *Zainuddin* (1990). There is an outside chance that this would not apply in Persephone's case, as she has arguably compromised herself by initially agreeing to settle the issue by the installation of double glazing. A plaintiff in a similar position was ordered to apply for an interlocutory injunction in *Blue Town Investments* v *Higgs & Hill* (1990), but there are doubts whether the judge had jurisdiction to make such an order.

Judges are reluctant to grant mandatory injunctions requiring the defendant to take positive steps, especially where these require the cooperation of others (not the case here) or long term policing. If Charon has covenanted to keep the fence in repair in a conveyance or lease of the land, this obligation would be specifically enforced if either Pluto or Persephone had the benefit of the covenant, and even if he has not, the existence of cases where this sort of order was made should persuade the court to grant an injunction in these terms if it is considered the appropriate way to resolve the problem.

Subject to the foregoing the court is likely to grant an injunction restraining use of the boats so as to cause a nuisance. This may fall short of an absolute ban, if a partial restriction produces a reasonable level of amenity for the plaintiffs: *Kennaway* v *Thompson*.

What is most unlikely is that the court will award damages in lieu under s. 50, Supreme Court Act 1981. Ever since *Shelfer* v *City of London Electric Lighting Co.* (1895) the courts have been reluctant to allow a defendant to buy out the right to cause a nuisance, even where there is a strong public interest in their activities. This was reiterated in *Kennaway* v *Thompson* where the facts were similar to the present. Virtually the only exception is where the plaintiff comes to the nuisance. This was the argument of Cumming-Bruce LJ in *Miller* v *Jackson*, and appears to be a more orthodox approach than that of Lord Denning MR.